The
Impossible
Dream

Recent Titles in
Contributions in Political Science
Series Editor: Bernard K. Johnpoll

The Italian Communist Party: Yesterday, Today, and Tomorrow
Simon Serfaty and Lawrence Gray, editors

The Fiscal Congress: Legislative Control of the Budget
Lance T. Leloup

Iran, Saudi Arabia, and the Law of the Sea: Political Interaction and
Legal Development in the Persian Gulf
Charles G. MacDonald

Improving Prosecution? The Inducement and Implementation of
Innovations for Prosecution Management
David Leo Weimer

Creating the Entangling Alliance: The Origins of the North Atlantic
Treaty Organization
Timothy P. Ireland

The State as Defendant: Governmental Accountability and the Redress of
Individual Grievances
Leon Hurwitz

Ethnic Identities in a Transnational World
John F. Stack, Jr., editor

Reasoned Argument in Social Science: Linking Research to Policy
Eugene J. Meehan

The Right Opposition: The Lovestoneites and the International Communist
Opposition of the 1930s
Robert J. Alexander

Quantification in the History of Political Thought: Toward a Qualitative Approach
Robert Schware

The Kent State Incident: Impact of Judicial Process on Public Attitudes
Thomas R. Hensley

Representation and Presidential Primaries: The Democratic Party in the
Post-Reform Era
James I. Lengle

Heroin and Politicians: The Failure of Public Policy to Control Addiction
in America
David J. Bellis

The Impossible Dream

The Rise and Demise of the American Left

**BERNARD K. JOHNPOLL
with LILLIAN JOHNPOLL**

Contributions in Political Science, Number 59

GREENWOOD PRESS
Westport, Connecticut • London England

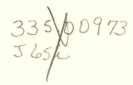

Library of Congress Cataloging in Publication Data

Johnpoll, Bernard K.
  The impossible dream.

  (Contributions in political science; no. 59
ISSN 0147-1066)
  Bibliography: p.
  Includes index.
  1.   Socialism in the United States—History.
2.   Radicalism—United States—History. I. Johnpoll,
Lillian, joint author. II. Title. III. Series.
HX83.J63   335′.00973   80-24829
ISBN 0-313-22488-9 (lib. bdg.)

Library of Congress Catalog Card Number: 80-24829
ISBN: 0-313-22488-9
ISSN: 0147-1066

First published in 1981

Greenwood Press
A division of Congressional Information Service, Inc.
88 Post Road West, Westport, Connecticut 06881

Printed in the United States of America

10 9 8 7 6 5 4 3 2 1

To our parents
who fought
the good fight

≈ Contents ≈

Preface	*ix*
1. Introduction	3
2. Owen and New Harmony	14
3. The Owenites	26
4. The Workies	50
5. The Individualists	69
6. The Associationists	84
7. The Burned-Over District	100
8. Labor Reform	115
9. Marxists and Lassalleans	129
10. The Road to Haymarket	147
11. The Henry George Interlude	166
12. Burnette G. Haskell: Firebrand or Fraud?	180
13. Nationalists and Populists	205
14. Christian Socialists	229
15. The SLP, 1890-1900	249
16. The Socialist Party	273

17. Decline of the Left   297

18. The Politics of Duplicity   323

19. The New Left   338

20. Ideals and Reality   345

    Bibliographic Note   *351*

    Index   *357*

❧ Preface ❧

All books are essentially autobiographical; this book is no exception. Most of my youth and a large part of my earlier adult life were spent in the radical movement. I could chant by rote the slogans that peppered the *Communist Manifesto* and debate for endless hours the minutiae that permeated the "intellectual" life of a young Marxist. Never did I question the essential justice of my Socialist ideals. My belief in them was an act of faith.

As I grew older, and as it became more apparent to me that the beliefs of my youth were less than perfect, I decided to reexamine those ideals. This book, like my previous works and my forthcoming studies of the American Socialist and Communist parties, is part of that reexamination. If my conclusions are at times harsh, it is because I am disillusioned. For the ideals of my youth have turned out to be a compound of nonsense, political egotism, and arrogance. Socialism, I have come to realize, is merely another in a long line of myths by which man has deluded himself into believing that "Thy will" could, in fact, "be done on earth as it is in heaven." It is difficult for an old man like myself to concede that "Thy will" can be done neither on earth nor in heaven. It is also difficult to concede that man's options are finite and that perfection is not one of them.

In the twilight of my years, I have discovered that humans continually improve their situation here on earth by solving individual problems as they occur, one at a time; no overall solution exists for all problems. Socialism has, in practice, become a subterfuge for oppressive totalitarianism; anarchism has proven to be an unfulfillable dream; and syndicalism has led to conservative business unionism and the corruption that power brings.

The preceding statement does not mean I have moved from radicalism to conservatism or reaction. A return to laissez fare would be no more successful or liberating than a revolutionary shift to socialism, anarchism, or syndicalism.

This book basically examines the important radical movements and thinkers of the nineteenth and early twentieth centuries. Some significant radicals have been omitted—most notably Emma Goldman and Alexander Berkman. Neither of those two great American Anarchists of the present century ever led a radical movement of any consequence. However, I basically agree with their positions on most issues. I have also devoted only a short chapter to the Communist party. This is, after all, a study of *American radical* movements, and long and arduous research has convinced me that the Communist party was never—except, perhaps, for a year of its early life—either an American or a radical movement. My forthcoming seven-volume history of the Communist party will discuss the party in detail. In addition, I have dealt briefly with the New Left, which had little theoretical base. Unfortunately, the New Left was a fleeting tragic-comedy, the product of all that was wrong in previous radical and quasi-radical movements.

Many of my friends and colleagues suggested that I use secondary sources essentially in researching this book. One colleague even listed several score of them for me. I have examined them carefully over the past ten or more years, and I am convinced that most of them should be avoided in any research into radical movements. The few that had some value I have cited in footnotes. Most were replete with errors of fact, and many were more polemical than scholarly.

I have thus, wherever possible, used primary sources in writing this book. This has meant examining records in all sections of the United States and abroad. The result has led to persistent delays, which no doubt has made for a more accurate discussion of the people and movements involved.

Among the major archives I examined in researching this work were Harvard University's Houghton Library; the International Institute for Social History in Amsterdam, The Netherlands; the University of Colorado; Duke University; the Wisconsin State Historical Society; the New York State Library; the Oklahoma Historical Society; the Hebrew Union College and American Jewish Archives; the New York Public Library; and especially the Tamiment Collection at New York University.

One of the problems encountered in researching American radical movements was the fact that much of the material was written and published originally in foreign languages, particularly German and Yiddish. This is especially true of the early Marxian-Lassallean organizations and the Anarcho-Communists, particularly, Johann Most. Both groups published material in German almost exclusively. Many of the factional and theoretical disputes within the early Socialist party (particularly 1898–1910) can best be followed through the pages of the Yiddish *Daily Forward*. Just as a book about Machiavelli can hardly be written without a working knowledge of Italian, or a major work about Socrates, Plato, or Aristotle without a working knowledge of Attic Greek, so is it impossible to do an adequate study of American radicalism without a knowledge of German and Yiddish.

I have employed history to explain what American radicals believed and accomplished. One of the great failings of contemporary political science is that it ignores history. Much current quantification is an effort to replace history with "science." Unfortunately, history remains the one true empirical science on which political scientists can rely. History cannot be denigrated to a secondary position unless we are to ignore reality. The attempt to ignore history has resulted in the quantification of the inconsequential on the part of most so-called empirical political scientists and in the contemplation of the navel on the part of most political theoreticians.

It must be understood, however, that history is not its own excuse. Unless historical facts can lead to truth, we are forced to accept the old Spanish aphorism: *Los hechos son los enemigos de la vardad* ("Realities are the enemies of truth").

Of those who assisted in this work, none deserves credit more than my wife, Lillian. She was virtually my co-author. Her research and editing prevented me from making several serious errrors. She, in effect, made my own "Impossible Dream" come true.

I owe special thanks to Mark Yerburgh, Sally Stevenson, Judith Wing, and Jackie Mitnick of the State University of New York at Albany Library. I am especially grateful to Dorothy Swanson of the Tamiment Collection at New York University's Bopst Library and to other librarians without whose cooperation this work would never have been completed.

Two scholars' advice was extremely helpful, although I did not necessarily agree with all of their views. Both Kathy Ferguson of Siena College and the late Howard Quint of the University of Massachusetts deserve my heartfelt thanks. Thanks are due also to my typists, Ann B. Wright, Mary P. Warburton, Addie Napolitano, Maxine H. Morman, and Ava Charne Avellino, whose ability to correct my outrageous spelling and to read my indecipherable handwriting was service above and beyond the call of duty.

A last word of thanks should go to the group of exceptional students in my 1979 seminar on American radical thought who helped me dissect this manuscript. I absolve all of those named above from any responsibility for any errors, which are all of my own making, and I take full responsibility.

$\approx$ *1* $\approx$

Introduction

- 1 -

For more than 150 years, the American radical Left has been assailing America's industrial (and preindustrial) society; for more than 150 years, it has been proposing revolutionary change in the social structure of the United States; for more than 150 years, it has found itself ignored by the very people it has attempted to reach; and for more than 150 years, its revolutionary plans have been frustrated. In all of this time, the radical Left has been engaged in what might be called an exercise in futility. Yet despite its obvious failures, it would be grossly unfair to assume that it has failed to leave its imprint on American society. For many of the democratic and welfare reforms enacted in the United States since the 1820s owe their origins to the organized American Left. Under radical leadership, the workers of America have "abolished the debtors' prison, won the franchise, abolished conspiracy laws, and won the right to associate together for the common good of their class."[1] Moreover, it was the radical Left in America that proposed and fought for social security, workmen's compensation, protection against long hours and unconscionably low wages, and the entire New Deal reform structure.

Yet although the radicals first proposed and later fought for these reforms, they were effectuated by nonradical, pragmatic politicians who invariably ignored or rejected the basic assumptions the American Left postulated. In fact, these victories for reform have generally resulted in the further decline of the radical movements that fought for them. The basic principles of the American radicals have been ignored by the majority of Americans. The complete overhauling of American society by a reorganization of its legal, political, and economic structure, which radicals of the Left all agreed was the only solution to America's social ills, has not been effectuated except by evolutionary technological changes over the past centuries that are beyond the political pale.

The failure of American radicalism to develop a viable long-term political movement or to win many converts to its ultimate goals has been a matter of scholarly research from the early days of the present century.[2] It is true that radical movements have at times flourished temporarily in the United States, but these movements were more expressions of immediate discontent than conscious revolutionary actions.

The American Left was not an importation. Its origins were neither British, nor German, nor French. However, many of the leading theoreticians of the American Left were foreign-born: Robert Owen was British, as was Frances Wright; Johann Most, August Spies, and Justus Schwab were German, as were most of the early Marxists; Emma Goldman and Alexander Berkman were both born in Russia; Daniel De Leon's place of birth is one of many mysteries about him, although he appears to have been of Dutch-Jewish backround. But the ideas these non-Americans brought to the United States were soon altered by conditions here until they became more the expression of native American discontent with the present system than distinctly German or British or Russian revolutionary doctrine. This is as true of the Marxian period as it is of the pre-1848 movements. In fact, the early American radical movements had a lot of influence on Karl Marx and Friedrich Engels (particularly Engels),[3] although this fact, like most American contributions to revolutionary thought, has been ignored.

Except for fugitive mention in occasional textbooks of Eugene Debs, Norman Thomas, or Daniel De Leon, most of the leading thinkers of these movements have been relegated to oblivion by political historians and political scientists. This has been their fate even though their analyses of existing society have generally been more incisive than those of conservative or liberal observers. The American radicals have been ignored largely because they have persisted in expostulating their views in their own esoteric journals and in books replete with jargon understood only by the initiated. They have also been ignored largely because their rhetoric often has been far more florid than their ideas. That they have been placed in oblivion is unfortunate, because they did add a great deal to political and social thought both in the United States and abroad. The rebellion against bureaucracy that reached its apex in individualist anarchism, first enunciated by Josiah Warren, has had a significant impact on world thought even if in modified form; the thesis of the permanently imminent revolution, expostulated by Burnette G. Haskell of California, has had a great influence, particularly on the more militant of the New Left, even if its author is now forgotten. The insistence that Christianity meant social revolution, which was the keystone of the Social Gospel of Walter Rauschenbusch, W. D. P. Bliss, and George Herron, has had a greater impact on the Christian church than any other postreformation movement. The quasi-Socialist near-totalitarianism of Laurence Gronlund and Edward Bellamy has helped mold Socialist thought both in the United States and abroad.

This book is thus aimed at rectifying an error of omission. It is directed primarily at examining the radical movements of the United States since 1820 and exposing their strengths and their weaknesses. It is not meant to be a complete history of these movements, although it uses history as a tool, for it is a historical analysis aimed at unearthing the roots and the fate of American radicalism.

- 2 -

Left-wing American radicalism—and Left-wing radicalism the world over—has been divided historically into three diametrically opposed tendencies: socialism, syndicalism, and anarchism. Although much of America's radical thought has been composed of a synthesis of these antithetical ideologies, each has produced its own distinct movements. American radicalism is unique primarily in the types of Anarchist, Syndicalist, and Socialist thinkers and movements it has nurtured and developed. The individualist Anarchist tradition of Josiah Warren, Stephen Pearl Andrews, Lysander Spooner, and Benjamin Tucker; the nonpartisan syndicalism of disparate movements such as the Knights of Labor, the early American Federation of Labor, and the Industrial Workers of the World; and the socialism of the Social Gospel, the conspiratorial and short-lived International Workingmen's Association (of Burnette Haskell), and the Bellamyite Nationalist movement—all of these thinkers and movements were rooted in America and its peculiar social, political, and economic milieu.

Socialists, Syndicalists, and Anarchists differ primarily in their views of the state. To the Socialist, the state is the essential instrument through which a new radical society will be effectuated. Thus the state is viewed as a positive good; and Socialists would increase the scope and power of the state. The Syndicalist views the state as an irrelevancy. Society, he or she assumes, will be revised by the workers in their "mines, mills, and workshops" through their unions. The state either could play no part in the revolution, could act as a protector of the workers as their unions take over society, or could defend by force the hated status quo, but it could not change the system of society. Those Syndicalists who agree with the first assumption refuse to become involved in partisan politics; those who accept the second possibility support a Socialist party but expect it merely to defend labor-union gains and not to effect radical social change. Those who believe the state is an instrumentality for defending the status quo have assumed a stance toward the state similar to that of the Anarchists who consider it to be, by its very nature, the enemy of the exploited and oppressed working class. They argue that the new society can come about only after the destruction of the state. Anarchists view the coercive state as the root of all evil.

Despite their sharp philosophical differences, Socialists, Syndicalists, and Anarchists have much in common. Occasionally, the same people have been Anarchists and Socialists at the same time. More frequently, Socialists, Syndicalists, and Anarchists have cooperated on specific issues. But this does not imply that their differences have been exaggerated—for they are philosophical opposites. It does point up the practical realities they faced. Even the most devout revolutionist has recognized that America has been unlikely to become a Socialist, Syndicalist, or an Anarchist heaven in the reasonably foreseeable future. The ideals that separate the radicals are thus theoretical. More important is the fact that all have agreed in their opposition to the existing system in the United States, which they concede to be the common enemy.[4] The American Left has cooperated to combat the existing state of American society. The practical cooperation between these movements should not, however, dim the great philosophical differences among them, particularly between socialism and anarchism. They are theoretical antitheses. Where Socialists assume that society is superior to the individual, Anarchists assume the individual to be the superior and dedicate themselves to freeing the individual from the fetters of society.[5]

Socialism is, in essence, "the advocacy of communal ownership of land and capital," to quote Bertrand Russell, and "communal ownership may mean ownership by a democratic state. . . ."[6] Under socialism the power of the state would tend to be increased. The public sphere would be extended, because communal ownership would require an expanded state power. This would not necessarily diminish the democratic nature of the state—until 1917 most Socialists were wedded to the idea of parliamentary democracy.[7] Marxists, no less than non-Marxian Socialists, have favored this increase in state power. In the *Communist Manifesto*, the bible of most late nineteenth- and early twentieth-century Socialists, Marx and Engels called for expansion of the centralization of credit, communication, and production in the hands of state. It is true that Marx and Engels declared the "Political power, properly so called, is merely the organized power of one class for oppressing another. . . ." and that Engels called for a stateless society in his Introduction to Marx's *The Civil War in France*. But he was speaking of a time centuries away when "a generation reared in new, free social conditions is able to throw the lumber of the state on the scrap heap."[8] Most twentieth-century Socialists do not even go so far as Engels; they rarely if ever speak of doing away with the state, and they declaim against the "state which stands for a class, and which promotes the interests of that class by repressive measures designed to keep down the other class. . . ."[9] Moreover, Marxism is merely one strain—and not the dominant one—in American socialism; and the other Socialist tendencies, particularly those based on Bellamy and Gronlund, reject the view that the state will disappear.

To the Syndicalist, the Socialist reliance on the state as the instrumentality for revolutionizing society is basically irrational. Since the revolution is to be industrial, the Syndicalists argue, economic rather than partisan political action should be employed. Thus the Syndicalists, who accept the class struggle as their essential doctrine, advocate the use of industrial methods—the strike, the union label, and the boycott—to overthrow the capitalist system. The ultimate weapon of the Syndicalists is neither the ballot box nor the barricades; it is the general strike.[10] Dyer D. Lum, a leading Syndicalist publicist, defined the Syndicalist position in 1892: "The cry is not for 'more legislation' but more unity and self-help!. . .Instead of depending upon a politician, he is becoming to the unionist as unnecessary a factor, in his work, as the priest."[11] These assumptions are, in great part, the result of the fact that syndicalism's origins are to be found not in an idea but in an organization, the labor union. The "fact of Trade Union organization came first," the British philosopher Bertrand Russell wrote, "and the ideas of Syndicalism are those which seemed appropriate to this organization."[12] The fundamental Syndicalist idea asserts that the classless society of the future will be built upon the labor union of the present. William E. Trautmann, the theoretician of the apolitical wing of the Industrial Workers of the World (IWW), delineated the Syndicalist position in 1903: "Industrial organizations are forerunners of the society established on Socialist foundations, and within them are the elements preparing for a more scientific management of the implements of production and distribution."[13] Thus the Syndicalists, particularly after they won control of the IWW in 1908, argued that labor unions carried within themselves all of the elements of a new classless society. They repudiated the idea of a political revolution and talked in terms of a general strike that would "lock out the capitalist class" while the workers, through their unions, assumed control of the nation's industries and ran them in the interest of the working class. The Syndicalists thus reject both the Socialist reliance on the state and the doctrinaire Anarchist antipathy toward the state. For they assume that the state is irrelevant to the key struggle of the day; "a strong, militant industrial organization will prove sufficient to overthrow capitalism and establish" a classless society.[14]

Samuel Gompers expressed one of the underlying reasons for the Syndicalist antipathy toward political Socialists, an antipathy he shared:

It is hard for those who have not been a factor in real production enterprises to appreciate the nature and the self-efficiency of economic power. A trade-union movement is inherently a self-dependent movement. The friendly outsider may contribute advice and assistance, but there is not opportunity for him to play a conspicuous part. Consciously or unconsciously, it is personal egotism that leads him to . . . socialism in which he may have a leading. . . .[15]

It was this fear that the middle-class intellectual, "the friendly outsider," would interfere in working-class affairs and, under the iron law of oligarchy, dominate them that led both conservative Syndicalists, such as

Gompers, and radical Syndicalists to exclude political Socialists from their midst.

Anarchism stems far less from any theoretical foundation than from the realities of American life of the first three-quarters of the nineteenth century. The American pioneer was basically an Anarchist, who fought vigorously against any governmental interference. His was a "do your own thing" philosophy that insisted upon total elimination of coercive restraints.[16] The basic doctrine of Anarchists is "no authority." It is thus basically a negative doctrine, significant primarily because it rebels against authority "wherever it appears most oppressive." The only authority Anarchists are prepared to accept is that "coming from within." Anarchism is thus an exceedingly optimistic philosophy that assumes man, given total freedom, will use it for the benefit of his fellow men. The primary cause of man's antisocial behavior, all Anarchists agree, is the state. The state, in the Anarchists' view, is destructive of freedom and harmony. Only its end and the end of all coercive rule could result in a harmonious society.[17] Alexander Berkman, a leading Anarchist idol of the early twentieth century, postulated,

All Anarchists agree on this fundamental position: that government means injustice and oppression, that it is invasive, enslaving, and the greatest hindrance to man's development and growth. They all believe that freedom can exist only in a society where there is no compulsion of any kind. All Anarchists are therefore at one on the basic principles of abolishing government. . . . Anarchism teaches that we can live in a society where there is no compulsion of any kind. . . . [thus] Anarchism means doing away with the state or government altogether.[18]

From the differences in their broad philosophical outlooks, a divergence of views also developed among Socialists, Syndicalists, and Anarchists on the need for immediate ameliorative relief from oppressive conditions through social reform. Socialists with few exceptions favor social reforms. Not only do social reforms meet immediate humanitarian needs, they also create conditions that allow the workers greater leisure time during which, Socialists assumed, they would study social problems and come to the conclusion that only socialism offers them a final answer to their oppression. Syndicalists, generally, favor reform, but reject the state as the instrumentality for achieving improved conditions. Such improvement could come only through industrial action, the Syndicalist argues, because the problems are industrial. The Anarchist, because he believes the state is the root of all social evil, denigrates all attempts at social reform. Improved conditions under capitalism, most Anarchists argue, will merely retard the revolution "by smothering the dissatisfaction of the workers with their present conditions."[19]

- 3 -

Modern American radicalism had its gestation period during the 1820s with the beginnngs of the Owenite movement in the United States. Attempts at organizing communities based on primitive Christian communism were made as early as the latter part of the seventeenth century, but these efforts were mainly religious and escapist rather than social and political. Although they are interesting to historians of early America, their influence on the modern Socialist, Anarchist, and Syndicalist movements were, at best, minimal. Declamations, called socialistic and anarchistic by latter day radicals, also were made, but these outcries are found, on closer examination, to have been merely rhetorical. Agrarian, pre-1820 America was hardly the place to nurture the forbears of a modern radical movement.

The colonial governments were dominated by the wealthier agrarian interests. All of the colonies had property restrictions on suffrage and office-holding. These restrictions ranged from 500 acres and ten slaves for membership in the South Carolina Assembly to $134 in property for the right to vote in Connecticut. Even the Declaration of Independence, with its glowing egalitarian platitudes, and the success of the Revolution did little to change the suffrage laws. Virtually all early state constitutions, after first declaring that "all men are created equal," included restrictive property qualifications.[20] Thus the earliest struggles were for suffrage rather than for a reorganization of society along radical lines.

Early settlers along the western frontier (western New York, and western Pennsylvania, Ohio, and Kentucky) lived in a form of "frontier communism," but this was a matter of necessity rather than ideology. Money was useless to them, but "mutual aid" made life possible. Virtually nothing was available to purchase, and merchants (except for an occasional peddler) were nonexistent. Yet houses had to be built, clothing sewn, wheat reaped, logs hewn into proper lengths. All of these activities required cooperative efforts without which life would have been impossible.[21] This cooperation did not, however, indicate a radical transformation of society; as soon as the frontier area became more easily accessible, merchants swarmed west, cities and villages developed, and "frontier communism" vanished.

The first, and most famous, of the primitive Christian communistic communities was organized about 1663 in that part of New Netherlands that is now Delaware. Its founder was a Dutch Collegiate Mennonite leader named Christopher Plockhoy. The Collegiate Mennonites rejected any dogmatic creed and favored unlimited discussion, religious freedom, and social concern. In 1663 Plockhoy and his Mennonite followers established their commune. A year later, the British seized New Netherlands and "destroyed the Quaking society to a naile."[22] The colony left no imprint on America, although Plockhoy lived in Philadelphia until his death in 1700. To quote his biographers: "Plockhoy's ideas are only significant in their historical context. It would not only be un-historical but quite unprofitable to remove them from the Seventeenth Century scene and examine them in isolation."[23]

None of the other pre-1820 attempts at religious colonization had any influence on latter-day American radicalism. It was not until 1819 that the first attempt at building a secular commune in the United States was undertaken. That colony, founded in Pennsylvania by a German, Ludwig Lampert Gall, was a dismal failure, and within a year Gall returned to Germany where he became an active revolutionist.[24]

Early efforts at organizing urban workers into unions were also of little significance in the development of modern left-wing American radicalism. The Colonies and the early United States had sporadic strikes as early as 1742 when journeymen bakers went on strike in New York. During the last decade of the eighteenth century, Philadelphia's shoemakers struck on three occasions. Between 1802 and 1805 sailors and shoemakers in New York had strikes, and twelve years later caulkers and shipwrights had a national strike. But these strikes were all reaction against specific grievances; the 1802 sailors' walkout involved a pay dispute of $4 a month. These early strikes were, to quote a Syndicalist historian, "more or less spontaneous and sporadic in character, instead of the reflex of a strong tendency toward conscious and deliberate organization."[25]

Despite this dearth of radical substance, no shortage of revolutionary rhetoric was evident before 1820. A "Connecticut Mechanic" could, in 1792, call upon the mechanics of the world to unite.[26] Thomas Jefferson declaimed, "God forbid that we should ever be twenty years without a rebellion. What country can preserve its liberties if its rulers are not warned from time to time that the people preserve the spirit of resistance? Let them take arms. What signify a few lives lost? The tree of liberty must be refreshed from time to time with the blood of patriots and tyrants. It is its natural manure."[27] The rhetoric of the statement is revolutionary, but the context in which it was made and Jefferson's own agrarianism during the late eighteenth century make it clear that it had no socially revolutionary intent.

The most rhetorically revolutionary writer of eighteenth-century America was Thomas Paine. He remained for more than 150 years the saint of American radicals whose name was invoked with those of Karl Marx and Mikhail Bakunin. Yet except for his rhetoric, his radicalism is much inflated. In his most significant theoretical tract, "Agrarian Justice" written in France in 1792, he criticized society in terms that would have done credit to a Marxist. "It is wrong to say God made *rich* and *poor*," Paine argued. "He made only *male* and *female*; and he gave them the earth for their inheritance." But rich and poor did exist, and poverty was a fact of life in late eighteenth-century America. Why was there poverty in the civilized world?

Paine blamed civilization itself. "Poverty . . . is a thing created by that which is called civilized life. It exists not in the natural [primitive] state." The conditions of millions of people in the civilized world of the late eighteenth century were, Paine declaimed, "far worse than if they had been born before civilization began." Therefore, the "present state of civilization is as odious as it is corrupt."[28] Paine blamed poverty on the accumulation of wealth by "paying too little for the labor that produced it; the consequences of which is that the working hand perished . . . and the employer abounds in affluence."[29] More important to Paine was the private ownership of land that should have been the common property of the human race. In a statement anticipating Henry George, Paine maintained that individual ownership could extend only to the improvements to the land and not to the land itself. "Every proprietor, therefore, of cultivated lands, owes to the community a *ground-rent* . . . for the land which he holds." Moreover, since "the landed monopoly" had usurped real property that belonged to more than half the population of every nation, Paine proposed that the landowners pay the dispossessed an indemnification for that loss. "It is not charity but a right, not bounty but justice, that I am pleading for."[30] The indemnification Paine proposed was to pay each person $15 at age twenty-one "for loss of his or her natural inheritance" and pay each person $10 a year for life from age fifty on. Moreover, he proposed a 10 percent tax on inherited land as a form of ground tax.[31] It thus should be apparent that Paine's radicalism was hardly more than rhetoric, and except for the rhetoric, its influence on modern American movements was minimal.

Although the roots of American radicalism do not stretch beyond 1820, it is historically inaccurate to accept the opinion of a German economic historian that the modern Socialist and radical movements owe their origins to the German Marxists who fled to the United States seeking asylum after the collapse of the 1848 revolution.[32] It is true that the Germans brought Marxism with them, but Marxism is only one thread, and hardly the major one, in American radicalism.

Notes

1. James Oneal, *The Workers in American History* (New York: Rand School of Social Science, 1921), p. 103. This book, originally written in 1910, is an almost totally ignored classic in economic deterministic history. It antedates Charles A. Beard's work in that field by three years. Oneal was a Socialist and a newspaper editor, not a scholar; the work suffers from that, but it remains a seminal study.

2. *See*, for example, Werner Sombart, *Warum gibt es in der Vereinigten Staaten keinen Sozialismus* (Tubingen: J. C. B. Mohr [P. Siebeck], 1906).

3. See particularly Lewis S. Feuer, "The Influence of American Communist Colonies on Marx and Engels," *The Western Political Quarterly* 19 (September 1966): 456–74.

4. Norman J. Ware, *The Labor Movement in the United States, 1860-1890* (New York: D. Appleton and Company, 1929), p. 304.

5. Morris Hillquit, *History of Socialism in the United States* (New York: Funk and Wagnalls, 1910), p. 209.

6. Bertrand Russell, *Proposed Roads to Freedom* (New York: Henry Holt, 1918), p. 1.

7. Laurence Gronlund, "A Reply to Heber Newton," *The Nationalist* 1 (September 1889): 159-60; Reginald Wright Kauffman, *What is Socialism* (New York: Moffat Yard and Company, 1910), pp. 16-18; Sidney and Beatrice Webb, *The Decay of Capitalist Civilization* (London: George Allen and Unwin, 1923), p. 247; Richard T. Ely, *Socialism and Social Reform* (New York: Thomas Y. Crowell, 1894), p. 19.

8. Karl Marx and Friedrich Engels, *The Communist Manifesto*, reprinted in Robert C. Tucker, ed., *The Marx-Engels Reader* (New York: W. W. Norton, 1972), p. 352; Friedrich Engels, Introduction to *Civil War in France*, by Karl Marx, in Tucker, *The Marx-Engels Reader*, pp. 536-37.

9. Ely, *Socialism and Social Reform*, p. 29.

10. Russell, *Proposed Roads to Freedom*, pp. 65-66; Louis Levine, "The Development of Syndicalism in America," *Political Science Quarterly* 28 (September 1913): 451.

11. Dyer D. Lum, *Philosophy of Trade Unions* (1892; reprint ed. Washington, D.C.: American Federation of Labor, 1914), p. 8.

12. Russell, *Proposed Roads to Freedom*, p. x.

13. Quoted in Levine, "The Development of Syndicalism," pp. 461-62.

14. Ibid., p. 473.

15. Samuel Gompers, *Seventy Years of Life and Labor*, 2 vols. (1925; reprint one-volume ed. New York: E. P. Dutton, 1948), p. 491.

16. Ware, *The Labor Movement*, p. 304.

17. Eunice Minette Schuster, "Native American Anarchism: A Study of Left-Wing American Individualism," *Smith College Studies in History* 17 (October 1931-July 1932): 179; Alexander Berkman, *Now and After: The ABC of Communist-Anarchism* (New York: Vanguard Press, 1929), p. vi.

18. Berkman, *Now and After*, pp. 182, 185, 211.

19. Hillquit, *History of Socialism*, pp. 211-12, Norman M. Thomas, "A Program for Unemployment," *World Tomorrow* 13 (May 1930): 216.

20. Oneal, *The Workers*, pp. 89-91.

21. Ibid., pp. 150-51.

22. By far the best work on Plockhoy is H. Leland and Marvin Harder, *Plockhoy from Zuider Zee: The Study of a Dutch Reformer in Puritan English and Colonial America* (Newton, Kans.; Board of Education and Publication, 1952), especially pp. 1-67.

23. Ibid., p. 84.

24. Arthur Bestor, *Backwoods Utopias: The Sectarian Origins of the Owenite Phase of Communitarian Socialism in America, 1663-1829* (Philadelphia: University of Pennsylvania Press, 1950), p. 100.

25. Justus Ebert, *Trades Unionism in the United States, 1742-1905* (New York: New York Labor News Company, 1905), pp. 2-3; Oneal, *The Workers*, pp. 159-62.

26. *Connecticut Courant*, August 6, 1792.

27. Charles Sotheran, *Horace Greeley and Other Pioneers of American Socialism* (1892; reprint ed. New York: Mitchell Kennerly, 1915), p. 59. Sotheran, a moderate Socialist, called Jefferson a Jacobin who "had in theory a decidedly Anarchist trend." Jefferson made his statement in commenting on Shay's Rebellion, an agrarian uprising in Massachusetts in 1786-1787. The rebellion itself is not pertinent to this study.

28. Thomas Paine, "Agrarian Justice," in *The Life and Works of Thomas Paine*, 10 vols. (New Rochelle: Thomas Paine National Historical Association, 1925), 10: 8, 10–11.

29. Ibid., vol. 10, p. 30.

30. Ibid., vol. 10, pp. 11, 12, 14–15, 24.

31. Ibid., vol. 10, pp. 15, 18.

32. August Sartorious (Freiherr von Waltershausen), *Der Moderne Socialismus in den Vereinigten Staaten von Amerika* (Berlin: Verlag von Hermann Bahr, 1890), pp. 29–30.

∾ 2 ∾

Owen and New Harmony

The 1820s was a decade of gigantic growth in American industrial urban development. The population of New York, for example, grew from 123, 706 to 202,589; Philadelphia's population increased from 112,772 to 161,410; and huge gains also were recorded in Baltimore, Boston, and New Orleans. Industrially, the number of cotton spindles in the United States increased fivefold, and basic iron manufactures had grown into a major industry.[1] With the growth of industries and cities came all of the ills attributed to the capitalist system: extreme poverty and extreme wealth, alienation, disease, and governmental corruption. These problems led to calls for a radical reorganization of society to reap the benefits of the new industrialization without suffering the ills. The America of the 1820s appeared to radical thinkers to be fertile ground for planting such ideas. The United States was still less than a half century away from its revolution for independence, the spirit that revolution represented reportedly still burned brightly in America, and the rights to disseminate radical ideas were protected by the United States Constitution. Radical reformers thus flocked to the United States.

Most of the radicals who came to the United States from 1820 until the 1840s were communitarians. They believed in organizing communities that would serve as experiments to be replicated indefinitely until the whole world would operate as either one large commune or a federation of small communities. The number of such communities attempted during the period, although impossible to determine exactly, was in excess of one hundred.[2] Most of the communitarians possessed an optimism and a self-righteous dogmatism that persisted in all later radical movements. Each was confident that he had found the ultimate truth, that it could be made to work in a small colony immediately, and that once the rest of the world saw his Utopia at work, it would become the model for a new system of society. Some of the Christian communes did not expect that their earthly Utopia would be the answer to man's search for final uncontradictory verity—that answer could be found only in heaven. But they assumed that the *only* key to that heaven lay in their particular community's life-style and theology. This was as true of the Rappites as it was of the Shakers or the Perfectionists. All of the communitarians assumed that they had found the "keys to the kingdom."

Of the radicals who came to the United States, none had a more lasting effect than Robert Owen. He influenced future Socialist, Anarchist, and, particularly, Syndicalist thought in America. Born into a middle-class artisan family in England in 1771, Owen, although poorly educated, amassed a fortune as a textile manufacturer in New Lanark, Scotland. His operation of the New Lanark mill was a model of humanitarianism: he ran schools, protected the health of the workers in his factory, and opened a social center in this town of some 2,000. Not only did Owen improve the conditions of his workers, he also improved the profits of the mill. While at New Lanark, Owen also published several tracts and wrote letters to London newspapers decrying the condition of the working class and proposing solutions.[3] He came to America in late 1824 to set up a community along the lines he had proposed in his writings, convinced that this would prove the practicality of his scheme. At the time of his arrival in late 1824, his work was known in Jeffersonian and intellectual circles. His *New View of Society* had been republished serially in the Philadelphia Jeffersonian newspaper *Aurora* in 1817, only three years after the tract's appearance in Britain.[4] John Grissom, a professor of chemistry at Columbia University, had visited Owen's model town in Scotland during 1819 and in 1823 reported that New Lanark proved that providing for the welfare of the poor was "far more effectual as . . . regards both their morals and their happiness . . . and infinitely less expensive and oppressive than the existing system of workhouses and poor laws, and forced maintenance."[5] In 1819 Cornelius Blatchly, a graduate of Columbia University's College of Physicians and Surgeons, formed the Owenite New York Society for Promoting Commonwealths. In 1822 Blatchly's tract *An Essay on Commonwealths* was published, and in 1823 a Philadelphia Society for Promoting Communities was formed. Blatchly wanted "the most spiritual and self-denying of every religious society to form separate communities, Friends, Methodists, etc., each by themselves."[6] By 1825 Owen's popularity was so great in the United States that the essay *A Lecture on Human Happiness*, by his British disciple John Grey, went into three editions in rapid succession. At Owen's request, the *National Gazette* published William Thompson's *An Inquiry Into the Principles of the Distribu-*

tion of Wealth Most Conducive to Human Happiness; Applied to the Newly Proposed System of Voluntary Equality of Wealth. Owen himself addressed Congress twice, with President James Monroe and his cabinet, ex-President James Madison, and President-elect John Quincy Adams in attendance.[7]

The theoretical underpinnings of the Owenite system that won a great following in the United States were not too different from those that most Marxists were to accept later. Owen expostulated these views in three major addresses in the United States, before Congress on February 25 and March 7, 1825 and at New Harmony, Indiana, on July 4, 1826.

Man, he argued, was entirely the product of society. Infants "at birth are ignorant of themselves, and of all things around them." External environment formed personality. Since "individuals were always formed by circumstances," it was necessary to "govern the circumstances; and thus by means imperceptible and unknown to the individuals" to form their characters.[8] Moreover, he argued that the increase in productive capacity wrought by the industrial revolution required major social and economic changes. He believed (1) that the basis for these changes should be cooperative industry in place of competitive labor and (2) that "society, discarding large cities and solitary homes, should resolve itself into associations of fifteen hundred or two thousand persons" in which residents should jointly own land and houses while working together for the good of the community. These cooperative methods would "tend to aid, not tend to oppress, the workman."[9] These Owenite arguments have been used ever since by American radicals. His assumptions that man is the product solely of his environment and that the industrial revolution made necessary a major reorientation of society in which cooperation would replace competition have been, for almost 150 years, the keystones of the American radicals' argument. Only Owen's plea for small communes has not been universally accepted by the American Left.

Despite his democratic protestations, an antidemocratic strain was evident in Owen's philosophy. He was opposed to parliamentary government and the electoral process. Instead of favoring an elected legislature, Owen favored a form of participatory democracy, limited to a specific age group—"for instance those between thirty-five and forty-five." This, he argued, would eliminate "all the numberless evils of elections and electioneering."[10]

Owen would not compromise—the revolution had to be complete. "I mean to carry these measures of amelioration to the full extent of my means and influence into immediate execution," he told America's political leaders in March 1825. By *amelioration* he meant a complete revolution, for as Karl Bernhard, Duke of Saxe-Weimar, a contemporary traveller reported, "Mr. Owen looks forward to nothing less than to remodel the world; to root out all crime; to abolish all punishments; to create similar views and similar wants, and in this manner to avoid all dissension and warfare. . . . He was too unalterably convinced of the results, to admit the slightest room for doubt." Nor did Owen believe that the change would be evolutionary. He spoke, at times, in terms of gradual change, but even then he explained: "The change cannot be effected in a week or a month—although much, very much can be put into action next year." More often Owen insisted that the change he proposed "could not be one of slow progression, but it must take place at once, and made an immediate, and almost instantaneous, revolution in the . . . manners of the society in which it shall be introduced."[11]

Man was the slave of "*a TRINITY of the most monstrous evils that could be combined to inflict mental and physical evil upon the whole race*," Owen told his followers. This trinity was composed of "PRIVATE OR INDIVIDUAL PROPERTY—ABSURD AND IRRATIONAL SYSTEMS OF RELIGION—AND MARRIAGE FOUNDED ON INDIVIDUAL PROPERTY COMBINED WITH SOME ONE OF THESE IRRATIONAL SYSTEMS OF RELIGIONS."[12] This unholy trinity, he argued, would disappear in his new system of society. The existing trading system of "buying cheap and selling dear" was one of deception, which necessarily trained participants to seek selfish advantage. The result of this system in which "the interest of all is opposed to each" was a maldistribution of wealth and power in which the small minority virtually monopolized both while the majority suffered in poverty and subjection. Under Owen's new system, he said, no drive for great wealth would occur, because for "a few hours daily of healthy and desirable employment," every resident would earn full security and there would be "a full supply, at all times, of the best of everything for everyone." The result would be that value would be set by actual worth, that goods would not be squandered, and that all products would be used for the benefit of society.[13] Owen believed that once this system was demonstrated in a commune, the old system would break up "from necessity and inclination." The new commune would undersell the individual farmers and manufacturers, thus making their economic existence untenable. Moreover, "it is scarcely to be supposed that anyone would continue to live under the miserable, anxious, individual system of opposition and counteraction, when they could with ease form themselves into, or become members of, one of these associations of union, intelligence, and kind feeling."[14] The optimistic suppositions of this argument followed directly from Owen's theory that man's behavior is determined exclusively by his social environment. Thus man would be avaricious in a society that considered individual gain to be the primary goal of life. But Owen believed that human avarice would vanish once society had changed along the lines he proposed. For humans had a natural love of truth and a desire to benefit fellow creatures. Only the nature of contemporary society had made mankind selfish and avaricious. A simple change of the social system would change humanity into a loving community whose chief ambition would be service. The new society was to achieve this end by its very mode of operation, by education, and by the development of a system of social welfare that would protect all from the vicissitudes of illness, old age, "or any other cause."[15]

Owen's attack on the socioeconomic structure was revolutionary, for it called for a complete restructuring of society. But it was far less radical than his assaults on two of the most sacred of American institutions: religion and marriage. He charged that all organized religions had degenerated into mere superstitions that made of man "the most abject slave through the fear of non-entities created solely by his own disordered imagination." These superstitions assumed the existence of an omniscient and omnipotent Being who could and did everything. Moreover, this Being was "all-wisdom and all-goodness and all-powerful." Yet despite these powers by the all-goodness Almighty, "evil and misery superabound." To argue that " this being, who makes and does all things, is not the direct or indirect author of evil," as most divines then maintained, was a contradiction that Owen could not tolerate. "Such is the foundation on which all the mysteries and ravings of superstition are erected." The results of the "inconsistency and inconceivable folly" called religion had been "to keep the world in continued wars, and massacres, to create private divisions leading to every imaginable evil; and . . . more than its . . . [share] of the crimes and sufferings of the human race."[16] Owen's argument, one of the most cogent against most organized religion, has remained a keystone of radical anticlericalism.

The second of the sacred institutions of early nineteenth-century America against which Owen declaimed was marriage. His stance was similar to that used decades later by Marx and Engels and bears a striking resemblance to the arguments of the militant feminists and the women's liberation movement.[17] Owen said that women were treated as property by the ruling class. At the time that property was divided among the few, marriage was devised—as a means "that could . . . permit them to retain their division of the public spoils, and create to themselves an aristocracy of wealth, of power and of learning." The women were treated basically as sex objects, he argued, because it gave the ruling class the most desirable women as part of their private property, thus enslaving them. Moreover, the institutions of marriage tended to aggravate the class divisions in society by keeping the children of the poor apart from the children of the wealthy.[18]

The seeds of modern radicalism were obvious in the Owenite philosophy: the postulates that man's personality has been shaped wholly by society; that a system that guaranteed economic equality and security to all would eliminate all of the contemporary social ills; that man is inately good; that organized religion is a superstition that has created little except evil; and that marriage is an institution created by the ruling class to enhance its own economic and social position and to make women into sex objects and slaves. The roots of the visceral radicalism best exemplified in the terrorist anarcho-communism of Johann Most and the latter-day "revolutionary factions" of the Students for a Democratic Society can likewise be found in the Owenite philosophy. For to quote Owen's son William, a devout follower of his father, "mankind could never be happy so long as they continued philosophers and acted from reflection; that a natural, happy character could only be produced when mankind shall have been so trained that his feelings, habits and impulses shall always lead to do the best *without the aid of reflection.*"[19]

- 2 -

Even before Owen came to the United States, attempts were made to establish Owenite colonies in the United States. About 1822 one was reportedly formed in Virginia, but it vanished without trace shortly thereafter. Another colony was rumored to exist in Kentucky about the same time, but one Owenite who walked to its supposed location reported that none existed.[20] Despite the previous failures of such colonies, Owen was determined to establish his new commonwealth in the United States. Several Shakers, members of the Communist-Christian sect, told him they doubted that his colony could be successful, because it was not based on any specific religious doctrine. "When my father talked of establishing communities," young William Owen wrote in his diary, "they asked: of Quakers? of Jews? or what? And shook their heads when they found it was for all sects."[21]

Owen purchased the successful Rappite religious community at Harmony, Indiana, which was being moved east to the Pittsburgh area, and proceeded to organize his colony there. New Harmony, Owen's community, was established in early 1825; it had a peak membership of from 800 to 900 and lasted slightly less than two years. From the outset, Owen's insistence on following his philosophy made it impossible for the experiment to succeed. Because he supposed that all men were good at heart, and that only the environment created wicked people, Owen "admitted all men, however ignorant or vicious . . . into his village." No introduction, no examination, no references, were required. As might have been expected, New Harmony attracted, according to Owen's son Robert Dale Owen, "waifs and sharps from surrounding society; men and women of crude, ill-considered, extravagant notions, nay, worse, vagrants who regard the latest heresy but as a stalking-horse for pecuniary gain, or a convenient cloak for immoral demeanor." The community attracted the erratic as well as the corrupt. One, for example, was "a page of nature, dressed all in green, who claimed he had in olden times been a page for King David." Now, in 1825, he told Owen's son, nature "talks to me, instructs me in the way I should go, and tells me how I can best benefit my fellow creatures." The community eccentric led one Owenite to ask, "Are we *all* crazy, do you think, Robert? Have we been poking into great subjects and thinking of a world's reform, until our brains are addled and we are fit inmates of a lunatic asylum?"[22] A probationary clause in the constitution of the community, in effect from June 1825 until June 1826, was never used. All were admitted to the colony who simply signed New Harmony's constitution. The "motley assemblage" was even allowed to elect its own committee of management, although Owen retained control, and twenty-three-year-old William Owen was in complete command from June 1825 until January 1826.[23] New Harmony's economy was stagnating, because Owen, by admitting all comers, had allowed in a disproportionate number of unskilled laborers, and thus a shortage of skilled workmen resulted. Thus the manufacturing establishments left intact by the Rappites were producing far below expectations.[24]

Despite its great weaknesses, positive accomplishments in the New Harmony experiment left a lasting imprint on America. True, New Harmony was hardly the "Canaan of my hopes" that young Robert Dale Owen expected to find when he first arrived in the United States in 1825. His optimistic view of mankind and his dreams of an Eden along the banks of the Wabash simply reflected his youthful exuberance. For a time, he did find life at New Harmony "wonderfully pleasant." After all, the community had "good-fellowship and . . . the absence of conventionalism." Moreover, among those who settled at New Harmony within two or three weeks after Robert Dale Owen's arrival were outstanding intellectuals such as the naturalist Thomas Say, a founder of the Academy of Natural Sciences in Philadelphia; Charles Lesueur, a French naturalist and designer; and Gerard Troost, noted Dutch chemist and geologist, who was to become a professor of chemistry at Vanderbilt University in Nashville.[25] Also, by June 1825 130 children were being educated, boarded, and clothed at the community's expense. The free schools of New Harmony were open on equal terms to all children. This was a decade before the free public school system was organized in Indiana. New Harmony's schools were of four types: the infant school (reputedly the first in America), the higher school (the equivalent of grade school), the school for adults (children over twelve years of age), and the industrial schools. The three key men who established New Harmony's innovative educational system were William Maclure, a Scottish scientist and educator; Joseph Neef, a protégé of Johann Heinrich Pestalozzi, whose teaching methods he brought to the Western Hemisphere; and Robert Dale Owen himself, who was fresh from work in the experimental schools of New Lanark.[26] Maclure, whose work was the most significant, was interested in Owen's colony primarily because it gave him the opportunity to establish his manual training school there. It was Maclure who brought the scientists and educators to New Harmony, thus giving that frontier village "both during the experiment and after, much of its intellectual significance."[27] As with all radical groups, other "educational" activities took place. One day each week the members met to discuss things in general, another day they met to hear a concert of vocal or instrumental music, and still another day they held a public ball. This dedication to *Kultur* would normally go unnoticed, except that the bandmaster, Josiah Warren, was a Yankee member of the community who was later to begin the Individualist Anarchist movement in America.[28]

Despite the talk of equality in New Harmony, despite Robert Owen's egalitarian philosophy, sharp class distinctions developed. Robert L. Jennings, who as a Universalist minister had preached absolute equality, treated the ordinary masses at New Harmony with such disdain that he was almost censured by a public meeting. The intellectuals generally found they could not associate on even terms with the ordinary members. Thus a form of social snobbishness at New Harmony created a deep, enduring cleavage that was never overcome.[29] The inability of intellectuals and ordinary working people to associate on equal terms has remained one of the insoluble problems faced by American radicals.

Owen, who left New Harmony shortly after it was organized, returned in January 1826 and was so impressed with its progress that he ordered it reorganized under absolute Communist lines—ostensibly getting from each according to his ability and giving to each according to his needs. The real property, which belonged to Owen, was to be held "in perpetual trust forever for use of the community." Actual control was to be in the hands of all adult members of the community. New Harmony was now, according to Robert Dale Owen, "Liberty, equality, and fraternity, in downright earnest!" The plan "found favor with that heterogeneous collection of radicals, enthusiastic devotees to principle, honest latitudinarians, and lazy theorists, with a sprinkling of unprincipled sharpers thrown in." But the new order was a catastrophe. Debate replaced work; arguments became endemic. Within three weeks the new constitution was abandoned, and Robert Owen, at the insistence of most of the residents, took over the reigns of the community, placing New Harmony under his personal control. Despite the end of "democratic rule," the community did not change. A month after Owen took over, the *New Harmony Gazette* boasted that talk had ended and work had begun again. As late as May 1826, Robert Owen still maintained that "The great experiment in New Harmony is still going on, to ascertain whether a large heterogeneous mass of persons, collected by chance can be amalgamated into one community." But this was merely wishful thinking. It was soon obvious that the experiment had failed. He delayed conveying the property to the association that technically controlled New Harmony. He proposed three classes a week on the principles of the community. But interest had been dissipated; residents of New Harmony turned to trading and speculation. The *Gazette* on November 8, 1826, reported a "Want of confidence in the good intentions of each other." Shortly thereafter the community dissolved. New Harmony, Robert Owen's dream, had failed.[30]

- 3 -

Why did New Harmony fail? His sons argued that he had ignored the antisocial conditions in which the residents had been reared. They were still convinced that man's personality was shaped exclusively by his environment. But it was more than the immediate environment that was responsible for human character; the surroundings of childhood were equally important. About fifty years later, Robert Dale Owen was to change his view and blame equality of reward. "What may be safely predicted is, that a plan which remunerates all alike will, in the present condition of society ultimately eliminate from a cooperative association the skilled, efficient, and industrious members, leaving an ineffective and sluggish residue in whose hands the experiment will fail both socially and pecuniarily."[31] Thomas Low Nichols, who was for a brief time a communitarian, although never at New Harmony, blamed the "interminable speeches on how they should cultivate their fertile lands [until] seed-time . . . passed, and they had no harvest. The discussions went on, and the time came when there was nothing to eat." One historian has blamed the unwillingness to work and the lack of strong leadership.[32] Instead of work, there were social events. The schools were fine and so was the *Gazette*, but these things were essentially peripheral to what Robert Owen was preaching. The schools did have major historical significance, but they were, of themselves, not a new social order. As with most radical movements, Owen's New Harmony did bring about major social improvements. In Owen's case, it was in the development of schools, primarily of Maclure's manual-training institution. But the changes wrought by Owen, as by all other radicals, were peripheral to their theoretical base.

Some of those who came to New Harmony lost all faith in socialism. One wrote to a Christian Socialist journal, a half century later: "I was in New Harmony for two months in 1826, and have no faith in Socialistic paradises. . . . I have no confidence in such a movement unless it originates in religious motives. The bonds of mere morality drop asunder under slight pressure. At New Harmony plenty were willing to teach, tend store, or even to dig in the garden, but hard work or menial labor agreed with hardly any."[33] Some others simply withdrew from the social struggle and sought only personal gain. All had lost faith in their fellow New Harmony communitarians. Most remained Owenites, albeit inactive.

Only one critic argued that New Harmony had failed because Owen was in reality "a brother speculator in land, power, influence, riches and the glories of this world" and not a true Socialist. That critic, Paul Brown, a Quaker teacher, had been lecturing about his version of socialism since 1817. Brown had been a member of the New York Society for Promoting Commonwealths. He had attempted to join nonreligious communities whereever he heard of them. But New Harmony was the first at which he actually spent time. Unfortunately, he came to New Harmony at a bad time, April 2, 1826, in the midst of one of the many crises that rent the community during its last months of existence.[34]

He found that "instead of a 'community of equality' organized and fully settled under their new [Socialist] constitution . . . the capital cancer of the lord proprietor seemed to be to get an assemblage of people that were willing to sign a contract to pay for the estate at an appraisal that had been made, with the interest, within a certain time." Soon Brown was leading the opposition to Owen: he attended the nightly meetings; he sent missives to the *Gazette*. New Harmony at first, by his own admission, had absolute freedom of speech and press. But then, as the situation became more critical, Owen began censoring the *Gazette*.[35] Brown soon left New Harmony, but he was still writing Socialist Missives as late as the 1840s.

Brown was critical primarily of Owen's attempt to salvage as much of his financial loss as possible. For the colony had cost him dearly. Besides, a serious theoretical disagreement had developed between Brown and Owen. Brown did not believe that a man's character could be changed simply by altering his environment. His faith was in education, which would be required of all applicants in each of his proposed communities, because "they must be founded on . . . knowledge and clear conviction." Nor did Brown believe that men joined communes in a conscious effort to reshape their characters by reshaping their social environment. They had been driven to become Socialists, he argued, by the troubles they had suffered under existing conditions. These troubles had led them to reflect and thus to see "the degeneracy of fashionable politics . . . [and] the corrupt deceitfulness of the present constitution of society, they sigh to introduce and to substantiate beyond the possibility of defeat, a new and better structure . . . even a new system of social life, more congenial to truth and to nature."[36]

Brown reasoned that the capitalist system alienated man: "Mercantile ideas produce mercantile feelings—mercantile feelings produce distrust, suspicion, and avarice—distrust, suspicion, and avarice produce litigous feelings—litigous feelings produce litigation, animosity, jangling, fighting, unequal division of property, and all the endless maze of mischiefs that the most corrupt stage of society is heir to." How could one end this alienation? Only by socialism, which is but a "sort of regeneration of human character."[37]

- 4 -

Other attempts were made at forming Owenite communities in the United States, but all were failures. Owen himself returned to Great Britain where he continued working for his new society, albeit with some modification. But this period of Owenism was now dead in America. Many scholars have asserted that Robert Owen's social theories had a "brief and insignificant influence in the United States."[38] But they err, for Robert Owen has given American radicalism its theoretical underpinnings. His views have permeated American socialism; with modifications by Frances Wright and Josiah Warren, they were the basis for American anarchism, and the Industrial Workers of the World owe whatever philosophy they have to Maclure's writings at New Harmony and to Owen's Grand National Consolidation Trades Union, formed in Britain seven years after New Harmony's collapse.

NOTES

1. These data are based on various sources, particularly the United States Department of Commerce, Bureau of the Census, *Historical Statistics of the United States, 1789–1945* (Washington, D.C.: U.S. Government Printing Office, 1952), p. 149; Robert Brooke Zevin, "The Growth of Cotton Textile Production in United States," in *The Reinterpretation of American Economic History*, ed. Robert W. Fogel and Stanley L. Engleman (New York: Harper and Row, 1971), pp. 123–24; See also Samuel Eliot Morrison, Henry Steele Commager, and William E. Leuchtenberg, *The Growth of the American Republic* (New York: Oxford University Press, 1969), pp. 453–56.

2. Arthur Bestor, *Backwoods Utopias: The Sectarian Origins of the Owenite Phase of Communitarian Socialism in America, 1663–1829* (Philadelphia: University of Pennsylvania Press, 1950), p. 231, estimates that ninety-nine communitarian experiments took place between 1805 and 1855. Although Bestor is by far the most reliable historian of these communities, his estimate appears to be low.

3. Robert Owen, *A New View of Society & Other Writings*, Introduction by G. D. H. Cole (London: Everyman's Library, J. W. Dent & Son, 1927), pp. 1–90, written originally 1813–1814; See also John F. C. Harrison, *Quest for a New Moral World: Robert Owen and the Owenites in Britain and America* (New York: Scribner's, 1969).

4. Joseph Dorfman, Introduction to *Observations on the Sources and Effects of Unequal Wealth*, by Langton Byllesby (New York: Russell and Russell, 1962), p. 6; Bestor, *Backwoods Utopias*, p. 96.

5. Dorfman, Introduction to *Observations*, pp. 7–8.

6. Ibid., pp. 7–8; David Harris, *Socialist Origins in the United States: American Forerunners of Marx, 1817–1832*, includes a complete discussion of Blatchly's two major essays, *Some Causes of Popular Poverty*, and *An Essay on Commonwealths* (Assen, Netherlands: Van Gorcum and Comp., N.V., 1966), pp. 10–19. Blatchly was later (1829–1830) active in the Working Men's party of New York. See chapter 4.

7. Dorfman, Introduction to *Observations*, pp. 8–9; Joel Hiatt, ed., "Diary of William Owen from November 10, 1824 to April 25, 1825," *Indiana Historical Society Publications* 4 (1906): 35.

8. Robert Owen, *A Discourse on a New System of Society, as delivered in the Hall of Representatives of the United States in the presence of the President of the United States, the President-elect, Heads of Departments, Members of Congress & c., & c., on the 25th of February, 1825* (Washington, D.C.: Gales & Seaton, 1825; reprinted in *Robert Owen in the United States*, Oakley C. Johnson (New York: Humanities Press for the American Institute for Marxist Studies, 1970), pp. 25–27. The original was used in preparing this book; pagination, however, is from the Johnson edition, which is more readily accessible.

9. Robert Dale Owen, *Threading My Way: Twenty-seven Years of Autobiography* (New York: G. W. Carleton & Co. Publishers, 1874), p. 256.

10. Robert Owen, *A Discourse on a New System of Society; As Delivered in the Hall of Representatives of the United States: In the Presence of the President of the United States, the Ex-President, Heads of Departments, Members of Congress & c. on the 7th of March, 1825*

(Washington, D.C.: Gales & Seaton, 1825), reprinted in Johnson, *Robert Owen*, p. 51; *New Moral World*, 12 (June 8, 1844): 402; quoted in Bestor, *Backwoods Utopias*, p. 64.

11. Karl Bernhard, Duke of Saxe-Weimar, "Travels Through North America During the Years 1825 and 1826" (extracts from his book by that title published in 1828), in *Indiana as Seen by Early Travellers*, ed. Harlow Lindley (Indianapolis: Indianapolis Historical Commission, 1916), p. 428; quoted in Bestor, *Backwoods Utopias*, pp. 73–74; Owen, *Discourse* (February 25, 1825), in Johnson, *Robert Owen*, pp. 31–35; Owen, *Discourse* (March 7, 1825), in Johnson, *Robert Owen*, p. 50.

12. Robert Owen, "Oration, containing (A Declaration of Mental Independence, Delivered in the Public Hall, at New Harmony, Indiana, at the Celebration of the Fourth of July 1826)," in Johnson, *Robert Owen*, p. 70. Italics and capitalization in original.

13. Owen, *Discourse* (February 25, 1825), in Johnson, *Robert Owen*, pp. 32–33.

14. Owen, *Discourse* (March 7, 1825), in Johnson, *Robert Owen*, p. 52.

15. Owen, *Discourse* (February 25, 1825), in Johnson, *Robert Owen*, pp. 29, 33, 62.

16. Owen, *Oration* (July 4, 1826), in Johnson, *Robert Owen*, p. 71.

17. See, for example, Karl Marx and Friedrich Engels, *The Communist Manifesto*, reprinted in Robert C. Tucker, ed., *The Marx-Engels Reader* (New York: W. W. Norton 1972), pp. 338–49; Friedrich Engels, *Socialism Utopian and Scientific*, in Tucker, *The Marx-Engels Reader*, p. 608.

18. Owen, *Oration* (July 4, 1826), in Johnson, *Robert Owen*, p. 81. Owen's position regarding religion is almost identical with that of Thomas Paine. See Paine, *The Age of Reason* (London: T. Williams, 1796).

19. Hiatt, "Diary of William Owen," p. 61.

20. Paul Brown, *Twelve Months at New Harmony* (Cincinnati: Wim. Hill Woodard, 1827), pp. 4–5.

21. Hiatt, "Diary of William Owen," p. 14.

22. Robert Dale Owen, *Threading My Way*, pp. 259, 264–68; George E. McNeill, ed., *The Labor Movement of Today* (Boston: A. M. Bridgman and Co., 1887), p. 72.

23. McNeill, *Labor Movement*, pp. 259–60; Bestor, *Backwoods Utopias*, pp. 122, 161.

24. Bestor, *Backwoods Utopias*, p. 162.

25. Robert Dale Owen, *Threading My Way*, pp. 263–64, 267–68, 270, 275–76.

26. Ibid., pp. 260, 283–84; Elinor Pancoast and Anne E. Lincoln, *The Incorrigible Idealist: Robert Dale Owen in America* (Bloomington, Ind.: The Principia Press, 1940), pp. 2–4.

27. Richard William Leopold, *Robert Dale Owen: A Biography* (Cambridge, Mass.: Harvard University Press, 1979), pp. 27–28.

28. Robert Dale Owen, *Threading My Way*, pp. 260, 276.

29. Bernhard, "Travels," p. 431; Bestor, *Backwoods Utopias*, pp. 178–79.

30. Robert Dale Owen, *Threading My Way*, pp. 285–88; *New Harmony Gazette* 1 (March 22, 1826): 207.

31. Quoted in Robert Dale Owen, *Threading My Way*, pp. 289–90.

32. Leopold, *Robert Dale Owen*, pp. 31–38; Thomas Low Nichols, *Forty Years of American Life* (New York: Stackpole Sons, 1937), p. 238.

33. *American Socialist* 1 (September 28, 1876): 213.

34. Paul Brown, *Twelve Months*, pp. 3–5, 9–11, 13–14.

35. Ibid., pp. 13–14, 16, 71.

36. Ibid., pp. 42–43.

37. Ibid., pp. 6, 17–18, 69.

38. See, for example, Leopold, *Robert Dale Owen*, pp. 26–27.

The Owenites

The failure of New Harmony did not dampen the ardor of all American radicals. A few attempted to set up new colonies; some turned to religious communities, convinced that man alone could not achieve the perfect universe, and others set about "righting" what they assumed to be Owen's errors. Six of the Owenites who tried to revise his system and, in so doing, left their own imprint on the American Left were Langdon Byllesby, Thomas Skidmore, Frances Wright, Robert Dale Owen, Orestes Brownson, and Josiah Warren.

- 1 -

Byllesby, a native of Philadelphia, was a printer and editor who wrote only one small book on socialism—in 1826. Yet the imprint he left on American socialism was great, and he was quoted by Socialists long after his death.[1]

Although basically an Owenite, Byllesby disagreed with his mentor in at least three particulars: (1) he rejected Owen's belief in the equality of the sexes; (2) although he favored communes, he warned that they failed to include the "immense and important interests with valuable uses embraced in the composition of large cities"; and (3) he favored hard money rather than "labor notes," which Owen preferred.[2] These were, however, minor differences when compared to the broad areas of agreement, for both believed that the industrial revolution had made the competitive system obsolete. Both agreed that a new cooperative system had to replace the outmoded capitalist order. Their chief points of difference were about means rather than ends.

Thus although Owen did not limit his following to members of the working class, Byllesby argued, in language foretelling the rhetoric of latter-day revolutionaries, that only the workers could win their own emancipation. He wrote in 1826:

. . . reform must receive its chief impulse . . . [from] those whose labor is the origin of wealth which they do not enjoy. . . . History does not furnish an instance wherein the depository of power voluntarily abrogated its prerogatives, or the oppressor relinquished his advantage in favor of the oppressed. . . . [When] a radical alteration has taken place, that went to ameliorate the general condition, or that of a particular section, it has uniformly been impelled, prosecuted and finally adjusted by the sufferers.[3]

He was convinced that the suffering workers could expect no support in their struggle against the competitive system from either the learned or the rich. The learned, in an effort to safeguard their monopoly of knowledge, would naturally oppose equality. The rich—who are interested primarily in increasing their own wealth—cannot understand the privation and suffering of the poor.[4] Since Byllesby believed that self-interest was a basic law of nature, it followed that he would not expect any help for the exploited workers from those who benefit from that exploitation.

Byllesby argued that although "hard money" ostensibly was based on gold or silver, and "labor notes" were based ostensibly on time worked, both really represented wealth, and wealth was a product of labor. Money and wealth were not the same. "Money is not intrinsically wealth; it is only an accredited representative of it." Thus it made little difference which type of money was made the representative of wealth; all were based essentially on labor.[5]

Instead of merely building rural communes, Byllesby proposed that the workers in a given industry form their own producer cooperatives and opt out of the capitalist system by refusing to work for employers. He suggested a somewhat complex system that called upon the workers in each industry to form small urban cooperatives in which each worker—and thus each stockholder—would own one share. These cooperatives, which he called associations, would form federations and finally, through "a general system of conference," a voluntary national body of associations.[6] In Byllesby's proposal can be found the roots of American Syndicalist thought: the basic essentials of the cooperative ventures of the National Labor Union under William Sylvis, the grand cooperative schemes that were discussed within the Knights of Labor, and the new industrial society of which the theoreticians of the post-1908 Industrial Workers of the World (IWW) dreamed.

Byllesby made two other contributions to radical theory. Although he was no pacifist, Byllesby rejected violence. Using language that recalled statements by Socialists one hundred years later, Byllesby declared that "though violence may change the operation of oppressive circumstances, yet the very means of violence plant anew the seeds from which it must again spring up and grow with renewed vigour."[7] About war, Byllesby took a position that would in more modern times be called Marxist. Writing twenty-two years before Marx and Engels produced the *Communist Manifesto*, Byllesby blamed war upon the competitive economic system. Wars may ostensibly be fought to regain lost possessions, or to extend domain, he said, but "these objects have no other uses, than as a source from whence to drive the means of extracting *wealth*, and its accompaniment, *power*, in order to influence the condition of others."[8]

Byllesby, unlike the other radicals, formed no movement; he lived in no commune; and except for a short period as editor and publisher of an anti-Jeffersonian journal in Easton, Pennsylvania, he was not particularly active in politics. Yet his theories have had a great deal of influence among radicals, few of whom ever heard his name.

- 2 -

In contrast to Byllesby, Thomas Skidmore was, at least during the latter part of his short life, a political activist and a founder of one of America's first labor parties.[9] Skidmore, a Connecticut Yankee, was born in 1790. As a young man he taught school for a few years in New Jersey, Virginia, and North Carolina. Skidmore also spent some time in chemical and mechanical research in Wilmington and Philadelphia before moving to New York in 1819. In New York he worked as a machinist, became active in radical politics, and wrote his major work, *The Rights of Man to Property!* in 1829. He died in 1832 during New York's cholera epidemic.[10]

Skidmore was antagonistic toward Owen, and he argued that New Harmony was in fact no experiment in Socialist living, "everything being in the proprietorship and under the dictation of a few Aristocratic speculating theorists."[11] The criticisms were reminiscent of those made previously by Paul Brown, whom he was apparently paraphrasing. Despite this outburst against New Harmony, a lot of Owenite influence could be seen in Skidmore's work, which may have come indirectly through the works of Cornelius Blatchly and Byllesby.[12] Also traces of individualist anarchism and a large dose of the Protestant ethic were evident in his works. Skidmore believed that all property should be redistributed to make absolute equality in ownership. Moreover, he suggested that property should belong to an individual during his lifetime only and that it should not be inheritable.

Lack of equality in property, he argued, was the cause of the downfall of nations. His was not a plan for collectivization; it was rather a plea for individualism, for he insisted that each person should own his own property and that each "should labor . . . *exclusively* for himself." He considered great wealth to be as dangerous "as a sword or a pistol" in a robber's hands, because it could be used to "extort from others their property in their personal qualities and efforts." He called upon the exploited to wrest excessive property from the exploiters—similar to the Marxists' call for expropriating the expropriators. The owners might have a right to their property, Skidmore said, but they "have no right to use it in such a manner as to extract from others the result of their labors." This followed naturally from Skidmore's postulate that "all men should live on their own labor, and not on the labor of others." The only way to eliminate the ills of the world, he maintained, was to eliminate "[these] dividends, these rents, these profits."[13] His simplistic version of what Marx was to call "surplus value" has continued to be echoed by Socialists until the present. His stance on exploitation as a form of robbery has remained unaltered in the radical's lexicon.

Man's right to property was thus the basic theme of Skidmore's theory. It was as "sacred or unalienable" as man's right to life or liberty. It was necessary to acquire property to pursue happiness. Did not man feel the need daily to endanger "both liberty and health and ultimately life, into the bargain" in his search for property? The very rights of life and liberty were precarious without property. The right to life and liberty was, therefore, "but an empty name" without property.[14]

If Skidmore's views of property were clear-cut, his theories about government were basically contradictory. He argued in Anarchist terms when he claimed that government was instituted among men as a means of formalizing inequitable ownership of property. Thus "all governments in the world have begun wrong." Since government had legitimized the evil of unequal property, it now had the duty of righting that wrong; else it would be an "unauthorized institution, alienating the 'inalienable right,' with which the creator has endowed all men." But Skidmore had grave doubts that government could right that wrong; in fact, he hinted broadly that as the conditions of the people worsened, as he was sure they would, the people would rebel against government. Only where "tyrants have sufficient discretion" to revolutionize the social structure gradually could government survive. Having thus shown his disdain for the state, Skidmore reversed his field and declared his faith in representative democracy. He argued that the people "hold in their hands, through the silent, peaceful, and irresistible operation of the ballot-boxes, the power to establish it [Skidmore's Utopia], as the basis of their social compact." Having called for peaceful, parliamentary methods of revolution, he again turned 360 degrees and argued for the right of the impoverished masses to take the law into their own hands. Should a new machine threaten to add to their economic woes, Skidmore called upon them to "LAY HOLD OF IT, AND MAKE IT THEIR OWN." He added, "LET THEM APPROPRIATE ALSO, in the same way, THE

COTTON FACTORIES, THE WOOLEN FACTORIES, THE IRON
FOUNDARIES, THE ROLLING MILLS, HOUSES, CHURCHES, SHIPS,
GOODS, STEAMBOATS, FIELDS OF AGRICULTURE, & c, & c."[15]

Having thus delineated his just society, Skidmore proposed a "practical"
plan for bringing it to fruition. He wanted the state of New York to call a
constitutional convention that would proclaim immediately an end to all
debts, renounce all property held by New Yorkers in other states, and seize
all property and redistribute it among all citizens on a basis as nearly equal
as possible. When New Yorkers died, their property was to be divided
among citizens coming of age. Since property would now be distributed
equally, Skidmore proposed that charity, gifts, and gambling be made fel-
ony crimes, because they might tend to create an imbalance of wealth, and
gifts could be used to circumvent laws against inheritance.[16]

Skidmore expected to accomplish his revolution within months after his
book appeared. He was convinced that once people were informed of his
plan, they would flock to join his crusade. He had great faith in his program
and in the ability of Americans to discern truth from error. Any just and
workable plan published "in clear and plain language," Skidmore argued,
would win the immediate support of the American people. "The *printing
press*, together with the population of the whole state or Empire being instructed and rendered capable of reading;—together, also, with the possession by every individual of such population, *of the right of sufferage*; put it
out of the power of a few to defeat, frustrate or delay for any considerable
time the wishes of the many."[17] Most radicals have been optimistic; some
have even dreamed of "socialism in our time," but few have equalled Skidmore's naivete.

Besides his plan to equalize property holdings, Skidmore suggested immediate political and social reforms, many of which have since been enacted in whole or part. He was an early advocate of suffrage for women and
blacks. He was vehemently opposed to child labor. He wanted the government to support all children, maintaining that the "tender years" should be
devoted to education. In addition, more than a hundred years before social
security, Skidmore maintained that the government was obligated to provide for the aged. In effect, Skidmore proposed a genuine cradle-to-grave
welfare state.[18]

He favored universal military service and objected to conscientious ob-
jectors on the ground that others had to fight to defend their property. Said
Skidmore:

He who will not defend his property; and in such manner as the government of his
country prescribes, *has abandoned it already*. Tell us not of the rights of conscience.
He has no conscience who, in the first place, would abandon that which is truly his

own to the invader, and then, after it has been defended against the enemy, by the blood of others, *would come and claim it again!* He has no conscience who desires to hold his own at the expense of the blood and treasure of another.[19]

His conservative contemporaries called Skidmore an agrarian, a term of derision in early nineteenth-century America derived from the aristocratic agrarian reformers of antiquity who seized and divided among serfs parts of great estates.[20] but the appellation was hardly deserved; Skidmore was no more an agrarian in his views than were many other reformers. At least one historian has attempted to link him to Henry George's "Single Tax" theory.[21] But this over-simplifies Skidmore's thesis, for property in the sense that he was using the word meant more than simply land and real property; it meant all goods including land. Skidmore was "a talented, bold, and honest reformer."[22] Hobart Berrian, who helped lead the opposition to him in the Workingmen's party, recalled that "though ultra in many of his political sentiments, [Skidmore] was an ardent supporter of the true interests of the working-classes and a never-tiring devotee in the worship of human liberty."[23] Moreover, he helped lay the foundation for the American radical movements that followed.

- 3 -

Frances Wright was the most notorious of the early American radicals. But her notoriety was based more on her rhetoric than her action. For despite her revolutionary speeches and writings, her actions—and she was as much an activist as a thinker—were invariably moderate, and they had a tempering effect on more radical activists. Her opposition to slavery was, despite her bold talk, limited to a circumspect plan that was conservative by comparison to proposals by even the least fiery of Abolitionists. In the Workingmen's party, Wright allied herself with the less-radical wing in opposition to Skidmore's revolutionary "agrarianism." Her brave talk of women's rights was, in reality, little more than talk. Yet she was a significant radical thinker, a precursor of the revolutionary anarchism later expostulated by Emma Goldman and Alexander Berkman and of the women's liberation movement of the 1960s and 1970s.

Fanny Wright, as she was known popularly, was born in Dundee, Scotland, in 1795. Her mother and father died when she was only two-and one-half years old, and she and her sister Camilla were raised in London by their grandparents. Her upbringing was proper for an upper middle-class English girl.[24]

In 1819 she and her sister sailed to America where they spent a year. This visit to America was crucial in her development as a radical intellectual. First, she stayed in New York at the home of the widow of Theobald Wolfe

Tone, leader of the ill-fated Irish revolutionary movement of 1798. Second, her play *Altorf*, a paean to liberty, was performed in New York while she was there and it was well received. Among those impressed with the play was Thomas Jefferson, who was to become an acquaintance. Finally, letters she sent to a friend in Glasgow, dealing with a trip she took across the northeastern United States, were published as a book, *Views of Society and Manners in America*.[25] The book was uncritical in its praise of the United States. Admittedly, she had not visited the southern states, because "slavery is revolting everywhere, but to inhale the impure breath of its pestilence in the free winds of America is odious beyond all the imagination can conceive." Wright had allowed her enthusiasm to blur her vision. The United States of 1819 was hardly the paradise she pictured. Corruption was rife, the franchise was limited, frontier crudeness abounded, and poverty was everywhere. But the twenty-three year-old romantic was so in love with the United States, she was blind to its faults.[26]

As a result of the publication of her book, she was invited to the London home of philosopher Jeremy Bentham, the lion of England's intellecttual society. There she met many of the most illustrious of London's literati, and the seventy-three-year-old Bentham became her fast friend. The book also brought her to the notice of the Marquis de Lafayette, who invited her to his summer home in France. He even proposed adopting Wright and her sister, but objections from his family prevented it.[27]

Lafayette convinced her to become involved, as he was, in the democratic revolutionary movement of the 1820s. Thus when the revolutions in Italy and Spain collapsed, she lost hope in Europe and returned to America, which she was convinced was the only country "in which human progress was rendered at once safe and certain, by the nature of its institutions, and the condition and character of its people."[28]

Upon her return to the United States, Frances Wright became engrossed in two issues: communitarianism and slavery. She set out to observe the cooperative communities and to study laws relating to slavery. In 1825, accompanied by her sister Camilla, she travelled west to the Rappite colonies at Economie, Pennsylvania, and Harmonie, Indiana, which Owen was about to take over, and to several other religious colonies. These religious communities antagonized her. She found in all of them that "Christian fanaticism and subjection were means employed to stultify the intelligence, and hold the physical man submitted to the will of others." She found no scientific advances, no laboratories, and no "scientific workshops devoted to aid the progress of invention and the sublime conquest of matter by mind." she found at these communities

no men and women, beaming with intelligence and that joy of the soul, the necessary result of worldly independence . . . and no rising generations trained to excellence . . . and promising to start ahead of their predecessors and to be themselves vanquished in their turn by successors profiting by their example and experience and by the ever accumulating knowledge and capital of society.[29]

Her interest in the slave question was as intense as it was recent. In *New Views of Society and Manners in America*, Wright discussed slavery in a cursory manner. She found the slaveholders in Virginia to be humane. Yet she believed it would be wise to end slavery completely, although she wanted it to be done gradually and after the slaves were prepared for freedom. To give "liberty to a slave before he understands its value is, perhaps, rather to impose a penalty than to bestow a blessing."[30] She had little sympathy with the Abolitionists, who she argued showed "much zeal with little knowledge." Moreover, they were prone to "carry all things with struggle and violence, and to believe that their own view of every subject is precisely the right one."[31] She blamed slavery on Britain, claiming that the colonies themselves, particularly Virginia, had attempted to outlaw the slave trade. Had not slavery itself been abolished by the Americans, except where "the number of slaves was sufficient to render an act of enfranchisement menacing to major interests of public order, industry, and the general welfare of the country."[32]

Once having decided to become involved in the attempt to end slavery in the United States, Wright devoted her whole energies to the task. During the winter of 1824–1825, she travelled to James Madison's home, Montpelier, Virginia, with Lafayette, to study the problem. She discussed it with planters in the region as well as with the former president. She decided, on the basis of these talks, that slavery could be abolished, without financial loss to the South, providing it was not done precipitously. Moreover, Wright believed that simply freeing the slaves would do them no good and might even harm them. Thus she decided that it would be necessary to prepare the blacks for freedom and pay the owners for their losses. To achieve this end, she decided it was necessary to organize colonies at which they would be trained and in which they could work until they could buy their freedom.

She published her plan in a tract called "A Plan for Gradual Abolition of Slavery in the United States Without Danger or Loss to Citizens of the South." It soon won the support of Madison, James Monroe, Chief Justice John Marshall, Thomas Jefferson, and Benjamin Lundy, the antislavery Quaker, editor of *The Genius of Universal Emancipation*, which was later to be instrumental in the downfall of her colony.[33]

Her proposal was neither original nor particularly revolutionary. Lafayette had organized a similar colony in his estate, La Belle Gabrielle, in Cayenne, French Guiana, that failed. The plan Wright proposed was almost a carbon copy of one suggested earlier by James Madison's long-time secretary Edward Coles.[34] Nor was the aim of her plan particularly radical. It was designed to make the end of slavery gradual and painless and to prevent the rebellion that some of the Abolitionists favored. As for the freed slaves, they were to be trained in the crafts and shipped to California or Texas—then barely civilized—or Haiti, a black nation whose primary attributes were poverty and violence, She was, in fact, more interested in avoiding dislocation for southern whites than in equality, opportunity, and freedom for the black slaves. Her stance was to change later, but her reasons for proposing and organizing the colony were basically conservative.

Within months after she had published her proposal, Wright was at work organizing the first colony. With moderate Abolitionist George Flower, she purchased 300 acres of Wolf River bottom land near Memphis, Tennessee, from William Lawrence and William A. Davis, who were friends and assignees of Andrew Jackson. Additional purchases soon increased the size of the plot to 1940 acres. Wright expected financial help from her friends and from others who opposed slavery, but she received almost none. Lafayette, despite rumors that he had contributed $10,000, gave her no money. Only a New York Quaker, Jeremiah Thompson, sent supplies as a gift. She and Flowers "had only their own funds to rely on."[35] Even Thomas Jefferson, who approved of her plan wholeheartedly, refused to get involved in Nasnoba—as her colony was known. He wrote her: "At the age of eighty-two, with one foot in the grave, and the other uplifted to follow, I do not permit myself to take part in any new enterprises . . . not even in the great one which has been through life that of my greatest anxieties."[36] Madison and Monroe both supported her work morally, although Madison doubted it would meet with speedy success.

She planned to teach the slaves "farming, stock-raising, carpenter-work, shoe-making, black-smithing, meat-curing, cooking, house-work, sewing, weaving, and spinning . . . according to the sex of the pupil with some rudimentary knowledge of reading and writing." The entire plan resembled what was already being done on the plantations of Virginia, where "useful crafts" were taught so slaves could be of greater use to their masters.[37]

Financial problems plagued Wright's plan from the beginning. She had hoped to build a colony for one hundred slaves, which she believed would be the minimum required to attract national attention, and thus become the nucleus of future colonies culminating in total emancipation. But this would have required $41,000, and Wright had only $17,000. She could, therefore, buy only ten slaves and begin construction of her community. In early 1826 the slaves and three white associates arrived at Nashoba and began the backbreaking job of transforming the uncultivated bottom land into tillable acreage. The white arrivals were to be the key figures in the operation of Nashoba. They were her sister Camilla, her Scottish friend James Richardson, and Richard Whitby, a long-time communitarian who had been a Shaker and a resident of New Harmony.[38]

None worked harder than the overenthusiastic Frances Wright. She toiled along with the slaves from early morning until late at night, until she was struck ill when an epidemic swept the colony. The illness forced her to withdraw from the active control of the community and move north to New Harmony. She turned the control of Nashoba over to a ten-man board of trustees, including illustrious names such as LaFayette; Robert Owen; Cadwallader Colden, a noted lawyer, who was later to be mayor of New York; and Robert Dale Owen. But the community was under the effective control of Camilla Wright; Richard Whitby, whom she was soon to marry; and James Richardson, the only trustees who lived there. When Robert Dale Owen visited Nashoba several months after Frances Wright had left, he found it a forbidding place, with poor soil, bad housing, and lackadaisical labor. He stayed only a short time and returned to New Harmony where Wright was still seriously ill. In May he and the ailing Wright sailed for France via New Orleans.[39]

Before she left for Europe, Frances Wright instructed her trustees to educate the black and white children on equal terms, and she insisted that all of the residents of Nashoba were to work on an equal basis. She also stipulated that each slave's labor should be paid for, and that when it reached a value of $6,000 plus 6 percent interest, he or she should be freed. But it was soon apparent that her plan was, at best, a dream. Whitby was a fanatical Quaker and communitarian, whose only background for his role as leader of Nashoba was a short apprenticeship as overseer in a Shaker community. He was also too deeply involved romantically with Camilla Wright to pay much heed to his responsibilities at Nashoba. Richardson, who became the de facto leader of the colony was a convinced and aggressive atheist and materialist who believed in absolute equality of all people and who opposed marriage. Moreover he believed in publicizing his nonconformism, and this was the immediate cause for the collapse of the community.[40]

Richardson organized daily meetings with the slaves at which they were lectured on their behavior or heard a talk in favor of free love or a discourse on the metaphysical differences between slaves and free men. He sent detailed reports on these meetings to Lundy's religious-abolitionist journal, *The Genius of Universal Emancipation.* The meetings from May 20 until June 17, 1827, are reported in the journal. On June 1 Richardson reported a meeting at which a slave girl had reported an attempt by a male slave to rape her. She asked for a lock on her door, but it was refused. Said the report to the *Genius,*

Our views on the sexual relation have repeatedly been given the slaves; Camilla

Wright again stated it, and informed the slaves that, as the conduct of Redrick [the male slave] which he did not deny, was a gross infringement of that view, a repetition of such conduct by him, or by any other of the men, ought in her opinion, to be punished by flogging. She repeated that we consider the proper basis of the sexual intercourse to be the unconstrained and unrestrained choice of both parties.

This report created considerable scandal among the puritanical Quaker Abolitionists who read Lundy's publication. The final crushing blow came sixteen days later when *The Genius* of *Universal Emancipation* reported: "Met the slaves—James Richardson informed them that, last night, Mademoiselle and he began to live together; and he took this occasion of repeating to them our views on color, and on the sexual relation." Mademoiselle Josephine was the free Octoroon daughter of Mademoiselle Lolotte, a New Orleans woman who taught at Nashoba. The openness with which Richardson boasted of his violating the mores against miscegenation and "unsanctified" marriage created a scandal of unprecedented proportions. Readers of the *Genius* cried out, "What is this but the creation of one great brothel." Even Lundy was upset by this latest escapade. Only Camilla Wright and Richardson stood fast.[41] When news of the scandal reached Frances Wright—in England—she left with her friend Frances M. Trollope almost immediately. She also wrote a long letter to the *Memphis Advocate and Western-District Advocate* in which she absolved the trustees and took full responsibility for the incident. She denied no charge. She criticized American political and social mores: True, the United States had political liberty, but that was less than half of genuine freedom, for the United States had no moral liberty. Freedom of speech, she argued, was being throttled by personal prejudice. Moreover, "liberty without equality, what is it but a chimera?" Her objective in Nashoba was to prove that moral liberty—liberty plus equality—could exist. To achieve this end, marriage had to be abolished and the races amalgamated.[42] Her support for miscegenation, although radical for the time, was hardly original. Her best friends in Memphis had been Marcus Winchester, the first mayor of Memphis, and his wife, Mary, a French Quadroon.[43]

On her return, Wright found Nashoba in shambles. Trollope reported that "one glance sufficed to convince me, that every idea I had formed of the place was as far as possible from the truth. Desolation was the only feeling, the only word that presented itself."[44] Not even a school had been established. Her former friends, including Madison, had turned against her. The community had run out of money. By mid-1828 Frances Wright conceded that her experiment had failed. In a last act of humanitarianism, she took the thirty-one slaves at Nashoba—eighteen adults and thirteen children—to Haiti, at her personal expense. There she freed them after first obtaining land for them from the Haitian government.[45] Thus ended the Nashoba experiment.

Nashoba has been called the model from which Booker T. Washington patterned Tuskegee Institute's vocational-professional educational system. It has been labeled "the first industrial training school for Negroes that was ever attempted in this country." Frances Wright's "experiment in self-emancipation," her biographer claimed, "was one of the few real efforts made to solve the problems of American slavery." In fact, it was none of these things, for although its founder spoke of vocational education, it offered virtually none; although it appeared to be an experiment in self-emancipation, it demonstrated little. It was merely an interesting exercise in futility. One result of Nashoba was to disillusion Frances Wright and eventually to turn her against the Negro.[46]

Although it dealt a blow to her ego, the demise of Nashoba was not as great a tragedy to Wright as might have been expected. For she had come to believe even before the end of the experiment that economic factors would end slavery in a few years.[47] By this time, she was also becoming involved in issues that now appeared to her to be of more significance than slavery. She became a momentary figure in New York City politics, and she was active in the struggle for free public education, against ecclesiastical domination, and for the amelioration of the condition of the working class. She also edited a newspaper in New York. Within a year after the collapse of Nashoba, Wright published a series of articles in which she expounded her political and social philosophy. She had, as Orestes Brownson pointed out, "hit upon a just medium between the individualism of Godwin and the communism of Owen." In so doing she developed revolutionary, or Communist, anarchism that Prince Peter Kropotkin was to enunciate some sixty years later.[48]

Frances Wright recognized the existence of a class war. "What distinguishes the present from every other struggle in which the human race has been engaged," she wrote in 1830, is

that the present is, evidently, openly, and acknowledgedly a war of class. . . . It is no longer nation pitched against nation . . . nor sect cutting the throats and roasting the carcasses of sect for the greater glory of God and satisfaction of priests. . . . No; it is now everywhere the oppressed millions who are making common cause against oppression . . . it is labor rising against idleness, industry against money, justice against law and against privilege . . . Until all classes shall be merged into one . . . by gradual and fundamental changes in the whole organization of society, much bad feeling must prevail everywhere.[49]

The class war, Wright argued, was caused by man's progress and two great evils: coercive government and inequality of condition. Progress had made it possible for man to see the "two great evils" she believed the laboring classes were destined to abolish. Thus progress plus the "two great evils" equalled class war.

She defined government by violence as any form of coercive rule. She opposed the constraining power of government, whether "administered in the form of despotic executive authority, coercive law, or terrifying superstition." Every government that had ever existed was a coercive government, because every government since time immemorial had three objectives: Obedience, restraint, and constraint. Forms of government had varied, but this did not matter, for the principle remained the same. Government presupposed that "man is a vicious animal in need of constraint . . . a tiger ever on the alert to tear his neighbor to pieces." Thus all laws ever enacted had started from this wrong principle, and "the root being rotten, the tree must be unsound."[50]

What of the law? Frances Wright considered law the worst product of an evil system. "It can make a bad cause a good one, and a good a bad one. It can imprison a wretch when poverty hath driven him to steal or hang another when passion has hurried him to murder. It can give to lies the solemnity of an oath, secure fraud within the forms of justice; substitute fraudulent bankruptcy for highway robbery, and prove right and might to be with the biggest purse." Her answer to the woes of the world was to end all government. She believed that "We are better off because we are less governed, [for] . . . coercion is a principle at war with the nature of all sentient existence."[51]

Regarding religion, Frances Wright was an agnostic rather than an atheist. She considered the question of God's existence to be beyond man's ken. No man could know anything of the issues raised by religion; thus the whole question was not worth discussing. It was all idle speculation. She argued that organized religion, which was based on something of which it knew nothing, and which ruled by coercion on that basis, was one of the gravest evils on earth. It replaced rationality with irrationality as the basis for human actions. She proposed that the study of religion be halted and that instead man study "your own body . . . your own mind, and . . . the fair material world which extends around you." Religion was the result of ignorance. "The less we know of this world, the more we imagine of others." The more man understood the world about him the less would he need supernatural agencies. She proposed turning all churches into halls of science—she did, in fact, purchase the Ebenezer Baptist Church in New York, which she turned into a lecture hall that she labeled "Hall of Science."[52]

The great hope for overthrowing the inequitous system was, according to Frances Wright, education. Unless the people were educated, "the churches may preach damnation, the legislatures enact penalties, and the city corporations erect prisons and poorhouses." The inequality of condition could not be eradicated unless the people realized their power. Then and only then could inequality and coercive government—law and organized religion—be eliminated. Despite her interest in education, Frances Wright despised many of the so-called learned professions. She argued that the "lawyer . . . lives by his quarrels" and the "physician . . . lives by his disease." What she meant by education was not the ordinary schooling of her day, but preparation for the remaking of society. She expected education to help level society by abolishing social distinctions in the classroom and by teaching "useful" trades. She proposed that physical science be the prime subject taught, because it was the best discipline for developing rational minds: "the only corrective . . . to superstition is physical science." She also wanted history studied so man could check the present with the past. Her plan called for "National, Rational, Republican Education; Free for All at the Expense of All; Conducted under the Guardianship of the State. And for The Honor, The Happiness, The Virtue, The Salvation of The State."[53]

Almost as radical as her views on education were her economic views. She cited Benjamin Franklin's estimate that four hours a day labor by each adult would insure abundance. Given the more developed state of industrial development, she surmised that only two hours labor would be needed each day. To achieve this end, it would be necessary to eliminate the nonproducing consumers: "priests, lawyers, soldiers, merchants, traders, bankers, brokers, capitalists, to say nothing of fine ladies and gentlemen." It would also be necessary to eliminate useless production of unneeded items "satisfying of artificial wants, supplying vain luxuries, and feeding vice, idleness, and intemperance." Moreover, she proposed ending the system of rewarding labor "in a reverse ratio to its utility." To achieve this end she proposed a five-point plan: (1) purchase of private property by society; (2) a free, universal educational system; (3) social security; (4) payment on the basis of work done; and (5) a press controlled by editors elected by the people.[54]

Educational reform, economic change, dismemberment of government, and abolition of organized religion were all vital issues, but on none was Wright as vehement as on women's rights. She was an early advocate of birthcontrol, arguing that big families meant starvation for working-class families. She described the loss of property rights by women at marriage as robbery. "I would ask every father not absolutely dead to all human feeling how he can permit his daughters blindly to immolate all their rights, liberties, and property by the simple utterance of a word, and thus place themselves in their tender, ignorant and unsuspecting youth, as completely at the disposal and mercy of an individual, as is the Negro slave who is bought for gold in the slave market of Kingston or New Orleans." She lashed out at the marriage laws, for which she blamed the church. The law, she maintained, was unfair to talented women who "shrink equally from the servitude of marriage and the approbrium stamped upon unlegalized connections." She wanted all marriage laws repealed, and until legal marriage was abolished, she favored easier divorce laws.[55]

Despite her objections to marriage, Frances Wright sailed to France in 1830 to marry Phiquepal Casimir Sylvan D'Arusmont, a French educator who had been in New Harmony. The marriage was unhappy, and after bearing two children, one of whom died, she returned to the United States in 1835. She eventually divorced D'Arusmont in Memphis.[56] By the time she married D'Arusmont, Wright was a tired and disillusioned revolutionary. "We have all sacrificed too much of our worldly ease in attempts to better human society," she wrote to the aging Robert Owen.[57] Although she still toured the country as a lecturer, and although she was still considered an anathema by conservatives and clergymen, Frances Wright was no longer interested in revolutions or radical schemes. At forty, she was a tired, old, ex-revolutionist, who had served her cause and left a heritage that remains viable more than 140 years later.

- 4 -

Two of the three remaining Owenites are only peripheral to the study of American radicalism, except insofar as they demonstrate the endemic nature of deradicalization in the American Left.[58] Both Robert Dale Owen and Orestes Brownson were briefly involved with American radicalism; both were tenuously allied for a few months in the Workingmen's party of New York. But neither remained in the American Left for any length of time: Owen went from radical reformer to western Democratic politician to Spiritualist; Brownson stopped only briefly in the Socialist ranks on his voyage from Presbyterian to liberal Universalist to Unitarian to conservative Roman Catholic convert.

Owen, born in New Lanark, Scotland, arrived in the United States in 1825, one day before his twenty-fourth birthday. He went almost immediately to his father's community at New Harmony, where he was active in the development of schools and the editing of its newspaper. His views during that period were almost identical with those of his father. He believed character was solely the product of environment and viewed education as a chief determinant of that environment. It was for this reason that he favored a system of compulsory boarding schools where children could learn under conditions of nearly absolute equality. Young Owen accepted his father's postulate that industrial capitalism had failed and that only the establishment of small, self-sufficient Socialistic communities—united in a loose federation—could solve the social problems engendered by modern society. He favored greater use of labor-saving machinery—in a Socialist society—but warned that it would be a curse in the existing social system where pecuniary profit was considered the primary human goal. He opposed marriage ceremonies as illogical and considered "indissoluble unions" to be dangerous. As editor of the *New Harmony Gazette*, he was critical of customs of modern society—proposing reforms of English grammar, medicine, and female fashions and assailing the government's proclivity for building roads rather than schools. Moreover, he questioned the basic theological precepts of organized religion—particularly Christianity—and assailed Sabbatarianism.[59]

The failure of New Harmony had a profound effect on young Owen. It turned him away from communitarianism—although he did not abandon his radical egalitarianism and socialism. He became a strong advocate of a national system of education that would teach men, from childhood, to regard their fellow men as equals, regardless of birth, nationality, or creed. He proposed schools that would teach manual arts and respect for community property. Owen had not yet turned from socialism, but his priorities had now been revised. Education became the prerequisite for the new system; selfishness could not be eliminated without education from earliest childhood. His attention turned almost completely toward education and free thought from earliest childhood. His reputation as a radical—particularly during his short tenure as a leader of the New York City Workingmen's party—was based on his educational and religious statements rather than on his socialism.[60] Thus when Owen came to New York in April 1829, he worked for his educational plan rather than for any grand proposal for economic reorganization. But he viewed education preimarily as a means to achieve a new social system rather than as an end in itself.

In New York Owen became an editor, with Frances Wright, of the *Free Enquirer*, an activist in the Workingmen's party, and founder of the Association for the Protection of Industry and for the Promotion of National Education. In forming his association, Owen declared: "I believe in a national system of Equal, Republican, Protective, Practical Education, the sole regenerator of a profligate age and the only redeemer of our suffering country from the equal curses of chilling poverty and corrupting riches, of gnawing want and destroying debauchery, of blind ignorance and unprincipled intrigue."[61]

Frances Wright, whose anticlerical and antimarriage writings had by this time earned her a reputation as a dangerous radical, joined him in the new association, winning for it the unwelcome appellation of "Fannie Wright Societies." The association was, in fact, less than radical in its practical program. It drew up a petition to the New York State legislature asking that $100,000 be appropriated for the establishment near the center of the state of a model boarding school—organized along the lines proposed by Owen, which he labelled the state guardianship system.[62]

The state guardianship education scheme was based on Plato's educational theories. They had been attempted, in part, years earlier by Philip Emanuel von Fallenberg, at his private school in Switzerland, which Owen had attended as a boy.[63] Basically, Owen's scheme called for all children between two and twenty-one to be provided with education, food, clothing, and lodging in boarding schools at public expense. All students, regardless of background, were to wear identical clothing, eat identical food, and live in identical lodgings. The education was to be in both manual and liberal subjects. Students in the higher schools were to work at industrial or agricultural tasks, thus making the schools self-sustaining.[64] Owen assumed that this new plan would make revolution unnecessary, that it would change the characters of members of the next generation so completely that they would work out all of society's future problems amicably. It was a Utopian view, which was to be buttressed in later generations by the Pavlovians. Moreover, many of the facets of modern education—particularly the idea of state financing, vocational training, and the attention to environment—had their origins in Robert Dale Owen's campaign for his guardianship scheme.[65]

Besides education, Owen had other interests, particularly women's rights and religious freedom. He was among the first journalists to raise his voice in favor of women's rights. "How should we male citizens of America like to lose our individual existence, as married women virtually do in this free country?" he asked in 1829. He favored equal educational opportunity for men and women and an end to the then existing disabilities in common law, which prevented married women from holding their own property.[66]

An atheist, Owen considered organized religion an absolute evil. He was particularly opposed to Sabbatarianism—the practice of enforcing the keeping of the Sabbath. This practice, he argued, robbed the worker of his sports and amusements and resulted in heavy drinking. His animosity toward religion was aggravated by the church-influenced schools, which he accused of hindering the advance of science and of causing discrimination in the dispensing of justice by the courts. He considered clergymen to be a danger to society, because they considered fear the primary human motive. Skepticism in place of Christianity was Owen's religious creed.[67]

Owen was to lose much of his radical tint after an unsuccessful interlude in radical politics in New York's Workingmen's party. He edited the left-wing *Daily Sentinel* in New York during 1830 and a radical journal in Britain in 1832–1833. By 1836 he had become a western Jacksonian and was elected to the Indiana legislature as a Democrat. His work in the state legislature indicated how far his radicalism had moderated. He favored a public school system but doubted that Indiana was yet ready for one equal to New England's common schools. He proposed that women retain their right to property after marriage, but settled for an easing of dower rights instead.

Despite his modified stands on most issues, Owen's earlier radicalism was to plague him in later politics. During his 1839 race for Congress, his earlier political writings were used by his opponent to smear and defeat him. When he was finally elected to Congress in 1842, Owen was a typical westerner who opposed a high tariff, favored the annexation of Texas, and urged a firm stand on the Oregon border dispute with Britain. He also played a significant role in the establishment of the Smithsonian Institution and served a term on its board. In 1850, at the Indiana State Constitutional Convention to which he was a delegate, he proposed bills that resulted in Indiana's public school and public library systems. During the Civil War, he helped write the Emancipation Proclamation. In his later years, Owen became a Spiritualist—as did many Socialists.[68] He died in 1877.

Robert Dale Owen's contributions to American life were many, particularly in education. He was instrumental in the development of the New York and Indiana public school systems. He helped secure for Indiana a system of public libraries. But his influence on American radicalism must be seen more as another example of middle-class interference in basically working-class problems. Owen's middle-class reformism alienated him from the working class. His educational scheme may have been a perfect solution to the problems of an alienated world, but it ignored the realities of working-class life during the first quarter of the nineteenth century. The workers were interested in solutions to immediate economic problems, not in long-range plans that might bring them a heaven on earth. Moreover, the guardianship proposal went directly counter to what the working people considered their best interests. They saw in his scheme a threat to the only thing they owned: their families. He thus became an anathema to the very people he tried to serve. This has been the fate of almost all middle-class, intellectual leaders of radical movements. They have been considered either irrelevant or with hostility by the working class to which they were purportedly appealing. In Owen's case, as with most other middle-class, intellectual radicals, the result of worker hostility was his own deradicalization and a resultant search for more personally rewarding political pursuits. He succeeded; most have failed.

- 5 -

Orestes Brownson's fame as a radical thinker and possible precursor of Marx hinges on a single essay he wrote in 1840. Its similarity to Marx and Engels's *Communist Manifesto* of 1848 is apparent, but only superficial. It was, in reality, a plea for Democratic votes in a particularly unpleasant presidential election—an election in which Brownson's Jacksonian favorite, Martin Van Buren, was defeated by "Tippecanoe and Tyler Too."

All of his life, Brownson was basically a pilgrim in search of an elusive eternal verity. Born and raised in a nonreligious atmosphere in Vermont,

Brownson early showed a great interest in theology and ecclesiastical affairs generally. He read voraciously every book he could find on religion, and in 1822, at nineteen, he joined the Presbyterian church. Within three years, he was ordained a Universalist minister. But soon the Universalist church became too restricting for Brownson, and he turned Unitarian. Even Unitarianism was too conservative, and so he formed his own, more liberal church. Then he turned to Democratic politics—until 1840 when the defeat of Van Buren led him to despair for America. So he returned to religion—but this time as a conservative Roman Catholic—his faith until his death in 1876.[69]

Brownson was first attracted to socialism by Robert Owen's writings, which he studied as a young man. They "drew my attention to the social evils which exist in every land, to the inequalities which obtain even in our own country, where political equality is secured by law, and to the question of reorganizing society and organizing a paradise on earth." Although Owen's writings did not transform Brownson into a communitarian, they did convert him into "What is now called a Socialist." Brownson was to claim later that the writings of William Godwin, the British precursor of anarchism, more than those of Owen influenced his early thinking. This is doubtful, however, since Brownson's writing contained virtually no anti-statism. He was, in fact, highly critical of Godwin's individualism.[70] Brownson claimed two other influences on his thinking: the Bible and the Comte de Saint Simon, the French Utopian. That he was influenced by the Bible is apparent, but Saint Simon's role is doubtful.

Brownson was an early advocate of what was later to be called the Social Gospel. His object was "to found a holy kingdom on earth, under the dominion of which all men should finally be brought. . . . We would establish the Kingdom of God on earth." To organize such a heaven on earth would require a complete reorientation of Christendom. He considered the church a hindrance to the establishment of the new Jerusalem. "The moral energy which is awakened it misdirects, and makes its deluded disciples think they have done their duty to God when they have joined the church, offered a prayer, sung a psalm, and contributed of their means to send out a missionary to preach unintelligible dogmas to the poor heathen, who, God knows, have unintelligible dogmas enough already, and more than enough." In place of this formalized, ritualistic religion divorced from social reality, Brownson wanted a church that would preach with simplicity and power the Christianity of Christ, which postulated that "no man can enter the kingdom of God, who does not labor with all his zeal and diligence to establish the kingdom of God on earth; who does not labor to bring down the high, and bring up the low." To be Christian, man had to reform society into what God had meant it to be. To achieve this, a true Christian had to be a Socialist. "No man can be a Christian who does not refrain from practices by which the rich grow richer and the poor grow poorer, and who does not do all in his power to elevate the laboring classes, so that one man shall not be doomed to toil while another enjoys the fruits."[71]

His early writings brought Brownson to the attention of Frances Wright. She met him in Auburn, New York, in the fall of 1829 and persuaded him to become a contributing editor of the *Free Enquirer*. He was inactive in that role.[72] Instead, he edited his own paper in Auburn and eventually moved to Boston where he started his *Quarterly Review* in 1838. *The Review* was designed to be the organ of the Christian Democratic—really Social Gospel—wing of the Democratic party.[73] It was in the *Review*, during the campaign of 1840, that he published "The Laboring Classes," his Yankee version of the *Communist Manifesto*.

In his magnum opus, Brownson argued that class wars had always existed; only the classes had changed with the changing systems. Thus the "old war between King and Barons is well nigh ended, and so is that between the Baron and the Merchant and the Manufacturers,—landed capital and commercial capital." Now the struggle was between the worker and his employer, "between wealth and labor."[74] By *workers*, he meant only those who owned "none of the funds of production," that is, those who had nothing to sell but their labor power. The middle class, the farmers, and the self-employed—"laborers on their own lands or in their own shop"—although not of the laboring class, would ally themselves with the workers in the current class war, for they, too, were the exploited in the capitalist society.[75]

The cause of the class warfare was the virtual robbery of the workingman's labor, he wrote. He also noted that "the workingman is poor and depressed, while a large portion of the non-workingmen . . . are wealthy. It may be laid as a general rule . . . that men are rewarded in inverse ratio to the amount of actual service they perform." So serious was this robbery of man's labor that it was basically a form of slavery—wage slavery; and wage slavery was—"except so far as the feelings are concerned"—more oppressive than chattel slavery. The worker, Brownson argued, had all of the disabilities of freedom, but none of the blessings. "We are no advocates of slavery, we are as heartily opposed to it as any modern abolitionist can be; but we say frankly that if there must always be a laboring population as distinct from the proprietors and employers, we regard the slave system as decidedly preferable to the system at wages." Employers, he argued, spent less in wages than slaveholders paid in food and lodging for their slaves.[76]

His criticism was wide ranging. The church, he claimed, was allied with Mammon against the working people. "If you will only allow me to keep thousands toiling for my pleasure," he quoted a mythical capitalist, "I will ever aid you in your pious efforts to convert their souls." The most vile employer "passes among us as a pattern of morality . . . [Our] clergy would not dare question his piety." A large enough donation toward the clergy's salary or to some charity, no matter how vile the person, was enough to win him status in the church. "Not a few of our churches rest on Mammon for their foundation."[77]

History could bear witness to the cause of the evils of modern society, for there had always been a "class distinct from the reigning class," he wrote. The evils were the product of society to rid itself of the wrongs it had produced. To achieve this end, he called upon government ("for the action of society is government") to repeal all laws detrimental to labor and the laboring classes and to enact new laws "necessary to enable them to maintain their equality." The first laws to be repealed had to be those that gave banks their great power; "Following the destruction of the Banks, must come that of all monopolies, of all privilege."[78] Admittedly, the conclusion Brownson reached was disappointing. Starting from a quasi-Marxian critique of society, he developed a simplistic solution for all of the system's woes. Yet his analysis was Socialist and, for 1840, uniquely revolutionary.

Unfortunately, it failed to help the Democrats. Martin Van Buren was defeated. William Henry Harrison and John Tyler were elected. It had been a campaign "carried on by doggerels, log cabins, and hard cider, by means utterly corrupt and corrupting." It disgusted Brownson. He decided that the people could no longer be trusted, and he questioned "the intelligence and instincts of the 'masses.' " His radical days were past. "I became henceforth a conservative in politics, instead of an impracticable radical, and through political conservatism I advanced rapidly towards religious conservatism."[79] Over the next 125 years, others were to follow Brownson's example.

NOTES

1. See, for example, editorial box, *The People* 1 (September 20, 1891): 4.

2. Joseph Dorfman, Introduction to *Observations on the Sources and Effects of Unequal Wealth*, Langton Byllesby (New York: Russell and Russell, 1962), p. 15; "Labor notes" are discussed in chapter 5. They were not crucial to Owen's theory.

3. Byllesby, *Observations*, p. 23.

4. Cited in David Harris, *Socialist Origins in the United States: American Forerunners of Marx, 1817–1832* (Assen, Netherlands: Van Gorcum and Comp., N.V., 1966), p. 36.

5. Ibid., pp. 28–29.

6. Ibid., pp. 110–16; Dorfman, Introduction to *Observations*, pp. 16–17, sees in these associations the beginnings of the corporation system, "although his corporation has wider social implications than its modern successor." See also Harris, *Socialist Origins*, p. 52. Dorfman's position appears to ignore the cooperative nature of Byllesby's association.

7. Byllesby, *Observations*. p. 98.

8. Ibid., p. 69.

9. The Workingmen's party, which Skidmore was instrumental in founding in New York in 1829, is discussed at length in chapter 4.

10. Biographical data from Edward Pessen, "Thomas Skidmore: Agrarian Reformer in the Early American Labor Movement," *New York History* 35 (September 1954): 280–81; Amos Gilbert, "A Sketch of the Life of Thomas Skidmore," *The Free Enquirer* 1, third series (April 6, 1834): 1.

11. Thomas Skidmore, *Moral Physiology Exposed and Refuted, Comprising the Entire Work of Robert Dale Owen on that subject, with Critical Notes showing its tendency to degrade and render still more unhappy than it is now, the condition of the Working Classes, by denying their right to increase the number of their Children; and recommending the same odious means to suppress such increase as are contained in Carlile's "What is Love, or Every Woman's Book"* (New York: Skidmore and Jacobus, 1831), p. 73.

12. Harris, *Socialist Origins*, p. 93.

13. Thomas Skidmore, *The Right of Man to Property!* (New York: Printed for the author by Alexander Ming, Jr., 1829), pp. 3–5, 29, 385–86. Also quoted in Justus Ebert, *Trades Unionism in the United States, 1742–1905* (New York: New York Labor News Company, 1905), p. 5.

14. Skidmore, *Moral Physiology*, pp. 58–62.

15. Ibid., pp. 15, 19, 126–27, 383–84. Capitals in original.

16. Ibid., pp. 137–44, 348.

17. Ibid., pp. 9–11. Italics in original.

18. Ibid., pp. 158–60, 266–67, 281–82.

19. Ibid., pp. 198–99.

20. Pessen, "Thomas Skidmore," pp. 286–87.

21. Ibid., pp. 288–89.

22. George H. Evans, "Of the Origins and Progess of the Workingmen's Party in New York," *The Radical* 2 (January 1842): 1.

23. Horbart Berrian, *A Brief Sketch of the Origin and Rise of the Workingmen's Party in the City of New York* (Washington, D.C.: The Workingmen's Advocate, 1840), p. 4

24. Data on her early life is from William Randall Waterman, *Frances Wright* (New York: Columbia University Studies in History, Philosophy, and Public Law, 1924), p. 14; F. M. Holland, "Frances Wright," *Open Court* 9 (September 5, 1895): 4623; O. B. Emerson, "Frances Wright and the Nashoba Experiment," *Tennessee Historical Quarterly* 6 (December 1947): 291.

25. Waterman, *Frances Wright*, pp. 33–41, 50.

26. Ibid., pp. 44, 45; Edd Winfield Parks, "Dreamer Vision: Frances Wright at Nashoba (1825–1830)," *Tennessee Historical Magazine*, 2d. ser. 2 (January 1932): 76.

27. Ibid., pp. 61, 63; Edd Winfield Parks, "Dreamer Vision: Frances Wright at Nashoba (1825–1830)," *Tennessee Historical Magazine*, 2d. ser. 2 (January 1932): 76.

28. [Frances Wright], *Biography and Notes of Frances Wright D'Arusmont* (Boston: J. P. Mendum, 1848), p. 18; see also Holland, "Frances Wright," p. 4623.

29. [Wright], *Biography*, pp. 24–25.

30. Frances Wright, *Views of Society and Manners in America* (Cambridge: Harvard University Press, 1963), pp. 268–70; Emerson, "Frances Wright," pp. 291–92.

31. [Wright], *Biography*, pp. 21–23. Although written in 1844, the views reflect her early thinking.

32. Ibid.

33. Waterman, *Frances Wright*, pp. 92–99; Holland, "Frances Wright," p. 4623; Parks, "Dreamer's Vision," p. 77 Emerson, "Frances Wright," pp. 294–96.

34. Waterman, *Frances Wright*, pp. 92–97; Wright, *Views of Society*, p. 269; Coles is an almost forgotten early Abolitionist. Born in Virginia in 1786, and a landed aristocrat, he freed his slaves and moved them to Illinois. He served as secretary to Madison (Wright erroneously claims he was Jefferson's secretary) and was later a special envoy to Russia, antislavery governor of Illinois, and an unsuccessful antislavery candidate for representative and senator. See Allen Johnson and Dumas Malone, eds., *Dictionary of American Biography*, 24 vols (New York: Charles Scribner and Son, 1933), 4: 296–97; E. B. Washburn, "Sketch of Edward Coles," *Collections of the Illinois State Historical Library* 15 (1920): 15–201.

35. Parks, "Dreamer's Vision," p. 78; Emerson, "Frances Wright," p. 297.

36. Thomas Jefferson to Miss Frances Wright, August 7, 1825, in *The Writings of Thomas Jefferson*, ed. Andrew A. Lipscomb and Albert Ellery Bergh (Washington, D.C.: The Thomas Jefferson Memorial Association, 1904), pp. 119–20.

37. Anna B. A. Brown, "A Dream of Emancipation," *New England Magazine* 24 (June 1904): 495–96; Parks, "Dreamer's Vision," pp. 76–77.

38. Ibid., 78; Waterman, *Frances Wright*, pp. 104–106.

39. Parks, "Dreamer's Vision," pp. 79–80; Emerson, "Francis Wright," p. 301; Brown, "A Dream," p. 497; Elinor Pancoast and Anne E. Lincoln, *The Incorrigible Idealist: Robert Dale Owen in America* (Bloomington, Ind.: The Principia Press, 1940), p. 7; Waterman, *Frances Wright*, pp. 111–23; John Humphrey Noyes, *History of American Socialisms* (1869; reprint ed. New York: Hillary House Publishers Ltd., 1961), pp. 69–70.

40. Emerson, "Frances Wright," pp. 302–3; Waterman, *Frances Wright*, pp. 106–7; Parks, "Dreamer's Vision," p. 79.

41. Waterman, *Frances Wright*, pp. 111–23; Parks, "Dreamer's Vision," pp. 80–83; Emerson, "Frances Wright," pp. 305–9.

42. Parks, "Dreamer's Vision," p. 83; Emerson, "Frances Wright," pp. 307, 309; Frances Wright's views on marriage are discussed later in this chapter.

43. For Frances Wright's relations with the Winchesters, see A. J. G. Perkins and Theresa Wolfson, *Frances Wright, Free Enquirer: The Study of a Temperament* (New York: Harper and Brothers, 1940), pp. 133–34, 144; Emerson, "Frances Wright," pp. 299–300.

44. Frances M. Trollope, *Domestic Manners of the Americans* (New York: Vintage Books, 1960), p. 27. Also cited in Emerson, "Frances Wright," pp. 310–11.

45. Emerson, "Frances Wright," pp. 311–13; Brown, "A Dream," p. 497; Waterman, *Frances Wright*, p. 129.

46. Brown, "A Dream," pp. 494–95; Waterman, *Frances Wright*, p. 133. In 1844 Frances Wright in *Biography* warned against admitting the Negro to full citizenship lest he "degrade the constituents to the level of his own moral and mental state," pp. 27–28.

47. Waterman, *Frances Wright*, p. 128; Holland, "Frances Wright," p. 4624.

48. Holland, "Frances Wright," p. 4624.

49. Thomas Low Nichols, *Forty Years of American Life* (New York: Stackpole Sons, 1937), p. 41; Orestes Brownson, *The Convert* (New York: Edward Dunigan & Brother, 1857), p. 120.

50. Frances Wright, "The People at War," *Free Enquirer* 2 (November 27, 1830): 38; also in James Oneal, *The Workers in American History* (New York: Rand School of Social Science, 1921), p. 165; John R. Commons et. al., *A Documentary History of American Industrial Society*, vols. 5, 6 (Cleveland: The Arthur H. Clark Company, 1910), 1: 178, 181.

51. Frances Wright, "On the Causes of Existing Evils," *The Free Enquirer* 1 (March 18, 1829): 166.

52. Ibid., March 25, 1829, p. 175.

53. Ibid., Waterman, *Frances Wright*, pp. 152–53, 176; Brown, "A Dream," p. 498.

54. Wright, "On the Causes," March 25, 1829, p. 175; April 1, 1829, p. 183; Waterman, *Frances Wright*, pp. 154–56, 249–54; Perkins and Wolfson, *Frances Wright*, p. 253; Holland, "Frances Wright," p. 4624. Wright used the words *state* and *society* interchangeably. It was a social and not a political entity as she used it. She could thus infer a state without government.

55. Wright, "On the Causes," April 1, 1829, p. 183.

56. Emerson, "Frances Wright," pp. 309–10, 313; Waterman, *Frances Wright*, pp. 156–60, 224; Perkins and Wolfson, *Frances Wright*, p. 312.

57. Frances Wright D'Arusmont to Robert Owen, November 11, 1831, cited in Richard William Leopold, *Robert Dale Owen: A Biography* (Cambridge: Harvard University Press, 1940), p. 114.

58. Josiah Warren, the sixth of the Owenites, is not discussed in this chapter because his position in American radicalism requires that he and his followers receive separate treatment. See chapter 5.

59. Leopold, *Robert Dale Owen*, pp. 8–9, 39.

60. Ibid., pp. 45–46; Oneal, *The Workers*, p. 163; Leopold's argument that Owen "could no longer be called a Socialist" within a year after the collapse of New Harmony overstates the case. He was to remain a Socialist into the early 1830s when he edited *The Crisis* (November 3, 1832 to April 20, 1833), but his primary interests had changed. His anti-clericalism left his political supporters open to charges to being "the Infidel Ticket" during the internal squabbles in the Workingmen's party, 1829–1830.

61. Quoted also in Perkins and Wolfson, *Frances Wright*, pp. 254–55.

62. Ibid.

63. Leopold, *Robert Dale Owen*, pp. 11–13; Waterman, *Frances Wright*, pp. 194–98; Plato, *Republic*, in Plato, *Five Great Dialogues* (New York: Walter J. Black, 1942), especially pp. 305–6; George Sabine, *A History of Political Theory* (New York: Holt, Rinehart, and Winston, 1961), pp. 39–63, is a concise exposition of Plato's views on education; Socialist interest in Plato has continued unabated; see, for example, Harry W. Laidler, *History of Socialism* (New York: Thomas Y. Crowell, 1968), pp. 9–15.

64. Waterman, *Frances Wright*, pp. 194–98; Leopold, *Robert Dale Owen*, pp. 11–13; Frank T. Carleton, "The Workingmen's Party of New York City, 1829–1831," *Political Science Quarterly* 22 (September 1907): 406; Holland, "Francis Wright," p. 4624.

65. Leopold, *Robert Dale Owen*, p. 100.

66. Quoted in Pancoast and Lincoln, *The Incorrigible Idealist*, p. 9; Leopold, *Robert Dale Owen*, p. 60, 76.

67. See Leopold, *Robert Dale Owen*, pp. 58–59.

68. Pancoast and Lincoln, *The Incorrigible Idealist*, pp. 29–30, 32, 34–35, 36–39, 44–45, 59; The relation of Socialists to spiritualism is virtually an unexplored facet of American history. See, for example, *The American Socialist* 1 (March 30, 1876): 1.

69. Biographical data from Brownson, *The Convert*, pp. 1–17, 60.

70. Ibid., pp. 89–90, 107, 110, 118–20.

71. Ibid., 237–42.

72. Leopold, *Robert Dale Owen*, p. 67.

73. Brownson, *The Convert*, p. 245.

74. Orestes Brownson, "The Laboring Classes" [from *Boston Quarterly Review*, 1840], in *American Philosophical Addresses*, ed. Joseph L. Blau (New York: Columbia University Press, 1946,), p. 181.

75. Ibid., p. 182.

76. Ibid., pp. 182–85.

77. Ibid., pp. 183–84, 187.

78. Ibid., pp. 201–3.

79. Brownson, *The Convert*, p. 267.

❦ *4* ❦

The Workies

- 1 -

The American labor movement of the early nineteenth century was more involved in political than economic activity. Occasional strikes were held and a few contracts were negotiated, but the chief interest of organized workingmen was the election of prolabor men to legislatures and "the furtherance and support of communistic and Socialistic enterprises of a Utopian character."[1] This was, however, not a matter of choice; the workers of that era had little alternative. Normal trade-union activity was considered a crime; between 1806 and 1829—in Pennsylvania, Maryland, and New York—eleven criminal cases were brought against workingmen for striking. In seven of these cases, the strikers were convicted of conspiracy. No decisions are recorded for the other five, although in at least one of them, the strike had to be abandoned after the striking journeymen were compelled to pay costs. It was not until 1829 that strike and trade-union activity were not considered conspiracies *per se*.[2]

The antitrade-union bias of the American judiciary during this period made it a matter of priority for workingmen that less prejudiced judges be named to the bench. Because the convictions were based on interpretations of the common law, it was considered necessary to write statute law to supersede the common law in labor relations. To achieve either of these ends required political action.

Even a cursory examination of the labor-conspiracy cases would expose the bias of the judiciary. The first such case, the notorious *Philadelphia Cordwainers* case of 1806, is a classic example.

The strike occurred in the first mass-production industry in America—the boot and shoe trade—when employers cut the price paid to journeymen on boots for the southern trade by 25 percent in 1805. The journeymen retaliated by "turning out." Almost immediately, eight of the strikers were arrested and charged with conspiracy. The result was the almost immediate collapse of the strike. At the trial, the cordwainers found themselves facing a hostile judge, Recorder Moses Levy. He told the jury that "a combination of workmen to raise their wages may be considered in a two-fold point of view: one is to benefit themselves . . . the other is to injure those who do not join their society. The rule of law condemns both." Levy argued further that such a combination interfered with the "natural" law of supply and demand, which, he maintained, regulated prices and wages. The jury found "the defendants guilty of a combination to raise their wages."[3]

Recorder Levy's prejudicial charge to the jury led William Duane, Jeffersonian editor of the Philadelphia *Aurora*, to cry out editorially:

A man who did not know the purposes for which a law contemplated the appointment of a *recorder* to preside in the mayor's court, would unquestionably have concluded that Mr. Recorder Levy had been paid by the master shoemakers for his discourse in the mayor's court on Friday last—never did we hear a charge to a jury delivered in a more prejudiced and partial manner—from such courts' recorders and juries, good Lord deliver us.[4]

The judges in many of the other conspiracy cases acted much like Recorder Levy. In a later case involving twenty-one striking tailors, the presiding judge assailed labor organizations as being of foreign origin, and proclaimed that: "This is not a mere struggle between master and workman; it is one on which the whole harmony" of the United States depended.[5]

In 1829, almost a quarter of a century after the *Philadelphia Cordwainers* case, the first acquittal was won in a labor-conspiracy case, and it was not until the reversal of a conviction by the Supreme Judicial Court of Massachusetts thirteen years later—in 1842—that the doctrine that workers combining in trade unions for higher wages and better conditions were involved in an illegal conspiracy was finally laid to rest.[6]

Although the early legal inhibitions against normal trade-union activity tended to prevent the formation of labor organizations in the United States, unions did exist and strikes did occur during this early period of American history, as the conspiracy cases, themselves, prove. These labor organizations were more than mere "reformers in every sense of the work"; their members were "among the first to denounce chattel slavery and capital punishment."[7] But the primary aim of the workingmen and their organizations was the alleviation of their own immediate distress, and their chief interest was higher wages and shorter hours. With strikes and other economic weapons virtually denied them, the workers' organizations found electoral activity—the formation of Workingmen's parties—the only expedient avenue open to them to win better conditions.

The three most significant political movements organized by labor during the first third of the nineteenth century were the Workingmen's parties of Philadelphia, New York, and Massachusetts. Although their accomplishments did not match their rhetoric, the "Workies," as they were popularly known, were instrumental in outlawing some of the grosser inequities in American society and law and in developing the public school system.

The Philadelphia Workingmen's party, the first labor party in history, was organized by William Heighton, a twenty-seven-year-old, British-born cordwainer who had come to Philadelphia as a youth. In 1827 he convinced the few labor organizations then in existence in Philadelphia to federate into the Mechanics Union of Trade Associations. Heighton, a Socialist, hoped the federation would become a vehicle for political action aimed at the Socialist transformation of American society.

The federation was active in aiding strikers and in organizing new trade unions. Heighton, who was primarily interested in the federation as a political propaganda organization, considered his chief contribution to be publishing and editing the official organ of the Mechanics Union—the *Mechanics Free Press*, the first labor publication edited by a workingman. Under Heighton's direction, the *Free Press* published, besides trade-union news, articles about social reform and excerpts from early British Socialist tracts.[8] Although he considered Robert Owen "a very eminent political economist" and although Owen reprinted one of his two major pamphlets in England,[9] Heighton was not an Owenite. He believed communities such as New Harmony were useless as instruments for revolutionizing society. Only the workers, by their own political action, could change the social and economic order to their advantage. His arguments of 1827–1828 are almost identical with the views expressed by American Socialists more than a century later.

In typical latter-day Socialist fashion, Heighton favored nominating a ticket even when little or no chance of victory existed. Election campaigns, he argued, should be educational and morale-building exercises. He conceded that the chances of electing a workingman to public office in 1828 were minimal, "but an attempt at this time, if nothing more, will at least afford a demonstration of our strength as regards point of numbers, talent and character. It will excite our friends, who have been indifferent to their interests, to laudable exertions, without which the best cause must be forever abandoned." Moreover, it would "disprove the notion that men of mechanical pursuits are unfitted for political and civil stations."[10]

His critique of the capitalist system was—despite its archaic phraseology—also a classic Socialist statement. The working class, he wrote,

are the authors of almost every thing that is generally deemed the most desirable for enjoyment, the most conducive to happiness, and that is universally sought after with the greatest avidity; and although through want of information relative to the *best method* of promoting their best interests, they are suffering themselves to be drained of the richest and choicest products of their industry, to be put off with a scanty portion of the coarsest and meanest of their own productions, to be deprived of almost everything which is calculated to confer delight and render life a blessing, and, as a *class*, to have no prospect before them than the gloomy one of endless toil and hopeless poverty; that they are, nevertheless, the sole authors of all the luxuries . . . and of all the property or wealth that is in existence.[11]

The whole of Heighton's thesis was based on this premise. Wealth being the product of labor alone, anyone who acquired wealth by any other means did so at the cost of his fellows. Likewise, anyone who rose above the laboring class did so "to the manifest injury of others." The employing and merchant classes, he argued, had reached their position of economic superiority by acquiring wealth produced by workers without "making an adequate compensation for it." Profit was basically a sales tax imposed by the merchant for his own benefit. Heighton maintained that the "system of profit . . . [is] to the working class, from the product of whose labour these profits are deducted . . . an iron chain of bondage." Law and "justice," he argued, are always on the side of the wealthy "accumulator" and against the poor "producer."[12]

His analysis of the causes of war was, in its oversimplification, an almost identical precursor of the antiwar Socialists' arguments against American participation in World War I. Said Heighton:

The labouring class toil incessantly to create property; which in every country called civilized is accumulated into the hands of a few individuals. These at last acquire so much, that they fall to quarrelling about where they shall carry it and what they shall do with it. The markets being all crammed, they have no longer any necessity for the services; for the poor, haggard, toil worn producers [;] and to settle the dispute they send a number of these poor creatures away to murder one another! While they stay at home and revel on the spoils accumulated.[13]

Heighton did not condemn individual capitalists; he assailed the profit system that allowed them to accumulate great wealth. He argued that the individual capitalists acted "from the same motives . . . that we and all men act from: the desire of happiness." All men, he said, acted in their own interest. "Was ever a class of men heard of who acted in direct opposition to what they conceived to be THEIR INTEREST? No never."[14]

If, as Heighton maintained, it was not the individual capitalist who was to blame for the inequitable system, and if, as he insisted, workers were the intellectual and moral equals of the successful capitalists, how did he explain the social and undeniable economic inequality? His answer was the superior information and education available to the capitalists as a class. In the struggle between the producing class—the workers—and the accumulating class—the capitalists—the class with the greater knowledge available to it would be victorious.

Let the great mass of mankind once become acquainted with the vast and continually increasing powers they possess for the creation of wealth. Let them once acquire *sufficient* KNOWLEDGE to enable them to form arrangements and establish institutions by which that wealth shall be retained in the hands of industrial producers, and the cry of 'hard times' shall die away from the lips of the working class, and poverty and wretchedness, and starvation [shall] be driven forever from the world.[15]

To achieve this end, Heighton proposed that the workers form their own organizations, where they *"would learn to speak for themselves,"* and that they found their own publications so "they would acquire the habit of *writing for themselves."* They would thus be able to discover who among them were most capable, and these persons they would nominate for public office. One of Heighton's cardinal principles was that only a worker, who would be "intimately acquainted with their wants and necessities," could represent the workers. It was the duty of the workers to free themselves; to achieve this end, they could only rely on their own efforts. "I think it is pretty clear . . . that we shall never reap any benefit from [legislatures] . . . until we have men of our own *nominating,* men *whose interests are in union with ours."*[16]

Heighton thus enunciated what was to become Socialist doctrine: the workers' salvation had to be achieved by a political overhaul of society. Unions and strikes might solve an immediate problem temporarily, but whatever temporary gains unions and strikes might achieve could soon be wrested from the workers by "avaricious accumulators and ungenerous employers." Strikes, he argued, had never won anything permanent for the working class.[17]

Although his political doctrine was identical with that of the latter-day Socialists, his Utopia was more nearly identical with that of the latter-day Anarcho-Communists and Syndicalists. Instead of nationalization of industry by government ownership, Heighton proposed the establishment of producers' cooperatives in each locality. The cooperatives would arrange nationally ("by arbitration or otherwise") for distribution. Moreover, the cooperatives would hire local "official labourers" to perform needed municipal and other community tasks—paying them at the same rate as the workers receive.[18] In effect, Heighton was proposing a community-oriented, decentralized, voluntary socialism that was to be the basis of the Anarchists' Pittsburgh Manifesto fifty-six years later.

Heighton's arguments were apparently effective, for in January 1828 the Mechanics Union of Trade Associations revised its bylaws to provide for the nomination of independent labor candidates for public office. These nominees were to be "such individuals as shall pledge themselves . . . to support and advance . . . the interests and enlightenment of the working classes . . . And [the federation proposed] to recommend to the members of the represented societies, and to the working classes generally, to support and promote the interests of the same [candidates] at the next ensuing general election." Moreover, the new bylaws specified that no candidate nominated by one of the old parties was to receive the union's support, "since the association ought to know no party that is opposed to the general interests of the working classes."[19]

Unfortunately, 1828 was not a good year for the formation of a labor party: John Quincy Adams ran against Andrew Jackson for the presidency; no secret ballot was provided, and voters could be easily intimidated. Moreover, rowdyism was the rule on election day. No possibility existed for a prolabor man to be nominated on any of the established tickets; a ruling clique in each of the major parties controlled nominations. The decision to contest the 1828 election with a new party under such unfavorable conditions was thus more the product of frustrating necessity than a principled conscious act.

The eight independent Workingmen's candidates campaigned by denouncing the capitalist accumulators, while ignoring labor's real key issues—free public education, abolition of militia duty, and the mechanics lien law. Adams's men accused the "Workies" of being Jacksonian straw men, and the Jacksonians accused them of being Adams's stooges. The poor campaign and the unpropitious times resulted in an electoral debacle: Workingmen's candidates polled an average of 250 to 539 votes each. The Jacksonians had averaged 4,500 a candidate and the Adams men had about 3,500.

Only Heighton was pleased with the campaign and the party's showing. Immediately after the election, he attempted to organize a permanent Workingmen's party. In December 1828 he formed the Republican Political Association of Workingmen in South Philadelphia. He expected it to be the basis for a major political movement. Heighton planned to use the club to dispense political and legal advice and to debate current issues, but by late 1829 the Mechanics Union, rent by internal disputes, disbanded. In 1830 the old parties adopted many of their key demands, and the Philadelphia "Workies" disappeared.[20] Heighton was to remain active in labor politics until his death in 1871.[21]

- 2 -

The short-lived Workingmen's party of New York City represented the political culmination of the Socialist agitation of the Owenite period. Among those whose names were connected with the party were Cornelius Blatchly, Thomas Skidmore, Robert Dale Owen, and, peripherally, Frances

Wright and Orestes Brownson. The party's accomplishments and failures were to represent in microcosm the accomplishments and failures of the multitude of Socialist parties that were to exist in the United States over the next 140 years.

The Workingmen's party proposed many major reforms considered radical in its time, which have come to be accepted as routine in the United States. Among the issues that agitated the working people in that period were public education, mechanics liens, imprisonment for debt, the militia system, and opposition to chartered banks and monopolies.[22]

New York in late 1829 was ripe for revolt. The winter had been severe; hunger and want were rampant among the workers. Employers frequently defaulted on wages due workingmen, and the workers had little legal recourse. An effort to enact a mechanics lien law, which would give the worker precedence in collecting his wages, was killed in legislative committee. The filthy, vermin-ridden debtors' prisons were full to overflowing. Prisoners had to purchase their own food, rely on private charity, or starve. Most of the jailings were for small debts—sometimes as low as twenty-seven cents.[23]

The Workingmen's party was organized as an indirect result of an attempt by employers to increase the daily hours of work from ten to eleven. Most of those in attendance at a meeting called to plan action against the increase wanted to strike. Skidmore, who was present, was opposed; he suggested, instead, a unique plan for frightening the employers into keeping the ten-hour day: the working men would call a meeting to discuss not only the ten-hour day but also the whole issue of the inequity of property. He suggested that raising the issue of the unfair distribution of property, particularly "of so dangerous a question as that of how they came to be rich without merit, and the great mass of their fellow citizens poor without crime," would force the "aristocratic oppressors" to give up their demand for an eleven-hour day. Skidmore was convincing; no strike was called. Instead, a committee of fifty was organized to set up a new labor organization, "but with no view to founding a separate party." The original objective of the newly formed organization was to "exchange opinions on the subject of their political and social grievances and devising some plan to escape or destroy them."[24] The founders soon decided that merely protecting the ten-hour day would not be worth the effort. "The ultimate object was a *Radical Revolution*," George H. Evans, editor of the *Workingmen's Advocate* reported, "which should secure to each man the fruit of his labor." But there was no plan for accomplishing the objective. The workingmen "had not investigated the matter sufficiently themselves."[25]

After almost six months of preparation, the Workingmen held a mass meeting on October 19, 1829. Skidmore was in the chair. Robert Dale Owen, who had only arrived in New York a few days previously, was secretary. The Committee of Fifty was by now convinced that the candidates of neither of the old parties would give the workers what they wanted. It was, therefore, decided to nominate an independent ticket dedicated to achieving the Workingmen's demands. Skidmore was in full command. He directed the composition of the party's platform; he controlled the meeting with little regard for democratic procedures. He refused to permit debate on crucial resolutions. The ten-hour question, which had been the spark that started the party, was ignored—it had already been settled in the workers' favor. Instead, the platform called for abolition of debtors' jails, the enactment of a mechanics lien law, the taxation of church property, an end to chartered monopolies and banking privileges, and—Skidmore's panacea—the abolition of inheritance and a redistribution of property. It was a radical platform, replete with revolutionary rhetoric. "Your committee are sensible," the report declared, "that, until a revolution take place, such as shall leave behind it no trace of that government which has denied to every human being an equal amount of property on arriving at the age of maturity, and previous thereto, equal food, clothing, and instruction at the public expense, nothing can save the great mass of the community from the evils under which they now suffer."[26]

With only $76.13 in its treasury, and only five days left before the election, the Workingmen's party nominated its legislative ticket—two machinists, two carpenters, one printer, one brass founder, one tinsmith, one cooper, one painter, one grocer and one physician. (The physician was Cornelius Blatchly.) The election—which took three days—was a scene of pandemonium. Tammany Hall brought in repeaters and used violence in an effort to keep the opposition from voting. When the ballots were finally counted, the Workingmen had elected one of the eleven assemblymen from the city—Ebenezer Ford, a carpenter. Two candidates, Thomas Skidmore and Alexander Ming, Sr., barely missed election. The party's candidates had averaged more than 6,000 votes each. It was a victory beyond the expectations of even the most optimistic party member.[27] The Workingmen were a political force to be reckoned with.

Tammany and its National Republican opposition were stunned. *The Journal of Commerce*, the voice of the business community, lamented that "we have placed the power in the hands of those who have neither property, talents, nor influence in other circumstances; and who require in their public officers no higher qualification than they possess themselves."[28] It inferred that the property qualification should be resurrected. Tammany's *Morning Courier and New York Enquirer*, was almost hysterical, "We are surrounded by danger—not only to the party, but to the country. The working ticket, got up by a few fanatics, supported by those who know not its origin, and led on by persons without religion or principle is sweeping everything before it."[29]

The leaders of Tammany, and the conservative old Federal faction, were alarmed at the strength of the "Workies." They moved to destroy the new party. Within a week after the election, Tammany Chieftain Mordecai Manuel Noah's *Courier and Enquirer* called for a mechanics lien law.[30] The *Courier and Enquirer* had previously opposed such a law. Tammany and the National Republicans sent skilled political operators to infiltrate the new party. They helped its leaders—particularly Owen and Skidmore—tear the party apart in a struggle over broad "principles" that few of their supporters understood.[31]

The internal squabbling followed quick on the heels of the election victory. Owen was to claim later that he had never approved the Skidmore platform's property planks. He argued that these planks were adopted without discussion and with no one fully examining them. But this was an ex post facto complaint. The pro-Owen *Working Man's Advocate*, edited by Evans, had inscribed as its motto during early November 1829: "All children are entitled to equal education; all adults to equal property, and all mankind to equal privileges." It was only after the feuding erupted, on November 21, that the *Advocate* deleted the second postulate—"all adults [are entitled] to equal property"—from its motto.[32] The split was a power play, for which the program differences were used as an excuse. By a series of maneuvers Owen won control of the December 29 meeting of the party. He prevented Skidmore from speaking. The Owen-controlled party membership passed resolutions at that meeting that denied any animosity toward private property or religion. They called for an end to imprisonment for debt, free and equal education in a "system that shall unite under the same roof the children of the poor man and the rich, the widow's charge and the orphan, where the road to distinction shall be superior industry, virtue and acquirements without reference to descent," the development of a civil service merit system, an end to the militia system under which workingmen had to serve a minimum of three days a year without pay—subject to fine—while the wealthy could buy their way out of serving, a more equitable court system, and restrictions on banking. Moreover, they proposed a new method for electing members of the legislature by districts instead of at large. Young Owen was now a major political figure; he had captured a potentially powerful political organization in New York. He was proving to be an apt student of political infighting. Skidmore's connection with the party was over. He organized his own Poor People's party, which remained little more than a minor sect for its two years of half-life.[33]

The Workingmen's party showed remarkable growth both in the city and in the upstate area. Pro-Workingmen newspapers were now published in Albany, Auburn, and Rochester.[34] But the internal feuding had become more intense. Skidmore accused Owen of being an aristocrat and of being a hypocrite in his prolabor statements. He charged that Owen's statements favoring birth control were insulting to the workers, and that birth control would have an adverse effect upon the economy of the working class. Skidmore reprinted Owen's probirth control book *Moral Physiology* with deprecating footnotes and a conclusion in which he attacked Owen unmercifully. Careful reading of the panegyric fails to explain Skidmore's reasoning. Owen said that it "would do its author no good and me no harm."[35] He was right.

Internal feuding was heightened after the ouster of Skidmore. A group of expert political operators who were sent into the party by leaders of the two old parties soon found themselves elected to the executive committee. Once on the committee, they split the party further. They realized that the education plank was barely understood by most workmen, although it was the basic fabric for Owen's grand design. Moreover, they knew that potential opposition to the guardianship plank existed within the party—particularly upstate.[36] The Albany *Farmer's Mechanics and Workingmen's Advocate*, for example, did not believe that the public was prepared for it. The *Advocate* believed that education should be of secondary importance to the workingmen, after "laws for the amelioration of the conditions of the laboring classes by securing to the laborer his hire and the implements of industry."[37] Thus the political hacks were able to slip through a resolution obviously aimed at forcing Owen from the party and splintering it further.

The resolution solemnly pledged the party never to support

any attempt to palm upon any man or set of men, the peculiar doctrines of infidelity [an obvious attack on Owen and Miss Wright]. . . . While your committees do not wish to induce any person to join our cause by the tempting doctrines . . . of boarding and clothing all children in the land, they strenuously contend for a republican system of education, but upon a plan that shall leave to the father and the affectionate mother the enjoyment of the society of their offspring.[38]

The resolution had its desired effect. A special party meeting was called—the Owen faction won a clear majority for its pro-guardianship education scheme. The anti-Owenite Cook-Guyon faction refused to accept the decision. Thus two Workingmen's parties were created plus Skidmore's Poor People's party. They were to spend more time fighting each other than they did fighting either Tammany or the National Republicans.

The Owen Workingmen nominated a statewide ticket in 1830; the Cook-Guyon faction, which first nominated a statewide ticket whose candidates refused to run, supported the anti-Jacksonian candidate. The Democratic candidate for governor polled 128,892 votes; the candidate of the National Republicans, supported by the Cook-Guyon faction, polled 120,361, and the candidate of the Workingmen polled 2,332. In New York City, the Workingmen polled 1,959 for their gubernatorial candidate. In the assembly race, Ebenezer Ford, the only member of the party in the legislature and an Owenite, polled 2,329 votes compared with 6,166 the year previous.[39] The splits and intrigues and Tammany's adoption of key Workingmen's planks had taken their toll. The Workingmen's party had come apart. It was to remain an electoral party until 1831. A small fragment went into the "Loco-Foco" faction of the Democrats five years later. Owen moved to England and later to Indiana, where he had a more successful political career. George H. Evans moved into land reform—he played a role in the development of the Homestead Act and in the formation of the Republican party.

The Workingmen's party—as all other radical parties—was a political failure. For one brief moment, it set the city on edge. It elected only one member to the state legislature. Its influence was limited to a two-year period. Yet it accomplished much that has had a lasting effect on American life. It set the pattern for all future radical parties in America: the internal dissension, the endless schisms over fine points of theory, the ease with which major parties adopted and enacted the nonideological planks that gave the radical parties whatever strength they had.

As early as December 1830, George H. Evans noted that "Many of the reforms called for by the Working Men are now admitted to be just and reasonable, and are even advocated by several of the presses which have hitherto supported the party in power, and there is little doubt that the ensuing Legislature will relieve them from a share of their oppressive burdens."[40] Enact them, they did. Almost immediately a mechanics lien law was placed on the statute books with Tammany's support; by May 1831 imprisonment for debt ended; public funds were soon finding their way, in ever increasing amounts, to education; the militia system was made more equitable. But the "key" planks of the "Workies" were never accomplished. Neither Skidmore's scheme for equal distribution of property nor Owen's plan for guardianship education was ever seriously considered. The professional politicians knew that few workers understood—or favored, if they understood—Skidmore's proposal. They voted for the Workingmen's party because they believed it would help alleviate their current condition. The same thing happened with Owen's educational ideas. If anything, workers would have been hostile to any idea that would have separated them from their children. But they did favor good education in public schools. Thus when the reforms that Owen and Skidmore considered to be peripheral to their platforms were enacted, the rest of their plans were irrelevant. This situation has caused the demise of the whole range of political movements of the Left. Most particularly was this true of the destruction of the American Socialist party in 1936—when the combination of the internal feuding, Communist-Trotskyite Trojan Horse maneuvering, and the New Deal Democrats' enactment of its pragmatic social reform demands led to its demise.

- 3 -

Of all of the workingmen's movements of the 1827–1837 decade, the one that was least ideological—and thus most pragmatic—was in Massachusetts. It began as a meeting of workingmen in 1831, emerged as a political party two years later, culminated in a national federation of labor by 1834, and vanished during the depression of 1837.

The movement began in 1831 at a Boston workingmen's meeting whose participants formed themselves into the New England Association of Farmers, Mechanics, and Workingmen. The association, which lasted for four years, first gained public notice at its second annual meeting, also in Boston, at which it began agitation aimed at organizing a national labor federation.

Included in the association's membership were representatives of agrarian, intellectual, and manual labor interests, all of whom were considered the producing classes. The idea of labor organization was still young in those days,[41] and allies were accepted wherever they could be found. Moreover, the factory system was still in its formative stage in Massachusetts, and most industrial labor was recruited from the farm population. Only in the larger eastern port cities was there a class of working people, apart from the agrarian rural population; these were mostly skilled journeymen, rather than factory hands.[42]

Conditions in factories were appalling. The most unfortunate of the factory hands were the children, many of them less than twelve years old. They worked as many as fourteen hours a day, despite laws that prohibited more than ten. Captain Basil Hall, who visited Lowell in 1828, reported that: "They work only from daylight to dark, having half an hour for breakfast and as much for dinner." The children were thus left with no time for education or playing in the sun. Moreover, they worked under dangerous conditions; no laws required the fencing out of machinery, and "corporal chastisement"—whipping—was common.[43]

It was against these abuses—plus the habit of masters who worked journeymen twelve to fourteen hours a day and then failed to pay them their wages—that the New England Association addressed itself. At its 1832 meeting, seven issues were considered: (1) the ten-hour work day; (2) the effect of banking and other monopolies on the condition of the working classes; (3) improvement of the educational system; (4) imprisonment for debt; (5) national bankrupt law; (6) extension of suffrage in states where it was restricted [particularly Rhode Island], and (7) the mechanics lien law. The participants passed strong resolutions calling for a lien law, the abolition of imprisonment for debt, and an end to the militia system. Moreover, they called for the ten-hour day, the extension of suffrage, and the establishment of schools in factories. Committees were set up to study the conditions in factories, particularly those affecting children and women. Plans were also formulated for establishing lyceums, for educating the working classes, and for calling a national convention of workingmen.[44]

The New England "Workies" 1832 platform was thus pragmatic; its rhetoric was far less revolutionary than that of its Philadelphia or New York predecessors. So were its political plans, for the New England Association was not expected to become a new political party. The meeting had voted to accomplish its moderate ends by rewarding its friends and punishing its enemies on election day. The address of the 1832 meeting called for "the selection from among the politicians of the respective parties to which workingmen may happen to belong, of those as the objects of our preference whose moral character, personal habits, relations and employments, as well as professions, afford us the best guarantee of their disposition to revise our social and political systems, and to introduce those improvements called for by us and demanded by the spirit of the age."[45]

The admittedly reformist, pragmatic Massachusetts movement, although it preferred to work within the existing party system, was prepared, if necessary, to nominate its own list of candidates. Thus when, in December 1831, a Lowell worker was fired for attending a Workingmen's convention in Providence, he was nominated as a Workingmen's candidate and elected to the legislature with Jacksonian backing.[46] When in 1833 the existing parties nominated two gubernatorial candidates who were not considered friendly to the association's 1832 program, a Workingmen's party was formed with Samuel C. Allen, a Harvard graduate and a Congregational minister, as its candidate for governor. His platform called for abolition of imprisonment for debt, a mechanics lien law, banking reform, and education of all classes. Allen polled 3,459 votes, 5.5 percent of the 62,375 votes cast. He carried six towns in rural western Massachusetts, one in Worcester County, one in Middlesex near Boston, and two on Cape Cod. Only 519 of the votes for Allen came from urban Boston; most came from the agricultural areas of the state.[47] By 1834 the Democrats, under the prodding of the radical Jacksonians, nominated for lieutenant governor W. W. Thompson, who was already the Workingmen's candidate. The independent labor party collapsed. Allen, who was again its gubernatorial candidate, polled less than half of the votes he had received the previous year, and the Workingmen's party disbanded.[48]

The man most responsible for the nonideological outlook of the Massachusetts workingmen's movement was Seth Luther, "an agitator of the early [eighteen] thirties," given to making "inflammatory albeit accurate statements about child labor, and one of the most tireless among those fighters who inspired New England labor to its first organizational awakening."[49] Born in Rhode Island in 1795, he moved to the western frontier in 1817, where he remained until about 1831. During his absence, industrial capital-

ism began its development in New England "with unparalleled speed, bringing with it new hardships for the wage earner."[50]

Upon his return to New England, Luther went to work in a mill, where he
was appalled at the dehumanization of the factory system. He was particularly upset by the inhuman conditions under which women and children
were employed there, and he began agitation for organization of factory
workers. He was the first labor agitator to show an interest in industrial
workers; previous trade unions were limited to organizations of skilled
journeymen.[51] In 1832 Luther moved to Boston where he worked as a lecturer and as a writer and subscription solicitor for the *New England Artisan*, the organ of the New England Association. From the beginning, he
pleaded with workers to unite behind a program of pragmatic reforms.[52]
"We are accused of a wish to divide property," he wrote. "I, in the name of
the workingmen, feel myself authorized to say, that this statement of our
views is false, utterly, totally, and maliciously false."[53] Luther proposed instead that inequities could be abolished by (1) developing a system of free,
publicly supported, compulsory, and equal schools "open alike to the children of the poor as well as the rich" in which manual arts as well as liberal
arts would be taught; (2) abolishing all "licensed monopolies"; (3) outlawing capital punishment; (4) doing away with imprisonment for debt; (5)
abolishing or, at least drastically revising, the militia system; (6) making the
legal system less expensive, thus allowing a poor workingman to defend
himself or to sue against inequitable treatment; (7) equalizing taxation of
property; (8) enacting of an effective mechanics lien law, and (9) granting
universal suffrage.[54]

Although his demands seem—at least by late twentieth-century standards—to be moderate, his basic premises were radical—even revolutionary in early nineteenth-century terms. "The history of the workingmen in
all ages of the world has been a history of oppression on the side of wealth,
and a base submission to that oppression on our part." As long as workers
continued to neglect their own interests, they would be deprived of their
"just station in society." He doubted that the workers could expect aid from
politicians. The leaders of the political parties were "robbing the workingmen by partial and unjust legislation." They had "neglected the producing
class and their interests." Only the workers, themselves, could end the oppression under which they labored.[55]

Luther equated freedom and justice with equality. It was a "self-evident
truth" that all men are created equal: "Some men are born kings and born
fools at the same time." The key to genuine equality, he argued, was an educational system that would inculcate all children, rich or poor alike, with the
realization that "wisdom, knowledge, virtue, and benevolence, are far better than diamonds, rubies and fine gold." He proposed that these ideals be

inculcated in schools from an early age on the assumption that children so educated would lose their materialistic, and thus selfish, outlook on life. If, Luther argued, "we do what we never have yet done, *'educate'* the *people*, we shall have no need for Jails and State-prisons, Penitentiaries and Alms-houses, Houses of correction and popular executions. Suicide would be a thing unknown, except as the history of the *'dark ages'* of the present day."[56]

Luther wanted schools also to serve a practical purpose—to teach young people how to earn a living. He wanted the rich to pay for the schools. He was, therefore, opposed to the then prevalent use of the lottery as the chief means of financing education. Most of those who supported the lottery were the poor "for the rich . . . seldom buy tickets." Yet most of the children at school came from wealthier families; poor children were too busy working to attend school. The lottery was drawing money "from the pockets of the *poor*, to be expended by the rich, on *their children*."[57]

Although Luther expected education to lead to a peaceful ballot box revolution, he was prepared to use extra-legal means, if necessary, to achieve the pragmatic changes he proposed. He did not accept the assumption that law was sacrosanct. "Law hung old women in Salem. . . . Law hung the Quakers in Boston. . . . Law laid the Stamp Act. . . . Must we be told to submit in silence to *law*, merely because it is law without reference to its constituent principles?" He told an audience of Brooklyn workers: "We will try the ballot box first; if that will not affect our righteous purpose, the next and last resort is the cartridge box." By 1836 he had begun to despair of the ballot box and predicted that "another revolution will be necessary."[58]

Luther worked selflessly in an effort to make his beliefs become realities. After the demise of the New England Association of Farmers, Mechanics, and other Workingmen in 1834, Luther helped organize the Trades Union of Boston, a federation of twenty-two skilled craft unions of the Boston area, which included in its membership employers as well as employees, particularly of the building and printing crafts. Later that year, he helped found the National Trades Union, composed of local federations in New York, Philadelphia, Boston, Baltimore, Louisville, and other cities. Luther attempted, unsuccessfully, to interest the trades in organizing unions of factory hands; the crafts unionists were opposed. Strikes broke out in 1835, and the craft unions grew in size and strength. But jurisdictional disputes soon erupted and the labor movement began to collapse. The depression of 1837 virtually killed it off.[59]

With the collapse of the trade-union movement, Luther turned his attention to political action again—this time in his native Rhode Island, where workers could not vote because of property qualifications. In 1840 Luther was sent on tour by the Rhode Island Suffrage Association. He found little support for universal suffrage among the state's middle-class intellectuals, so he turned his efforts to organizing the state's workers to win full voting rights "peaceably if we can, forcibly if we must." In 1842 a comic-opera armed uprising against the property qualification broke out. Named after the rebels' choice for governor, Thomas Dorr, it collapsed almost as soon as the first shot was fired. Luther was among its leaders. Most of the others, almost all of whom were middle class and educated, fled. Luther held his ground, was captured, and imprisoned for high treason. Kept in filthy prison conditions for over a year, Luther attempted unsuccessfully to escape by setting fire to his cell. He was pardoned in 1843.[60] Luther again became active in the New England labor movement. In 1846, at age fifty-one, he attempted to enlist in the army during the Mexican War, but he was rejected. In June 1846 he was committed to the lunatic asylum at East Cambridge, Massachusetts, where he soon died.[61]

Luther was the father of the American industrial unionism. He was the first American to show any interest in the organization of factory hands as well as skilled craftsmen. Less rhetorically radical than latter-day Syndicalists, his ideas of organization, his insistence that the oppressed must free themselves, his rejection of law as sacrosanct, and his personal courage in the cauuse set the standards they would—consciously or unconsciously— emulate.

- 4 -

Workingmen's parties after the demise of the Massachusetts movement were anticlimactic. In New York, for example, the Equal Rights party, a coalition of dissident working-class Democrats and middle-class antimonopolists, elected Ely Moore, a former president of the New York Trades Union, to Congress in 1834 and 1836.[62] But he was a Democrat who soon reverted to his old party. Other short-lived Workingmen's parties were of little significance. Beginning with 1834, strikes and boycotts replaced politics as the chief means employed in the struggle for the amelioration of the conditions of the working class.

Trade unions per se were no longer viewed as conspiracies. From 1829 until 1842 three more convictions for labor conspiracy were imposed, but these three were offset by five acquittals. Moreover, the real aims of the workingmen's political movements had been achieved by the 1840s. The skilled workmen—who formed the backbone of the workingmen's movement—saw no reason to struggle for the improvement of conditions of the unskilled, many of whom were women, children, and foreigners.

Although short lived, the achievements of the "Workies" between 1827 and 1837 were monumental. During the period, imprisonment for debt was almost totally abolished; mechanics lien laws were enacted in almost all states; the ten-hour day was becoming the rule; and the free public school system was becoming universal.[63] Admittedly, the conditions of factory workers remained abysmal, and child labor remained the rule for another hundred years. But these issues were considered peripheral to their genuine interests by the skilled mechanics and farmers who dominated the working-men's movement. The rhetoric of revolution of most of their leaders—except in Massachusetts—proved to be mere rhetoric, mere exercises in intellectual self-delusion. The practical accomplishments of the movement bore little resemblance to the Utopias some of the leaders envisioned.

NOTES

1. Justus Ebert, *Trade Unionism in the United States, 1742-1905* (New York: New York Labor News Company, [1905]), p. 4.

2. For a list of the cases and their dispositions, see Marjorie S. Turner, *The Early American Labor Conspiracy Cases, Their Place in Labor Law: A Reinterpretation* (San Diego: San Diego State College Press, 1967), pp. 2-3.

3. *Commonwealth v. Pullis,* in *A Selection of Cases and Other Authorities on Labor Law,* by Francis Bowes Sayre (Cambridge: Harvard University Press, 1922), p. 101; also in Nicholas S. Falcone, *Labor Law* (New York: John Wiley and Sons, 1962), p. 35. For an interesting analysis of the case, see Walter Nelles, "The First American Labor Case," *Yale Law Journal* 41 (December 1931): 165-200.

4. Ibid., p. 192.

5. Quoted in George E. McNeill, *The Labor Movement: The Problem of Today* (Boston: A. M. Bridgman & Co., 1887), p. 184.

6. *Commonwealth v. Hunt,* 4 Metcalf 111 (1842), in Falcone, *Labor Law,* pp. 39-42, and Sayre, *Selection,* pp. 100-04, Turner, *Early American Labor Conspiracy Cases,* pp. 58-72, takes an opposing view of the *Hunt* case, but this does not affect the point here made.

7. McNeill, *Labor Movement,* pp. 71-72.

8. Louis H. Arky, "The Mechanics' Union of Trade Associations and the Formation of the Philadelphia Workingmen's Movement," *Pennsylvania Magazine of History and Biography* 76 (April 1952): 144, 152-53, 158-61, 163.

9. [William Heighton], *An Address to the Members of Trade Societies and to the Working Classes Generally* (Philadelphia: Published by the Author, 1827), p. 19; *Arno Press Announces Publication of BRITISH LABOUR STRUGGLES: Contemporary Pamphlets, 1727-1850: From the Kress Library, Graduate School of Business Administration, Harvard University* (New York: Arno Press, 1972), p. 24.

10. *Mechanics' Free Press,* August 9, 1828, quoted in Arky, "Mechanics Union," p. 166.

11. Heighton, *Address to Members,* pp. 3-4.

12. (William Heighton], *An Address Delivered Before the Mechanics and Working Classes Generally, of the City and County of Philadelphia At the Universalist Church in Callowhill Street on Wednesday Evening November 21, 1827 [by an Unlettered Mechanic]* (Philadelphia: Mechanics Gazette, [1827]), p. 5; Heighton, *Address to Members,* pp. 9, 12, 41.

13. Heighton, *Address to Members,* p. 29.

14. Ibid., pp. 33, 42.

15. Ibid., pp. 8, 25.

16. Ibid., pp. 34-35, 44.

17. Heighton, *Address to Mechanics,* p. 8.

18. Heighton, *Address to Members,* p. 13.

19. Arky, "Mechanics Union," p. 20.

20. Ibid., pp. 164, 167-70, 173-75; John R. Commons, "Labor Organization and Labor Politics, 1827-37," *Quarterly Journal of Economics* 21 (August 1907): 326. For a more recent criti-

cism of Socialist candidates who ignore immediate issues for ideological pronouncements, see Reinhold Niebuhr to Norman Thomas, October 27, 1944, cited in Bernard K. Johnpoll, *Pacifist's Progress* (Chicago: Quadrangle Books, 1970), pp. 247–48.

21. See William Heighton to George L. Stearns, February 27, 1865, reprinted in William Darrah Kelly, *The Equality of All Men Before the Law, Claimed and Defended* (Boston: C. C. Rand and Avery, 1865), pp. 42–43.

22. James Oneal, *The Workers in American History* (New York: Rand School of Social Science, 1921), pp. 156–57; *Albany Argus*, February 16, 1830, reported that the Albany Workingmen's party, affiliated with the more conservative wing, considered the key reforms needed to be (1) a mechanics lien law, (2) reform in appropriations for education, (3) abolition of all monopolies, (4) abolition of imprisonment for debt, and (5) a more equitable administration of justice. The Troy party adopted virtually the same platform—particularly emphasizing the mechanics lien law. See *Albany Argus*, November 21, 1829 and February 12, 1830. See also Hobart Berrian, *A Brief Sketch of the Origin and Rise of the Workingmen's Party in the City of New York* (Washington D.C.: The Workingmen's Advocate, 1840), p. 2.

23. McNeill, *Labor Movement* pp. 75–76; Oneal, *The Workers*, pp. 99–102; *Free Enquirer* 1, series 2 (March 11, 1829).

24. George H. Evans, "Of the Origins and Progress of the Workingmen's Party in New York," *The Radical* 2 (January 1842): 2; Berrian, *Brief Sketch*, p. 3. Both Evans and Berrian played leading roles in the party.

25. Evans, "Of the Origins," p. 5.

26. "The Report and Resolutions of the Committee of Fifty," *Workingman's Advocate*, October 31, 1829 quoted in John R. Commons, et. al., *A Documentary History of American Industrial Society*, vols. 5 and 6 (Cleveland: The Arthur H. Clark Company, 1910) 1: 150–54.

27. Frank T. Carleton, "The Workingmen's Party of New York City, 1829–1831," *Political Science Quarterly* 22 (September 1907): 404; Evans, "Of the Origins," p. 17; Berrian, *Brief Sketch*, pp. 3–4.

28. *New York Journal of Commerce*, November 7, 1829, quoted in Commons, *Documentary History*, 1: 154–55.

29. *Morning Courier and New York Enquirer*, November 4, 1829, quoted in Commons, *Documentary History*, 1: 156.

30. November 9, 1829.

31. Carleton, "Workingmen's Party," p. 402, blames the dissension on the leaders of the older parties. It was, in fact, internal squabbling, between Skidmore and Owen, that broke out before the older parties intervened in Workingmen's party affairs, that resulted in the beginning of the party's end.

32. Ibid., pp. 403–4, 406; Edward Pessen, "Thomas Skidmore: Agrarian Reformer in the Early American Labor Movement," *New York History* 35 (September 1954): 284–86.

33. Berrian, *Brief Sketch*, pp. 5–9, 11; Arthur Bestor, *Backwoods Utopias: The Sectarian Origins of the Owenite phase of Communitarian Socialism in America, 1663–1829* (Philadelphia: University of Pennsylvania Press, 1950), p. 226. See also "Proceedings of a Meeting of Mechanics and other Working Men held at Military Hall, Wooster Street, New York, on Thursday evening, December 29, 1829," pamphlet (New York, 1830), in Commons, *Documentary History*, pp. 157–61.

34. *Free Enquirer*, 2d ser. 2 (November 21, 1829); also cited in William Randall Waterman, *Frances Wright* (New York: Columbia University Studies in History, Philosophy, and Public Law, 1924), p. 202; Edward Pessen, *Most Uncommon Jacksonians: The Radical Leaders of the Early Labor Movement* (Albany: State University of New York Press, 1967), p. 68.

35. Quoted in Waterman, *Frances Wright*, p. 203.

36. Richard William Leopold, *Robert Dale Owen: A Biography* (Cambridge: Harvard University Press, 1940), pp. 77, 81–82.

37. *Farmers, Mechanics, and Workingmen's Advocate* 1 (May 29, 1830).

38. *Working Men's Advocate*, May 29, 1830, quoted in Carleton, "Workingmen's Party," pp. 407–8.

39. Carleton, "Workingmen's Party," pp. 411–12.

40. *Working Man's Advocate*, December 11, 1830, quoted in Commons, *Documentary History*, vol. 1, p. 182.

41. Samuel Whitcomb, Jr., "An Address Before the Workingmen's Society (Dedham, Massachusetts, 1831)," quoted in Richard T. Ely, *The Labor Movement in America* (New York: Thomas Y. Crowell, 1886), p. 47.

42. Arthur P. Darling, *Political Changes in Massachusetts, 1824-1848* (New Haven: Yale University Press, 1925), pp. 98–99, 167.

43. Edith Abbot, "A Study of the Early History of Child Labor in America," *American Journal of Sociology* 14 (July 1908): 32–34.

44. Ely, *The Labor Movement*, pp. 50–51; Charles S. Persons, "The Early History of Factory Legislation in Massachusetts from 1825 to the Passage of the Ten-Hour Law in 1874," *in Labor Laws and Their Enforcement: With Special Reference to Massachusetts*, ed. Susan M. Kingsbury (New York: Longman Green and Co., 1911), pp. 11–12; Massachusetts Bureau of Statistics of Labor, *Report of the Bureau of Statistics of Labor* (Boston: Wright & Potter, 1870), pp. 93–96.

45. Quoted in Ely, *The Labor Movement*, p. 51.

46. Seth Luther, *An Address to the Working Men of New England* (New York: George H. Evans, 1883), pp. 24–25.

47. Darling, *Political Changes*, p. 115; Arthur P. Darling, "The Workingmen's Party in Massachusetts," *American Historical Review* 29 (October 1923): 82–86.

48. Darling, "Workingmen's Party," p. 84.

49. Abbott, "A Study," p. 34 (footnote); Louis Hartz, "Seth Luther: The Story of a Working Class Rebel," *New England Quarterly*, 13 (September 1940): 401.

50. Ibid., pp. 401–3; A sympathetic, but often inaccurate biography of Luther can be found in Dumas Malone, ed., *Dictionary of American Biography*, 24 vols. (New York: Chas. Scribner's Sons, 1933), 6: 511. No full-length study of Luther exists.

51. Hartz, "Seth Luther," pp. 403, 417.

52. Ibid., pp. 403–5, 411.

53. Quoted in ibid., p. 411.

54. Ibid., pp. 416–17; Seth Luther, *An Address on the Origin and Progress of Avarice* (Boston: Published by the Author, 1834), p. 43.

55. Ibid., p. 12; Seth Luther, *An Address Delivered Before the Mechanics and Workingmen of the City of Brooklyn* (Brooklyn: Alden Spooner and Sons, 1836), pp. 7, 12.

56. Luther, *An Address on the Origin and Progress of Avarice*, pp. 35, 36; see also Luther, *An Address Delivered before the Mechanics and Workingmen of the City of Brooklyn*, pp. 16–17.

57. Luther, *An Address on the Origin and Progress of Avarice*, pp. 35–36; Luther, *An Address to the Working Men of New England*, p. 22.

58. Luther, *An Address Delivered Before the Mechanics and Workingmen of the City of Brooklyn*, pp. 9–11, 17–18.

59. John Commons, "Labor Organization and Labor Politics, 1827–1837," *Quarterly Journal of Economics* 21 (August 1907): 324–28; *Documentary History*, John R. Commons, et. al., 6: 90–99; Hartz, "Seth Luther," p. 406.

60. Hartz, "Seth Luther," pp. 406–9. The rebellion was an interesting, romantic occurence in American history, which has received minimal study from most historians. The best study is Arthur May Mowry, *The Dorr War* (Providence: Preston and Rounds Co., 1901), which is outdated.

61. Hartz, "Seth Luther," pp. 409–10; Malone, *Dictionary of American Biography*, 6: 511.

62. Evans Woollen, "Labor Trouble Between 1834 and 1837," *Yale Review* 1 (May 1892): 88.

63. Commons, "Labor Organization," p. 329; Persons in Kingsbury, *Labor Laws*, pp. 19–20.

∾ 5 ∾

The Individualists

- 1 -

Complete individualism, the total rejection of all authority, spiritual or temporal, was another outgrowth of the Owenite movement. Its roots were deep in American tradition, tracing back at least to the religious dissenters who fled Britain to set up colonies in New England and some of the Middle Atlantic states.[1] Its first overt expression as a political ideal was developed as an aftermath of the collapse of the Owenite experiment at New Harmony by Josiah Warren.

This "ingenious, thoughtful little man" was a Boston Yankee born in 1798 who earned a precarious living variously as a musician and as an inventor of printing methods and lamps. Although no trained scholar, Warren developed an economic theory similar to Marx's surplus value, some twenty years before the *Communist Manifesto* was published. And about "twelve years before Joseph Proudhon published his views, Josiah Warren reached similar conclusions in America."[2]

Warren was an active participant in Owen's New Harmony from 1825 to 1827. Unlike other Owenites, he did not blame its failure on personalities, for he believed that the community had failed because of theoretical weaknesses. He argued that excessive paternalistic authority and majoritarianism had combined to cause its demise. They had undermined individualism, initiative, and responsibility, which he considered the true road to Utopian success. Warren argued that the collapse could have been averted if total individualism had prevailed, if each individual had possessed the right to do with himself, his property, his time, and his reputation as he saw fit. The only inhibition he placed on total freedom was the fact that an individual had to be prepared to accept the consequences for his actions.[3]

Warren agreed with Owen's basic assumption that man was the product of his environment. "Surrounding circumstances alone produce the difference between the people of different nations," he wrote, and "it is the influence of surrounding circumstances which makes one man a king, and another a beggar, which divides society into rich and poor, which enables some to command, and others to do otherwise than obey. It is the influence of circumstances which produces different classes in society."[4] To achieve an environment in which circumstances would allow men to develop to their fullest potential—and thus create the best possible society—Warren suggested that is was necessary to solve six basic problems: (1) the assurance of a proper reward for labor; (2) a guarantee of the security of each person and his—or her—property; (3) unlimited personal liberty; (4) proper means of production and uses of wealth; (5) ownership of land and other wealth by each individual and (6) voluntary cooperation among people. His solution to these problems called for an individualist-Anarchist society, which he termed "sovereignty of the individual," and an economic system, which he called "equitable commerce" or "equity," in which cost would be the limit of price, the labor dollar would replace money based on metallic or government-ordered value, and supply would be adapted to demand.[5]

Warren maintained that government was unnecessary, that individuals who associated voluntarily could perform community services more economically and more efficiently. Such services would, moreover, develop naturally to meet specific needs. Protection of life and property, the administration of justice, education, sanitation, even defense, could best be handled voluntarily by individuals. In fact, Warren considered government to be the chief enemy of a free and just society: "To establish the sovereignty of the individual all governments must be dispensed with."[6] Nor did he believe in the "forming of societies or other artificial combinations." Such organizations would require that the individual surrender to the group a portion of his own control over his person, property, or time; and the very act of giving up some of the individual's sovereignty would defeat the purposes for which the combination had been formed. "*Individuality* is the great prevailing fact in all persons and things: this never fails."[7] Warren carried his individualism to extremes—it even precluded, in his view, personal friendships, for he equated such relationships with combination. "I entirely decline all personal friendships," he wrote to a sympathizer, "for they only amount to partyism. The very best thing the friends of Equity can do is befriend Equity *strictly* and solely—in this way I shall get the only kind and quantity of friends that I am willing to leave."[8]

Individualism, as Warren defined it, meant that each person was a society unto himself. This precluded any attempt by a person—or group—to govern another in any particular. All customs and institutions that demanded conformity—even in the least degree—were, therefore, false and unjust.

Any effort to regulate the commerce or relationships between individuals was, likewise, unacceptable to him. Moreover, all law or regulation based on language—that is, any written or oral law—was perforce a wrong, for language is not universal; "each individual has a right to interpret language according to his individuality."[9]

Warren's argument for individualist anarchism derived from his understanding of music. He claimed that individualism represented harmonious relationships—on which Utopia would be based. In music, individuality was the basis for "all that we enjoy." So, too, was it to the "equally indestructible individuality of man that he is indebted for the harmony of society." Differences between men—and their beliefs—he compared to "the admissable discords in music [which] are a valuable part of harmony."[10]

His extreme individualism created a dilemma for Warren: How could there be some order in the world without government or organization? How could one human be prevented from injuring another? Warren believed the solution lay in mass communications, for "public influence is the real government of the world." Since public influence was the product of mass communication, simplification of printing methods would make it simple to mobilize public sentiment for order and against violations of individual rights.[11]

Warren conceded one other major impediment to total individualism: "sovereignty of the individual" could not be achieved unless the economic system were altered to assure a just reward for labor, that "each may receive the full fruits of his industry."[12]

Warren's economic views followed directly from his political. If he rejected government, it was necessary for him to eliminate administration as well. This he claimed for his economic system. To quote Warren: "Equitable commerce furnishes no offices to be filled by the ambitious and aspiring, no possible chance for the elevation of some over the persons or property of others." Warren's economic order was devised specifically with his political system in mind.[13]

The fundamental basis of Warren's economic theory was that the price that could be charged for an item would be exactly what it cost to produce and distribute it. Utility would have no relation to price; the sole determinant of price would be the cost—and the only cost would be the amount and repugnance of labor involved in production and distribution. This would eliminate all profit, all rent, and all interest.

He saw no other way to measure price. He agreed that water was an invaluable product, but if no labor was involved in obtaining, purifying, and delivering it, water should be free. Its value could not be determined equitably on any basis other than labor cost, for value was a relative matter. "The *value* of a loaf of bread to a starving man," he said, "is equivalent to the value of his life, and if the 'price of a thing' should be 'what it will bring' then one might properly demand of the starving man, his whole future life in servitude as the price of the loaf."[14]

To guarantee that cost would be the limit of price, Warren proposed that the circulating medium be changed, so all money would be based on labor, that all money would reflect actual time spent at work. Gold, silver, and other precious metals would have no exchange value. Since these labor dollars were to be issued "only by those who labor," Warren believed they would create an immediate revolution, since the workers would hold all the wealth, and the former employing class would lose both wealth and power. Moreover, the labor dollar would gradually make all money useless, since everyone would now work as the equal of everyone else. It would "sweep away all the crushing masses of fraud, iniquity, cruelty, corruption, and imposition that are built on" money.[15]

Warren was not a mere theorizer; he believed in carrying his ideas into practice. Almost as soon as New Harmony collapsed, he organized a new enterprise, a retail store in Cincinnati based on his economic ideas. Goods were sold at labor value—plus the time spent by the salesperson in dealing with the customer. The latter was achieved by the simple device of having a clock, in back of the sales counter, that the clerk would set going as soon as the customer began to make the sale. It would stop as soon as the sale was completed. Payment was in labor notes, which would specify, for example, "Due to Josiah Warren, on demand, thirty minutes of carpentry work. John Smith."

The store was successful. Its prices were substantially below those of most Cincinnati merchants, because it had eliminated the profits of the middle man. After less than three years, however, Warren closed the store "for the purpose of carrying the principles into all the commerce of life."[16]

At the invitation of Robert Dale Owen, Warren came to New York in 1830 to establish a new community based on equitable commerce. But Owen, who had promised to finance the experiment, was called to Europe, and Warren returned to Cincinnati. He continued efforts to spread his ideas and put them into practice. He attempted to organize a "Time Store" in New Harmony, Indiana, in 1842, but the local merchants cut their prices and offered credit to force the Time Store out of existence. In 1847 Warren reorganized a failing Fourierite community near Cincinnati into one based on "equitable commerce." By exchanging their labor, the residents of the community built their own homes and grist and sawmills. From near starvation, they advanced to prosperity. Success killed the experiment and values soared; speculators bought out the community in 1850. The residents went to Minnesota where they became successful individual farmers.[17]

Warren returned to New York where his followers had for some time been preparing to organize a community based on "sovereignty of the individual" and "equitable commerce." Warren, on his return to the city after a twenty-year absence, doubted he could undertake the task of organizing the community. Fortunately, he met and converted Stephen Pearl Andrews,[18] who undertook the task under Warren's tutelage.

They chose a desolate, poorly settled scrub area on Long Island, forty miles from New York, as the site for their colony. Within a few months, the tract was laid out in lots, which sold at $22 each, and the first houses were built. Each settler was limited to three lots. The community, which was named Modern Times, attracted various types of eccentrics including militant nudists, women who insisted on wearing men's apparel, believers in (but not practitioners of) free love and polygamy, and food faddists, including one woman who starved to death on a diet of beans without salt. Given the basic assumptions of "sovereignty of the individual," they had no alternative but to admit such people into the community and to allow them to act without restraint.

The result was an exceptionally bad press. One news story claimed that the people at Modern Times were committing suicide by food faddism. Another reported—accurately—that a blind German man paraded naked in the streets of the community. When a reporter asked a resident: "Do you hold to Marriage?" the Modern Times citizen replied:

Marriage! Well, folks ask no questions in regard to that among us. We, or at least some of us, do not believe in life partnerships when the parties cannot live happily. Every person here is supposed to know his or her own interest best. We don't interfere; there is no eavesdropping or prying. . . . The individual is sovereign and independent, and all laws tending to restrict the liberty he or she should enjoy are founded on error and should not be regarded.[19]

The interview raised a storm, especially among the clergy. To avoid further difficulties, the community changed its name to Brentwood but continued the experiment in "equitable living." Despite the strange conglomeration of members and the bad publicity, it was successful socially and economically.

Modern Times had a post office, an excellent six-mile road, pleasant and well-built green and white clapboard houses in which the 100 to 200 residents lived, and a railroad station. They had lectures on heterodox and unorthodox topics ranging from Unitarianism and Positivism to nonresistant pacifism. Dancing, amateur theatricals, madrigal singing, and readings from Warren and Andrews rounded out the full range of cultural activities. Moreover, they had "no demand for jails—No Grog shops—No Houses of Prostitution—no fighting about politics. . . . The Gardens and Strawberry beds are mostly without fences, yet no one (*belonging to the village*) is seen in them without the owner's consent. Few, if any doors are locked at night, and the fear of robbers and *fire* probably disturbs no one's sleep."[20]

When, in 1857, the national economy collapsed, the economy of the community also became untenable. It continued to exist until the outbreak of the Civil War in 1861, which exposed the ideological schism among its residents. Some joined the Union army in what they considered to be the "great crusade" against the evil of slavery; others—pacifists, in particular—fled abroad.[21]

Warren, now in his sixties, returned to his native Massachusetts, where he continued to write and speak for individualist anarchism, until his death in 1874.

- 2 -

Warren was the father of individualist anarchism, and Stephen Pearl Andrews was his prophet.

Born in Templeton, in north central Massachusetts, in 1812, the son of a Baptist minister, Andrews moved south to Louisiana as a teenager. There he studied and practiced law before moving west to Texas in 1839. In Texas he resumed his legal career, but his opposition to slavery forced him to return to the North in the early 1840s.[22] Andrews was not an Abolitionist. He had no ties—organizationally or ideologically—with the northern antislavery militants. His active opposition to slavery, based on pragmatic considerations, dated from the 1840s and related to the falling price of land near Houston. To stem the decline in real property values, Andrews proposed that slavery be abolished in Texas so the land there could be opened to free, white settlers. His suggestion won support from Houston land speculators who arranged for him to tour the state propagandizing for it. In Galveston, however, the proslavery politicians forced him to leave town and the scheme failed. He then went to England in an unsuccessful attempt to win financial and political support for his scheme.[23]

His abolitionism has been exaggerated by his biographers, but his other accomplishments have not. He became an expert on "phonography," the shorthand system devised by Isaac Pitman in England, and imported it into the United States. His original interest in bringing shorthand to America was to teach illiterates—primarily slaves—"to overcome the perplexities and absurdities of conventional spelling." His efforts did not end illiteracy, but they did simplify office procedures. He was also a philologist—especially of Chinese—and a language reformer, who developed an international language, Alwato.[24]

In 1850 Andrews heard a lecture by Warren in Boston, was immediately converted to "equitable commerce" and "sovereignty of the individual," and became an enthusiastic missionary for the ideas. He turned lecturer for individualist anarchism, wrote *The Science of Society*, the most systematic exposition of the theories, and helped found Modern Times.[25]

Andrews added a "scientific" dimension to Warren's theory. He argued that scientific inquiry was the basis of all truth, and he considered the study of society a genuine science, for "if researches into the habits of beetles and tadpoles, and their localities and conditions of existence, are entitled to the dignified appellation of Science, certainly similar researches into the nature, the wants, the adaptations and the true or requisite moral and social *habitat* of the spiritual animal called Man, must be . . . equally entitled to that distinction." From this study of society could be devised a "perfect order of human society . . . a Social Providence, subserving all the wants, developing all the faculties, utilizing all the powers of every creature from the cradle to the grave."[26] Andrews considered himself—and Warren—a true social scientist.

His "scientific" study convinced Andrews that two basic and antagonistic principles were at work in society. The first of these, which he labelled "order through subordination" was the conservative principle. The second, "the principle of freedom through individuality" was the root of progressivism. The sovereignty of the individual was the ultimate development of the principle of "freedom through individuality." It thus followed that "The sovereignty of the individual is the foundation principle of social order and harmony."[27]

Andrews's argument for "sovereignty of the individual" differed a great deal from Warren's simple explanation. Andrews, as a seeker after what he considered scientific truth and as a trained attorney, felt constrained to build a logical case in as convincing and irrefutable a manner as possible. He began from the premise that freedom "consists of the right to do wrong"; he considered freedom to mean, essentially, the right to choose between good and evil. Thus an individual had the right to do what others—or even his own conscience—considered wrong. This was merely the assertion of his civic or political right. Because right or wrong are concepts in ethics or morality, Andrews argued, the choice between them is solely a matter of individual judgment. Society could not legislate morals, and thus the individual had a civic right to commit a moral wrong. He considered evil consequences to be the only impediment to wrongdoing. No civic—or public—action could be taken to prevent a person from committing an immoral act. In only one instance did Andrews believe society could interfere with an individual's action: when someone committed an "actual encroachment" against another individual. But Andrews assumed this could not happen in a society that accepted the sovereignty of the individual. "It is nothing more and nothing less than that simple dictate of common sense and good breeding which requires that every one should abstain from intrusion in other people's affairs."[28]

He equated "sovereignty of the individual" with sovereignty of the nation. "I claim individually to be my own nation," Andrews wrote in a newspaper debate with Henry James and Horace Greeley. "I take this opportunity to declare my national independence. . . . I may have to fight to establish my claim, but the claim I make."[29] Since the individual was sovereign, it followed from Andrews's reasoning that representative democracy was "a mockery and a cheat." Under the American form of democracy, he wrote, the individual submitted to the will of a majority, and nothing could be more foreign to true democracy. "Democracy asserts that all men are born free and equal, that is, that every individual is of right free from the governing control of every other or of all others. [True] Democracy asserts, also, that the right is inalienable—that it can neither be surrendered nor forfeited to another individual, nor to a majority of individuals."[30]

Andrews carried his "sovereignty" of the individual further than Warren on one key issue: marriage. Whereas Warren opposed free love because he feared it would be "more troublesome than a crown of thorns," Andrews, although happily married for more than twenty years at the time of the disagreement, favored free love and opposed the institution of marriage. He believed legal marriage turned a wife into a private whore and encouraged public prostitution. Wives, he argued, were slaves, and he felt constrained to fight against the slavery of wives. It was an impertinence, he argued, for anyone to meddle in the personal affairs of another. No man or institution had a right to dictate whom a person should love "well enough or purely enough to live with." But having proclaimed his belief in sexual freedom, Andrews warned that "It is futile . . . to talk of removing the restraints of law from marriage . . . before . . . a positive [economic] security of condition for women and children" is achieved. The achievement of such security would require a new economic order.[31]

Andrews's economic views were identical with Warren's, but his arguments were far more sophisticated. He considered profitmaking a form of slaveholding and argued that it would be necessary to eliminate profit before the economic order could be rationalized. He agreed that in several ways this could be achieved: cooperative communities, communist division of resources, and socialism, among others. The simplest and most effective of all, he said, would be adoption of "Cost as the limit of Price," which would allow full individual freedom plus competition for excellence among producers. But he doubted the system would be established before society passed through a transitional stage of authoritarian Social Democracy.[32]

With the coming of the Civil War, Andrews abandoned temporarily his individualist anarchism and devoted his entire energies to fighting against the slaveholding South. He described the national character of the South as that of the "gentlemanly blackleg, bully, and desperado." The slaves, he said, were "too far depressed in the scale of humanity" to rise against their inhuman masters. Only an absolute military victory against the slaveholders could end the South's barbarism. He doubted the northern leaders wanted such a total victory, for to achieve it they would have had to rely on the use of guerilla warfare and slave revolts in "the spirit of John Brown or Nat Turner."[33] He saw no middle ground. It was strange that an individualist-Anarchist should support a government in a military adventure. But faced with the reality of the situation, with an imperative choice between two absolute evils—and with no other alternative—Andrews chose to fight against slavery even if it meant supporting the institution of government.

After the Civil War, Andrews formed a new group called the New Democracy, which preached a form of voluntary socialism and was affiliated for a short time with Karl Marx's International Workingmen's Association. The group attracted to itself Victoria Woodhull. She became the nominal leader of the movement; Andrews was its guiding brain. Woodhull, an attractive, young, midwestern woman of questionable background, had been a favorite of the aging Commodore Cornelius Vanderbilt. He helped her and her younger sister Tennessee Claflin organize a Wall Street brokerage house and, later, assisted them in founding a New York newspaper, *Woodhull and Claflin's Weekly*. Andrews, who was officially a minor editor of the weekly, was, in fact, its editorial director. Moreover, he wrote virtually everything that bore Woodhull's name from 1870 to 1876.[34]

Andrews thus became the intellectual genius of the most militant of women's rights movements. He was the mental father of the latter-day women's liberation movement. His involvement with that cause followed logically from his radical views of marriage. Writing in Victoria Woodhull's name in the *New York Herald*, Andrews delared: "As soon as the [female] sex is prepared to perform all the calls and duties of life, the right to do so cannot be withheld, and if so, we ourselves propose to fight for it, if need be. Without secession, we propose revolution, whenever the chains of conservatism drop too slowly and leave us chafing under their restraints too long, or deny us the means of applying possessed capacity."[35]

Woodhull proclaimed in a speech that unless Congress granted women "all legitimate results of citizenship," she would call a revolution. "We mean treason! . . . We will overthrow the bogus republic and plant a government of righteousness in its stead." She went to Washington and claimed for women the right to vote under the Fourteenth and Fifteenth amendments. Although the House Judiciary Committee rejected her claim, two members, Benjamin Butler of Massachusetts and William Longbridge of Iowa, supported it. The argument, which a latter-day biographer called "one of the strongest arguments even written on woman's right to vote under the Constitution," although delivered by Victoria Woodhull, was the work of a trained attorney—Stephen Pearl Andrews. Even in her declarations on free love in the *New York Times* and *New York Herald*—"I advocate free love . . . [in] the highest and purest sense, as the only cure for the immorality . . . by which men corrupt . . . sexual relations"—and sex education—"When sexual science is introduced into the schools, as assuredly it will be, sexual ills that now beset the young will vanish"—she was merely signing what Andrews had written.[36]

Victoria tried her hand at communism—but not for long. She assumed the nominal leadership of Andrews's Section 12 of the International Work-ingmen's Association (IWA). She headed the New York parade of IWA members commemorating the deaths of two leaders of the Paris Commune. But communism was not nearly so newsworthy a subject as sexual freedom. So she led Section 12 in proclaiming its belief in women's rights and free love. Soon Section 12, after first getting itself ousted from the IWA, vanished. Victoria Woodhull resumed her campaign for women's rights and sexual freedom—under the tutelage of Stephen Pearl Andrews.[37]

In 1872 an assorted band of radicals ranging from free lovers to Spiritual-ists to Communists united in the Equal Rights party and nominated Victoria C. Woodhull as the first female candidate for president of the United States. Her vice-presidential running mate was the black fighter for freedom Frederick Douglass. Andrews was the grey eminence of the party and the campaign. In her opening speech, written by Andrews, Woodhull pro-claimed: "From this convention will go forth a tide of revolution that will sweep over the whole world. . . . shall we be slaves to escape such revolu-tion? . . . Away with such weak stupidity! . . . [A] revolution . . . shall sweep over the whole world. . . . Shall we be slaves to escape such revolu-political trickery, despotic assumption, and all industrial injustice." She polled more than 30,000 votes.[38]

But Woodhull soon tired of revolution. After a long series of speaking tours, and romantic interludes, she turned to religion. The flaming, unin-hibited radical became a thoroughgoing prude and conservative. She went to Britain where she married an English gentleman, John Martin, and turned against her former mentor. She called Andrews "the high priest of debauch-ery" and charged that he "actually had the audacity and unblushing effron-tery to affix Mrs. Woodhull's signature to his effusions." A week later, she cried out: "Stephen Pearl Andrews! I impeach thee before the judgment bar. Pure hearts, which might have communed with their maker in the spir-itual Sinai, hast thou by infernal wiles tempted to bow down before the idol of the flesh. . . . Arch-blasphemer."[39] The diatribe had some truth; An-drews had, in fact, written almost all that bore Woodhull's name in public print during the early 1870s, but she had not been duped into signing the ar-ticles; she did so knowingly and agreed with their sentiments.[40]

Andrews continued writing in radical periodicals until his death in 1884.

- 3 -

During the time that Warren and Andrews were propagating their brand of individualist anarchism, another New Englander, Lysander Spooner, was developing his. Warren developed his theories from a psychophilosophic base rooted in Robert Owen's thesis on the effect of environment on charac-ter, and Andrews developed his on the basis of his own "scientific" investi-gation of society, but Spooner evolved his conclusions from his own philos-ophy of law. His was a "legalistic brand of anarchism."[41]

Spooner was born in 1808 in Athol in north central Massachusetts, only a few miles from Andrews's birthplace. He read law for two years and then practiced in Massachusetts before being admitted to the bar. At twenty-eight he moved to western Ohio, where he remained for seven years. On his return to the East, Spooner became involved in the protest against high mail rates. He founded a private mail firm that transmitted letters at less than half the price the government service was charging. Although his American Letter Mail Company was a financial success, it went out of business under the pressure of government prosecutions. Significantly, Spooner's competition helped force the government to reduce its mail charges. With the failure of his mail company, Spooner resumed his legal practice and became an active Abolitionist. His pamphlet *The Unconstitutionality of Slavery*, a concise, legalistic argument, was adopted by the Liberty party in 1849 as "a perfectly conclusive legal argument against the constitutionality of slavery," although other Abolitionists, notably William Lloyd Garrison and Wendell Phillips, were unimpressed. After the Civil War, Spooner turned to writing Anarchist materials, composing his last missive, *A Letter to Grover Cleveland on His False Inaugural Address, The Usurpation and Crimes of Lawbreakers, and Judges, and the Consequent Poverty, Ignorance, and Servitude of the People*, shortly before his death in 1887.[42]

Spooner defined law as "that *natural*, permanent, unalterable principle, which governs any particular thing or class of things." Law was, therefore, a "natural, universal, impartial, and inflexible principle." Its object was natural justice; thus any law that violated natural justice would be invalid. Moreover, natural law, and thus natural justice, was not an obscure notion. It was self-evident; it could be understood instinctively.[43]

Since, in Spooner's view, justice was a natural principle, man could neither make it, unmake it, or alter it. Moreover, it was the supreme law, and as such "it is everywhere and always the only law." All human legislation is, therefore, bereft of authority or obligation. "They are all necessarily either the impudent, fraudulent, and criminal usurpations of tyrants, robbers, and murderers, or the senseless work of ignorant or thoughtless men, who do not know, or certainly do not realize, what they are doing." He considered natural social law to be the equivalent of natural biological law and as immutable.[44] Thus when a number of men combined to declare themselves a government, they were in effect a conspiracy who had no rights over any other men, "And whenever any number of men, calling themselves a government, do anything to another man, or to his property, they thereby declare themselves trespassers, robbers, or murderers, according to the nature of their acts." From this argument, it followed naturally that Spooner could reach the conclusion that the only inhibition upon a man's actions was justice, which no man could legislate or, in fact, define, but could know only by intuition.[45]

Since he considered all human government a criminal conspiracy, good government was not possible. To call the United States government the best in the world was not to say it was a good government; it simply indicated how much worse the others were. Likewise, he doubted the American Constitution was an ideal or permanent contract. At best, it was a contract between persons long dead. "And the Constitution, so far as it was their contract, died with them." The Constitution was thus null and void because it violated natural law by attempting to legislate for future generations.[46]

Government, Spooner insisted, served only one purpose—to "arbitrarily forbid" the poor working people to obtain the capital they needed to work for themselves. This was done "to reduce them to the condition of servants; and subject them to all such extortions as their employers—the holders of privileged money—may choose to practice upon them." Government was thus the tool of the greedy monopoly capitalist. How could this be ended? Spooner wanted every man to have the right to issue his own money, secured by his own property or his own labor or anything else he had that had any value. But this could not be achieved by the ballot box, for man-made governments, upon which elections were based, were by their nature criminal conspiracies. Instead, Spooner proposed that the working people should refuse to pay taxes—"refuse to pay for being cheated, plundered, enslaved and murdered, they will cease to have cheats and usurpers, and robbers, and murderers, and blood-money loan-mongers for masters."[47]

- 4 -

Individualist anarchism was to continue as a minor tendency in the American Left. But by the midtwentieth century, it had been adopted by the so-called New Right that, after emasculating its economic base, used it as a defense for a selfish form of Social Darwinism.

Two sympathetic critics have noted the serious weaknesses that allowed extreme libertarianism—based on voluntary socialism—to become a basis for latter-day conservatism. Catholic Social-Gospel activist T. Wharton Collens argued that Warren "could show no way of carrying his formula into practice. Practically, he left things as they were since he would have every man demand his own price for his labor or goods, put his own estimate on it, and obtain that estimate if he could. . . . The consequence [of Warren's individualism] was that selfishness and competition were to be untrammelled and meet with no check but an abstraction."[48]

Dyer D. Lum, an Anarcho-Syndicalist of the latter half of the nineteenth century, argued—with particular reference to Andrews—that "I don't like to let my imagination run riot about what might be when I know it can't"[49] The criticism has a lot of truth in it, although Collens and Lum exaggerated the impracticality of Warren and Andrews. Both recognized that the "sovereignty of the individual" could not be viable without economic and educational changes. Andrews decried the profit system as an impediment in the path of true freedom, and Warren designed his new economic system as a necessary precursor of total individualism. Moreover, both recognized that they were describing an ideal; Andrews, in particular, did not delude himself into assuming that his Utopia was at hand—or, perhaps, even attainable.[50] He suspected that an authoritarian socialism would have to precede anarchism (an idea still espoused by many Marxists.) Yet the humane political and economic ideas of Warren, Andrews, and Spooner lend themselves to the inhuman, selfish, egotistical purposes of the conservative New Right. Total Social Darwinists, like the individual Anarchists, assumed that the only legitimate law was the natural law. To Social Darwinists, natural law implied "survival of the fittest" at the social level. To them, any regulation of man's relationships with his fellow men that modifies this "natural law" is a violation of that immutable law. Thus the New Right reasons that even community action aimed at social amelioration—welfare legislation to assure minimal needs to persons unable to take care of their own—is a violation of natural law. That the lack of such action might result in human suffering would have troubled Warren, Andrews, Spooner, and their followers, and it was for this reason that Warren developed his voluntary Socialist system. Yet by making "sovereignty of the individual" the keystone of their theoretical structure, the individualist Anarchists were preparing the way for the extreme Social Darwinist New Right, who ignore their economic theories and accept their political. The road to reaction is paved with the best of revolutions.

NOTES

1. Eunice Minnette Schuster, "Native American Anarchism," *Smith College Studies in History* 17 (October 1931-June 1932), maintained that individualist anarchism had its roots in the Antinomian rebellion in Puritan Boston during the 1630s (see particularly pp. 14-35). for an interesting and impressive opposite view, see James J. Martin, *Men Against the State* (Colorado Springs: Ralph Myles, 1970), pp. viii-ix.

2. Thomas Low Nichols, *Forty Years of American Life, 1821-1861* (New York: Stackpole Sons, 1937), pp. 238-39; Herbert L. Osgood, "Scientific Anarchism," *Political Science Quarterly* 4 (March 1889): 2; Victor S. Yarros, "Philosophical Anarchism, 1880-1910," *Journal of Social Philosophy and Jurisprudence* 6 (April 1941): 256; William Bailie, *Josiah Warren: The First American Anarchist* (Boston: Small-Maynard, 1906), pp. xii, 1-8, 46-47, 83-90.

3. Bailie, *First American*, pp. 1-8; Josiah Warren, *Manifesto* (Berkeley Heights, N.J.: Oriole Press, 1952), pp. 3-4. A photocopy of the original, issued on November 27, 1841, is at Houghton Library, Harvard University, Cambridge, Massachusetts; Pagination is from the easily accessible 1952 edition.

4. *The Peaceful Revolutionist* 1 (February 5, 1833): 1. Copy at Houghton Library.

5. George E. McNeill, *The Labor Movement: The Problem of Today* (Boston: A. M. Bridgman and Co., 1887), pp. 72-73. McNeill listed a seventh problem, a change in human nature, but this is the basic point of all of the problems and a redundancy not found in Warren's writings.

6. Josiah Warren, *Equitable Commerce* (Utopia, Ohio: Amos E. Sentner, 1849), p. 19; Josiah Warren to Stephen Pearl Andrews, *Woodhull and Claflin's Weekly*, 3 (August 19, 1871); Bailie, *Josiah Warren*, pp. 104-5.

7. Warren, *Manifesto*, pp. 1, 3–4; Josiah Warren, *Practical Applications of the Elementary Principles of True Civilization to the Minute Details of Every Day Life* (Princeton, Mass.: Printed by the Author, 1873), pp. 22–23.

8. Josiah Warren to "Dear Blocker," June 9 [1842], in Autograph File, Houghton Library.

9. Warren, *Equitable Commerce*, pp. 4, 18.

10. Ibid., p. 7; quoted in Bailie, *Josiah Warren*, pp. 54–55.

11. Warren, *Manifesto*, p. 6.

12. Bailie, *Josiah Warren*, p. 105; Warren, *Manifesto*, p. 6.

13. Warren, *Manifesto*, p. 6. For an interestingly similar view, see Karl Marx, *The Civil War in France*, in *The Marx–Engels Reader*, Robert C. Tucker, ed. (New York: W. W. Norton, 1972), particularly p. 556.

14. Warren, *Equitable Commerce*, p. 10; Bailie, *Josiah Warren*, pp. 9–13, 108–9, see also, Josiah Warren, "Cost, the Limit of Price," *Equity* 1 (May 1874): 12–13.

15. Warren, *Manifesto*, p. 7.

16. Ibid., pp. 4–5; Bailie, *Josiah Warren*, pp. 9–13, 17, 22–23. Louis H. Arky, "The Mechanics' Union of Trade Associations and the Formation of the Philadelphia Workingmen's Movement," *Pennsylvania Magazine of History and Biography* 76 (April 1952): 143, reports that a "Labour for Labour Association" in Philadelphia emulated Warren about the same time and operated three "Time Stores."

17. Bailie, *Josiah Warren*, pp. 25, 42–46, 50–56; the Fourierite Phalanx was named Claremont; Warren changed the name to Utopia.

18. Andrews is discussed in the next section of this chapter.

19. Bailie, *Josiah Warren*, pp. 59–63; Warren, *Practical Applications*, pp. 16–17; Madeline B. Stern, "Stephen Pearl Andrews and Modern Times, Long Island," *Journal of Long Island History* 4 (Fall 1964): 2–4.

20. Stern, "Stephen Pearl Andrews," pp. 7–8; Warren, *Practical Applications*, p. 22, Bailie, *Josiah Warren*, p. 68.

21. Stern, "Stephen Pearl Andrews," pp. 10–12; Bailie, *Josiah Warren*, pp. 77–78.

22. Biographical data on Andrews can be found in Stern, "Stephen Pearl Andrews," pp. 1–2; William C. Andrews, "Sketch of the Life of Stephen Pearl Andrews." *Woodhull and Claflin's Weekly* 4 (December 9, 1871): 13; Harvey Wish, "Stephen Pearl Andrews. American Pioneer Sociologist," *Social Forces* 19 (May 1940).

23. Andrews, "Sketch," p. 13.

24. Stern, "Stephen Pearl Andrews," pp. 1–2; Wish, "Stephen Pearl Andrews," pp. 477–79.

25. Stern, "Stephen Pearl Andrews," pp. 1–2.

26. Stephen Pearl Andrews, "Civilization a Failure," *Woodhull and Claflin's Weekly* 2 (May 13, 1871): 4; Stephen Pearl Andrews, *The Science of Society* (New York: Fowlers and Wells, 1853), p. vi.

27. S[tephen] P[earl] A[ndrews], "The Sovereignty of the Individual," *Woodhull and Claflin's Weekly* 3 (June 3, 1871): 5; Stephen Pearl Andrews, "The Great American Crisis," *The Continental Monthly* 5 (March 1864): 315.

28. Andrews, "The Sovereignty," p. 5.

29. Ibid.; Henry James, Horace Greeley, and Stephen Pearl Andrews, *Love, Marriage, and Divorce: A Discussion* (1853; reprint ed. Boston: Benjamin R. Tucker, 1889), p. 65.

30. Andrews, *The Science of Society*, p. 38.

31. Ibid., p. 37; James, Greeley, and Andrews, *Love, Marriage, and Divorce*, p. 69; Stern, "Stephen Pearl Andrews," p. 8.

32. S[tephen] P[earl] A[ndrews], "Review of J. N. Larned, *Talks About Labour and the Evolution of Justice Between Labourers and Capitalists*," *The Radical Review*, 1 (May 1877): 168–69.

33. Stephen Pearl Andrews, "The Great American Crisis," *The Continental Monthly* 4 (December 1863): 660, 663–65; 5 (January 1864): 93.

34. Emanie Sachs, *The Terrible Siren: Victoria Woodhull (1838–1927)* (New York: Harper and Brothers, 1928), pp. 81–82; Johanna Johnston, *Mrs. Satan* (New York: G. P. Putnam's Sons, 1967), pp. 63, 65–68, 122; *New York Herald*, February 13, 1870. p. 7; Mrs. Woodhull admitted, ten years later, that Andrews had written all of her material, see Johnston, *Mrs. Satan*, p. 267. One journalistic scoop by *Woodhull and Claflin's Weekly* was the first publication in America of Karl Marx's *Communist Manifesto* in English. It went virtually unnoticed.

35. Sachs, *The Terrible Siren*, p. 55; Although Mrs. Woodhull's husband, Colonel Blood, appears to have helped Andrews in the authoring of the letters to the *Herald*, which later appeared in *The Origins, Tendencies, and Principles of Government* (New York: Woodhull, Claflin & Co., 1871), Andrews was the intellect behind them. The book lists Victoria Woodhull as author.

36. M. Marion Marbury, *Vicky: A Biography of Victoria C. Woodhull* (New York: Funk and Wagnalls, 1967), pp. 27–28; Sachs, *The Terrible Siren*, pp. 80, 87, 97, 224; Woodhull, *Origins*, pp. 36–40.

37. Woodhull, *Origins*, p. 123; Marbury, *Vicky*, pp. 53–54.

38. Sachs, *The Terrible Siren*, pp. 157–59.

39. Quoted in Johnston, *Mrs. Satan*, p. 267.

40. Sachs, *The Terrible Siren*, p. 266; for an interesting description by Benjamin Tucker of his seduction at the age of nineteen by the thirty-three-year-old Vicky Woodhull, see pp. 238–66.

41. A. John Alexander, "The Ideas of Lysander Spooner," *New England Quarterly* 23 (June 1950): 216.

42. For biographical material on Spooner, see ibid., pp. 200–203; see also Schuster, "Native American Anarchism," p. 145.

43. Schuster, "Native American Anarchism," p. 145; Alexander, "Ideas," p. 207.

44. Lysander Spooner, "A Letter to Grover Cleveland on His False, Absurd, Self-Contradictory, and Ridiculous Inaugural Address," *Liberty*, June 20, 1885–May 22, 1886, reprinted in Henry J. Silverman, *American Radical Thought* (Lexington, Mass.: D. C. Heath & Co., 1970), pp. 110–11. Pagination is from Silverman edition.

45. Ibid., p. 113.

46. Lysander Spooner, "No Treason: The Constitution of No Authority," typescript, Houghton Library, dated 1870, pp. 1–2, 6.

47. Ibid., [p. 30]; Spooner, "A Letter," pp. 123–24, 126.

48. T. Wharton Collens, "Labor Time or Cost," *Labor Balance* 1 (October 1877): 13.

49. Dyer D. Lum to Voltairaine de Cleyre, September 25, 1889, Houghton Library.

50. It is, however, inaccurate to assume that he ceased believing in his ideal after a major disagreement with Warren in 1870. See his praise of Warren's system seven years after the disagreement, and three years after Warren's death, in Andrews, "Review of J. N. Larned," p. 165.

~ 6 ~

The Associationists

- 1 -

America of the 1840s has been called a country of nostrums, a nation abounding in social, economic, and political cure-alls. Its broad, open land, replete with almost unlimited possibilities, became the happy hunting ground for grandiose schemes aimed at the total reformation of mankind. The 1840s was the era when phrenology flourished and the water cure was in vogue. During the decade, Reverend Sylvester Graham led a popular crusade against white bread; "Robert Owen flitted back and forth across the Atlantic and about the cities of the New World catechizing prince and pauper in the true laws of life"; land reformers called for the abandonment of big cities and a return to the land where "every man [would live] under his own vine and fig tree on a ten-acre lot or a quarter-section farm"; women in bloomers shocked the sensibilities of staid Americans, and the Americanized version of Association—the Utopian dream of the French philosopher Charles Fourier—blossomed, withered, and died. The decade was "the hot-air period . . . an era of lost causes."[1]

The simplistic Utopianism of the 1840s was the product of a revivalism that had swept the nation during the latter half of the preceding decade and of transcendentalism. The revivalists—particularly Charles G. Finney, who preached anti-Calvinist doctrine of "free and full salvation" across New York State and New England—had as their primary goal the regeneration of the soul of the individual. From rebirth of the individual soul, it was a short intellectual journey to socialism—or Utopianism—whose primary objective was the regeneration of society, "the soul's environment."[2]

Like revivalism, transcendentalism was interested primarily in the individual. It was, basically, "an assertion of the inalienable worth of man . . . of the immanence of divinity in instinct, the transference of supernatural attributes to the natural constitution of mankind." Its origins were German, but it had little influence on German society or social institutions. It had been popular earlier in Britain, where its influence was limited to poetry and art. In early nineteenth-century New England, "it took root in the native soil and blossomed out in every form of social life."[3]

Before 1837 the Transcendentalists ignored or were hostile toward organized labor, for 1827–1837 was the decade of labor's aggressiveness, defiance, political activism, and, finally, strikes; Transcendentalists were opposed to militancy. But beginning with the economic crisis of 1837, and the long depression that followed, during which the labor movement became virtually dormant, the younger Transcendentalists, almost none of whom came from the working class, attempted to ally themselves with the workers.[4] It was thus natural that the movement with which they would become allied would be basically nonmilitant, apolitical, ideological, and more grandiose than practical; that it would be a "Socialist" movement that would reject the class struggle and ameliorative social reform. They allied themselves with Fourierism, as imported and Americanized by Albert Brisbane, a wealthy, young intellectual who had no experience or connection with the working class.[5]

- 2 -

Brisbane was born in 1809 to wealthy merchant parents in the small western New York State town of Batavia. He studied in Europe from 1828 until 1834 under teachers such as Victor Cousin and Georg Wilhelm Friedrich Hegel. Hegel, in particular, left him unimpressed. "I found in Hegel and his disciples no idea of a higher social order than the European civilization," he complained. During his six years in Europe, he travelled to Turkey, Greece, Ireland, Italy, England, and Scotland and met Goethe, Heine, Liszt, and Felix Mendelsohn. On the basis of his observations in Europe and the Near East, he decided that political systems had less influence on society than did economic and social systems. "I discovered," he wrote later, "that the American Republic was simply a new dress on old institutions. It retained the same system of social relations, the same system of commerce, the same rights of property and capital." Brisbane first became a follower of Comte Henri Saint-Simon, the French Utopian who proposed reorganizing society for greater productive efficiency by turning its direction over to technicians and scientists. But he soon tired of this nostrum and found another in the rambling, almost incoherent writings of Francois Marie Charles Fourier. After personal instructions from the aging Frenchman at $2.50 a lesson, he decided to devote his life to Fourier's ideals. By 1839, five years after his return to America, Brisbane had become an active propagandist for Fourier's system, and a year later he published *Social Destiny of Man*, a distillation of Fourier's ideas from which he deleted segments—particularly on marriage—that might shock Puritan America's sensibilities.[6]

Brisbane argued that Association, Fourier's system, would create the "most perfect system [of democracy] that can be conceived. It will extend Liberty and Equality, now restricted to the narrow field of Politics, to every department of Society and human life, and render them *Social and Universal.*" Moreover, it would achieve all of this without descending into political action, for Brisbane maintained that politics and legislatures dealt only with superficial issues and could thus achieve no practical results. He equated politics with party strife and argued that politicians were interested primarily in "seeking an ephemeral reputation." Fourierites, on the contrary, were interested in "the future." Because society's problems were not political problems, it was obvious to him that politics could not solve them. The "evil, misery, and injustice now predominant on the earth" were the product of the organization of society itself because the structure of society was out of harmony with man. This social malorganization was thus the cause of avarice, deceit, injustice, crime, and all other social ills. It followed that merely rectifying political or administrative errors, the imperfection of a single human institution, the "depravity of the passions," or some facet of human nature could not solve the universal social problem. Only a complete reorganization of society itself could rectify the situation.[7]

Nor would Brisbane's social revolution involve class warfare or class antagonisms. It would instead pit all of society against the "invidious social mechanism, which like a Divinity, stands undoubted and unsuspected." It was not one class exploiting another that caused social dislocation; it was rather the inefficient, hence unjust, system itself.[8] Nor was private ownership of property at the root of the system's evil. In fact, lack of private property had, Brisbane wrote, been the basic weakness in previous Utopian systems, secular and religious. The absence of private property, although well intentioned, had, he argued, led to a monotony in the Owenite and religious communities, which the Fourierites would avoid. In Association, the ownership of individual property would be extended "so that no one will be subjected to galling pecuniary dependence."[9]

The system Brisbane propagated was designed primarily to increase efficiency with justice. He expected capitalist and worker to cooperate, which would be impossible in a laissez faire society where each would work for his own interest, even when that interest might be in conflict with "public good."[10]

Brisbane proposed that communities, called Phalanxes, be built as models for a restructuring of society, and he envisioned a world composed of countless such communities. Approximately 2,000 persons "of different degrees of fortune, of different ages, of varied theoretical and practical knowledge" would reside in each Phalanx, and each would consist of about three square miles of land, through which should flow "a fine stream of water," whose terrain should be "undulating," and whose soil should be fertile for a variety of crops. He wanted each Phalanx to adjoin a forest, but he also wanted each to be near a large city. The first would assure timber, the second transportation and a market for products. Although agriculture would be the primary pursuit of the residents, each Phalanx would have "three types of manufactures," to "afford occupation during rainy days and the winter months." Seven-eighths of the residents would be farmers and workers, the rest would be "capitalists, men of science, and artists." Control of the Phalanx would be in the hands of a council "composed of stockholders, distinguished for their wealth or their industrial and scientific acquirements."[11] Moreover, Brisbane expected that enlightened capitalists, realizing the social advantages inherent in his system, would invest in the Phalanxes and thus share in the profits. Labor was to receive five-twelfths of a Phalanx's earnings; capital, four-twelfths; and "practical and theoretical knowledge," a Brisbane euphemism for management, three-twelfths.[12]

Class distinctions were to remain: each Phalanx dining hall would have "tables of three different prices." But the discrimination was not to be based on sex, for women would have equal status with men "in all business matters," as long as they had the requisite knowledge.[13] Children—particularly between ages ten and twelve—would not fare as well as women. Brisbane suggested that they be organized into Corporations of Little Hordes that would undertake the most filthy occupations: they would clean sinks, sewers, and privies, would manage the manure piles, and would hunt down and kill insects and reptiles. Brisbane rationalized that since children love filth, these jobs would offer them an opportunity to help maintain what he called social unity, while they entertained themselves. He predicted that these "repugnant occupations will become for children the sport of a *compound indirect* Attraction."[14]

Brisbane convinced many Americans that this system would rid the world of its social ills. It was the vision of a social order in which "a population living at their ease and imbued with honorable feelings, would not think of" crime. This was the system he preached on the lecture platform throughout the United States and in his column in Horace Greeley's *New York Tribune*. But Brisbane's role as the leader of the Fourierite movement in the United States was short lived—from 1839 until 1844. In the latter year, a tactical dispute rent the movement and Brisbane sailed to Europe. Thereafter, he was without major influence—an historical museum piece at thirty-five. The Association movement now came under the control of Horace Greeley and the New England Transcendentalists centered in Brook Farm.[15]

Although Brisbane imported and propagated Fourierism, its early success in the United States was primarily due to the efforts of Horace Greeley, whom John Humphrey Noyes called "Brisbane's other and better half." Fourier's ideas did not win widespread support until Greeley threw his support behind it by opening the columns in his popular daily, the *New York Tribune*, to the propagation of Association. At first the *Tribune*, with a circulation of about 20,000, printed only notices of Brisbane's lectures, and finally, in March 1842, a daily column on Association by Brisbane began appearing in Greeley's newspaper. It was this publicity, and this column, that spread American Fourierism.[16] The content of Brisbane's columns were unimportant; most of them were little more than rehashes of his *Social Destiny of Man*. But their appearance in a mass-circulation newspaper made the Fourierite ideas available to tens of thousands who would otherwise not have known of them. The publicity was effective: within a year after the column first appeared, American interest in Fourierism surpassed the fondest dreams of Brisbane and Greeley.[17]

Despite his dedication to Fourierism during the 1840s, Greeley was, in fact, a conservative journalist and politician whose rhetoric seemed at times to proclaim revolutionary ideas, which on closer examination were meaningless phrases, and who sought escape from reality in Utopia. On key issues, his views were more reactionary than radical.[18]

Born in 1811 to a poor farm family in New Hampshire, Greeley was apprenticed at seventeen to a printer in Vermont. Three years later, his apprenticeship completed, he walked to New York in search of a job. Within three years, Greeley had acquired enough capital to start his own weekly newspaper, *The New Yorker*, a quality journal of literature and politics that soon attained a circulation of 9,000. Seven years later, he started a one-cent Whig daily, *The New York Tribune*, of which he was editor and part owner.[19]

In October 1840 Greeley read Brisbane's book and claimed he was converted to Fourierism. Three months later, he proclaimed in *The New Yorker* that

our conviction is strong that the frame-work of society may be beneficially remodelled by the introduction of Association. . . . It cannot be doubted that one hundred families heartily united to promote the common good, under the guidance of the wisest, most skilled and liable of their number, living in common so far as would be found advantageous, and sharing the products of industry among them according to the contribution of capital, skill, and labor of each might enjoy in plenty the means of physical comfort and intellectual progress, and at the same time accumulate wealth with far greater rapidity than under the present discordant system.[20]

For the next eight years, until 1849 when the Fourierite movement collapsed completely, Greeley remained active in its cause.[21]

Greeley's sympathy for the workingman was limited to platitudinous statements: "Labor . . . must be guaranteed to all, so that each may know that he can never starve or be forced to beg while able and willing to work." But he had little sympathy with any effort by workingmen to improve their conditions by direct political or economic action—particularly strikes. He believed that employers were at least as kind, considerate, and humane as their employees. He considered most workingmen to be dullards, especially since they did not always agree with him politically.[22] When the pro-Labor Democrats in New York formed their own Equal Rights (or Loco-Foco) party in 1836, he led the journalistic assault against them. The workers were not the "miserable and hopeless slaves" pictured by the Loco-Focos, he said. The workers' hardships were not nearly so severe as those that an entrepreneur—particularly a publisher—faced. "The wages of labor have advanced ten to twenty-five percent with the increased cost of living, but the price of newspapers must remain substantially the same." The Equal Rights party's class appeal roused his opposition; the solution to the economic dislocation, he argued, "is by unity and concord—by the joint efforts of cool heads and strong arms."[23] Greeley was thus invariably hostile to the strikers and generally sympathetic with the employers—no matter how niggardly and intransigent. When the carpenters walked off their jobs in 1836, Greeley wrote: "There is a limit to all things—to the recompense of labor as well as to the profits of capital and enterprise—and there can certainly be no moral obligation resting on employers to accede to prices which must ensure bankruptcy to themselves and beggary to their children." When in 1845 the girls in a Pittsburgh textile plant struck for a ten-hour day, Greeley sided with the employer, who, he proclaimed, would go bankrupt if he yielded. When a year later Connecticut carpet mill workers went on strike against a sharp cut in pay, Greeley again defended the employer and attacked the workers, arguing that the pay cut was economically necessary.[24] Even when he agreed with the strikers' demands, Greeley opposed the strike. Thus during the 1844 strike of tablecloth weavers in Paterson, New Jersey, whose demands he agreed were justified, Greeley was vehement in his condemnation of the workers whom he accused of fomenting class conflict. He persistently pleaded with labor leaders to avoid class conflict, even if it meant surrender.[25]

His rhetoric did not always match his actions, for even as he denounced workers' efforts to improve their conditions by strikes, he spoke in radical terms about the plight of the workers. "Labor," he told his fellow printers, "has . . . doubled and quadrupled its own efficacy in production of whatever is needful to the physical sustenance, intellectual improvement and social enjoyment of Man." But "I do not find that there has been a corresponding melioration in the condition of the laborer." Nor did he accept the conservative view that overproduction was the cause of economic crises. "Can there be overproduction of Food, when so many . . . are suffering the pangs of famine? 'Overproduction' of Clothing and Fabrics, while our streets swarm with women and children who are not half-clad, and who shiver through the night beneath the clothing they have worn by day?

'Overproduction' of Dwellings, when not half the families of our city have adequate and comfortable habitations." Yet despite his rhetoric, Greeley invariably proposed a conservative and illusory solution that placed the burden on the workers themselves. In 1850, for example, he urged the workers to set up Laborer's Exchanges where they could list their availability and skills so employers could locate and hire them.[26]

Greeley's views on governmental responsibility for alleviating the conditions of the poor were, likewise, conservative. In October 1837, months after the economic depression had begun, he appealed for concerted action on the part of the "wealthy and benevolent" to give employment to those in need of work. He appealed to residents of rural areas to stay out of the cities where jobs were few. He wanted the urban workers to "scatter through the country—to the great West." It was not until the depression was twenty months old and it became obvious that the "wealthy and benevolent" would not make jobs available, and the city proletariat could not go west, that Greeley finally appealed for government assistance for the starving working people in the cities.[27] His general view of labor legislation was, likewise, conservative. As late as 1844, Greeley staunchly proclaimed: "Government cannot intermeddle with them [labor relations], without doing great mischief. They are too delicate, complex, and vitally important to be trusted [to] the clumsy handling of raw and shallow legislators." It was not until 1845 that he supported even a ten-hour law, and that halfheartedly and only after his failure to convince any employers to offer to reduce hours voluntarily.[28]

At root in Greeley's antipathy for strikes, labor political action, and labor welfare legislation was the low esteem in which he held workingmen and his exalted view of successful businessmen. "All human beings will work when pressed by hunger and cold," he wrote, "[but] only the minority will persist in working after their present needs have been fully satisfied." A worker was willing to produce for his employer only because he expected "to find his advantage in so doing." The employer was, therefore, under no obligation to consider a worker's needs in fixing his wages. The employer, on the other hand, who had risen out of the laboring class by his "energy, industry, frugality, and good management" was benefitting the "class from which he has risen" by "ceasing to compete for existing jobs and by offering employment to others."[29]

Labor, he argued, was not exploited. "Thousands who habitually assert that Hired Labor is inadequately recompensed act as though they knew this to be a lie," he wrote.

They persist in working for wages when they might be their own employers if they chose. . . . If he really believed the employing class [to be] oppressors of their workmen, he would relieve one of the number by employing himself. . . . But it is notorious that the greater number of thrifty, provident workmen choose to remain where they are, earning and receiving wages, when they might be proffering and paying them. They fancy their present condition one of less risk and less care. . . .[30]

In politics, Greeley was a Whig, an opponent of woman's suffrage, and an elitist, and he was a believer in party regularity. His Whiggism led Greeley to condemn Frances Wright's pleas for reform as "belchings" that disgusted him. She was, after all, a free thinker, who disliked the institution of marriage, and—worst of all—a Democrat. Nor did Greeley allow ethics or honesty to modify his partisanship. During the 1854 gubernatorial election, he claimed that the "Know-Nothing" American party candidate Daniel Ullman was a German-Jew born in Calcutta. This bit of pandering to nativist anti-Semitism was based on a lie, for Ullman was a Protestant born in Delaware. Neither did his role in the pre-Civil War Republican party signify a turn toward political progressivism by Greeley. At the 1856 national convention, he served as spokesman for the conservative wing of the party and opposed Salmon P. Chase as potential candidate for president, because he considered him too radical. He told Thurlow Weed, boss of the New York Whigs, that the party could win support of the working masses if it could convince them that the Whigs advocated Association.[31]

His attitude toward women reflected his overall political conservatism; Greeley classed votes for women as an abomination on a par with divorce and spiritualism. He also opposed egalitarian democracy, although he did occasionally pay lip service to broader suffrage. Yet when the working people of Rhode Island rose in rebellion to achieve the right to vote, he condemned them. Admittedly, the fact that the leader of the uprising, Thomas Dorr, was a Democrat played a part in shaping his opposition. Greeley favored the life sentence meted out to Dorr after the rebellion collapsed. In 1845, while he was the leading Fourierist, Greeley condemned the release of Dorr.[32]

Greeley's animosity toward egalitarian democracy stemmed from the low esteem in which he held the common people. "I am . . . well aware . . . that the mass of the ignorant and destitute are, at present, incapable of so much as understanding the Social Order I propose," he declared in 1847. He told an audience at Hamilton College that true democracy would be possible when the "aristocrats of intellect" could instruct the common masses.[33]

Stephen Pearl Andrews aptly described Greeley as "suggestive, inspiring, and disappointing."[34] Greeley was, in fact, a conservative in radical clothing.

- 3 -

Among the leading American Fourierites was at least one who attempted to examine social ills from a revolutionary perspective. Parke Godwin

believed in the class struggle and originated a theory of capitalist development that antedated by almost a decade the almost identical view of the latter-day Marxian Socialists. Godwin, who was born in New York City in
1816 and graduated from Princeton in 1834, was, like Greeley, a
journalist.[35] But unlike Greeley, he was interested in analyzing the root
causes of social and economic injustice rather than in making bold and
meaningless pronunciomentos.

Godwin premised his argument on the fact that population was multi-
plying rapidly "without any due provision by society for its employment or
support." As a result, he said, the workers, "who are a majority everywhere," were being forced by the increased competition for jobs, into "pick-
ing each others pockets and cutting each others throats." The situation was
further exacerbated by the rapid development of laborsaving machinery,
which threw more workers out of jobs. As a result, the condition of the
working class was deteriorating. At the same time, the power of the capitalist class was growing, and that power was being concentrated in ever fewer
hands.[36] Thus the working class—"the class without wealth, talent or education"—was completely subjugated to the "well-provisioned and equipped"
capitalists. Moreover, he argued that the middle class was disappearing into
the working class and further increasing the competition for menial factory
jobs. "Small properties—master mechanics on a small scale— . . . are destined to be crushed under the colossal wheels of larger properties and enterprises. Steam, machinery, large manufacturers are everywhere supplanting
the meaner kind of workshops. Employers are sinking into the class of the
employed." This growing misery of the working class and the middle class
he blamed on planless laissez faire capitalism.[37]

Godwin feared that the growing conflict of interests between the workers
and the capitalists could soon lead to open class war. The workers were
"getting restless under their long discipline of a thin diet and hard labor."
They were beginning to demand that society alleviate their plight but society was ignoring them. He warned of the danger of "a terrific [social] explosion." The disaster could yet be avoided, but only if the social system were
totally reorganized. Nor could the needed change be achieved by simple political means. Godwin maintained that "no political party has as yet proposed any measure that in the remotest degree touches the root of these
evils." Even if a political party should adopt a program aimed at revolutionizing society, it would be a useless gesture, for "the money power is mightier
than the legislative power." All governments, he observed, had become
subservient to the capitalist class; they had become "the vile, miserable
vassals of their superiors—the Money Lords, bound hand and foot . . . to
the capitalists . . . who are their owners and masters.[38]"

What then was Godwin's solution? It was "Association, on the basis of attractive industry," a unity of capital, labor, and talent. Thus Godwin's analysis of the social system was revolutionary, but his solution to its problems was not.

- 4 -

During the Fourierite excitement, at least thirty-four Utopian communities were organized in the United States. None is more famous than the 200-acre Brook Farm of West Roxbury, a suburb of Boston. This most romantic interlude in New England transcendentalism lasted only five years; yet its fame has outlived Association, the social theory its members eventually espoused but never practiced.[39]

Brook Farm started its life in 1841 as a Transcendentalist haven from the realities of a less-than-perfect world. Its founders believed man to be a self-determined being; they asserted, as their first principle, the supreme dignity of the individual. They blamed the world's social evils on "the lust of accumulation of personal objects," and they believed these ills could be cured only by withdrawing from competitive, institutional society and setting up a new community, free of competition, commerce, and the desire for accumulation. By so doing, the founders believed they would be planting the seeds for a new social order based on the dignity of the individual and in sympathy with his loftier aspirations. The new social order was thus to be based on Christian principles—for the ultimate objective of Brook Farm's founders was the establishment of Christ's kingdom on earth.[40]

George Ripley, Brook Farm's leader during most of its existence, expected it

to insure a more natural union between intellectual and manual labor than now exists; to combine the thinker and the worker, as far as possible, in the same individual; to guarantee the highest mental freedom, by providing all with labor adopted to their tastes and talents, and securing to them the fruits of their industry; to do away with the necessity of menial services by opening the benefits of education, and profits of labor to all; and thus to prepare a society of liberal, intelligent, and cultivated persons, whose relations with each other would permit a more wholesome and simple life than can be led amidst the pressures of competitive institutions.[41]

He thus proposed that Brook Farm lead the way in remaking the world in the Transcendentalists' own image. Menial labor was to serve as a means by which free time could be assured to all for intellectual pursuits; intellectual pursuits were, in their view, the primary purpose of life.[42]

It was this devotion to the intellect that gave Brook Farm its unique status. Thus its most successful undertaking, and its primary source of income, was its school. Even Harvard College advised students in need of more educational preparation before entering its ivy halls, to attend the Brook

Farm school. Its roster of teachers included names such as Charles Dana, who later gained fame as founder of the *New York Sun*; John S. Dwight, who was to become a leading music critic; and George Ripley. The school's educational policy was as unique as its faculty; teacher and student had freedom of discussion between them, each pupil could study when and where he desired, and older students—who did some manual labor—had their classes arranged at convenient periods of the day. Unfortunately, the mental strength of Brook Farm's residents was matched by their physical weakness. They had a permanent shortage of "hands" for farm work but always more than enough personnel available for the school.[43]

The dearth of manual workers and lack of financial practicality among the members of Brook Farm caused continuing crises. Samuel Osgood, a friend of the organizers, feared that the souls of the Brook Farmers would be "evaporated by the hot summer suns, that are to shine down upon their toils." Moreover, overborrowing led to perpetual financial difficulties. The farm had at least four mortgages against it during most of its life.[44]

The dominance of intellectuals also led the Brook Farm residents into its fatal Fourierite phase. The philosophic basis of Brook Farm, at its foundation, was antithetical to Fourierism. Its founders warned against three dangers: (1) organization, "which begins by being an instrument and ends by being a master"; (2) financial endowment, which was seen as a deterrent to self-reliance; and (3) "coterie," the development of cliques and small factions, which was considered an anathema to brotherhood.[45] At least the first should have made Association unacceptable to Brook Farm's residents, and most Transcendentalists were highly critical of Fourier's ideas when they were first presented to America by Brisbane.

Elizabeth Peabody, writing in the Transcendentalist quarterly *The Dial* in October 1841, condemned Fourierism for being spiritually deficient and oppressive of moral independence and declared that Association would "circumvent moral freedom and imprison it in his [Fourier's] Phalanx."[46] As late as July 1842, the Transcendentalist journal was highly critical of Fourier and his Utopia:

. . . He treats man as a plastic thing, something that may be put down, ripened or retarded, moulded, polished, made into solid, or fluid or gas, at the will of the leader; or perhaps as a vegetable from which, though now a poor crab, a very good peach can by manure and exposure be in time produced, but skips the faculty of life, which spawns and scorns systems and system-makers, which eludes all conditions, which makes or supplants a thousand phalanxes and New Harmonies with each pulsation.[47]

Yet Fourierism was fast becoming a fad among America's intellectuals. Moreover, by 1843–1844 few of the Transcendentalists who had started

Brook Farm remained in it; nearly all of the original residents had left. The life of cooperative community labor did not appeal to them in practice. For example, Nathaniel Hawthorne, one of the founders, resigned because he wrote an inquirer, "it is my present belief that I can best attain the higher ends of life, by retaining the ordinary relation to society." Also, Brisbane was a frequent visitor and lecturer at Brook Farm.[48] It was thus inevitable that Brook Farm's residents would be caught in the popular intellectual wave of the moment and swept into the Fourierite camp.

Brook Farm's formal change from transcendentalism to Association occurred during the Christmas season of 1843–1844 at a Boston convention of representatives from Massachusetts Utopian communities. The convention, William H. Channing reported, "marked an era in the history of New England." The delegates hailed Association and derided social reformers; society could not be reformed until after the achievement of Association. Only one delegate doubted that Association was the ultimate answer to man's plight; this heretic viewed it as a mere step on the path to communism. He was ignored, Association was in its ascendency, and Brook Farm began the work of changing from an "educational establishment" into a Phalanx.[49]

But all that changed at Brook Farm was the rhetoric. In 1845 the members promised that "We shall suffer no attachment to literature, no taste for abstract discussion, no love of purely intellectual theories, to seduce us from devotion to the cause."[50] But the primary interest at Brook Farm remained intellectual; its chief contribution to the cause was the publication of a well-edited, literate Fourierite journal, *The Harbinger*. Although George Ripley persisted in issuing optimistic reports about Brook Farm to his friends, he conceded that it was "merely preparing for Association." The financial problem was exacerbated when the residents decided to construct a Phalanstry, a residence plus refectory. Thus when a fire destroyed the Phalanstry in 1846, the community was bankrupt. Moreover, the tide of Fourierism had receded, it was no longer fashionable, and Brook Farm dissolved. Two months later, in May 1846, the American Union of Associationists discarded Fourierism. The movement was dead.[51]

- 5 -

Fourierism in America was little more than a passing fad. Few of the Phalanxes lasted more than a year; only the North American Phalanx in Red Bank, New Jersey, continued for eleven years, and it was hardly a Fourierite community. The Phalanxes failed because they were artificial attempts to create a new society overnight without regard to the social environment. Ezra H. Heywood, an individualist-Anarchist and social critic, blamed their failure on the Fourierist "delusion that a mere form of organization will cure individual or collective sin."[52] More important perhaps than the social environment or the organizational delusions of Fourierism—although either would on its own be fatal to a movement—was the failure of the Associationists to attract any working-class support.

Association was basically a middle-class movement. The Fourierites intruded themselves into labor movements, but virtually no workers were involved in the Phalanxes. Few were interested in any Utopian schemes. During the 1840s, the only truly working-class movement was the struggle for a ten-hour day, which Utopians either ignored or denigrated. The Fourierites invariably opposed the very things the workers needed. At the time when starvation was a way of life for American workers, William H. Channing denounced government welfare measures charging they would "aggravate the very evil they are expected to heal." Channing, a Unitarian Transcendentalist turned Fourierite, suggested that the only cure for the workers' sufferings could be found in a system where *"all energies* [are] united in Production"* to eliminate waste.[53]

Whenever the Fourierites appeared as "workingmen" at labor conventions, they interposed their own nostrum while opposing pragmatic reforms. Thus at the 1845 convention of the New England Workingmen's Association in Fall River, Massachusetts, Brook Farmer L. W. Ryckman opposed support for a cooperative store, insisting that the Workingmen's Association should be organized on a "broader and nobler basis . . . aimed at something more fundamental, that shall not merely ameliorate the working classes, but disenthrall the laborer from the power of misused capital." Nor were the Fourierites democratic in their opposition to ameliorative measures—they would invariably gain control of the meetings by "packing" them with their followers in order to refuse the floor to delegates who favored reform.[54] The results of the Fourierite intervention in the labor movement were (1) its impotence during the mid-1840s and (2) the eventual rejection by the workers of any long-range aims. Thus when genuine workingmen recaptured the New England Workingmen's Association from the intellectuals in 1846, they vehemently rejected even Seth Luther's suggestion that the ten-hour demand was merely a stepping stone on the road to a new social order.[55]

The Fourierite movement was essentially conservative. It has been considered part of the American radical Left by Socialist historians on the basis of faulty and scant research.[56] Some of the rhetoric of the movement was admittedly radical, even revolutionary, but this was mere rhetoric. The very essence of Fourierism was a continued division of society into classes, with capital remaining dominant. It guaranteed the worker his job, but only part of the earnings of the Phalanx; control remained in the hands of the "most able"—the managers and capitalists. The primary aim of Fourierism was a more efficient capitalist society; its chief purpose was to avoid working-class revolution.[57] It was essentially an interlude in American history that emphasized the inability of intellectuals to comprehend the needs and aspirations of the working class.

NOTES

1. Leo Brophy, "Horace Greeley: Whig or Socialist" (Ph.D. diss., Fordham University, 1939), pp. 20–21, 37–38; John R. Commons, "Horace Greeley and the Working Class Origins of the Republican Party," *Political Science Quarterly* 24 (September 1909): 468–69; Norman Ware, *The Industrial Worker, 1840–1860* (1842; reprint ed. Chicago: Quadrangle Books, 1964), p. 18.

2. John Humphrey Noyes, *History of American Socialism* (1870; reprint ed. New York: Hillary House Publications, 1961), p. 26.

3. Octavius Brooks Frothingham, *Transcendentalism in New England: A History* (New York: G. Putnam's Sons, 1876), pp. 105, 136.

4. Commons, "Horace Greeley", 476.

5. Ware, *Industrial Worker*, pp. 164–65. See section 5 of this chapter.

6. Arthur Eugene Bestor, Jr., "Albert Brisbane—Propagandist for Socialism in the 1840s," *New York History* 28 (April 1947): 131–50.

7. Quoted in ibid., Albert Brisbane, *Social Destiny of Man: Or Association and Reorganization of Society* (Philadelphia: C. F. Stollmeyer, 1840), pp. viii–ix, 2.

8. Brisbane, *Social Destiny*, p. 4.

9. Ibid., pp. 29, 353; Albert Brisbane, *A Concise Exposition of the Doctrine of Association* (New York: J. S. Redfield, 1843), p. 9 (column 2).

10. Ware, *Industrial Worker*, p. 169; Brisbane, *Social Destiny of Man*, p. 10.

11. Brisbane, *Social Destiny*, pp. 350–53.

12. Ibid., p. 354.

13. Ibid., pp. 353, 355.

14. Ibid., pp. 443–46.

15. Bestor, "Albert Brisbane," Cecilia Koretsky Michael, "Horace Greeley and Fourierism in the United States" (M. A. Thesis, University of Rochester, 1949), pp. 61–85, 147; Brisbane continued to write for Fourierite journals, particularly the *Harbinger*, from 1845 until 1847; his name appeared, as a contributor, in the annual index of that journal from volume 1, 1845, through volume 4, 1847. He also spoke at a May 13, 1845, public meeting of the New York Associationists and visited the North American Phalanx in New Jersey that month. See *Harbinger* 2 (May 30, 1846): 397–99. He also addressed the 1847 dinner in New York honoring Fourier's birthday. See *Harbinger* 4 (April 24, 1847). He was interested in other quasi-Fourierite endeavors during the 1850s and 1870s, none of which was significant. For bibliographic notice of these activities, see Bestor, "Albert Brisbane," p. 158. He was, however, after 1844, no longer a leader of the Fourierite movement; the effective leadership was in the hands of Greeley and the Brook Farmers.

16. Cecelia Koretsky Michael, "Horace Greeley", pp. 49–53, 56; "Fourierism in the United States," *The Dial* 3 (July 1842): 86; Noyes, *History*, p. 231.

17. Michael, "Horace Greeley," pp. 80–83.

18. Glydon G. Van Deusen, *Horace Greeley: Nineteeth-Century Crusader* (Philadelphia: University of Pennsylvania Press, 1953), pp. 72, 75–76.

19. Michael, "Horace Greeley," pp. 36–38.

20. *The New Yorker* 10 (January 16, 1841): 281–82.

21. Michael, "Horace Greeley," pp. 91–92; *The Harbinger*, October 1845, quoted in Noyes, *History*, pp. 231–32.

22. Charles Sotheran, *Horace Greeley and Other Pioneers of American Socialism* (New York: Mitchell Kennerly, 1915), pp. 192–97, 200–201; Van Deusen, *Horace Greeley*, pp. 76–78.

23. *The New Yorker* 3 (March 25, 1837): 9. Date erroneously printed on page as March 25, 1835.

24. *The New Yorker* 2 (June 25, 1836), quoted in Brophy, "Horace Greeley," p. 71; *New York Tribune*, May 18, 1843, p. 2; October 14, 1845, p. 2; September 4, 1846, p. 2.

25. *New York Tribune,* June 21, 1841, p. 2.

26. Horace Greeley, "The Union of Workers," in *Hints Toward Reforms in Lectures, Addresses, and Other Writings* (New York: Harper and Brothers, 1850), pp. 336–38, 374.

27. *The New Yorker* 3 (June 3, 1837): 169; 4 (October 7, 1837): 457; 5–6 (January 12, 1839): 265.

28. *New York Tribune*, January 25, 1844, p. 2; February 16, 1844, p. 2; also quoted in Commons, "Horace Greeley," p. 485.

29. Horace Greeley, "Capital and Labor," *Wood's Household Magazine* 9 (November 1871): 211; Horace Greeley, *Recollections of a Busy Life* (New York: J. C. Ford & Co., 1868), pp. 156–57.

30. Greeley, "Capital and Labor," 211–12.

31. Brophy, "Horace Greeley," pp. 41–44, 138–41; Van Deusen, *Horace Greeley*, pp. 73–74, 79–80; Jeter Allen Isely, "Horace Greeley: Apostle of Social Democracy, 1853–1881, (Ph.D. diss., Princeton University, Princeton, N.J., 1941), ch. 3: 48, ch. 5: 4–5, ch. 6: 6; Commons, "Horace Greeley," p. 488.

32. Van Deusen, *Horace Greeley*, pp. 74–76; Emanie Sachs, *The Terrible Siren: Victoria Woodhull (1838–1927)* (New York: Harper and Brothers, 1928), p. 113.

33. Horace Greeley, "The Relation of Learning to Labor," in *Hints*, pp. 140–42; quoted in Sotheran, *Horace Greeley*, p. 209.

34. Quoted in Van Deusen, *Horace Greeley*, p. 81.

35. Parke Godwin, *Democracy, Constructive and Pacific* (New York: J. Winchester, 1844), p. 14.

36. Quoted in Sotheran, *Horace Greeley*, pp. 139–40.

37. Parke Godwin, "Constructive and Pacific Democracy," *The Present* 1 (December 15, 1843): 185–93.

38. Ibid., See also Sotheran, *Horace Greeley*, pp. 139–40.

39. Noyes, *History*, pp. 14, 104; Lindsey Swift, *Brook Farm: Its Members, Scholars, and Visitors* (New York: The Macmillan Company, 1900)., p. vi.

40. Frothingham, *Transcendentalism*, pp. 156, 164; *The Dial* 1 (October 1840): 254–55, as quoted in Michael, "Horace Greeley," p. 17; Elizabeth P. Peabody, "Plan of the West Roxbury Community," *The Dial*, January 1842, extracted in Noyes, *History* p. 114; Elizabeth P. Peabody, "A Glimpse of Christ's Idea of Society," *The Dial*, October 1841, extracted in Noyes, *History*, pp. 109–12.

41. George Ripley to Ralph Waldo Emerson, November 9, 1840, quoted in Swift, *Brook Farm*, pp. 15–16.

42. Peabody, "Plan of the West Roxbury Community," p. 114.

43. Swift, *Brook Farm*, pp. 69–70, 72.

44. Samuel Osgood to John S. Dwight, April 9, 1841, *Brook Farm Collections*, Dwight Papers, Boston Public Library; William H. Channing to John S. Dwight, January 18, 1846, *Brook Farm Collections*, Boston Public Library; Swift, *Brook Farm*, pp. 24–25.

45. Frothingham, *Transcendentalism*, pp. 157–58.

46. Peabody, "A Glimpse of Christ's Idea of Society," p. 112.

47. "Fourierism and the Socialists," *The Dial* 3 (July 1842): 88–89.

48. Samuel Osgood to John S. Dwight, November 21, 1840, *Brook Farm Collections*, Boston Public Library; Nathaniel Hawthorne to "My Dear Sir," May 25, 1842, *Brook Farm Collections*, Boston Public Library; Swift, *Brook Farm*, pp. 118, 280.

49. "Signs of the Times," *The Present* 1 (December 15, 1843): 207–10; Noyes, *History*, pp. 512–17, 527.

50. Quoted in Sotheran, *Horace Greeley*, pp. xlvii–xlviii.

51. George Ripley to "Dear Sir," September 11, 1844, *Brook Farm Collections*, Boston Public Library; Swift, *Brook Farm*, pp. vii, 280–81.

52. Ware, *Industrial Worker*, p. 174; *The American Socialist* 1 (June 29, 1876): 106–7.

53. "Signs of the Times," *The Present* 1 (November 15, 1843): 143–44; Brophy, "Horace Greeley," p. 137; Ware, *Industrial Worker*, pp. 164, 178, 199.

54. Ware, *Industrial Worker*, pp. 163, 177, 178, 205, 207; *The Harbinger* 1 (September 27, 1845): 255.

55. Ware, *Industrial Worker*, pp. 206, 218–19.

56. See, for example, Morris Hillquit, *History of Socialism in the United States* (New York: Funk and Wagnalls, 1910), and Sotheran, *Horace Greeley*.

57. See, for example, Ware, *Industrial Worker*, pp. 167, 169.

∽ 7 ∽

The Burned-Over District

- 1 -

Transcendentalism and Fourierism suited their Boston and New York intellectual clientele. They were sedate, their religious base was Unitarian and anti-Fundamentalist, and their revolution would hardly have upset the social structure that made the middle class comfortable. But neither was fitted for the early nineteenth-century semifrontier environment in the upstate New York area known as the "Burned-Over District." This was an area populated primarily by farmers who had migrated from the hill country of western New England. The Burned-Over District was the scene of religious revival that was unmatched in the rest of the nation. Enthusiasm and emotionalism greeted each new idea of salvation. Stretching from the Hudson to Lake Erie, and from Lake Ontario to the Delaware, the Burned-Over District was a huge, sparsely populated region, with good farm lands and plentiful timber. It was in this region that the most radical of movements developed. Most of its radicals, like most of its inhabitants, were hill country New Englanders. The two most notable residents, John Anderson Collins and John Humphrey Noyes, were Vermonters. Both disliked transcendentalism, both rejected orthodox religion—one as an agnostic, the other as the leader of his own sect—and both organized communistic communities. One community failed after approximately two years of stormy life; the other existed for more than thirty years.

- 2 -

The shorter lived community was the Owenite community at Skaneateles. Its founder was John Anderson Collins, an erstwhile Abolitionist, who abandoned the antislavery crusade to organize a Utopia designed as a model for reshaping society into an Owenite heaven.

Born in 1810 in Manchester, Vermont, Collins was educated at Middlebury College and Andover Theological Seminary. Shortly after completing his studies at Andover, he joined the William Lloyd Garrison wing of the Abolitionist movement, becoming in 1839 general agent for the Massachusetts Anti-Slavery Society. Garrison was so impressed with Collins that he sent the younger man to England in 1840 on a fund-raising mission for the society, which was then in dire financial straits because of internal feuding among the Abolitionists. Collins's one-year stay in Britain failed financially, but it turned him from a simple Abolitionist into a confirmed Owenite. The poverty he found among Britain's working class appalled him. He attended Chartist meetings and rallies, and he met Owen, who convinced him of the justice of the elderly Utopian's social theories.[1]

Upon his return to the United States, Collins was appointed general agent for the American Anti-Slavery Society in upstate New York. In that post, he recruited the famed black Abolitionist Frederick Douglass as an orator for the Garrison wing of the movement and accompanied him on his speaking tour. But Collins was no longer dedicated to abolition alone; in fact, he believed that the "anti-slavery cause is a mere dabbling with effects." To abolish only chattel slavery, he told an antiproperty convention in Syracuse, would change the form of slavery, but not its fact, for property was the basic evil that enslaved men. Thus the only solution to the problem of slavery was "universal reform." By 1843 Collins refused to accept his salary from the Anti-Slavery Society and became "almost entirely absorbed" in working for a total reformation of society. William Lloyd Garrison reported that Collins "goes for a community of interest, and against all individual possessions whether of land or its fruits—of labor or its products." Moreover, Collins now agreed with Owen that man was "the creature of circumstances and therefore not deserving of praise or blame for what he does," a position diametrically opposed to the Abolitionist view that held slaveholders to be individually to blame for the misery of the slaves.[2]

Collins premised his thesis on the assumption that property and its products, although actually the joint property of all human beings, had been monopolized by a small class that had gained political and economic power by the use of force or trade. This class, he said, controlled government and had made of it "the mere instruments . . . to protect them in their wholesale plunder." All of his other views developed from this assumption; from it he also developed the thesis that partial meliorative reform would be futile, that only a total reorganization of society could remedy the situation. "The times demand," he wrote to an abolitionist", an association which will not be satisfied with the pruning off of the branches of the tree of evil, but will, with a giant's power, lay the axe at its root, that root, trunk and branches may perish together."[3] To set in motion the wheels of needed change, Collins organized his community at Mottville, near Skaneateles, New York. It was to be a cooperative, joint stock association capitalized at $50,000, each share to cost $50. Membership would be limited to shareholders who would eschew the use of liquor and win the approval of 75 percent of the other members. All members would vote on all expenditures, and the community's officers were to be elected by the membership. Although the property would be owned in common, the deed would be held in trust by the elected trustees.[4] The community was thus organized on a contradictory basis—it was both egalitarian and elitist: all members were to have equal rights and responsibilities, but membership was to be limited to those elected by the existing membership.

The community began its organizational phase at a mass meeting in a barn on the Skaneateles property. Present besides Collins were Ernestine Rose, Polish-Jewish radical; Nathaniel Peabody, editor of the *Herald of Freedom*; and other militant reformers. The audience was enthusiastically in favor of the proposal to create the new Owenite colony, but not all of those present agreed with Collins's blueprint for Utopia. Quincy A. Johnson, one of two trustees (the other was Collins), opposed social ownership, a disagreement that was to help lead to the community's demise.[5]

In November 1843 Collins proclaimed the "Articles of Belief and Disbelief and Creed" for the Skaneateles Community. The articles rejected religion as being based on falsehood. Collins admired the ideals of Jesus, because they were "best adapted to promote the happiness of the race," but he denied that their author was divine or superhuman. Biblical miracles were, he argued, unphilosophical; he denied the possibility of salvation from sin or from punishment after death through a crucified Christ. It thus followed that he would consider the clergy an "imposition" and organized religion a sower of strife and contention rather than of peace and love.[6]

Collins also proclaimed his antipathy toward all coercive governments, which, he declared, were organized of "bands of banditti." Therefore, he urged his followers to ignore government, by not voting, petitioning their governments, doing military service, sitting on juries, paying personal or property taxes, testifying in court, or appealing to the law for redress of grievances. Instead, he urged them to use all "peaceful and moral means to secure their [governments] complete destruction."[7] He also denied the right to private property, "that the idea of mine and thine, as regards the earth and its products" was to be disregarded. Moreover Collins wanted "all buying and selling" to be disavowed. In effect, the articles called for "no-religion, no-government, no-individual property, and vegetarianism."[8]

Proclamation of the articles created serious dissent both within and without his coterie of followers. Some of his adherents were absolutist-Anarchists who opposed any creed; others, who were not convinced Socialists, rejected his "no-property" stand. Those who were on the outside were repelled by his rhetoric. Faced with such oppositions, Collins eased his stance.

In an editorial in his newspaper, the *Communitist*, he denied that the articles represented the community's position. In the editorial, he renounced all "creeds, sects, . . . parties," constitutions, and declarations of belief or disbelief. Each individual in the community was free to believe as "he or she may be moved by knowledge, habit, or spontaneous impulse."[9] But Collins had merely yielded to pressure, for despite his ostensible change, he remained a firm believer in the principles he enunciated in his articles. In the "Preamble and Constitution" of the New England Social Reform Society, which he founded in 1844 "to assist in carrying into practical operation the community of property partially commenced in Skaneateles, New York," he reiterated and expanded on his positions proclaimed in the Skaneateles Articles of 1843. He now charged that a society based on competition—as was capitalist America—placed a premium on selfishness, cant, and strength; that it created two classes, the capitalist and the laborer—the rich and the poor. This "disparity of possession," which he attributed to the socioeconomic system, was at root in the internal strife that plagued society. Moreover, by placing a premium on selfish interest, the social order encouraged "fraud, deception, and crime." Laborsaving machinery, which should have been a boon to mankind, became under the system of private property "instruments of tyranny and toil," which forced wages down by eliminating the need for skills and created unemployment, and thus misery, by eliminating jobs. Moreover, private ownership of property made of the products of man's industry objects of *speculation, of barter, and sale*"; this, Collins argued, "is the greatest outrage that can be inflicted upon the race, and is the fruitful source of all the evils of civilized society."[10]

His solution called for nothing less than the elimination of the private ownership of property, and with it the elimination of commerce, and "hence [there would be] no temptation to fraud, theft, slavery, piracy, or war." When such a social system would be constituted, he declared, society would be in harmony with man's natural wants, and "disease, vice and ignorance must soon disappear." The achievement of such a system would, he argued, change man's mode from "idleness, selfishness and vice" to "industry, benevolence and virtue."[11] Collins's position paralleled Robert Owen's, for he assumed that man, as the product of his environment, would change once the social system—man's environment—had been reordered.

Nor did Collins abandon his anarchistic view of law and government. All law, "written, traditional, and oral," all creeds and sects, all governments based upon coercion, and all political parties were antagonistic to freedom of thought and action, which he considered "indispensable to intelligence, purity, and peace." Moreover, the state legitimized inequality—particularly of women and the church—"the handmaiden of the state—sanctified."[12]

The Skaneateles Community began operation in January 1844 with about ninety members. It consisted of some small workshops, particularly a sawmill, and a lot of agriculture. The houses were good and, so were the location and the crops. Cultural and intellectual life was active at Skaneateles, which provided lectures and a good school. No church was on the premises, nor any active clergy. Although marriage was by free choice and without benefit of clergy, no promiscuity occurred. Success appeared attainable, as Robert Owen, who visited the colony in 1845, believed. But external and internal strife intervened.

Externally, the opposition came from conservative neighbors and Fourierites. The neighbors called the members knaves, fanatics, and hypocrites; clergymen damned it for Collins's antipathy toward religion. The Fourierites damned it for Collins's views on property and religion. The Fourierites journal *The Harbinger* ridiculed his "No-God, No-Government, No-Marriage, No-Money, No-Meat, No-Salt, No-Pepper system of community." From within, Collins's rejection of coercion and his opposition to private property created insoluble problems. The Skaneateles Community soon attracted what the Owenite writer John Finch described as an "indolent, unprincipled, and selfish class of 'reformers' as they termed themselves." Although Collins asked them to leave, he would not, as an opponent of coercion, force them out. Also, since his co-trustee Johnson opposed Collins's no-property ideal, legal difficulties developed, but Collins refused to go to court. He did eventually convince Johnson to leave, but it was too late. The internal squabbling had already disillusioned Collins, and after a fruitless effort to incorporate, he turned the farm over to the remaining members in 1846 and left. The members soon dissolved the community.[13]

After Skaneateles, Collins abandoned reform. He went to Cincinnati where he published a short-lived journal called *Queen City*, which, to quote *The Harbinger*, "threw cold water on the social movement." After serving as an agent for the Sons of Temperance, he moved to California in 1860 to earn his fortune. An Abolitionist acquaintance reported that Collins now devoted himself to "Muck-rake, the gross worship of Mammon, the brazen-faced denial of his earlier and better life." Some reports said he had become a gold-mine speculator and auctioneer. These reports were inaccurate; Collins did become wealthy, but as a successful attorney in San Francisco and not as a speculator. Nor did he abandon all of his ideals; he represented the antireligious Freethought Publishing Company—without charge. As late as 1879, when most white Californians were violently opposed to Oriental immigration, he supported William Lloyd Garrison in the latter's protest against the Chinese exclusion bills in Congress. But he was totally disillusioned with Utopias. In 1889 he was "cool if not indifferent" toward the Edward Bellamy-inspired Nationalism. "I went through all this turmoil and excitement fifty years ago," he told an acquaintance.[14]

- 3 -

The demise of Collins's Skaneateles Community left the "Burned-Over District" without a major community for only about two years; by 1848 a new commune was founded near Oneida Lake, in Madison County. The Oneida Community, which lasted more than thirty years, was the most successful and most unique of American Utopias.

Oneida was a product of religious fanaticism and Yankee initiative—the two outstanding characteristics of its founder and leader, John Humphrey Noyes. The son of a well-to-do Vermont political leader, Noyes was born in 1811 in Brattleboro; he was raised in nearby Putney. His mother was a pious woman, but his father, who was too busy earning a living and serving in the state legislature or Congress, had little time, or interest, in religion. The younger Noyes was likewise little interested in the church or religion until after he had graduated from Dartmouth—where he was elected to Phi Beta Kappa and delivered a commencement oration—and had read law for a year. Then Noyes was converted during a revival. He dropped his study of the law, entered Andover Theological School, and prepared to become a missionary. At the end of one year, he transferred to the more prestigious Yale Divinity School, where he came under the influence of Dr. Nathaniel W. Taylor, who argued that sinless perfection was attainable on earth. While at Yale, he became a friend of James Boyle, a "Perfectionist" evangelist who converted him. Noyes became an active member of Boyle's sect—which was considered heretical by Yale's orthodox faculty—and his preaching license was revoked. He emerged shortly thereafter as leader of the New Haven Perfectionist Free Church.[15]

Perfectionism, as John Humphrey Noyes preached it, postulated that it was necessary for man to achieve perfection on earth. This was the true meaning of the Biblical injunction: "Thy will be done on earth as it is in heaven." It was beyond question that God willed that man should be perfect. Moreover, Noyes argued that man's perfectibility was possible because Christ had actually returned to earth in 70 A.D., the year of the destruction of the Temple. The Second Coming was a dispensation from sin, and those who wished could live in a sinless state. This belief in potential human sinlessness was the central theme of Noye's theology.[16]

Although Noyes was not a social radical while at New Haven, his orthodox religious views led him early to revolutionary social ideas. By 1837, only four years after his conversion to Perfectionism, he publicly condemned the United States government for allowing slavery to exist and for the maltreatment of Indians. Unfortunately, he wrote in the Abolitionist *Liberator*, "every other country is under the same reprobate authority." He called for a virtual revolution so that "in the end, Jesus Christ, instead of bloodthirsty Napoleon, will ascend the throne of the world."[17]

That same year, he expanded his Perfectionist thesis to denounce marriage. From Ithaca, New York, where he was then publishing a journal, he
wrote a personal letter to a Connecticut friend, in which he maintained that
*"In a holy community there is no more reason why sexual intercourse
should be restrained by law, than why eating or drinking should be—and
there is as little occasion for shame in one case as in the other."* The "wall of
partition between man and woman" was established during "the apostasy,"
he argued in the letter, but once the "apostasy" had ended, once the Second
Coming had been accepted, the partition would be broken down. "But woe
to him who abolishes the law of the apostasy before he stands in the
holiness of the resurrection!" Sexual freedom was thus to be granted only to
those who had achieved sinlessness. But once perfection had been achieved,
marriage was sinful. "The marriage supper of the Lamb is a feast at which
every dish is free to every guest. Exclusiveness, jealousy, quarrelling, have
no place there, for the same reason as that which forbids the guests at a
thanksgiving dinner to claim each separate dish." Thus "I call a certain
woman my wife. She is yours, she is Christ's, and in Him she is the bride of
all saints."[18]

Although written as a private letter, it fell into the hands of Theophilus
Gates, an eccentric religious radical in Philadelphia, who published it in his
journal *The Battle Axe*. The letter created a storm in religious circles. Because Gates deleted Noye's signature, it was first attributed to James Boyle.
Noyes, however, made it clear in his own publication *Witness* that he was
its author. With the publication of the "Battle Axe Letter," Noyes's movement
became an anathema to "good" Christians. He ceased his Ithaca publishing
activities and returned to Putney, where he gathered his followers in a small
community.[19]

Noyes's chief interests during the first years of his return to Putney were
his publishing and the spreading of his religion; his interest in organizing a
communistic community was secondary at best. But he eventually became
convinced of the need for communal living in an Augustinian City of God,
"which symbolizes the unity of all believers, the blessed and the angels."
The objective of his followers at Putney was to revert to pre-Nicaen Christianity. They rejected legalism, which meant to them restraint and compulsion, as well as antinomianism, a nihilistic religious ideology they equated
with licentiousness and lawlessness. Instead, the Putney Perfectionists
asserted their belief in rule by the spirit—in rule by grace. Noyes defined
these beliefs as

an assertion of human rights; first, the right of man to be governed by God and to
live in a social state of heaven; second, the right of woman to dispose of her sexual
nature by attraction instead of by law and routine and to bear children only when

she chooses; third, the right of all to diminish labors and increase the advantages of life by association.[20]

Noyes's economic and religious declarations were not likely to create violent antipathy toward the Perfectionists, although they did lead townsfolk to consider them mentally unbalanced. But his sexual teachings created serious difficulties that led to the demise of that community. Although Noyes denounced both the celibate Shakers and the libertines for overestimating the significance of physical sex, he believed that copulation would exist even in heaven. Moreover, sex played a dominant role in Noyes's teachings, especially after he had read Robert Dale Owen's pioneer birth-control tract *Moral Physiology* and developed his own form of contraception, male continence, in 1844. With birth control, unwanted pregnancies could be avoided and complex marriage—in effect, sexual relations on a nonexclusive basis among residents of the community—practiced.[21]

The fact that the Putney Perfectionists practiced complex marriage and attempted to convert others to it—and Perfectionism—led to the demise of the community. In 1847 Noyes was indicted for adultery. He fled Vermont; his followers, fearful of persecution, disbanded and scattered. For the next year, Noyes resumed his travels, finally settling near the present city of Shelton, New York, where he took over the farm of Perfectionist Jonathan Burt and organized the Oneida Community. This farm was to become for the next thirty years the center for experiments in eugenics, sexual equality and liberty, communal living, canning—it was among the first farms to can fruits in glass jars for sale—and manufacturing—the Oneida Community was a leading manufacturer of wolf traps.[22] It was here that Noyes expounded his social theories and practiced them.

Reaffirming his belief that the Second Coming of Christ occurred in 70 A.D., Noyes proclaimed that since that date, a unity existed among believers in heaven, on earth, and in Hades. This unity, which he called the resurrection of the spirit, would overcome disease, restore youth, and abolish death. The Second Coming also made possible a heaven on earth, and such a heaven required a community of all property and its distribution by inspiration. Moreover, all in the heavenly city were to dwell together in a system of complex marriage and as a single complex family. To achieve these ends, Noyes called for daily meetings, "home churches and home schools," communion at every meal, free criticism "the regulator of society," horticulture as the basic business of the community, and "a daily press divorced from Mammon and devoted to God."[23]

It was assumed that every member of the community would agree with each of the points, for Noyes spoke by inspiration "from God to Christ; from Christ to Paul; from Paul to John Humphrey Noyes." Noyes was thus

Oneida's absolute ruler, although he was not a despot. The procedures were democratic, and he never employed tyrannical methods. Noyes used tact and persuasion to achieve his ends. Community business was discussed and acted upon at daily meetings. Although technically a form of participatory democracy, these meetings invariably endorsed decisions already made by Noyes. The result was a high degree of voluntary discipline achieved without formal bylaws or statute books. One of the chief instruments for maintaining the discipline and preventing recalcitrance was "free criticism."[24]

"Free criticism" was considered a cure for moral—and at times physical—ills. The methods would vary according to the particular case. Basically, it meant telling an errant member "plainly and kindly" how he had erred. At times the member would be criticized at a general meeting; in such a case, almost all of the other members would join in the criticism. Under other conditions, the criticism would be made by a committee or an individual at a private meeting. The criticism might have dealt with the person's general character, or it might have involved only a single facet of his or her character, or a particular offense. The sessions, although they were brutally frank, were not resented—in fact, many criticisms were initiated by the subjects themselves. The Oneidans believed these sessions could purge the body as well as the soul of evil. A committee would criticize a sick member at his bedside on the assumption that they were thus stimulating the body to resist disease. A general assumption in Oneida was that "free criticism" had cured many physical ailments—including as epidemic of diphtheria—after all other methods had failed.[25]

Unlike other dictatorships, Noyes's rule at Oneida did not include any form of censorship. The community library was kept current with the most significant periodicals, newspapers, and books. Almost all political, religious, or social outlooks were represented. News items were read and discussed at community meetings. Nor was general education ignored. In fact, residents had an enthusiasm for education at Oneida, and grown men and women, some in their middle and late years, made up for early lack of schooling by studying "the three R's and more advanced subjects earnestly and persistently." The younger men were sent to Yale, where they studied medicine, science, and engineering.[26]

The use of criticism, the lack of censorship, and the positive attitude toward education created a democratic facade for Noyes's dictatorial rule of Oneida. This was necessary to avoid dissension and win compliance with some of the harsher regulations. Special—or exclusive—love between two members of the opposite sex, for example, was considered a heinous sin. So, too, was any friendship that excluded others. Those guilty, or suspected of being guilty, of these sins were subjected to censure. Noyes believed in acting quickly to uproot the exclusive affection, and so he moved as soon as the first signs appeared. More difficult was the problem of mothers and children. The Oneida youngsters lived apart from their parents, in a special house. Mothers could visit them only once a week. "Stickiness"—great affection between parents and children—was considered a serious "error." Parents, particularly mothers, who showed too great an affection for their offspring faced severe criticism and censure. Despite the criticism and censure, mothers often showed special affection for their own children. This upset Noyes, who argued that the rule was for the mother's own benefit. "Philopregenitiveness," he wrote, "is so strong a passion, particularly in women, that one who has had a family needs rather to devote her after life to recovering herself from the disorders which it has brought upon her."

Noyes's sympathy for women was no idle gesture; he was genuinely interested in their liberation from the disabilities placed upon them by the mores of nineteenth-century American society. At his insistence, men and women worked together and held equal status at Oneida. By his order, a "mingling of the sexes" occurred at work—an unusual thing in the midnineteenth century. His actions were pragmatic as well as idealistic, for Noyes found that "the great secret of securing enthusiasm in labor and producing a free, healthy, social equilibrium, is contained in the proposition, loving companionship and labor, and especially the mingling of the sexes." But it was not practicality alone that led Noyes to favor dismantling "the partition between the sexes"; he wanted society to cease simply to bear children—they were made for God and themselves. Moreover, this view bolstered his antipathy toward marriage—monogamous or polygamous—for in either case the woman remained an unequal partner, and sex was controlled by law with propagation as its main aim. He wanted sex for nonprocreative purposes to be divorced from shame and for women to have equal rights with men.[27]

Childbearing was accepted by Noyes as a necessary part of life, but he argued for scientific procreation to produce genetically superior children. He thus undertook in 1858 an experiment in *stirpiculture*—controlled breeding—at Oneida. He based the experiment in eugenics on Charles Darwin's theory of natural selection and maintained that "the survival of the fittest leads right on to the idea of improvement of man by voluntary selection." Thirty-eight young men and fifty-three young women at Oneida agreed to mate with specified partners, because "we have no rights or personal feelings in regard to childbearing." The girls offered themselves as "living sacrifices to God and true Communism." A committee headed by Theodore Noyes, the leader's son and a medical doctor from Yale, decided which couple could mate for the purposes of having a child. Before a couple was allowed to conceive a child, a check was made of the heredity of each partner and of their attributes. The plan was acceptable to the Oneidans—only four of fifty-eight children born at Oneida Community after 1858 were not planned.[28]

The problem of sex was significant at Oneida, but it was only one aspect of community life. Another aspect was its total communism—a primitive communism in which all of the members lived together like a family and owned all things in common. Noyes's communism was totally unpolitical, it was based on his assumption that selfishness was the prime enemy of Christianity, and that this "demon" could not be destroyed within a system based on love of money. It was for this reason that he withdrew from the mundane materialistic environment with his followers and sought to reach perfection in a society in which the individual would forget his own desires while striving for the happiness of his fellows. The communism practiced was almost total—even most clothing, especially children's going-away apparel, was common property. Anyone making a journey to New York or Syracuse, or even to the satellite community at Wallingford, Connecticut, was given a suit from the stock kept on hand for that purpose.[29] Along with the communism went a responsibility for sick and disabled members; should a member become ill, or should he or she be injured, "he does not need to worry, and think that his work is suffering for attention, and his family becoming destitute." Sick or well, the members' needs were looked after. Oneida communism worked well. None of the members was a malingerer or lazy; some had to be chastized for working too much. Within three years after its founding, the community was self-sustaining.[30]

Despite its communism and its separation from the materialistic capitalistic world about it, Oneida Community was not free from class distinction. Members of the ruling board received preferential treatment, two made European trips, and Noyes, himself, visited London during the early meager years. Members of the board had preference in choosing their sexual partners. Moreover, workers brought in from the outside during the early 1860s, because of a shortage in labor among the members, were not considered participants in the community. Although their wages were relatively high, and their conditions good, they were considered socially inferior.[31] The communism of Oneida was thus a communism for the elect, which precluded the rest of humanity.

This elitism of Oneida was, in part, indirectly to blame for its destruction. In the twenty years between 1851 and 1871, its membership grew from 150 to 270 (of whom 50 were children). Many more applied for admission but were refused entrance because the Oneidans were unwilling to share their good fortune. Noyes claimed the community was at its optimal size and suggested that "earnest disciples . . . wait until the Spirit of Pentecost shall come over their neighbors and give them communities right where they are."[32] Noyes had hoped that the rising generation of young Oneidans would replenish the community so outsiders would not be needed. He even dreamt that with greater education, the young Oneidans would expand the community's horizons. But he erred—education led them away from Perfectionism; their studies of Darwin and the other scientists led them to question fundamentalism—orthodox or Perfectionist. Instead of Perfectionism and communism, they chose agnosticism.[33] Other elements caused the disintegration of the Oneida Perfectionist-Communist Community: internal disputes involving its oligarchic control, outside attack by orthodox clergymen in the area, and Noyes's own growing interest in secular socialism—each played a part.

In 1876 Noyes turned the *Circular*, the community's newspaper, into the *American Socialist*, a weekly that would "watch, report, and assist the evolution of the civilized world from an old and very defective social system to one adapted to the present needs of mankind, and to discuss the principles which would govern the transition."[34] The next year he resigned the presidency of the Oneida Community. At the same time, the community itself changed its character: it moved into the manufacture of silverware and dropped complex marriage, and in 1881 it abandoned its communism, disbanded as a community, and became a joint stock company. But Noyes had already left.[35]

Noyes did not abandon his search for a Utopia. In 1876 he thought the time was ripe for the emergence of a major Socialist political movement in America. But he was repelled by the idea of class struggle: "We have no inclination to take part in any war of classes," he wrote. In fact, he felt sorry for capitalists, because he believed any man whose sole objective was making money to be a mere hireling. His antipathy for class war led him to oppose labor unions. He believed they were fighting capital without offering a plan "whereby the laborers may sustain themselves without the aid of capital." Despite his sympathy for political socialism, he refused to join the Marxist Workingmen's party, because it proclaimed its belief in the class struggle. He offered to join the party when its members "work out for themselves an original American platform, which will commend itself to the reason and conscience of those who have learned to think in American schools and under American institutions." By 1878 he announced his support of the New Socialistic Labor party "a Party of Peace; seeking a peaceful revolution."[36]

Personal difficulties made it impossible for him to join the party. He left Oneida in 1879, in the midst of internal strife, and organized a small community on the Niagara frontier.[37] But the day of religious and social ferment that gave rise to John Humphrey Noyes's community at Oneida had passed, and the new community never developed. At the time of Noyes's death in 1886, his Oneida community had become a major materialistic corporation producing silverware. The Burned-Over District had become a center of New York State conservatism. Mammon had conquered.

4

Why did Skaneateles fail after only two years, and why did Oneida last for more than thirty? One failed and the other succeeded primarily because of the difference in the aims and ideologies their leaders espoused. Noyes led a religious crusade; Collins was hostile to religion. Noyes realized the significance of religion as a social myth; Collins did not. Moreover, Collins rejected coercion; he assumed all men to be reasonable. Noyes used coercion where necessary—albeit the coercion was never physical.

At Oneida all of the members assumed they were among God's anointed. Their sex relations were considered sinful in mundane society, but at Oneida they were following God's law. Physical love, they argued, could not be selfish in Christ's heaven; therefore complex marriage was God's way. Since they considered the Oneida Community to be heaven on earth, ruled over by Christ's own messenger—Noyes—they were above the laws of man. It was their belief that they were, in fact, God's elect that made the Oneidans willing to work under hostile conditions. The collapse of the community came only after the new generation rejected its religious fervor. Noyes recognized this truth; during the period of decline, less than five years before the final collapse occurred, he warned that "we who have labored in it (Oneida) our whole lives must be admitted to know how necessary its religion is to its existence. We have often said that without religion it would fail."[38] Religion gave the members of Oneida an immediate goal for which to strive—the goal of a heaven on earth where selfishness, suffering, war, and hatred would be replaced by love, peace, eternal youth, and health. Collins could offer only the dream of Utopia on earth—a dream that was based only on his intellectual assumptions, but lacked any sacred myth.

Moreover, the religion at Oneida made it possible to enforce discipline. A recalcitrant member faced the ordeal of criticism. Because he believed that this was God's way, the Perfectionist at Oneida was willing to be demeaned by his confreres. At Skaneateles the opposite was true. Collins rejected all forms of religion and all forms of coercion. He refused to force anyone to do anything. Malingerers could be asked to leave, but they faced no punishment if they refused. Skaneateles had no shortage of those unwilling to work.

Significantly, the experiences at Oneida and Skaneateles were not unique. The Rappites succeeded in their religious-Communist society at New Harmony; the Owenites failed. The Shakers were successful, until the iron law of celibacy depleted their ranks to zero—all of the nonreligious communities failed. Even in contemporary times, the Israeli *Kibbutzim* succeeded as long as the nationalist-secular religion of Zionism was dominant among them. But with the decline of Zionism as a myth after the establishment of Israel, the *Kibbutzim* have been changing into less Socialist settlements, and they have been declining.

That religion—or myth of religion—is a necessary prerequisite for a successful Utopian community is borne out by the Skaneateles and Oneida experience. The failures of communes founded without a religious base are legion.

Significantly, the heritage of Collins is unimportant. Collins, disillusioned by his experience, withdrew from social radicalism. His was a classic case—often repeated among radicals. Like them, he is almost forgotten. As for Noyes, the corporation that replaced his community differs little from any other middle-sized manufacturing enterprise in its social outlook; his Perfectionist religion is long dead and forgotten. Of his ideas, only "free criticism" plays a significant role, primarily on Israeli *Kibbutzim.*

NOTES

1. William Lloyd Garrison and Francis Jackson Garrison, *William Lloyd Garrison, 1805-1879: The Story of His Life Told by His Children,* 4 vols. (New York: Negro Universities Press, 1969) 2: 277, 278, 292, 415, 416; 4: 363; John L. Thomas, "Antislavery and Utopia," in *The Antislavery Vanguard: New Essays on the Abolitionists,* ed. Martin Duberman (Princeton, N.J.: Princeton University Press, 1965), p. 254; Lester Grosvenor Wells, *The Skaneateles Communal Experiment, 1843-1846* (Syracuse: Onondaga Historical Association, 1953), p. 2.

2. Garrison and Garrison, *William Lloyd Garrison,* 3: 20, 64, 94–95; Philip S. Foner, ed. *The Life and Writings of Frederick Douglass* (New York: International Publishers, 1950), pp. 47, 53; F[rederick] Douglass to Maria [Weston] Chapman, September 10, 1853, Anti-Slavery Collections, Boston Public Library, also reprinted in Foner, *Life and Writings,* pp. 110–12; William Lloyd Garrison to Mrs. Maria W. Chapman, September 9, 1843, Anti-Slavery Collection, Boston Public Library.

3. John A. Collins to Mrs. M[aria] Chapman, February 28, 1843, Anti-Slavery Collection, Boston Public Library.

4. *Onondaga Standard,* May 3, 1843, quoted by Wells, *Skaneateles,* pp. 1, 3.

5. Ibid., pp. 4–5; Yuri Suhl, *Ernestine L. Rose and the Battle for Human Rights* (New York: Reynal & Company, 1959), pp. 77–81.

6. William A. Hinds, *American Communities* (Chicago: Charles H. Kerr and Co., 1902), pp. 294–95; John Humphrey Noyes, *History of American Socialism* (1870; reprinted New York: Hillary House Publications, 1961), pp. 163–64.

7. Noyes, *History,* pp. 163–64.

8. Wells, *Skaneateles,* p. 5; Albert Post, *Popular Freethought in America, 1825-1850* (New York: Columbia University Press, 1943) p. 182.

9. Noyes, *History,* pp. 167–68, 170; Hinds, *American Communities,* p. 295; Wells, *Skaneateles,* p. 6; Thomas, "Antislavery," p. 257.

10. Noyes, *History,* p. 168; [John A. Collins], "Preamble and Constitution of the New England Social Reform Society" (1844). A copy of this broadside is in the Anti-Slavery Collection, Boston Public Library.

11. Ibid.

12. Ibid.

13. Post, *Popular Freethought,* p. 181; George Ripley, "The Skaneateles Community," *The Harbinger* 1 (September 27, 1845): 253–54; *The Harbinger* 5 (September 18, 1847): 239; Frederic A. Bushee, "Communistic Societies in the United States," *Political Science Quarterly* 20 (December 1905): 662; Whitney Cross, *The Burned-Over District: The Social and Intellectual History of Enthusiastic Religion in Western New York, 1800–1850* (Ithaca, N.Y.: Cornell University Press, 1950), p. 332; Foner, *Life and Writings,* p. 438, says that Collins organized the colony on Fourieristic principles. He cites no evidence for his statement, which is apparently in error.

14. Wells, *Skaneateles,* pp. 6–19; *The Harbinger* 5 (September 18, 1847): 240; Samuel May, Jr., to "Dear Friend R. D. Webb," July 12, 1864, Anti-Slavery Collection, Boston Public Library; Post, *Popular Freethought,* p. 183; Garrison and Garrison, *William Lloyd Garrison,*

4: 301; George E. MacDonald, *Fifty Years of Freethought* (New York: The Truth Seeker Company, 1929), pp. 478, 502; Foner, *Life and Writings*, p. 438, gives the year of Collins's death as 1899. This is an error; he died in 1890.

15. Carl Carmer, "Children of the Kingdom," *The New Yorker* 12 (March 21, 1936): 26–28; *Circular*, November 30, 1851, reproduced in Constance Noyes Robertson, *Oneida Community: An Autobiography, 1851–1876* (Syracuse: Syracuse University Press, 1970), p. 54; Robert Allerton Parker, *A Yankee Saint: John Humphrey Noyes and the Oneida Community* (New York: G. P. Putnam's Sons, 1936), pp. 9–27.

16. Parker, *Yankee Saint*, pp. 22–27, 112–13; Carmer, "Children," pp. 27–28.

17. Carmer, "Children," pp. 27–28; quoted in Parker, *Yankee Saint*, pp. 48–50.

18. Quoted in Hubbard Eastman, *Noyesism Unveiled* (Brattleboro, Vt.: Published by the Author, 1849), p. 90. Italics in original.

19. Ibid., quoted in Cross, *Burned-Over District*, pp. 247–48; Parker, *Yankee Saint*, p. 56.

20. Parker, *Yankee Saint*, pp. 107–8; quoted in Cross, *Burned-Over District*, p. 335.

21. Ibid.

22. Ibid., pp. 128–30, 132–42; Carmer, "Children," pp. 28–29.

23. *Circular*, January 17, 1854, in Robertson, *Oneida Community*, p. 105.

24. Pierrepont Noyes, *My Father's House* (New York: Farrar and Rinehart, 1937), pp. 132–33; Maria Lockwood Carden, *Oneida: Utopian Community to Modern Corporation* (Baltimore: The Johns Hopkins Press, 1969), p. 85; Cross, *Burned-Over District*, p. 336; *Circular*, November 30, 1851, in Robertson, *Oneida Community*, p. 54.

25. *Circular*, November 30, 1851, in Robertson, *Oneida Community*; Pierrepont Noyes, *My Father's House*, p. 136; Carmer, "Children," pp. 30–33; Carden, *Oneida*, pp. 72–73.

26. Pierrepont Noyes, *My Father's House*, pp. 68, 133.

27. Ibid., pp. 49, 64-65; *Circular*, May 2, 1864, in Robertson, *Oneida Community*, pp. 75–76. See also Raymond Muncy, *Sex and Marriage in Utopian Communities* (Bloomington: Indiana University Press, 1973).

28. Carmer, "Children," pp. 30, 36, and March 28, 1936, p. 43; Robertson, *Oneida Community*, p. 336; *Circular*, October 8, 1853, in Robertson, *Oneida Community*, p. 58; *Circular*, January 23, 1858, in Robertson, *Oneida Community*, pp. 340-41; *Circular*, March 21, 1870, in Robertson, *Oneida Community*, p. 340; Noyes, *History*, p. 636.

29. Pierrepont Noyes, *My Father's House*, pp. 125–27; Noyes, *History*, p. 615.

30. *Circular*, November 30, 1851, in Robertson, *Oneida Community*, pp. 55–56; *Circular*, January 2, 1863, in Robertson, *Oneida Community*, p. 83.

31. Carden, *Oneida*, pp. 83, 87; *Circular*, October 1, 1863, in Robertson, *Oneida Community*, p. 73.

32. *Circular*, November 30, 1851, in Robertson, *Oneida Community*, pp. 53–56; *Circular*, November 21, 1870, in Robertson, *Oneida Community*, p. 89; *Circular*, July 10, 1871, in Robertson, *Oneida Community*, p. 90.

33. Carmer, "Children," March 28, 1936, pp. 46, 48; Robertson, *Oneida Community*, p. 356.

34. Carden, *Oneida*, p. 91; Robertson, *Oneida Community*, p. 360; Parker, *Yankee Saint*, p. 274.

35. Pierrepont Noyes, *My Father's House*, pp. 150, 163–64, 170–71, 175–76; Parker, *Yankee Saint*, pp. 174, 276, 284–85, 287, 291.

36. *Circular*, December 13, 1875, in Robertson, *Oneida Community*, pp. 125–26; *The American Socialist* 1 (March 30, 1876): 1, 2; (August 3, 1876): 148; 2 (November 15, 1877): 364; (December 20, 1877): 404; 3 (June 27, 1878): 205.

37. Pierrepont Noyes, *My Father's House*, pp. 158–59, 297.

38. *Circular*, August 31, 1874, in Robertson, *Oneida Community*, p. 96.

$\approx 8 \approx$

Labor Reform

- 1 -

The American Left was in the doldrums during the 1850s and early 1860s. A few radicals proclaimed socialism or anarchism, but they were almost universally ignored. Dreams of Utopian communities had virtually all ended in failure during the preceding two decades. Josiah Warren and Stephen Pearl Andrews's Modern Times and John Humphrey Noyes's Oneida were exceptions. But neither one of them was a mass movement designed to alter the relationships of society as were the Utopian movements based on the teachings of Robert Owen and Charles Fourier, and they had, in effect, ceased to exist. The labor unionists of the 1850s and early 1860s were disdainful of the rhetoric of the radical Left; some of the union leaders had even declared an anathema upon the idea of a class struggle. The delegates to the first national convention of the Machinists and Blacksmiths Union proclaimed in 1859 "that so far as encouraging a spirit of hostility to employers, all properly organized unions recognize an identity of interests between employer and employee, and we give no countenance or support to any project or enterprise that will interfere with the promotion of the perfect harmony between them."[1] William Sylvis, the model militant labor activist, favored nonideological pure-and-simple trade unionism that would "limit your supply of labor until scarcity has raised its price."[2] Even the arrival of European Socialist emigres from the revolutions and counterrevolutions of 1848 failed to revive the American radical movement. The Europeans were too deeply involved in plotting new revolutions on the Continent to be interested in the United States.

Radicalism was out of style in America at that time, because the issues that were dividing the country did not lend themselves to the rhetoric of

Utopia. They required immediate, practical results. Radicals have historically had a tendency to take strong—and divergent—views when faced with urgent, practical issues that require action instead of rhetoric. This was especially true of slavery and war—the leading problems confronting the United States. Some American Socialists, like John Francis Bray, accused the Abolitionists of raising the false issue of chattel slavery while ignoring the real problem: the degradation of the free, industrial worker of the North.[3] Others—Stephen Pearl Andrews and Wendell Phillips, for example—were themselves militant Abolitionists. Even among Socialist Abolitionists, divisions were exacerbated by the Civil War. Some of them were pacifists, and when faced with the choice between war and slavery, some, particularly Christian-Socialist Adin Ballou, chose to countenance slavery rather than sanction a war.[4] Others, like Phillips, supported the war, claiming slavery was the greater evil.

It was only after the Civil War had ended and America again faced the primary issue of industrial society—labor versus capital—that the radical Left revived. The conflict between the working class and the employing class is the lifeblood of radical movements.

- 2 -

In growing capitalist America, the conflict was unequal. It was heavily weighted in favor of capital. With the end of the war, demand for manufactured goods slackened, and the need for labor declined. Employers took advantage of the changed conditions by cutting wages. Labor attempted to retaliate by calling strikes or organizing producers' cooperatives. Because labor was in easy supply, the strikes invariably failed; because the cooperatives were formed without sufficient study of the potential market, or proper organization, they soon collapsed. With the failure of the strikes and the cooperatives, friends of labor turned to the only available means remaining to them in the war with capital: political action. During the late 1860s, "labor reform" political conventions abounded. The organizations founded at these conventions were generally peripheral to the development of the American Left. Most had little if any immediate or permanent impact on American life. One of the few that did affect later American life was the National Labor Union, (NLU), a labor federation organized by William Sylvis.

Founded in 1867, the NLU early proclaimed its belief in the need for labor political action. Sylvis argued that trade unions were at best purely defensive, aimed at preventing a worsening of workers' conditions. Any improvement in the workers' position in their struggle with the employers would, he believed, require political action. Moreover, labor-union action was too slow and too costly. The workers could solve their problems only through the ballot box. It thus followed that the NLU, which was essentially his creature, would favor political action. From the beginning, the NLU urged workers to vote against any political candidate who opposed labor's demands and to support any in public office who favored labor's demands, particularly the eight-hour day.[5] By 1868 the NLU leadership, ignored by Republicans and Democrats, despaired of achieving their ends by supporting political friends and punishing political enemies in the existing parties. They therefore proclaimed their aim to be the formation of a labor party. The aim of that new party would be to gain control of the Congress and the state legislatures in order to enact laws that would assure a more equitable distribution of "the products of labor between non-producing capital and labor."[6]

The chief plank of the NLU political platform was monetary reform. The NLU leaders assumed that such reform would end the inequities inherent in the existing social system. Of course, other planks were in the platform—one demanding fair treatment of Indians, another urging equal pay for women, and a third proclaiming that "the highest interests of our colored fellow-citizens is with the workingmen, who, like themselves, are slaves of capital and politicians, and strike for liberty."[7] Despite its emphasis on monetary reform, the NLU impressed no less a revolutionist than Karl Marx, who wrote from London that he was very pleased with the NLU especially since he conceived the main slogan of the organization to be "organization for struggle against capital," and he believed that NLU demands were similar to those he had incorporated in the 1864 program of the International Workingmen's Association (IWA).[8]

Marx even attempted to win the NLU to membership in his international. The NLU was interested, but financial difficulties prevented the federation from sending a delegation to an IWA meeting until 1869, the year after Sylvis had died. That year a contribution from a wealthy reformer made it possible for A. C. Cameron to attend the Basel congress. Unfortunately, Cameron took no part in the discussions except to present a wildly exaggerated report of the NLU's strength. A year later, at the suggestions of Friedrich Sorge, Marx's friend in America, the NLU voted to affiliate with the IWA. But the union was disintegrating, and it never joined the international.[9] Ambitious middle-class politicians had moved into the NLU and its Labor Reform party. They alienated the trade unionists who were unwilling to become involved in grandiose political schemes. These trade unionists refused to allow their organizations to become stepping stones for those whom they considered to be politically ambitious intellectuals. By 1872 only seven delegates were at the NLU convention.[10]

- 3 -

Wendell Phillips was the typical middle-class, intellectual radical. A Boston Brahmin, a Harvard graduate, an attorney, he was for most of his

adult life a full-time revolutionist fighting against the slave system, the oppression of the working class, British rule in Ireland, or denial of human
rights to women. He participated with all his might in all of the "good"
causes of the Left. Eventually, all of the causes he espoused were won by
those for whom he fought—but, except in the case of slavery, long after he
had died.

Phillips believed all of his struggles had the same aim—establishment of
the Christian Commonwealth on earth. Moreover, he believed that the
struggle was never ending and that it required eternal vigilance. Thus when
William Lloyd Garrison proposed disbanding the Anti-Slavery Society immediately after the Civil War ended and all slaves were proclaimed free,
Phillips opposed him. He doubted that slavery had, in fact, been abolished
in the United States. Even if it had been, he expected the proslavery forces
to reestablish it.[11]

Phillips's uncompromising opposition to slavery and racial inequality
was only one aspect of his belief in a general, peaceful social revolution. His
political philosophy was based on his devout faith, which viewed Christianity as the instrumentality for the social regeneration of mankind and Jesus
as the ultimate agitator for the revolution. Phillips equated Christianity
with the activism found "in the Peace Society, the Temperance Organization, . . . in Anti-Slavery, in Woman's Rights, in the eight-hour
movement." It was a religion that "was never yet at peace with its age"; it
was a revolutionary Christianity aimed at curing—not simply alleviating—the wrongs of society.[12]

Despite his belief in the need for a revolutionary reshaping of society,
Phillips ignored the Associationist and land-reform movements of the preceding decades. His primary interest then was the abolition of slavery. He
rejected the thesis that workers were in the same position as slaves. The free
workingmen, he argued, were capable of affecting their own ends; slaves
were not. He did, however, believe that labor was unfairly exploited. After
the war, and the emancipation of the chattel slaves, Phillips proclaimed:
"The wage system cheats and enslaves the workingman."[13] To achieve an
end to the corrupt and corrupting wage system, Phillips believed it would
be necessary to abolish by political—that is, electoral—action the profit
system and all monopolies.[14]

He believed that political action went beyond simply campaigning for
public office; it was also a demonstration of strength and will. "A political
movement [of labor] saying 'we will have our rights,' is a mass meeting in
perpetual session," he told an 1865 rally of the eight-hour movement. The
failure of the old-line political leaders to alleviate the workers' sufferings
during the 1868 depression bolstered his faith in the need for an independent
labor party. The leaders in Washington were "weak and shortsighted"; they
had by their ineptitude given the working class the golden opportunity to

form its own political movement, he wrote to a friend. Two years later, Phillips helped form the Labor Reform party of Massachusetts and ran as its candidate for governor. He polled a respectable 20,000 votes (the winner garnered only 72,000). But a year later, with his friend General Benjamin Butler as the party's candidate, the Labor Reform vote was down to 10,000, and the party virtually disappeared.[15]

On the basis of Phillips's political activity and his acceptance of the theory of the class struggle, it has been suggested that he was basically a Marxist.[16] But Phillips was a Social-Gospel activist, not a Marxist. Although he accepted the labor theory of value—in simplistic terms—and spoke of the struggle between labor and capital, he had little if any understanding of the historical forces that had caused the development of the contemporary political and social system. He viewed the struggle between labor and capital in Christian moral terms. Phillips could not comprehend that the labor movement was an outgrowth of objective historical conditions. He called it the "last noble protest of the American people against the power of incorporated wealth." It was a moral, not historical, instrument. Labor was militant, even aggressive, only because capital was also militantly aggressive. The means by which labor and capital confronted each other was determined, according to Phillips, by malevolent capital and was not the natural outcome of the mode and relationships of production. It was capital that immorally and unilaterally controlled the conditions of the workers. It was against this arbitrary immorality that labor had to unite. The solution to this iniquitous state of affairs was a new social order in which wealth would be redistributed by taxation. A new system would be devised in which "the rich man shall have a lesser income in proportion as he is rich" and "the poor man shall have a larger income in proportion as he is poor." It was to be a system of peace and order without riots in the streets or disorder or revolution. It was to be a system where all men and women would go to school to develop their tastes, where each would work eight hours a day and would have a garden, good books to read, and beautiful things to see. As a result, poverty and intemperance would disappear and men would no longer steal, nor would women turn to prostitution.[17] Phillips summed up his idea of the perfect society thus:

My idea of a civilization is a very high one, but the approach to it is a New England town of some two thousand inhabitants, with no rich man and no poor man in it; all mingling in the same society, every child at the same school, no poor house, no beggar, opportunities equal, nobody too proud to stand aloof, nobody too humble to shut out. That's New England as it was fifty years ago. . . . [The] civilization that lingers beautifully on the hillsides of New England, nestles sweetly in the valleys of Vermont, the moment it approaches a crowd like Boston, or a million men gathered in one place like New York, it rots.[18]

What Phillips sought was a return to the past. He doubted he would live to see his ideal realized. He wrote to the British reformer G. J. Holyoake in 1874 that he would probably not "live long enough to see a marked result of our labor movement here."[19] But he was sure that the seeds he had helped sow in the 1870s would bear fruit.

- 4 -

Ira Steward was essentially a pragmatic reformer, with a basic one-issue program, but his plank was significant enough to unite under its banner radicals, apolitical workingmen, and pure-and-simple trade unionists. His chief interest was in achieving the eight-hour day—a demand he pursued to the virtual disregard of all others.

Steward came by his pragmatism naturally; he was a workingman, a machinist, untrained in the niceties of the theoretical construction of Utopias. A Bostonian, he began his career as an active member of that city's local of the Machinists and Blacksmiths Union, who had experienced the long hours that late nineteenth-century workers toiled.[20]

Steward did not assume that the reduction in the hours of labor would be the panacea for all of the problems confronting labor. It was to be merely the first step in the emancipation of labor from "the slavery and ignorance of poverty." He founded the Boston Eight-Hour League and worked hard with his closest collaborators, the Reverend Jesse H. Jones and George E. McNeill, to form a major national Eight-Hour League, but he conceded that the eight-hour day was not the cure-all for society's ills. The ultimate solution for the problems was beyond his ken. Certainly, it could not be found in popular nostrums such as currency reform, interest protection, free trade, or an end to the franking privilege for congressmen, or civil service reform and the merit system. These things would still leave "the laborer a laborer and the capitalist a capitalist." Between the worker and the capitalist was an irrepressible conflict "which must continue until all are laborers or all are capitalists."[21]

This was the most radical statement Steward ever uttered. It followed directly from his analysis of the American class structure. He believed America had two classes: the workers, who owned nothing but their labor power; and the capitalists, who bought that labor power at the lowest price possible. Labor was thus a commodity; the workers could only sell their persons. This was, according to Steward, the cause of labor's low social and economic estate. The capitalist system—and thus the capitalist class—was responsible for labor's plight. Therefore, in the class struggle, the capitalists "have no rights, whatever, that any human being is bound to respect."

Despite his radical rhetoric, Steward was basically interested in the achievement of the eight-hour day, which he considered a realistic goal. For this end, he worked ceaselessly. Unfortunately, the labor reformers were more interested in other panaceas. Even the National Labor Congress of 1880, which Steward had helped organize, paid scant heed to the eight-hour day. It was more interested in other significant labor problems such as repeal of the conspiracy laws, an end to the use of convict contract labor, establishment of a national bureau of labor statistics, compulsory education up to age fourteen, ventilation of mines and factories, extension of mechanics lien laws, incorporation of labor unions, and the most popular issue among workers of the day—a prohibition against Chinese immigration.[22]

Steward was a unique leader of labor reform—a worker himself, dedicated to improving the lot of his fellow workers, and an excellent organizer, with a long-range vision of a classless society—but enough of a pragmatist to recognize the limits of what could be done effectively. His work for the eight-hour day, unlike the work of most "labor-reform" panacea peddlers, had a lasting impact on the American society.

- 5 -

The relations between the so-called labor reformers and the few Socialists in America were friendly and generally cooperative. Steward, in particular, worked closely with the Socialists, most of whom were German. But none of the major labor reformers except John Francis Bray was directly involved in any of the Socialist movements. Bray's carreer in the American Left stretched from 1843 until 1897, and his involvement included the Owenites, the Social Democratic Workingmen's party, the Socialist Labor party, the Knights of Labor, and the Populists. Despite his long involvement with the American movement, he and his work have been almost totally ignored.

One of the chief reasons for this oversight is that Bray has been erroneously considered an Englishman—even though he was born in the United States and most of his Socialist activity was in this country. The error is due to a mistake by Karl Marx. Marx had, in quoting from Bray's most famous work *Labour's Wrongs and Labour's Remedy*, called Bray "an English" Communist. The book was written and published in England, but its author was an American residing in Great Britain.

Bray was born in Washington, D.C., in 1809 of an English father and an American mother, both theatrical. He was raised in Boston until 1822, when his father became ill and went to England in search of a cure. John, the eldest of seven children, accompanied him on the journey, expecting to return to the United States shortly. Unfortunately, the elder Bray died almost immediately after arriving in his native Leeds, and the British relatives did not have the money for John's return fare. He, therefore, remained with a paternal aunt who eventually adopted him.

Young Bray, after a short stint at a British grammar school, was apprenticed by his aunt to a printer. After completing his apprenticeship, he went "on tramp" throughout England looking for an elusive job. He was thus able to observe the poverty of early industrial Britain firsthand. The jobs he did get were invariably of short duration and included work on illegal publications. In 1833, for example, he was the temporary publisher of a newspaper whose actual publisher was serving a term in the local jail for violation of the British stamp act. Shortly thereafter, Bray began writing letters to the editors of Leeds newspapers. Originally republican and antimonarchical, the letters soon began to attack the class divisions in society. In late 1835 and early 1836, he wrote a series of five Socialist letters to the *Leeds Times*. These letters won for him notoriety and a short period of leadership in the Chartist Leeds Working Men's Association. A series of lectures he delivered to that association resulted in his famous book. But he was soon disillusioned with the Chartists, particularly after the bombastic, non-Socialist wing won control of the Leeds organization.[23]

Labour's Wrongs and Labour's Remedy, which appeared in 1839, received little notice, except in the *Leeds Times*, which called it Utopian. The review irritated Bray into writing a reply in the form of a new book, *A Voyage from Utopia to Several Unknown Regions of the World*. It was intended to demonstrate "what existed outside Utopia." Bray, in this heavy-handed fantasy, ridiculed the existing institutions in Brydone (Great Britain), Franco, (France), and Amrico, (The United States), primarily the first. His description of the Western capitalist world was similar to Edward Bellamy's picture of the United States in the 1880s. The Americans, Bray noted, "talked of liberty and the equal brotherhood of man," but they understood neither, for they were as exploited as the British or French. He blamed the evil conditions in the Western world on private property.

The new book was completely ignored until about sixty years after his death, for Bray could not arrange for its publication. It was finally published in 1957 as a historical curiosity.[24]

Unhappy at his failure to win a mass following for his ideas, and unable to earn a respectable living in Britain, Bray returned to Boston in late 1842. He soon moved to Michigan, where he remained until his death in 1897. In America he worked as a printer, farmer, and photographer, and he wrote and agitated for socialism.

His first American publications were two pamphlets of a never-completed series called *The Coming Age*. Published in 1855, when spiritualism was the rage among radicals, they debunked belief in a spirit world.[25] His next work was an attack on the Union cause in the Civil War, *American Destiny—what Shall It Be, Republican or Cossack? An Argument Addressed to the People of the Late Union*, published in 1864. His basic premise was the right of a state to secede. Bray argued that the South, by withdrawing from the Union, sought to carry forward the American revolutionary idea. The North, "on the contrary, endeavored to maintain the principle of governmental inviolability which the revolution overthrew."[26] As for slavery,

Bray did not believe it was an absolute evil, nor was he convinced that blacks wanted their freedom. He charged that the Abolitionists "would enslave eight millions of a developed race to give a thankless freedom to four millions of an undeveloped one." He warned that "the actual condition of the free black might . . . be no better than that of the slaves."[27] As with most anti-Union writings during the Civil War, Bray's pamphlet had little readership.

With the end of the war, Bray resumed his Socialist activity—writing articles for Socialist and labor papers in Detroit, Chicago, Cincinnati, Milwaukee, Paterson, San Francisco, Denver, Hartford, and Princeton, Massachusetts. He also wrote another pamphlet, *God and Man a Unity and All Mankind a Unity—A Basis for a New Dispensation, Social and Religious*. He was active as a speaker for the Socialistic Labor party. He was the Socialist choice for vice-president on the Greenback-Labor ticket in 1880—but the Socialists walked out of the Greenbackers convention, and his name was never placed before it.[28]

Bray's view of American society was almost identical with that held by the Socialists generally. He saw society divided into three classes: the employers, the workers, and the self-employed farmers. Of these three, the workers composed the exploited class. But they were neither helpless nor hopeless. They were, in fact, already participating in a class war aimed at their emancipation from the despotism of capital. The victory of the workers in that class war would result in an end to the plunder of one class by another. This warfare might result in violence, for he accepted the assumption that the government was the tool of the class in power, and capital would call on its subservient tool to use its military force to put down the social revolution. But labor need not despair; the military could be won over to the cause of the revolution. "What does all military and police force consist of? Why, wage workers. Men that capital has reduced to beggary and slavery."[29]

Bray was not anxious for the class war to erupt into an outright battle between labor and capital. He preferred to have compromise replace warfare, melioration replace confrontation, and harmony prevail. Even his proposed "Socialist" system was not totally revolutionary. He suggested that the Socialist society would see all workingmen and workingwomen in business for themselves, working together through a cooperative system under governmental management. The establishment of such a system of voluntary cooperatives should be labor's chief interest. He rejected the idea of a fair day's work, because that meant continued servitude for the workers. Only socialism could assure the workers of all of the advantages of industrial independence and self-employment; only these advantages could assure that the workers would no longer be mere commodities in the marketplace.[30]

The great strikes of 1877, and the bloodshed that accompanied them, proved to Bray the stupidity of the capitalist rulers. As with the French Revolution and the American Civil War, the industrial uprising of 1877 came only after warning signs had been discerned. Yet the ruling class in each case failed to recognize their implications. Instead of trying to avoid the conflict by attempting to ease the situation, the ruling powers turned to coercion to maintain their position. All they could do, he said, "is to bark like frightened dogs at the new light appearing on the horizon." Instead of seeking a permanent, workable solution, they attempted to "once more try repression," and they would again "fail at ruinous cost." The industrial reformation—the social revolution—grew out of historical necessity, exactly in the same manner as the religious reformation. He doubted that mortal man could prevent it. If thoughtful men guided it, the reformation could lead to conciliation.[31]

The means Bray proposed for achieving his Utopia were political, the use of the ballot. Toward this end, he proposed the formation of a political party composed of all labor reformers that would gradually institute a Socialist social system in the United States. Such a party would appeal to all who favored genuine labor reform, in spite of their own economic class. The class war was aimed at the system and not at individuals. In fact, capitalism was against the best interests of all, not only of the workers. "I see no hope for society except in a perfect union of labor with capital . . . a union that is equitable and equalitarian so far as men are equal," he wrote to the third annual convention of the American Labor Reform League. Because he favored such a union against the "tyranny of money," Bray early supported uniting the discontented farmers with the discontented workers in a joint struggle against the existing system.[32]

During the 1870s and 1880s, Bray was optimistic about the outlook for radical social change. At age seventy, he still expected a revolution during his lifetime. The first phase of that revolution was already begun, he claimed. This was a revolution in the thinking of the working class. All that the revolution required to become a reality was the leadership of "the best minds and hearts of the age." At a Detroit Socialistic Labor party rally for the eight-hour day at which he was the honored speaker, Bray warned again against putting too much stock in mere melioration; socialism was the sole answer. He believed socialism was on its way.[33]

But his optimism did not last long. By 1883 he was upset by "the apathy of the dronish and swinish multitudes" and despaired of any revolution. He still believed that the revolution would have to come by the force of history, but he was no longer sure it would come in the foreseeable future. The public was still solidly behind "law and order." Moreover, the workers had little or no understanding of the purposes of the revolution, and they could therefore not take advantage of it. It was up to the Socialists, "the advanced guard of the Revolution," to educate and prepare the masses. But even the Socialists were disappointing him.[34]

Despite his disenchantment with the working class and the Socialist movement, Bray remained active in the party and the labor-reform movement generally. He joined the Knights of Labor—whose Pontiac organization promptly became the John F. Bray Assembly in his honor. But he doubted the Knights of Labor would succeed in remaking American society. It had grown too fast to be permanent, he warned. Moreover, it would have "to go outside and beyond its present demands" to win permanent support. The Knights of Labor could succeed, he believed, only if it became a Socialist political organization.[35]

His belief in the ultimate failure of the Knights of Labor followed directly from his view of labor reform generally. Such reform was useful only insofar as it was a step in the direction of socialism. Reform for its own sake was useless. He believed that reformers were interested in peripheral measures when they should be dedicated to the chief reform—a complete reshaping of society that would give labor control of hours, wages, and conditions of work.[36] He continued working for this new social order all of his life. At eighty-three, he urged a simplification of the legislative system as a means of giving government power to the working class. In 1894, at the age of eighty-five, he pleaded for labor to take independent political action. As late as five months before his death, in 1896, Bray was still actively advocating revolutionary change, although his allegiance had by this time shifted from the Socialist Labor party to the Populists.[37]

- 6 -

The Labor Reform movement of post-Civil War America was a complex of many divergent groups and ideals. It was in great part a moral outcry against the rapaciousness of growing American industrial capital. The intellectuals who moved from abolition to reform were motivated by their Christian-moral abhorrence of the crass materialism of the era. Wendell Phillips, the most notable of these reformers, was typical. This Harvard-educated Brahmin fought for the oppressed, because he accepted the Christian injunction, "As ye do unto the least of these My brethren, so also do ye unto Me." Thus he fought for the rights of blacks—before and after slavery. When the chief struggle shifted from the plantation South to the industrial North, he fought for the workers of the North. In all of his struggles, Phillips was the true Puritan, fighting God's battle as he sought to build His City on a Hill.

William Sylvis, on the contrary, was a labor union organizer whose ideals were "a fair day's pay for a fair day's work." He was directly and personally involved in the struggle for better working conditions. His views were not far different from those of latter-day labor unionists. But unlike them, because his unions were unable to win strikes, he favored partisan political action. That he and his successors failed at politics was to have been expected. They were neophytes in the art and thus easy prey for skilled professionals. Their failure did serve a purpose: it helped steer the latter-day labor movement away from independent political action.

John Francis Bray was a Socialist, who was also a labor reformer. He saw reform as a step on the road to revolution, and he proclaimed the need for revolution as the only solution for the woes of society and of the working class.

Each of the labor reformers left his mark on the latter-day Left. Phillips is the model for the many intellectuals and Social-Gospel Christians who became Socialists for moral and religious reasons—men such as Abraham J. Muste and Norman M. Thomas; Sylvis has had his emulators among labor leaders of the twentieth century—Walter Reuther, for example. Steward and Bray are typical of the Social Democrats whose Marxist rhetoric was a simplistic basis for a commitment to needed reform.

NOTES

1. Terence V. Powderly, *Thirty Years of Labor* (Columbus, Ohio: Excelsior Publishing House, 1889), p. 25.

2. Jonathan Grossman, *William Sylvis, Pioneer of American Labor* (New York: Columbia University Press, 1945), p. 121.

3. [John Francis Bray], *American Destiny: What Shall it Be, Republican or Cossack? An Argument Addressed to the People of the Late Union, North and South* (New York: The Columbian Association, 1864), p. 26.

4. Adin Ballou, *History of the Hopedale Community from its Inception to its Virtual Submergence in the Hopedale Parish* (Lowell, Mass.: Thompson and Hill, the Vox Populi Press, 1897), pp. 310-12.

5. Quoted in Powderly, *Thirty Years*, p. 45.

6. Ibid., pp. 38-39, 47, 52.

7. Ibid., pp. 50-51, 57.

8. Charlotte Todes, *William H. Sylvis and the National Labor Union* (New York: International Publishers, 1942), p. 88.

9. Ibid., pp. 89-90; August Sartorius (Freiherrn von Waltershausen), *Der Moderene Socialisumus in den Vereinigten Staaten von Amerika* (Berlin: Verlag von Hermann Bahr, 1890), p. 56.

10. Powderly *Thirty Years*, pp. 54-55, Morris Hillquit, *History of Socialism in the United States* (New York: Funk and Wagnalls, 1910), p. 174; Norman J. Ware, *The Labor Movement in the United States, 1860-1895* (New York: D. Appleton and Company, 1929), p. 10.

11. William Lloyd Garrison to "Dear Wife," May 10, 1865, Anti-Slavery Collection, Boston Public Library [hereafter cited as (BPL)]; William Lloyd Garrison to "My Darling" [daughter Fanny], January 27, 1866, Anti-Slavery Collection, (BPL); [William Lloyd Garrison] to [Oliver] Johnson, January 25, 1867, Anti-Slavery Collection, (BPL); [Ann Phillips] to Henry C. Wright, December 7, 1868, Anti-Slavery Collection, (BPL); James J. Green, *Wendell Phillips* (New York: International Publishers, 1943), pp. 29-31.

12. Wendell Phillips, "Christianity a Battle, Not a Dream" (Speech at Horticultural Hall, Boston, April 11, 1869), reprinted in *The Dawn* 2 (October 1891): 4-6.

13. Robert D. Marcus, "Wendell Phillips and American Institutions," *Journal of American History* 56 (June 1969): 47; Wendell Phillips, "Speech Delivered October 13, 1871, in the Music Hall, Boston," *The Labor Enquirer* 3 (April 5, 1884): 1; Charles Sotheran, *Horace Greeley and Other Pioneers of American Socialism* (New York: Mitchell Kennerly, 1915), p. 57.

14. Quoted in Green, *Wendell Phillips*, pp. 34-35; [Wendell Phillips], Letter to *The Advertiser* quoted in *The Labor Enquirer* 2 (October 6, 1883):2.

15. Wendell Phillips to Henry [C. Wright], February 16, 1868, Anti-Slavery Collection, (BPL); Samuel May, Jr., to "Dear Friend Webb," November 8, 1871, Anti-Slavery Collection, (BPL); Green, *Wendell Phillips*, pp. 33–34.

16. Vernon Louis Parrington, *The Beginnings of Critical Realism in America, 1860–1920*, vol. 3, *Main Currents in American Thought* (New York: Harcourt, Brace and World, 1930), p. 145.

17. Wendell Phillips, "Speech Delivered October 31, 1871 . . . ," *The Labor Enquirer* 3 (April 5, 1884): 1; Wendell Phillips, letter to *New York Herald*, September 13, 1877, reprinted in *Labor Enquirer* (Chicago) 1 (April 30, 1887): 2; "Resolution Presented by Wendell Phillips at Labor Reform Convention, Worcester, Massachusetts, September 4, 1871," *The Dawn* 3 (October 1891): 7; Wendell Phillips, "Address to the International Grand Lodge, Knights of St. Crispin, April 1872," *The Dawn* 3 (October 1891): 9.

18. Wendell Phillips, "Speech delivered October 31, 1871, in Music Hall, Boston," *The Labor Enquirer* 3 (April 5, 1884): 1.

19. Wendell Phillips to G. J. Holyoake, July 22, 1874, *Equity* 1 (December 1874), p. 2.

20. Friedrich Sorge, "Die Arbeiterbewegung in den Vereinigten Staaten," *Neue Zeit* 9, pt. 2 (1890–1891): 398.

21. Quoted in George E. McNeill, *The Labor Movement: The Problem of Today* (Boston: A. M. Bridgmen, 1887), p. 144; *Equity* 1 (June 1874): 20; *The Labor Balance* 1 (April 1878): 16.

22. McNeill, *Labor Movement*, p. 167; *The American Socialist* 1 (June 29, 1876): 109; during the period beginning about 1876, Steward worked closely with the Workingmen's party, the Germanic predecessor of the Socialist Labor party.

23. W. D. P. Bliss, *A Handbook of Socialism* (London: Swan Sonnenschein and Company, 1907), p. 214, calls Bray an "English Communist of the School of Owen. . . ."; Karl Marx, *The Poverty of Philosophy* (New York: International Publishers, 1963), p. 69; M[uriel] F[rances] Jolliffe, "Fresh Light on John Francis Bray, author of *Labour's Wrongs and Labour's Remedy*," *Economic History* 3 (February 1939): 241; John Francis Bray, *A Voyage from Utopia* (London: Lawrence and Wishart, 1957), pp. 140–41; H. E. Wade, "John Francis Bray" (Ph.D. diss., St. Louis University, 1967); also see John Francis Bray, "A Brief Sketch of the Life of John Francis Bray, Social, Political, and Religious Reformer" (Handwritten manuscript, original at London School of Economics Library; microfilm copy at library of State University of New York at Albany, undated).

24. Wade, "John Francis Bray," pp. 58–83, 92.

25. Jolliffe, "Fresh Light," p. 242.

26. Ibid., p. 243; Bray, *American Destiny*, pp. 2–4.

27. Bray, *American Destiny*, p. 26.

28. Jolliffe, "Fresh Light," pp. 242–43; Wade, "John Francis Bray," p. 121, quoting *Detroit News*, July 25, 1885.

29. J[ohn] F[rancis] Bray, "Co-operation or Confiscation," *Truth*, n.s. 1 (November–December 1884): 322–24.

30. J[ohn] F[rancis] Bray, "The Workingmen's Party," *American Socialist* 3 (January 3, 1878): 2; J[ohn] F[rancis] Bray, "The Inevitable," *The American Socialist* 2 (December 6, 1877): 387.

31. Bray, "The Inevitable," p. 387.

32. John Francis Bray, Letter to *The Word* 2 (May 1873), reprinted in M[uriel] F[rancis] Jolliffe, "John Francis Bray," *International Journal of Social History* 4 (1939): 16; J. F. Bray, "What is the Way," *Detroit Labor Leaf*, 1 (September 30, 1885), reprinted in Jolliffe, "Fresh Light," p. 24; J. F. Bray, "Letter to the Third Annual Convention of American Labor Reform League, New York, May 4–5, 1873," *The Word* 4 (June 1873), reprinted in Jolliffe, "Fresh Light," p. 17.

33. [John Francis Bray], *God and Man a Unity, and All Mankind a Unity: A Basis for a New Dispensation, Social and Religious* (Chicago: Western News Company, 1879), p. 90; J. F. Bray, "The Revolution," *Detroit Labor Leaf* 1 (October 28, 1885), reprinted in Jolliffe, "Fresh

Light," p. 25; *Chicago Socialist*, July 12, 1879, and *The Trades* (Philadelphia, July 12, 1879), cited in Ware, *Labor Movement*, pp. 120–21.

34. J. F. B[ray] to "Dear Friend Pyne" [editor, *The Examiner*, Hartford,], April 14, 1883, reprinted in Jolliffe, "Fresh Light," p. 23; J. F. Bray, "The Revolution," *Detroit Labor Leaf* 1 (October 28, 1885), reprinted in Jolliffe, "Fresh Light," pp. 25–26; J. F. Bray, "Set It all Down," *Detroit Labor Leaf* 2 (June 16, 1886), reprinted in Jolliffe, "Fresh Light," p. 28; Bray, "Co-operation or Confiscation, p. 322.

35. *Detroit Labor Leaf*, June 30, 1886, quoted in Wade, "John Francis Bray," pp. 125; J. F. Bray, "The Knights of Labor," *Detroit Labor Leaf* 1 (November 11, 1885), reprinted in Jolliffe, "Fresh Light," pp. 26–27.

36. Bray, "Co-operation or Confiscation," pp. 322–23; J. F. Bray, letter, *John Swinton's Paper* 4 (January 2, 1887), reprinted in Jolliffe, "Fresh Light," pp. 29–30; J. F. Bray, "A Platform for Farmers and Wage Workers," Paterson (New Jersey) *Labor Standard*, December 31, 1892, reprinted in Jolliffe, "Fresh Light," pp. 31–32.

37. J. F. Bray, "What Will You Do About It," Paterson (New Jersey) *Labor Standard* October 2, 1894, reprinted in Jolliffe, "Fresh Light," p. 33; J. F. Bray, "A Sound Dollar," Paterson (New Jersey) *Labor Standard*, September 12, 1896, reprinted in Jolliffe, "Fresh Light," p. 35.

∾ 9 ∾

Marxists and Lassalleans

- 1 -

The emigres from the unsuccessful European revolutions of the midnine-teenth century, commonly called '48ers, have generally been credited with the founding of the American Socialist, Anarchist, and Syndicalist move-ments.[1] This is an exaggeration.[2] The role of the emigres in the origin of these movements was primarily organizational; they had, at most, a slight influence on the intellectual and theoretical bases of the more contemporary movements.

The earliest of the refugees to organize in the United States were followers of the non-Marxian, Socialist, theoretician-activist Wilhelm Weitling, whose American Socialist career was replete with internal feuds, bursts of activity, and sudden withdrawal from the movement. Weitling, who was like most of the '48ers a German, first came to America in 1846 at the age of thirty-eight. He returned to Germany two years later to participate in the revolution. When that uprising failed, Weitling fled from the postrevolu-tionary persecutions and returned to the United States. On his return, he founded two organizations—the *Befreiungsbund* and the *Arbeiter-bund*—and he began publication of a short-lived newspaper, *Die Republik der Arbeiter*. Internal squabbling led to the demise of his newspaper and organizations in 1853 and to his own estrangement from the Socialists.

Weitling's basic theoretical assumptions were a synthesis of the ideas first expounded by Karl Marx, Comte de Saint-Simon, François Marie Charles Fourier, and Robert Owen. He recognized the existence of a class struggle, which he considered to be a moral wrong rather than a historical dynamic. To right the wrong, he proposed the establishment of a highly centralized state, ruled by technocrats, similar to the society suggested by Saint-Simon. He believed that such a state would make possible a universal Utopia in which the "governing of men" would be replaced by the "administration of things." In place of money, the new society would use labor notes—à la Josiah Warren and Owen. This centralized rule was to know no national boundaries.

The theory vanished with Weitling's organizations. Except for an appearance at a meeting of the International Workingmen's Association—a few days before he died—he ignored the Socialist movement from 1853 until his death in 1872.[3]

- 2 -

Unlike Weitling and his followers, the early German Marxists formed more permanent and more practical organizations. The largest were the *Turnverein*, or gymnastic unions. Organized about 1850, they were intellectual as well as recreational centers for radical German emigres. Besides tumbling and other sports, the *Turnverein* offered intellectual sessions where members debated political, social, and cultural issues relating to both the United States and Germany. Seventeen of the *Turnverein* were federated in the *Turnerbund*, with a Socialist platform that included planks calling for abolition of the presidency and the Senate and the introduction of legislation by referendum. These planks and talk of forming a Social Democratic party in the United States were, however, little more than a facade, for the *Turners* were interested primarily in freeing Germany from the thralls of autocratic government and had little interest in American society and politics. As the Germans became more Americanized, as the dream of a revolution in the *Vaterland* became more remote, and as the emigres prospered in their country of refuge, the *Turnverein* lost their Socialist complexion until, by the end of the Civil War, they were purely social and atheletic associations.[4]

Like the *Turnverein*, the other pre-Civil War, German Socialist groups in America were almost totally detached from American reality. The *Kommunisten Klub*, a discussion group of left-wing intellectuals, ignored the political and social conflicts in the United States while they argued fine points of Socialist and Anarchist principles. Although commited to equality of races and sexes—and to opposition to all organized religion—they eschewed any involvement in the political process.[5]

On only one American issue—slavery—did the emigres evince great interest. The marginality of the German Socialists' interest in their home in exile did not blind them to the struggle that was rending America at that time. Thus when the debate over the slavery issue erupted into the Civil War, the German Socialists—unlike native American radicals—were virtually unanimous in support of the antislavery cause. Almost half of the eligible members of the *Turnerbund*, for example, joined the Union army. Many died in combat; others won decorations for heroism.[6]

- 3 -

Their involvement in the Civil War ended the isolation of the German Socialists. They became more directly involved in American issues. Socialist groups were founded throughout the East and Middle West. They were divided between followers of Ferdinand Lassalle,[7] who wanted to eschew economic for immediate political action, and disciples of Karl Marx, who believed economic—labor-union—organization had to precede political action. The Lassalleans, who had joined William Sylvis's National Labor Union by 1866, were instrumental in directing it into labor-reform politics. The Marxists, who recognized their political and economic impotence, limited their activity to the formation of propaganda groups, most notably the German Workers Educational Association. During the postwar recession of 1868, the Marxists and Lassalleans of New York City united for a short-lived foray into electoral politics. They nominated municipal candidates, proposed a platform of civic reform, and ran a lacklustre campaign under the banner of the Social party. The party polled a negligible vote and immediately after the election gave up.[8]

With the collapse of the Social party, the Socialists abandoned electoral activity and turned their attention to the International Workingmen's Association (IWA), which Marx had been instrumental in founding in 1864 "to serve as a medium between workingmen of different countries, to arbitrate all international disputes between labor organizations, [and] to keep members informed of the progress of the labor movement in all countries." Marx's International proclaimed the economic emancipation of the working class to be "the great end to which every [Socialist] political movement must be subordinated as a simple auxiliary." The IWA had affiliates in France, Britain, Germany, Austria, Belgium, Holland, Denmark, Spain, Portugal, Italy, Switzerland, Poland, and Australia. The first American branch was organized in New York in 1867 by Friedrich A. Sorge, an emigre friend of Marx. Within three years, IWA branches were in all of the major cities of the United States. Most of them were German speaking, although a few sections were French, Scandinavian, Czech, and English speaking. Although composed of Socialists, the American IWA was active primarily in reform movements—especially the drive for the eight-hour day.

By 1872, just as the IWA was showing signs of life in America, the international organization was rent by internal strife; it became the forum for vituperative debate between Marx and the Russian Anarchist Mikhail Bakhunin. The struggle became so intense that Marx arranged to move its headquarters to New York, where he expected it to have a quiet burial.[9] The IWA did die in the United States—but it was hardly a quiet burial. C. Osborne Ward, a leading native-born Socialist of the period, joined Frenchman Eduard David in refusing to serve on the General Council to which they had been elected. The treasurer, E. Levielle, vanished with the International's meager funds. Moreover, the international organization had to compete for funds with persistent appeals to the "affluent" American Socialists for financial aid for jailed strikers and revolutionaries in Europe. Besides the financial plight of the International, serious internal disputes developed within the American branches of the IWA. This was particularly true in San Francisco, then in the throes of serious anti-Chinese agitation. The statutes and principles of the International called for racial equality and brotherhood, but the San Francisco labor unions, with whom the Socialists sought close ties, demanded the ouster of the Chinese immigrants who were competing, at less than normal wages, with American workers on the Pacific coast. The dilemma of opposing Chinese immigration while preaching Socialist internationalism split the San Francisco section.[10] The realities of American life had apparently doomed the early American Socialist movement to impotence and probable demise, but a major depression, beginning in 1873, and a near-revolution, in 1877, intervened.

- 4 -

The 1873–1876 panic "of unmatched fury" was one "in which the workers suffered from want that is beyond description." Thousands were without work and hunger was common.[11] Under such conditions, a revolutionary movement, such as the International, might have been expected to win converts. But it was composed almost exclusively of foreigners—primarily German, many of whom had "neither a vote or a knowledge of the English language." To quote Jessie Wallace Hughan, a leading Socialist-pacifist of the first half of the twentieth century, their socialism was "interpreted by the principles of the German working class movement, with . . . no specific application to the needs of the American proletariat."[12]

Despite this fact, the Socialists' appeal for meliorative measures did win a strong response from the unemployed and the hungry masses. In December 1873 approximately 20,000 Chicago workingmen, organized by the Socialists, paraded to demand food for the hungry and jobs for the unemployed. That same month, a New York meeting drew 5,000 workingmen. The meetings failed to win genuine relief; instead, they created a backlash by impressing the authorities with fears of a new Paris Commune. Thus when the Socialists called a rally for New York's Tompkins Square, the police attacked them brutally, although the meeting was orderly and legal. The police attack led to a public outcry instigated by journalist John Swinton—who had by this time become radicalized by his observations of the hunger pervading the working class. A legislative investigation was ordered, but it "became stuck in the quicksand and swamp of party politics."[13]

The Socialists won a great deal of sympathy among the working people and intellectuals repelled by the brutality of the New York police—but little else.

- 5 -

By this time, the United States had two emigre-organized Socialist move-ments—the Lassalleans, in the loosely structured Social Democratic Work-ingmen's party, and the Marxists, in the IWA. Their primary disagreement was over the efficacy of immediate electoral activity, which the Lassalleans favored and the Marxists opposed. Despite their differences, the two groups maintained friendly relations; the Lassallean weekly newspaper, for example, published a thirteen-part condensation of Marx's *Das Kapital*.[14] Yet serious points of theoretical disagreement arose. Lassalleans devoted their energies to political organization; the IWA members were interested primarily in labor union work. One relatively major group of English-speaking IWAers formed the Association of United Workers of America, whose primary aim was the organization of a united federation of labor. Their declaration of principles was a mere paraphrasing of the IWA postulate:

The emancipation of the working class can be achieved through their own efforts and that emancipation will not bring class rule and class privileges for them but equal rights and equal duties for all members of society. Economic betterment is the first step to the desired end; to its achievement all political effort must be subor-dinated. Political action can be effective only by constituting the labor class a separate political party. The emancipation of labor is not merely local or national, it is international.

Beyond that, the United Workers' official journal, *United Workingmen*, an-nounced that it was "Devoted to the advancement of trades organizations and the economic advancement of the working class."[15] It was this view that dominated most of the IWA leaders. Many of the members of the United Workers were later to play significant roles in the establishment of the American Federation of Labor.

The members of the Lassallean Social Democratic Workingmen's party (SDWP) were little interested in labor-union organization, for they did not believe that economic organization could be an effective instrument in changing the social system. Their position was stated succinctly by John Francis Bray, who was a member of the party, when he argued that the ballot box was the only hope of the working class. "The ballot renders out-breaks, riots, and revolutions unnecessary. It is imperative, therefore, that labor should organize as a great political party, with fundamental principles and policies adopted to its conditions and wants."[16]

The minuscule size of both organizations, their isolation from the American workingmen, the failure of the IWA to organize a major labor federation, and the inability of the SDWP to become an effective political party soon narrowed the differences between them and made Socialist unity necessary. By 1876 the Lassalleans amended their party's platform to include a plank calling for the organization of trade unions and declaring that "every member of our party is duty bound to join the union of his trade." It also called upon those in trades where no unions existed to organize them.[17] Stirrings of political unrest were also occurring, dominated by the money reformers, commonly called the Greenbackers, which posed a threat to both Socialist organizations and thus tended to unite them.

The money reformers had wide support among labor leaders, especially in the Knights of Labor. A national "labor-reform" convention in April 1876 called by the Junior Sons of '76, one of the myraid of Greenbacker organizations, was dominated by representatives of the Knights. Several Socialists were active at the meeting, among them Peter J. McGuire, a leader of the Lassalleans, and Otto Wedemeyer, a Marxian. Wedemeyer, who was elected a secretary at the convention, pleaded for trade-union organization of producer cooperatives aided by the government. The convention rejected both proposals and proceeded to enact a Greenback monetary reform program. Both Socialist factions then withdrew. This meeting apparently convinced the Socialists of the futility of division, and a week later they united into the Workingmen's party.[18]

The new party adopted a program that was basically Marxist. Its platform asserted that the party would not participate in elections until it was strong enough, but called for the organization of powerful national and international labor unions as a means of meliorating the condition of the working class and—primarily—as a forum for spreading Socialist principles. Not all Socialists were convinced; some Lassalleans still insisted that immediate political action was necessary. But most of the members of both groups accepted the basic principles—the Marxists because they represented their point of view; the Lassalleans because they were convinced no viable alternative was open to them. Most Socialists agreed with Louis Berliner, a leader of the New York section, that the new party's program was based upon reality, that few workers were prepared to vote for the abolition of the capitalist system, and that even fewer understood the meaning of so drastic a step. "But they all understand what eight hours and more pay means." Under such conditions, only one successful type of working-class organization could exist—the labor union. Moreover, when the entire working class is organized by the unions into "one solid Phalanx," the whole capitalist system will be abolished "without the use of one ballot."[19]

With the emphasis placed on trade-union organization, the Socialists found it simple to deemphasize politics totally. Members of the New York organization of the Workingmen's party considered confining themselves to the economic struggle for an eight-hour day. So did the English-speaking American section in Philadelphia. New York and Philadelphia Socialists also favored turning the party into an "auxiliary to Trades Unions." The party organ changed its name from *The Socialist* to *The Labor Standard*, and its new editor, J. P. McDonnell, was an Irish-born founder of the United Workers. He filled its columns with the writings of eight-hour advocate Ira Steward and labor-union pioneer George E. McNeill.[20]

This emphasis on trade unionism turned the Workingmen's party into a quasi-Syndicalist movement. Berliner's assumption that the capitalist system would be abolished by economically organized workers without political action was expanded by McDonnell. The workers' problems were economic problems could be solved only by economic organization. Moreover, labor unions would be the basis for the new society once the capitalist system was abolished. "The entire society of the times to come will consist of cooperative laborers' unions, each one responsible to the state and to its members."[21]

The theoretical rationale for the Syndicalist orientation was expanded in a series of lectures by David Kronberg, published over a three-week period in April 1877 in the columns of *The Labor Standard*. His argument was basically that economics and politics were two unrelated issues that "like oil and water can never coalesce." It was thus necessary to concentrate upon one or the other. Since the workers suffered from economic rather than political deprivation, they required economic—not political—organization. Economic issues were practical; political issues were ephemeral, he argued. The problems confronting the workers were practical problems and thus required practical, not ephemeral or sentimental solutions.[22]

The dominant position during the first two years of the Workingmen's party's existence was based on three essentially Syndicalist postulates: (1) that labor could emancipate itself only through labor unions; (2) that labor unions offered immediate benefits for the working class, whereas political action could offer only eventual emancipation; and (3) that trade unions would form the basis for the new Socialist order. These same arguments would be raised some thirty-five years later—in somewhat more militant rhetoric—by the leaders of the Industrial Workers of the World (IWW). Like the 1876–1877 Socialists, many of the leaders of the IWW were Syndicalists who belonged to a Socialist party.

Not all Socialists agreed with the Kronberg-McDonnell-Berliner position. A large minority of both Lassalleans and Marxists insisted that politics and economics could not be divided, that one followed from the other. The leader of this group was Peter J. McGuire, an Irish-American who would a few years later abandon socialism completely and gain fame as the president of the United Brotherhood of Carpenters. The New Haven party, under his leadership, nominated a full ticket in the 1876 municipal election. The Workingmen's ticket polled a mere 500 votes after a vigorous—albeit low-cost—campaign. He also toured the New England states and organized party branches—generally committed to political action—in Massachusetts, Connecticut, and Rhode Island. McGuire maintained (1) that a political campaign offered Socialists a valuable forum for agitation, and (2) that union officials were basically defenders of the capitalist system, opponents of socialism, and exploiters of Socialists' sympathy with labor for their own ends. This argument had its mirror image among the followers of Kronberg and McDonnell, who feared that middle-class politicians entered the Socialist party to corrupt it for their own political advantage.[23]

The official antielectoral stance of the Workingmen's party created a dilemma for the Socialists. The party leadership had, during the 1876 presidential election, advised the membership to vote for no one. The election, they said, was essentially between two representatives of entrenched capital—Democrat Samuel J. Tilden and Republican Rutherford B. Hayes—and an ineffective, irresponsible Greenbacker, Peter Cooper, who was himself a capitalist. Although agreeing with the party's assessment of the three candidates, many party members insisted that as citizens they were duty-bound to vote, and as Socialists they wanted an opportunity to vote for a Socialist.[24]

The party leaders rejected the argument. They insisted that the time was not ripe to organize an electoral campaign. The first task was to organize labor unions and to agitate in them for socialism; "There is absolutely no other way to a *future* victorious political action." Even McGuire had second thoughts after the election: "The Workingmen's Party is more an educational than a political one; we do not desire to enter politics until we know what we are going to strike for."[25]

- 6 -

The Socialist movement of the period had few theoreticians of stature in its midst. Most of the party's members were skilled workingmen—which helps to explain the dominance of the trade-union wing—and had little time to spare on the fine points of Socialist doctrine. It was thus a period devoid of major philosophic discussions within the movement; the debates involved practical problems of organization or tactics. Only occasionally was a theoretical idea put forward, but these fugitive declarations were often totally ignored. Debate within the Workingmen's party was limited generally to tactics, primarily to the issue of electoral versus trade-union activity. Few Socialist ideas were developed or propagated. Only two party leaders made regular forays into the field of Socialist theory; they were W. G. H. Smart, a leader of the Boston party, and Friedrich A. Sorge, the Hoboken, New Jersey, piano teacher who was a confidante of Marx.

Smart believed that "individual ownership and control of commonwealth . . . will soon be consigned to the limbo of [the] past" and that democracy "in the sphere of politics and the *sphere of wealth*" would soon reign. He called himself a Social Democrat, because he believed in the social ownership of the means of production only but not in the collective ownership of the end product. The means of production, he argued, were essentially social wealth; the products were essentially individual wealth. The objective of social ownership of social wealth was the redistribution—but not the socialization—of individual wealth to eliminate the inequalities existing under capitalism. He argued that no man had the right to own the means of production to enrich himself. Social Democracy, in eliminating these inequities, threatened property rights; but so, too, had "the abolitionists *denied the right* of white men to hold black men as property for the purpose of enriching themselves by enslaved labor."[26]

Sorge addressed himself primarily to the growth of monopoly. He viewed the trend toward combination as a step toward socialism. The basic difference between monopoly capitalism and socialism was, he wrote, selfishness. Under either system, mass production in rationally organized industries would be the economic base of society. Under capitalism, Sorge argued, "everybody looks out for his own interest, even at the cost of his fellow-men." Under socialism, the common interest would dominate, and mass production would be for the benefit of society as a whole. This would be as true for farming as for manufacturing. Small farmers, "seeing that farming on a small scale cannot compete with farming on a large scale," would cultivate their farms in common and divide the products among themselves.

Sorge's view of socialism, however, was simplistic. For he discerned signs that socialism was triumphing in the growing use of institutions for public rather than private interest. He pointed to schools, churches, roads, public waterworks, public baths, public hospitals, and the post office as examples of this trend. The expansion of this system, he believed, was irresistible, and once this system became universal, a complete change would occur in social interests. Work would be compulsory. Laziness would not be tolerated. It "is everybody's duty to work . . . whoever is able to work and is not willing to do it, has no right to enjoy the fruits of the industry and labour of others." Nor would work be wasted on conspicuous consumption: "Labor will not be wasted in making luxuries for the idle, but be usefully employed in making the necessaries of life for the workers." Who would decide what was a luxury for the idle? On this Sorge was silent.

The new system was not to be created cataclysmically; it was to develop gradually. "There is a natural process of development in this as in all changes that history has recorded so far." Sorge did not rule out violence and repression as ingredients of the revolution. It was possible that some capitalists might refuse to cooperate with the socialization process. They would have to perish, "overwhelmed by the newly formed organization of the state." It was likewise possible, he said, that some might consent to the social takeover of their industries. Such capitalists would be honored for their patriotism "and remunerated deservedly."

But all of this was a long-range vision. Sorge conceded that "Nobody is able to state the development will go on exactly in the way we sketched out." It was thus necessary to alleviate the poverty and oppression of the working class immediately. He called, therefore, for immediate meliorative measures—primarily the eight-hour day and higher wages. To achieve these ends, workers would have to organize against rapacious, egotistical capital. "If working people would only learn to comprehend the solidarity of their interest!"[27]

Most Socialists, like Sorge and Smart, were overtly democratic and egalitarian, but, in fact, they reflected most of the mores and prejudices of the period. Although Richard T. Ely reported that Socialists generally favored equal rights for women, membership in the party was limited to men. The Philadelphia American section, for example, favored admitting women, but only in a separate section "under the same regulations as the others." One Socialist woman called for the organization of workwomen, but not for specific women's rights. Instead, she suggested that they organize against "the rapacity of the common enemy of workmen and workwomen—the capitalist class." The executive committee of the party called for equality of women, but only as part of the emancipation of the working class as a whole.[28] The same was true of the issue of race. The party was officially in favor of racial equality, but the Socialist press was replete with anti-Chinese articles. "The efforts the toilers are making will be in vain if this country is to become a Chinese province," a California Socialist wrote to the party newspaper in 1876.[29]

- 7 -

By 1877 the membership of Workingmen's party had grown to 6,000, preponderantly German, in 360 sections.[30] But it was still an insignificant party. A series of violent strikes, tantamount to a "revolution without revolutionary intent," however, won it temporary notoriety and short-lived political power.

The first of a wave of railroad strikes during the summer of 1877 was called originally by underpaid workers on the Baltimore and Ohio Railroad in protest against a proposed new wage cut. That strike was soon put down by military and police force. But others quickly spread across America; riots caused by the strikes left death and destruction in their wake. The Socialists had nothing to do with calling the strikes; they were, in fact, unaware that the railroad workers contemplated such action and were unprepared when the workers walked off their jobs. But the Socialists did eventually assume positions of leadership among the strikers in several cities. The labor uprisings won for the Socialists short-lived political power and turned the Workingmen's party into a political movement. To quote J. A. Dacus, the chronicler of the strikes, the Socialists, "an association with which the American people had heretofore had small acquaintance became suddenly extremely active, and dangerously bold" in many of America's major cities.[31]

Although unprepared, the Socialists were immediately enthusiastic supporters of the strike. The Socialist weekly thundered, in its first issue after the labor revolt began:

WAR!!!
Plundered Labor in Arms

The story that followed described the walkout at Martinsville in strident, almost hysterical terms. The article called for financial help for the strikers and "warned" President Hayes against sending federal troops to aid the railroads.[32] In Baltimore the Workingmen's party drew a huge crowd to a meeting in support of the strikers. The theme of the meeting was proclaimed by Christopher Hess, a local party leader who demanded that the "government should own the railroads and workingmen should constitute the government." In Philadelphia, where the Workingmen's party assumed leadership of the strike, police shot a seventeen-year-old youth to death at an outdoor party rally and invaded and dispersed a private meeting of the party's German section.[33] In Chicago, which was the center of Socialist activity, mass meetings were the order of the day. Although the Socialists' demands were moderate—an eight-hour day and government operation of the railroads—newspapers charged that the Socialists were inciting the workers to a "red rebellion." Police attacked Socialist meetings, even though they were orderly. The key speakers at the Chicago rallies, Albert R. Parsons, then a Socialist trade unionist, and Philip Van Patten, national secretary of the party, called for calm. The workers heeded the call; the police did not.

In St. Louis the Socialists organized an executive committee of strikers and sympathizers that dominated the city's life during the strike. The committee called for an eight-hour day, an end to child labor, reasonable wages, and food for the hungry. Its aim was to assure that members of labor organizations "will hold themselves individually and collectively responsible to pay for all food procured by their order," to avoid riots, and to "faithfully maintain the dignity of the law." The Socialist rallies drew 8,000 to 10,000 supporters, and as many as 2,000 of them marched in a torchlight procession supporting the strikers. The show of strength and discipline frightened the "ruling citizens" of the city. They raised a vigilante force of 15,000 men to put down the executive committee, and with the aid of police, infantry, and cavalry, the vigilantes stormed the Workingmen's party headquarters, attacked all people gathered in the street outside the hall, and arrested seventy-three Socialists and sympathizers. All were eventually freed by the courts, but the raid effectively broke the strike.[34]

The wave of strikes was finally ended by the use of federal troops dispatched by President Hayes, who considered the strikes to be an insurrection.[35] The Socialists protested Hayes suppression of the strikes. At a huge meeting in Tompkins Square, New York Workingmen's party speakers blamed the police for the death and destruction and warned that money had become the dominant power behind the operation of the federal government. "Think you, Mr. President," the New York Socialist leaders rhetorically asked President Hayes, "these [military power and coercion] are effective and permanent remedies that will insure henceforth peace and good order in Society? We think not." What was needed to secure economic and social tranquility was legislation to benefit labor. "Had legislation afforded the same opportunities and guaranteed the same rights and privileges to labor that it has to capital, these evil days would not have befallen us."[36]

The protest and appeal were futile. The strikes were broken by the brute force of government. *The Labor Standard*, still wedded to syndicalism, editorialized that the "strike has shown the world, at all events, what the organization of trades can effect." But the majority of Socialists, having experienced the repressive power of government, shifted their tactics. They now set out to seize political power—by ballot if possible—to use the state for, rather than against, the workers in their struggle with the rapacious capitalists. They saw in the ballot a surer and more peaceful alternative to strikes as a means of winning improved conditions for labor.

The move into electoral politics was an immediate success. In city after city, Socialists won victories in the fall municipal elections of 1877. In New York State, Workingmen's party candidates swept into power in Utica, Auburn, Oswego, and Elmira. Other cities won by the Socialists were Altoona, Pennsylvania, and Louisville, Kentucky. Even in Chicago, Parsons polled more than 7,000 votes and barely missed election from his aldermanic district. Wherever railroad men lived, Socialists candidates showed great strength.

But the electoral successes were only temporary. Within two years, virtually all of the Socialists were out of office. Why did the Socialists fail so soon after making such a strong showing? They failed primarily because they were unprepared for political power. Louisville was a typical example. The five Workingmen's candidates elected to the Kentucky State legislature "never succeeded in impressing themselves upon the history of the times through the introduction of any useful legislation."[37]

Other problems plagued the party after the great strikes of 1877. The working people seemed less interested in Socialist solutions to their problems than in the blandishments of immediate panaceas. In California a rabble-rousing racist politician, Dennis Kearney, won virtually unanimous labor support on a program that was basically limited to "driving out the Mongolians." So strong was the support of Kearney's anti-Chinese party, that he barely missed gaining political control of the state. Although his party adopted the Workingmen's name, its program was almost totally bereft of any measures aimed at alleviating the economic misery of the workers. Yet Kearney had become so powerful that the Socialists found it necessary in December 1877 to change the name of their organization to Socialistic Labor party (soon modified to the less Germanic Socialist Labor party) lest they be too closely identified with the California movement.[38]

The Kearney problem was minor compared with the internal strife that soon rent the party over the Chicago-based *Lehr and Wehr Verein* ("Educational and Defense Union"). Chartered in 1875 "for the purpose of improving the mental and bodily condition of its members so as to qualify them for the duties of citizens of the republic," it was basically a military drill team whose members were "instructed in military and gymnastic exercises." During 1875 and 1876 the *Verein* was almost exclusively ceremonial. Its members marched in the Chicago parade honoring the centennial of American independence on July 4, 1876. According to a contemporary Socialist report, they wore "white pants, blue blouses, and black hats. Drilled as corps of light infantry, they marched with fixed bayonets and won golden opinions by their solid and martial appearance."

During the 1877 upheaval, an unprovoked police attack on a peaceful gathering of journeymen cabinetmakers in Chicago's Turner Hall turned the *Verein* into an armed activist group. The meeting, which was not related to the strikes or with the disturbances, was attacked without reason. Those in attendance were primarily members of the Harmonia Association of Joiners, a craft union, and their employers. It was called to ratify a wage scale for the cabinetmakers. Police, apparently mistaking it for a strike rally, attacked suddenly and without warning. They wantonly clubbed those in attendance as they left the hall. Unsatisfied with merely clubbing their victims, the police fired into the crowd, killing one youth. The police attack was so brutal and unprovoked that an Illinois judge ruled that it amounted "to a criminal riot."[39]

Immediately after this riot, the *Lehr und Wehr Verein* began drilling in earnest with arms. Few Socialists joined the *Verein*; neither did many outside Chicago support it. An investigation by a leading "Red scare" newspaper in New York found neither drilling nor arms among the 1,300 members of the Socialist Labor party (SLP) in Brooklyn and New York. But this did not matter, the word *Socialist* became "synonymous with murder, arson, destruction, and other delectable terms." Most Socialists abhorred violence: "Our party plants itself decidedly on the grounds of lawful agitation by means of the right of suffrage," the *Ohio Volkszeitung*, an official party organ, proclaimed. Moreover, some Socialists were pacifists, and one of them, Theodore L. Pitt, opposed the *Verein* because "Socialism and war are incompatible, irreconcilable." Finally, the national executive committee ruled that the *Lehr und Wehr Verein* occupied "a position of hostility to the principles and policy of the Socialistic Labor Party." It ordered all sections to "avoid any official connection with such bodies and to require that no arms be carried in their processions."[40] But the order was ignored. The extreme revolutionary wing of the party, now moving toward anarcho-communism, and a large group of less revolutionary Socialists, led by Paul Grottkau of Milwaukee, defied the national executive. It was, after all, still a legal organization. Only after the *Lehr und Wehr Verein* marched fully armed in 1879 did the state of Illinois, fearful of armed rebellion, outlaw the group. The state's action had little effect; the *Verein* remained in existence for seven more years—albeit in secret.[41]

- 8 -

The experience of the great strikes of 1877 and the collapse of Socialist political power in 1878 turned most Socialists into reformers. The SLP platform, after paying homage to the idea of socialism and internationalism in a five-paragraph preamble, proposed a fifteen-plank program of social reforms that could have been accepted by any Progressive thirty years later—and most of which was to be enacted into law within the next sixty years. The platform called for (1) the eight-hour day; (2) sanitary inspections of factories, stores, and tenements; (3) an elected bureau of labor statistics; (4) a ban on convict labor; (5) a legal prohibition against labor by children under age fourteen; (6) compulsory and free education up to age fourteen; (7) "Prohibition of the employment of female labor in occupations detrimental to health or morality, and *equalization of women's wages with those of men where equal service is performed*"; (8) employers to be liable for accidental injury to men in their employ; (9) wages to be paid in cash; (10) repeal of antilabor conspiracy laws; (11) free administration of justice; (12) a graduated income tax and an end to all indirect taxes; (13) government ownership of banking and insurance; (14) "*The right to suffrage shall in no wise be abridged*"; and (15) initiative, referendum, and recall to be instituted. Almost as an afterthought, the Socialists added to their platform: "We acknowledge the perfect equality of rights of both sexes."[42]

Even this moderate platform failed to attract any mass of workers to the Socialist banner. The party remained small and basically German. Disappointed by the lack of support they were winning from labor union leaders, the Socialists became alienated from them. Frank Roney, a pioneer of both the Socialist and labor movements in California, recalled that "They [Socialists] regarded them [trade unions] as only pseudo-agencies for the attainment of benefits for the workers. Socialists denounced them because by the limitation of their demands they obscured the view and retarded the progress that would otherwise be made in the realization of Universal Cooperation in the production and distribution of the products of labor."[43]

For the party that only three years earlier announced as its main aim the organization of labor, this was a sharp reversal of policy. Many of the pro-union members of the party left. Their alienation from the labor movement led the Socialists into a disastrous venture in coalition politics.

In 1878 the political prairie fire of the Greenback party was sweeping the nation. The pro-Socialist *Labor Balance* editorialized that "there is more likelihood that it [the Greenback party] will elect the President in 1880 than there was in 1854 that the Free Soil Party would rise to such a mighty power in 1856." Many Socialists were themselves caught up in the Greenback fever. What did it matter that Socialists had argued only two years earlier that the Greenback party was "just as much a capitalistic party as the two old ones," or that it was "doomed to fail, to discourage its followers and to retard the ultimate victory of the common cause of labor?" A White House was waiting at the end of the political rainbow, and the Socialists wanted to be part of the victory. In 1880, after making a vain attempt to have John F. Bray nominated for vice-president by the Greenbackers, most Socialists—and the Socialist Labor Party, officially—backed the Greenback ticket headed by General James B. Weaver of Iowa.[44]

The Greenbackers did not win the election—they polled only 303,000 votes. But the SLP was left in a shambles. Some moderate Socialists insisted that they had virtually nothing in common with the monetary reformers and agrarians. The more radical revolutionaries considered the support of the Greenbackers to be a betrayal of socialism. Most of the dissenters on both sides abandoned the party: the more moderate dropped out of reform and Socialist politics generally (some to return ten years later in the Nationalist movement); the more radical turned to anarcho-communism and "the propaganda of the deed," whose leading German advocate—Johann Most—was soon to come to the United States.[45]

The best Friedrich Engels could say about his factionalized, opportunistic, and politically inept American followers in 1883 was that "all mistakes must be experienced in practice."[46]

NOTES

1. See, for example, Jessie Wallace Hughan, *American Socialism of the Present Day* (New York: John Lane Company, 1911), pp. 33–34; August Sartorius, (Freiherrn von Waltershausen), *Der Moderne Socialisumus in den Vereinigten Staaten von Amerika* (Berlin: Verlag von Hermann Bahr, 1890), pp. 30–31.

2. This point is one of the key themes of Howard H. Quint's excellent study, *The Forging of American Socialism* (Columbia: University of South Carolina Press, 1953; paperback ed. Indianapolis: Bobbs Merrill, 1964).

3. Sartorius, pp. 30–31; Morris Hillquit, *History of Socialism in the United States* (New York: Funk and Wagnalls, 1910), pp. 144–53; See also Carl F. Wittke, *The Utopian Communist: A Biography of Wilhelm Weitling* (Baton Rouge: Louisiana State University Press, 1950).

4. Sartorius, *Moderne Socialisumus*, pp. 33–34.

5. Ibid., pp. 32–33.

6. Ibid., pp. 31–32; Hillquit, *History of Socialism*, pp. 151, 154–55.

7. Ferdinand Lassalle (1825–1864) was a German-Jewish contemporary of Marx and the founding genius of what was to become, after his death, the German Social Democratic party. He believed that political power had to precede economic power. He thus eschewed trade unions and was active in forming the political General German Workers Union, the forerunner of the Social Democratic party of Germany. As a means of establishing a Socialist society, he favored the organization of state-aided producers' cooperatives that would be federated in national associations. The standard works on Lassalle are Georg Brandes's 1875 study, *Ferdinand Lasselle* (New York: Bernard G. Richards Company, 1925); Arno Schirokauer, *Lassalle* (New York: The Century Company, 1932); David Footman, *Ferdinand Lassalle* (New Haven: Yale University Press, 1947); and Eduard Bernstein, *Lassalle as Social Reformer* (London: Swan Sonnenschein & Sons, 1893). Few of Lassalle's books and pamphlets have been translated into English. His *Gesammelte Reden and Schriften*, edited by Eduard Bernstein, was published in twelve volumes by Paul Cassirer in Berlin in 1919–1920. An eight-volume collection of his letters, edited by Gustav Mayer, is also available in German. His most significant letters are to Karl Johan Rodbertus. For Karl Marx's criticism of Lassalle, see his letter to Johan Baptist von Schneitzer, October 13, 1868, in Karl Marx and Friedrich Engels, *Werke*, 39 vols. (Berlin: Dietz Verlag, 1965), 32: 568–71.

8. Friedrich Sorge, *Neue Zeit* 9 (1890–1891): 439; 11 (1891–1892): 389; Sartorius, *Moderne Socialisumus*, pp. 37–39.

9. Sartorius, *Moderne Socialisumus*, pp. 48–49; Hillquit, *History of Socialism*, pp. 156–63; Friedrich Sorge, *Neue Zeit*, 10 (1891–1892): 390.

10. F. A. Sorge, "Circulaire confidentielle aux federationes etc.," October 27, 1872, in *Papers of the General Council of the International Workingmen's Association, New York, 1872–1876,* ed. Samuel Bernstein (Milan: Feltrinelli Editore, 1962), p. 18; F. A. Sorge to North American [Federal Council], December 30, 1872, in ibid., p. 38; Sartorius, *Moderne Socialisumus*, pp. 48–49, 55–56. The San Francisco section was one of the strongest in the IWA, publishing its own newspaper. It should not be confused with the latter-day International Workingmen's Association founded ten years later by Burnette G. Haskell.

Other schisms were evident within the IWA at this time, particularly in New York. These schisms, however, are irrelevant to this study. They are covered in detail in Samuel Bernstein, *The First International in America* (New York: Augustus M. Kelley, 1962), especially pp. 112–24.

11. United States Senate, Committee on Education and Labor, *Report of the Committee of the Senate Upon the Relations Between Labor and Capital and Testimony Taken By the Committee,* 4 vols. (Washington, D.C.: U.S. Government Printing Office, 1885), 1: 1094–95; Sorge, *Neue Zeit* 10 (1891–1892): 210.

12. Hughan, *American Socialism*, p. 36.

13. Sorge, *Neue Zeit* 10 (1891–1892): 210; Robert V. Bruce, *1877: Year of Violence* (Chicago: Quadrangle Books, 1970), pp. 227–28.

14. *The Socialist* 1 (July 29, 1876). [n.p.]

15. Samuel Gompers, *Seventy Years of Life and Labor*, 2 vols., (New York: E. P. Dutton and Company, 1948), 1: 102–3; Bernstein, *The First International*, pp. 241–42.

16. *The Socialist* 1 (May 6, 1876, and May 13, 1876).

17. See Minute Books, Social Democratic Workingmen's Party, Philadelphia, November 15, 1873, until January 1876, Library of Congress. They are in German and are called "Protokoll." The American section, that is, the section of the party that used English as its language, first appeared on January 30, 1876. *The Socialist* 1 (May 15, 1876).

18. Norman Ware, *The Labor Movement in the United States, 1860-1895* (New York: D. Appleton and Company, 1929; paperback ed. (New York: Vintage Books, n.d.), pp. 35–36. Pagination follows paperback edition; *The Socialist* 1 (April 29, 1876, and July 29, 1876).

19. The Workingmen's party platform is reprinted in full in *The Labor Standard* 1 (September 23, 1876); the "Address of the Executive" of the Workingmen's party is in *The Labor Standard* 1 (September 2, 1876); See Louis Berliner's letter, *The Labor Standard* 1 (December 9, 1876).

20. Minutes, Philadelphia American Section, Workingmen's Party, U.S.A., November 21, 1876, and February 20, 1877, Library of Congress; Ira Steward to M. Doyle, November 27, 1876, in *The Labor Standard* 1 (December 9, 1876); see also *The Labor Standard* 1 (November 28, 1876).

21. Editorial, "Political Action," *The Labor Standard* 1 (September 23, 1876); editorial, *The Labor Standard* 1 (November 8, 1876).

22. Kronberg's lecture was reprinted in full as "Labor Real and Ideal," *The Labor Standard* 2 (April 7, April 14, and April 21, 1877).

23. *The Socialist* 1 (April 15, 1876); *The Labor Standard* 1 (October 21, 1876, November 18, 1876, and November 25, 1876); *The Labor Standard* 2 (January 6, 1877, February 24, 1877, March 24, 1877, and April 7, 1877).

24. Letter of William Haller in *The Labor Standard* 1 (November 25, 1876); Editorial, *The Labor Standard* 1 (November 11, 1876).

25. *Boston Herald*, quoted in *The Labor Standard* 2 (April 14, 1877).

26. W. G. H. Smart, "Universal Co-operation," *The Labor Standard* 1 (April 15, 1876); W. G. H. Smart, "Is the Workingmen's Party Communistic," *The American Socialist* 2 (December 20, 1877): 400.

27. Friedrich A. Sorge, *Socialism and the Worker* (1876; reprint ed. London: The Modern Press, 1885), pp. 4–8, 10–11, 13.

28. Minutes, Philadelphia American Section of Workingmen's Party, U.S.A., October 22, 1876, Library of Congress; Richard T. Ely, *Recent American Socialism* (Baltimore: Johns Hopkins University, 1885), p. 58; *The Labor Standard* 1 (September 2, 1876, September 16, 1876).

29. *The Socialist* 1 (April 15, 1876, June 24, 1876, July 8, 1876).

30. J. A. Dacus, *Annals of the Great Strikes in the United States* (Chicago: L. T. Palmer, 1877), pp. 82–83; Minutes, Philadelphia American Section, Workingmen's Party, October 10, 1876, Library of Congress.

31. Ware, *Labor Movement*, p. 45; Bruce, *1877: Year of Violence*, p. 229, Dacus, *Annals*, p. 57.

32. The Labor Standard 2 (July 28, 1877).

33. Dacus, *Annals*, pp. 65, 185; Minutes, Agitation Meetings of Philadelphia American Section, Workingmen's Party, U.S.A., July 25, 1877 and August 2, 1877, Library of Congress.

34. Dacus, *Annals*, pp. 308, 319-20, 322-23, 377-78; *The Labor Standard* 3 (August 4, 1877); Philip Van Patten was national secretary of the Workingmen's party from its founding in 1876 until 1883. He was also prominent in the Knights of Labor, serving on its general executive board from 1879 until 1880. He was an educated, native-born American. Van Patten was made secretary of the party primarily because there was a paucity of party members who could write English well. Van Patten was neither a Marxist nor a Lassallean; he was basically a Utopian. The party feuding, his miserly $10 a week salary, and the apparent futility of attempting to organize an American party, plus his own financial plight, led Van Patten to quit his post in 1883, leaving behind a false suicide note. See Ware, *Labor Movement*, p. 105; Terrence V. Powderly, *Thirty Years of Labor* (Columbus, Ohio: Excelsior Publishing House, 1889), p. 328; Bruce, *1877: Year of Violence*, pp. 229–31, Hillquit, *History of Socialism*, p. 217.

35. Dacus, *Annals*, p. 164.

36. Ibid., pp. 247–50; Editorial, *The Labor Standard* 3 (August 11, 1877).

37. Ware, *Labor Movements*, p. 49; *The Labor Standard* 3 (October 21, 1877, October 28, 1877, November 4, 1877, November 11, 1877, November 18, 1877, November 25, 1877, December 9, 1877); Bruce, *1877: Year of Violence*, pp. 317–18; *The American Socialist* 3 (March 14, 1878): 84; Ely, *Recent American Socialism*, p. 56; Charles Dobbs to Morris Hillquit, September 28, 1909, Morris Hillquit Papers, Wisconsin State Historical Society, Madison, Wisconsin.

38. Frank Roney, *Frank Roney: Irish Rebel and California Labor Leader*, ed. Ira B. Cross (Berkeley: University of California Press, 1931), pp. 295, 300, 303; Minutes, Philadelphia American Section, Socialistic Labor Party, February 25, 1878, Library of Congress; Ware, *Labor Movements*, p. 306.

39. *The Socialist* 1 (July 15, 1876): "Address of Messrs. [William M.] Salter, [Henry Demarest] Lloyd, and [J.P.] McConnell to Governor Richard J. Oglesby, November 10, 1887," *The Labor Enquirer* 1 (Chicago) (November 14, 1887). "Harmonia Association of Joiners v. Michael C. Hickey et al., Circuit Court of Cook County, Illinois, May 5, 1879," reprinted in *The Labor Enquirer* 1 (Chicago) (December 10, 1887).

40. "Address of Slater, Lloyd, and McConnell. . . . "; 'The Socialistic Labor Party," *The American Socialist* 3 (June 27, 1878):205; Roney, *Frank Roney*, p. 322; *The American Socialist* 3 (December 6, 1877), has a quote from the *Ohio Volkszeitung*; see also, letter of Theo. L. Pitt, *The American Socialist* 3 (June 27, 1878):205.

41. Frederic Heath, ed., *Social Democracy Red Book* (Terre Haute, Ind.: Debs Publishing Company, 1900), pp. 34–35.

42. "Platform of the Socialistic Labor Party," *Labor Balance* 1 (April 1878):14–15.

43. Roney, *Frank Roney*, pp. 317, 327–28.

44. *The Labor Balance* 1 (April 1878): 16; Editorial, *The Labor Standard* 1 (October 28, 1876); Ware, *Labor Movement*, p. 306.

45. "Reminiscences," in Charles Sotheran, *Horace Greeley and Other Pioneers of American Socialism* (New York: Mitchell Kennerly, 1915), p. xv; *John Swinton's Paper* 1 (September 14, 1884); August Spies, *Autobiography, His Speech in Court, and General Notes* (Chicago: Nina Van Zandt, 1887), pp. 25–26.

46. Friedrich Engels to Friedrich Sorge, June 29, 1883, in Leonard E. Mins, ed. and trans., "Unpublished Letters of Karl Marx and Friedrich Engels to Americans," *Science and Society* 2 (Spring 1938):231.

The Road to Haymarket

- 1 -

The decision of the Socialist Labor party (SLP) leaders to support James B. Weaver was the last straw for the more radical Socialists. Their faith in the electoral system had begun to wane at least a year earlier when the Socialist aldermanic candidate had apparently been elected in Chicago's Ward 14 only to be counted out. The Socialists went to court despite legal obstacles and prohibitive costs—more than $2,000—and won. But it took a year to obtain a verdict, and by the time the court had ruled, the term of the duly-elected Socialist had expired.[1] August Spies, a leader of the revolutionary wing of the Chicago party, claimed that this incident proved that a conspiracy existed to rob the workingmen of any electoral victory, and that he, therefore, looked upon the ballot "with disgust" and considered it a fraud.[2]

The 1880 decision to support Weaver thus merely exacerbated an already developing antipathy toward peaceful, parliamentary revolution. Just as the strikes of 1877 had destroyed the Socialists' faith in trade unionism by proving that the coercive force of the state was uniquely available to the capitalists in their struggle with labor, so did the electoral fraud of 1879 and the Greenbacker deal of 1880 convince the revolutionary Socialists that the ballot was useless as a means for achieving a Socialist revolution. Moreover, a new wave of radical German immigrants, fleeing Bismarck's anti-Socialist laws, had just arrived in America. Many of these refugees were also disillusioned with the electoral process, for their powerful Social Democratic party had been effectively emasculated by Bismarck's autocratic decrees.

Thus in 1881, the central committee of the Chicago Socialist Labor party issued a call for armed resistance to capitalism. That same year, a group of New York Socialists formed a new revolutionary organization, and shortly thereafter the two groups, plus a few supporters in other cities, formed a loose federation: the Revolutionary Socialist party, which proclaimed its belief in direct revolutionary action. The new movement was centered in Chicago, where its leaders, Spies and Albert R. Parsons, resided.

Although they disagreed on tactics, the revolutionary Socialists cooperated with the more moderate members of the Socialist Labor party during 1881 and early 1882. Their basic long-range aims were identical, and their tactical differences, although sharp, were considered unimportant when compared with their parallel beliefs. All of this changed, however, in late 1882 with the arrival in America of the German revolutionary firebrand, Johann Most.

When Most arrived in the United States, he was already well known in radical circles. A former Social Democratic member of the German Reichstag, he was forced to flee his native land after Bismark enacted the anti-Socialist laws. The decision of the leaders of the Social Democratic party to acquiesce to Bismarck's edicts, instead of fighting them by violent, underground action, led to Most's resignation from the party.

An inflammatory speaker, Most's orations had, before his departure for America, resulted in six years imprisonment in three countries: Austria (1869), Germany (1870, 1872, 1874, 1877), and England (1881–1882). He came to New York fresh from his British imprisonment. His arrival in America was a scene of rejoicing; thousands of Socialists cheered him at a Cooper Union welcome. Almost immediately after that meeting, Most embarked on a speaking tour of the United States, drawing huge crowds and frightening the authorities with his bombastic rhetoric. Most used the speaking tour to solidify his influence among the most radical of the Socialists and to unite them into an organization under his control.[3]

Although his revolutionary rhetoric and abrasive personality endeared him to the most radical elements of the German-American Left, these attributes soon created an unbreechable chasm between the revolutionary and the moderate Socialists. He ridiculed electoral and democratic processes in favor of revolutionary violence; he proclaimed himself an anarchist, belittling the term Socialist or Social Democrat. The revolutionary Socialists emulated him, and although they proclaimed that "anarchism and socialism are as much alike as one egg to another," the movements fast became antagonistic.[4]

- 2 -

Most worked unceasingly at unifying the various revolutionary Socialist and Anarchist units throughout the country. As a result of his efforts, a congress of representatives of the various revolutionary groups was held at Pittsburgh in October 1883. The delegates were preponderantly Germans—the records were kept in English and German—representing units in fifteen cities in nine states. The delegates were all united in their rejection of electoral politics and in their conviction that the workers had to arm for the impending revolution. Unlike Most, who opposed any but "revolutionary" activity, Spies and Parsons favored trade-union work and wanted to "warn the workers against false methods of agitation" leading to electoral activity or political accommodation. Parsons, in particular, urged trade-union organization, especially among the unskilled and unorganized. He expected that union struggles would "break down the capitalistic system, and create such disorder and hardship that the social revolution would become a necessity."[5]

Because Most's primary interest was the organization of a national movement dedicated to the violent overthrow of the capitalist system, and not arguments over fine points of revolutionary dogma, he did not debate trade unionism with Parsons and Spies.

All of the delegates accepted Most's views of violence. The delegate from the Chicago *Jaegerverein* ("Hunters' Federation") urged the "speedy arming of the proletariat and the adoption of all new scientific developments, especially chemistry" useful for making explosives. The Milwaukee Revolutionary Socialists' delegate called for "arming of our comrades." A representative of the Pittsburgh organization urged "arming and other progressive measures." The spokesman for the Communistic Workingmen's Educational Society of St. Louis proposed that the new national movement devote its time to the "furthering of chemical knowledge among our comrades." A member of the Astoria, New York, revolutionists proposed that the new organization obtain weapons immediately.[6]

The congress was thus as harmonious as it was bombastic. Its final manifesto, issued without dissenting vote, soon became the classic statement of the aims of revolutionary anarchism. It called for the "destruction of existing class rule, by all means, that is by energetic relentless, revolutionary and international action"; it urged the establishment of "a free society based upon co-operative organization of production" with free barter between the independent, federated cooperatives "without commerce and profit mongering." The manifesto also demanded education for all "on a secular, scientific and equal basis for both sexes" and urged equal rights for all "without distinction to sex or race." Finally, the delegates voted in favor of society in which all public affairs would be regulated by "free contracts between . . . autonomous communes and associations, resting on a federalistic basis."[7] The congress also formed a permanent national organization, the International Working People's Association (IWPA), based ideologically on the manifesto.

One result of the Pittsburgh Congress was the increase in bombast on the part of the revolutionaries. Their rhetoric was now loaded with calls for "propaganda of the deed" and for armed action. The slogan of the IWPA soon became "gunpowder and dynamite will set mankind free."[8]

Bombast proved to be more popular than moderation; by 1884 the IWPA had twice the membership of the Socialist Labor party, although the official IWPA claims of 25,000 armed members was a boastful exaggeration, as was the claim of 3,000 armed IWPAers in Chicago alone in 1886. The IWPA actually had about 7,000 members nationally; they were organized in eighty branches, of which only twelve were English speaking. In Chicago a German daily, three German weeklies, and one English biweekly were published by the IWPA. Many trade unionists in the midwestern metropolis supported the revolutionists.[9]

The long-term economic views of the IWPAers were generally identical with those of the Socialist-Laborites. They differed mainly on the issue of reform under capitalism, which the revolutionaries generally rejected and the Socialist-Laborites generally favored. The Anarchist-Communists, as the IWPAers were labelled, argued that reform movements "did not strike at the root of the evil." Thus they rejected the persistent invitations to join the eight-hour movement, arguing that it was, by its very existence, a vote of confidence in the capitalist system. "Either our position that the capitalists have no right to the exclusive ownership of the means of life is a true one, or it is not," an editorial in the official IWPA organ *Alarm* argued. "If we are correct, then to accede the point that capitalists have the right to eight hours of our labor is more than a compromise, it is a virtual concession that the wage system is right." Moreover, August Spies maintained that the workers would gain little or nothing even if the eight-hour day were instituted, because the workers would remain the "slaves of their masters."[10]

In place of reform, the IWPAers favored a total social revolution, the substitution of cooperative, humane socialism for competitive, dehumanizing capitalism. Yet their economic views were vague and difficult to describe precisely. The basic system they proposed would require the destruction "of existing class rule . . . by energetic, pitiless, international revolution." In its place would be organized a series of cooperative colonies that would have a community of goods. These communities or associations would be allied in a federated organization and would trade with each other—"without middle men or profits"—in a system of barter. The new system would do away with all private property, for, according to Most, the "beast of property" was the root of the inequitable class structure that was the hallmark of capitalist society; this class structure was the cause of current social evil. The elimination of class differentiation was thus the basic social change that Anarchist-Communists proposed to achieve.[11]

The Anarchists-Communists' analysis of the economic system derived from a simplistic reading of Marx and Engels, particularly of the *Communist Manifesto*. Borrowing from that revolutionary classic, the IWPAers argued that labor "is the foundation of all wealth," and nothing could have value except to the extent that it required labor to produce it. Thus the

IWPAers reasoned, all that was added to price that did not represent labor value—profit, rent, interest—was theft. This oversimplified version of the labor theory of value was only one of several borrowed from the Marxists. Another was the assumption that the mode of production controlled the relationships of society. Spies, for example, told a gathering of clergymen that "economic conditions and institutions of a people form the groundwork of all their social conditions, of their ideas—aye even of their religion."[12]

The Anarchist-Communists' debt to the Marxists also included the theory of the class struggle, which both accepted. Every advance for mankind, Spies said, was the result of "the struggles between the dominating and dominated class in different ages." The Anarchist-Communists likewise accepted the Marxian *immiseration thesis*, which postulated that as capitalism developed, technological advance and its concomitant economic concentration would cause the conditions of the working class to become progressively worse while the middle class would disappear into the working class, thus further impoverishing the workers as labor competition increased in a contracting job market.[13] This last argument had a ring of truth to it in late nineteenth-century America, where technological advance was creating monopoly and was causing the economic dislocation of much of the middle class and unemployment among working people, particularly those whose skills had become obsolete. Their belief in the immiseration thesis led the Anarchist-Communists to become determinists. They believed that socialism, which they never defined fully, was inevitable. "To quarrel with socialism," Parsons argued, "is to quarrel with history; to denounce the logic of events." Perhaps it could be put off, perhaps "Napoleons and Bismarcks may stifle it in blood," but it could not be avoided. Charles James, one of the few native-born American intellectuals in the movement, urged the rulers of America to accept the inevitable. "That only is wise statesmanship which gives up moribund institutions to die. That only is reform which anticipates in a less painful manner the work of revolution."[14]

- 3 -

If their economic analysis was borrowed from Marx, the Anarchist-Communists' political analysis was based largely on the teachings of Josiah Warren, Stephen Pearl Andrews, and Lysander Spooner, plus some of the ideas of Marx's long-time antagonist, the Russian Anarchist Mikhail Bakhunin, as synthesized by Most. Socialism, they argued, would be achieved "in the name of the people" rather than in the name of the state as Socialist-Laborites believed, or of religion, as Christian Socialists claimed. Like the latter-day New Left—whose catch-phrase slogan "Power to the People" was borrowed directly from Most—the Anarchist-Communists never defined what was meant by the "people." The Anarchists were obliged to pin their Socialist revolution on this amorphous mass—the "people"—because they proposed to dismember the state, which Socialist-Laborites proposed to use as the instrumentality through which socialism would be effectuated. The IWPAers argued that the state would, by its very nature, become despotic, especially since it would have to become centralized in an industrial state. Centralization, they believed, would remove government from the masses, thus making rulers less responsive and more powerful and thus despotic.[15]

The basic rationale for the Anarchist political views of the IWPAers was the premise of sovereignty of the individual as espoused by Warren half a century earlier. "The natural and the inprescriptible right of all is the right of each to control himself," Parsons wrote. From this it followed that any restriction upon an individual's control over himself would be an infringement upon that person's natural rights. Statute law would, according to Parsons, violate man's natural right and should thus be eliminated. Parsons did not, however, believe that all law was by its nature evil; some law—natural law—was discernible rather than enacted. But statute law was made by man and was thus "an insult to divine intelligence." He argued that statute law was based on power, that power "is might and might always makes its own right. Thus in the very nature of things, might makes itself right." Thus the state, being rooted in statute law, tended to center power in the hands of a few rulers "who dominate, dictate, rule, degrade, and enslave the many."[16]

To speak of men being free under a democratic parliamentary form of government was, therefore, in Parson's view, a contradiction. No man could be free as long as he submitted to government, which was by its very nature a domineering power and as such an enemy of freedom. Parsons argued that man could have personal liberty only under anarchism—the absence of government and of man-made law. The Anarchists insisted that their Utopia would be orderly, because poverty would be unknown, education would be free and universal, and competition for property would have disappeared.[17]

Had the Anarchist-Communists limited their attack to parliamentary institutions, they might have found an ally in the more radical Socialist-Laborites. Paul Grottkau, a leader of the Milwaukee SLP, for example, insisted that organized government—"the executive committee of the class in power"—would be superfluous in a Socialist society in which classes would no longer exist. But the IWPAers opposed more than mere government; they proposed abolishing many other social institutions, primarily marriage, which they considered needless state interference in a private matter—immoral interference, in fact, in cases where either of the parties no longer felt affection for the other. Most argued that the family itself was a repressive institution, that it was the model from which the state was designed.[18]

The Anarchist commonwealth would be free of laws—and free of exploitation and class distinction. It was a Utopia that rivaled any previously designed, and its spokesmen believed that its emergence would bring with it a worldly paradise free of all the trials and tribulations of mundane history. Most argued that: "Vice and crime will have disappeared with their virginal causes, private property and general misery." So, too, would disease vanish, "because bad lodgings, murderous workshops, impure food and drink, over-exertions etc., etc. [will] have become things unknown."[19]

- 4 -

The members of the IWPA dreamt of a totally free society in which people would live at peace and in which no man would rule another. But their immediate aim was violently authoritarian, the absolute antithesis of their long-term dream. This was less of a contradiction than it would appear on the surface, for the Anarchist-Communists believed the new libertarian political system could be organized only after the economic system had been socialized. Since those who profited from the present order would fight socialism, the most important task facing the revolutionists, once the rebellion had succeeded, was the establishment of a short-term, transitional rule during which the capitalist class would be destroyed. As Most pictured it, this interim period would be a veritable reign of terror. Armed revolutionary committees would be set up in each community to carry out orders issued by the revolutionary army, "reinforced by armed workingmen, [who] now rule like a new conqueror of the world." Capitalists and their adherents would be annihilated, "since if the people do not crush them they will crush the people." Literal massacres of the capitalists and their adherents would be instituted. All property would be absorbed into communes; men would either work or starve; schools would be set up—as agitational arms of the revolution; churches would teach revolutionary "truth and knowledge," and "no priestly cant will be tolerated." The press would have no freedom; the media would serve the revolution.[20] No time limit was placed on the transitional period, nor was any blueprint prepared for phasing it out.

The transition was to be well directed—as was the revolution that preceded it—by a well-trained, totally dedicated vanguard of full-time revolutionists. Most held the masses in low esteem; he argued that workers were generally gullible and ignorant. Except for the small group of conscious Socialists, most workers were politically indifferent, because they were inherently dull and interested only in short-term economic benefits. Nor would education of the workers solve the problem, for Most believed that education's primary role should be to incite the masses to revolt when economic conditions become unbearable. A well-trained revolutionary nucleus was thus a prerequisite for a successful, properly directed revolution, because, he argued, the masses were incapable of carrying out a social revolution.[21]

Twenty years later, a Russian revolutionary emigre in Switzerland, Vladimir Ilyich Ulyanov—Lenin—was to parrot Most's vanguard theory, without crediting his source. Almost thirty-five years later, Most's tactical prescription for revolution was to prove viable—in Russia under Lenin's leadership. His "transitional" dictatorship proved to be permanent in the Soviet Union.

- 5 -

It followed from their analysis of society that the IWPAers "glorified physical force and magnified 'the propaganda of the deed.' "[22]

The Anarchists argued that they would favor a peaceful parliamentary revolution if it were possible—but it was not. Samuel Fielden, an English-born leader of the Chicago IWPA, told reformer Henry Demarest Lloyd that he agreed with the latter in favoring the use of peaceful, legal means to accomplish the revolution, but he doubted "the enemy would allow it." Parsons also did not believe that "capital will quietly or peacefully permit the economic emancipation of their wage slaves." August Spies preached the use of dynamite by the workers only because the capitalists would not listen to reason; the capitalists would use brute force "to stay the wheels of progress."[23]

Not all of the IWPAers were convinced that a bloodless revolution was impossible, but even they insisted that an armed working class was a prerequisite for a peaceful revolution. *Alarm*, the IWPA organ edited by Parsons, urged the workers to study chemistry in order to manufacture explosives and thus make themselves and their revolution too strong for the capitalists to oppose with arms. "This alone can insure against bloodshed."[24] Arms were the only effective weapon in the workers' revolutionary arsenal. The Anarchist-Communists argued that without arms, the workers would be easy prey for the violent and rapacious capitalists. The latter had many weapons, not only guns and clubs, but also economic power to force the workers into submission by hunger, exposure, and general economic suffering. Thus the use of revolutionary violence was humane, for in comparison with captalism's "starving, freezing, exposing, and depriving tens of thousands . . . the application of force would" be less torturous. Moreover, it would eliminate the cause of mass misery. Thus the Anarchists argued: "It is clearly more humane to blow ten men into eternity than to make ten men starve to death."[25]

The Anarchists reasoned that violence was excusable as a necessary means for erasing an iniquitous state of society. Moreover, they argued that all historical advances had required force, that none had been achieved by peaceful means. Advances in weaponry had gone hand in hand with social

improvements. Anarchists, therefore, hailed the development of dynamite—a relatively inexpensive, effective, deadly, and obtainable explosive,
because—to quote Lucy Parsons—"dynamite is the voice of force, the only
voice tyranny has been able to understand." August Spies believed that
dynamite guaranteed the revolutionists' victory.[26]

With justice, humanity, and history on their side—by their own proclamation—the IWPAers' rhetoric rang ever more militantly bloodthirsty.
Workers were openly advised to purchase easy-to-obtain daggers and
revolvers, to make their own low-cost hand grenades, and to obtain explosives of all sorts. *Alarm* published a series of articles on the manufacture of
dynamite. Most brought out a manual for the manufacture and use "of
Nitro-Glycerine, Dynamite, Gun Cotton, Fulminating Mercury, Bombs,
Fuses, Poisons, etc., etc."[27]

At first the Anarchist-Communists' appeal to violence was limited to a
call for organized force as a tactic for overthrowing the capitalist system.
But from 1884 on, calls for the use of individual terror became common-
place in IWPA-affiliated publications. Instant death to anyone who claimed
ownership in any property was considered a legitimate means for abolishing
"this infernal monster called 'the right of property.' " Finally, *Alarm* called
for the assassination of all heads of government on the assumption that if
enough of them were slain, all governments would disappear, since "no
government can exist without a head."[28]

The calls for violence of Most, Parsons, and Spies, and their rationales,
were to be repeated for the next ninety years by Anarchists, Communists,
members of the Weatherman faction of the Students for a Democratic Society, and others interested in ending class oppression in the United States.
They were to repeat Parson's ringing declaration that "against tyrants and
tyranny all means are not only justifiable but necessary."[29] Unfortunately
for the radicals, they could—and can—hardly compete with the state in
means of violence and repression. The ability of the state to suppress vocal
opposition, and the willingness of its rulers to use whatever means appear
necessary to eliminate militant opposition, is well documented. From the
very beginning of the United States, radical and labor organizations have
been restrained legally or, when necessary, restricted forcibly by the coercive force available to the state. In the least oppressive of these acts, the
state has imposed limitations against free speech and assembly. In the more
serious cases, police and military forces have employed armed might
against labor and Socialist opposition.[30]

The memory of the government's military intervention against the railroad strikers of 1877 should still have been fresh in the minds of the radicals
of the 1880s. It should have been apparent to the Anarchist-Communists
that the leaders of the state would not tolerate any open, militant defiance.
History should have proven to the IWPA members that rulers would not

permit moral scruples to interfere with the elimination of serious militant opposition. Moreover, it should have been obvious that public appeals for violence against the all-powerful state, and the class it served, would be inviting doom. Yet the IWPA members, and their latter-day imitators, were so enamored of their rhetoric that they forgot the obvious lessons of history. The result, in 1886, was Haymarket.

- 6 -

The tragedy called Haymarket began as a simple labor demonstration for the right to organize and for an eight-hour day. The IWPA leaders became involved in the demonstration despite their lack of enthusiasm for reform, because they realized that to have done otherwise would have isolated them from the mass of the workers to whom the right to organize and the eight-hour day—not revolution—were key issues. Moreover, because the most powerful unions in Chicago were also the most militant, and because they were closely tied to the IWPA, the Anarchist-Communists played leading roles in the demonstrations. The immediate precursor of the Haymarket affair was a May 3, 1886 mass demonstration in support of the union employees of the McCormick Harvester plant, who had been locked out of their jobs in an effort by management to destroy their union. It was unusually large—the crowd has been estimated as high as 25,000 people—because a general strike for the eight-hour day was then in progress in Chicago. The unions and their leaders had earned the enmity of the business and political community in Chicago, because they demonstrated the potential power of the labor movement in that city. *The Chicago Daily Mail*, which echoed the views of the dominant business and political interests, wanted the laborers' leaders "driven from the city" and insisted that they should be held "personally responsible for any trouble that occurs. *Make an example of them if trouble does occur.*" William Barth, president of the City National Bank, suggested that the city authorities "ought to run out the gatling guns and shoot down the strikers."

A few minor skirmishes had occurred between union and nonunion employees at the meeting when suddenly, without warning, a phalanx of several hundred armed police and gun-wielding Pinkerton agency private guards in the employ of McCormick Harvester attacked a part of the crowd. A rock-throwing scuffle ensued; the police and guards fired a fussillade into the crowd; six workmen lay dead. The crowd dispersed, but civil war was in the air.[31]

Almost immediately after the riot, August Spies composed a rhetorically militant handbill that read,

Workingmen to arms. Your masters sent out their bloodhounds the police. They killed six of your brothers at McCormick this afternoon; they killed the poor wretches because they had the courage to disobey the supreme will of your bosses; they killed them because they dared to ask for the shortening of the hours of toil; they killed them to show you, free American citizens, that you must be contented with whatever your bosses consent to allow you or you will get killed. You have for years suffered unmeasurable iniquities; you have worked yourselves to death; you have endured the pangs of want and hunger; your children you have sacrificed to the factory lords—in short you have been miserable and obedient slaves all these years. Why? To satisfy the insatiable greed, to fill the coffers of your lazy, thieving masters. When you ask them now to lessen the burden they send their bloodhounds out to shoot you—kill you. If you are men, if you are the sons of your grandsires who have shed their blood to free you, then you will rise in your might, Hercules, and destroy the hideous monster that seeks to destroy you! To Arms! We call you to arms!

Your Brothers.[32]

As if there were not enough hyperbole in the handbill as written, Hermann Podeva, a compositor at the *Arbeiter-Zeitung*, which printed it, added as a salutation the word *REVENGE!*[33]

The executive committee of the IWPA called a mass meeting for the next evening at the Haymarket to protest the police massacre at the McCormick Harvester plant. The call for the demonstration was published in a bilingual (German and English) handbill, which had been written by Adolph Fischer, and which read:

ATTENTION WORKINGMEN! *Great Mass-Meeting to-night* at 7:30 o'clock, at the Haymarket, Randolph St., bet. Desplaines and Halsted. Good speaders will be present to denounce the latest atrocious act, the shooting of our fellow-workmen yesterday afternoon. Workmen arm yourselves and appear in full force!

The Executive Committee

Spies deleted the words "Workmen arm yourselves and appear in full force!" from the handbill. That provocative sentence appeared in none of the handbills that were distributed.[34]

The Haymarket meeting was hardly a rousing success. A combination of threatening late spring weather, and fear of a repetition of the previous day's police slaughter, kept the audience to between 800 and 1,000 persons. Later in the evening, the growing threat of rain cut the crowd to about 250. The meeting was peaceful, and the speakers cautioned against precipitous steps. Order was maintained by a "counterpolice" of IWPA members. Spies told the crowd that the "monsters who destroy the lives and happiness of the citizens (for their own aggrandizement) will be dealt with like wild beasts." But he warned his listeners, the time for such action had not yet come. "When it has come you will no longer make threats, but you will go and 'do it.'" Parsons pleaded with the crowd not to beat scabs, but to pity them, for they were merely unemployed workers who were forced to become strikebreakers by poor conditions. Admittedly, Parsons ridiculed the ballot as an instrument for liberating the worker, "a man who could not control his bread stood a poor chance to control his ballot"; he had called upon the workers to arm: "Americans, as you love liberty and independence, arm, arm yourselves." But nowhere did he call for immediate violence or make any remarks that could have roused the crowd to a fever pitch. In fact, the speakers and the crowd were so peaceful and lacklustre when compared to previous Anarchist rhetoric that Mayor Carter Harrison, who attended because he expected violence, ordered Inspector John Bonfield to send the police reserves home and then left Haymarket himself.[35]

But the order was ignored. The police were not interested in keeping order. Inspector Bonfield had previously told a non-Socialist salesman, Barton Simonson, that the police at Haymarket intended to make "short work of the Socialists." The *Chicago Times*, hardly a friend of the IWPA, or of the labor movement, reported that the police were at Haymarket to arrest Spies, Parsons, Michael Schwab, another German Anarchist, and Samuel Fielden, an English-born member of the IWPA. Spies believed that "detectives had been stationed in the crowd to kill the obnoxious speakers at the instant the police would charge upon the crowd."[36]

No sooner had the mayor departed than Bonfield, in direct contravention of his superior's order, directed his men to end the meeting. Captain William Ward and a squad of police approached Samuel Fielden who was addressing the crowd. The captain ordered the meeting to disperse. Fielden protested that the rally was peaceful. Ward was adamant, and the police moved in as if to seize Fielden. Suddenly, without warning, a bomb exploded. Immediately, the police went berserk; to quote the *Chicago Tribune*, they became "as dangerous as any band of Communists." They fired their pistols into the crowd; they clubbed and felled innocent bystanders. When the dust had cleared, seven policemen and four demonstrators were killed, and sixty policemen and fifty demonstrators and bystanders were wounded. No one knew who threw the bomb—an Anarchist, an apolitical madman, an *agent provacateur*, or an undercover policeman.[37] Nor was the mystery ever solved.

Within hours after the explosion, the police arrested hundreds of Anarchists, Socialists, trade unionists and innocent bystanders in raids on offices and meeting halls of labor and radical organizations and newspapers. Among those who were seized was the entire staff of the *Arbeiter Zeitung*, the IWPA daily newspaper. Unable to find Parsons at home, the police arrested his wife and a female friend. It was apparent that the police were determined to use the Haymarket bombing as an excuse for eliminating the Anarchist-Communist threat. The police claimed that they found a bag of dynamite in a "greasy closet" at the *Arbeiter-Zeitung* office, about thirty-six hours after the explosion. But a mason who had calcimined the closet that same day "found no bundle, no large package, no dynamite on the shelf." He also saw "no indication of greasiness there." It was apparent that Chicago's authorities were determined to extract the penalty for the tragedy from the Anarchists, regardless of their guilt.[38]

Although hundreds had been arrested, only nine—all leaders of the IWPA—had been charged with complicity in the crime. Besides Spies, Parsons, Fischer, and Fielden, the men accused of the crime were George Engel, Louis Lingg, Oscar W. Neebe, Michael Schwab, and Rudolph Schnaubelt. This was an unlikely crew to face a trial for murder. All of them were working-men—Engel, the eldest, had worked at many trades, Fielden was a teamster, Lingg was a carpenter, Neebe was an organizer of the Brewery Workers Union and a brewer, Parsons was a compositor, Spies and Schwab and Fischer were journalists. All of them were basically idealists, who talked of violence, but who had never been involved in a violent act. Schnaubelt avoided the police and fled the country. Parsons could also have escaped arrest. He fled to Waukesha, Wisconsin, and police were unable to find him. But he refused to allow his fellow radicals to stand trial alone and he walked into court voluntarily on the first day of the trial.[39]

The trial of the eight Anarchists was a travesty on justice. Questioning of the jurors made it clear that the court was determined to hang the Anarchists. The defense was forced to use all of its preemptory challenges against jurors, who admitted they were biased against the defendants, but whom the court refused to disqualify. At least one of the jurors had said before the trial that Spies "and the whole damned crowd" should be hanged. Another was quoted as saying that the police should have shot "them all down." The entire panel of 1,000 from whom the jury was chosen was antagonistic to all radicals. The jury was composed entirely of upper middle-class, Protestant conservatives who believed their social position depended upon "law and order," which they equated with the existing political, social, and economic system.

The charge against the defendants was murder, but the state did not claim that any of the defendants threw the bomb or even knew who threw the bomb. The charge was basically that the conspiracy existed between the defendants, the "general object and design" of which was "the overthrow of the existing social order and of the constituted authorities of the law by force," and that because of this conspiracy, Mathias J. Degan, one of the policemen killed in the explosion, had lost his life. The question of whether any of the defendants was directly involved in the killing of Degan was thus irrelevant. All that had to be proven was that any act by all or any one of the conspirators could have helped instigate the action that led to Degan's death. "If you show that some man threw one of these bombs without the knowledge, or authority, or approval of any of these defendants is that murder?" a defense attorney asked. "Under the law of the State of Illinois *it is* murder," the prosecutor replied. But there was a great deal of doubt that a conspiracy actually existed. Lingg had never met Spies or Parsons.[40]

The prosecution's case was based primarily upon contradictory testimony. The defense was unable to present a plausible case because of prejudicial rulings from the bench, Judge Joseph E. Gary being, by his own admission, prejudiced against the defendants. Some prosecution witnesses said Fielden fired a shot at Haymarket; others said he did not. He was said to be seen in various places by various witnesses. Detective John Bonfield admitted that his search of the *Arbeiter-Zeitung* office was done without a warrant. He also admitted that the piece of pipe, fulminating cap, fuse, and pistol he supposedly found in the office were quite old and probably useless. What evidence was presented merely affirmed that Most's pamphlet, *Science of Revolutionary Warfare*, was sold at IWPA picnics and that some of the defendants had, quite some time before the explosion, urged the use of arms and violence.[41]

Eight murderers were not on trial: "Law is on trial! Anarchy is on trial!" Julius Grinnell, the prosecutor, cried out in his summation. Judge Gary told the defendants: "Not because you have caused the Haymarket bomb, but because you are Anarchists, you are on trial." Yet Judge Gary prevented Charles L. James, a scholarly anarchist of Eau Claire, Wisconsin, from explaining *anarchism* to the jury.[42]

At the end of the trial, all eight defendants were found guilty. Seven—Spies, Parsons, Schwab, Fielden, Fischer, Engell, and Lingg—were condemned to death. Neebe was sentenced to fifteen years in the state penitentiary. The defendants hardly flinched. Spies, speaking for all of them, told Gary: "You may pronounce the sentence upon me, honorable judge, but let the world know that in A.D. 1886, in the state of Illinois, eight men [he had expected Neebe also to be doomed] were sentenced to death because they believed in a better future; because they had not lost faith in the ultimate victory of liberty and justice!"[43]

The sentences were appealed up to the United States Supreme Court, to no avail. One Illinois appeals court justice told a businessman friend before he ruled on the case that no reversal was possible under any conditions. Pleas went for nought.

Labor and radical support for the eight men was not unanimous. Although Samuel Gompers, the head of the new, relatively conservative American Federation of Labor, pleaded for the men, erstwhile Socialist Terrence V. Powderly, grand master workman of the Knights of Labor, refused to defend them. "It is not the individuals who are in prison at Chicago that I speak against," he told the Knights' 1887 General Convention in Minneapolis. "It is the hellish doctrine which found vent on the streets of Chicago. . . . [If] I could I would forever wipe from the face of the earth its double damned presence." Henry George also favored their execution. But thousands of Knights of Labor and Single-Taxers disagreed with their leaders and signed petitions for commutation of the death sentences.

It was all in vain. Governor Richard J. Oglesby commuted the sentences of only Schwab and Fielden to life imprisonment. On November 10, 1887, Lingg escaped the hangman's noose by committing suicide. The next day Spies, Parsons, Fischer, and Engell were hanged.[44]

Almost six years after the execution of the four Anarchists, Populist-Democratic Governor John P. Altgeld freed the three remaining Haymarket defendants. His pardon statement condemned the trial, pointed out the prejudice against the Anarchists, and reaffirmed the Anglo-American principle of a fair trial. Much of the evidence, Altgeld declared, "was a pure fabrication; . . . some of the police officials in their zeal not only terrorized ignorant men by throwing them into prison and terrorizing them with torture if they refused to swear to everything desired, but that they offered money to those who would consent to do this." He quoted the bailiff—second hand—as admitting that "I am managing this case and know what I am about. Those fellows are going to be hanged as certain as death." He also cited the bailiff's comment on jury selection: "I am calling such men as defendants will have to challenge pre-emptorily and waste their time and challenges. Then they will have to take such men as the prosecution wants."[45]

- 7 -

Spies, Parsons, Fischer, and Engell, had died as heroes; they were given honored places in Socialist and Anarchist hagiographia; the great labor and Socialist holiday, May 1, was originally dedicated to their memory. Their funeral drew 200,000 mourners who heard Thomas J. Morgan, a Socialist labor leader, who predicted that the mourners would yet have their revenge with the imminent collapse of the capitalist system. But Haymarket effectively destroyed the American revolutionary Socialist and Anarchist movements. The IWPA disbanded. The once-revolutionary *Labor Enquirer* of Denver now declared that the "ballot box is the only battlefield" where labor can fight capital. Samuel Gompers reported that the "throwing of the bomb has killed the eight-hour movement."[46] Only Johann Most did not believe that the time for violent rhetoric had passed. He told a New York memorial meeting for the four executed anarchists: "The day of revolution will soon come. First of all will be Grinnell; then comes Judge Gary; then the Supreme Court of Illinois; then the highest murderers of the land, the Supreme Court of the United States. . . . I again urge you to arm yourself as the day of revolution is not far off . . . and when it comes, see that you are ready to resist and kill those hirelings of the capitalists." For this speech, Most was arrested and jailed for almost a year on charges of inciting to riot. At the end of his sentence, he was greeted by a crowd of 5,000 at Cooper Union. His tone was now changed; his rhetoric was no longer militant. Haymarket had ended even his excursion into the dream world. Five years later, when a young Russian-born Anarchist, Alexander Berkman, shot Henry Clay Frick, the steel baron, Most repudicated the action and condemned violence and terror in an article in his journal *Freiheit*.[47]

Nor was the lesson of Haymarket lost on those most directly involved. In 1894 Michael Schwab—one of the pardoned Anarchists—appeared as a delegate at the Illinois Federation of Labor's political conference. He told the assembled delegates that he and all of the other editors of the *Arbeiter-Zeitung* now rejected violence. He also announced that the *Arbeiter-Zeitung* was now committed editorially to peaceful political action, and that virtually all of the old Anarchist-Communists conceded that they had erred in advocating violence during the period from 1881 to 1897.[48]

Haymarket was one of the great tragedies of American history. Four men were executed after a travesty called a trial; one man committed suicide rather than face the hangman's noose, and three others spent almost seven years in the penitentiary. None of them was ever proven guilty of any capital crime. Yet the lesson of Haymarket—that the state is more potent in violence than the revolutionists—was soon forgotten. Revolutionists—in the United States, at least—have historically allowed their emotions to dominate their reason to the detriment of the revolution they purport to favor.

NOTES

1. "George Engells on Anarchism," in Albert R. Parsons, *Anarchism: Its Philosophy and Scientific Basis as Defined by Some of Its Apostles* (Chicago: Mrs. A. R. Parsons, Publisher, [1887]), p. 87; Michael R. Johnson, "Albert R. Parsons: An American Architect of Syndicalism," *Midwest Quarterly* 9 (1968): 199.

2. August Spies, *Autobiography* (Chicago: Nina Van Zandt, 1887), pp. 1–11, 27; Spies was born in Germany of middle-class Protestant parents. He was educated at a polytechnical institute. After his father's death, when young Spies was seventeen, he went to New York, where he had some wealthy relatives. He worked at the furniture trade and travelled extensively in the United States, finally settling in Chicago. Spies joined the SLP during the strikes of 1877 and soon also became a leader of the *Lehr und Wehr Verein*. He was editor of the daily *Arbeiter-Zeitung*. Despite his libertarian anarchism, and his intellectual development, Spies was an anti-Semite. In fact, anti-Semitism was prevalent among American, German, and British radicals during the later nineteenth century.

3. Norman J. Ware, *The Labor Movement in the United States, 1860–1895* (New York: D. Appleton and Company, 1929; paperback ed. Vintage Books, n.d.), pp. 51, 307–10. Pagination follows paperback edition. Albert R. Parsons was born in Montgomery, Alabama, in 1848, of New England parents. His father died when Albert was only four, and he moved to Texas, where he lived with a brother. He served in the Confederate army from 1862 to 1865. Parsons later became a compositor and editor. He married a Mexican-American girl in 1871. For one year (1870), he was a secretary of the Texas Senate, and for a short time, he worked as a collector of internal revenue in Texas. He moved to Chicago in 1873 and worked there as newspaper compositor. Parsons joined the SLP in 1876, was a leader during the 1877 strikes, ran for various offices, and was the choice of some Socialists as presidential candidate in 1880, before the party backed Weaver. He left the SLP after it made the alliance with the Greenbackers. See "Views of General Parsons," in Parsons, *Anarchism*, p. 188; Johnson, "Albert R. Parsons," p. 197; Robert V. Bruce, *1877: Year of Violence* (Chicago: Quadrangle Books, 1970), p. 235; Dyer D. Lum, *A Concise History of the Great Trial of the Chicago Anarchists in 1886* (Chicago: Socialistic Publishing Company, [1887]), p. 13; Henry David, *The History of the Haymarket Affairs* (New York: Ferrar and Rinehart, [1936]).

4. J. S. Hertz, *Di Idishe Sotsialistishe Bavegung in Amerika* [The Jewish Socialist Movement in America] (New York: Der Wecker, 1954), pp. 57–58; Richard T. Ely, *Recent American*

Socialism (Baltimore: Johns Hopkins University Studies in Historical and Political Science), pp. 26–27; Paul Grottkau and Joh[ann] Most, *Discussion uber das Thema Anarchismus oder Socialismus* [Discussion on the Theme of Anarchism or Socialism] (Chicago: Das Centrale-Comitre der Chicagoer Gruppen der I.A.A., 1884), pp. 2, 3, 607; *Socialism and Anarchism, Antagonistic Opposites*, quoted in Terrence V. Powderly, *Thirty Years of Labor* (Columbus, Ohio: Excelsior Publishing House, 1889), p. 288; Charles Sotheran, *Horace Greeley and Other of Pioneers of American Socialism* (New York: Mitchell Kennerly, 1915), p. 11; Hippolyte Havel, "Anarchists: John Most—The Stormy Petrel," *Man!* January 1934, p. 5; *The Labor Enquirer* (Chicago), 1 (December 3, 1887); *Truth* 4 (December 27, 1882): 2. A post card addressed to Burnette G. Haskell and signed by Most is in the Haskell Family Papers, Bancroft Library, University of California, Berkeley. It may, however, be a forgery by Haskell, made to impress his followers. It is a reply to an invitation. "George Engell on Anarchism," in Parsons, *Anarchism*, p. 88; see also Frederic Trautmann, *The Voice of Terror: A Biography of Johann Most* (Westport, Ct., Greenwood Press, 1980).

5. Carl Nold, "Fifty Years Ago," *Man!* January 1934, pp. 5, 8; *Freiheit*, October 20, 1883; *Alarm*, April 3, 1886, as quoted in *Spies and Others v. People*, 12 *Northeast Reporter*: 888. The delegates represented organizations in Cincinnati; Chicago; Allegheny, Pennsylvania; Omaha; Philadelphia; Milwaukee; Guttenberg, New Jersey; New York City; Meriden, Connecticut; Sallinvale, Ohio; Brooklyn; Jersey City; Saint Louis; Saint Joseph, Missouri; and Cleveland.

6. *Freiheit*, October 20, 1883. The term *Communists* was used by anarchists to indicate revolutionary Socialists or supporters of Most.

7. The Pittsburgh manifesto was published in full in *Freiheit*, October 20, 1883. It is also reprinted in Richard T. Ely, *The Labor Movement in America* (New York: Thomas Y. Crowell, 1886), pp. 358–63.

8. Hertz, *Di Idishe Sotsialistishe Bavegung*, p. 59.

9. Ely, *Recent American Socialism*, pp. 57–59; *Alarm*, March 7, 1885, as cited in 12 *Northeast Reporter*: 887; *Spies and Others v. People*, p. 868; Andre Tridon, *The New Unionism* (New York: B. W. Huebsch, 1913), p. 93; Johnson, "Albert R. Parsons," p. 198.

10. Ely, *Recent American Socialism*, p. 31; Lum, *Concise History*, pp. 16–19.

11. John [Johann] Most, *The Beast of Property* (New Haven: The International Workingmen's Association, Group New Haven [1885], pp. 7, 9–10; *Freiheit*, October 13, 1883.

12. Herbert L. Osgood, *Socialism and Anarchism* (Boston: Ginn & Company, 1889), p. 25; "Address of Michael Schwab," in Parsons, *Anarchism*, p. 70.

13. *Alarm*, January 9, 1886; Charles James, "Anarchy from an Anarchist's Standpoint," in Parsons, *Anarchism*, p. 52.

14. James, "Anarchy from an Anarchist's Standpoint," in Parsons, *Anarchism*, p. 52; also see "Parsons' Plea for Anarchy," *New York Herald*, August 30, 1886, reprinted in Parsons, *Anarchism*, p. 109.

15. "Adolph Fischer," in Parsons, *Anarchism*, pp. 78–79. "Lucy Parsons on Anarchy," in Parsons, *Anarchism*, p. 111; William D. P. Bliss, *A Handbook of Socialism* (1895); reprint ed. (London: Swan Sonenschein, 1905), p. 15; *Freiheit*, December 15, 1883 as cited in Osgood *Socialism*, p. 27.

16. "Albert R. Parsons on Anarchy," in Parsons, *Anarchism*, p. 93; Spies, *Autobiography*, p. 20.

17. *Alarm*, March 21, 1885, as quoted in 12 *Northeast Reporter*: 887; "Parsons Plea for Anarchy," in Parsons, *Anarchism*, pp. 107–9; Address of Michael Schwab," in Parsons, *Anarchism*, p. 72; "Adolph Fischer," in Parsons, *Anarchism*, p. 81; Lum, *Concise History*, p. 6.

18. Grottkau and Most, *Discussion*, p. 6; *Vorbote*, May 12, 1883, reprinted in Ely, *Recent American Socialism*, p. 33; Ely, *Recent American Socialism*, p. 34.

19. Most, *Beast*, p. 14.

20. "August Spies on Anarchy," in Parsons, *Anarchism*, pp. 64–65; "Lucy E. Parsons on Anarchy," in Parsons, *Anarchism*, p. 110; Most, *Beast*, pp. 12–14.

21. Most, *Beast*, pp. 11–12; *The Labor Enquirer* 2 (September 29, 1883).

22. Bliss, *Handbook*, p. 15.

23. Caro Lloyd, *Henry Demarest Lloyd, 1847–1903: A Biography*, 2 vols, (New York: G. P. Putnam's Sons, 1912), 1: 88–89; "A. R. Parsons on the Eight-Hour Movement," *Chicago Daily News*, March 13, 1886, reprinted in Lum, *Concise History*, pp. 190–91; Spies, *Autobiography*, pp. 51–52.

24. *Alarm*, October 25, 1884, cited in *Spies and Others v. People*, p. 884; *Arbeiter-Zeitung*, April 29, 1886, in 12 *Northeast Reporter*: 879–80.

25. *Alarm*, January 13, 1885, cited in 12 *Northeast Reporter*: 885–86; *Arbeiter-Zeitung*, May 5, 1885, and June 19, 1885, cited in 12 *Northeast Reporter*: 875–76.

26. Lucy E. Parsons, "Dynamite," *The Labor Enquirer* 5 (April 4, 1885): 1; "August Spies on Anarchy," in Parsons, *Anarchism*, pp. 55–56; "George Engell on Anarchism," in Parsons, *Anarchism*, p. 87; *Arbeiter-Zeitung*, May 4, 1886, reprinted in Lum, *Concise History*, pp. 25–26.

27. *Arbeiter-Zeitung*, March 23, 1885, cited in 12 *Northeast Reporter*: 875; *Alarm*, March 21, 1885, cited in 12 *Northeast Reporter*: 887; Johann Most, *Science of Revolutionary Warfare: Manual for Instruction in the Use and Preparation of Nitro-Glycerine, Dynamite, Gun-Cotton, Fulminating Mercury, Bombs, Fuses, Poisons, etc.* (New York: International Zeitung Verein, [1885]), reprinted in 12 *Northeast Reporter*: 894–901; citations and pagination are from 12 *Northeast Reporter*: 899.

28. *Alarm*, November 1, 1884, November 29, 1884, and March 21, 1885, quoted in 12 *Northeast Reporter*: 884–85, 887.

29. Johnson, "Albert R. Parsons," pp. 203–4.

30. See, for example, Arthur Bestor, *Backwoods Utopias: The Sectarian Origins of the Owentite Phase of Communitarian Socialism in America, 1663–1829* (Philadelphia: University of Pennsylvania Press, 1950), p. 42. Bestor cited a letter from Thomas Jefferson to Albert Gallatin, dated June 12, 1817; see also, George E. McNeill, *The Labor Movement: The Problem of Today* (Boston: A. M. Bridgman & Co., 1887), p. 147.

31. Lum, *Concise History*, pp. 19–23; *The Labor Enquirer* 6 (June 5, 1886).

32. Lum, *Concise History*, p. 24.

33. Ibid., p. 86.

34. Joseph E. Gary, "The Chicago Anarchists of 1886: The Crime, the Trial, and the Punishment," *The Century Magazine* 45 (April 1893): 826–28, italics in original; Lum, *Concise History*, pp. 96–97.

35. Lum, *Concise History*, pp. 29–31, 37–48, 150; *Workmen's Advocate*, May 13, 1888.

36. Spies, *Autobiography*, p. 45; Lum, *Concise History*, p. 31–32.

37. *Chicago Tribune*, May 5, 1886, cited in Lum, *Concise History*, p. 34; Morris Hillquit, *History of Socialism in the United States* (New York: Funk and Wagnalls, 1910), p. 224.

38. Lum, *Concise History*, pp. 34–35, 126; *The Labor Enquirer* 6 (May 15, 1886); William Holmes, "The Chicago Anarchists," *Twentieth Century* 2 (June 15, 1889): 228.

39. Frank Roney, *Frank Roney: Irish Rebel and California Labor Leader*, ed. Ira B. Cross (Berkeley: University of California Press, 1931), p. 481; Lloyd, *Henry Demarest Lloyd*, 1: 85; Lum, *Concise History*, pp. 48–49.

40. Lum, *Concise History*, pp. 50–59, 73; Lloyd, *Henry Demarest Lloyd*, p. 87; see also Alan Calmer, *Labor Agitator: The Story of Albert R. Parsons* (New York: International Publishers, 1937), p. 96.

41. Lum, *Concise History*, pp. 67–102, particularly pp. 87–88.

42. Ibid., p. 174; Parsons, "Dynamite," pp. 51–52; Emma Goldman, "The Psychology of Political Violence," in Emma Goldman, *Anarchism and Other Essays* (1911; reprint ed. New York: Dover Publications, 1969), p. 87.

43. Gary, "Chicago," pp. 807, 809; Lloyd, *Henry Demarest Lloyd*, 1: 86; Spies, *Autobiography*, pp. 59–61.

44. Henry D. Dement to E. M. Chamberlain (secretary of state of Illinois), October 31, 1887, Massachusetts Labor Party Papers, Boston Public Library; *The Labor Enquirer* 6 (July 17, 1886, November 27, 1887); 7 (January 1, 1887, August 6, 1887); Samuel Gompers, *Seventy Years of Life and Labor*, 2 vols. (New York: E. P. Dutton and Company, 1948), 1:178–79; Powderly, *Thirty Years of Labor*, p. 284; *The Labor Enquirer* (Chicago) 1 (October 27, 1887, November 14, 1887): Gary, "Chicago," p. 837.

45. *The Labor Enquirer* (Chicago) 1 (November 14, 1887); *The People* 3 (July 9, 1893) reprints in full Governor Altgeld's statement.

46. Lloyd, *Henry Demarest Lloyd*, 1: 99; *The Labor Enquirer* (Chicago) 1 (April 23, 1887); *The Labor Enquirer* 7 (December 31, 1887).

47. *People v. Most*, 128 New York Reporter 109–11; *The Labor Enquirer* 7 (April 16, 1887); Emma Goldman, *Living My Life* (New York: Alfred Knopf, 1931), p. 105.

48. Lloyd, *Henry Demarest Lloyd*, 1: 243.

❧ 11 ❧

The Henry George Interlude

- 1 -

Those Socialists who remained faithful to the social, political, and economic ideals of the Socialist Labor party (SLP) during the early 1880s found themselves almost completely isolated and powerless. The party was still basically "a German colony, a branch of the German Social Democracy." Of the sixty-eight party branches in New York, only fifteen conducted their meetings in English. The majority of the others used German. The few English-speaking branches were themselves divided by race: Negroes generally belonged to separate party organizations.

The interests of the party reflected its ethnic makeup. The chief activity of the American Socialists between 1880 and 1886 was the organization of speaking tours for German—or other European—Socialists. Thus in 1886 Karl Marx's daughter Eleanor and her husband, Edward Aveling, toured the United States as representatives of the Socialist League of Great Britain, and Wilhelm Liebknecht spoke in a number of American cities as the representative of the German Social Democratic party.[1] Although a new wave of immigrants—this time Jews fleeing religious persecution in Czarist Russia—was to swell the ranks of the SLP during the next decade, its effect on the Socialist movement would be minimal during the 1880s. As late as 1885, almost all of the SLP correspondence was in German; less than 1 percent was in English.[2]

The party's alien complexion was apparent even to Friedrich Engels in Great Britain. He treated the American party and its press with disdain: "The gentlemen of the *Volkszeitung* [German-language Socialist daily in New York] must be satisfied," he wrote to his friend Friedrich Sorge. "They have gained control of the whole movement among the Germans and their business must be flourishing." The party leadership was, he told Sorge, incompetent at best; he called its weekly journal, *Sozialist*, "a model of what a paper should not be."

Despite his distaste for the German leadership of the party in the United States, he did not despair, for he had no doubt that the American working class would soon become class conscious, and the American revolutionary movement would grow "faster than anywhere else in the world." But this, he said, would come from the native American workers and not from the German Socialists in America.[3]

Not only was the SLP small, isolated, and basically inactive during the early 1880s, it was also composed of ideologically disparate groups. The eastern membership, centered in New York, Boston, Cincinnati, and Milwaukee, was basically reformist and dedicated to democracy and eventual electoral activity. The western Socialists, who were centered in San Francisco and Denver, looked with disdain on electoral activity and proclaimed their belief in the use of violence as the only effective means for overthrowing the capitalist system. Thus Charles Sotheran, a leading New York Socialist suggested that the followers of Johann Most "should be placed under restraint the same as other irresponsible persons, before they are allowed an opportunity of being dangerous." Moreover, he argued, "American Socialism, if it be nothing else, is a constitutional party or rallying point for loyal American citizens to protest against universal political corruption." San Francisco's SLP branches were at the same time proclaiming that "it is beyond doubt that if 'universal suffrage' had been capable of emancipating our people (the proletariat), our enemies would have suppressed it long ago. In our opinion the abolition of the LOAFING CLASSES can never be effected by the ballot." The declaration went on to berate electoral politics as a dirty business, replete with betrayals. It concluded with a cry to the workers to prepare for physical conflict, for "it is self-evident that the dirty pool of politics can never thus elevate or refine us."[4] These differences were so great that the delegates to the national party convention of 1883 found it necessary to compromise their differences; they called for electoral activity in addition to proclaiming that force would be necessary to effectuate the revolution, because the capitalist class would be unwilling to give up power peacefully. It would thus be necessary for the workers to employ "that old prime lever of all revolutions FORCE . . . in order to place the working masses in control of the state."[5]

Nor was this the only problem confronting the Socialists. Although they had no Socialist candidate, party members were prohibited, on threat of expulsion, from supporting any of the three candidates for president. Not all Socialists obeyed the edict. John Swinton, then editing his own Socialist-labor weekly, openly supported Benjamin Butler on the Greenback ticket. Even the social revolutionary Dyer D. Lum supported Butler, hoping a large

Greenbacker vote would "decide the fate of both old parties, a fate they both richly merit."[6] But most Socialists "sat out" the election; they opposed all of the candidates. They were thus neither pleased nor distressed by the election of Grover Cleveland, a conservative Democrat, or the small vote for Butler, whose rhetoric, at least, was prolabor. It was apparent, however, that the isolation of the Socialists could not continue much longer if the party was to become a viable movement. The isolation ended—in New York, at least—temporarily with the Henry George campaign of 1886.

- 2 -

During the 1880s, the courts—particularly in New York—became increasingly hostile toward labor unions. Decisions invariably opposed labor and favored the employers. Economic action, particularly strikes, became more difficult to organize. The leaders of the Central Labor Union, the federation of trade unions in New York City, decided that, with economic action virtually precluded, they would use their political power to achieve their ends—primarily more equitable treatment in the courts. They assumed that a huge vote for labor candidates would assure them of fairer treatment from the courts, whose judges were almost all political hacks closely tied to the corrupt Tammany Democratic machine. The conditions that led to the rise of the United Labor party of New York duplicated those that gave birth to the New York Workingmen's party of 1829–1831.[7]

Attempts at organizing a United Labor party had been made early in the 1880s, but none of them had succeeded. The labor movement lacked a charismatic leader capable of winning the political support of a significant number of New Yorkers. In 1886 the trade-union leaders finally found a candidate who appeared to have all of the attributes they required. Henry George was basically prolabor, he had a large following, and he proposed a simple cure for all of labor's ills—a complete reform of land ownership. He argued that undeveloped land derived its value from society and not from individual investment of labor or capital. Private gain from such land was therefore an unearned increment. To eliminate that unjust and economically unviable condition, he proposed a 100 percent tax on land, thus in effect confiscating it. This single tax on land would, he argued, make all other taxes unnecessary and would create a virtual Utopia without upsetting the other aspects of the capitalist system, for George opposed the abolition of profits, interest, or rents from buildings—apart from land—or other improvements.[8]

George's proposal appealed to American labor for several reasons. First, land reform was an old idea among Americans. Second, most foreign-born workers had come to America in search of land. They accepted urban employment, because their poverty made it impossible for most of them to travel west. Third, much of the land made available under the Homestead Act of 1862 had been obtained by railroad speculators rather than actual settlers. This added to the clamor for radical reform of land ownership. George's proposal was also trusted by the average workingman, because its author had been a worker himself. As an editor in California, George had backed almost all of their aims—particularly the eight-hour day and the right to organize.[9]

George's writings were well known to many New York workingmen. *Progress and Poverty*, his most significant work, first published in 1879, appeared in daily installments in the New York prolabor daily *Truth* during 1881 and 1882. Enthusiasm for his ideas among trade unionists had reached such a high point in 1882 that the Central Labor Union (CLU) officially hailed him on his return from the United Kingdom with an address that said his name "had become a household name to millions who recognized in him a leader whose teachings would yet lead labor out of the house of bondage in which it had so long sojourned." Edward King of the Type-Founders Union added that George had proven that possession of land determined labor's share of wealth. Robert Blisset, president of the CLU, agreed, informing George that the workers of the city considered *Progress and Poverty* to be "the holiest Bible they ever received." He announced that his organization was now based upon George's principles, since the first plank of the CLU's platform called for the nationalization of land. George reaffirmed his dedication to labor and proclaimed: "Every man who desires to labor should be permitted to receive that which he produces. . . . The labor question must be brought into politics. It is not charity but justice that is wanted. Move forward for that."[10]

Although George was not a Socialist, his support among trade unionists made it imperative that the Socialists abstain from opposing him. To have done otherwise might have alienated the union workingmen while the SLP was attempting to win them over. Thus the Socialists participated in trade-union rallies at which Georgeite slogans dominated. Nor were George's views alien to the Socialists' interpretation of the land question. The 1883 Declaration of Principles of the SLP had proclaimed that the "land of every country is the common inheritance of the people in that country." The Socialists were impressed with George's theory after it had become popular. "Warning! Landowners look out!" one Socialist publication declared.

This is the new law governing the price of land in both city and country. The price of land is determined by the sale of Henry George's "Progress and Poverty," falling as it rises, and rising as it falls. It is now past its hundredth edition, and it is going faster than ever. In ten years from now, town lots will not be worth more than the taxes! Private property and land is doomed!

Both the progressive economist Richard T. Ely and the radical publicist John Swinton called George a revolutionist. Moreover, the majority of Socialists were convinced that George was on his way to becoming a

Socialist himself—it was apparent to them that George's land scheme led inexorably to socialism. True, Karl Marx had called George's nostrum "a last attempt to save the capitalist regime," but few of the Socialists knew or cared about what their prophet had said. A scent of political victory was in the air—United Labor parties were cropping up all over the nation—in Wisconsin, California, Connecticut, Massachusetts, among others. In New York the labor unions were entering politics, with Henry George as their hero. The American Socialists had no intention of being left in the cold.[11]

George was eager to enter politics, but he was not interested in fighting a losing battle. Thus when the Central Labor Union leaders approached George with the proposition that he run for mayor of New York, he set one condition: he insisted upon 30,000 valid signatures on his nominating petition. Labor proved up to the task and presented him with the petitions, and their 30,000 signatures, in time to assure his acceptance of the nomination.[12] Almost immediately, George began remaking the labor party into his own personal organ. The platform of the United Labor party had originally contained all of the so-called immediate demands—the reform proposals—of the SLP platform and concluded with Marx's dictum in his inaugural program of the International Workingmen's Association that "the emancipation of the working class can only be accomplished by the working class itself." George deleted all of that; the platform finally adopted—at his behest—called for George's land tax and ballot reform, and it assailed monopolies and political corruption. It was a platform that disappointed the Socialists—platitudes had replaced genuine calls for ameliorative reform. But the Socialists swallowed their ideals and worked selflessly for George's election.[13]

The campaign was one of the most heated in New York history. The Democrats nominated Abram S. Hewitt, a wealthy philanthropist and son-in-law of Peter Cooper, 1876 presidential candidate of the Greenback Labor party. The Republicans chose a rising young politician, Theodore Roosevelt. The battle was between Hewitt and George; Roosevelt was largely ignored. The *New York Herald* reported that "the Republican mayoralty candidate seemed to be disregarded and all interest seemed to be centered on Hewitt and George as the Giants in the field."[14]

The center of the campaign was a series of well-publicized letters between George and Hewitt. George had challenged Hewitt to a debate, the latter refused, and the series of letters followed. Hewitt argued that George's supporters were "anarchists, nihilists, communists, socialists, and mere theorists for the democratic principles of individual liberty." He accused George of preaching hate to the working class and of attempting to array one class against the other. "As mayor," he wrote to George, "neither you nor I can do anything to introduce new principles of legislation, but the moral effect of your election would be an endorsement of your peculiar views." Hewitt conceded that his one purpose in the election was to prevent George—and his "radical" followers—from seizing control of the city. Even the *New York Times*, which was antagonistic toward George, conceded that "absolutely the only blessing which Mr. Hewitt promises to confer upon the city of New York through his election as Mayor is the defeat of Henry George."[15]

George replied by denying that his movement sprang from a "desire to substitute the ideas of Anarchists, Nihilists, Communists, Socialists, and mere theorists for the democratic principle of individual liberty which involves the right to private property." Such a notion, he wrote to Hewitt, was based upon a misunderstanding "which will be dissipated if you will read the platform of the convention which nominated me." In fact, he argued, neither he nor his followers had any interest in changing the social or the political system in the United States. His intent was, he said, to assure that the system that "affords the best possible machinery for carrying into effect the will of the people" should be preserved.[16]

George's declaration in favor of the "American system" and his anti-Socialist statements would under normal conditions have alienated the Socialists from his campaign. But this was not the case; only a small group of moderate Socialists refused to work for him. Among them was Charles Sotheran, who warned that

Nothing but harm came from pooling interests with the Greenbackers; and I feel the same results will follow fusing with the Single-Taxers. Should George win or poll a very large vote, all will be attributed to the popularity of the candidate and belief in his land-taxing scheme. So whichever way the election goes the Socialists may find themselves left out in the cold.[17]

But Sotheran was almost alone. Virtually all of the other Socialists worked feverishly for his election. The German sections of the party supplied speakers in neighborhoods where that language was spoken. The *Volks-zeitung* was one of only two newspapers supporting his election (it became a virtual propaganda organ during the last week of the campaign). The only other newspaper that endorsed George was the *Leader*, a daily organized specifically to aid in the vote drive. In Jewish areas, the pro-Socialist Jewish Workers League abandoned all other activity to bring out the vote for George. Socialists played a significant role in naturalizing 7,000 alien workingmen during September and October 1886, almost all of whom supported George. On the Saturday before election day, Socialists helped organize a parade of 25,000 New Yorkers crying "Hi! Ho! The leeches—must—go!" and "Vote-Vote-Vote for George!"[18]

Election day brought out one of the biggest votes in New York's history. With the huge vote came the most flagrant cases of election fraud. Votes were bought at the polling places. Poll watchers and workers were bought off, abused verbally, and terrorized physically. Police cooperated with Tammany toughs in keeping all but Hewitt voters from the polling booths. A writer in the presitgious *North American Review* reported that "the Anarchists . . . in Chicago have not so sinned against society as have the political leaders."[19] Despite the wholesale cases of fraud perpetrated against George, he polled 68,110 votes, approximately 31 percent of the total 219,097 cast. Hewitt polled 90,552 votes, approximately 41 percent of the total, and Roosevelt polled only 60,435. It was obvious that George and the United Labor party were now a power in New York politics. "I did not want the office; I did want the fight," George told his supporters on election night. He talked of a new era in the United States based on his principles as enunciated in *Progress and Poverty*. George expected a new national party to be formed. His followers raised the cry of "Henry George our next Governor!" and "Henry George our next President!" It was a moment of great exhilaration. Nor were the Socialists ignored. Soon after the election, they held a huge rally at Cooper Union to celebrate the "victory." George attended the meeting and thanked them for their "warm and steady support" during the campaign. "I want especially to thank my socialistic friends for their support . . . because I know I do not represent their principles . . . because they sank all their differences for a common cause. . . . This is as it ought to be and as I hope it will continue to be in the future. . . . I ask no man to abrogate his right to opinion."[20] But the unity was short lived; the ideological and political differences were too great.

- 3 -

No sooner was the election over than the struggle for control of the United Labor party began. Henry George's followers struck first. The only banner that greeted participants at the first postelection meeting of the United Labor party read: "Abolish all Taxes But One on Land." Socialists, annoyed by this Georgeite display, retaliated. The *Volkszeitung* opened the counterattack by declaring editorially that the Socialists had supported George despite his single-tax panacea rather than because of it. They had backed him, the editorial explained, because he represented the working class against capital. Their support did not, however, signify any modification of the Socialist insistence that "the burning issue is not a land-tax, but the *abolition of all private property in instruments of production*." Without the Socialists' support, the editorial inferred, George would be politically impotent.[21]

The party leaders then arranged for Laurence Gronlund, the Danish-born Socialist publicist, to produce a small monograph criticizing George from a Socialist position. George, Gronlund argued in the booklet, began with a solution before examining the cause. George exclaimed he was seeking in *Progress and Poverty* to answer the social question of "What produces poverty amid advancing wealth." He was, in fact, merely using that question as an excuse for proclaiming his nostrum. George's solution "is, and probably for a long time previous to writing his book was, a foregone conclusion in his mind. . . . [Moreover,] the foregone conclusion has not merely blinded his one eye but 'inextricably' twisted his mind."[22] Gronlund did not mean to imply that George was a dishonest man. In fact, Gronlund considered George "the forerunner of Socialism in the United States, and the entering wedge for our ideas into American minds"; but George's doctrines were, by themselves, "altogether too narrow and one-sided," and they were "in every way impracticable and inadequate."[23]

George had based his theory on the inequity of private income derived from unimproved land. Gronlund agreed that this was a condition that should be remedied. But, he argued, "bare, valuable land stands exactly on the same footing as capital. *The value of both is created by labor—not of their possessors, but—OF OTHER PEOPLE.*" Was it not true that land increased in value as the result of improvements in surrounding areas—street paving, grading, railroad construction—which makes it possible for people to live, work, and trade in the area. This being so, he wrote, it followed that the unearned increment on land was merely another facet of the general accumulation of wealth on the part of the capitalist class at the expense of those who work: *"land and capital . . . are twin sisters."* It was thus illogical to confiscate unimproved land by means of a 100 percent tax while leaving "all other capitalist classes in quiet enjoyment of their wealth." Such action was "in fact, nothing but downright robbery." Moreover, confiscation of unimproved land alone would accomplish little if anything. Gronlund agreed that land should be nationalized—"but only as part of an overall program of socialization of the means of production and distribution."[24] Gronlund concluded that Henry George was attempting, by limiting his attack to ownership of unimproved land, to deny the existence of a struggle between the capitalists and the workers. He was thus trying, "by hook or by crook, to make Capital and Labor *twin-sisters*—which they are if the horse leech and the horse can be called twin-sisters."[25]

Gronlund's attack on George was needlessly harsh, but it was not inconsistent with basic Socialist postulates. Even the editors of the anti-Socialist *New York Sun* agreed that the Socialist critique had some merit. The Socialists had a logical system, the *Sun* editor declared, whereas George did not. "They propose to deal radically with the evils of society by constructing it on a new basis. He proposes only a single measure of relief and inconsistently refuses to carry his land theory to its logical conclusions. If the state may take the land, why may it not go further and take all property and control and conduct human affairs as the Socialists propose?"[26]

The Socialist attacks tore the United Labor party into two warring factions. George accused the Socialists—he called them "State or German Socialists"—of trying to "impress their personal views" on the United Labor party. He then forced them out of the organization. As his first act, he convinced members of the party executive, almost all of whom were his followers, to ignore a national meeting called for February 1887 to form a national farmer-labor party. Socialists were not directly involved in it—the meeting had been called by Knights of Labor, Grangers, members of the Farmers Alliance, antimonopolists, and former Greenbackers—but George and his followers saw it as a Socialist stepping stone.[27]

Socialists did not leave the party despite George's action; instead they showed unusual strength in the voting for delegates to the party's 1887 state convention. George, who was determined that the Socialists should be ousted from the Labor party, chose a technicality, the fact that most Socialists were members of the Socialist Labor party, which, although it ran no candidates, spoke of itself as a party, and the constitution of the United Labor party prohibited its members from belonging to any other political party. This was merely a facade, however; George made it clear that he wanted the Socialists out of *his* party; he told the *New York Herald* reporter that the United Labor party "is not and never has been a socialistic party and we should be false to our principles if we allowed them to be given a socialistic color."[28] Duly elected delegates to the convention, who happened to be Socialists, were thus denied their seats. Nor were all of those barred from the convention Socialists; at least one was a non-Socialist trade unionist: George C. Block, editor of the Bakers' Union magazine, who opposed George's domination of the labor party. He was denied his seat—by a vote of ninety-one to eighty-six; many of those who voted against Block came from the poorly organized upstate rural districts.[29] Following his ouster, Block accused George of turning the United Labor party from a workingman's political organization into "a tax reform party of the middle classes." The SLP national executive committee agreed and declared that George and his followers had, by their action, deprived the United Labor party "of its rudder; without it the ship of the new party, laden with such splendid promises, will surely suffer shipwreck on the shoals of trifling half measures."[30]

Ousted from the Labor party they had helped to build, the Socialists organized a new electoral organization aimed primarily at siphoning off votes from George's party, which they now called the party of "office seekers, free traders, and deadheads." At the founding mass meeting of the new party—the Progressive Labor party—they assailed George and "his personal political machine" and accused him of "pandering to the hatreds and prejudice of the capitalistic class in attempting to cast odium upon that earnest body of wage-workers and advanced thinkers who for fifty years have fought the battles of humanity and progress on two continents."[31]

The schism was to cost George dearly. *John Swinton's Paper*, the finest labor paper in the country at that time, which had since 1884 urged the election of George for president "on a platform of the principles of 'Progress

and Poverty,' " changed its stance and by June 1887 suggested either Robert
Lincoln or A. J. Streeter for president. The editorial masthead of the leading
Western labor paper had proclaimed in 1886:

> For President in 1888
> HENRY GEORGE
> of the United States

The editor took his stand because he believed that George "more than any
other man in the country can unite all the different branches of organized
labor and can come nearer than any other to receiving the endorsement of
the leading advocates of the various isms in the agitation of the labor question." By the summer of 1887, the masthead no longer mentioned Henry
George; it pleaded instead for *"Any Man* who will go as a SERVANT of the
people not as the *BOSS* and who understands that poverty can be abolished
by the Abolition of the competitive wage-system and the inauguration of
State Socialism."[32] In London Friedrich Engels breathed a sigh of relief after
the schism. "Henry George was an unavoidable evil," he wrote to Friedrich
A. Sorge, "but he will soon be obliterated." He saw George's repudiation of
the Socialists as "the greatest good fortune that could happen to us. Making
him the standard bearer last November was an unavoidable mistake for
which we had to suffer."[33]

The 1887 statewide, off-year election campaign was dirty and, at times,
brutal. For example, police attacked a Socialist meeting at Union
Square—reportedly at the instigation of some pro-George politicians. The
Progressive Labor campaign was devoted almost exclusively to assailing
George and his followers.[34] The battle took its toll: George polled only
72,781 votes throughout the state as United Labor's candidate for New York
State secretary of state. In Manhattan, where he had a year earlier polled
68,000 votes, he polled fewer than 34,000 in 1887. Progressive Labor won
only 5,000 votes throughout the state.[35] Within six months, both parties
had virtually disappeared—the Progressive Labor party voted in 1888 to
dissolve, advising its members to join the SLP, if they were not already
members.[36]

The Socialists had gained little from their affiliation with Henry George.
The Single-Taxers had gained even less from their short-lived alliance with
the Socialists. But the elections of 1886 and 1887 have great significance in
the history of the American Left, for they marked the beginning of the long
process that was to result in the Socialists turning to independent electoral
politics.

- 4 -

The New York experience was not unique. In other cities—particularly
Milwaukee—the Socialists learned they could expect little from affiliation

with political movements they could not control. A Labor party backed by the Socialists, although dominated by non-Socialist trade unionists, won the local election in 1887. Paul Grottkau, editor of the Socialist *Arbeiter-Zeitung*, was arrested by police under control of the labor mayor for leading a demonstration of unemployed. Moreover, he was prosecuted by a "labor" district attorney and sentenced to a year in prison. The conviction was overturned on appeal—but after Grottkau had served a month of the sentence. The Socialists retaliated for Grottkau's arrest by running a candidate against the Labor mayor and thus bringing about the defeat in 1888 of the entire Labor ticket.[37]

By 1888 the Socialists were no longer interested in electoral alliances with non-Socialist labor men. They would resist efforts aimed at forming labor parties for the next thirty-six years. To quote Abraham Cahan, the

duty of the Socialist party should be to work hand-in-hand with a trade-union labor party. But that should be done only when the American unions are sincere about the labor party. Thus far they are too closely tied to capitalist policies. At any rate, when they [trade unionists] talk about a labor party they intend only to use their influence among the workers to win votes for Republicans or Democrats, in order to win for themselves personal political gain.[38]

By 1888 the leaders of the Socialist Labor party had decided to run their own candidates, although they still considered the party incapable of actively fielding a national ticket. But the party did issue a national electoral platform and an appeal to the voters in the nation's largest city. The platform, after proclaiming its dedication to a "cooperative system of society" and declaring its faith in legislation as an alternative to violence, listed seventeen demands aimed at ameliorating the condition of the working class under capitalism. The demands were to become standard in future Socialist election documents. Included were calls for a legal cut in hours to eight a day; government ownership of transportation and communications systems; the inviolability of public lands; legal incorporation of labor unions; public works to alleviate the economic distress of the unemployed workers; a government monopoly on the issuance of currency; an end to patents—inventors to be paid by the government; progressive income taxes; free and compulsory education to age fourteen; repeal of all pauper, tramp, and conspiracy laws; unlimited right of labor to organize; a prohibition of the use of convict or child labor in competition with adult labor; the prohibition of women working in certain dangerous crafts; all wages to be paid in cash; equal pay for equal work for men and women; employers' liability for injuries to workingmen; proper safety measures; uniform national marriage laws; simple consent divorce laws and government protection of the rights of children in the event of a divorce. Political demands were made, too, such as the initiative and recall; the referendum; the abolition of the presidency; a unicameral legislature; municipal self-government; direct, secret ballot; woman's suffrage; a ban on racial or religious tests on elections; a nationally uniform code of law; free administration of justice; abolition of capital punishment, and separation of church and state with taxation of church property.

The platform was hardly revolutionary. Many of its planks have since been adopted or surpassed; others are now obsolete. But it was a daring document for 1888. So, too, was the call to the voters of New York that year. That call recognized that socialism could not yet "be wrought." Therefore, the party's city committee urged the adoption of "a number of real, earnest reforms which are now capable of realization." The reforms were duplicates of those in the national platform.[39] But the SLP was fighting what appeared to be a futile battle. In New York, SLP candidates polled only 2,339 votes in the 1888 municipal election.

- 5 -

The Socialists had, it appeared, failed miserably in America. They had won few native recruits; their alliances had invariably turned out to be failures—or worse. All that the Socialists appeared to have remaining to them was a faith that they had found the truth and the way. What difference did it make that so few people followed their path:"it is the minority who, in times of great struggles, are always right. Only a coward or a knave will shield himself behind a 'majority.' "[40] Moreover, the Socialists were so certain of their Utopia that they were convinced they would, sooner or later, win over all intelligent human beings who were exposed to it.

To a great extent, it was this assumption that led the Socialists into their alliances from which they invariably emerged badly damaged. They entered these coalitions in the hope and expectation of converting followers of their allies into true believers in socialism. The Socialists of the last two decades of the nineteenth century were, in fact, a missionary church militant rather than a political party. Their arrogant, almost religious zeal led them into the alliance with Henry George, and their failure to convert him or his followers helped lead to the demise of the movement—a demise that exposed their failure. Only the rise of an unrelated native American Utopian collectivist movement prevented the Socialist organization from disappearing into the dustbin of history immediately thereafter.

NOTES

1. "Report of the National Executive Committee of the Socialist Labor Party," *New York Leader*, October 1, 1887, reprinted in the *Labor Enquirer* (Denver) 7 (October 1, 1887); Samuel-List: Fonds für die Bebel-Liebknecht'sche Agitations Reise," SLP Collection, Wisconsin State Historical Society, Madison, Wisconsin (micro-film edition); Handbill for Aveling-Liebknecht meeting at Cooper Union, September 20, 1886, SLP Collection (microfilm edition); Richard T. Ely, *Recent American Socialism*, (Baltimore: Johns Hopkins University, 1885), p. 53; Joseph Armstead, secretary, "Report of Colored Section of the Socialistic Labor Party, 12th Ward Club, St. Louis," SLP Collection.

2. J. S. Hertz, *Di Idishe Sotsialistishe Bavegung in America* (Yiddish) (New York: Der Vecker, 1954), p. 31. Hertz reported that of 114 SLP branches organized between 1889 and 1893, 43 used German as their language, 14 used Yiddish, and the other 18 were divided among French-, Czech-, Polish-, and Italian-speaking members. Only 39 branches used English as the language for transaction of business. Of the 70 branches organized before 1889, and still in existence that year, almost all were German speaking. Thus 113 of 184 branches of the SLP were, as late as 1893, German speaking. The SLP collection at the Wisconsin State Historical Society (microfilm edition) file for 1885 contains fewer than 1 percent English-language letters.

3. Friedrich Engels to Friedrich A. Sorge, April 24, 1886, in Leonard E. Mins [editor and translator], "Unpublished Letters of Karl Marx and Friedrich A. Engels to Americans," *Science and Society* 2 (Spring 1938): 354; Friedrich Engels to Friedrich A. Sorge, ibid., pp. 358–59. The *Volkszeitung* (technically, *New Yorker Volkszeitung*) was an extremely influential Socialist daily newspaper.

4. Hugo Vogt to San Francisco Section, S. Robert Wilson, Secretary, November 25, 1883, SLP Collection (microfilm edition); Charles Sotheran, *Horace Greeley and Other Pioneers of American Socialism* (New York: Mitchell Kennerly, 1915), pp. 11, 15; *Truth* n. s. 96 (December 8, 1883); Emil Kreis, Secretary, Socialistic Labor Party, to [H.] W. Roewer, June 6, 1883, SLP Collection; Hugo Vogt to S. Robert Wilson, January 14, 1884, SLP Collection.

5. *John Swinton's Paper* 1 (August 24, 1884); *John Swinton's Paper* 2 (October 19, 1884); Ely, *Recent American Socialism*, pp. 48–50.

6. Letter by Dyer D. Lum, *John Swinton's Paper* 1 (September 14, 1884). (Lum was then secretary of the National Eight-Hour Committee in Washington, D.C.)

7. Arthur Nichols Young, *The Single Tax Movement in the United States* (Princeton, N.J.: Princeton University Press, 1916), p. 95.

8. Henry George's theories are, at most, peripheral to this study. They are thus limited to an oversimplified mention. For a full exposition of his ideas, see Henry George, *Complete Works* (New York: Doubleday and Page, 1898–1901) 10 volumes; Charles A. Barker, *Henry George* (New York: Oxford University Press, 1955).

9. Henry George (1839–1897) was born in Philadelphia, left school at fourteen, and traveled to San Francisco five years later. Originally a printer, he educated himself on the job and became an editor. His first book, *Our Land Policy*, appeared in 1871, and his *magnum opus*, *Progress and Poverty*, appeared eight years later. Young, *Single Tax Movement*, pp. 90–91.

10. Young, *Single Tax Movement*, pp. 92–94.

11. Ely, *Recent American Socialism*, p. 20.

12. Ibid., pp. 19–20; *John Swinton's Paper* 2 (November 16, 1884); *John Swinton's Paper* 4 (October 17, 1886); "Platform Union Labor Party," handbill, Boston Public Library; "Report of National Executive Committee of the Socialist Labor Party," *New York Leader*, September 21, 1887, reprinted in *The Labor Enquirer* (Denver) 7 (October 1, 1887); George never became a Socialist, but some of his followers, most notably Daniel De Leon and Lucien Sanial, did. De Leon is discussed in chapter 15; for Sanial, see *John Swinton's Paper* 1 (March 30, 1884). Karl Marx to John Swinton, June 2, 1881, in Mins, "Unpublished Letters," p. 228. Young, *Single Tax Movement*, pp. 95–96.

13. Morris Hillquit, *History of Socialism in the United States* (New York: Funk and Wagnalls, 1910), p. 254: *John Swinton's Paper* 3 (October 3, 1886); Young, *Single Tax Movement*, p. 96.

14. *New York Herald*, October 22, 1886, p. 2.

15. Young, *Single Tax Movement*, pp. 98–100; Louis F. Post and Fred C. Leubuscher, *Henry George's 1886 Campaign* (New York: John W. Lovell Company, 1887), p. 52. The campaign occurred during the hysteria over the Haymarket bombing, and this allowed Hewitt to use his "Red scare" tactics so successfully.

16. Post and Leubuscher, *George's 1886 Campaign*, p. 47.

17. "Reminiscences," in Sotheran, *Horace Greeley*, pp. xviii–xix.

18. Hertz, *Di Idishe Sotsialistishce Bavegung*, p. 25; Young, *Single Tax Movement*, pp. 99–102.

19. Edgar J. Levey, "An Election in New York," *The North American Review* 145 (December 1887): 679–81; Young, *Single Tax Movement*, pp. 102, 104; Post and Leubuscher, *George's 1886 Campaign*, p. 44.

20. *New York Herald*, November 11, 1886, p. 8.

21. Lester Luntz, "Daniel De Leon and the Movement for Social Reform" (Manuscript, n.p., 1939), pp. 1, 7, Edward Bellamy Collection, Houghton Library, Harvard University, Cambridge, Massachusetts; Young, *Single Tax Movement*, pp. 118–19.

22. Laurence Gronlund, *The Insufficiency of Henry George's Theory* (New York: New York Labor News Company, 1886), pp. 2–7.

23. Ibid., pp. 1, 7.

24. Ibid., pp. 7–8, 12.

25. Ibid., p. 11.

26. *The Labor Enquirer* (Denver) 7 (August 13, 1887, August 20, 1887).

27. *John Swinton's Paper* 4 (May 8, 1887).

28. Young, *Single Tax Movement*, pp. 119–20.

29. *The Labor Enquirer* (Denver) 7 (August 27, 1887, September 27, 1887).

30. *The Labor Enquirer* (Denver) 7 (August 20, 1887).

31. *New York Herald*, August 23, 1887, p. 1; see also Young, *Single Tax Movement*, p. 121.

32. *John Swinton's Paper* 1 (February 10, 1884); *John Swinton's Paper* 4 (October 24, 1886); *John Swinton's Paper* 4 (June 12, 1887); *The Labor Enquirer* (Denver) 6 (November 13, 1886); *The Labor Enquirer* (Denver) 7 (August 8, 1887).

33. Friedrich Engels to Friedrich A. Sorge, August 8, 1887, and September 16, 1887, in Mins, "Unpublished Letters," pp. 361–62.

34. *The Labor Enquirer* (Denver) 7 (October 22, 1887).

35. Young, *Single Tax Movement*, pp. 122–23. The Socialists were the least of George's defections. The loss of Catholic support was far more serious. That loss was caused by the excommunication of Father Edward McGlynn by the conservative archbishop of New York because he supported George. *The New York Tribune*, November 10, 1887, said that he was also hurt by charges of corruption. See ibid. For Progressive Labor party vote, see *Workmen's Advocate* 3 (November 12, 1887).

36. *Workmen's Advocate* 4 (May 12, 1888).

37. *The Labor Enquirer* (Chicago) 2 (April 7, 1888); *Workmen's Advocate* 4 (April 7, 1888, April 14, 1888, May 28, 1888).

38. Abraham Cahan, *Bleter fun Mein Lebn* [Leaves from My Life] (Yiddish), 5 vols. (New York: Forward Association, 1926–1931), 3: 367.

39. The platform was published virtually weekly in the *Workmen's Advocate*; see example, 5 (February 2, 1889); "To Voters of New York: Address of the City Committee [Socialist Labor party]," *Workmen's Advocate* 4 (November 3, 1888); *Workmen's Advocate* 4 (November 10, 1888).

40. *The Labor Enquirer* (Denver) 7 (January 1, 1887). The author of this editorial was Burnette G. Haskell, who is discussed in detail in chapter 12. It reflected, however, the views of most Socialists. A striking similarity can be seen between this statement and some of Lenin's arguments for his vanguard theory, particularly in *What is to be Done* (1902).

∾ 12 ∾
Burnette G. Haskell: Firebrand or Fraud?

- 1 -

The Socialist Labor party (SLP), unable to attract the support of native-born Americans and thus precluded from becoming a political force, remained, throughout the 1880s, an insignificant, impotent, and alien organization. All of its efforts aimed at winning support from the broad masses of American labor had failed miserably: its alliances with the Greenbackers and the Single-Taxers had only sapped its strength; its members' attempts at labor-union organization had resulted in strong trade unions in some crafts, but little gain for socialism. The SLP was an esoteric German colony in America.

If socialism was to make any headway in America, it was apparent that a new movement, rooted in the peculiar American traditions and social conditions, would have to be formed. Its leaders and spokesmen would have to speak in the language of the land: English. In sum, it would have to be an American movement. Such movements did arise in the United States during the 1880s and 1890s, and they had considerable short-lived intellectual impact on the country and long-term effect on the American Socialist movement.

- 2 -

California, far from the normal centers of Socialist organizations—the immigrant-flooded eastern and midwestern cities, notably New York, Chicago, and Milwaukee—was the site for the first such movement. The new locale should hardly have been a surprise; even Karl Marx, as early as 1880, had prophesied it, for "nowhere else has the upheaval caused by capitalist centralization taken place with such speed."[1] Moreover, because the Pacific Coast was an area with a rapidly growing population and comparatively few Central European immigrants, the Socialist movement that developed there had, from the outset, a number of native-born Americans as members. They were also independent of the Teutonic party organization of the East and thus ignored its internal disputes. Because they were native-born Americans, and because the SLP isolated them in separate American, that is, English-speaking branches, their organizations bore the imprint of American social life. These California Socialists superimposed their revolutionary ardor on secret rites that imitated those of Freemasonry—a fraternity popular among Anglo-Saxon Americans. Their theoretical base was more visceral than intellectual.

The moving spirit of the new movement was a typical California radical of the era: an erratic, if brilliant, young lawyer and publicist named Burnette G. Haskell, a white, Anglo-Saxon Protestant of unimpeachable American ancestry. Haskell was descended on both sides from Puritans. On his maternal side, he had one ancestor who was a Revolutionary War hero and another who was the first Anglo-American fruit producer in California. Haskell's Peak, the mountain in northern California's Sierra County near which Burnett Haskell was born in 1857, was named for his great-grandfather.

Haskell's parents, who were considered wealthy by midnineteenth-century California standards, sent their son to prestigious Oberlin College in Ohio for his university education. But he had little interest in liberal education and soon left. He also attended the University of Illinois and the University of California, for short periods, but he never earned a degree. Instead, he read law in an attorney's office and was admitted to the bar in 1879. Haskell soon found the practice of law—he represented primarily railroads and land speculators—boring, and developed an intense dislike for his profession. Early in 1882, a politically ambitious uncle started a weekly newspaper in San Francisco and turned its operation over to Haskell.[2] Shortly thereafter, Haskell embarked on his carrer as a revolutionist.

Before assuming the editorship of *Truth*, the journal his uncle had organized, Haskell had been apolitical but conservative; he had had no previous contact with the labor or Socialist movement. His first contact came when, in the course of his reporting, Haskell attended meetings of the San Francisco Trades Assembly, the federation of trade unions in the city. In early 1882, when *Truth* was on the verge of collapse—its circulation was minute and its influence almost nonexistent—Haskell sought a cause that could rescue his publication. He found it in the labor movement in San Francisco, which then had no organ, and convinced Frank Roney, president of the Trades Assembly, to have *Truth* named as its official organ. The young editor, who had little knowledge of the labor or Socialist movement, almost immediately immersed himself in labor and radical literature "and became without a doubt the best-read man in the local labor movement."[3] For the next ten years, Haskell was to be the leading radical of San Francisco and the West.

- 3 -

The members of the English-speaking American section of the San Francisco Socialist Labor party were the most radical in the national movement. Almost all of them believed that socialism could be achieved by force of arms alone; they rejected the moderate Socialists' reliance on labor-union organization and the ballot box. By the time Haskell became involved in the labor and radical movements, they had virtually withdrawn from the national SLP. They had, in fact, changed the name of their section to the International Workingmen's Association, although Marx's old federation of the same name had been dead for six years.[4] Haskell's entry into the organization was viewed as a godsend by the other members, for he owned a newspaper and thus gave it an organ of propaganda. Moreover, Haskell was an exceedingly brilliant and resourceful leader; he was enthusiastic, intelligent, and a good speaker and writer. That he was also unstable and ephemeral was not yet known to the Socialists.[5]

One of Haskell's first actions in the Socialist movement was to propose its reorganization. He was a perceptive observer of organizations and of radical groups in particular. He early observed that more than 75 percent of all dues collected was spent by most organizations on operational expenses—salaries of paid functionaries, postage, and rent. He argued that this was a waste; the money could better serve the cause if it were used for propaganda or agitational purposes. Moreover, he noticed that 90 percent of all time spent at meetings was wasted on routine organizational business. This, he maintained, tended to bore and alienate new members, and it resulted in either lethargy or large-scale turnover of membership. Haskell claimed that the excessive expense and involvement in organizational matters was caused by the large size of most organizations. Moreover, they were thus easy prey for unscrupulous leaders. He therefore proposed limiting membership in each unit to 8. Each member was expected to organize a new unit of 8. Thus if 50 members would each organize a group of 8, there would be 400 members; if each of the 400 would organize a new unit of 8 members, there would be 3,200 members; if each of the 3,200 members would organize a unit of 8, there would be 25,600 members; and if each of the 25,600 would organize a new unit of 8, the International Workmen's Association (IWA) would have 204,800 members. This would assure a major force organized in small, manageable units that would waste little or no time or money on organizational matters. His critique showed insight, although his alternative scheme was admittedly harebrained. Haskell believed in it; he assumed that "in plain words, one year's effort would organize the whole West Coast." Despite his Herculean efforts, this grandiose scheme did not succeed.[6]

The reorganized, Haskell-led IWA was a secret organization, each member of which was compelled to sign a secret pledge "in the name of

Liberty and Equality to aid the agitation, organization, and fraternization of the producers of the world" and to "bind myself to secrecy concerning the membership of the International Workingmen's Association and pledge to it my foremost and highest duty." Moreover, a new member upon entering the IWA agreed (1) to protect all other members; (2) to defend all other workingmen; (3) to assist all trade unions and work for their unity; (4) to work for an alliance between industrial workers and farmers; (5) to encourage international working-class solidarity; (6) "to ascertain, segregate, classify, and study our enemies, their habits and acts"; (7) to educate the working class to "prepare the way for the direction of the coming revolution by an enlightened and intelligent" leadership; (8) to eliminate national and sectional boundaries and differences; and (9) "to eradicate the false impression of the people that redress could be obtained by the ballot."[7]

The organization Haskell fashioned was thus a cross between a conspiratorial revolutionary society with a program for the radical restructuring of society and a fraternal order. Names were never used among members; each was assigned a code number, and all communications were made by using that number. The organization also had secret handshakes and secret initiations and passwords. It had three levels of affiliations. Ordinary members had red cards, which indicated that they were still unprepared educationally to assume positions of leadership; their principal duty was to study socialism. Those members who completed their studies were promoted to white-card membership; they were acknowledged Socialists and were considered organizers and agitators for the movement. Blue-card members, of whom there were few, were the acknowledged leaders of the IWA.[8]

The IWA was never large. Haskell, who was "a labor editor with a habit of making extravagant statements," claimed the IWA had "millions of members." This was obviously impossible. Morris Hillquit in his *History of Socialism in the United States* estimated that the IWA had about 6,000 members at its height—about 2,000 in Washington and Oregon; 1,800 in California; 2,000 in Montana, Colorado, Utah, Wyoming, and the Dakotas; and about 200 in the South and East. These figures, which Hillquit obtained from Haskell about 1902, are not reliable. Records indicate that the IWA had, at its peak, about sixty groups—or about 480 members. Occasionally, local spurts of membership occurred in specific areas, but these were ephemeral; they never led to permanent organizations. In Humbolt County, California, for example, sixty active IWA groups were organized; they had a membership of almost 300. But the spurt was caused by a struggle between local workingmen and a lumbering magnate. As soon as the dispute was settled, the IWA units disappeared.[9]

- 4 -

The IWA was, despite, its Socialist rhetoric, a Populist organization. Each red membership card called for "The reorganization of society independent of Priest, King, Capitalist, or Loafer." The pledge proclaimed that "Every man is entitled to the full product of his labor, and to his proportionate share of all of the natural advantages of the earth."[10] But not all men were to share in the Utopia Haskell proclaimed, especially if they happened to be Orientals. Haskell and his followers, reflecting the views of their non-Socialist working-class neighbors, wanted them sent back where they came from. Thus in 1882 he led the opposition to the organization of a union of Chinese carpenters, because "the right to incorporate ought to be . . . limited to citizens." He blamed big business for the influx of Chinese labor and believed that the "Mongolian race is being silently but surely armed for the deadly race-struggle that coming years will bring." He demanded that all Chinese immigration be prohibited and that Mongolians already in the United States should be deported. The Chinese, he argued, were uncivilized barbarians who lived like savages and animals. They "are cruel, relentless, deceitful, tricky, avaricious, sensual and in every moral sense utterly debased. . . . They murder their infant children, abandon their aged and poor to death by starvation, and observe the most horrible customs in private and public life." He charged that cheap Chinese labor was the basis of the "accursed, unjust, cruel, relentless, and infamous aristocracy" that ruled America. The only hope for American workers was the expulsion of the Chinese "AT ANY HAZARD AND AT ANY COST." [11] Although he remained anti-Chinese, Haskell ended his almost hysterical campaign against them without explanation less than a year after it started.

- 5 -

Haskell wasted little time with issues of theory; he was more interested in action. "Let us be organized first and then we will decide how best to remove the wrongs we suffer under," he wrote in 1882. What theory he did develop was limited to tactics and organization. The first platform of the IWA was replete with demands for economic reforms—calling for an eight-hour day, and end to child labor, equal pay for men and women, expulsion of the Chinese, civil service reform, safety inspection of workshops and mines—but it contained not a single plank calling for socialization of the means of production and distribution. Admittedly, the IWA newspaper *Truth* published works by noted Socialists including an abridged version of the *Communist Manifesto*, but these were not offered for theoretical elucidation; rather they were published because of their revolutionary rhetoric.[12] The only theoretical articles published in *Truth* were those devoted to discussing the relative merits of an electoral or a violent revolution, for the IWA members were more interested in agitation and organization than in education.

In the debate over peaceful versus violent revolutions, Haskell and his IWA followers supported the latter; they were convinced that elections were useless. They believed that workingmen could accomplish little except by force of arms. Throughout 1883 *Truth* appealed to each of its readers to "arm yourself at once. The day of battle will be upon us before we are prepared." Haskell doubted any reforms that aided labor—even the nationalization of land as proposed by Henry George—could be achieved by the ballot. Elections, he maintained, were invariably "rigged," and most of those who voted were members of the "whiskey-soaked . . . pseudo-Christian" element of the population. As for elected legislators, they were invariably "perjured, vile, bribed . . . representatives of the loafings classes." Should Socialists or genuine reformers win an election, Haskell insisted, they would never be allowed to rule; the landowners and capitalists would seize power by a coup.[13] The IWA position on violence as enunciated by Haskell was thus similar to that of the Anarcho-Communists led by Johann Most. Haskell acknowledged the similarity and published works by Anarchists Peter Kropotkin and Mikhail Bakhunin alongside those of Marx and Ferdinand Lassalle.

"I am neither an Anarchist nor a Marx-State Socialist," he editorialized. . . .Anarchism has many truths and so also has state Socialism." Haskell's primary interest he now claimed was forming a unity between Socialists and Anarchists, for "the honest Anarchists are in reality nothing more or less than Revolutionary Socialists." He urged individualist-Anarchist Benjamin Tucker to accept his view that a modified Marxism could be the basis for a new Socialist-Anarchist movement. But Tucker was not interested.[14]

The Chicago Anarcho-Communists, who were interested in Haskell's attempt at forging a united revolutionary movement, arranged for him to be invited to the Pittsburgh Congress of 1883 at which the revolutionary International Working People's Association was born. Haskell could not attend; instead, he sent a memorandum to August Spies and individualist Jo Labadie in which he again proposed the formation of a united revolutionary movement composed of Socialists, Anarchists, and radical trade unionists, which would be organized into a carbon copy of the IWA. The "day has come for solidarity. Ho! Reds and Blacks [Socialists were labeled Reds; Anarchists were called Blacks], thy flags are flying side by side," he wrote. He then repeated what he claimed was a quote from Bismarck: "Crowned heads, wealth and privilege well may tremble should ever again the Black and Red unite!" The memorandum was taken seriously by the delegates at Pittsburgh; they debated it at a lengthy secret session before rejecting it.[15] The rejection of his plan by the Anarcho-Communists did not alienate Haskell from them. In fact, he moved closer to their position. His journal *Truth* published the entire "Pittsburgh Manifesto" in a leading position on its first page. Calls for violence became more strident in the IWA.

An article on street violence was given two columns on page one of *Truth*. Haskell noted "the fallacy of peaceable action" in his diary, citing the Gracchi of ancient Rome, the late medieval Roman reformer Cola di Rienzi, and the dates"1776, 1789, 1861" to bolster his argument. George D. Coleman, a leader of the IWA living in Chihuahua, Mexico, wrote to Haskell: "With a little high grade powder, a galvanic electric battery, and some insulated wire, troops can be blown up in blocks, and buildings and roads [made] impregnable."[16] As part of the overall antipolitical bias that permeated the IWA immediately after the Pittsburgh congress, the central committee ruled that "members engaged in party politics . . . surrender their [IWA] cards at once." "Science proves," Haskell wrote, "that your wages depend not on politics but upon a law of political economy, and that not altered legislation but changed *conditions* are necessary to destroy the operation of their rule of social relations." So violent was Haskell's antipolitical stance by mid-1884 that he proposed the publication of a pamphlet calling for a ticket composed of Benedict Arnold, the Revolutionary War traitor, for president and convicted Tammany Hall grafter William M. (Boss) Tweed for vice-president. He called James G. Blaine, the Republican candidate for president, a "corruptionist" and Grover Cleveland, the successful Democratic candidate, "a seducer."[17]

Haskell's rationale for violence was similar to that later enunciated by August Spies, the Anarchist leader and later Haymarket martyr. "The time is coming," Haskell claimed, "when journals like *Truth* will be forcibly suppressed, when meetings of honest citizens will be dispersed at the point of the bayonet, when the producers will be shot down like dogs in every street. When that day does dawn, the hour for using DYNAMITE will have struck." His journal carried the admonition: "*Truth*" is five cents a copy, and dynamite forty cents a pound." In his IWA membership book, Haskell wrote: "Seize Mint, Armories, Sub-Treasury, Custom House, Government steamer, Alcatraz, Presidio, newspapers." He told an inquirer years later that he had made bombs and secreted valises full of them in areas where they could hardly be found. He had a plan worked out for blowing up the land records office so radicals could seize and claim valuable real property.[18]

Haskell believed that an armed uprising was unavoidable, that the "insolent rich and the ignorant poor" were on a collision course that was preordained by the very nature of the exploitative capitalist society. But he and his followers had little faith in the working class; in fact, the IWAers held the workers in contempt and assumed that they had to be treated like recalcitrant children. Most of the members of the IWA were "men of education in the commercial and professional world." They considered any attempt to educate the workers "a hopeless task." The inevitable class conflict would end in chaos unless the Socialists intervened and directed the rebellious workers toward establishing a Socialist Utopia. One leader of the IWA wrote to Haskell: "The history of revolutions of the world tell us that it is an organization among a few resolute men of action that excites a following among the masses who are generally incapable of anything but to feel the wrong without any idea of means to remedy them." Haskell echoed the sentiments, but not so crudely. In his letter to the Pittsburgh Congress, he argued that the mass of the workers were almost always prepared to revolt. Any pretext could be used to rouse them, but that the workers "will not know what they are fighting for." It would thus be necessary for committed radical leaders, who were generally not members of the working class, to "assume and hold control." The Socialists were thus to be the surrogate rulers for the working class. Once the workers, led by the Socialists, had seized the press, the railroads, the telegraph, all shipping and production facilities, and all military stores, Haskell proposed that all capitalists be arrested, that goods be rationed, and that Socialist cadres be organized into paramilitary units to prevent disorder. In effect, Haskell proposed that a small cadre of dedicated revolutionists control the uprising and the social revolution that would follow. In a classic statement of the vanguard theory, popularized twenty years later by Lenin, Haskell wrote: "It [the revolution] only needs leaders who are able, heroic and self-sacrificing in order to fan the slumbering discontent into a flame. Let us therefore concentrate our energies upon the task of providing such *leaders* rather than in vainly trying to educate the whole sluggish world before we strike."[19]

The time was not yet ripe for an uprising, he wrote in 1885. "To strike this year would be to uselessly slaughter our best people and put back the cause a hundred years." He proposed, instead, that the members of the IWA act as "peaceful as doves" for the next four years, until 1889, while the IWA high command perfected its plans. "Then may we strike and strike to win."[20]

But Haskell was not quiescent during the four years. He was involved in quixotic plans and plots. One of these led Terrence V. Powderly, leader of the Knights of Labor, to accuse Haskell of having been a police spy. Although Powderly's charge is suspect, he offers evidence to support his claim. During the 1883 strike of telegraphers, Haskell reportedly informed some IWA members that he had been asked by the union to supply some volunteers who would destroy some valuable Western Union Telegraph Company property. A number of IWA members agreed to the plan and met on the night assigned. They then went to Haskell's house—a development Haskell had not expected—only to discover that their leader was in bed, asleep. Had they gone to the Western Union property without first stopping at Haskell's home, it is probable, according to Powderly, that they would have been arrested.[21] Powderly's charge, made for political reasons during a major fight for control of the Knights of Labor between himself and Haskell's ally Joseph R. Buchanan, is suspect, but it does indicate Haskell's irresponsibility.

- 6 -

Despite his overt hostility toward pure-and-simple trade unionism, Haskell was instrumental in organizing one of the great labor institutions of the Pacific Coast, the Sailors Union of the Pacific. He also founded what was later to become the California Federation of Labor and local labor federations.

Haskell maintained that strikes for higher pay or fewer hours were futile, even counterproductive. He argued that the workers actually lost a strike for higher pay even if they ostensibly won it, for "the employer adds the extra wage into the price of the product and forces the *consumer* to pay it." Who was the consumer? The workingman. "Thus you pay your own advance out of your own pocket and are not a whit better off." Moreover, he insisted, wages could not increase so long as competition between workers existed. Under those conditions, workers would vie with each other for jobs, and "he who will work for the least, and live the cheapest, gets the job." This did not mean that Haskell opposed strikes; in fact, he favored them because they might foster a spirit of unity and awaken an interest in the root causes of their misery among the working people. That misery could only be alleviated by eliminating it, and the only way of eliminating it was by the working class taking over the capitalist monopoly in land, natural resources, and the tools and machinery of production.[22] He and his followers thus saw unions as purely agitational organizations. But despite the revolutionary rhetoric, members of the IWA played significant roles in organizing and leading trade unions, particularly in northern California.[23]

Haskell's first successful organizational effort came almost as a countervailing action against the extremely conservative leadership of the California Knights of Labor. Haskell led the radical wing at an anti-Chinese convention called in 1885 by San Francisco District Assembly 53. About 200 delegates were at the convention. They represented most of the labor unions in the Bay Area, the German Socialists, the IWA, and even some units of the Turnverein. Haskell and his followers controlled a majority of the delegates and turned the convention into an organizing session for a permanent statewide federation of labor organizations. He was later to be instrumental in organizing similar federations in Sacramento, Visalia, Oakland, Tulare, and Hanford.[24]

His most impressive work in labor organization came later that same year when he was instrumental in forming what was later to become the Sailors Union of the Pacific. Haskell and two associates in the IWA devoted months of tireless labor during 1885 and 1886 to organize the coastwise sailors into the Coast Seamen's Union and the ocean-going seamen into the Steamship Sailors Union. Neither Haskell nor his associates received any reward for their effective organization. The unions soon had a huge following among the seamen. Both the Coastwise and Steamship Sailors Union were originally under the direct control of the IWA, but by late 1886 they were made independent and the union lost its Socialist character. Haskell, shortly thereafter, was instrumental in calling a bloody seafarers' strike, which ended in failure. As a result of that strike, for which he was blamed, Haskell lost his power in the union. He remained an attorney for the maritime unions in San Francisco until 1889,[25] but he no longer had any say in its affairs. Five years later, the union was again to call for his free services, which he gave willingly and well.

On Christmas night 1893, a valise loaded with dynamite exploded in front of a boarding house used for recruiting strikebreaking seamen. Six men died instantly, two died later, and several men suffered serious injuries. John Tyrrell, a union seaman, was accused of the murders. Haskell defended him, for no pay, and won Tyrrell's acquittal.[26] He was to have no further contact with the seamen's unions (which later merged to become the Sailors Union of the Pacific).

- 7 -

Haskell's relations with other Socialists was in a constant state of flux. The Socialist Labor party convention of 1883 voted unanimously to declare Haskell's newspaper *Truth* the best labor organ written in the English language. The national secretary of the party reported that *"Truth* is well known here as a true workingmen's organ and is fully appreciated as such." But Haskell's antielectoral bias prevented it from being endorsed officially. Instead, the Socialist Labor party (SLP) decided in 1884 to publish its own newspaper—a decision that helped kill *Truth.*[27]

Even after the 1884 rebuke, Haskell continued his efforts to unite the various Socialist factions. He appealed to Peter J. McGuire, one-time Lassallean leader turned union official, for help. Haskell sugggested that the various Socialist groups form a federation of the masses. He predicted that the revolution would inevitably require violence, although he did not insist that belief in the use of force was a prerequisite for federation. McGuire was less than impressed:

You favor a Federation of Socialists beginning in New York and stretching across the continent. And I care not where it starts from. But the question arises: Upon what basis? There must be a certain unity of thought, or, in its absence, a catholicity of spirit among Socialists, before we get any 100 or 200 of them to federate. Now let us see if we can find any common basis of action. One contends for remedial measures and ballot box agencies, another for communities and co-operative experiments, a third for Revolution and Dynamite, a fourth for Peaceful Propaganda of Socialist thought to educate the masses.

It was obvious that McGuire considered Haskell's effort to be futile, although he favored a unified Socialist movement.[28]

Except on the issue of violence, Haskell's IWA comrades were in basic theoretical agreement with the members of the SLP. Admittedly, the list of required readings for new IWA members was a conglomeration of standard late nineteenth-century Left-radical literature; it ran the gamut from the anarchism of Kropotkin to the moderate socialism of William Morris to the simplistic Marxian analyses of Laurence Gronlund and H. M. Hyndman to the nihilistic terrorism of Sergius Stepniak. But the few theoretical writings of Haskell himself were hardly different from standard Socialist epistles. The Socialist's work, he said, should be "to save, purify and remodel the people of this land." The Socialists wanted to do this in Britain, but they faced insurmountable legal obstacles there, obstacles that led the Pilgrims to America; however, had "no hospitable America been open to them, they would have remained at home—and fought." Now, they had no new continent to which to flee, and thus given the oppressive conditions in late nineteenth-century society, "the grand revolution is imminent in every land." Social conditions had, he argued, already reached the point in America where no social alternative to socialism was available. The revolution of 1776 had established bourgeois rule in America, when social conditions required it; now, under new social conditions, the new revolution would replace that rule with a socialist state. He repeated the long-held Marxian prophecy that as capitalism developed, the proletariat would grow, as members of the *petit bourgeoisie* are forced into its ranks, thus further immiserating the workers by adding to competition for jobs.[29] These were his public pronouncements; in private, Haskell was less circumspect. To the question, "What should be our aim as individuals to secure universal happiness?" he answered: "To practice the Jesuits' motto 'The end justifies the means.' " His mission was, he wrote in his diary, "To know all. To rule all."[30]

The tactical differences between Haskell and the other Socialists had begun to narrow by 1886. The IWA program of 1885 was a strange mixture of Socialist and Anarchist planks. It called for the instantaneous abolition of all profits, a guarantee that all who supported the community would receive a job, and—finally—a plank calling for the abolition of money that would be replaced by labor notes based on the principle that cost is the limit of price. But the bombast was gone; there no longer was any call for instantaneous violence. By 1886 the IWA leaders, at Haskell's suggestion, announced that they were opposed to violence, that the organization's sole interest was propaganda. The action came less from ideological reassessment than from practical considerations. Although its official pronouncements, from 1882 to 1885, proclaimed its faith in violence, the IWA was prey to police spies and *agents provocateurs*. Moreover, the Haymarket bombing had created a violent antipathy toward radicals, especially those who preached the use of force. "I have come to believe that the cause of labor must pass through a political stage," Haskell wrote shortly after the Haymarket trial began in Chicago. Within a year, the once antipolitical Haskell was openly calling for electoral activity at the municipal level.[31] In 1887 the IWA and Haskell abandoned violence—and Haskell abandoned San Francisco temporarily.

- 8 -

In late 1886, Joseph R. Buchanan, leader of the radical wing of the Knights of Labor, member of the IWA, and editor of the Denver labor weekly *Labor Enquirer*, left the Rocky Mountain West to establish a daily labor newspaper in Chicago and appointed Haskell as his successor on the Colorado paper. Haskell arrived in Denver with letters of praise from California labor organizations. The Coast Seamen's Union and the Federated Trade and Labor Organizations of the Pacific Coast congratulated the workingmen of Colorado on "having secured so fearless and tried a champion of the labor cause; being assured that he will in Colorado, as he has done heretofore on this coast, make the struggle of the workers his own and the sole object of all his energies and endeavors."[32]

No sooner had Haskell assumed the editorship of the *Labor Enquirer* than he resumed his almost forgotten crusade to oust the Chinese from the United States. He called the Chinese "a race devoid absolutely as a race of the power to *recognize a moral obligation*." He accused each of them of coming from a civilization with "so low a *moral* grade that association with him means corruption and degradation to us without the possibility of any elevation to him." He called the Chinese a cruel, treacherous, selfish, deceitful, and cowardly people. "Such a race coming in conflict with the Aryian [sic!] creates an issue that will be arbitrated only by the sword." Haskell argued that for these reasons, "thoughtful radicals" want all Chinese expelled from the United States.[33] His attack provoked a sharp reply from Dyer D. Lum, then a leading light in the New York Assembly of the Knights of Labor, one of the few units of the national labor movement then organizing Chinese workers. Lum did not deny that the Chinese were leprous, rat eaters, and semihuman. But they were not the real villains in the importation; the real villians were the capitalists who brought them here as a cheap commodity. The solution was thus to organize these "subhuman monsters" so they could no longer be used as strikebreakers.[34] But most Socialists, particularly in the western states, agreed with Haskell, and at least one Socialist-controlled organization within the Knights warned that "many good men" would be leaving the Knights of Labor in the West if any eastern unit allowed them to enter.[35]

Besides the anti-Chinese crusade, Haskell's primary interest during his stay in Denver was uniting the IWA with the SLP. The reason behind this effort was the virtual collapse of the IWA. By 1887 it was a shadow of its old self, rapidly vanishing into nothingness. The depression that began in 1883 had ended and with it the revolutionary fervor. Haskell's persistent disputes drove others out of the movement. Moreover, the *Labor Enquirer* was in extremely poor financial condition and Haskell hoped the SLP could salvage it. But Haskell's appeals to the SLP were greeted with little enthusiasm by the eastern Socialists. His approach, which lacked any humility, won him few friends. He sent a missive to the party's convention in Buffalo urging the formation of a new Socialist party that would be composed basically of the old SLP and the IWA. "We who have all along insisted on the whole truth being spoken out," he wrote to the convention, "We who have borne the brunt of the battle in the Western states,—we on our part must put ourselves more boldly to the front even than before." A lot of opposition to his plan developed. Some of the delegates were old-time Socialists who recalled Haskell's former alliance with the Anarchists. The delegates rejected Haskell's proposal; they passed a resolution instead suggesting that IWA members who accepted the SLP program[36] join the party as individuals. Haskell reported the convention, but he misrepresented the facts. He wrote that the convention had decided to admit the IWA and that he had been named the SLP organizer for the West Coast.[37] The ruse failed, and within a month, Haskell resigned as editor of the *Labor Enquirer*[38] and departed for the Kaweah Co-operative Colony he had helped found in the Sierra Nevada mountains.

- 9 -

Kaweah owed its birth to a picnic of members of the IWA and the Coastwise Sailors Union in San Francisco late in 1885. It was at that picnic that Haskell and his followers decided to establish a colony based on Laurence Gronlund's *Co-operative Commonwealth*, a new—albeit hardly successful—quasi-Marxian work by the Danish-American publicist and lawyer. Its founders claimed that the aims of the proposed colony were "to insure their members against want, provide comfortable homes for them, and maintain co-operation among themselves on the principles of justice and fraternity." They hoped to replace political government with simple administration of operations by competent experts.[39] The colony was to be an example of how men could live on earth in peace, harmony, and plenty. Its founders hoped that the Socialist system would spread out from Kaweah "until it embraces, in time, the whole world." To quote Haskell, "It was for propaganda" that Kaweah was organized.[40]

The site chosen for the new colony—on the north fork of the Kaweah River, Tulare County, in the Sierra Nevadas—was in one of the most beautiful, although inaccessible, portions of California. It included some of the finest forests in the United States with huge areas of salable pine, fir, and redwood, plus the giant Sequoias—the largest living things in the world. Lumber companies had explored but later ignored the forests because of their inaccessability. A careful exploration of the area by several of Haskell's associates led them to conclude that the forest could, in fact, be reached by construction of a road. Once the road was built and the forest opened to exploitation, the prospective colonists assumed that it would be possible for Kaweahns to earn a good living. The nearby San Joaquin

Valley was then developing rapidly and had an urgent need for construction lumber. Haskell and forty-two of his followers filed a claim for each of the forty-three plots that made up the proposed colony.

News of the filing alarmed the residents of nearby Visalia. They suspected that the claimants were actually agents for the hated land and lumber barons, particularly the Southern Pacific Railroad. A large number of Visalians protested, and the federal government suspended the claims for five years. Despite the suspension of their claims, Haskell and his followers went ahead with the organization of the colony; they were sure that the protests would be withdrawn and the suspension lifted as soon as the Visalians would realize that they had erred. The Socialists relied "upon the faith of the government, so often pledged, to protect the actual settler." The colony was thus organized on unapproved land claims.[41]

Kaweah, during his lifetime, attracted about 400 settlers. At its peak, it had some 300 residents; at the end, 150 colonists were still there. The first settlers came early in 1887, and they lived in tents. The first permanent building was erected in 1889.[42] Kaweah was to be "a collective . . . ruled by no class, but by the people." In many ways, it succeeded, albeit superficially. The Kaweah trustees established an eight-hour day, a minimum wage of thirty cents an hour (payable in scrip acceptable for all transactions in the colony). Moreover, there was equality in pay; everyone was given the same amount—thirty cents an hour. Gronlund's doctrine of "No interest, no rent, no profit" was the keystone of Kaweah's operation.[43] No interest was paid or charged, nor was any rent or profit realized.

As if to prove the feasibility of socialism, the Kaweahns built the "impossible" road into the "impenetrable" Sequoia forest. This was done under extremely adverse conditions. With the crudest of tools and at the expenditure of only $50,000, they built an eighteen-mile-long road over almost impassable terrain, at a grade of 8 in 100 feet, rising to an elevation of more than 8,000 feet. It took slightly less than four years, from October 1886 to June 1890, to complete the job. Land agents who examined the project admitted that the colonists had overcome insurmountable difficulties; government engineers estimated that it would have cost at least $300,000 for contractors to have built it.[44]

The reports that reached the rest of the Socialist world from Kaweah were enthusiastically optimistic. In 1889, when Edward Bellamy's Socialist novel *Looking Backward* was becoming a bestseller, Haskell called Kaweah "a practical attempt to realize in practice the ideas of Bellamy's novel." By 1890 Haskell was claiming that Kaweah was "a successful operation on Bellamyite principles." J. J. Martin, one of the trustees, reported that the social effect of living in a cooperative colony such as Kaweah "has been remarkable; a more peaceable, orderly, and intelligent camp of workingmen never existed." Friendly relations were the rule, he reported. "Each one feels the responsibility of upholding the social integrity of the colony; and, as a result, an inoffensive and charming rivalry exists to outdo the other in neighborly acts."[45]

Despite these glowing reports of life at Kaweah, it was beset with serious difficulties: political, economic, and legal. The legal problems were the most obvious causes of the demise of the community. They were caused by the settlement of the area while the original colonists' claims were under suspension. The immediate cause of the difficulties was an 1890 decision by the federal government, apparently at the instigation of Harry Crocker, president of the Southern Pacific, to establish a national park at the site of Kaweah. Crocker's animosity toward Kaweah was based on a report that Haskell and his supporters planned to build a short-haul railroad from the Sequoia forest into Visalia that Crocker feared would compete with his railroad. By creating a national park, the federal government would bar the Kaweah settlers from cutting any more timber. They would thus have no need—or legal right—to build a short-haul railroad. Authorization for the national park—to be named Sequoia—was included as an amendment to the Yosemite National Park Bill. The first the colonists knew of the new park was when their trustees—including Haskell—were arrested for illegally cutting timber on federal land. The charges against them were merely that they had ordered some timber cut. A hostile press reported erroneously that among the trees cut were several giant Sequoias. After a long and costly trial, each of the trustees was fined a nominal amount. The fines were appealed in vain; President William McKinley pardoned each of the trustees eleven years later. The government's action in seizing the property was appealed by the original colonists for the next forty-four years. It was not until April 1935 that the Department of the Interior issued its final report upholding the 1891 action against Kaweah.[46]

Even if no legal problem had arisen, Kaweah could not have survived. Despite the optimistic reports of life at the colony, it was beset with problems, strife, and struggle almost from the beginning. An attempt was made, for example, to organize a band. But the population was too transient and the rate of turnover too great for so permanent an institution as a band to be formed. A Sunday school and a church were formed, but they failed; classes were attempted to educate the adult settlers, but few attended; meetings of mothers ended in bickering disputes; attempts at organizing dances met with opposition from religious members who considered dancing sinful. "Instead of fraternal, friendly feelings," Haskell wrote ten years later, "one found Kaweah divided into factions and fractions of factions." A tendency to gossip was evident; teachers were hounded out of the school by parents and students with often fictitious complaints. "It was," Haskell complained, "kick, kick, kick, until one longed again for the large city, where one's next-door neighbor is unknown." The feuding became so intense that more than half of the members of the colony left. A letter from a group of colonists complained: "One by one our comrades who came here in good faith to carry out the noble purposes for which we organized have gone away discouraged and disheartened."[47]

Economic problems, caused for the most part by indolence, plagued Kaweah. Soon after the road was completed, a sawmill was erected. It was capable of sawing 3,000 feet a day. In three months, it cut only 22,000 feet. The workers were poorly organized, no leadership was available, and attempts at rationalizing production failed. Most of those who came to Kaweah believed that they had been denied full use of their talents in the capitalist world. They, therefore, saw no reason why they should waste these talents in the new order performing mundane tasks. They expected instantaneous recognition at Kaweah. If the recognition of their talents were denied them at Kaweah, they argued that the corrupt influences of capitalism had pursued them and had affected the management of the colony. Few of the men were more than average in ability or talent, many were basically lazy, others were dreamers, and almost none of them understood management. Work was often done poorly—except for the road—and was often useless. A ditch was built in an area where water did not flow; a mill foundation was laid in a region without water power; trees and vines were planted and then left to die for lack of care. Bookkeeping was so bad, it was almost impossible to understand. Overall, excuses abounded, but little work was accomplished.[48]

In November 1891, the combination of legal harrassment, indolence, and incompetence forced the Kaweahns to admit defeat and dissolve the colony. A disheartened, disillusioned Haskell wrote:

The enterprise is a dreary failure, . . . and so will any other similar attempt. . . . Under the competitive system men produce because they must work to the highest pitch or starve, and they are under competent leadership. Under the co-operative [system] there is no such prodding incentive to toil, no probability of such leadership, and men are not yet civilized enough to do right for right's sake alone and to labor for the sake of production itself[49]

Haskell withdrew from futile efforts at creating a new system. He still believed, hoped, and trusted in socialism,[50] but he now proposed to join the Socialist mainstream—the Nationalist and Populist movements.

- 10 -

The Nationalist movement, of which Haskell became a California leader in 1889, was based on a novel, *Looking Backward*, written by a New England author, Edward Bellamy. The novel and the movement were quasi-Socialist, opposed to the profit system but rejecting the concept of class struggle. The Nationalists were known as "kid glove Socialists."[51] Haskell, the one-time firebrand, had by 1889 moderated his views to the point where he could become a Nationalist. His revolutionary rhetoric of the early years of the decade had availed him and his movement little. His attempt at colonization was by that time an obvious failure, although it was to exist for another year and a half. Failure tended to moderate Haskell's zeal; he now preached moderate, peaceful, political action.

Haskell called for the evolution of the competitive capitalist system into a cooperative Socialist system as rapidly as possible through the nationalization of industry. He rejected "riot, anarchy, disorder," and proclaimed himself a collectivist, "which is the exact opposite of 'Anarchy.'" He preached evolution rather than revolution and urged his followers to challenge argument and criticism rather than "policemen's clubs and gatling guns." Haskell proclaimed that he was no longer a romantic revolutionist, but a social scientist. "We stand not as a band of dreamers and cranks," he told a meeting of his followers, "but as scientists in our line, representing the tendencies of historic evolution." But his new-found science did not keep Haskell from promising his followers "two hours work per day, luxuries for the poorest equal to those now enjoyed by the richest, rare exotics in every man's front yard, carpets in the house ten inches thick" and a $12 railroad fare to New York.[52]

His first assault on the capitalist system as a Nationalist came in the San Francisco municipal election of 1889. Haskell formed his own Common Sense party, which pledged an end to poverty in San Francisco by the employment of unemployed workers to build a municipal water works. He proposed to pay the workers with "labor notes" a la Josiah Warren, thus costing the taxpayers of the city no money. He also suggested that the city build its own electric power plant using the tides of the harbor for turning the turbines, and that the city operate its own bakeries, slaughterhouses, street-car lines, bathing houses, and laundries. Moreover, he wanted the municipality of San Francisco to issue its own scrip, which would be acceptable in all of these municipal businesses. This, Haskell argued, would give the scrip full currency value and would undermine the capitalist system. Haskell's dream of socialism in one city was similar to the Epic Plan proposed in the same state by Upton Sinclair forty-five years later. Like the Sinclair plan, it failed to win electoral support.[53]

Despite his failure to win control of the government of San Francisco, Haskell emerged from the election as a power in California politics. By May of that year, California had 48 Nationalist clubs (of a total of 113 nationally). Burnette Haskell was the man chiefly responsible for Nationalism's rapid growth; he was the publicist and organizer of the movement in the area of its greatest strength. Haskell had joined the Nationalists almost immediately after Eugene Hough, a Bay Area labor leader, had founded the first club in

Oakland. Within a matter of months, Haskell emerged as a key figure in the statewide organization. By February 1890 he could proclaim to a public meeting of San Francisco Nationalists that "we have here . . . an organization in every one of the 176 precincts." Although the organization was to collapse within a year, the report was accurate; the Nationalists had become a major power in California politics.[54]

The Nationalism of Haskell was an amalgamation of the socialism of the SLP and the Utopia of Bellamy. Nationalism, he said, was based on the philosophic doctrines of Hegel and Marx to which Bellamy had added a practical plan for solution of the social problem. *"Looking Backward,"* he wrote "was to the cause of Nationalism, what *Uncle Tom's Cabin* was to emancipation." The misery of the working people, Haskell opined, was caused by neither a belief in God nor a belief in the state, as revolutionary Socialists and Anarchists claimed. In fact, that "misery is far less than it was a hundred, a thousand, or ten thousand years ago. What exists now exists solely because it is a survival from barbaric conditions." The state was, he argued, a developing organism moving toward perfection. The individual was, at the same time, also evolving into a more perfect being—"the specialized portion of a greater societary organism." Under these conditions, the individual became more dependent on the state *"for its very life and being."* The state, as it becomes perfect, will inevitably meet the needs of each individual. It, therefore, "becomes my duty to so shape my individual life that I shall fit in as one piece of the future social mechanism if I would survive." Haskell rejected the idea of individual rights, which he called tying "selfish strings . . . around our fingers to impede the collective circulation." He pleaded for an end to self-interest, for man's surrender to the perfecting state, so future generations would be free from economic and social misery. "I am myself too little to be an 'Anarchist' and boss the world," he wrote, "and so perforce—or no! by choice—I whisper 'Not *rights*, but duties!' and behold, I am a Nationalist."[55] The Nationalism that Haskell preached was a prescription for authoritarian rule. It denied individual rights and proclaimed collective responsibility as the alternative. His Nationalism resembled in many ways Stalin's latter day "socialism."

Not all Nationalists agreed with Haskell's interpretation of Bellamy's work. Some, in fact, were little interested in Bellamy or Nationalism but saw in the fast-growing Nationalist movement a means to achieve political success. Among such politicians was a former New Jersey Democrat, Thomas V. Cator, and his ally James H. Barry, a Single-Taxer and editor of the weekly *San Francisco Star*. Barry had been an enemy of Haskell and of socialism for many years. No sooner had Haskell emerged as a leader of the Nationalist movement in California than Barry opened a public assault against him. Thus in early 1890, Barry charged that Haskell and his friend Thomas G. Ashton, financial secretary of the club, had embezzled the club's treasury. Barry also arranged for the San Francisco *Freethought*, an antire-ligious journal, to publish the report. He then sent copies of *Freethought* to each of the residents of Kaweah—with which Haskell was still affili-ated—and to leading Nationalists. An investigation by the Nationalist clubs proved the allegations to be untrue; the Nationalist clubs actually owed Haskell $700 for legal fees.[56] When this attempt failed, Barry turned to a more direct assault. He reprinted much of Haskell's earlier IWA material calling for armed uprising and terror.

Burnette G. Haskell is thoroughly on record as an advocate and teacher of murder and arson—of assassination in its worst form. . . . Haskell said in print that Gould, Vanderbilt, Huntington, Stanford, Sage, Field [noted capitalists of the 1880s and 1890s], and so on "are deserving of dynamite and dagger at the hands of the people!" . . . We say that Burnette G. Haskell is a systematic teacher of arson and assassination, and if there is any excuse for his conduct it is that he is mad.

The *Star* compared him editorially to the violent anti-Chinese rabble-rouser Denis Kearney and *Freethought* called him "tonguey" but not profound.[57]

At the 1890 statewide convention of the Nationalists' United Labor party, Haskell's followers were in the majority; Cator and his adherents made up the minority. The debate waxed hot and heavy—the struggle was over personalities not issues. Efforts at compromise—one suggesting Cator run for governor and Haskell for United States senator—failed. On other votes, primarily over proxies, Haskell's faction won sixty-three to forty. The Cator faction bolted and held its own convention and formed a new "Popu-list" party, which formed an alliance with the California Farmers' Alliance and the old Greenbackers. Cator eventually became the leader of the Cali-fornia People's party until 1898 when he joined the Republicans. Haskell and his followers attempted to keep the Nationalist movement alive after the split, but the internal bickering involved in the struggle between Haskell and the Barry-Cator faction left most of his supporters dispirited. More-over, by late 1890 and early 1891, Haskell was too preoccupied with his Kaweah-related difficulties to spend much time or effort with the splintered Nationalist movement. Most of the remaining members of the Nationalist clubs in California joined the Socialist Labor party. Haskell withdrew from Socialist and labor activity—except to defend John Tyrell of the Sailors Union of the Pacific during his murder trial in 1894.[58]

- 11 -

Haskell made several unsuccessful attempts to reenter politics during the 1890s. In 1892 he made an effort to gain control of the San Francisco Demo-cratic party by forming the Neptune Club, "The Democratic Club on the [Water] Front." It was composed chiefly of members of the Sailor's Union of the Pacific; it failed. Later that year, he ran as an independent candidate for police judge and polled a respectable 3,000 votes. The next year, he ran as a Populist, and the next year he tried, but failed, to win the Populist nomination for superior court justice. In 1894 he again failed to win the Populist nomination for judgeship. In 1896 he was again active, this time as a leading light at the state convention of the People's party.[59] That was to be his last attempt at partisan politics.

In 1900 President McKinley appointed Haskell a notary in Alaska. He stayed in the North only a short time. Within two years, he was back in San Francisco—now searching for employment. To his high school friend George C. Pardee, a conservative Republican who was elected governor in 1902, Haskell replied: "I was a Socialist, a Nationalist, a Populist. What of that? . . . I'm back again in Republican ranks." His pleas went for nought; Pardee refused to name him to any post. By 1906 Haskell was in dire financial straits; he appealed to Socialist labor leader Frank Roney for help in obtaining the job as Socialist member of the San Francisco Board of Elections at $83 a month. He assured Roney that he had voted for Debs in 1904. Roney did not help him. After the earthquake and fire of 1906, Haskell worked as a proofreader on the *Oakland Tribune*, but his health was now failing. A year later, after living in poverty the last five years of his life, friendless, and forgotten, Burnette G. Haskell died. He was buried in a plot of ground donated by the Sailors' Union of the Pacific—the only payment he had ever received from a labor or Socialist organization.[60]

- 12 -

Haskell was an enigmatic character. He was undoubtedly a brilliant organizer, a fine publicist, an impressive speaker, and a charismatic leader. Yet he was a personal failure as a radical leader. Admittedly, he was instrumental in organizing a major labor union that exists some ninety years after he founded it. True, the Kaweah Colony, which he established in the Sierra Nevadas, opened that area to settlement. The road his followers built is still usable. But both he and his ideas have virtually been forgotten. The union he founded is a pure-and-simple trade union, part of a large and conservative international union. Its members and officials know little and care less about the ideals that led him and his friends to organize the union. As for Kaweah, it is forgotten even in the area where it existed. Except for records at the Sequoia National Park archives, his connection with the area is totally ignored. The IWA was a flash that left virtually no mark on American socialism or California society. Admittedly, the Nationalist movement in California was the base on which the once powerful Socialist party of that state was to be built. But the Nationalists became Socialist partisans after he had left the movement. Haskell is significant only as a symbol, for he illustrates a pattern in American radicalism, an excess of rhetoric and a minimum of viable Socialist achievement. He was not, as George E. Mac-Donald, the radical free thinker argued, "a four-flusher." True, as Mac-Donald pointed out, there was "confirmatory evidence on that point from persons having knowledge of Haskell's past performances."[61] But no verifiable evidence suggests that Haskell was dishonest or corrupt. He died in penury; his life was spent impoverished, although as an attorney and publicist, he could have lived in luxury. The obvious fact is that Haskell was a self-deluded intellectual who saw himself as the leader of a cursade for a new world order. As with most other middle-class, radical, intellectual crusaders, Haskell could not accept the fact that rhetoric could not feed a starving human. He was so enamored of his own intellect and the rhetoric it produced that he could not understand simple pragmatic reality.

NOTES

1. Karl Marx to Friedrich Sorge, November 5, 1880, in Leonard E. Mins [editor and translation], "Unpublished Letters of Karl Marx and Friedrich Engels to Americans," *Science and Society* 2 (Spring 1938): 226.

2. Ira B. Cross, *A History of the Labor Movement of California* (Berkeley: University of California Press, 1935), pp. 153–58; Joseph R. Buchanan, *The Story of a Labor Agitator* (New York: The Outlook Company, 1903), pp. 266–67; Commonwealth of Massachusetts, Office of the Secretary, "Revolutionary War Service of Abel Briggs," Copy Certified by Wm. M. Olin, July 8, 1896, Haskell Family Papers, Bancroft Library, University of California, Berkeley, California; [Burnette G. Haskell], "Burnette G. Haskell's Record," [1894], typescript, Haskell Family Papers; Hyman Weintraub, *Andrew Furuseth: Emancipator of the Seamen* (Berkeley: University of California Press, 1959), pp. 17–18.

3. Cross, *History*, pp. 153–58; "Burnette G. Haskell's Record" is an interesting—if inaccurate—autobiographical note that Haskell hoped to use in the 1894 election. It lists among Haskell's personal friends the British Socialist H. M. Hyndman, John Swinton, labor editor and organizer Joseph R. Buchanan, Eugene V. Debs, Wendell Phillips, Walt Whitman, Irish patriot Charles S. Parnell, Populist leader James G. Weaver, Danish-American Utopian Socialist Laurence Gronlund, Edward Bellamy, Stephen Pearl Andrews, Russian Anarchist Prince Peter Kropotkin, and Victor Hugo. Except for Buchanan, and possibly Hyndman, most of the reputed friendships appear to have been figments of Haskell's fertile imagination. Weintraub, *Andrew Furuseth*, pp. 17–18; Frank Roney, *Frank Roney: Irish Rebel and California Labor Leader*, ed. Ira B. Cross (Berkeley: University of California Press, 1931), p. 390.

4. *The Workmen's Advocate*, June 9, 1888; Cross, *History*, p. 156; "Shall Red and Black Unite? An American Revolutionary Document of 1883," in Chester McArthur Destler, *American Radicalism, 1865–1901* (Chicago: Quadrangle Paperbacks, 1966), p. 84, quoted Haskell as saying that he founded the IWA on the advice of Henry M. Hyndman, the British Socialist. No other evidence points to this except that letters from Hyndman to Thomas Davidson in the Thomas Davidson Papers at the Yale University Library indicate Hyndman's involvement in efforts aimed at organizing a strong American Socialist movement.

5. Cross, *History*, pp. 164–65.

6. *Truth* 6 (May 19, 1883): 1; Destler, *American Radicalism*, pp. 82–88.

7. Buchanan, *Labor Agitator*, 267–73; Burnette G. Haskell, *What the I.W.A. Is* (San Francisco: National Executive, Headquarters, International Workingmen's Association, 1885), n. p.; "Pledging Allegiance to I.W.A.," original document, Haskell Family Papers.

8. Cross, *History*, pp. 159–61.

9. Ibid., p. 153, 160–70; Morris Hillquit, *History of Socialism in the United States* (New York: Funk and Wagnalls, 1910), p. 231; "To the Laboring Men of Humboldt County," broadside, Haskell Family Papers.

10. Cross, *History*, pp. 159, 162.

11. *Truth* 1 (February 11, 1882): 4; (February 18, 1882): 2; (February 25, 1882): 2; (March 4, 1882): 4; (April 15, 1882): 1; (April 22, 1882): 2; (April 24, 1882): broadside extra edition; (May 17, 1882): 1.

12. *Truth* 3 (July 19, 1882): 2; *Truth* 4 (November 29, 1882): 2; *Truth* 6 (June 16, 1883): 1.

13. *Truth*, n.s. 90 (October 27, 1883): 1; *Truth*, n.s. 93 (November 17, 1883): 2; see also, for example *Truth*, n.s. 94 (November 24, 1883): 2.

14. *Truth* 5 (January 17, 1883): 1; *Truth* 5 (January 24, 1883): 2; *Truth* 7 (September 8, 1883): 1; *Truth*, n.s. 90 (October 27, 1883).

15. Destler, *American Radicalism*, pp. 80–81, 91–100, 102; *Truth* 7 (September 15, 1883): 1–4; the actual declaration is carried in *The Labor Enquirer* (Denver) 2 (September 22, 1883): 4. A crucial passage from that declaration reads:

There exists now no great obstacle to . . . unity. The work of peaceful education and revolutionary conspiracy well can and ought to run in parallel lines. . . . Tremble! Oppressors of the World! Not far beyond your purblind sight there dawns the scarlet and sable lights of the judgment day.

Tucker considered Haskell's plea to be self-contradictory. "This document," he wrote, "does not reconcile in the least but simply and summarily places liberty and authority side by side and arbitrarily says: 'These twain are one flesh.' We will be parties to no such marriage." The letter appeared in *Truth*, n.s. 90 (October 27, 1883): 1.

16. *Truth*, n.s. 95 (December 1, 1883): 1; *Truth*, n.s. 97 (December 15, 1883): 1; Roney, *Frank Roney*, p. 474, reported that "he [Haskell] might arrange for a band of daring simpletons to blow up the Hall of Records, while he himself should slip to San Jose to have a safe alibi during the day when the explosion was to be." "Burnette G. Haskell's diary for September 19, 1883-February 1, 1884," Haskell Family Papers; George D. Coleman to Burnette G. Haskell, October 17, 1883, Haskell Family Papers.

17. "Minute Book of International Workingmen's Association Central Committee," meeting of June 27, 1884, p. 7, and meeting of July 27, 1884, p. 15, Haskell Family Papers; Burnette G. Haskell, "Strikes," *Truth* n.s. 1 (October 1884): 298.

18. *Truth* 6 (June 30, 1883): 1; Cross, *History*, pp. 163–64.

19. "Aims and Purposes of the Anarchists," *Chicago Daily Star*, April 25, 1887, reprinted in Terrence V. Powderly, *Thirty Years of Labor*, (Columbus, Ohio: Excelsior Publishing House, 1889), pp. 367–68, 371. *The Chicago Daily Star* was published by a Chicago group of conservative allies of Powderly. The editor of the paper was Ethelbert Stewart. The anti-Powderly members of the Knights of Labor in Chicago started their own daily newspaper, *The Labor Enquirer*, edited by Haskell's friend and IWA member Joseph R. Buchanan. Buchanan, *Labor Agitator*, p. 266; Destler, *American Radicalism*, pp. 85–87; Burnette G. Haskell, "The Development of American Socialism," *Truth* n.s. 1 (August 1884): 158; also reprinted in Powderly, *Thirty Years of Labor*, p. 274; George D. Coleman to William Bluhm, September 20, 1883, Haskell Family Papers.

20. Destler, *American Radicalism*, pp. 101–2.

21. Powderly, *Thirty Years of Labor*, pp. 275–76.

22. Burnette G. Haskell, "Strikes," *Truth* n.s. 1 (October 1884): 297–99.

23. Weintraub, *Andrew Furuseth*, p. 18.

24. Cross, *History*, pp. 175–77.

25. Weintraub, *Andrew Furuseth*, pp. 11, 18–20; Roney, *Frank Roney*, pp. 345, 406–7; Cross, *History*, p. 183; Letter, *San Francisco Daily Report*, by Edward Crangle, secretary, and

Edward Anderson and Edward Carpenter, patrol of "Coasting Sailors," February 6, 1886, clipping, "Personal Reminiscences, Memoranda of Burnette G. Haskell," Haskell Family Papers; "An Easy Way to Get Rich," broadside (San Francisco: Common Sense Party, April 10, 1889), Haskell Family Papers.

26. Cross, *History*, p. 213; clipping, *The Examiner* (San Francisco), March 7, 1894, in "Personal Notes: Burnette G. Haskell," p. 70, Haskell Family Papers.

27. Emil Kreis to S. Robert Wilson, August 24, 1883; Hugo Vogt to S. Robert Wilson, January 14, 1884; Hugo Vogt to S. Robert Wilson, March 5, 1884, all in SLP Collection, Wisconsin State Historical Society, Madison, Wisconsin (microfilm edition).

28. P[eter] J. McGuire to Burnette G. Haskell, February 20, 1884, Haskell Family Papers; also see handwritten notation by "P. J. McGuire," August 13, 1884, on printed circular letter signed "Burnette G. Haskell," June 1, 1884, Haskell Family Papers.

29. Haskell, *What the I.W.A. Is*, lists the required reading for new IWA members as follows: Henry George, *The Land Question*; Peter Kropotkin, *Letters to Young People*; W. C. O[wens], *The Manifesto*; [Thomas Paine], *The Rights of Man*; A. J. Starkweather and S. R. Wilson, *Socialism: Evolution or Revolution*; H. M. Hyndman, William Morris, and Burnette G. Haskell, *The Historical Development of Socialism in England and America*; Sergius Stepniak, *Underground Russia*; and Laurence Gronlund, *The Cooperative Commonwealth; The Labor Enquirer* (Denver) 7 (February 12, 1887); Burnette G. Haskell, "The Development of American Socialism," *Truth* n.s. 1 (August 1884): 150–51; "Burnette G. Haskell Diary, September 19, 1883–February 1, 1884," dated November 16, 1883, captioned "To Professor Sumner, the capitalist looter of Yale College and his fellow craftsmen," Haskell Family Papers.

30. "Personal Reminiscences, Memoranda of Burnette G. Haskell" (handwritten), vol. 9, p. 22, dated January 29, 1886, and vol. 9, p. 21, dated January 29, 1886, Haskell Family Papers.

31. "Aims and Purposes of the Anarchists," *The Chicago Star*, April 25, 1887, reproduced in Powderly, *Thirty Years of Labor*, pp. 368–69; *Workmen's Advocate* 4 (June 9, 1888); editorial in *The Labor Enquirer* (Denver) 6 (November 13, 1886); Burnette G. Haskell, *The Truth Shall Set You Free* (Denver: The Labor Enquirer Print, 1887), n.p.

32. *The Labor Enquirer* (Denver) 7 (February 5, 1887).

33. *The Labor Enquirer* (Denver) 7 (July 9, 1887).

34. Letter of Dyer D. Lum, *The Labor Enquirer* (Denver) 7 (July 9, 1887).

35. *The Labor Enquirer* (Chicago) 1 (July 16, 1887).

36. *Report of the Proceedings of the National Convention of the Socialistic Labor Party held at Buffalo, N.Y., on September 17, 19, 20 and 21, 1887* (New York: John Oehler, 1887), pp. 6–7, 13; *The Labor Enquirer* (Denver) 7 (August 20, 1887).

37. *The Labor Enquirer* (Denver) 7 (October 1, 1887).

38. *The Labor Enquirer* (Denver) 7 (September 10, 1887).

39. Ruth R[onnie Krandis] Lewis, "Kaweah: An Experiment in Cooperative Colonization," *Pacific Historical Review* 17 (November 1948): 429–30, 436; F. I. Vassault, "Nationalism in California," *Overland Monthly* 2d ser. 15 (June 1890): 661; Roney, *Frank Roney*, p. 409; see also Arthur W. Johns, "The Kaweah Cooperative Colony" (M. A. thesis, Stanford University, 1913), and Ruth Ronnie Krandis Lewis, "The Rise and Fall of Kaweah: An Experiment in Cooperative Colonization" (M. A. thesis, University of California, Berkeley, 1942). For a discussion of Gronlund, see chapter 13. Robert V. Hines, *California's Utopian Communities* (New York: W. W. Norton, 1966), pp. 78–100.

40. J. J. Martin, "A Co-operative Commonwealth: The Kaweah Colony," *The Nationalist* 1 (October 1889): 208; Burnette G. Haskell, "Kaweah: How and Why the Colony Died," *Out West* 17 (September 1902): 303.

41. *Kaweah* is an Indian word for "here we rest," *Commonwealth* 1 (June 20, 1888): 4; Haskell, "Kaweah," pp. 311–15; Lewis, "Kaweah," p. 430.

42. Lewis, "Kaweah," p. 431; Haskell, "Kaweah," p. 317.

43. Haskell, "Kaweah," p. 319; Lewis, "Kaweah," pp. 431–32; Martin, "Co-operative Commonwealth," pp. 207–8.

44. Lewis, "Kaweah," p. 431; Haskell, "Kaweah," pp. 311, 316.

45. *The Commonwealth* 2 (April 24, 1889); *Kaweah Commonwealth* 1 (January 18, 1890); Martin, "Co-operative Commonwealth, pp. 206–7. For discussion of Bellamy see chapter 13.

46. Lewis, "Kaweah," pp. 436–37, 441; Martin's letter is in the files of the Sequoia National Park Office at Three Rivers, California; see also Haskell, "Kaweah," p. 321 and letter of J. J. Martin to Frank Been, March 3, 1933, in Sequoia National Park Office library archives.

47. Haskell, "Kaweah," pp. 317–18; Lewis, "Kaweah," pp. 432–33; See also *Treanor Farm News* 1 (October 1955), and Charles Keller's reminiscences in typescript at the Sequoia National Park office library archives. The General Grant Tree, the largest living thing, which is within the Kaweah boundaries, was named the Carl Marx Tree by Haskell, and the second largest living being, General Sherman Tree, was named by the Kaweahns for John Swinton.

48. Lewis, "Kaweah," p. 436; Haskell, "Kaweah," pp. 320–21.

49. Burnette G. Haskell, "How Kaweah Fell," *The Examiner* (San Francisco), November 29, 1891.

50. John P. Cosgrove, *San Francisco Call*, May 11, 1896, quoted in *Haskell Journal* 1 (1898), [The *Haskell Journal* was a short-lived genealogical magazine edited and published by Burnette G. Haskell. Its contents were limited to reports about the Haskell family], clipping, Haskell Family Papers; Haskell, "Kaweah," pp. 321–22.

51. Donald Edgar Walters, "Populism in California, 1889–1900" (Ph. D. diss., University of California, Berkeley, 1952), p. 19.

52. Burnette G. Haskell, "A Plan of Action," *The Nationalist* 2 (December 1889): 30; *The Commonwealth* 2 (June 24, 1889): 85–86; *The Examiner* (San Francisco), August 25, 1889, clipping in "Scraps Collected by Anna Haskell in relation to the Nationalist Movement, San Francisco, 1889," 117, Haskell Family Papers; George E. MacDonald, *Fifty Years of Freethought* (New York: The Truth Seeker Company, 1929), pp. 478–79; *Kaweah Commonwealth* 1 (November 15, 1890).

53. Haskell, "A Plan for Action," pp. 30–32; *The Commonwealth* 2 (April 24, 1889): 63; "An Easy Way To Get Rich," Haskell Family Papers; Walters, "Populism in California," p. 30 (note).

54. Walters, "Populism in California," p. 20, "San Francisco Nationalists: Accounts of Meetings of the Club Since the Thirteenth Public Reception," February 21, 1890, Haskell Family Papers.

55. *Oakland Daily Bulletin*, July 9, 1889, clipping in "Personal Reminiscences, Memoranda of Burnette G. Haskell," p. 153, Haskell Family Papers; "San Francisco Nationalists: Accounts of Meetings of the Club Since the Thirteenth Public Reception," Haskell Family Papers, February 21, 1890; Burnette G. Haskell, "Why I Am a Nationalist," in Hugo O. Pentecost *The Why I Ams*, ed. Hugo O. Pentecost (New York: Humboldt Publishing Co., 1892), pp. 29–31, 33, 34.

56. *Workmen's Advocate* 6 (May 17, 1890, May 31, 1890, and September 13, 1890); M.A. Hildebrand, corresponding secretary, San Francisco Nationalist Club, to the Officers and Members of Kaweah Colony, July 3, 1890, reprinted in *Kaweah Commonwealth* 1 (July 12, 1890).

57. "Dynamite Haskell," *San Francisco Star*, May 3, 1890, clipping in "Personal Notes: B. G. Haskell," pp. 93–94, Haskell Family Papers; *San Francisco Star*, March 22, 1890, in "Scraps Collected by Anna Haskell in Relation to the Nationalist Movement, San Francisco, 1889," p. 266, Haskell Family Papers; *Freethought*, November 9, 1889, clipping in "Scraps Collected by Anna Haskell in Relation to the Nationalist Movement, San Francisco, 1889," p. 150, Haskell Family Papers.

58. Royce D. Delmatier, Clarence F. McIntosh, and Earl G. Waters, *The Rumble of California Politics, 1849–1970* (New York: John Wiley & Sons, 1970), pp. 100–102; *San Francisco*

Chronicle, April 10, 1890, clipping in "Personal Notes: Burnette G. Haskell," pp. 8–9, Haskell Haskell Family Papers: *San Francisco Call,* April 10, 1890, clipping in "Personal Notes," p. 11,: Burnette G. Haskell," Haskell Family Papers; "Call for a State Convention of the National United Labor Party of California at Fresno, July 4, 1890," in "Personal Notes: Burnette G. Haskell," p. 103, Haskell Family Papers; *The People* 1 (April 3, 1892).

59. Burnette G. Haskell to "My Dear Wife," August 2, 1892, and Burnette G. Haskell to "My Dearest Wife," August 8, 1892, in "Personal Reminiscences, Memoranda of Burnette G. Haskell," Haskell Family Papers; Campaign handbills, Haskell Family Papers; *San Francisco Examiner,* August 4, 1894, clipping in "Personal Notes: Burnette G. Haskell," p. 106, Haskell Family Papers; *Examiner* (San Francisco), October 6, 1904, in "Personal Notes: Burnette G. Haskell," p. 111, Haskell Family Papers; Cosgrove, *San Francisco Call.*

60. Burnette G. Haskell to George C. Pardee, October 6, 1902, November 14, 1903; April 17, 1904, April 26, 1904, May 5, 1904, May 17, 1904, September 26, 1904, October 6, 1904, March 21, 1905, April 18, 1905, April 20, 1905 (telegram), December 26, 1905, October 25, 1906, all in George C. Pardee Papers, Bancroft Library, University of California, Berkeley; Burnette G. Haskell to Frank Roney, April 15, 1906, in Haskell Family Papers; Weintraub, *Andrew Furuseth,* p. 18.

61. MacDonald, *Fifty Years of Freethought,* pp. 478–79.

☙ *13* ❧

Nationalists and Populists

The Americanization of the Socialist movement was a complex process involving at least four distinct and, at times, antithetical aspects. The first was the rising quasi-Socialist-Nationalist movement, which had its basis in the writings of Edward Bellamy and, to a lesser extent, Laurence Gronlund. The second was the People's party, particularly its left wing in which Nationalists and nonparty Socialists played a significant role. The third was the more radical wing of the Social-Gospel movement in Protestant Christianity commonly called Christian Socialism. The fourth was the arrogant, despotic Daniel De Leon who helped speed the disintegration of the old Socialist Labor party (SLP).[1]

- 1 -

The first Socialist book to reach a major English-speaking American audience was a pedantic polemic, *The Co-operative Commonwealth*, written in 1884 by Danish-born lawyer-journalist Laurence Gronlund. It was, to quote long-time Milwaukee Socialist leader Frederic C. Heath, "the first . . . to place the new theory ['scientific' socialism] before American readers in a popular way." It was also the book that converted Eugene V. Debs to socialism as he testified in 1894.[2]

Gronlund, born in Copenhagen in 1846, had earned a law degree at the university in his home city at the age of nineteen. He came to the United States two years later and studied American law and taught school in Milwaukee until 1869, when he was admitted to the Illinois bar. After practicing law for a short time, he turned to journalism. During the great depression of the 1870s, Gronlund became a Socialist, joined the Socialist Labor party, and became an active Socialist agitator. His first major effort at pamphleteering, *The Coming Revolution*, was enlarged in 1884 into *The Co-operative Commonwealth*. This book, like the pamphlet, was a conglomeration of simplistic Marxian socialism, Social-Gospel Christianity, and authoritarian elitism.[3]

The basis for Gronlund's socialism was his assumption that under capitalism workers were basically slaves, and capitalists their masters. The workers'—or wage slaves'—position differed from that of chattel slaves in only two particulars: (1) the chattel slave sold all of his time to the master; the wage slave sold only about half of his time to the capitalist; (2) the chattel slave's master was obligated to care for him or her in sickness an in old age; the capitalist was under no such obligation to his workers. "In buying the labor, the employer thus buys virtually the body and soul of the worker for the time being." He thus "pockets a gain from the workingman without rendering an equivalent in return to society." Everyone who pockets gains without rendering an equivalent to society is a criminal. Therefore, "every millionaire is a criminal."[4] Socialism was thus a moral necessity, for it alone could eliminate the slavery of one class and the criminality of the other.

Gronlund's socialism involved more than mere morality. Socialism was more than a mere social system; it was also a philosophy of history that analyzed human affairs since the dawn of time. History was a series of logical progressions with each social system "a necessary step to each succeeding step." Capitalism was merely a transition to "the Golden Age ahead on whose threshold we stand." This simplistic, quasi-Marxist theory of history was based almost completely on the *Communist Manifesto*, which Gronlund paraphrased: "First slavery, then serfdom, then the wage system, and at last social cooperation."[5]

Since the revolution for which Gronlund agitated was historically inevitable, he assumed it would be peaceful. But he doubted it could be brought to full fruition without the use of coercive state power. The state's authority was, in Gronlund's view, limitless; it could do "anything whatsoever which is shown to be expedient" to achieve the new system. As far as the state was concerned, the end justified the means.[6]

The form a state took mattered little to Gronlund. What did matter was the economic system. The political structure, he maintained, was merely the inert machinery of society; the power to move it rested in economic conditions. Thus the political institutions were merely reflective of the economic system. In Gronlund's new Socialist system, the whole governmental structure would have to be revised. The parliamentary system—"a rude device for securing power to our *leading classes*"—would be dismantled, and presidents and governors would be eliminated. In fact, government as we now understand it would disappear. "The '*whole* people' does not want, or need, any 'government,' at all," Gronlund wrote. "It simply wants *administra-*

tion—good administration." The ideal system that Gronlund proposed was thus a world ruled by bureaucrats, for to him democracy meant *"Administration by the Competent."*[7] What about those who might object to "administration by the competent?" "When the Co-operative Commonwealth is achieved," Gronlund declared, "there will be no room for any more revolutions."[8]

Gronlund's view of the state was only one of several of his ideas that bear a striking resemblance to the ideas and practices of the Leninist and Stalinist movements. Gronlund also advocated the vanguard theory that postulates that only a small dedicated minority can make a revolution. He was basically an elitist.[9] The Communist concept of "democratic centralism" also originated with Gronlund.[10]

His socialism was thus a mixture of disparate theories, some humane, others oppressive; some egalitarian, others elitist. Most significantly, however, Gronlund was a product of his background; he was basically a middle-class North European who reflected the biases and myths of his class. Despite his Socialist pretentions, he was both an anti-Semite and an opponent of equality of the sexes. He considered Jews to be "speculators." He believed women to be different from men "in intellect . . . in temperament . . . in muscles." Moreover, he opposed sexual freedom and assumed that "sexual irregularities . . . will hardly be heard of as soon as . . . every young pair can marry without any fear of consequences."[11]

Gronlund's Utopia was thus a puritanic Victorian land ruled by bureaucrats enforcing political and social uniformity.

- 2 -

Industrial development reached fever pitch in the United States during the last quarter of the nineteenth century, bringing with it unbridled urban growth and population increase. At the same time, farm prices were declining and farm debt was increasing, forcing many rural residents into unpleasant urban environments. The result was severe social dislocation and economic suffering. These things, in turn, caused a growing sense of frustration, alienation, and rebelliousness among workers and farmers.

Whenever such disquiet and dissatisfaction permeate a society, attempts are made "to discover an escape from the conditions" that exist. Such attempts have almost invariably taken the form of romantic novels depicting a Utopia in which all the wrongs of contemporary society are corrected and where everyone lives in a condition of love, peace, and cooperation. The last quarter of the nineteenth century was no exception: between 1884 and 1900, at least fifty such novels were published.[12] Among the most popular was Edward Bellamy's *Looking Backward*, written in 1887, "the year of ten thousand strikes."[13]

The Bellamy book was probably the most influential single work in the development of an American Socialist movement. At the time of its appearance, it was hailed by virtually all radicals except the Anarchists. Burnette G. Haskell described *Looking Backward* as being for socialism what *Uncle Tom's Cabin* had been for antislavery movement thirty years earlier. The Socialist Labor party's National Executive Committee endorsed it and recommended it to its members. Stephen Leacock said that "No single influence ever brought its [socialism's] ideas and its propaganda so forcibly and clearly before the public mind as" had *Looking Backward*. Historian Charles A. Beard, philosopher John Dewey, and editor Edward Weeks of the *Atlantic Monthly* called it the most influential American book written between 1885 and 1935. Among the thousands of Americans influenced by the book were Mark Twain; Norman Thomas, national leader of the Socialist party from 1928 until his death in 1968; Jasper McLevy, long-time Socialist mayor of Bridgeport, Connecticut; and Gaylord Wilshire, Socialist publicist during the pre-World War I years. *Looking Backward's* role in winning Americans to socialism is without equal.[14]

The author of *Looking Backward*, Edward Bellamy, was a member of one of the oldest families in New England. His paternal ancestors settled in Connecticut in 1635, and on his maternal side, he descended from old-line Vermonters. His great-grandfather, a noted pre-Revolutionary War clergyman, was a lifelong friend of Jonathan Edwards. Bellamy's father was a Baptist minister, as was his maternal grandfather. Edward was born and lived most of his life in Chicopee Falls, Massachusetts, where his father had his church. Chicopee Falls is a section of the small, western Massachusetts manufacturing city of Chicopee. Its primary products during Bellamy's boyhood were cotton goods, armaments, paper, leather goods, bronze casting, and some farm machinery. During the midnineteenth century, when Bellamy was growing up, it was still basically a Yankee city, with a substantial French Canadian population—mainly sent to work in the mills. Eastern European migrants were to come to Chicopee later in the century.

The Bellamy home was religiously rigid, although Edward's father, The Reverend Rufus Bellamy, was considered a theological liberal by midnineteenth-century standards. Edward and his brothers—he was the third of four—attended two church services and Sunday School each Sunday and prayer services at least once daily. At fourteen, Bellamy accepted Christianity and was baptized.[15]

The Civil War raged during Bellamy's most impressionable years—he was eleven years old when it began and fifteen when it ended. The parades and martial atmosphere of the war years impressed Bellamy, who decided to make the military his career. His health, however, was poor, and when he attempted to enter West Point in 1867, he failed the physical examination after passing all other entrance tests. His rejection at West Point was a severe blow to young Bellamy. He attempted for a short time to study at Union College, but he soon dropped out.[16]

He went to Europe in the fall of 1868 and spent a lot of time in Germany and Britain, primarily in their industrial cities. He was disturbed by the poverty of the working class and peasantry in both countries. From 1869, when he returned to the United States, until 1871, when he was admitted to the Massachusetts bar, Bellamy read law. But his first case disillusioned him, and he abandoned the practice of law and turned to journalism. He worked first on the *New York Evening Post* and then on the *Springfield Daily Union*. In 1877 Bellamy's health failed, and he went to Hawaii. After a year, he returned to the mainland and turned to the writing of fiction. Most of his books were of little importance. [17]

One book, *The Duke of Stockbridge: A Romance of Shays' Rebellion*, serialized in 1879 in the Great Barrington, Massachusetts, *Berkshire Current*, has at times been cited as proof that Bellamy had become a social radical years before *Looking Backward* first appeared. But a careful reading of the work would not support this contention. First, the novel was written for publication in an area where many—probably most—of the residents descended from participants in Shays's Rebellion, a farmers' uprising against high taxes in 1786–1787, and where the population tended to be sympathetic with their rebellious ancestors. Second, although the novel is sympathetic to the farmer-rebels and antagonistic to the moneylenders and lawyers, it is hardly a call to social revolution—it was basically a romantic "pot-boiler," typical of the late 1870s.[18]

Although the *Duke of Stockbridge* did not portend Bellamy's later radicalism, he was no doubt inclined toward socialism years before he wrote *Looking Backward*. Bellamy's own testimony about the origins of his socialism is contradictory. "I have never been in any sense a student of Socialistic literature, or have known more of the various Socialist schemes than any readers on newspapers might," he wrote to William Dean Howells a few months after *Looking Backward* appeared. A year later, he denied that he had any intention of "attempting a serious contribution to the movement for social reform" with the writing of the book; it was a "mere literary fantasy, a fairy tale of social felicity." He told Abraham Cahan that he first became acquainted with socialism after he had completed most of *Looking Backward*.

Bellamy was being less than candid. He had already been introduced to socialism by reading Gronlund's *Co-operative Commonwealth*. In 1894 Bellamy himself conceded that he wrote the book as a Socialist work: "I sat down to my desk with the definite purpose of trying to reason out a method of economic organization by which the republic might guarantee the livelihood and material welfare of its citizens on a basis of equality corresponding to and supplementing their political equality."[19] Moreover, he wrote in his personal journal in 1868 that his eyes had been "opened [in Europe] to the extent and consequences of man's inhumanity to man." As early as 1873, he wrote an editorial against child labor: "Civilization does not deserve the name in any land, if it cannot run its business enterprises of whatever kind, indoor or outdoor, without such a sacrifice of human rights and well being." The same year, Bellamy said it was the "dream of socialism to introduce democracy into the industrial world." He was, however, not certain that socialism was realizable; "experience only can show." During the late 1870s, he spoke of the need for a social reform that would eliminate the oppression of workingmen by the "classes privileged by wealth." He believed that it was now possible to establish a Socialist system. Three years before *Looking Backward* appeared, Bellamy told acquaintances that he "was developing with the eloquence of sincerity, his philosophy of the insignificance of the individual and the greatness of the commonwealth."[20]

Some conservative critics called *Looking Backward* a satire on socialism. But Bellamy considered it a serious work of propaganda. It was written as a "forecast, in accordance with the principles of evolution, of the next stage in the industrial and social development of humanity." So sure was Bellamy of the book's propaganda value that he wrote his publisher six months after publication, "If you will kindly sell 5,000 copies of *Looking Backward* for me, I will engage to give the voters a platform worth voting for, and the votes, too."[21]

The book sold well over 5,000 copies, and Bellamy and his associates devised a platform "worth voting for." When *Looking Backward* first appeared, in January 1888, it received critical attention, but its sales were slow. By the end of the year, it had sold only 10,000 copies. But during 1889 it became a best-seller: about 210,000 copies were bought that year, and demand reached 10,000 copies a week by December. Its success can be attributed to the fact that it offered an apparently practical plan for solving the problems of the period without too much disruption. Unlike most other Utopias, *Looking Backward* happened in a familiar place, was based upon possible happenings, and used inventions already known—and some already in use during the late nineteenth century—and it evolved historically. It was a conceivable Utopia. Bellamy was not "a romantic poet"; he was basically a pragmatic social theorist. The great muckraker Ida M. Tarbell put it succinctly: "Of all Utopias which men, revolting against the bitter world in which we live, have created to stir the imagination and raise the hopes of the people of the earth, none has ever been so substantial, so realistic, so seemingly practical. A dream—yes—but a dream built upon materials in our hands."[22]

- 3 -

Written in the form of a novel, *Looking Backward* was basically a polemic against Social Darwinism, the quasi-scientific rationalization for the rapacious laissez faire capitalism then prevalent in the United States. During the nineteenth century, Bellamy wrote, "it was firmly and sincerely believed that there was no other way [than laissez faire capitalism] in which society could get along . . . that no very radical improvement even was possible. . . . It had always been as it was, and it always would be."[23] It was to prove that this was wrong, that Bellamy created *Looking Backward*.

The "awkward and pretentious" novel tells a simple story: Julian West, a thirty-year-old Bostonian falls asleep on May 30, 1887, and awakens 113 years later in the year 2000—still in Boston. But it is a much changed city—music is piped into every home; there is no poverty, nor are there any banks.[24] The changes had been achieved early in the twentieth century by a peaceful revolution that had transformed society from an inefficient, capitalist social and economic order into a new, efficient, cooperative commonwealth. The change had occurred without violence; Labor parties, Socialist parties, and strikes had played no part in the peaceful revolution. Actually, Bellamy claimed, radicals had, because of their immoderate, often violent, rhetoric, hindered rather than aided the cause. The new epoch came into being only after the American people had voted the Nationalist party into power. Moreover, the change had occurred with a minimum of dislocation, because the public had been prepared for it by economic conditions. Thus all classes of society favored the new social order, by the time it was effectuated, and it was achieved without bitterness.[25] The peacefulness of the revolution had in great part been due to the industrial monopolies, whose growth, Bellamy argued, had proven "the feasibility of organizing and centralizing the administration of capital on a scale of corresponding magnitude." He cited the Knights of Labor, the Federation of Trades (as the American Federation of Labor was then known), the Grangers, and the Farmers' Alliance as proof that the workers and farmers had also been drawn into huge economic organizations. Economic concentration was the basis on which socialism had been built during the twentieth century in Bellamy's Boston. The only differences between the monopolies in the late nineteenth century and those in the new epoch were ownership and purpose. Monopolies under the capitalist system were privately owned; those in Bellamy's Utopia were owned by the nation. The chief objective of the privately owned monopolies was profit; under Bellamy's system, production would be motivated solely by social need. Monopolies were thus the logical antecedents of socialism.[26]

The manpower for the new nationalized "Great Trust" would come from an "Industrial Army" composed of every able-bodied citizen between the ages of twenty-one and forty-five. The idea of an Industrial Army reflected Bellamy's lifelong infatuation with the military. "All able-bodied citizens are held bound to fight for the nation," he said. "Why not extend this accepted principle to industry and hold every able-bodied citizen bound to work for the nation." The Industrial Army would be organized along military lines. Most workers would be in the ranks. Their superiors would hold titles of assistant foreman, the equivalent of a lieutenant; foreman, for captain; superintendency, for colonel; general of guild, for major general; chief of one of the ten divisions, for lieutenant general; and general in chief for the president. Appointments would be from lower ranks to higher ranks on the basis of excellence. General of guild would be elected by retirees more than forty-five years of age; workers under the age of forty-five could not vote. The general in chief—the president—would also be chosen from among former department heads by a vote of the retirees only.[27] The new system would be an administrative state—a bureaucratic heaven. The legislature would meet every five years; its sole power would be to receive a report from the president, which it could either accept or condemn. The real power would be in the hands of "minor" civil service officials.

The new system would have a free press, privately controlled. The government would not interfere with it. Readers would have the right to hire and fire editors.[28] But little opposition to the system would be allowed. Any person who neglected his work, did "bad work," or showed other "remissness" would discover that the discipline in the Industrial Army was exceedingly strict. "A person able to do duty, and persistently refusing is sentenced to solitary imprisonment on bread and water till he consents."[29]

Nor would women be placed on an absolutely equal footing with men. They would be freed from the drudgery of housework and would be drafted automatically into the Industrial Army, where they would serve for ten to fifteen years, with time out for maternity. But women, "being inferior in strength to men, and further disqualified industrially in special ways," would be limited to specific jobs. Their pay would equal that of men, but they would not participate in the rule of the state. In fact, a separate president and other public officials would look after women's interests. Women would, in effect, be auxiliaries to the Industrial Army.[30]

Looking Backward described a society where economic security would be assured to each individual from the cradle to the grave. Each citizen would be assured of exactly the same income as his neighbor; his education would be free, uniform, and compulsory; his health would be guaranteed, and his physical well-being assured. Society would have no private charity, for it would not be needed. Bellamy believed that "the right of a man to maintenance at the nation's table depends on the fact that he is a man, and not on the amount of health and strength he may have, so long as he does his best." In effect, Bellamy proposed that the nation "write for every member [of society] an endowment policy."[31]

Bellamy's Utopia for 2000 A.D. was thus a well-regimented, albeit happy, welfare state dominated by bureaucrats.

- 4 -

In view of the conditions of industrial and social discontent prevalent in the United States, it was natural that *Looking Backward* became an almost instantaneous best-seller with great and immediate political impact. Even before *Looking Backward* appeared, educated, native-born Americans had attempted to form Socialistic societies divested of the Germanic attributes of the SLP. One of these societies, organized by retired Civil War Captain Charles E. Bowers and General A. F. Devereaux, both of whom had been converted to socialism by Gronlund's *Co-operative Commonwealth*, was the immediate predecessor of the Nationalist Clubs, the Bellamyite political organizations. It was one of the elements from which the first Nationalist Club was formed in Boston in late 1888. The other came from suggestions by two Boston journalists, Cyrus Field Willard and Sylvester Baxter, that Bellamy help form such a club. Bellamy agreed. At the same time, the pro-Socialist, retired, Civil War officers informed Bellamy that their club had adopted his book as its own. At Bellamy's suggestion, Baxter and Willard contacted the military men and after long negotiation united with them to form the First Nationalist Club of Boston in December 1888.[32]

The First Club was to be a model for all future Nationalist groups. Its membership was composed almost exclusively of upper middle-class professionals; virtually no one from the working class was a member (except in California, where Burnette G. Haskell was to be one of the organization's leaders during its shortlived heyday). Membership was generally limited by design to "the intelligent and the educated." The upper middle-class intellectuals who dominated the Nationalist movement made it an implied condition of membership that an applicant be "successful in the present fierce competitive struggle." It was thus expected that the clubs could bar the "crank and uneducated foreigner importing ideas declared to be 'exotic.' " Cyrus F. Willard reported in 1889 that "Men and women of wealth, brains and of heart are interested." The largest professional groups in the clubs were clergymen, lawyers, journalists, and physicians; a majority of the members were women. W. D. P. Bliss, the Christian Socialist, reported that most of the Nationalists were as worried by the militant leaders of labor unions as they were by the "grasping tycoons of finance and industry."[33]

Among the members of the Boston club were famous persons such as Edward Everett Hale, the Unitarian minister and author; William Dean Howells; Colonel Thomas Wentworth Higginson, writer, poet, and Civil War hero; Frances Willard, leader of the Women's Christian Temperance Union; Lucy Stone and Mary A. Livemore, both leaders in the woman's rights movement; Rabbi Solomon Schindler; Laurence Gronlund; and John Boyle O'Reilly, poet and editor of *The Pilot*, official publication of the Boston Roman Catholic Archdiocese. Many of the 200 members of the club were Theosophists, members of a mystic religious movement led by Helen Blavatsky, who favored Nationalism, as defined by Bellamy, but who rejected mundane political or social action. *Looking Backward* had evoked a "mild form of hysteria" throughout the United States among professionals with humanitarian instincts—"that neurotic crowd that invades all new catchy movements and abandons them when the novelty has passed," to quote Frank Roney, the California labor leader of that period. To a rabbi, who was soon to abandon his pulpit to preach Nationalism to "both Jew and Gentile," Bellamy's Utopia was Judaism come to fruition; to followers of Mary Baker Eddy, "it was Christian Science." Theosophists saw in it Theosophy, some Spiritualists claimed that it was in harmony with their beliefs, and Christian ministers "were heard to affirm they were Nationalists because they were Christians." The range of beliefs was great, and they grew with the increasing membership. By mid-1889 Nationalist organizations were established in Boston, Hartford, New York, Chicago, Portsmouth (New Hampshire), Albany, Springfield (Massachusetts), Lehigh (Iowa), Independence (Kansas), Los Angeles, San Francisco, San Diego, Oakland, Lynn (Massachusetts), Minneapolis, Brooklyn, Kansas City, and throughout California. In San Francisco the Nationalist Club operated reading rooms that were open all day. Nor were all of the Nationalists members of the "Neurotic crowd." Among the Nationalists were General Abner Doubleday, the "father of baseball"; Thomas Davidson, founder of the Fellowship of the New Life, from which Britain's Fabian Society developed; Florence Kelley, who was later to gain fame as a social worker; Clarence Darrow, the great attorney; and future Socialist leaders such as Jesse Cox and Corrine Brown of Chicago, Algernon Lee and A. S. Edwards, of Minneapolis, and H. Gaylord Wilshire of Los Angeles.[34]

Nor were those who "found" elements of their own religions in Nationalism unjustified. Bellamy himself said that "The platform of Nationalism [is] 'Thy kingdom come; Thy will be done on earth as it is in heaven.' "[35] A careful reading of the platform of the First Nationalist Club of Boston, which became the movement's universally accepted official statement of principles, would show elements of Theosophy, Unitarianism, Social-Gospel Protestant Christianity, Prophetic Judaism, and Fabian Socialism. Its chief thrust, however, was its assault upon Social Darwinism and predatory capitalism. It differed little from any standard Socialist platform of the period, except for its religious passages. The platform called competition "simply the application of the brutal law of the survival of the strongest and most cunning." It decried the wrongs and inefficiencies created by that system. In its stead, the Nationalists pledged to replace wage slavery and the whole competitive capitalist system with a new cooperative Socialist social order.[36]

The Nationalist movement was a loosely federated group of clubs, with no central organization, linked together by a common belief in Bellamy's Utopia, which each interpreted in his own way.[37] Its intellectual diversity and lack of organization were to be key factors in the movement's early demise.

- 5 -

The leaders of the Socialist Labor party were elated at the appearance of the Nationalist Clubs. The fact that Friedrich Engels had denigrated the Bellamy followers made little difference. Nor did the fact that Bellamy's views were in many ways identical with those of the non-Marxian Socialist Wilhelm Weitling modify the enthusiasm of the American Marxists. The Socialists had great hopes that the Nationalist movement would swell their ranks and Americanize their movement. Within a year after its publication, *Looking Backward* had become the predominant topic for the educational propaganda meetings of the SLP.[38] Serge Shevitch, a leader of the party, assured the delegates to the party's 1889 national convention in Chicago that "The essentially American movement known under the name of 'Nationalism' . . . is in reality nothing else but socialism pure and simple."[39] When the Nationalist Club of Boston adopted its declaration of principles, the SLP organ, *Workmen's Advocate*, reported that it "embodies the principles of the S.L.P." Its Boston correspondent assured its readers that the Nationalist Clubs were "no *dilletante* movement but an organized force of honest and educated men who are willing to suffer for their ideas. Although not of us [working class], they are for and with us and will be a potent factor in the remodeling of society."[40] Gaylord Wilshire, who was active in both the Nationalist and Socialist organizations, told the Philadelphia SLP that the two movements were essentially the same, except that the membership of the Socialist Labor party came from the working class, and the followers of Bellamy came primarily from the middle class.[41]

Most American Marxists realized the propaganda potential of the Nationalist Clubs, and many joined. Florence Kelley and Charles Sotheran became members of the New York Nationalist Club, and in San Francisco, SLP members enlisted in Burnette G. Haskell's Nationalist movement.[42] In other cities, too, wherever the SLP and Nationalists both existed, dual membership was a common phenomenon. The results were gratifying to the SLPers. In Los Angeles a Socialist Labor party organization was formed from members of the Nationalist Clubs. In Cleveland the SLP and the Nationalists ran a joint election campaign. In Rhode Island the Nationalists adopted word for word the platform of the Socialist Labor party. At the same time, the Chicago Nationalists voted unanimously to endorse the local SLP platform and support trade unionist Thomas J. Morgan, the Socialist Labor party candidate for mayor. Daniel De Leon, a recent convert to socialism and a member of both the Socialist Labor party and the Nationalist Club of New York, was elated by the Chicago endorsement; Nationalist support and agitation, he argued, were an effective means of "disarming opposition." Moreover, the Nationalists "have access to . . . men and women and societies which the Socialists cannot reach, and where they [can] sow a seed that never could otherwise have been sowed."[43]

Just as the Socialists saw the propaganda advantages inherent in a native American movement agreeing with their aims, so Bellamy and his lieutenants realized the problems the Socialists could cause them. The Nationalist leadership feared contamination by the foreign Marxists, whom they suspected of atheism, belief in violence, and "sexual novelties."[44] However, some agreement existed among Nationalists that Marx was an outstanding Socialist thinker. W. C. Owen, a Marxist-Nationalist and one-time close associate of Burnette G. Haskell, wrote a laudatory review of Marx's *magnum opus, Das Kapital,* in Bellamy's weekly, *The New Nation.* It was, he said, "the leading classic on the [labor] question."[45] But Bellamy and the more devout of his followers were generally hostile to the Marxists. Bellamy was willing to concede that both he and the members of the SLP were Socialists. But he argued that *socialism* was a basically indefinite term; "to say one is a socialist or believes in socialism is not . . . a sufficiently accurate definition of his position." Nationalism was only one of many species of socialism. Bellamy insisted that it differed from Marxian socialism on four vital issues: (1) how socialized industries were to be administered; (2) economic equality; (3) violence; and (4) the class struggle.[46]

Bellamy claimed that the Marxists proposed placing the administration of each industry in the hands of associations of its workingmen, loosely united in a "sort of confederation of guilds, each controlling for its own benefit some province of industry." He claimed this proposal had been made originally by Marx's International Workingmen's Association. Bellamy wanted the industries to be controlled by existing municipal, state, and national governments. Bellamy was inaccurate. Neither Marx, nor his international had ever proposed such an organization of industry. The only plan similar to the one mentioned by Bellamy had been proposed by the Anarchist International Working People's Association in Pittsburgh in 1883. In fact, no difference could be seen on this issue between Bellamy and the Marxists; the disagreement had been manufactured by the Nationalist leader.[47] As for economic equality, it was, likewise, a nonissue. True, the Nationalists did insist upon absolute economic equality. All workers, no matter their jobs, sex, or efficiency, were to receive the same pay under Nationalism. But it was not true, as Sylvester Baxter would argue, that Marxists would continue "distinctions and gradations . . . now dominant . . . with all their baneful effects." In fact, members of the SLP disagreed a lot on this issue; most appear to have supported Bellamy's stance.[48] On the issue of revolution and violence, too, only minimal disagreement was evident. True, the Socialist-Laborites, although they favored peaceful means, were prepared to use violent methods to prevent a counterrevolutionary force from seizing power after the Socialists had been elected into office. But virtually all of the Marxists opposed the use of extra-legal means to achieve power—in fact, they had fought against Johann Most and his Anarcho-Communists over precisely that issue. Unlike Bellamy, however, they did not equate their peaceful revolution with Christianity. Socialists spoke of socialism in material terms and opposed violence on material grounds; Bellamy, on the contrary, maintained that nationalism was "the express doctrine of Jesus Christ, and the very heart and essence of his religion." He thus rejected violence as a Christian. Moreover, he argued that socialism, being an ideal of eternal peace, could be achieved only by peaceful means, because means invariably became ends. Except for the religious orientation of Bellamy's argument, it differed little from the American Marxists' position.[49]

On the issue of the class struggle, an apparent difference could be seen between the Marxists and the Nationalists. But even on this issue, the disagreement was theoretical rather than practical. "Nationalism knows no class feeling," Bellamy wrote, "but appeals equally to all classes to join in abolishing class." Bellamy argued, "We war with systems, not with men." It was not the private capitalist whom the Nationalists viewed as their enemy; "we fully recognize the dependence upon his initiative of the working masses at present." Bellamy believed that the wealthy capitalists, just like the workers, were enslaved by the system. The Nationalists had no bitterness toward the individual or classes; their sole aim was to destroy a system and construct a new one. Laurence Gronlund, in arguing for Nationalism, emphasized the differences with regard to the class struggle. He charged that the Marxists, whom he called German Socialists, "lay undue stress on Socialism being a class-movement." He accused the SLPers of artificially dividing the world into workers and capitalists and then preaching a virtual class war between them. The Nationalists, on the contrary, divided the world between the "poor, the suffering," and their allies—"the noble, the progressive, and the patriotic on one side"; and "the ignorant and the selfish who find their advantage in the present social anarchy" on the opposite side.[50] The Nationalist disagreement with the Socialists on the issue of the class struggle was obviously exaggerated; both were essentially at war with the system. In fact, they had only two differences between them: the Nationalists appealed primarily to the educated segment of the middle class; the Socialists appealed to the working class. The Nationalists expected that the revolution could be accomplished by "our intellectual classes"; the Marxists anticipated that the working class would "emancipate" itself.[51] Thus although Socialists were active in the labor movement, most of Bellamy's followers were indifferent to it. Some were even hostile. Generally, Nationalists believed that the time had passed for labor unions to have any effect on social conditions. "The question which the masses are interested in now is not whether they are a little better or worse off than at some other time, but whether they are as well off as they might be under different industrial and social arrangements," *The New Nation* editorialized. Michael Lynch, a leader of the Boston plasterers local, confessed after his conversion to Nationalism that he now had "but little faith in the promises of Trade Unionists." Bellamy's position was less severe; he insisted only that "no mere organizations of labor . . . will alone solve the problem of securing permanent employment on favorable terms."[52]

Although Bellamy supported the strikers during the bloody walkout of steel mill hands at Homestead, Pennsylvania, in 1892, he still insisted that unions were of little use, that only a Socialist system could be of any use to the workers.[53]

The differences between the Marxists and the Nationalists were thus greatly exaggerated by Bellamy. They agreed on almost all issues. On those where they did not concur—the class struggle and trade unions—the disagreements were more theoretical than real. Why then did Bellamy exaggerate the differences? Why did he attempt to build so wide a chasm between his movement and the Socialist Labor party? Bellamy inadvertently conceded the real reason during an interview with Abraham Cahan, the future Socialist leader, journalist, and novelist: Bellamy doubted that a Marxist-Socialist movement could ever succeed in the United States,[54] but that a new political party, with genuine mass support, was being born. Bellamy was intent on playing a significant role in the organization of this new People's party, whose followers were predominantly native-born farmers, merchants, and workingmen. The alien Marxian Socialists might prove embarrassing for him among the People's followers.

- 6 -

Bellamy often derided social reform. He proclaimed that Nationalism "takes the place of all other reforms."[55] But that was mere rhetoric. In fact, the Nationalists were active in innumerable causes during the movement's heyday. The Los Angeles clubs were active in the struggle for the Australian ballot, direct legislation, and the abolition of private municipal franchises; the Oakland group was at the forefront in the battle against child labor; New York City Nationalists agitated for better school laws, municipal ownership of the city's rapid transit system, factory legislation that would protect the city's children, and laws that would outlaw the tenement sweat shops; the Philadelphia organization was commended for its work in investigating public works deficiencies and industrial conditions; and the Massachusetts clubs campaigned for lower utilities rates and for municipal ownership of gas, electric, and transit systems.[56]

As long as Nationalists spoke in terms of Utopia alone, they could ignore partisan political action and devote themselves to intellectual polemicizing. But once they became engaged in pragmatic reform, most Nationalists turned to practical partisan politics. The first result was a wave of defections from the movement; the Theosophists, who made up a sizeable minority of the membership and who controlled the movement's monthly magazine, *The Nationalists*, left. Their magazine went out of existence, and, in its stead, Bellamy published a weekly, *The New Nation*.[57]

The Nationalists were optimistic about the political outlook. They forecast that Nationalists would be in control of the United States by 1950. Bellamy proclaimed as early as 1889 that "Fifty years will see our entire program accomplished." Nationalists generally spoke of "The American Revolution of 1950." In 1891, after the Nationalists entered their first statewide election contest in Rhode Island, the *New Bedford Evening Journal* editorialized that the "Nationalists have better prospects of becoming a strong third party than any of the third parties now in the field." But the election results contradicted the optimistic predictions: the Nationalists polled only 472 votes, after raising only $25 for campaign expenses. An avowed Socialist, Gaylord Wilshire, who ran for Congress in Los Angeles on the Nationalist ticket polled a respectable 1,000 votes. But the party in California was soon torn asunder in a struggle for power between the Socialist faction headed by Burnette G. Haskell and the anti-Socialist faction of politicians attracted to the movement by its high vote. The latter were aided by a group of anti-Haskell Marxists.[58]

Neither the dismal showing in Rhode Island nor the internal dissension engendered by the respectable vote in California dampened the Nationalist's ardor for political action. By 1891 they were no longer alone, for they had become part of the new People's party. The new party was itself an alliance of some basically disparate groups: the Farmers' Alliances of the West and South—including black southern agrarians—Knights of Labor, impoverished small merchants, victims of the trusts, and western Socialists and followers of Bellamy. Although the Nationalists, at best, were a secondary source of strength for the Populist movement, Bellamy's book was hailed as its literary godfather. Populist strength was greatest in the newly admitted states on the prairies and the Pacific Coast where "the reception of 'Looking Backward' was most general and enthusiastic." Van B. Prather, state lecturer of the Kansas Farmers' Alliance, called Bellamy's *Looking Backward* the ideological substructure of the People's party. One "brawny farmer" assured Bellamy at the 1892 St. Louis conference of Populists, "Talk about Nationalism, why, west of the Mississippi we are all Nationalists."[59]

The influence of the Nationalists on the People's party and its program, however, was minimal. Despite a preamble that could have won support of even the most doctrinaire Marxist, the platforms themselves were, at best, reformist. "Wealth belongs to him who creates it," the declaration of the St. Louis national conference of 1892 proclaimed. "Every dollar taken from industry without its equivalent is robbery. 'If any will not work neither shall they eat.' The interests of rural and urban labor are the same; their enemies are identical." But the program merely called for a national currency; a sub-treasury system; $50 per capita in circulating currency; economy in government; an end to land monopoly; and restrictions against the liquor trade. The four most radical, and most ignored, planks urged a graduated income tax, a postal savings system, full universal suffrage without regard to race or sex for all over twenty-one years of age, and nationalization of communications and transportation. The platform adopted at the later Omaha convention was little changed from the St. Louis document, except for a strong stand against immigration and alien land ownership. The convention at Omaha had a few new prolabor planks—one calling for the outlawing of company and private police forces, another for an enforced eight-hour day on government work—and a call for political reforms. But none was Socialist.[60]

Bellamy was disappointed. He was particularly distressed that the Populists failed to call for public ownership of monopolies "when they become oppressive," and because the party platform ignored the coal operators' control of supply, which they reduced to increase prices at the same time that they "oppress their employees in a way that is a national disgrace." But Bellamy did not waver from his support of the new party, although he conceded that it was not an "ideal organization from the standpoint of Nationalism." He argued, however, that the party platform could eventually be made more Nationalist. But this could be achieved only "by cordially joining hands with the People's Party and lending our efforts to secure its success." He saw the People's party as a fertile field in which "to do Nationalistic missionary work among its membership."[61] In fact, Populism had the opposite effect; the People's party was responsible, in great part, for the final, total collapse of the Nationalist movement. Although almost a third of the 1,654 delegates at the Omaha convention were Nationalists, they formed no cohesive body. Nationalists had no national organization to unite and lead them. An impromtu meeting of 200 or 300 Bellamyites held at the convention accomplished little and organized no continuing body. Moreover, once the campaign began, Nationalists became so deeply committed to the Populists that they ceased their Nationalist activity. As a result, virtually all of the clubs disappeared.[62] Besides destroying the clubs, the Populist campaigns succeeded in driving the SLP and the remaining Nationalists apart. The Bellamy-dominated Massachusetts Populists ran a full slate in the 1891 Massachusetts state election against the Socialist-Laborites. Neither party did particularly well: the Populists polled 2,832 votes statewide, the SLP candidates polled only 1,798. But it infuriated the Marxists—particularly their newfound leader, ex-Nationalist Daniel De Leon. The "People's Party drew its first and last breath," De Leon wrote after the election. "The capitalists know they have nothing to fear for their stolen goods and their criminal system but from the Socialists."[63] Not all Socialists, of course, agreed.

Julius A. Wayland, the future publisher of the *Appeal to Reason*, the largest Socialist journal ever published in the United States, wrote: "All [Populist] leaders and practically all the followers are as true and earnest Socialists as you eastern chaps." The Populists were merely giving "the patient a few doses of the money problem to get him in a condition to absorb" Socialist propaganda. Christian Socialist W. D. P. Bliss also reported that the Populists were "coming to favour a complete Socialist programme." Even SLPer Charles A. Sotheran was deeply impressed by the more than one million votes cast by the People's party and worked for a merger of the two parties.[64] Similarly, reciprocity came from the agrarian wing of the Populists. The *Farmer's Alliance*, the Populist newspaper in Lincoln, Nebraska, declared that an actual irreconcilable state of war existed under the capitalist system. Peace could only come after the present competitive system was abolished, for "Competition is only another name for war."[65]

As a result, less doctrinaire Socialists, especially in the West, left the SLP and went into the Populists. In 1894 the Chicago Socialists virtually disbanded to support the Populist campaign of Henry Demarest Lloyd. So, too, did other Socialists repelled by the dogmatism that permeated the SLP.[66] The Milwaukee party, for example, became a Populist organization headed by Victor Berger, and in Iowa a group of Populist-Socialists, led by John Work, formed the Iowa Socialist party.

As Bellamy became more involved in the Populist movement, he became more deeply committed to social reform. But his movement had disappeared, and by 1894 he was forced to abandon his weekly newspaper. Even Christian Socialists were now abandoning his movement, which they labelled Utopian.[67] By 1895 the People's party itself had become "boss-ridden, ring-ruled, gang-gangrened." Professional politicians who had neither ideals nor morals had moved into positions of control and the Socialist-Nationalist position disintegrated. Although the politicians failed to rid the 1895 platform of all Socialist or Nationalist planks, they succeeded by the 1896 convention. The delegates, at that convention, were a disparate collection of Greenbackers, antimonopolists, Socialists, Nationalists, third-party people who simply opposed the two major parties, and politicians who had abandoned whatever principles they once had in the hope of electoral victory. They were united on one thing only, to quote from the report in the *New York Sun*: an "extraordinary hatred of Jews . . . and of particular Jews who happen to have prospered in the world."[68] The politicians controlled the convention from the start by a series of maneuvers. The resolution committee was packed, any pro-Socialist plank was deleted. The chairman refused to recognize any opponent of the ruling clique. The platform and resolutions were adopted amid noise well orchestrated from the 1,500 delegates and thousands of spectators. An effort, initiated by starving, blacklisted Pullman strikers, to nominate their leader, Eugene V. Debs, for president was dropped after Debs wired that he would not run. The convention then nominated the grandiloquent, but hardly radical, Democratic nominee, William Jennings Bryan, who promised to support free silver. With his nomination, the People's party died.[69]

Bellamy supported Bryan in the 1896 campaign. Some of his friends and supporters—most notably Henry Demarest Lloyd—refused and voted for the Socialist Labor party. But most, including Bliss, Debs, and William E. Foster, who was later to gain fame as William Z. Foster, supported Bryan.[70]

Bryan lost the election. Bellamy was left with no organization and no political party. He was sorely disappointed; he wrote to Lloyd asking that they jointly call a conference of leading radicals to form a new distinctly Socialist party. "We do not want any more fooling; and the country is ready for plain talk." Victor Berger, leader of the pro-Socialist Milwaukee Populists, also appealed to Lloyd to help form a new Socialist party. But Lloyd was not interested in organization, and Bellamy's health was failing.[71]

Bellamy made one last effort to rouse the American people. Despite a debilitating illness, he wrote a new book, *Equality*. It argued that the chief determinant in a man's future was neither race nor education nor social origins nor his morality nor whether "beautiful or ugly, saint or scamp." The single most important factor was a man's wealth. The time had now come, he wrote, when men could control their economic status socially; and this revolution was possible because of the "unending diffusion of knowledge."[72] But the book failed—it reached few readers. Except for Socialist reprints of an interesting passage from the book—"The Parable of the Water Tank"—it is virtually forgotten. Bellamy never knew that his last book was a failure: he died in May 1898, about a year after the book appeared.[73]

By the time of his death, Bellamy's movement had virtually disappeared. Occasional books and pamphlets came from the Bureau of Nationalist Literature in Philadelphia, but few clubs existed, and these few were spread throughout the world. An effort to form an American Fabian Society composed of Nationalists, Christian Socialists, and Marxists failed, although it did produce a short-lived, albeit interesting, Socialist magazine.[74] During the depression of the 1930s, Bellamy clubs again sprang up throughout the United States, particularly in California where they filled the Hollywood Bowl for a mass meeting in 1934, and where they spearheaded Upton Sinclair's unsuccessful End Poverty in California (EPIC) campaign for governor in 1934. That year Nationalist clubs reported 600,000 members in seventeen states. But dissension soon permeated the movement and it disintegrated again.[75]

Bellamy, and his romantic novel, did more than any other writer to spread socialism in America. His book helped convert thousands of Americans to a recognition of social responsibility and occasionally socialism.

The Nationalist movement, albeit short lived, was a major factor in the early years of the Populist movement that swept the country in the early 1890s. The book plus the movement it helped organize played a leading role in the birth of the Socialist party of America and thus in the Americanization of socialism in the United States.

NOTES

1. See, for example, Howard H. Quint, *The Forging of American Socialism: Origins of the Modern Movement* (Columbia, S.C.: University of South Carolina Press, 1953).

2. Frederic Heath, ed., *Social Democracy Red Book* (Terre Haute, Ind.: Debs Publishing Company, 1900), p. 42; Ray Ginger, *The Bending Cross* (New Brunswick, N.J.: Rutgers University Press, 1949), pp. 155–56. Debs argued, at the 1894 Pullman Strike hearing, that he was *not* a Socialist, because he had been converted to belief in a cooperative commonwealth by Gronlund rather than by Marx.

3. Heath, *Social Democracy*, pp. 101–2; *The Labor Enquirer* (Chicago) 1 (September 10, 1887): 1; Stow Persons, Introduction to *The Co-operative Commonwealth*, by Laurence Gronlund (Cambridge, Mass.: Harvard University Press, 1965), pp. x–xii, xxi; Laurence Gronlund to "Comrades," November 10, 1879, SLP Collection, Wisconsin State Historical Society, Madison, Wisconsin. Gronlund remained active in the Socialist Labor party until 1890 when he joined the Nationalist movement. He wrote three books after *The Co-operative Commonwealth*. None was successful. Gronlund revised *The Co-operative Commonwealth* in 1890, eliminating any reference to the class struggle. At the time of his death in 1899, he was employed with the Department of Statistics of Labor under Carroll Wright. He was by then a Social-Gospel Christian, closely allied with The Reverend W. D. P. Bliss in the American Fabian Society and the Social Reform Union. Joseph Buchanan, the radical editor of the Chicago *Labor Enquirer*, said of Gronlund that he exhibited "the mild virtues of a Melancthon rather than the fiery zeal of a Luther."

4. Laurence Gronlund, "The Nationalization of Industry," *The Nationalist* 1 (June 1889): 35–36; Gronlund, *The Co-operative Commonwealth*, p. 213.

5. Laurence Gronlund, "Why I am a Socialist," in *The Why I Ams: An Economic Symposium*, ed. Hugh O. Pentecost (New York: Humboldt Publishing Company, 1892), p. 24; Gronlund, "The Nationalization of Industry," p. 36; see also *The Labor Enquirer* (Denver) 7 (February 5, 1887): 2.

6. Gronlund, "The Nationalization of Industry," p. 36; Gronlund, *The Co-operative Commonwealth*, pp. 67–74.

7. Gronlund, *The Co-operative Commonwealth*, pp. 143, 147, 149, 154.

8. Ibid., 247.

9. Ibid., 247–48.

10. Ibid., 160–61.

11. Ibid., pp. 44, 179. Gronlund wrote: "Jewism to our mind best expresses the special curse of our age, *Speculation*, the transfer of wealth from others to themselves by chicanery without giving an equivalent."

12. Allyn B. Forbes, "The Literary Quest for Utopia, 1880–1900," *Social Forces* 6 (December,1927): 179, 188–89. Forbes listed only forty-nine Utopias. He ignored John Macnie, *The Diothas*, published in 1884, an especially significant work that has been cited as the model for Bellamy's work. Elizabeth Sadler, "One Book's Influence: Edward Bellamy's 'Looking Backward,' " *New England Quarterly* 17 (December 1944): 541, claims that only five Utopian novels appeared in America between 1798 and 1880.

13. Albert William Levi, "Edward Bellamy: Utopian," *Ethics* 55 (January 1945): 133.

14. San Francisco *Freethought*, November 11, 1889, clipping in "Scraps Collected by Anna Haskell in Relation to the Nationalist Movement," Haskell Family Papers, Bancroft Library, University of California, Berkeley; *Oakland Tribune*, July 9, 1889, as cited in Donald Edgar Walters, "Populism in California" (Ph.D. diss., University of California, Berkeley, 1952), p. 31; Heath, *Social Democracy Red Book*, p. 42; Stephen Leacock, *The Unsolved Riddle of Social Justice* (New York: John Lang Company, 1920), pp. 104–5, see also Sadler, "One Book's Influence," pp. 551, 553; *Workmen's Advocate* 4 (June 2, 1888): 3; (June 9, 1888): 2; (July 17, 1888): 1; Arthur E. Morgan, *Edward Bellamy*, (New York: Columbia University Press, 1944), p. xii; Levi, "Edward Bellamy," p. 132.

15. Edward Bellamy to "Dear Mr. Ticknor," June 15, 1888, Edward Bellamy Collection, Houghton Library, Harvard University, Cambridge, Massachusetts; Morgan, *Edward Bellamy*, pp. 5–8, 13–17, 55; Collins G. Burnham, "The City of Chicopee," *New England Magazine* 18 (May 1898): 372–75. Chicopee was formed from a merger of Chicopee Falls, where Bellamy was born, and Chicopee Center shortly before Bellamy was born; see also W. D. P. Bliss, *A Handbook of Socialism* (1895; reprint ed. London: Swan Sonenschein and Company, 1907), p. 211.

16. Morgan, *Edward Bellamy*, pp. 31–32, 41; see also Sadler, "One Book's Influence," p. 532; Edward Bellamy to Council of Delta Kappa Epsilon, [May 24, 1887], Edward Bellamy Collection.

17. Edward Bellamy to Council of Delta Kappa Epsilon, [May 24, 1887], Edward Bellamy Collection; Morgan, *Edward Bellamy*, pp. 43–44; That Bellamy's interest in social problems, and his interest in social reform, began when he was still a young man can be attested by some of his early writings. See, for example, Edward Bellamy, "Article in Reunion of Nations," manuscript, Edward Bellamy Collection.

18. Edward Bellamy, *The Duke of Stockbridge: A Romance of Shays' Rebellion* (New York: Silver Burdette, 1901). The novel was not published in book form until three years after Bellamy's death. Bellamy apparently planned rewriting it before allowing it to be published as a book. See also Charles A. Madison, *Critics and Crusaders*, (New York: Henry Holt and Company, 1948), p. 447; Morgan, *Edward Bellamy*, pp. 57, 62.

19. Edward Bellamy, "How I Came to Write 'Looking Backward,' " *The Nationalist* 1 (May 1889): 1–4; Abraham Cahan, *Bleter fun Mein Lebn* [Leaves from My Life] (Yiddish), 5 vols. (New York: Forward Association, 1926–1931), 3: 254–55; Edward Bellamy to William Dean Howells, June 17, 1888, cited in Quint, *The Forging of American Socialism*, p. 78; John Hope Franklin, "Edward Bellamy and the Nationalist Movement," *New England Quarterly*. (11 December 1938): 746.

20. Edward Page Mitchell, *Memoirs of an Editor: Fifty Years of American Journalism* (New York: Charles Scribner's Sons, 1924), p. 438; [Edward Bellamy], "Overworked Children in our Mills," editorial, *Springfield Union*, June 5, 1873, reprinted in Morgan, *Edward Bellamy*, p. 105 [Edward Bellamy], "Feudalism in Modern Times," *Springfield Union*, November 3, 1873, as quoted in Morgan, *Edward Bellamy*, p. 108; quoted in Madison, *Critics and Crusaders*, pp. 445–46; Morgan, *Edward Bellamy*, pp. 127, 139; Edward Bellamy to William Dean Howells, June 17, 1888, as quoted in Quint, *The Forging of American Socialism*, p. 78; Franklin, "Edward Bellamy . . ." p. 746; Levi, "Edward Bellamy," p. 131, claims Bellamy was influenced by reading Marx. "The Millenium of Socialism," *Boston Evening Transcript*, March 30, 1888, notes the many similarities between John McNie's *The Diothas, or a Far Look Ahead*, published in 1884, and *Looking Backward*. Arthur Morgan has written a pamphlet attempting to refute the charge of plagiarism against Bellamy. Arthur Morgan, *Plagiarism in Utopia* (Yellow Springs, Ohio: The Author, 1944). It is less than convincing.

21. Edward Bellamy to Hugh O. Pentecost, April 25, 1890, Edward Bellamy Collection; Edward Bellamy to "Dear Mr. Ticknor," June 15, 1888, Edward Bellamy Collection; Edward Bellamy, "The Progress of Nationalism," *North American Review* 154 (June 1892): 746; Ed-

ward Bellamy to *Boston Transcript*, April 1888, reprinted in Edward Bellamy, *Looking Backward* (New York: Modern Library, 1951), p. 273.

22. Sadler, "One Book's Influence," pp. 530, 533; Forbes, "Literary Quest," p. 184; Ida M. Tarbell, "New Dealers of the Seventies: Henry George and Edward Bellamy," *The Forum and Century* 92 (September 1934): 133; Levi, "Edward Bellamy," p. 132; Morgan, *Edward Bellamy*, p. ix.

23. Levi, "Edward Bellamy," p. 144; Bellamy, *Looking Backward*, pp. 5-6.

24. Bellamy, *Looking Backward*, pp. 36, 41, 66, 87-90, 116.

25. Ibid., pp. 42-43; See also Quint, *The Forging of American Socialism*, pp. 42-43.

26. Bellamy, *Looking Backward*, pp. 35, 41; Edward Bellamy, "The Progress of Nationalism," pp. 744-46; Edward Bellamy, "How Shall We Get There," *Twentieth Century* 2 (May 11, 1889: 166; Cahan, *Bleter*, 3: 249; Sadler, "One Book's Influence," p. 533; *The New York World*, March 2, 1890, p. 19.

27. Bellamy, *Looking Backward*, pp. 101, 152-56; *The New Nation* 2 (August 6, 1892): 499.

28. Bellamy, *Looking Backward*, p. 101.

29. Ibid., pp. 134-35.

30. Ibid., pp. 208-10, Edward Bellamy, "Address at Nationalist Club Anniversary, December, 19, 1889, Tremont Temple, Boston," *The Nationalist* 1 (April 1889): 179.

31. Bellamy, *Looking Backward*, pp. 70-105; Edward Bellamy, *Talks on Nationalism* (Chicago: The Peerage Press, 1938), p. 93.

32. Bellamy, "The Progress of Nationalism," p. 742; *The Commonwealth* 2 (February 24, 1889): 42; Cyrus Field Willard, "The Nationalist Club of Boston (A Chapter of History)," *The Nationalist* 1 (May 1889): 16-20.

33. Cyrus F. Willard, quoted in Franklin, "Edward Bellamy," p. 754; Francis A. Walker, "Mr. Bellamy and the New Nationalist Party," *The Atlantic Monthly* 65 (February 1890): 248-62; Sadler, "One Book's Influence," p. 535; Nicholas Gilman, "Nationalism in the United States," *Quarterly Journal of Economics* 4 (October 1889): 64-65; W. D. P. Bliss, quoted in Quint, *The Forging of American Socialism*, p. 79, Cyrus P. Willard, quoted in Quint, *The Forging of American Socialism*, p. 85; Howard Quint, "Gaylord Wilshire and Socialism's First Congressional Campaign," *Pacific Historical Review* 26 (November 1951): 328; F. I. Vassault, "Nationalism in California," *Overland Monthly*, 2d ser. 15 (June 1890): 660-61: Burnette G. Haskell, *The Commonwealth* 3 (September 1, 1889): 57, boasted that: "The San Francisco Nationalist Club . . . already numbers in its ranks some of the best people of this city"; Lester Luntz, "Daniel De Leon and the Movement for Social Reform, 1886-1892," manuscript, Edward Bellamy Collection, [1939]; Morgan, *Edward Bellamy*, pp. 247-49.

34. Among the active members of the Boston Nationalist Clubs were Abby Morton Diaz (1821-1904), a writer of children's stories and active participant in the fight for women's rights, whose father had been a trustee of Brook Farm. See *Dictionary of American Biography*, (New York, Charles Scribner and Sons, 1933), 5: 24 vols. 284-85; Edward Everett Hale (1822-1909), minister of South Congregational Church and author of "The Man Without a Country" and other articles and books. *Dictionary of American Biography*, 7: 99-100; Colonel Thomas Wentworth Higginson (1823-1911), minister, Civil War hero, founder of the nontheological Free Church, fighter for women's suffrage, author, member of Massachusetts legislature (he left the Nationalist Club within a year and became highly critical of Bellamy's plan—particularly of its coercive aspects). *Dictionary of American Biography*, 8: 16-18; Mary Ashton Rice Livermore (1820-1905), reformer, social worker, suffragette, author, early worker in workers' education movement, active temperance worker. *Dictionary of American Biography*, 11: 306; Anne Whitney, a noted sculptress, *Dictionary of American Biography*, 20: 155; Frances E. C. Willard (1839-1898), president of the Women's Christian Temperance Union, organizer of the Prohibition party, president (1871-1874) of Evanston, Illinois, College for Ladies, *Dictionary of American Biography*, 20: 233-34; and Rabbi Solomon Schindler (1842-1915), one of the

more effective leaders of the movement, German-born spiritual leader of one of the first reform Jewish synagogues in Boston, elected member of Boston School Committee, 1888–1894, special European correspondent of *The Boston Globe* (in which he praised Bismarck's social welfare state), and founder of the Federation of Jewish Charities. Schindler's socialism was much more oriented toward the working class than was Bellamy's Nationalism; see his *Young West* (Boston: Arena Publishing Company, 1894). For an excellent biographical study of Schindler, see Arthur Mann, "Solomon Schindler: Boston Radical," *The New England Quarterly* 23 (December 1950): especially 453–57, 471–74; Morgan, *Edward Bellamy*, pp. 260–75. Among Theosophists who held leading positions in the Boston First Nationalist Club were Cyrus F. Willard, Arthur B. Griggs, George D. Ayers, and Sylvester Baxter. They were instrumental in drawing up the Statement of Principles; see Morgan, *Edward Bellamy*, pp. 260–75. Theosophists were merely one of the major elements in the Nationalist movement: by 1890 a non-Theosophist Nationalist candidate, Gaylord Wilshire, polled a respectable 1,000 votes in a California congressional race, and Christian Socialists were joining the Nationalist Clubs. See Morgan, *Edward Bellamy*, p. 277; Frank Roney, *Frank Roney: Irish Rebel and California Labor Leader*, ed. Ira B. Cross (Berkeley: University of California Press, 1931), p. 409; George E. MacDonald, *Fifty Years of Freethought* (New York: The Truth Seeker Company, 1929), p. 478; Franklin, "Edward Bellamy," pp. 751–54; Quint, *The Forging of American Socialism*, p. 83.

35. *The New Nation* 1 (April 11, 1891): 172.

36. W. D. P. Bliss, ed, *Encyclopedia of Social Reform* (New York: Funk and Wagnall, 1897), p. 918; Charles Sotheran, *Horace Greeley and Other Pioneers of American Socialism* (New York: Mitchell Kennerly, 1915), p. 25. *Workmen's Advocate* 4 (December 15, 1888):1.

37. Bellamy, "Progress of Nationalism," p. 746, conceded that the Nationalists had "little, if any mutual organization." He boasted: "There never was, perhaps, a reform movement that got along with less management than that of Nationalists."

38. William H. Gray to William Hickstein, May 14, 1889, SLP Collection (microfilm); Friedrich Engels to Hermann Schlüter, January 29, 1891, in Leonard E. Mins [editor and translator], "Unpublished Letters of Karl Marx and Friedrich A. Engels to Americans," *Science and Society* 2 (Spring 1938): 365 [Schlüter was editor of the daily *New Yorker Volkszeitung*]; see Max Beer, *Social Struggles and Modern Socialism* (Boston: Small, Maynard and Company, 1926), p. 36; see also, Morgan *Edward Bellamy*, p. 370.

39. *Workmen's Advocate* 5 (October 26, 1889): 1.

40. *Workmen's Advocate* 4 (December 8, 1888): 1; (December 15, 1888): 1.

41. *The New Nation* 1, (March 7, 1891): 99.

42. "Reminiscences," in Sotheran, *Horace Greeley*, p. xxiv; F. I. Vassault, "Nationalism in California," *Overland Monthly*, 2d ser. 15 (June 1890): 659.

43. *Workmen's Advocate* 6 (September 20, 1890): 1; (November 29, 1890): 4; *The New Nation* 1 (March 21, 1891): 131; (April 4, 1891): 150.

44. See, especially, Quint, *The Forging of American Socialism*, pp. 86–87.

45. *The New Nation* 1 (August 22, 1891): 474–75.

46. [Edward Bellamy], "Is 'Socialism' a Definite or an Indefinite Term?" *The New Nation* 2 (January 2, 1892): 1; [Edward Bellamy], "Four Distinctive Features of Nationalism," *The New Nation* 2 (January 9, 1892): 17–18; *The New Nation* 2 (August 6, 1892): 499.

47. *The People* 1 (December 20, 1891): 2; (January 17, 1892): 2.

48. Sylvester Baxter, "Why the Name Nationalism," *The Nationalist* 1 (July 1889): 83; Lucien Sanial to George H. Wrightson, December 1, 1891, reprinted in *The People* 1 (December 6, 1891): 2.

49. *The New Nation* 1 (July 11, 1891): 374; Bellamy, *Talks on Nationalism*, p. 190; *The [New York] World*, March 2, 1890, p. 18; Edward Bellamy, "Looking Forward," *The Nationalist* 2 (December 1889): 4; Cahan, *Bleter*, 3: 255.

50. *The New Nation* 2 (August 8, 1892): 499; Bellamy, "The Progress of Nationalism," p. 743; Edward Bellamy, "Memorandum on Nationalism," [1889], manuscript, Edward Bellamy Collection; Morgan, *Edward Bellamy*, p. 87; *Workmen's Advocate* 5 (December 28, 1889): 1; Cahan, *Bleter*, 3: 247–48; Lucien Sanial to George H. Wrightson; Laurence Gronlund, "Nationalism," *The Arena* 1 (January 1890): 156–58.

51. Gronlund, "Nationalism," p. 165.

52. Cahan, *Bleter*, 3: 250–51; *The New Nation* 1 (April 11, 1891): 173; (July 11, 1891): 374; Michael Lynch, "A Workingman's View of Nationalism," *The Nationalist* 1 (August 1889): 108–9; [Edward Bellamy], "Trade Unionism, a Bird With One Wing," *The New Nation* 2 (October 1, 1892): 602.

53. [Bellamy], "Trade Unionism, a Bird With One Wing," p. 602; [Edward Bellamy], "The Homestead Tragedy," *The New Nation* 2 (July 16, 1892): 450; Edward Bellamy, "Labor, Politics, and Nationalism," *New York Herald*, August 28, 1892, reprinted in *The New Nation* 2 (September 10, 1892): 568; Interview of Edward Bellamy in *The Boston Globe*, July 7, 1892, reprinted as "A Nationalist View of the Homestead Situation," *The New Nation* 2 (July 16, 1892): 453; [Edward Bellamy], "The Trials of the Homestead Men," *The New Nation* 2 (October 8, 1892): 615.

54. Cahan, *Bleter*, 3: 255.

55. Edward Bellamy to John Lloyd Thomas, July 29, 1891, Edward Bellamy Collection; Bellamy, "Labor, Politics, and Nationalism," p. 568.

56. Quint, *The Forging of American Socialism*, pp. 95–96.

57. *The New Nation* 1 (April 11, 1891): 172; Morgan, *Edward Bellamy*, p. 66, reports that "toward the end of 1890 . . . Bellamy became convinced that *The Nationalist* magazine lacked the vitality necessary to give effective expression to his ideas, and he decided to publish a weekly newspaper of his own. . . . *The Nationalist* expired with the March-April [1891] number. With its death, the interest of Theosophists in the movement faded."

58. *The Nationalist* 1 (May 1889): 21; *New Bedford Evening Journal* quoted in *The New Nation* 1 (March 14, 1891): 101, 109; *The New Nation* 1 (March 14, 1891): 103, and (April 11, 1891): 172; F. I. Vassault, "Nationalism in California," p. 661; Howard Quint, "Gaylord Wilshire and Socialism's First Congressional Campaign," p. 327, 331; one Marxist who supported Haskell was Job Harriman, president of the San Francisco California Club, who was later to become a leader of the Socialist party and its candidate for vice-president. See *The Abolitionist* 1 (May 12, 1890): 2; also see Walters, "Populism in California," p. 36; Royce D. Delmatier, Clarence F. McIntosh, and Earl G. Waters, *The Rumble of California Politics, 1848–1970* (New York: John Wiley and Sons, 1970), p. 100.

59. William Dean Howells, *Literature and Life Studies* (New York: Harper and Brothers, 1902), p. 294; see also Sadler, "One Book's Influence," pp. 537–38; Bellamy, "Progress of Nationalism," pp. 750–51; *The New Nation* 1 (July 4, 1891).

60. Norman Pollack, *The Populist Response to Industrial America: Midwest Populist Thought* (Cambridge, Mass.: Harvard University Press, 1962), p. 12, claims that: "Had Populism succeeded, it could have fundamentally altered American society in a socialist direction." His evidence is limited, however, to the pro-Socialist wing of the People's party, particularly Henry Demarest Lloyd. A careful examination of a broad spectrum of Populist press and documents, however, disputes his assumption. See also, *The People* 1 (February 28, 1892), for the first Populist platform; for the official 1892 Populist election platform, see "The Omaha Preamble, Platform, and Resolutions," *The New Nation*, 2 (July 16, 1892): 457–58.

61. [Edward Bellamy], "The St. Louis Convention and The New Nation," *The New Nation* 2 (March 5, 1892): 146–47; *The New Nation* 1 (May 30, 1891): 277–78; (December 5, 1891): 716; *The New Nation* 2 (September 17, 1892): 577.

62. *The People* 2 (July 10, 1892): 2; *The New Nation* 2 (July 16, 1892): 454–55; Quint, *The Forging of American Socialism*, p. 101.

63. *The People* 1 (November 15, 1891): 1; (November 29, 1891): 1.

64. *The People* 2 (December 4, 1892): 3; J. A. Wayland, "The Farmers of West Falling into Line," *The New Nation* 2 (December 24, 1892): 755; Bliss, *Handbook*, p. 147; "Reminiscences," in Sotheran, *Horace Greeley*, pp. xxiv–xxv.

65. Quoted in Pollack, *The Populist Response*, p. 27.

66. Heath, *Social Democracy Red Book*, p. 53; Caro Lloyd, *Henry Demarest Lloyd: 1847–1903, A Biography*, 2 vols. (New York: G. P. Putnam's Sons, 1912), 1: 254.

67. Edward Bellamy to [Horace Elisha] Scudder, September 15, 1893, Edward Bellamy Collection; Bliss, *Handbook*, pp. 25, 144–45; Bellamy was a unique Utopian: he opposed the establishing of Socialistic communities. See a quotation from Bellamy's *Equality* in Charles P. Le Warne, "Equality Colony: The Plan to Socialize Washington," *Pacific Northwest Quarterly* 59 (July 1968): 145.

68. Caro Lloyd, *Henry Demarest Lloyd*, pp. 257, 259; *New York Sun*, July 23, 1896, p. 2, reported: "St. Louis, July 22—One of the striking things about the Populist convention . . . here and the crowd attending them, is the extraordinary hatred of the Jewish race. It is not possible to go into any hotel in the city without hearing the most bitter denunciations of the Jews as a class and of particular Jews who happen to have prospered in the world." The anti-Semitism may have been selectively against bankers, although there is no evidence that this is the case. See also, Henry Demarest Lloyd, "The Populists at St. Louis," *Review of Reviews* 14 (September 1896): 301.

69. Caro Lloyd, *Henry Demarest Lloyd*, pp. 161–62; Henry Demarest Lloyd, "The Populists at St. Louis," pp. 299, 301.

70. Caro Lloyd, *Henry Demarest Lloyd*, p. 265.

71. Ibid., p. 280; Edward Bellamy to Henry Demarest Lloyd, December 5, 1896, Edward Bellamy Collection; Franklin, "Edward Bellamy," pp. 770–71.

72. Edward Bellamy, "Original Introduction to Equality," manuscript, Edward Bellamy Collection, pp. v, x–xi, 1.

73. Franklin, "Edward Bellamy," p. 772.

74. Quint, *The Forging of American Socialism*, p. 102; "Constitution of the Fabian Society of Boston," *The American Fabian* 1 (June 1895): 5–6.

75. Sadler, "One Book's Influence," pp. 547–48.

∽ *14* ∽

Christian Socialists

- 1 -

Religion played a key role in the development of the American Left: the roots of the earliest Socialist and Anarchist movements were to be found in the radical utterances of the Old Testament prophets and the social teachings of Jesus.[1] Almost all of the successful communities were rooted in socialistic passages in the Holy Bible; most labor reform movements before, or immediately following, the Civil War were based in large part on the social creed of the pre-Nicaean Christian church. With the rise of industrial America, especially between 1870 and 1940, an increasing number of clergymen turned to socialism as the answer to the social problems of the times. They attempted to combine militant socialism with pacifist Christian ethics. Their influence in the Americanization of the Socialist movement was significant.

The Christian Socialists were neither clear nor united in their aims. A critic noted that socialism as defined by most Christian Socialists was "used in such a catholic sense that—even Proudhon's definition—'every aspiration for the amelioration of society' " was included.[2] Their ideological declarations contained pious and meaningless cliches such as the publication *The Social Gospel's* definition of its purpose to be "to inspire faith in the economic teaching of Jesus, and courage into life." The journal's editors declared the Christian Socialists' aim to be "the proclamation of the kingdom of heaven, a divinely ordered society *to be realized on earth.*" Philo W. Sprague, a leading turn-of-the-century Christian Socialist, defined his *socialism* to mean "the effort of society to perfect its own life and accomplish its own destiny."[3] Likewise, the Christian Socialists' aims ranged from a belief in labor unions to Marxism.[4]

Some Christian Socialists were Christians in name only. Most were true believers, but others were agnostics or even atheists; their only tie to organized Christianity was that they had at one time been ordained ministers or active denominational lay leaders.[5]

- 2 -

The first of the modern Christian Socialist organizations was the small and basically ineffective Christian Labor Union (CLU) of Boston, an association of churchmen interested in social reform. It was organized and dominated by Jesse H. Jones, a Congregational minister from North Abington, Massachusetts, and it was supported financially by T. Wharton Collens, a Roman Catholic layman from New Orleans. The union was founded in 1872 and lasted until Collens's death in 1878.[6] The CLU's most lasting contribution to the American Left was the publication of two journals, *Equity* and *Labor Balance*.

Jones, a veteran of the Battle of Gettysburg, began his labor reform career as an advocate of the eight-hour day shortly after the Civil War. Jones's chief contribution to the eight-hour day was a song, *Eight Hours*, for which he composed the music in 1867. By 1872 he had decided that an eight-hour day was not by itself a solution to the inequities of the current social system, that a complete overhaul was necessary. It was at this time that he organized the Christian Labor Union.[7]

Jones proclaimed the union's objective to be the establishment of a Christian Commonwealth on earth. To achieve this end, he proposed that the church become an instrument of social revolution. "Do not the teachings of Jesus require of His churches . . . that there shculd be mutual care . . . for the help of those who have need?" Jones asked, "Do they not now require the Church to establish labor partnerships and other industrial corporations?" Finally, he inquired, was it not necessary for the church to further Josiah Warren's economic thesis that "Cost is the limit of Price?"[8] The church would merely be spreading its own teachings if it did become the instrumentality for change, he argued, since "communism is Congregationalism applied to the management of work and wealth."[9]

Jones admitted that a class struggle existed. He blamed its existence on the capitalist economic system in which the stronger nonworking class gained wealth, power, and luxury at the expense of the weaker working class, which received suffering and pain for its efforts. Political parties, all of which, he insisted, represented economic classes, were also the products of the inequitable, anti-Christian capitalist system. Jones was certain that only the "righteous settlement of the labor problem" could remove the socially debilitating class and party structure of the American economic, political, and social system.[10]

Any "righteous settlement of the labor problem," he argued, would require acceptance of what he considered a basic Christian tenet: that "riches cannot be accumulated except by violating the principle of brotherhood, as when one man fraudulently or even by express contract retains a part of the labor of many." This accumulation is the basic principle of the capitalist system, Jones said. "In capitalism, the Golden Rule [is] REVERSED." He considered capitalism to be like a leech that "has fastened itself upon the body industrial, and there greedily devours the profit of industry, leaving but a bare pittance for the common toiler, while it gives luxury and plenty to the favored few."[11] During his early Christian Socialist days, Jones called upon enlightened and "energetic businessmen" to devote their zeal toward easing the burden of the poor workingmen. But he soon discovered that few if any altruistic capitalists were willing to devote their lives to easing the burden of the working class. He feared that the workingmen, therefore, would turn to violence to achieve improved conditions. He was certain that the "right will triumph *in the end*," but he feared that the way to freedom would, due to the selfishness of capitalists, be as terrible as the "way through to the abolition of slavery." Despite this, he believed violence to be needless, for the workers could appeal to the "Supreme Court of public opinion," where a favorable verdict was certain.[12]

By the latter part of the decade, other ministers were also calling for a social revolution. Some had gone far beyond Jones in militancy. Even as conservative an anti-Socialist as Professor Roswell D. Hitchcock of New York's Union Theological Seminary assailed the church for its support of predatory capitalism.

Is it any wonder that infidelity increases and that the red flag Communists are atheists when the relative condition of those who toil is steadily growing worse, *and the church, which contains all the religion they know gives her whole strength to sustain the system by which this effort is wrought?* For as the Church was the "great bulwark of slavery" in past days, so now is it the chief support of the Mammon-worshipping system by which the rich are growing richer and the poor poorer with fearful rapidity.[13]

Jones agreed with Hitchcock's assessment, but he disagreed with his forecast of bloody class warfare in which the labor movement would be wiped out and a dictator would rule America. Jones, whose patriotism was boundless, believed that America was God's chosen nation "just as the children of Israel were," and that God would not permit the freedom of His people to be abridged. "The Christian intelligence of the country at last will dethrone the capitalist classes, and *establish a republic of property as a century ago it established a republic of political affairs.*"[14]

How was the new Christian Commonwealth to be established? Jones expected that it would be voted into office, and he advocated formation of a new political party dedicated to the establishment of the new social order.[15] Labor would also require the aid of the deity; its victories could be won only through "one name—one title deed—" Jesus Christ. Reform movements and labor unions were, he believed, "secular churches," and he insisted that "Jesus Christ is the only solution to the Labor problem."[16]

His fundamentalism kept Jones out of the secular Socialist movement, although he was sympathetic to the Socialist Labor party (SLP) and published its platform in his journal. His pietistic patriotism—which bordered on jingoism—made him hostile to some of the harmless displays of militancy by SLPers. When in March 1878 the Cincinnati Socialists were barred by police from carrying the red flag at the head of a parade, Jesse Jones was delighted. "The red flag," he wrote, "is not the emblem of freedom and the standard of humanity;—*but it is the emblem of fury and the standard of anarchy.* . . . It never sprang up among American-born people, and never can. . . . And if the police refuse it a place in any procession they infringe on no real liberty of the people."[17]

Little came of the Christian Labor Union. Jones was soon forgotten, as was the rest of the movement. But the ideas he first espoused were to continue to evoke support among committed Christians. Jones's significance in the American Left is primarily historical, for he was a precursor of a major movement that helped shape the American Socialist movement of the twentieth century.

- 3 -

Hugh Owen Pentecost was both an atheist and a leading Christian Socialist during the last decade of the nineteenth century. Pentecost, born in New Harmony, Indiana, of Socialist parents who had been members of the by then defunct colony of Robert Owen (his middle name was in honor of the British Socialist pioneer), had only one claim to the appellation *Christian*: he had been ordained a Congregational minister in 1885.

His only pastorate was in the largely working-class Belleville Congregational Church in Newark, New Jersey, where he observed poverty firsthand. The sight of the abject suffering of his neighbors plus his early Socialist upbringing in New Harmony led Pentecost to the radical Left. During his first year in Newark, he became an active labor-union organizer. In 1886 he was elected president of the Newark Central Labor Union. That same year, when the Haymarket Anarchists were arrested, and the next year when they were hanged, Pentecost led the Newark protests. His congregation supported him in his outcry against injustice, but Pentecost had by this time become disillusioned with the church and with religion generally.[18]

Shortly after the Haymarket executions, Pentecost resigned his pulpit. His choice, he told his congregation in his farewell sermon, was between remaining a practicing Christian or being a follower of Jesus. "A minister or priest who becomes a follower of Jesus, as I understand him," he told his congregation, "can neither get nor keep a pulpit of organized Christianity." The church, he argued, was interested primarily in strengthening and perpetuating herself. "Instead of using herself for the betterment of the world, the church seems to me more willing to use this world for her own aggrandizement." Pentecost called organized Christianity a tool used by the capitalists to maintain their power. The Christian church was thus a partner in fraud, for "no man gets rich except by defrauding, legally or illegally, someone else." He charged that the charities of organized religion were keeping workers docile and thus poor and powerless, and "when it comes to righting the wrongs of the oppressed and defrauded or even seriously attempting to discover if there are wrongs to right, the church always shows that she has no such love for the poor as Jesus had." Pentecost accused formal Christianity of worshipping Jesus while, in effect, repudiating His doctrinal teachings as impractical. Moreover, he considered the defects of the church to be incurable. After the farewell sermon, his congregants pleaded with him to remain. He refused.[19]

Following his departure from the ministry, Pentecost read law and edited the *Twentieth Century*, a radical journal. He married the daughter of Richard Gatling, developer of the Gatling gun. His marriage gained him financial security and thus allowed him to become more active than previously in labor and Socialist movements. For a short time, Pentecost supported Henry George, who he insisted "goes to the bottom of the difficulty and removes the single cause of the whole complication of disorders." When Bellamy's *Looking Backward* appeared, Pentecost conceded that the book forecast the "final outcome of the 'logic of events.' " But he insisted that Henry George was still the "safe and sure guide" of how to achieve Bellamy's Utopia. Within a year, Pentecost abandoned the Single-Tax movement and turned to anarchism. He lectured at the Masonic Temple in New York and won a large following.

Samuel Gompers, founding president of the American Federation of Labor, attended one of the lectures titled "Trade Unions No Remedy." Gompers met with Pentecost after the lecture and convinced the latter—temporarily—that trade unionism was the answer to society's ills.[20] Pentecost then tried his hand at organizing workingmen into trade unions, but his effort ended in failure. Workers were generally unwilling to join in his crusades. By 1891 he abandoned all hope in the working class, and he retired—except for one last attempt in 1906—from the radical Left. "One of the lessons I have learned is that the working people, as a class, are in the

unfortunate position they are in because, as a class they are incapable of being better off," Pentecost wrote in *Twentieth Century*.

> They are wedded to the Clergyman and the politicians. They will follow a black
> gown and a brass band into slavery, and they enjoy their servitude. They like to be
> humbugged, robbed, and ruled; and they love the men who humbug, rob, and rule
> them. . . . I did not know this once. I know it now. When I did not know it I was
> willing to suffer, if need be, for the working people. Now that I know it I am not.[21]

For the next fifteen years, Pentecost wrote for the anticlerical *Truth Seeker*
and delivered weekly lectures attacking organized religion. In 1906 he
resumed his interrupted venture into left-wing radicalism: he joined the
Socialist party, for which he became an active propagandist for the last year
of his life. Pentecost's entry into the Socialist party did not signify that he
had become convinced of the correctness and justice of its doctrines; it was,
to quote a friend, "the social spirit which aroused Mr. Pentecost's enthusiasm." He favored the movement rather than its program.[22]

As a Socialist, Pentecost argued that the primary objective of man was
"the securing of . . . happiness," which was unavailable to most people
because of their economic distress. Poverty would be abolished with the fall
of capitalism, and happiness would reign throughout the earth. He denied
that he was urging the working class to find happiness as the capitalists had
found it "in killing and stealing and covetousness and envy and idleness and
drunkenness." Nor did he believe that man should endure suffering in this
world in return for luxury in some other world after death, as some religions taught. He argued that this doctrine constituted a cruel hoax: there was
no world but this one.[23]

His new venture in radicalism was short lived: he died in 1907.[24]

Many men and women were to emulate Pentecost: like him, they would
come to socialism because they believed in the social teachings of Jesus, and
like him, they would leave their churches and their religious faith after they
had became convinced that the church was a counterrevolutionary organ of
repression. Some turned to militant socialism and, having discovered that
the Socialists and the workingmen were themselves less than pure, abandoned
their socialism and became crass materialists. Others left their churches and
became active leaders in one of the Socialist or Communist movements during the first half of the twentieth century.

- 4 -

The Episcopal church has historically been one of the leading centers of
Christian Socialism. Organizationally, the American offspring of the
Church of England is, as its name implies, hierarchical. Doctrinally, it is one
of the more democratic of ecclesiastical organizations, allowing for a broad
spectrum of theological and social viewpoints within the church.

The church unity, which resulted from the hierarchical organization, plus the intellectual freedom of the Episcopal church, led William Dwight Porter Bliss to abandon Congregationalism. Born in Constantinople in 1856, the son of missionaries, he was educated at Amherst College and the Hartford Theological Seminary. Ordained in the Congregational church in 1882, Bliss served in only two pastorates of that church—one in Denver and the other in South Natick, Massachusetts. Two years after his ordination, Bliss resigned his charge and joined the Episcopal church. He immediately became a lay reader, a prelude to ordination in his new church, in the small Western Massachusetts industrial town of Lee. The sufferings of the working-class population in that town roused him to action. He helped organize the local lodge of the Knights of Labor and served as its master workman in 1886.

A year later when he was called to become rector of Boston's Grace Church Missions, he continued his prolabor activity, organizing the Church Association for the Advancement of the Interests of Labor, which agitated for labor unions, cooperatives, profitsharing, the eight-hour day, civil service, ballot, and land reforms. Bliss, who was early impressed with Bellamy, also helped found the First Nationalist Club in Boston. The ethereal nature of the Theosophist leadership of the club soon alienated him, and he left to found the multidenominational Society of Christian Socialists.[25] Bliss also began publication at that time of a Christian Socialist journal, *Dawn*.[26]

Socialism and the social teachings of Christ were synonymous to Bliss. The former was merely the practical application of the latter. Jesus would have been a Socialist had He lived in turn-of-the-century America, he maintained. The socialism Bliss preached was intended to promote the brotherhood of humanity as envisioned by Jesus. Nationalization would thus be limited to major industries; to extend it beyond that point would "merely . . . extend tyranny and . . . develop slavery." Moreover, it would be useless to nationalize industry under most existing governments; only in a genuine democracy, which was "the organic unity of a people organized to do the complete business of the people," could nationalization be aimed at brotherhood. It was because the Bellamyites did not, in his view, genuinely believe in these precepts that Bliss left the Nationalsits. He warned that the "rich . . . take up Nationalism and exploit it for their own private purposes, turning everything over to the state, and seeing that they themselves are the state."[27]

The Society of Christian Socialists' proclaimed objective was the establishment of a Socialist—hence a Christian—social order on earth. Its program anathematized capitalism, and every other competitive social system, for being contrary to God's order. Modern industrialism was proclaimed as a God-given opportunity for man to develop a cooperative commonwealth. The "new order" would mark a return to the pre-Niceaen Christian idea;

"Christian socialism . . . is simply another name for primitive Christianity," James Whiton, a follower of Bliss, wrote.[28]

The Society was dedicated solely to the propagation of socialism. It was not competing for preeminence with any other Socialist group, Bliss assured both the Socialist Labor party and the Nationalist Clubs. Its sole aim was to further belief in the "fatherhood of God and the brotherhood of man" as the basis of society, for Jesus "taught us not to compete each for his own good, but to be members one to another." The SLP leaders recognized the prestige an American clergyman could bring to their movement, and Bliss became a frequent speaker at party meetings. His talks were reasoned attempts to divorce socialism from revolutionary, often authoritarian, rhetoric.[29] He argued that political democracy was a prerequisite for genuine socialism, for, in a nondemocratic state, power would be wielded by a small and self-ish minority no matter the economic system.[30] Nor could true socialism exist in an Anarchist political system, according to Bliss. Man could not escape from organized society, which was, he argued, man's natural condition. The objective of socialism would thus have to be human domination over social organization. Anarchists, by attempting to destroy the state—and thus organized society—were struggling in vain against a mirage. Bliss believed the state to be an evolving, steadily improving, social reality. During a debate with anarchist-individualist Benjamin Tucker, Bliss declared:

. . . The State is; and the State is stronger, better, wiser than it was. . . .

Not only does this evolution stand out in history, but sometimes it seems the main bequest of history.

. . . The evolution of society organized seems at times the foremost fact of history.[31]

The Society of Christian Socialists was, despite Bliss's efforts, a failure: it attracted few followers and had limited influence. After less than two years, the society disbanded. But Bliss refused to surrender; almost immediately he formed the Guild of the Brotherhood of the Carpenter, an organization aimed at applying Christian principles to social problems. The brotherhood proclaimed itself to be a Christian organization based on "ethical and democratic socialism." The new organization's statement of principles rejected the idea of "any Utopia in the clouds, any Oceanica within the West, any Boston of the year 2000; any Kaweah colony, any ideal paradise conceived on earth." Behind Bliss's anti-Utopianism was a retreat from socialism; he now favored a basically pragmatic reformation of society that would assure each man an honest day's work. Bliss's Christian Socialism had evolved into little more than labor reform.[32] He now abandoned political socialism, and in its place, he advocated trade-union organization. Trade unions represented to him "the natural unity of men." Impressed, apparently, by his friend George McNeill, a trade-union organizer and publicist, Bliss proclaimed that "Side by side with the Nation, with the Church, with the Family, must the Trade Union take . . . its place as a natural, divine, local function, as necessary to society as the unity of the hand in the unity of the body." Between 1890 and 1894, he supported the most militant of labor struggles: the New York Central strike of 1890, the Homestead strike of 1892, and the American Railway Union's strike against the Pullman Corporation in 1894.[33]

Bliss did not, like the Syndicalists, lose faith in the efficacy of political action. He was merely alienated from all existing political parties; he could find no political vehicle for his views. He held the Republicans and Democrats responsible for perpetuating the inequitable, cruel, and anti-Christian capitalist system. The Socialist Labor party had by 1892 fallen under the domination of Daniel DeLeon, whose imperious, despotic rule and dogmatic theorizing repelled the Episcopal priest. Bliss found a temporary political haven in the People's party, after he had met some impressive Populist leaders during a speaking tour in the prairie states. He was, in fact, a delegate to a national conference of the party in early 1892. He toured the East and Midwest for the party. But the failure of the Populists to support women's suffrage dampened Bliss's enthusiasm for the party. The party politicians had failed to call for an end to women's "slavery." It was, he said, "the disgrace of our modern society that she is . . . left a slave after slavery has been destroyed. As man's slave, man's tool, or man's toy, woman has been equally dishonored." The failure of the People's party conference to recognize this fact disappointed Bliss. He voted for the party, but he was not active in its campaign. He believed that the Populists were doomed to failure, that they could not improve society.[34]

Bliss failed to influence the direction of the People's party; the reformers in the People's party, on the contrary, influenced Bliss considerably. By 1894 Bliss had become little more than a moderate social reformer. Despite occasional excursions into militant Socialist rhetoric, he wanted little more than civil service reform—with higher salaries for bureaucrats—the initiative, the referendum, and proportional representation. He still favored shorter hours for labor on the assumption that it meant longer hours in the home, library, and church. But even on reform, Bliss favored gradualism. His Socialist zeal was dissipated.

In 1895 Bliss made his last foray into organized "socialism." He helped found the publication *American Fabian* and attempted to organize an American Fabian Society. Both the journal and the society were short lived, and neither had a significant following.[35] In 1896 Bliss supported William Jennings Bryan for president and assailed the Socialists for opposing the "Great Commoner."[36] Thereafter, he lectured extensively on social reform, wrote an almost forgotten, but still significant, *Handbook of Socialism*, and edited the monumental *Encyclopaedia of Social Reform*. As late as 1899, he still called Christ "the greatest Socialist of which I know" and argued that "Modern business and modern city life is, I think, pretty nearly our modern hell."[37] But he was no longer a Socialist-activist. In 1917 the Reverend William Dwight Porter Bliss was involved in secret work with the Allied powers for the United States government. Nine years later, he was dead.

Bliss, during his thirteen-year sojourn as a Socialist, sought to develop a synthesis of Judeo-Christian morality and Marxian materialism. He failed, as did others who tried to accomplish the same feat later. Like him, they became tired and disillusioned and gave up the apparently futile struggle.

- 5 -

The outstanding theoretician of Christian Socialism was a Baptist theologian and professor of church history, Walter Rauschenbusch.

Born in Rochester in 1861, Rauschenbusch spent most of his life in that city. He was educated at Rochester Free Academy, the Gymnasium (higher secondary school) at Guteslöh, Germany, the University of Rochester, and the Rochester Theological Seminary. He intended originally to become a missionary, but his theological liberalism prevented him from obtaining an appointment in that field. His only parish was the Second Baptist Church on West 45th Street in the poverty-stricken Hell's Kitchen district of New York City, where his Christian conscience forced Rauschenbusch to speak out against the condition of the working people in his parish and in the city generally. In 1886 he supported Henry George actively. Two years later, Rauschenbusch joined Leighton Williams, Elizabeth Post, and J. E. Raymond in editing *For the Right*, a prolabor Social Christian journal he helped found. Rochester Theological Seminary appointed him to its faculty in 1897, and five years later, he was named professor of church history there. He first came to public notice in 1907 with the publication of his *magnum opus, Christianity and the Social Crisis*. For the next eleven years—he died in 1918—Rauschenbusch was a leading spokesman for Christian Socialism, although he joined neither the Socialist party nor any other organization of the radical Left.

The basis for Rauschenbusch's socialism was a passage from the Lord's Prayer in the Gospel of Matthew: "Thy will be done on earth. . . ."[38] The kingdom of God was, he said, a transformation of life on earth "into the harmony of heaven." The early Christian hope for Christ's return to earth, he argued, was premised on the assumption that He would build there the kingdom of God. Such a kingdom would require "the overthrow of the present world powers" so social perfection could exist. The new society would substitute love, service, and equality for coercion, exploitation, and inequality.[39]

His theology was basically rooted in the Old Testament, particularly the prophets. "The great prophets whom we revere . . . were the men of the opposition and of the radical minority," he wrote. They were not interested in piety or detached private morality; their primary concern was the social morality of the nation—of humankind as a whole. "They said less about the pure heart for the individual than of just institutions for the nation." The "Day of Jehovah" meant the social revolution to the prophets, as Rauschenbusch interpreted them.[40]

Jesus, he believed, was a prophet who spoke for his own age about concrete problems of that period. "Jesus . . . lived in the hope of a great transformation of the national, social, and religious life about him." His was thus a "Jewish hope . . . a human hope with universal scope." Jesus's teachings were thus revolutionary rather than ascetic.[41]

Rauschenbusch's Social Gospel also had a strong element of Marxism. He agreed with Marx that history had been a continuum of class struggles of which that between workers and capitalists was only the most recent. Moreover, each social class had used whatever weapons were available to it—violence, clerical anathemas, law, or ostracism. The working class, which was fighting its own struggle against capitalism, could use only organization, through which it could gain political and social strength. Working people, as exploited and poor individuals, were powerless, but united they could, through strikes and political action, achieve genuine power.[42] Even before it was fashionable, Rauschenbusch believed the capitalist system caused man to be alienated from himself, his society, and his product. This alienation was, in fact, one of the "greatest accusations against our industrial system." It was "like a corrosive chemical that disintegrates [the workers'] self-respect."[43]

Rauschenbusch blamed the church's decline on its failure to fight the evils of the existing social order. "Other organizations may conceivably be indifferent when confronted with the chronic or acute poverty of our cities. The Christian Church cannot."[44] He was not upset by the decline of the organized church, for it had lost its social revolutionary aim and thus its Christianity almost at the outset, when control fell permanently to an institutionalized, ecclesiastical oligarchy, which he virtually equated with the anti-Christ. "There was no higher exercise of piety than to build churches or endow monasteries. Avarice was refusal to enrich the Church. Charity to the Church covered a multitude of sins."[45] But Christianity was ignored; the church had become an organization antithetical to Christianity. "The Kingdom of God can never be advanced by cruelty and trickery; [yet] the power of the paganized church can be and has been advanced by persecution and forgery."[46]

According to Rauschenbusch, the Christianity of the pre-Nicaean church caused some to throw down their tools and quit work . . . stirred women to break down the restraints of custom and modesty . . . invaded the intimacies of domestic relations and threatened families with disruption . . . awakened the slaves to a feeling of worth and a longing for freedom . . . disturbed the patriotism and loyalty of citizens for their country, and intervened between the sovereign state and its subjects.[47]

Some Socialists did not welcome Rauschenbusch's Social Gospel. George Herron, who considered himself a leading Christian Socialist, claimed that Rauschenbusch's primary interest was in winning the working class to the church "in order that the church may save itself by bridling and saddling the working class." Heron warned that Rauschenbusch's relation to the Socialist movement would be "wholly parasitical."[48] Despite the antagonism, Rauschenbusch, although he never joined the party, remained active in its behalf.

In a 1916 lecture, Rauschenbusch proclaimed his fealty to socialism and the Socialist movement. He argued that socialism was the Christian social order, that like Christianity, it created a unity—a solidarity—based on love and forgiveness. Socialism offered the workingmen the sole hope of freedom and emancipation from poverty, and it offered Christians moral and spiritual justice. A genuine Christian would perforce have to be a Socialist.[49]

Rauschenbusch attempted to synthesize the teachings of Christ and Marx. "Christianity and Socialism both are 'concerned for the lost,' for the derelicts of society," he said. "Christianity by evangelism and by charity has dealt with single cases, but society manufactures the lost faster than the church can heal them. Socialism has concentrated attention on child labor and prostitution, on the choking of the family by high rent and long hours and low wages. I stand for combining the methods of Christianity and Socialism."[50]

The synthesis Rauschenbusch attempted to create continued to elude Christian Socialists long after his death, but his influence on the Socialist movement was monumental. Literally thousands of clergymen became active Socialists under the influence of his writings and teachings.

- 6 -

Rauschenbusch was a Socialist, although he never became a party member. His contemporary, George D. Herron, was a party member, but he was never a genuine Socialist. Herron was primarily a reformer and Social Gospeleer with an immense ego.

Herron was born in Indiana in 1862 of a Scot father and southern mother. His family was poor, and Herron went to work at the age of ten. He earned a living as a printers' devil and later as a printer. During his spare time, he read the Greek classics. While still working as a printer, he attended Ripon College in Wisconsin and was ordained in 1883 as a Congregational minister. He had a lacklustre early career in small Ohio and Michigan churches, until he delivered, in 1890, a Social-Gospel sermon to the Minnesota Congregational Club in Minneapolis, which caused an instant sensation and won for Herron a major pulpit, the Congregational Church in Burlington, Iowa. He began his Social-Gospel ministry there, delivering sermons on labor, capital, and the injustice of the capitalist system. In Burlington he also met Mrs. E. D. Rand, an extremely wealthy parishioner, and her daughter Carrie. Both were impressed with the young minister, and Mrs. Rand endowed a chair in applied Christianity at Iowa College in Grinnell (now known as Grinnell College), which was awarded to Herron. At the same time, Mrs. Rand's daughter was named dean of women at the college.

Herron was active both as a teacher at the college and as a lecturer throughout the country. A journal, *The Kingdom*, was organized by his friends, his sermons were published in book form, and large crowds were attracted to his lecturers. During his short tenure as professor, Herron's talks became steadily more political and more Socialistic. Some donors protested.

At the same time, Herron, a married man, became romantically involved with Carrie Rand. The trustees brought action to oust Herron. He denied the charges, claiming that the real issue was: "Shall the Churches allow the Christianity of Christ and the early Church to be taught in their schools." He proclaimed: "I will not resign. If I go the trustees must put me out, and the people will know why." Then, suddenly, he resigned under fire.[51] He sent the trustees a conciliatory note:

I do believe that our system of private ownership of natural resources is a crime against God and man and nature. . . . But I recognize that the constituency of this college is equally sincere in believing such teaching to be dangerous and untrue. . . . I have a right to make any sacrifice of myself that I may think worthwhile, for what I believe to be the truth, but I have no right to keep others in a position of sacrifice for that which is other than their chosen work.[52]

After being forced from his chair, Herron went on a speaking tour, supported the Socialist party then in its formative stage, and became active in J. Stitt Wilson's Social Crusade.

In 1901 he divorced his wife, married Carrie Rand, and left the United States permanently to live in Italy. In 1906 he arranged for the endowment of the Socialist Rand School of Social Sciences—named for his mother-in-law—in New York, but he had little else to do with the American movement. With the outbreak of the war in Europe in 1914, Herron broke with the Socialists and supported the Allied cause. He later represented the United States government in dealing with European Socialist rulers, particularly in Germany. He died in 1925.[53]

Herron's Christian Socialism differed from most other brands, because he denied that Jesus was a Socialist or "a believer of any outward government." But he conceded that Jesus was revolutionist, "the most radical revolutionist that ever came to earth," for He proposed to bring the Kingdom of Heaven to earth, and the Kingdom of Heaven meant a society in which all humans should be "equal in opportunity and freedom to live their full lives; in which each should live for the common good."[54] This kingdom could, moreover, be achieved only by revolution.

The hallmark of a Christian was, in Herron's view, sacrifice, the bearing away of the sins of the world. It thus followed that a Christian had to be a revolutionist. Revolution was perforce part of a divine movement. Turn-of-the-century Christians were no exception: they, too, had to be revolutionists. The social system in which they lived was an aberration; the time had arrived for a new revolution; the only question facing the world was "what kind of revolution."[55]

The Christian society Herron hoped the revolution would bring to the earth was best exemplified, in his view, by the orderly medieval monastery. The monks, because they lived in a pure Communist society, were able to preserve for the future intellectual and cultural materials such as those that were developed during the Dark Ages. Also, they gave refuge to the sufferers of injustice, the poor, the dispossessed, and the robbed. Thus to be in accord with God, society would have to be devoid of ambition and competition. "You will hear people talking about honorable ambition, honorable competition. From Christ's point-of-view you can just as well talk about honorable burglary or honorable bigamy." A Christian civilization would require that all would work for the common good, and each "would receive according to every kind of need."[56]

Herron's contribution to the American Left was peripheral, except during the few years he was active in it. His writings were, unlike those of Rauschenbusch, soon forgotten. True, he was primarily responsible for the establishment of the Rand School in which two generations of Socialists were educated. But his own activities were, in the long run, insignificant. His "socialism" won little following.

- 7 -

Some Christian Socialists could not wait for the political process to bring them God's kingdom on earth. They formed communities in which they assumed they could live the "true" Christian life no matter what social system prevailed in the world at large. Among these communities was the Christian Commonwealth, organized in 1897 near Columbus, Georgia.

Fewer than one hundred members lived in the more than 930-acre commune where they raised plums, peaches, sweet potatoes, and other crops; did some dairying; and built a sawmill. All of them pledged to "obey the teachings of Jesus Christ in all matters of life and liberty and the use of property." Moreover, each member pledged to live the Socialist life and to "use, hold, or dispose of all my property, my labor, and my income according to the dictates of love for the happiness of all who need."[57]

But the unity that was necessary for the community to survive was short lived. In short order—after only a year of existence—the colonists were struggling over control of a journal they published called *The Social Gospel*. After two years of feuding, half of the members left the community, taking with them all of the printing equipment.[58] The disagreements generally involved petty, personal matters. But occasional issues of principle also divided them, for example, their reaction to the Spanish American War. Some members of the commonwealth believed that: "No argument whatever is admissable in its [war's] behalf, and only on the plea of . . . insanity can the lips that defend it be recognized as other than savage and pagan."[59] Others defended the war, and saw it bringing order out of anarchy among the "savage . . . half-civilized . . . densely ignorant and superstitious people" in Cuba, Puerto Rico, and the Philippines.[60]

The demise of the commonwealth hardly discouraged others from founding new ones. All of the others failed too, for the lessons of the Christian Commonwealth were neither heeded nor even studied.

- 8 -

All Christian Socialist movements before the turn of the century avoided party affiliation—some of their leaders and members supported the Socialist-Laborites during electoral campaigns; a few even became members of the SLP, although few remained after 1892, and most supported the People's party while it lasted. Beginning with the turn of the century, however, this changed. Christian Socialists in large numbers became active members of the newly formed Socialist party of America. The most significant of the Christian Socialist politicians during the first quarter of the twentieth century was a Canadian-born, Methodist-Episcopal minister, J. Stitt Wilson. His first venture into socialism was the Social Crusade, which he organized in 1898 while serving a Chicago slum parish. The crusade aimed at propagandizing for socialism to trade unions, churches, cooperatives, and study groups. Wilson's socialism was based on a Pollyannalike view of the world. He began with the assumption that evil was vanishing, and mankind was constantly developing a better and more just society. Jesus died so man might realize this society. Just as Jesus had sacrificed Himself, so would contemporary man have to be prepared to bear the burden to achieve the just society, which represented the ultimate "triumph of social man over the savage man." The just society could be achieved only through the abolition of social and economic competition and the development of a cooperative commonwealth. All of this was to come from the "Inspiration of the Divine Spirit."[61]

The crusade had a large following, but like most Christian Socialist movements of that period, it was only temporary. In 1903 Wilson moved to Berkeley, California, and the crusade disappeared. Three years later, a group of his followers, all of whom were also members of the Socialist party, formed a new organization—the Christian Socialist Fellowship.[62] Its proclaimed aim was: "To permeate churches, denominations, and other religious institutions with the social message of Jesus; to show that socialism is the necessary economic of the Christian life; to end the class-struggle by establishing industrial democracy and to hasten the reign of justice and brotherhood upon earth." As dues-paying Socialists, the members of the fellowship assured their less religious comrades that they wanted the party itself to "avoid every form of religious or anti-religious theory or dogma."[63]

The fellowship was active; it held conferences and meetings throughout the country and published pamphlets and journals. Its journal *Christian Socialist* was devoted to political socialism, although its most successful single issue was a special edition on temperance, which reached a circulation of 75,000.

In 1908 the fellowship arranged for 161 ministers to issue a Christian manifesto that declared socialism to be the fulfillment of the economic teachings of the Scriptures and called upon all ministers to join them in working for socialism. George H. Strobell wrote a pamphlet, which the Fellowship published, called *A Christian View of Socialism*, in which he argued that with socialism there would be "for the first time in history . . . an intelligent and systematized movement toward the conscious organization of a just society."[64] But the fellowship soon was torn asunder by an internal squabble over the role of New Yorkers in the organization, and in 1908 it split.[65]

The split and the near demise of the fellowship did little to dampen the ardor for socialism on the part of many Protestant ministers. The Church Socialist Union, an Episcopal group, and new Christian Socialist fellowships, and unions of Christian Socialists were soon organized. Some survived for decades; others soon vanished.

Wilson remained an active Socialist for many years. He preached Christian Socialism throughout the Bay Area. In 1911 Wilson was elected mayor of Berkeley on a Socialist ticket pledging municipal ownership of light, power, water, phone, gas, incinerator, and transit systems in the city, and he pledged to work for lower utility rates, trade-union conditions and higher wages for municipal workers, night schools for adults, kindergartens for children, low-cost school meals for all children, and free textbooks. He also spoke of higher taxes on the unused increment of land values, beautification of the city, uniform assessments, and reduction in municipal expenses. Unfortunately, Wilson served only two years. During his entire term, a majority on the city council was opposed to his program. Little came of it.[66]

During World War I, Wilson broke with the Socialist party and supported the Allied cause. After the war, he rejoined the party, but he resigned permanently in 1934 to support Upton Sinclair's End Poverty in California (EPIC) campaign for governor of California.

- 9 -

The early Christian Socialist movement died with Wilson in 1942. The latter-day Christian Socialists—Norman Thomas, Devere Allen, Sherwood Eddy, and A. J. Muste—were the spiritual progeny of the movements and ideas spawned by Jones, Pentecost, Bliss, Rauschenbusch, Wilson, and, to a lesser extent, Herron.

The Christian Socialists—like the Gronlund-Bellamy-inspired Nationalists—helped give the American Left its uniqueness. The Nationalists' influence was significant, because so many of them eventually did become Socialist party members, and because so many Americans were converted to socialism by Edward Bellamy's book. The Christian Socialists were important, because they laid much of the moral groundwork for American socialism. The leading Socialists in the United States—except for a small group in New York—were hardly Marxists. Their arguments against capitalism were based primarily on what they considered to be the immorality—the violation of the Christian ethic—inherent in the competive industrial society they called capitalism. The speeches of Eugene V. Debs or Norman Thomas, the two great leaders of the Socialist party, read more like sermons against the anti-Christ of capitalism than like "scientific" Marxian social analyses.

A careful examination of the background of Socialist leaders indicates that, with few exceptions, they were more influenced by the Social Gospel than by *Das Kapital*. Even a cursory examination of party convention delegate lists between 1900 and 1912 indicates that at least one in four Socialist party leaders came out of the Christian Socialist movement. In the latter-day movement—especially from 1930 to 1940—the ratio was probably higher.

NOTES

1. See, for example, Arthur Bestor, *Backwoods Utopias: The Sectarian Origins of the Owenite Phase of Communitarian Socialism in America,* 1663–1829 (Philadelphia: University of Pennsylvania Press, 1950), p. 37.

2. Paul Monroe, "English and American Christian Socialism: An Estimate," *American Journal of Sociology* 1 (July 1895): 51–52.

3. *The Social Gospel* 1 (February 1898); Philo Woodruff Sprague, *Christian Socialism, What and Why* (New York: E. P. Dutton Company, 1891), p. 16. This is one of the basic works in early American Christian Socialism. It has, unfortunately, been largely ignored. Cited also in Monroe, "Christian Socialism," p. 56.

4. Monroe, "Christian Socialism," pp. 51–52.

5. See, for example, ibid., p. 68.

6. George E. McNeill, *The Labor Movement: The Problem of Today* (Boston, A. M. Bridgman & Company, 1887), pp. 146–47. Collens was an unusual Christian Socialist in several ways. He was a southerner, a native of New Orleans, and a Roman Catholic; almost all of the other Christian Socialists were northerners and Protestants, primarily Baptists, Episcopalians, Methodists, and Congregationalists. He was a leader in the political and legal community in New Orleans; most of the other Christian Socialists were clergymen. He was also a playwright and novelist of sorts; his only political opus was his last, *The Eden of Labor; or The Christian Utopia*. See *Dictionary of American Biography*, 1958 ed., 2: 300–301.

7. *The Labor Balance* 1 (April 1878): 16; (July 1878): 16.

8. McNeill, *Labor Movement*, pp. 146–47.

9. *The Labor Balance* 1 (April 1878): 16.

10. [Jesse H. Jones], "Our Ideal," *Equity* 1 (April 1874):1; "Report of the Labor Bureau" (editorial), *Equity* 1 (May 1874); [Jesse H. Jones], "Our Political Need," *Equity* 1 (August 1874): 36.

11. [Jesse H. Jones], "In Whose Name," *Equity* 1 (May 1874): 14; see also *Equity* 1 (April 1874):4.

12. *Equity* 1 (April 1874): 6; [Jesse H. Jones], "The Outlook," *Equity* 1 (April 1874): 3; "Report of the Labor Bureau," p. 13.

13. *The Labor Balance* 1 (July 1878): 15. Hitchcock was a conservative theologian who was later to become president of Union Theological Seminary. For his anti-Socialist views, see his *Socialism* (New York: A.D.F. Randolph and Company, 1879).

14. [Jesse H. Jones], "Our Political Need," *Equity* 1 (August 1874): 36.

15. *Equity* 1 (April 1874): 5; (September 1874): 41.

16. [Jones], "In Whose Name," p. 13.

17. *The Labor Balance* 1 (April 1876): 16. Jones published the party platform in the same issue of *The Labor Balance*, pp. 14–15.

18. *The Labor Enquirer* (Chicago) 2 (December 10, 1887): 4; (December 17, 1887): 1; *The Labor Enquirer* (Denver) 7 (December 3, 1887): 1; (December 17, 1887): 4; (December 31, 1887): 4; (January 8, 1887): 2; Oakley Johnson, *An American Century: The Recollections of Bertha Howe, 1866–1966* (New York: Humanities Press for American Institute for Marxist Studies, 1966), p. 125, errs in calling Pentecost a Baptist minister, he was a Congregationalist. Johnson is also inaccurate in blaming Pentecost's defense of the Haymarket defendants for his being "forced" to leave his church.

19. The sermon is reprinted in *The Labor Enquirer* (Denver) 8 (December 17, 1887): 4; (December 31, 1887): 4; (January 1, 1888):2.

20. *The Labor Enquirer* (Chicago) 1 (July 23, 1887); *Workmen's Advocate* 4 (July 28, 1888): 1; *The Commonwealth* 2 (February 15, 1890): 2; Abraham Cahan, *Bleter fun Mein Lebn* [Leaves from My Life] (Yiddish), 5 vols. (New York: Forward Association, 1926–1931), 3: 369; Samuel Gompers, *Seventy Years of Life and Labor*, 2 vols. (New York: E.P. Dutton and Company, 1948), 1: 324–26; Johnson, *An American Century*, p. 40.

21. *The New Nation* 1 (November 7, 1891): 645–46, quoting an article in *Twentieth Century*, October 29, 1891.

22. Johnson, *An American Century*, p. 125. Johnson's book is, unfortunately, replete with errors. His claim that Pentecost, after abandoning the Henry George movement, became an opponent of "rent, interest, and profits" is inaccurate. Pentecost, in fact, abandoned the political Left; he did not return until 1906.

23. Hugh O. Pentecost, "The Pursuit of Happiness," a speech delivered in New York and published in the antireligious *Truth Seeker*, November 3, 1906, is reprinted in Johnson, *An American Century*, see particularly pp. 117–21, 124.

24. Ibid., p. 124.

25. Howard H. Quint, *The Forging of American Socialism: Origins of the Modern Movement* (Columbia, S.C.: University of South Carolina Press, 1953), pp. 109–12; James Dombrowski, *The Early Days of Christian Socialism in America* (New York: Columbia University Press, 1936), pp. 96–107; Charles Howard Hopkins, *The Rise of the Social Gospel in America, 1865–1915,* (New Haven: Yale University Press, 1940), p. 173; W.D.P. Bliss, *A Handbook of Socialism* (1895; reprint ed. London: Swan Sonnenschein and Company, 1907), pp. 145, 214.

26. Quint, *The Forging of American Socialism*, pp. 109–12.

27. W. D. P. Bliss, "Nationalism and Christianity," *The Nationalist* 1 (August 1898): 98–99; W. D. P. Bliss, "What to Do Now," *Dawn* (July-August 1890): 114.

28. Bliss, *Handbook*, p. 145; Philo Woodruff Sprague, *Christian Socialism, What and Why* (New York: E. P. Dutton and Company, 1891), pp. 144–45; James M. Whiton, "Why Christians Should Be Socialists," *Dawn* 2 (May 1890): 2–4.

29. *The Workmen's Advocate* 5 (January 26, 1889).

30. *The Workmen's Advocate* 5 (November 9, 1889).

31. Bliss, *Handbook*, p. 13; Benjamin R. Tucker, W. D. P. Bliss, and E. B. Andrews, "A Symposium Upon the Relation of the State to the Individual" (Papers read at the Ministers' Institute, Salem, Massachusetts, October 14, 1890), reprinted in *Dawn* 2 (November 1890): 276–77.

32. *The New Nation* 1 (April 1891): 154; Bliss, *Handbook*, pp. 109–11; Tucker, Bliss, and Andrews, "Symposium."

33. *Dawn* 6 (July 1894): 128; see also *Dawn* 2 (October 1890): 253; *Dawn* 3 (October 1892): 2; *Dawn* 6 (August 1894): 101.

34. Bliss, "What to Do Now," p. 112; W. D. P. Bliss, "A Study of the Present Situation," *Dawn* 3 (April 1892): 5–9; W. D. P. Bliss, "Socialism and Woman," *Dawn* 2 (October 1890): 247.

35. Dombrowski, *The Early Days*, p. 105; Contributing editors of the *American Fabian* were Henry Demarest Lloyd, Edward Bellamy, and Frank Parsons; *American Fabian* 1 (April 1895): 5.

36. W. D. P. Bliss, "Facts vs. Exaggerations on: Why Socialists Should Vote for Mr. Bryan," *American Fabian* 2 (October 1896): 2–3, 9.

37. Rev. W. D. P. Bliss, "Self-Serving Colonies Condemned," *The Social Gospel* 2 (March 1899): 14–17; see also Bliss, *Handbook*, pp. vii–viii, 17, 23.

38. For Rauschenbusch's biography, see Hopkins, *"The Rise,"* pp. 216–20; Rauschenbusch's final book, *A Theology for the Social Gospel* (New York: The Macmillan Company, 1917), originally written as the Nathaniel W. Taylor Lectures at Yale Divinity School, is probably the most cogent theological rationale for Christian Socialism. Walter Rauschenbusch, dedication in *Christianity and the Social Crisis* (New York: The Macmillan Company, 1907).

39. Rauschenbusch, *Christianity*, pp. 65, 70–71, 111.

40. Ibid., pp. 8, 11, 34, 39–40.

41. Ibid., pp. 47, 49, 64–65, 81.

42. Ibid., pp. 213–19, 234, 239, 318–19, 327.

43. Ibid., pp. 237, 340–41.

44. Ibid., p. 304.

45. Ibid., pp. 179–80.

46. Ibid., pp. 181–82.

47. Ibid., p. 133.

48. George D. Herron to Morris Hillquit, February 5, 1908, Morris Hillquit Papers, Wisconsin State Historical Society, Madison, Wisconsin.

49. Walter Rauschenbusch, "The Appeal of Socialism to the Christian Mind," *Intercollegiate Socialist* 5 (December 1916-January 1917): 8–9.

50. Ibid., p. 8.

51. Hopkins, *The Rise*, pp. 185–98, is probably the best source for material about Herron. Dombrowski, *The Early Days*, contains serious errors, particularly of dates; for data about his role in establishing the Rand School, see Dombrowski, *The Early Days*, p. 174; for his role during and after the war, see pp. 175–77; W. H. Dennison, "Professor George D. Herron, D. D.—A Sketch of His Life and Character," *The Social Gospel* 1 (July 1898): 14–20; *The Social Gospel* 2 (February 1898): 26–27; George D. Herron to Editor of *The Social Gospel*, February 15, 1899, reprinted in *The Social Gospel* 2 (February 1899): 3.

52. George D. Herron to the Trustees of Iowa College, October 13, 1899, reprinted in supplement to *The Social Gospel* 2 (November 1899): n.p.

53. See Hopkins, *The Rise*, pp. 198–99; see also Dombrowski, *The Early Days*, pp. 174–77.

54. George D. Herron, "Christianity and Trusts," *The Social Gospel* 2 (October 1899): 20; George D. Herron, "The Quality of Revolution," *The Social Gospel* 1 (June 1898): 8–10.

55. Ibid.; George D. Herron, "What is a Christian," *The Social Gospel* 2 (January 1899): 7.

56. George D. Herron, "The Economics of the Monastery," *The Social Gospel* 2 (February 1899): 31–32; George D. Herron, "Christ's Economics of Distribution" (a classroom lecture at Iowa College), *The Social Gospel* 1 (February 1898): 6–7; Herron, quoted in *The Social Gospel* 1 (November 1898): 18.

57. "A Brotherhood Organization," *The Social Gospel* 1 (February 1898): 21–23.

58. *The Social Gospel* 3 (June 1900): 23–26.

59. Ernest H. Crosby, "War and Christianity," *The Social Gospel* 1 (July 1898): 5–6.

60. *The Social Gospel* 2 (January 1899): 19.

61. "The Social Crusade," *The Social Gospel* 1 (May 1898): 26–28; Obituary of J. Stitt Wilson, *Berkeley Gazette*, August 29, 1942.

62. Eliot White, "The Christian Socialist Fellowship," *Arena* 41 (January 1909): 47. White was an Episcopal priest who later gained notoreity in New York as an advocate of marriage reform; he was later religion columnist of the official Communist party publication *The Daily Worker*. See also Hopkins, *The Rise*, p. 237.

63. White, "Christian Socialist Fellowship," pp. 47–52.

64. Ibid., pp. 48–50.

65. Hopkins, *The Rise*, p. 239.

66. *Berkeley Gazette*, March 4, 1911, March 8, 1911, March 18, 1911; Hal Johnson, "A Good Man Passes," *Berkeley Gazette*, August 29, 1942. Wilson refused to run for reelection in 1913.

❧ 𝟣𝟧 ❧

The SLP, 1890-1900

- 1 -

The late nineteenth-century efforts of the native Western radicals, of Edward Bellamy and his followers, and of the Christian Socialists failed to change the nature of the Socialist movement. It remained an alien enclave until the turn of the century, when the movement was Americanized despite, rather than because of, the established Socialist leadership. In the end, the imperious rule of the Socialist Labor party (SLP) by Daniel De Leon did more to unite the various trends among American Socialists than did the combined efforts of the Nationalists, Christian Socialists, left-wing Populists, and moderate Marxists. De Leon's autocratic, divisive, and dishonest personality drove almost all of the hitherto divided American radicals to combine—often against their wills—into a new organization dedicated to the cooperative commonwealth but devoid of the political duplicity, ideological dogmatism, and the authoritarian organizational discipline that were the hallmarks of his rule of the SLP. He had, in effect, turned the SLP into a political religion that deified himself personally;[1] by so doing, he forced other Socialists—who might have disagreed with him on some minor particular—to unite into a less doctrinaire Socialist party.

De Leon was, to a great extent, a product of his own myths. His early life is shrouded in mystery; his claims regarding place of birth, ancestry, name, and education are often contradictory—and more often untrue or questionable.[2] What is known about him is that he graduated with high honors from Columbia University's Law School, and that he served from 1883 until 1889 as a lecturer in international law at Columbia University Law School. He had earlier practiced law in New York and Texas.[3]

He was active in Henry George's 1886 attempt to win the mayoralty of New York[4] and remained active in the movement until 1888. He supported the Single-Taxers against the Socialists during the 1887 election.[5] George's stand against the Haymarket defendants, whom De Leon defended, was the only major issue on which they disagreed until 1888.[6] That year De Leon was converted to socialism by reading Bellamy's newly published *Looking Backward* and Gronlund's *Co-operative Commonwealth*. He almost immediately dissociated himself from the Single-Tax movement and joined the New York District Assembly 49 of the Knights of Labor.[7] He also became an active member of the New York Nationalist Club. He now argued against the single tax, claiming that it could not end selfishness, because it would perpetuate capitalism under which each individual would still look out "for himself alone." Each man would still have to keep an "eye peeled" lest another take advantage of him. Capitalism was, De Leon wrote, a "noble system best symbolized by two brawny pugilists holding their clenched fists under each other's noses."[8] His vision of socialism was pure Bellamy Nationalism: "The Central socialistic principle [is] that the state should own, control, and operate the wealth of the community."[9]

Because of his status as a lawyer and university law school teacher, De Leon was an influential member of the New York Nationalist Club. Moreover, the New York Nationalists, unlike the Boston group, cooperated with the local SLP. In October 1890, for example, "Professor" Daniel De Leon represented the city Nationalist organization at the SLP nominating convention. A few weeks later, having cooperated with the Socialists during the election campaign, several New York Nationalists—Daniel De Leon among them—joined the Socialist Labor party.[10]

The Socialists considered De Leon's entry into the party "a major gain for socialism." He was after all, an American of great formal education—a self-proclaimed "professor" at Columbia.[11] (Although a part-time lecturer at Columbia University Law School, De Leon was at no time a professor or a member of the faculty.)

- 2 -

The party De Leon joined was little different from what it had been for twenty years previously—a basically German organization in an English-speaking country. Only seventeen of the party's seventy-seven branches used English as their basic language—most of the rest used German. Minutes of the party conventions were kept in German as well as in English, and convention debates were conducted in both languages. English was adopted as the party's official language only a year before De Leon joined. Even this was more official than real. As late as 1890, only two members of the party's national executive committee, Benjamin J. Gretsch and Henry Kuhn, spoke English fluently.[12]

During the 1890s, the party underwent some ethnic change and some growth. These developments were due to two phenomena: (1) Bellamy and Populist movements and (2) the arrival of non-German, European, Socialist emigres. But the SLP still retained its basically alien nature. Between 1893 and 1896, the membership of the SLP grew from 1,300 to 4,000, but it was still "based on foreign workingmen." As late as 1896, the party press consisted of a small English weekly, *The People*; a large German daily, *New Yorker Volkszeitung*; a German weekly, *Vorwaerts*; a Yiddish daily, *Abendblatt*; and small weeklies in Swedish, Dutch, Italian, and Polish.[13]

The most significant of the new immigrant groups joining the SLP was the East European Jews. Many had arrived as Anarchists fleeing the brutal, anti-Semitic Czarist rule during the 1880s. By the mid-1890s, most of them had become Social Democrats.[14] The Jewish Socialists, who were generally active in organizing trade unions, particularly in the New York garment industry, were to have a significant influence on the Socialist movement's later development.

Although Populists, Nationalists, and new immigrants joined the SLP, it remained a pathetically small party. The slow growth had many reasons, not the least of which was the ideological arrogance, Marxian hair splitting, and Byzantine intrigue that permeated its ranks. One leading member found the "arrogance and . . . intolerable conceit," which existed so often "among my comrades," to be unbearable. He complained that Socialists "rudely reject all fraternity on account of differences which result only in hair splitting" and accused many party members of treating socialism as though it were a religious dogma. Most of all, he decried "the canonization of theories and set phrases, the intolerant sectarian spirit [which] is altogether wrong and damaging to our cause."[15] His criticism, applicable to most other radical movements, was generally ignored.

- 3 -

Ideologically, the SLP was hardly revolutionary during this period. Abraham Cahan, who was emerging as a Jewish party leader by 1891, considered socialism's primary functions to be the elimination of speculation and the creation of conditions that would make it possible for all workingmen to earn an honest living by honest and productive labor. Almost all Socialists agreed with Cahan that the change would come about peacefully, by constitutional means, although some capitalists might employ violence to prevent the revolution from succeeding. "Violence is always started by the class in power," Cahan argued; "revolutionists just stand ready to repel the violent enemy."[16]

Socialists generally assumed that the social revolution was a long way off. It was, therefore, necessary to improve the conditions of the working class under capitalism by economic and social reforms. Morris Hillkowitz, who was to become the intellectual leader of the Socialist party under the name of Morris Hillquit, believed that the social revolution would be the product of such reforms. "We must fight relentlessly to improve the living conditions [of the working class] and for reforms. Every additional cent in wages and every hour less of work are important, not only because they improve the unfortunate lot of the workers, but also because such improvements will bring the worker a step closer to the revolution."[17]

Almost all Socialists agreed with Hillkowitz. Only the Anarchists opposed reforms, and they vehemently condemned the Socialists for favoring them. The Anarchists called the Socialists "betrayers of the people" and "tools of the capitalist class."[18] These charges were to be reiterated at the turn of the century by De Leon and during the 1920s and 1930s by the Communists.

The Socialists ignored the Anarchists interpretation—just as they were later to ignore De Leon and the Communists. Between 1889 and 1900 the SLP platform, although it began with a call for a Socialist revolution, was essentially a program for social reform. Its fourteen economic planks called for a reduction in the hours of labor "in proportion to the progress of production"; government ownership of railroads, canals, telegraphs, and telephones; municipal ownership of public utilities; inviolability of public lands in perpetuity; legal incorporation of local labor unions by states; the United States treasury to be the sole issuer of money; natural resources to be managed scientifically; inventors to be paid by the government and inventions to be free to all; a progressive income tax; free and compulsory education for all up to age fourteen, plus public aid "in meals, clothing, books, etc., where necessary"; repeal of all pauper, tramp, conspiracy and sumptuary laws; publication of official labor statistics; child labor to be outlawed, convict contract labor to be prohibited, and women to be barred from working at trades that are "detrimental to health or morality"; work for unemployed on public projects; all wages to be paid in legal tender; men and women to receive the same pay for the same work; and workmen's compensation laws, insuring workers against injury on the job.[19] The reforms were barely revolutionary—many were to be adopted less than half a century later by an American government whose chief aim was the salvation of the capitalist system, and some were to appear in the platforms of non-Socialist, Populist, and Progressive candidates for the presidency in 1892 and 1924.

As for political demands, which composed a separate section of the platform, they were typically Populist-Progressive. Included were calls for the initiative; the referendum; municipal self-rule; abolition of the executive veto; direct vote; the secret ballot; equal franchise for all regardless of race, color, sex, or creed; proportional representation; the recall of unsatisfactory or dishonest elected officials; uniform civil and criminal law; free administration of justice; and abolition of capital punishment.[20]

This platform adopted originally in 1889, showed the influence of Christian Socialists and followers of Edward Bellamy. The Socialists had eliminated two planks that had been anathemas to most devout Christians: (1) a call for easy divorce for consenting adults and (2) taxation of church property by the state.[21] But these were essentially minor deletions, for the Socialist thrust remained one of reforming the capitalist system to ameliorate the conditions of the working masses. True, Lucien Sanial, the Belgian-born Socialist editor, argued that "the reduction in the hours of work, the compulsory education of children, the regulation of female labor, and any other [immediate] demand . . . are to be considered only as first and necessary steps in the direction of our ultimate object."[22] But most Socialists believed socialism to be a far-off Utopia, and they preached reform. Socialism was, to quote one party spokesman in San Francisco, "fundamentally a bread and butter issue."[23] In Elizabeth, New Jersey, in 1891, SLP candidates ran on a platform of municipal reform that would have been acceptable to most Progressives.[24]

Not all party members or sympathizers were pleased with the omissions in the platforms. J. Howard Sharp, a Socialist in Tennessee, upbraided the party leadership for ignoring black workers. He reported that the Negroes were "as much dependent upon the property owners as they were before the war." He suggested that the SLP make converts among "the more intelligent and honest negroes," who would in turn become agitators for socialism. Sharp blamed the capitalist system for the fact that "the same conditions of family life" as those that prevailed during slavery remained after emancipation. He charged that the blacks remained uneducated, because of "a deliberate and concerted effort on the part of the ruling class to prevent his enlightenment."[25]

Particularly after the 1887 Henry George debacle, Socialists refused to join any alliance, no matter how similar their views were to those of the other coalition partners. In fact, they considered all other parties to be "one reactionary mass." It thus followed that when leaders of the Farmers Alliance and the Knights of Labor met in late 1889 to lay the foundation for the People's party, most SLP members were unenthusiastic. They, in fact, prohibited other SLPers from cooperating with the Populists on pain of expulsion. A few Socialists who disagreed with the edict resigned and supported the Populists. Most remained, convinced that the SLP represented the wave of the future.[26]

Their expectations were not without basis. In 1890 the Socialist state ticket in New York polled a surprising 13,704 votes.[27] In 1892, when the SLP ran its first national ticket—Christian Socialist Simon Wing for president and Nationalist Charles H. Matchett for vice-president—it polled an amazing 21,877 votes. Of this total, 18,147 were in New York State.[28] In 1894 an SLP candidate, Matthew Maguire, was elected an alderman in Paterson, New Jersey—the first candidate of the party to be elected to office. But the victory failed to arouse much enthusiasm, for although the party platform remained essentially the same as it had been in 1889, and divergent opinions were still tolerated in the party,[29] a new leadership was in the process of taking over, and by 1894 the SLP bore the stamp of De Leonism, and most Socialists were looking for another home.

- 4 -

So delighted were the Socialists with their acquisition of De Leon, that they sent him on a speaking tour of the United States almost immediately. That tour, to quote one of his disciples, "was the beginning of the change that was to transform the Socialist Labor Party." De Leon visited about sixty cities. His route took him from New York to Seattle and then back via California and Denver. De Leon used the speaking tour to develop his own following and to build his power base in the SLP.[30]

During his first year in the party, De Leon demonstrated his boundless energy. He attended branch meetings of the party throughout New York City, no matter the weather. "So long as there were five members present at a meeting, De Leon was the sixth."[31]

Within a year after De Leon joined the party, Lucien Sanial editor of *The People*, developed eye difficulties, and De Leon was named his successor.[32] He almost immediately turned *The People* into an instrument for expanding his control of the pary. He published insulting attacks on his opponents in the party. The word *fakir* abounded in its columns, and dissident Socialists were open to accusations of some of the most heinous crimes against socialism. Proof that De Leon's charges were inaccurate—as they were—were useless. "We never retract anything," De Leon told Bernard Weinstein, when the latter pointed out that a victim of De Leon's vitriol was innocent. Loyalty took on a new meaning. "Although it inferred loyalty to the party, it actually meant loyalty to De Leon." Anyone who disdained his leadership, particularly if he was a union official, was labeled "a boodler, a fakir, a swindler." De Leon's tactics "were the tactics of a man who burns with the desire for power."[33] They resembled the tactics Stalin was to use in the Soviet Union some thirty-five years later in his successful quest for power. But there was a difference: Stalin drove his opponents and rivals from the party and thus won genuine power, because the party controlled a country. De Leon forced his opponents and rivals from the party and in the process virtually destroyed the party, for it was a minuscule organization that could ill afford to lose any members.

De Leon's war against any who disagreed with him on even the most minor point included personal vituperation. Thus when an SLP member named Goldenstick asked a sticky question of De Leon, at one of the first lectures he gave in New York, De Leon twisted the questioner's name to "Goldenstink." Even after it had been pointed out to De Leon that he was mispronouncing the man's name, he persisted in calling the man by the insulting name.[34]

- 5 -

The first victim of De Leon's purge was an old-time, English-born Socialist, Charles Sotheran. An editor of bibliographic dictionaries and journals, Sotheran had been active in the Social Democratic Workingmen's party and the SLP since 1874. De Leon had originally praised Sotheran, calling him "solid as steel." But in 1892, Sotheran edited a souvenir journal from which De Leon's name was accidentally missing. De Leon immediately opened clandestine warfare against Sotheran. He assailed Sotheran's book on Horace Greeley and accused him of being anti-Socialist on the basis of that book. Anonymous attacks against Sotheran began to appear in *The People*. Anyone who attempted to defend him was the immediate target of vituperative attack. Finally, De Leon accused Sotheran of misappropriating seventy cents of party funds. He charged that Sotheran had debated from a Populist and not a Socialist point of view for twenty minutes at a party debate. Since the hall cost six dollars to rent, De Leon calculated that Sotheran's argument had used up seventy cents worth of time. Sotheran had also the temerity to assail what Sanial was later to call the "burlesque reign of terror" in the SLP. De Leon used his position on *The People* to retaliate. He accused Sotheran of writing an anti-SLP article in the *New York Sunday Advertiser*, which he knew Sotheran did not write. Finally, he claimed that the English-born Socialist veteran had shown "too wide a tolerance" for Progressive movements outside the Socialist Labor party. By a series of deals and maneuvers, De Leon was able to force Sotheran out of the party.[35]

- 6 -

About the same time as the Sotheran ouster was taking place, De Leon became involved in a struggle for power within the Arbeiter Zeitung Publishing Association, the publishers of the Yiddish-language Socialist weekly *Arbeiter Zeitung*. The struggle involved no principles; it was based solely on petty, personal issues. It was triggered by a supposed personal slight of some of the association's leading lights at the 1893 conference of the Jewish sections of the SLP. The only issue involved was the membership of the association. The leadership wanted it to remain a small association answerable to no one but its officials. The opposition group proposed that the association be restructured into an organization representing all Socialist and pro-Socialist labor groups.[36] The Boston Jewish Socialists became so disenamored by the feuding that they published their own competing weekly, *Der Emes*.[37]

De Leon, whose theoretical position was closer to that of the opposition, nevertheless became involved in the struggle on behalf of the leadership in 1895. He reached an agreement with the leaders of the association that he would support them in their struggle with the opposition—headed by Abraham Cahan, Louis Miller, and Morris Winchevsky, all three of whom were to become significant figures in Yiddish journalism—if they would support him in his internal party disputes. About a year later, De Leon and his allies forced the opposition out of the Arbeiter Zeitung Publishing Association. The Cahan-led opposition began immediate planning for the publication of a new newspaper. De Leon and the association leadership accused the Cahan group of treason and moved to oust the nine ringleaders from the SLP. When the charges were rejected by the Jewish branches, De Leon arranged for the party secretary, Henry Kuhn, who was closely associated with him, to "reorganize" the Jewish branches thus ousting 300 SLP members in one fell swoop.[38]

"The Socialist Labor Party was to us equal to what a religion is to a devout man," Cahan recalled. "We were bitterly opposed to De Leon . . . his machine, and his intrigues, but the party was our party. We could not picture ourselves without the party anymore than a devout Jew could picture himself without a synagogue."

The ouster gave De Leon the opportunity to vent his spleen on the Jewish Socialists who rejected his edicts. In a sly, anti-Semitic editorial, he assailed the "moral, physical and intellectual riff-raff from Russia in this city" and accused the Jewish Socialists of organizing an opposition party, because they were "unable to use the Socialist Labor Party for their own crooked purposes." They were, he wrote, "Polish Jew Anarchists."[39]

The fight against the Jewish Socialists was, to a great extent, a calculated Machiavellian maneuver. De Leon assumed, incorrectly, that the Arbeiter Zeitung Publishing Association leadership would win the struggle with the opposition. Unfortunately for De Leon, the opposition's newspaper, the *Jewish Daily Forward*, became the dominant Yiddish daily in America within five years and the *Arbeiter Zeitung* and its daily version, the *Abendblatt*, disappeared.

- 7 -

Even more vituperative than his assault on the Jewish opposition was De Leon's attack on the Socialist Newspaper Union (SNU), a cooperative publishing association owned by several SPL sections, which published the weekly *St. Louis Labor* and its satellite editions in several middle western cities. The SNU posed a direct threat to De Leon's hegemony over the party press. First, the SNU papers were formally endorsed in 1893 by the national executive committee of the party. Second, at the suggestion of the party's executive committee, the SNU, which owned its own plant, offered to publish *The People*. The proposal was made in good faith, but it failed to recognize De Leon's personal stake in the *The People*, which had by this time become his personal organ and power base. De Leon answered the suggestion with a series of attacks against the SNU, its newspapers, and their staffs.

The American section of the New York SLP voted fourteen to thirteen to censure De Leon for these attacks on the St. Louis Socialist publishing organization. De Leon rejected the censure and charged the fourteen who voted for it "so far forgot themselves as to lay upon the S.L.P. such Kangaroo court proceedings." At the 1896 convention—having forced many of his opponents from the party—he forced through a regulation giving control of the party press to the national executive committee, which he now dominated, who would name the editors of all party newspapers.[40] This eliminated another threat to his control of the party.

Thus in less than six years, Daniel De Leon had cemented his rule of the SLP. He controlled the party secretary, the party executive committee, and the party press. But it was a party with no future, for he had alienated most Socialists. The editor of the *American Fabian* wrote in December 1895 that although "he has always favored the principles of the Socialist Labor Party . . . he has objected to some of its tactics, and especially to the—in his opinion—needlessly censorious and vindictive utterances of the party's principal English-speaking organ."[41] Even the editor of the Yiddish Socialist daily *Abendblatt* found his accusations and attacks "too excessive." The editor warned that "Such warlike and intolerant tactics are in every respect unfortunate for our party and have raised enemies for it among the friends of socialism."[42] His tactics forced Fred E. Martin and Harry Glyn, both members of the party's national executive committee, to resign from the party. Martin charged that De Leon's "unreasonable . . . indiscriminate" attacks had "hopelessly estranged the hundreds of thousands of organized American workingmen whose close relations with machinery, the greatest modern factor of production, make these bodies logically the most prolific field in this country for the propagation of the truths of Socialism." Martin concluded by charging that the party's tactics under De Leon "constitute an object lesson which cannot fail to dishonor the noblest idea of the 19th Century."[43]

- 8 -

Almost all Socialists believed in labor unions, which they considered to be the economic arm of the social revolution, just as they assumed the SLP was the political arm. But not all Socialists agreed on the relation between the two. Some favored "boring from within" existing trade unions—that is, of working within the existing labor organizations and trying to win the leadership—and membership—over to socialism. Others believed that trade unionists could not be won to socialism except in Socialist trade unions. They thus favored the organization of Socialist labor unions that would compete for members with the existing organizations.

From the outset, American Socialists generally favored "boring from within." First, the Socialist movement was so small that it could not successfully form new unions. Second, the trade-union movement itself was so weak that Socialists feared they would be accused of being enemies of organized labor if they formed competing organizations.

During the 1880s, the SLP worked closely with the labor-union movement. In 1888, for example, Charles Sotheran, a leader of the SPL, was the delegate of the New York Central Labor Union to the convention of the American Federation of Labor.[44] A year earlier, Socialists had hailed the re-election of Samuel Gompers as president of the AF of L. They called it a guarantee that "the organization intends to stay in the path of progress." Gompers was then considered pro-Socialist because the AF of L unions were open to Socialist propaganda, and many of their leaders were nominal Socialists.[45]

But the friendship was short lived. In 1889 Gompers, who had political ambitions, was approached by both the Democratic and Republican parties and offered a joint nomination for the New York State Senate. He appealed to the Central Labor Federation (CLF) for advice on whether to accept the nomination. Although the SLP would enter no ticket that year, pro-Socialist delegates prevailed upon the federation to advise Gompers to reject it. By a vote of forty to eight, the CLF delegates passed a resolution that condemned the two parties "who have nominated him" as "the ones who today oppress labor." The delegates called the Senate a "chamber of prostitution, not to be touched by workmen unless elected upon a labor ticket for the direct purpose of putting an end to such prostitution." Gompers accepted the decision reluctantly.[46] He blamed the Socialists for short-circuiting his political career.

A year later, he got his revenge. The New York Central Labor Federation, which included among its affiliates the American section of the Socialist Labor party, attempted to obtain the charter as the official AF of L organization for New York City. The newly formed and more conservative Central Labor Union also applied. Gompers backed the CLU; he noted that the SLP was officially in the federation. "I cannot bring myself to understand how a political party as such can be represented in a central trade union organization," he wrote to the CLF. He insisted that "the representation of that party or any other political party in a purely trade union central organization is to my mind not permissible."[47]

Lucien Sanial, who was then the leader of the SLP, answered that the admission of the SLP was proof that the CLF had put an end to "political scabbery" by trade unions. It "meant that no wage-worker would be deemed a good trade unionist, who after fighting capitalism in his shop the whole year proved a political scab on the last day and contributed his vote to the perpetuation of the capitalist system." Sanial called for a merger of the "economic and political labor movements . . . into one great comprehensive movement."[48]

Sanial's argument won the CLF delegates' support. One, representing the cloakmakers union, told the meeting that "The Socialists have performed more labor for the workingman than did the officers of the A.F.L. They fought for all the toilers against the capitalist. We could better dispense with the [AF of L] charter than with the Socialists."[49] Not only did the Central Labor Federation members support the Socialist position, they also selected Sanial, the delegate from the SLP, as their representative at the AF of L convention.[50]

Gompers had invited the CLF to send its representative to the convention to explain its position. "I am satisfied all courtesies will be extended to him for the purpose of presenting his case," he wrote to Ernest Boehm, secretary of the CLF. Gompers proved to be a man of his word. The Credentials Committee took no action on the seating of Sanial; it turned the matter over to the entire convention. The result was a day of acrimonious debate. Sanial pleaded with the delegates to recognize that there "is a fundamental difference between the old plutocratic parties and the S.L.P., that the former are notoriously the political machines of the employing class . . . whereas the Socialist Labor Party is owned and controlled by wage workers like yourselves, who are in full sympathy with you upon all the economic principles thus far advanced." He pointed out that trade unions of Europe were organized by the Socialists and inferred that the SLP would be an invaluable ally in organizational work by the trade unions. But his plea went for naught. Eighty-one delegates, representing 1,690 votes, backed Gompers; only ten delegates, with 535 votes, supported Sanial. The SLP was barred from the AF of L.[51]

Gompers action, which earned him the enmity of most Socialists, was defended by Friedrich Engels: "His Federation is, as far as I know, an association of trade-unions and nothing but trade unions. Hence they have the *formal* right to reject anyone coming as the representative of a labor organization that is not a trade union . . . [it] was beyond the question that it had to come, and I, for one, cannot blame Gompers for it."[52]

The delegates to the Bakers and Confectioners Journeymen International Union's 1891 convention condemned Gompers for his action and endorsed the SLP. Even Gompers's own Cigarmakers' International Union was unhappy with his stance, and Gompers was forced to explain to its 1891 convention that he was "not in opposition to the principles of the Socialistic Labor Party," but that he and "the party named could not agree on tactics." Moreover, since the great majority of working people were opposed to socialism, he was obliged to support "pure-and-simple" trade unionism.[53]

The AF of L was to be the target for "borers from within" for many more years, but never again would the SLP be directly involved. In 1894 a pro-Socialist plank was passed at an AF of L convention, but it was never officially enacted, and it was eliminated—by questionable means—at the next year's convention.[54]

Gompers was, from 1890 on, a target for the Socialists. De Leon and his followers called him a "fakir," an "ignoramus," and dishonest. One SLPer charged later that Gompers had founded the AF of L "at the instigation and under the patronage of Andrew Carnegie."[55]

Barred from the AF of L after the 1890 convention, the SLPers turned their attention to "capturing" the rapidly declining Knights of Labor. The Knights of Labor appeared to be a far more likely target for Socialist "boring from within" than the AF of L. Its organization was open to anyone except members of some professions—most notably lawyers—and its organization was built along community and industrial rather than along craft lines. Moreover, its rhetoric sounded far more Socialist than did the pure-and-simple trade union jargon of the AF of L.[56] Pro-De Leon Socialist-Laborites generally argued that the philosophy of the Knights was more in accord with the class struggle than were the teachings of the AF of L.[57]

Some justification could be found for the SLPers' views. Many of the Knights of Labor lodges, particularly in the West, were controlled by Socialists. The Eureka [Oregon] Lodge, for example, had proclaimed: "We believe that the Knights of Labor is a fundamentally Socialistic organization and should . . . be deeply interested in . . . bringing into closer relations those imbued with the Socialistic spirit."[58] A New York Knight went even further and called for an immediate social revolution that would replace "the system of capitalistic spoliation by one of universal co-operation."[59]

But by 1893 the Knights had become a shell of an organization. The growth of the AF of L and the growing conservatism and incompetence of the top leadership of the order had resulted in a decline in membership from almost 750,000 in 1886 to slightly more than 250,000 two years later, to 100,000 by 1890, and down to less than 75,000 in 1893 when the SLPers made their move to gain control of the order.[60]

The chief target of the Socialists in the Knights of Labor was Terrence V. Powderly, grand master workman of the order since 1879. Only thirty years old when he became grand master workman, Powderly had worked on railroads as a machinist before his election in 1878 as Greenback-Labor mayor of Scranton, a post he held until 1884. During his tenure as mayor he had—despite later denials—accepted a membership card in the Socialist Labor party. Although he was never active in the party, he called himself a Socialist as late as 1892 when he supported the Populists. He was a Populist, he said, because "the methods of the Socialists prove to be unsuccessful."[61]

Despite his Socialist rhetoric, Powderly was an indecisive, bungling conservative. He led the Knights during a period of gravest labor unrest, although he was an opponent of the strike as an instrument for improving conditions of the workingman. After a series of victories in railroad strikes between 1882 and 1885, the Knights suffered a serious reverse in 1886, losing a strike against the Jay Gould railroads of the Southwest. The loss was, in part at least, due to the vaccilation of Powderly and his executive board. A strike shortly thereafter at the Chicago stockyards was lost by the Knights because of apparent betrayal by Powderly.[62]

As early as 1887, the organized Socialists in the Knights opposed Powderly's rule. That year Powderly had supported the execution of the Haymarket Anarchists and had declared war against all radicals within the order. Most of the western lodges, then under the influence of Joseph Buchanan and, to a lesser extent, Burnette G. Haskell, opposed Powderly. But most of the western lodges by 1890 had disappeared or, like Buchanan, had been absorbed into the AF of L. It was not until 1893 that the Socialists, then under the influence of Daniel De Leon, were in a position to challenge Powderly. The Socialists by then had a major base: they had captured control of District Assembly 49, the Knights' New York district assembly. Moreover, they had found an ambitious ally in James R. Sovereign, leader of the agrarian wing of the Knights. Although an agrarian, Sovereign used Socialist rhetoric, arguing that the Knights "is not founded on the question of adjusting wages, but on the question of abolishing the wage system and the establishment of a cooperative industrial system. When its real mission is accomplished, poverty will be reduced to a minimum and the land dotted with peaceful happy homes."[63] At the 1893 convention, the Socialist-agrarian alliance was able to oust Powderly. Sovereign replaced him.[64]

For the next year, continuous bickering took place between the pro-Sovereign forces and the Socialists who claimed the "blundering political economy and false sociology" preached by the "agrarians" was hampering the Knights. The "blundering political economy and false sociology" that De Leon and his followers accused the Knights of Labor leadership of practicing was simple labor politics; Sovereign had said that the Knights would work to defeat any congressman who had voted against Knights of Labor-supported measures. De Leon castigated Sovereign for his statement: "If the workers were to endeavor to defeat the Republican Reed in Maine by supporting his Democratic adversary, and to defeat the Democrat Bailey in Texas by supporting his Republican adversary, then, whichever way the elections turned out the workers would be the only losers."[65] A serious effort by supporters of Powderly to recapture what was left of the order forced Sovereign and De Leon to remain united at the 1894 convention, where the De Leonites supported Sovereign for reelection. But as the price for their support, they extracted a promise that De Leon-controlled District Assembly 49 would name the new editor of the *Journal of the Knights of Labor*.[66]

Sovereign could not keep the promise; the order was in bad financial straits. Fortuitously, scandal broke over Daniel De Leon's head. Charles Sotheran, the long-time Socialist-Laborite who had earned the enmity of De Leon by omitting his name from a souvenir program, sent a letter to the leaders of District Assembly 49, charging that De Leon was not eligible for membership, because he was an attorney. He pointed out that even law students were barred from membership. De Leon had, in fact, practiced law in both Texas and New York and had taught at the Columbia Law School. "He is still technically a member of the New York Bar," Sotheran concluded. The letter could not be taken lightly; Sotheran was the past master workman of the Excelsior Labor Club, the mixed assembly composed chiefly of New York intellectuals. Sovereign now had the excuse he sought; he expelled De Leon. When District Assembly 49 ignored the expulsion, it was ousted, and with it the troublesome New York Socialist-Laborites.[67] But it was a Pyrrhic victory for Sovereign. By 1895 hardly enough was left in the Knights of Labor to make it worth fighting over. The total membership of the order had declined to less than 30,000.[68] Twenty-four years later, a De Leon supporter was to write that "it was found in the end that the whole fabric of the organization [Knights of Labor] was rotten to the core and nothing could be gained by capturing what had been reduced to a nest of crooks."[69] But this was reflection after almost a quarter of a century had elapsed. In 1895 the Knights of Labor appeared to be a valuable prize to De Leon. His defeat ended the SLPers venture into "boring from within."

"We tried it," De Leon claimed, but "finally, we landed on the outside." Anyone who "bored" for the purpose would "land on the outside," he maintained. The alternative would be to knuckle under the "labor lieutenants of the capitalists" and thus become a "silent supporter of the felonies" they commit. "Boring from within" was, he argued, little more than a synonym for surrender. "Boring from within meant to throw up the sponge, sheath the sword, and become a traitor to the working class. Boring from within meant that you had to keep quiet, and get the applause of the labor fakir, so that he might do what he wanted to do."[70]

Instead of working within existing unions, De Leon and his followers decided, almost immediately, to form dual unions that would compete with existing AF of L or Knights of Labor organizations. The officials of District Assembly 49, The Central Labor Federations of New York, Brooklyn, and Newark, and the United Hebrew Trades met in December 1895 and organized the Socialist Trade and Labor Alliance (ST and LA). The first meeting merely drew a rough outline of what the new organization would represent, but it was apparent that its founders wanted it "on the economic field . . . [to]

stand toward the corruptionists of the fake Knights of Labor, on the one hand, and the played-out scarecrow of the American Federation of Labor on the other, in the same uncompromising attitude as the SLP stands in the political field towards all the parties of capital."[71] De Leon claimed that the ST and LA was a truly American labor organization, that pure-and-simple trade unionism was an import from Britain. Instead of fighting for immediate alleviation of conditions, as trade unions would normally do, De Leon said the ST and LA would accept the Socialist thesis that "there was no such thing as establishing permanent relations between the proletariat and the capitalist, but that the system had to be overthrown and substituted by the Co-operative Commonwealth."[72] The main task of the ST and LA would be to transfer the main bout in the class struggle "to the political arena where the proletariat is omnipotent." The working class was, according to De Leon, virtually helpless in the economic or industrial arena "where at best it can offer only temporary resistance owing to lack of CAPITAL—the weapon there in use." But in the political arena, the proletariat would be supreme "owing to its ownership of the BALLOT the only weapon there needed." Since the proletariat was larger than the capitalist class by one hundred to one, it was only logical to De Leon that the working class could rout its adversaries at the ballot box with little trouble.[73]

De Leon's argument apparently convinced almost all of the other Socialist-Laborites. They voted overwhelmingly at the 1896 convention to endorse the ST and LA. In moving the resolution of support, De Leon called the existing unions buffers for capitalism, and the ST and LA the shield of the SLP's sword. He took the occasion to assail those who questioned the wisdom of dual unionism. "As is the case everytime an important step is to be taken, there are some in our own ranks who would favor a faint-hearted and noncommital attitude on the part of the party, fearing . . . that a firm and decided stand would involve us in conflicts. They seem to forget that the whole Socialist movement is the child of conflict," De Leon wrote in the name of the party's national executive committee.[74]

Almost immediately, the ST and LA became De Leon's weapon aimed at destroying the existing trade unions. "These unions cannot be ignored," he declared. "They must be battered to pieces from without. . . . [Some] will have to be taken by storm."[75] His militant antipathy toward existing unions soon drove the Central Labor Federation of New York to leave the ST and LA.[76] The United Hebrew Trades and the other Central Labor Federations followed suit.

The alliance was never a significant factor in the American labor movement. But it was in a few cases an irritant, and in at least one case—at the Seidenberg shop—it helped break a cigarmakers strike. De Leon never hid his disdain for economic strikes, nor was he above urging workers to break a strike if it served his purpose. The ST and LA, be believed, had an obligation to organize the workers, "enlighten them, and whenever a conflict breaks out in which their brothers are being fooled and used as food for cannon, to have the S.T. and L.A. throw itself in the midst of the fray and sound the note of sense."[77]

The Socialist Trade and Labor Alliance remained a minuscule organization of De Leonites until 1906, when it was, for a short time, amalgamated into the Industrial Workers of the World.

- 9 -

Daniel De Leon's contribution as a Socialist theorist has been acclaimed by most radicals, even those who detested him personally. Yet De Leon was not a systematic thinker; his philosophy must be culled from reading his editorials—written weekly between 1892 and 1900—or his speeches delivered during this period. De Leon did not write a single major work, nor did he ever attempt to arrange his writings systematically. Moreover, De Leon addressed himself to immediate and particular incidents; his editorials and speeches were *not* intended to be theoretical works. The issues to which De Leon addressed himself during the 1890s were the Populist movement, cooperative communities, the war with Spain, and social reform.

De Leon's position on the Populist movement developed from one of enthusiastic optimism to belligerent antipathy within a year. In 1891 he saw the Populists as a recruiting ground for Socialists. "All that the Socialists have to do is to push their wagon up into the Alliance districts and they will capture the whole movement," he said then. Moreover, he hailed the Populist movement because it would, at least, remove political apathy "—the greatest difficulty we have had to contend against."[78] But later that year when he spoke in the farm districts, he roused little interest and made few if any converts to socialism. He then decided that Populism was a farmers' movement designed to rescue capitalism. He called the People's party platform "farm bourgeois" and argued that it was aimed at salvaging the doomed position of the farming class. "Far from being revolutionary it is one of the most conservative and even retrograde . . . in the history of economic evolution," he editorialized in *The People*. "Its object is to perpetuate a class that modern progress has doomed, and the only result can be to prolong the agony of the poor people who belong to it by deferring the day of their complete emancipation. [Its supporters] mistake blind rebellion for intelligent revolution."[79]

In De Leon's view, the middle class and the working class could have no alliance. "All middle class movements are grafts upon the rotten trunk of capitalism; the polluted sap they draw from that trunk infects their very being—the result in all cases must be mortification, decomposition, and death." The farmers, of all middle-class elements, were the least likely to form a viable working coalition with the workers, because their interests are often diametrically opposed; the farmers are often the employers of under-paid and overworked hands.[80] The only interest such middle-class men could have would be in reforming the capitalist system to serve their own purposes better. Socialists, "who in their overwhelming majority are wage workers," could therefore not join the "small-fry farmers and tradesmen" in their struggle against the trusts.

"Beware of the People's Party," De Leon warned an outdoor audience at Faneuil Hall, Boston. "The party is bound to disappear, because it is made up of middle class men." Edward Bellamy, then active in the Populist movement, rejoined in print:

There scarcely is or ever has been any important leader of the socialistic movement who did not come from the middle class or the wealthy class. . . . The respected gentleman who uttered the . . . words before Faneuil Hall . . . is a former professor at Columbia University and a gentleman who neither is nor ever was identified, save by sympathy, with the proletarian class. . . . Are we to understand that Socialists may safely accept middle class and upper class men as leaders and as candidates for office, but must beware of them as comrades and voters.[81]

Despite his disagreement with Bellamy over the People's party, De Leon's socialism remained, at least until the end of the century, deeply rooted in *Looking Backward* and *Equality*. He considered the industrial trust to be an advanced form of capitalism and a step in the direction of socialism. In fact, he considered monopoly capitalism—the economic system based on privately owned trusts—to be "socialism for the few at the expense of the many." The Socialists proposed the socialization of the existing trusts, thus turning the rapacious capitalist system into euphoric socialism. Under a Socialist state the trust would seek to "preserve it [civilization] and improve it, and open it to all."[82] This change could be achieved only politically and nationally. Cooperative communities, such as those organized by Owen or Haskell, he believed, were worse than useless; they were actually anti-Socialist. In De Leon's view, they denied a basic tenet of socialism, the interdependence of contemporary man. Today "the co-operative commonwealth must be coextensive with the nation's boundaries."[83] Only a national system of socialism would do—and that required political change. Generally, De Leon assumed that political change meant a Socialist victory at the polls, but at times he inferred that other methods might be necessary. "The Socialist movement is a movement of peace," he wrote in 1897. "It does not, however, ignore that force is at times the midwife of peace."[84]

De Leon assumed that the capitalist class was more class conscious than the working class. It was this assumption that gradually turned him from a sanguine Socialist into a pessimist. The workers were the majority of the population, but the class-conscious capitalists could by stealth turn their attention from social revolution to other useless, deleterious interests.

Nowhere was this view more apparent than in the war against Spain in 1898.

De Leon recognized nationalism as a normal drive among civilized men. He even considered it a virtue, although he warned that driven to excess, nationalism could become a vice. He had also been a paid propagandist for a group of Cuban Nationalist revolutionaries in New York. Moreover, the Socialist Labor party's organ *Workmen's Advocate* had only ten years previously urged the United States to aid the Cubans win their freedom from Spain. Yet when war broke out between Spain and the United States, with Cuba's freedom as the ostensible issue, De Leon opposed both sides. This was not, in his opinion, a true war for national liberation; it was a struggle between "capitalistic schemers calling themselves 'Cuban patriots' " and Spanish capitalists attempting to hold on to a source of revenue. In the end, he argued, the American sugar and tobacco trusts—"and other American sharks"—would take "actual possession of the island in the name of King Dollar." The war was also being used, according to De Leon, to divert the attention of the masses from their own dire straits and as a means of getting rid of the "turbulent elements at home." But the imperialists' hopes would fail, he wrote, for the war against Spain, and the invasion of the Philippines that followed, proved that capitalism was in its final stages and that socialism was near.[85]

De Leon's stand was not unique among Socialists; they were sharply divided on the issue. William J. Ghent, editor of the *American Fabian*, called on the United States to intervene in behalf of "their helpless and oppressed neighbors." The supporters of the Jewish daily *Forward*, who had been forced from the SLP the previous year, carried signs reading *Cuba Libre* ("Free Cuba") in the 1898 May Day parade. Victor Berger's *Vorwaerts* of Milwaukee opposed militarism and war generally but saw some advantage to this conflict, because it would advance Cuba to a higher stage of capitalism and thus closer to socialism. But Eugene V. Debs, the railway labor leader turned Socialist, was vehemently opposed to the war, which he blamed on American capitalist greed. Julius A. Wayland, the Socialist publisher, claimed that the war would aid American financial interests without helping the Cubans, and Thomas J. Morgan, Chicago trade unionist and Socialist leader, warned that American intervention in the Philippines would reduce the Filipinos to the level of the disfranchised Negroes of America's South. Moreover, some non-Marxists—particularly A. S. Edwards, editor of the *Coming Nation* and Herbert Casson, pastor of the Lynn, Massachusetts, Labor Church—were vehement in their opposition to the war and to the militarism they feared would develop from it.[86]

The philosophy that emerged from De Leon's writings on war, Populism, and revolution was similar to that which emerged from most European Social Democrats of the period. It is in his two major speeches of the late

1890s—"Reform and Revolution," 1896, and "What Means This Strike," 1898—that he delineates his hallmark: revolutinary authoritarianism.

The overriding purpose of strikes, according to De Leon, was inspirational. The New Bedford strikers he addressed in "What Means This Strike" were, he told them, chasing after illusions in seeking higher wages and shorter hours. Despite this, "You preserve manhood enough not to submit to oppression, but rise in the rebellion that is implied in a strike. The attitude of workingmen engaged in a strike is an inspiring one."[87] But the labor movement had more to it than the Sorelian myth implied in the above statement; a new system was being born that needed the support of the working class. It was a revolution for economic and social justice.

Capitalism was based on theft, according to De Leon. All wealth, he argued, was founded on labor, but labor only received a small part of its own product. Most wealth was stolen by the capitalists in the form of profit. This booty was allowed to accumulate in the form of capital, the cornerstone of the present system.[88] It was on the basis of this simplistic version of Marx's theory of surplus value, his distrust of amelioration without revolution, and his belief in the revolutionary myth that De Leon built his political theory—such as it was.

Reform of capitalism, he believed was futile. It was the system itself that perpetuated the robbing of the worker by the capitalist, and it was the system that had to be changed. The change had to be internal—the whole workings of society had to be changed—for the injustice to end. To leave the internal mechanism untouched while reforming some external forms was useless. Thus "Socialists are not reformers; we are revolutionists. We . . . do not propose to change forms. . . . We want a change of the inside of the mechanism of society; let the form take care of itself." No reform, he insisted, could bridge the gap between the interests of the capitalist and the working classes. "It is a struggle that will not down and must be ended only by either the total subjugation of the working class or the abolition of the capitalist class." There was no middle way.[89]

He considered socialism to be the product of pure science. Just as Darwin understood the ongoing struggle between the species, so Socialists understood that an irrepressible conflict existed between the classes, and they recognized that "the line that divides the combatants is . . . [an] economic line." All intelligent workingmen thus would be conscious of the class and thus would favor a social revolution that would overthrow the system of "private ownership in the tools of production, because the system keeps them in wage slavery."[90]

Any changes that came about before the working class had seized political power through its own party according to De Leon, would be delusory. "So long as the capitalist class held the government, all . . . laws [favorable to labor] were a snare and a delusion." Thus the workingman had to become publicly allied with the party of his class—De Leon's SLP—and struggle for political power for labor. To those who argued that a working-man's politics, like his religion, was a private matter, De Leon answered that they were no more private than were "the wages and the hours of a working man . . . his private concern." Just as his wages and hours were the concern of his class, so too were his politics.[91]

From these assumptions, De Leon developed his authoritarianism. He believed socialism to be neither ethical nor unethical, neither "an aspiration of angels nor a plot of devils"; it was essentially a product of science and went "whithersoever she [science] points." Just as science was intolerant of error, just as science insisted "that two and two make four," so Socialists had "under no circumstances [to] allow that they make five." No compromise could be made with anything that did not accept the rule of science as defined by De Leon. To achieve a scientific society would require organization, and "organization implies directing authority."[92] Thus De Leon favored "collective freedom" under a "central directing authority." To those who argued that he was preaching bossism or dictatorship, De Leon answered that "the cry of 'Bossism' is as absent from the revolutionist's lips as it is a feature on those of the reformer." He believed a revolutionary party required disciplinary firmness and control from above. Above all else, the revolutionary party could not allow any tampering with its discipline.[93]

- 10 -

By 1897 the SLP was in a state of disintegration. De Leon had driven more than half the membership out of the party. The issue of the Socialist Trade and Labor Alliance—Socialist versus pure-and-simple trade union-ism—was forcing many other Socialists—particularly union men—to consider dissociating themselves from the SLP. By 1899 De Leon's rule made it impossible for the party to remain even nominally united and led to the final split in July of that year. The ostensible issue was the use by the anti-De Leon *New Yorker Volkszeitung* of *The People*'s mailing list to publicize its own monthly English edition.[94] But that was only an excuse; the party was already torn asunder. By July 1899 the SLP was no longer a potential political force in America.

At the next year's convention, it was decided to exclude from membership any official in any pure-and-simple trade union. All mention of immediate demands was deleted from the platform. It was now Daniel De Leon's personal party. During the next few years, almost all of those who had remained with De Leon after the 1899 split left his party: among them were Lucien Sanial, former editor of *The People* and SLP delegate to the Socialist International Meeting of 1900; Hugo Vogt, De Leon's chief adviser; Julian Pierce, manager of New York Labor News Company, the party publishing house; and James P. Reid and Thomas Curran, leaders of the party in Rhode Island.[95]

Except for a brief excursion into syndicalism, the SLP was virtually dead. All that remained of it was Daniel De Leon and a corporal's guard of adulators. Most Socialists had found a new party.

NOTES

1. Even in a eulogy for De Leon, Louis Fraina conceded that he was "temperamentally a Jesuit, consistently acting on the principle that the end justifies the means." See Louis Fraina, "Daniel De Leon," *New Review* 2 (July 1914): 397.

2. See Bernard K. Johnpoll, "A Note on Daniel De Leon," *Labor History* 17 (Fall 1976): 606–12.

3. *New York World*, October 26, 1886, p. 3.

4. *New York World*, October 2, 1886, p. 2. De Leon listed himself as Dr. Daniel De Leon.

5. *New York Tribune*, October 24, 1887, p. 1. De Leon is listed erroneously as Professor Daniel De Lisle.

6. *The Labor Enquirer* (Denver) 7 (October 29, 1887): 8.

7. Lester Luntz, "Daniel De Leon and the Movement for Social Reform, 1886-1896" [1939], p. 10, typescript, Edward Bellamy Collection, Houghton Library, Harvard University, Cambridge, Massachusetts.

8. Daniel De Leon, "A Criticism of the Single Tax," *Twentieth Century* 2 (February 2, 1889): 31. The article is signed "Daniel De Leon, Ph.D." De Leon had no such degree.

9. Daniel De Leon, "Mental Phenomena," *Twentieth Century* 2 (March 23, 1889): 87.

10. *Workmen's Advocate* 5 (August 24, 1889): 3; 6 (October 4, 1890): 1.

11. Abraham Cahan, *Bleter fun Mein Lebn* [Leaves from My Life] (Yiddish), 4 vols. (New York: Forward Association, 1926–1931), 3: 282.

12. *Workmen's Advocate* 5 (February 2, 1889): 3; (October 26, 1889): 1; Henry Kuhn, "Reminiscences of Daniel De Leon," in *The Man and His Work: A Symposium*, Daniel De Leon, 2 vols. (New York: New York Labor News Company, 1919), 1: 4–5.

13. Lester Luntz, "Daniel De Leon and the Movement for Social Reform" (Manuscript, n.p., 1939), pp. 21–22, 24, Edward Bellamy Collection; *The People* 6 (July 12, 1896).

14. For a discussion of the intricacies in the development of the Jewish Socialist movement in the United States during the late 1880s and early 1890s, see J. S. Hertz, *Di Idishe Sotsialistishe Bavegung in Amerika* (Yiddish) (New York: Der Wecker, 1954), especially pp. 22–23. The Jewish Anarchist movement did not evaporate. It continued as a tiny sect, publishing its own weekly, *Freie Arbeiter Stimme*.

15. Letter of Philip Rapoport in *Workmen's Advocate* 5 (October 12, 1889): 3. Friedrich Engels agreed with much of the criticism. See his letter to Friedrich A. Sorge, January 6, 1892, reprinted in Leonard E. Mins [editor and translator], "Unpublished Letters of Karl Marx and Friedrich Engels to Americans," *Science and Society* 2 (Summer 1938): 367.

16. *The New Nation* 1 (February 21, 1891): 67; Charles Sotheran, *Horace Greeley and Other Pioneers of American Socialism* (New York: Mitchell Kennerly, 1915), p. 15; *The People* 6 (June 21, 1896): 3.

17. Hertz, *Di Idishe Sotsialistishe Bavegung*, p. 58; *Arbeiter Zeitung*, September 12, 1890, quoted in ibid., p. 59.

18. Hertz, *Di Idishe Sotsialistishe Bavegung*, p. 58.

19. The 1889 Socialist Labor party platform appeared regularly in *The People* during 1891 and 1892; it is reprinted in Sotheran, *Horace Greeley*, pp. 20–23; see also Richard T. Ely, *Socialism; An Examination of its Nature, its Strength and its Weakness, With Suggestions for Social Reform* (New York: Thomas Y. Crowell, 1894).

20. Ely, *Socialism*.

21. *Workmen's Advocate* 5 (October 19, 1889): 1.

22. *Workmen's Advocate* 5 (November 23, 1889): 2.

23. G. B. Benham, *Patriotism and Socialism* (San Francisco: American Section, Socialist Labor Party, 1895), p. 13.

24. *The People* 2 (November 29, 1891).

25. *The People* 7 (August 29, 1897): 3.

26. *Workmen's Advocate* 5 (February 2, 1889): 3; *Workmen's Advocate* 5 (December 14, 1889): 1; *The People* 1 (September 20, 1891): 1; *The People* 1 (October 11, 1891): 5.

27. *Workmen's Advocate* 6 (December 13, 1890): 1; *The People* 1 (May 24, 1891): 5.

28. *The People* 2 (September 4, 1892): 1; *The People* 2 (October 30, 1892): 1; (November 6, 1892): 1; (December 18, 1892): 2.

29. Cahan, *Bleter*, 3: 374; *The People* 6 (July 19, 1896): 1; William School McClure, *Socialism [Paper read before the Albany Press Club]* (New York: National Executive Committee, Socialist Labor Party, 1896), p. 42.

30. Henry Kuhn, "Reminiscences of Daniel De Leon, Leader-Teacher-Pathfinder," in *Daniel De Leon*, p. 4; *Workmen's Advocate* 7 (January 24, 1891): 1; Cahan, *Bleter*, 3: 284.

31. Cahan, *Bleter*, 3: 400.

32. *The People* 1 (February 14, 1892): 3.

33. Cahan, *Bleter*, 3: 400.

34. Ibid., 3: 283.

35. Ibid., 3: 389–94; Sotheran, "Reminiscences," in *Horace Greeley*, pp. ix–xv, xxv–xxviii, xxxii, xxxviii–xxxix; the ouster of Sotheran cost De Leon dearly in the Knights of Labor; see *New York Herald*, July 29, 1894, sect. 1: 7.

36. Cahan, *Bleter*, 3: 378–79; Hertz, *Di Idishe Sotsialistishe Bavegung*, pp. 54–55.

37. Hertz, *Di Idishe Sotsialistishe Bavegung*, p. 58.

38. Cahan, *Bleter*, 3: 415, 441–46, 483–87.

39. Ibid., 3: 383; *The People* 7 (August 8, 1897): 2.

40. "Statement by Daniel De Leon," June 26, 1894, in SLP Collection, Wisconsin State Historical Society, Madison, Wisconsin; "Proceedings of the Ninth Annual Convention of the Socialist Labor Party Held at Grand Central Palace, 43rd Street and Lexington Avenue, New York City, July 4th to July 10, 1896" (n.p., n.d.), p. 19.

41. "The Socialist Labor Party," editorial, *The American Fabian* 1 (December 1895).

42. New York *Abendblatt* (Yiddish), November 15, 1895, quoted in *The People* 5 (December 5, 1895): 3.

43. Fred E. Martin to the Organizer of Section New York, Socialist Labor Party, February 2, 1895, SLP Collection; *New York Populist*, February 9, 1895, clipping in SLP Collection.

44. *Workmen's Advocate* 4 (December 1, 1888): 3. A year later the Central Labor Union became the Central Labor Federation.

45. *The Labor Enquirer* (Denver) 7 (December 24, 1887); Sotheran, "Reminiscences," in *Horace Greeley*, p. xxi.

46. *Workmen's Advocate* 5 (November 2, 1889):1.

47. *Workmen's Advocate* 6 (July 5, 1890): 1.

48. De Leon was not directly involved in the 1890 events. For details of these events, see Samuel Gompers to Ernest Boehm, secretary of the Central Labor Federation, September 11, 1890, reprinted in Workmen's Advocate 6 (September 20, 1890): 1; *Workmen's Advocate* 6 (November 15, 1890): 1.

49. *Workmen's Advocate* 6 (September 27, 1890); 1.

50. *Workmen's Advocate* 6 (November 8, 1890): 1; Samuel Gompers to Ernest Boehm, November 7, 1890, reprinted in *Workmen's Advocate* 6 (November 15, 1890): 1.

51. *Workmen's Advocate* 6 (December 13, 1890): 1; for Sanial's speech, see *Workmen's Advocate* 6 (December 20, 1890): 1.

52. Friedrich Engels to [Hermann] Schlüter, January 29, 1891, reprinted in Mins, "Unpublished Letters," p. 366.

53. A copy of the resolution is in SLP Collection (microfilm, Reel 6, #0674), reprinted in *The People* 1 (September 27, 1891): 1.

54. W. D. P. Bliss, *A Handbook of Socialism* (1895; reprinted. London: Swan Sonnenschein and Company, 1907), pp. 146–47.

55. Justus Ebert, *Trades Unions in the United States, 1742-1905* (New York: New York Labor News Company, [1905]), p. 8; Sotheran, "Reminiscences, in *Horace Greeley*, pp. xxii–xxiii; see also Kuhn, "Reminiscences," in *Daniel De Leon*, p. 8.

56. William Kirk, "The Knights of Labor and the American Federation of Labor," in *Studies in American Trade Unions*, ed. Jacob H. Hollander and George E. Barnett (New York: Henry Holt & Company, 1905), p. 366; see also Kuhn, "Reminiscences," in *Daniel De Leon*, pp. 7–8.

57. Ebert, *Trades Unions*, p. 7.

58. *The Labor Enquirer* (Denver) 7 (March 19, 1887): 2.

59. "A Knight of Labor," *Capitalism on Trial* (New York: J. Franz, 1886), p. 5; a copy of this extremely rare pamphlet is in the Polemic Pamphlet Collection, New York State Library, Albany, N.Y.

60. Norman Ware, *The Labor Movement in the United States, 1860-1895* (New York: D. Appleton and Company, 1929; paperback ed. New York: Vintage Books, n.d.), p. 66. Pagination follows paperback edition.

61. Ibid., pp. 134–46; Terrence V. Powderly, *Thirty Years of Labor* (Columbus, Ohio: Excelsior Publishing House, 1889), p. 276; Ware, *The Labor Movement*, pp. 82, 105; *The People* 2 (April 17, 1892): 1; see also interview by Alexander Jonas of Powderly in *The People* 2 (October 23, 1892): 1.

62. Foster Rhea Dulles, *Labor in America* (New York: Thomas Y. Crowell, 1966), pp. 144–47.

63. Ibid., p. 147; see also, Sotheran, "Reminiscences," in *Horace Greeley*, pp. xx–xxi.

64. Sotheran, "Reminiscences," in *Horace Greeley*, pp. xx–xxi.

65. *The People* 3 (August 5, 1894): 2; *The People* 5 (April 21, 1895): 2; *The People* 5 (December 1, 1895): 1.

66. *The People* 6 (December 1, 1895): 1.

67. Ibid., Charles H. Sotheran to G. W. McCadden, July 21, 1894, reproduced in the *New York Herald*, July 29, 1894, sect. 1: 7. The charge is accurate. De Leon was a practicing attorney for several years. He listed his occupation as "lawyer" when he married Sarah de David Lobo at the Reform Jewish Community Temple in Curacao, in 1882, and he gave his office address as 132 Nassau Street, New York. See Isaac S. and Suzanne A. Emmanuel, *History of the Jews of the Netherlands Antilles* (Cincinnati: American Jewish Archives, 1970), p. 450. Sotheran, "Reminiscences," in *Horace Greeley*, pp. xx–xxi, erroneously lists 1893 as the date for De Leon's ouster from the Knights. Ware, *The Labor Movement*, p. 112.

68. Ware, *The Labor Movement*, p. 112; *New Yorker Vorwaerts*, quoted in *The People* 5 (December 9, 1895); De Leon and his followers retaliated by ousting 687 pro-Sovereign members—including two major officers—from District Assembly 49, which they controlled.

69. Kuhn, "Reminiscences," in *Daniel De Leon*, p. 8.

70. Daniel De Leon and Job Harriman, *A Debate on the Tactics of the S.T. & L.A. Towards Trade Unions between Daniel De Leon of the Socialist Labor Party and Job Hariman of the Social Democratic Party, Held at New Haven, Connecticut, November 23, 1900* (New York: Job Harriman, 1900), pp. 7–8.

71. *The People* 5 (December 15, 1895): 1; Rudolph Katz, "With De Leon Since '89," in *Daniel De Leon*, 2: 30; the United Hebrew Trades was organized in 1888 by Jewish SLPers. It had 15,000 members in thirty-two unions by 1890. See Hertz, *Di Idishe Sotsialistishe Bavegung*, pp. 33–34.

72. W. G. H. Smart, "Is the Workingmen's Party Communistic," *American Socialist* 1 (December 20, 1877): 402; *The People* 5 (December 22, 1895): 2.

73. Katz, "With De Leon," in *Daniel De Leon*, 2: 31–32; *The People* 5 (December 15, 1895): 2.

74. The resolution in De Leon's handwriting is on page 30 of his copy of the "Proceedings of

the Ninth Annual Convention," SLP Collection (microfilm, Reel 35, #s 716–719); see also "Proceedings of the Ninth Convention," p. 11.

75. De Leon and Harriman, *A Debate*, p. 9.

76. Katz, "With De Leon," in *Daniel De Leon*, pp. 76–77.

77. Daniel De Leon and Job Harriman, *A Debate*, pp. 9–10; *The People* 7 (March 27, 1898): 3.

78. De Leon, quoted in Sotheran, *Horace Greeley*, p. 278.

79. *The People* 1 (November 29, 1891): 2; *The People* 2 (April 3, 1892): 2; (April 17, 1892): 2; (July 10, 1892): 2.

80. *The People* 3 (March 5, 1893).

81. *The People* 2 (November 6, 1892): 2; "If Middle Class May, Lead, Middle Class May Follow," *The New Nation* 2 (October 29, 1892): 650.

82. De Leon quoted in Sotheran, *Horace Greeley*, pp. 8–9; Luntz, "Daniel De Leon," pp. 19–20; *The People* 6 (March 14, 1897): 2.

83. *The People* 4 (January 6, 1895): 2.

84. *The People* 7 (June 20, 1897).

85. *The People* 7 (December 19, 1897): 3; Howard H. Quint, "American Socialists and the Spanish-American War," *American Quarterly* 5 (Summer 1958): 132–34; *The People* 7 (March 20, 1898): 2; Daniel De Leon, *Capitalism Means War* [Articles from *The People and the Daily People*], (New York: New York Labor News Company, 1941), pp. 9–11, 19, 26–28; *The People* 8 (May 1, 1898): 1.

86. *American Fabian* 4 (April 1898): 4; Quint, "The American Socialists," pp. 134, 137, 139; *Speeches of E. V. Debs, Social Democratic Candidate for President and Professor George D. Herron, Central Music Hall*, Chicago, September 29, 1900 (Chicago: [Social Democratic Herald], 1900), p. 2.

87. Daniel De Leon, "What Means This Strike" (Address, New Bedford, Massachusetts, February 11, 1898), in *Socialist Landmarks* (New York: New York Labor News Company, 1952), p. 83.

88. Ibid., p. 96.

89. Daniel De Leon, "Reform or Revolution" (Address, Boston, January 26, 1896), in *Socialist Landmarks*, pp. 33–34; De Leon, "What Means This Strike," pp. 93–94; for a diametrically opposite statement by De Leon, see Daniel De Leon and Job Harriman, *A Debate*, p. 4.

90. De Leon, "Reform and Revolution," p. 43; De Leon, "What Means This Strike," p. 104.

91. De Leon, "What Means This Strike," pp. 109, 112; Daniel De Leon and Job Harriman, *A Debate*, p. 4.

92. De Leon, "Reform and Revolutin," pp. 34, 38, 42.

93. Ibid., pp. 51–52, 57, 60.

94. Kuhn, "Reminiscences," in *Daniel De Leon*, pp. 18–23.

95. "Proceedings of the Tenth National Convention of the Socialist Labor Party Held in New York City, June 2 to June 8, 1900," pp. vi, 255–56; Katz, "With De Leon," in *Daniel De Leon*, pp. 90–96.

∾ *16* ∾

The Socialist Party

- 1 -

The Socialist party of America was born amid high expectations in 1897 and died an abysmal failure seventy-five years later. Only sixty years before the party's demise, the Socialists were considered a threat to the hegemony of the two major parties. Yet for more than half a century before the party ceased to exist as a political entity, it was impotent; its death went almost unnoticed in the nation's press.[1]

Even at its high point, in 1912, the Socialist party garnered barely 6 percent of the national vote; that vote was less an affirmation of support than a protest against Theodore Roosevelt's usurpation of the Progressive label. In no state did the Socialists ever win power, although individual candidates did garner as many as a third of the votes cast in some statewide elections. At its strongest, the party could elect only thirty-one members to thirteen state legislatures. Only a single Socialist ever sat in the Congress at any one time—Victor Berger from Milwaukee between 1911 and 1913, and 1923 and 1929, and Meyer London from New York's Lower East Side between 1915 and 1919, and 1921 and 1923. Socialists also served as mayors of a few major cities, notably Milwaukee, Wisconsin; Schenectady, New York; Butte, Montana; Berkeley, California; Minneapolis, Minnesota; Reading, Pennsylvania; and Bridgeport, Connecticut. But Socialist election victories were generally insignificant; the party was never a political force nationally.[2]

Socialists did, however, indirectly influence latter-day American social and political life. The New Deal, enacted by a Democratic president, was in many ways closer to the platform on which Norman Thomas, the unsuccessful Socialist candidate, ran in 1932 than the platform on which Franklin D. Roosevelt was elected president that year. Socialist election platforms from 1900 on proposed many of the more significant New Deal reforms, including Social Security, public works, minimum-wage and minimum-hour laws, and the right of workers to organize and bargain collectively.[3] But the basic ideals Socialists professed were almost totally ignored by the majority of the American public.

The failure of the party to develop into a major political force perplexed Socialists from the outset. Karl Marx, the patron saint of socialism, had, at times, expressed the opinion that America would be the home of the first Socialist revolution. He feared, in 1852, that "the revolution [in America] may come too soon," and in 1877 he speculated that the wave of violent strikes that swept seventeen states might be the "point of departure for organization of a serious labor party."[4] Neither happened. In fact, the Socialist party, the most significant Socialist organization in American history, was by 1916—only nineteen years after its birth—a failure.[5]

The cause of the party's failure is superficially complex—theoretical and tactical nuances abound.[6] In reality, the reason for its demise is simple; it relates to the theoretical schizophrenia that was its hallmark. The Socialist party of America was at the same time a revolutionary and a reform party.

- 2 -

The Socialists proclaimed their aim to be the establishment of socialism in the United States. All reforms were mere palliatives aimed at making life in a capitalist society bearable for the working class. Social reforms, they claimed, neither solved basic problems nor were they of any long-range value; only socialism could solve the problems engendered by industrialization.

Socialism, as defined by the Socialists themselves, called for the social ownership of the means of production and distribution. Morris Hillquit, the theoretician of the party, defined it simply in 1909 when he wrote that "Socialism advocates the transfer of ownership in the social tools of production—the land, factories, machinery, railroads, mines, etc.—from the individual capitalists to the people, to be operated for the benefit of all."[7]

This definition was universally accepted by Socialists. As early as 1880, Karl Marx, in a program drawn up for the French Parti Ouvrier (Workers' party), called for the collectivization of all means of production.[8] James Keir Hardie, patron saint of the British Labour party, believed that "in one form or another public must be substituted for private ownership of land and capital."[9] This common ownership was to be limited to means of production and distribution; Karl Kautsky, the heir to Marx's intellectual throne, made clear that means of consumption and personal enjoyment of goods purchased with the rewards of production were individual.[10] Socialists generally agreed that the state would probably—but not necessarily—be the instrument by which the means of production would be socialized.[11]

The American Socialists had from the beginning proclaimed their belief that the ills of society could be cured only by the establishment of a new collectivist social order. "The Social Democratic Party of America . . . reaffirms its adherence to the principles of International Socialism," the 1901 platform proclaimed, "and declares its aim to be the organization of the working class, and those in sympathy with it, into a political party, with the object of conquering the powers of government and using them for the purpose of transforming the present system of private ownership of the means of production and distribution into collective ownership by the whole people."[12] The 1912 platform put it more succinctly: "The Socialist party . . . purposes that, since all social necessities today are socially produced, the means of their production and distribution shall be socially owned and democratically controlled."[13]

In 1914 Hillquit proclaimed the Socialists' sole objective to be the collectivization of the primary tools and resources for the production of wealth.[14] This was to be the basic principle of American—and world—socialism during the life of the movement. The Socialist party's primary aim was the abolition of "exploitation by means of the collective ownership and democratic management of production and distribution."[15] Only socialism, Socialists insisted, could end exploitation and class division, the causes of all economic distress.[16]

Unfortunately, socialism could not be built instantaneously. "We fully realize," Hillquit argued, "that social evolution is gradual; that social institutions are products of historical growth and development; that no system of society can be changed in a day just because a certain number of individuals think it ought to be changed." For this reason, most Socialists favored ameliorative reforms of capitalist society. But the Socialists limited the reforms they favored; only two types were acceptable to them: (1) those that might aid in the gradual socialization of industry—as, for example, nationalization of telephone or railroad systems or municipal ownership of electric power plants, and (2) measures calculated to improve the immediate condition of workers under capitalism—laws establishing state or national insurance against old-age, unemployment, injury, and illness.[17]

In declaring for social reform, the Socialists denied that they were abandoning socialism or even Marxism. Had not Marx and Engels, in the *Communist Manifesto*, called for such reforms as the graduated income tax, free and universal education, abolition of child labor, and governmental monopolies in transport, communciations, and banking?[18] Were not the planks Socialists proposed invariably designed to follow those suggested by Marx and Engels?[19]

A minority of American Socialists disapproved of reform planks; a majority favored them. All agreed that socialism was the essential premise around which the party was organized, that reform was merely peripheral.

- 3 -

Sharp—often vitriolic—disagreement occurred among Socialists regarding many issues. At first the only cause for such dissension was the question of the extent to which Socialists should exert themselves to ameliorate the condition of the working class under capitalism. Then the party membership divided on whether to work within or without the conservative and, at times, corrupt trade-union movement. Between 1914 and 1917, Socialists disagreed on how best to oppose American involvement in World War I; from 1917 through 1918, they argued about whether to support the United States after it had entered the war. During 1919 and 1920, the party was torn asunder in an acrimonious, and at times violent, debate on the issue of political democracy versus proletarian dictatorship. After the argument had been solved by splitting the party into three separate and warring organizations, a new dispute arose within the part on the problem of supporting Robert M. La Follette in his 1924 Progress party campaign for the presidency. The issue of a united front with the Communists further divided the party and so, too, did Franklin D. Roosevelt's New Deal and World War II.

Nor were all of the disputes based upon divergence of opinion; some were caused by personality conflicts. The birth of the party was, in great part, the result of a personality conflict caused by Daniel De Leon's high-handed and dishonest rule of the old Socialist Labor party (SLP). Other conflicts of personality involving Victor Berger, Eugene V. Debs, Morris Hillquit, Daniel W. Hoan, and Norman Thomas rent the party during its lifetime.[20]

Socialist disputes make for interesting and often amusing reading. But they cannot by themselves explain the party's demise. Factionalism may have exacerbated the problems that led to the failure of the American Socialist party, but it was not the cause.

- 4 -

In a country as huge and diverse as the United States, with a federal structure,[21] it was only natural that a political party would be based on state and local organizations. It was also certain that the interests of each of the regions would differ, and that the Socialist party would reflect these regional differences. The result was a party that, despite a uniformly professed ideology, was divided—often against itself—on almost all issues.

The centers of Socialist strength included economically and socially incompatible areas. In Massachusetts, where the party had its first successes, its strength was centered in the industrial, primarily shoemaking, cities of Haverhill and Brockton. Montana, where Socialists represented a major political force from 1911 until 1916, the party's main strength was among copper miners in the Butte area. Metal miners in Nevada were also the base of the party in that state. Skilled German workmen were the core of Milwaukee's Socialist organization. Farmers and farm laborers dominated the party in Oklahoma and North Dakota, where it had considerable following in the years immediately preceding Amerian intervention in World War I. Stevedores, farm laborers, and lumberjacks were the dominant groups in the Washington state party. Native-born skilled and semiskilled building craftsmen, railroaders, and industrial workers were the backbone of the party in California. In New York, the most significant Socialist organizations were in the districts of New York City where immigrant East European Jews made up most of the population. Also, a sizeable, albeit short-lived (1911–1915), Socialist segment was found among the skilled craftsmen—heavily Yankee Protestant—of Schenectady. Later Socialist centers would develop among Protestant, Pennsylvania-German cigar and hosiery workers in Reading, Pennsylvania, and the middle-class, heavily ethnic, Catholic population in Bridgeport, Connecticut.[22]

The obvious differences of opinion among the American Socialists were, in great part, attributable to the regional interests among its various constituencies. For example, an attempt by the Industrial Workers of the World to organize farm workers in North Dakota was opposed, because of the adverse effect such organization would have on the economic well being of the Socialist farmers in that state. In the mining states, feuding between opposing unions affected the party adversely. The issues of Bolshevism and Zionism played significant roles in areas where Russian Jews abounded. Among Germans, the need to prove loyalty to America in a war against the fatherland was of great significance.[23]

- 5 -

Moreover, the Socialist party of America was born of the union of several diverse radical tendencies. Its creators included Social Gospeleers, trade-union radicals, Populists, Bellamyites, former associates of Burnette G. Haskell, orthodox Marxist refugees from De Leon's autocratic control of the Socialist Labor party, and a myriad of other fragments. All were united on only three issues: they opposed turn-of-the-century capitalism and favored its replacement with some form of vaguely defined socialism; they opposed the oligarchic control of the Germanic Socialist Labor party; and they agreed on the need for a united Socialist party.

The movement's dominant leaders, like the movement itself, represented diametrically opposite types. Eugene Victor Debs was a charismatic labor-union leader who made up for his lack of erudition with humaneness that won for him the affection of hundreds of thousands of working people; Victor Berger was an able political organizer who disdained theoretical discourse and emotionalism for practical politics, and Morris Hillquit was a Socialist intellectual whose forte was the popularization of Marxian theory. They were not competing leaders; Berger, Debs, and Hillquit complemented each other. Each of the three had his role in the development of early twentieth-century American socialism: Debs attracted workers to the banner of socialism by winning their hearts; Berger organized the party into a political organization capable of delivering votes and electing Socialists to office; and Hillquit expostulated the long-range view of the Utopia that party members promised to deliver, thus enforcing the myths that were so essential for a Socialist movement. Each of the leaders represented a different clientele within the early party; each came from a different movement. Debs came from the American Railway Union, a short-lived, militant, industrial organization he had formed in the early 1890s; Berger came from the *Sozialistischer Verein*, a Milwaukee organization that had broken with De Leon in the early 1890s, and Hillquit led the anti-De Leon wing that had split off from the New York Socialist Labor party at the end of the century. Each appealed to a different geographic and social segment of radical society, and each performed a unique task necessary for the gestation and development of the party. Hillquit's following was predominantly among the intellectuals and the immigrant masses of the Eastern Seaboard. Debs and Berger were both influential among middle westerners: Berger among the politically more practical radicals and Debs among labor unionists and workingmen.[24]

- 6 -

A large number of the middle-western Socialists had come out of the Populist movement, which one writer had described as "the great training school for socialism in the United States."[25] Others previously had been affiliated with one of the communitarian movements of nineteenth-century America. Most had been converted to socialism by reading Gronlund or Bellamy and others, by perusing Julius Wayland's popular weekly *Appeal to Reason*, after first being inspired to fight capitalism by *Coin's Financial School*, the most popular of the monetary reform books of the era.[26]

Of equal importance with any of these leaders was Eugene V. Debs, American socialism's hero, martyr, leader, and symbol. Born of middle-class Alsatian immigrant parents in Terre Haute, Indiana, in 1855, Debs grew up in a typical middle-American environment. His education was limited—public schools and a short course at a business college. At fifteen he went to work on the railroad, and at nineteen he labored in a grocery store. He turned to politics in 1880 and was elected city clerk and later state legislator—on the Democratic ticket—but he was so repelled by the corruption in Indiana government that he withdrew from politics after only two years. In the meantime, he became grand secretary of the Brotherhood of Locomotive Firemen and associate editor of its journal. Debs soon disagreed with the exclusivity of the railroad brotherhoods, and in 1892 he proceeded to organize an industrial union that would include all white railroad workers—skilled, semiskilled, and unskilled.[27]

The American Railway Union (ARU) was a basically conservative union. Its leader opposed strikes and favored conciliation between the railroads and the workers. The ARU engaged in little raiding of Brotherhood membership; Debs's primary aim was the organization of most of the railroad employees who were not in any union. The ARU's policies proved successful during the first few months of its existence. The Great Northern was forced by its workers to sign a contract with the union under terms favorable to them. By 1894 the ARU membership had reached 150,000.[28] Then catastrophe struck: the workers at the Pullman Corporation went on strike against the advice of Debs and his associates.

Debs attempted to have the dispute settled by arbitration, but Thomas H. Wilkes, a corporation vice-president, declared, "We have nothing to arbitrate." The company, supported by the General Managers Association, the organization of all the major railroads out of Chicago, proclaimed that it would have nothing to do with the union. Its aim was to destroy the union before it became too powerful.

Some violence occurred during the strike, but little of it was caused by strikers, who were advised by Debs to protect corporate property. Some of the disorder was instigated by the railroads, which the *New York Morning Journal* pointed out "had everything to gain by a little well-advertised rioting which could be attributed to the strikers."[29]

Workingmen generally supported the strikers. A call for a boycott of all trains carrying Pullman cars won the backing of railroadmen throughout the country. The success of the boycott led to federal intervention. United States Attorney General Richard Olney had represented railroads before he was appointed by President Grover Cleveland. Federal troops and federal marshals were called into service to break the strike—on the grounds that the boycott was interfering with the mail. Rioting by hoodlums, who had been deputized as federal marshals, followed. Thirteen people were killed (8 by United States marshals and 5 by soliders) and 53 were wounded. Moreover, the marshals arrested strikers, sympathizers, and passersby indiscriminately. Of 190 arrested by the marshals, only 71 were indicted,and of those indicted, most were subsequently cleared.[30]

Among those arrested were Debs and his three closet collaborators in the ARU. Debs and the other officials were found guilty of contempt by the judge, although a jury of "hostile" farmers voted eleven to one against convicting them of conspiracy. Debs was given six months for contempt; his cohorts drew three each.

The failure of the strike and its aftermath convinced Debs that the combined power of concerted wealth and the government of the United States, with which it was closely allied, made unions powerless. He thus had the ARU dissolved into a new political movement.[31]

Before the Pullman strike, Debs considered independent labor political action useful, but only of secondary importance. The strike changed all that, and his move toward politics was strengthened by a visit from Victor Berger in his jail cell in Woodstock, Illinois. Berger convinced Debs that the ballot gave labor "redeeming power."[32]

In the 1896 election, Debs, although he now considered himself a Socialist, supported William Jennings Bryan, the Populist-Democrat. He refused to support De Leon's candidate. "Such men as Bryan will bring socialism on," he argued, but "the [De Leon] S.L.P. will not." He was repelled by the dogmatism of De Leon and his followers; he doubted they could appeal to the working people; he objected to their villification of labor leaders and to the ouster from the SLP of any Socialist who dared disagree with De Leon on any issue. "I look upon the S.L.P. in the light of striflers who drive many would-be good Socialists out of their ranks by their intemperate language and actions." He saw little hope for the SLP and believed a new Socialist party was necessary. Debs expected the Populists to form the embryo for such a party.[33]

The 1896 defeat of Bryan proved to Debs the futility of Populist politics. Immediately after the election, he proposed that a new organization be formed to propagandize politically for socialism and to develop Socialist communes throughout the United States. In June 1897 the remnants of the American Railway Union united with the Brotherhood of the Co-operative Commonwealth, a small communitarian organization, to form the Social Democracy of America.

The Social Democracy's platform was modeled after the 1892 Omaha Program of the Populists. Its leaders were primarily ex-Populists and Christian Socialists. All of them believed in socialism but disagreed about the means for achieving Utopia. Berger—and eventually Debs—favored political means; most of the others preferred colonization.[34] the Social Democracy officially compromised the differences. It urged that a number of cooperative colonies be established in the sparsely populated state of Washington where the colonists would, besides setting up farms and factories, proselytize their neighbors. It was assumed that they could win the state for socialism in short order and that the state's congressional delegation would work toward converting the rest of the United States to socialism.

Berger recognized from the start that the scheme was unworkable; within a month, he had convinced Debs that the plan was illusory. Debs soon proclaimed: "The Social Democracy is not a colonization scheme. It is a political movement."[35]

Despite disagreements within the Social Democracy, a lot of optimism was evident. It was winning unexpected interest and support. A large contingent of northeastern Socialists—including the founders of the *Jewish Daily*

Forward—abandoned the De Leon-ruled SLP and joined the Social Democracy en masse. So did most Massachusetts Socialists.[36] By the end of 1897, it was apparent that a major Socialist movement had been born.

- 7 -

Gene Debs has been described as a "typical American revolutionist of the new kind; unconventional, with immense energy, dreaming on things to come, and yet with a certain practical turn that differentiates the true Westerner from the European Red." He has been called gentle, intensely earnest, a man who could win the complete confidence of his working-class listeners, and highly imaginative.[37] But Debs was neither a great intellect nor a political organizer. He was described in 1899 as "more sympathetic than logical [and] more rhapsodical than reasonable." The pace of his rhetoric was "so rapid as to quicken sensibility and to expel analysis or reason."[38] Morris Hillquit was the party's intellectual giant during the early days, and Victor Berger was its organizational genius.

Berger was a Jew, born in the Austro-Hungarian empire. He had been educated at the University of Vienna before coming to the United States in 1879 at the age of twenty-three. After a short sojourn in the West, he moved to Milwaukee in 1882 to teach German in the public schools. His politics were Socialist almost from the start, although he had been a follower of Henry George for a short period. His primary personality traits were his bluntness and his assertiveness.[39]

He was the leader of the well-organized, heavily German, Socialist movement in Milwaukee. It broke off from De Leon's party before the major schisms, because its members, who despite their German origin considered themselves to be good and tolerant Americans, despised his dogmatic, autocratic rule. Moreover, they had a close working relationship with the local Populists and the local American Federation of Labor (AF of L) Federated Trades Council, with whom they had formed an electoral coalition during the 1893 mayoral elections. The alliance with the Populists lasted only three years—it ended when Berger refused to support Bryan and free silver—but the alliance with the Trades Council remained intact for more than fifty years.[40] The Milwaukee party—and Berger's—creed was that: "Nothing more ought to be demanded than is attainable at a given time and under given conditions."[41]

Support for the colonization scheme within the new organization was too powerful in 1897 for Berger to oppose it openly. By 1898 the situation had changed, and Berger united with Debs, the *Jewish Daily Forward* group, and the Massachusetts Socialists in an effort to turn the Social Democracy into a purely political party. The antipolitical, procolonization wing had a majority of the delegates at the 1898 convention, but despite the support of Laurence Gronlund and the brilliant Anarchist Emma Goldman, it lacked leadership. It had no spokesman with the charisma of Debs or the political acumen of Berger. Thus when, in 1898, the Debs-Berger political wing withdrew, the Social Democracy was doomed to an early demise.[42]

Debs, Berger, and their followers formed a new party, the Social Democratic party (SDP) of America, immediately after leaving the Social Democracy of America. They adopted a new platform, which virtually duplicated the old, except that it deleted all reference to Utopian communities. It declared that "control of political power by the Social Democratic party will be tantamount to the abolition of capitalism and class rule." Until that day came, however, the Social Democratic party pledged to work for reforms in the capitalist system. It proposed to struggle for a comprehensive system of social security, including insurance against old age, unemployment, and injury. This plank, which would recur in every future Socialist national platform through 1932, played a significant role in the adoption of Social Security by a Democratic president and Congress thirty-seven years later.[43]

The first two years of the Social Democratic party's life were almost euphoric. SDP members were elected mayors in Haverhill and Brockton, Massachusetts, and James C. Carey, Lewis Scates, and the Reverend Frederic O. McCartney were elected to the Massachusetts legislature. All signs pointed to continued growth and eventual power. In Milwaukee, Social Democrats polled a respectable 2,400 votes—5 percent of the total cast—in 1898, their first election. Moreover, the party had a lot of following in the American Federation of Labor, polling 20 percent of the vote at its national convention.[44]

- 8 -

The other major element of what would, in 1901, become the Socialist party was the anti-De Leon wing of the Socialist Labor party. The leader of that segment was Morris Hillquit, a Russian-born Germanophile and a Jew. Hillquit, born in 1869, had arrived in the United States at age seventeen. He had, as a young man, worked as a waistmaker, a shirtmaker, a laborer in a picture frame factory, a clerk in the office of the Socialist Labor party, and as business manager, associate editor, and bookkeeper of the *Arbeiter Zeitung*, a Yiddish-language Socialist weekly he had helped found—although he knew little Yiddish. Hillquit had also helped organize the United Hebrew Trades, a federation of predominantly Jewish trade unions, and a Socialist school for teaching English to immigrant Jewish workers. He had, in the meantime, also earned a high school diploma and a law degree from New York University. By 1900 Hillquit was a successful labor lawyer.[45]

When the Hillquit-led anti-De Leon faction left the SLP in 1899, it continued to call itself the Socialist Labor party, and it called its newspaper *The People*. The De Leon faction also called itself the Socialist Labor party and published a newspaper called *The People*. In the fall of 1899, both factions nominated Socialist Labor party candidates for the forthcoming elections. A "capitalist" judge ruled in favor of De Leon, although Hillquit had support of a majority of the old SLP's members.

The Kangaroos—as De Leonites labelled the Hillquit followers—were then forced to organize a new Socialist political organization. They called a convention with that end in mind. The convention, held in Rochester, New York, represented a heavily Eastern membership. As with most Socialist organizations of the time, its ethnic composition was heavily German (the crucial resolution on trade unionism was written originally in German) with a healthy sprinkling of East European Jews.[46]

Ideologically, the Hillquit SLP and the Debs-Berger SDP did not differ. Both called for the abolition of private ownership of the means of production and distribution and its replacement by "the Socialist cooperative commonwealth." Both party programs were heavily laced with proposals to reform capitalism.

Nowhere was the similarity more apparent than in the resolution on trade unions. Hillquit sounded the keynote when he told the convention that the trade-union movement was an "inevitable manifestation of the struggle between labor and capital." Moreover, "any organization of workingmen in trade union is, consciously or unconsciously, battling in the field of class struggle," and its members are thus more susceptible to Socialist propaganda. The convention declared trade unions to be absolutely necessary "to resist the superior economic power of capital and to improve and maintain conditions and standards of workers." The delegates declared that trade unions tend to "develop the sense of solidarity and political independence" in workers by organizing them as a "class antagonistic to the capitalist class." The convention called all Socialists "To participate in all struggles of organized labor . . . without preference to one type union or the other."[47]

Three Socialist parties were now vying for dominance of the American Left. The outlook was for internecine struggles that would decimate the Socialist movement. To avoid such an event, Hillquit and his followers nominated Job Harriman for president and Max Hayes for vice-president, but made the nominations tentative. A move was afoot to unite with the new Social Democratic party.

Unfortunately, the desire for unity was stronger among Hillquit's followers than among the disciples of Debs or Berger. An inquiry from Hillquit brought a reply from Debs in which he disdained organic unity. The "better element" among Hillquit's followers would come into the Social Democratic party voluntarily, he argued. Jesse Cox, chairman of the SDP national executive board, and Seymour Steadman, the board's secretary, invited the members of Hillquit's party to abandon their organization and "join the Social Democratic Party in the struggle to emancipate humanity from class rule and the slavery of capitalism by the establishment of the cooperative commonwealth." But the former Socialist-Laborites would not be rejected that easily. They appointed a committee to negotiate on unity at the forthcoming SDP convention.[48]

- 9 -

On the surface, the obstacles in the path to unification of the two Socialist parties were merely the issues of name and location of headquarters. In fact, the actual obstacles were more geographic and historic than semantic. Berger, it is true, insisted that any united organization be called the Social Democratic party exactly like its German counterpart. This was an issue on which he refused to bend. Hillquit hoped, but did not insist, that a united party would be called simply Socialist. Berger, Debs, and their allies wanted the national headquarters to be located in Chicago; the Hillquit faction preferred that it be in the East.[49] But these were all insignificant differences that ignored the real distinctions between the two parties.

Virtually all of the predominantely East Coast Socialists who followed Hillquit had come out of the Socialist movement. The majority of SDPers had been Populists and were midwesterners. Of fifty-nine delegates at the Social Democrats' 1900 Indianapolis convention, thirty-seven represented organizations in the Midwest; only eighteen came from eastern states. Of the five members of the national executive board, three had supported the Populists in 1892 and 1896, and all five were midwesterners—one member came from Indiana, and two each represented Illinois and Wisconsin.[50]

Both parties were small—the Social Democratic party claimed 4,556 members, although convention figures indicate 2,120 was more accurate. The membership, which was reflected accurately by the delegates, was generally young and working class. Delegates to the 1900 SDP convention ranged in age from twenty-two to sixty-five, averaging twenty-eight. Sixty-two percent of them were workers, 22 percent were professionals, and 16 percent were businessmen. Four of the delegates were women.[51]

Despite their geographic and historic differences, the leaders of the two parties agreed in detail on program and organization. Both parties strongly opposed coalitions with other prolabor parties, and both insisted that Socialists elected to municipal, state, or federal positions would be under strict party control.[52]

A great deal of haggling went on between the two parties, but they did agree to run a joint national ticket in 1900, with Debs the nominee for president and Harriman the designee for vice-president. Both were native Indianans, although Harriman had lived in California for more than a decade. In the course of the joint campaign, members of both parties discovered that they could cooperate, and the result of such joint action could be gratifying. Debs and Harriman polled a record 97,730 Socialist votes in thirty states.

The vote was as strong in the states where Hillquit's party dominated as in those where Berger and Debs were dominant.[53]

Forty-eight percent of the Debs-Harriman vote was cast in the Midwest; 42.5 percent on the Eastern Seaboard; 5 percent on the Pacific Coast; 3 percent in the South, and 2.5 percent in the mountain West. The largest Socialist votes were polled in four eastern states (New York, New Jersey, Massachusetts, and Pennsylvania) and six midwestern states (Illinois, Michigan, Minnesota, Missouri, Ohio, and Wisconsin). The highest Socialist percentage of overall vote was in Massachusetts (2.3 percent) and Oregon (1.7 percent).[54] The vote seemed to indicate that the Socialist appeal was national rather than regional.

Despite the sanguine outlook, unity remained elusive. Morris Hillquit, one of the more ardent enthusiasts of a single Socialist party, was disheartened. A unified organization appeared impossible because of squabbling over party name and the location of national headquarters. But these "prolonged and, at times, heated controversies" were overcome by demands by the rank-and-file. American Socialists, except for the few remaining followers of De Leon, joined together at the 1901 Unity Convention of the Socialist party of America.

- 10 -

Three distinct groups of Socialists merged at the 1901 Unity Convention; the anti-Leon SLPers, the Social Democrats, and the members of independent Socialist parties, composed primarily of former Populists, in Texas, Kentucky, Iowa, Kansas, and Nebraska—into the Socialist party. The largest was the Hillquit-led party, which had about 7,000 members. The Debs-Berger SDP claimed more than 4,000. All told, the new party had approximately 12,000 members.[55]

Sharp differences arose at the convention, but they had little to do with former affiliation. Delegates from all three groups divided among themselves on all major issues. Berger and Hillquit were in agreement on virtually all issues—except party name. Neither did former affiliation play a major role in deciding how a delegate voted on the most divisive question before the convention—the issue of "immediate demands," a problem that would rend the party for the next twenty years.

"Immediate demands" are those planks in the Socialist platform that propose ameliorative measures under capitalism. The delusion of almost immediate Socialist victory was by 1901 so strong that some Socialists saw no need for reform planks. These Socialists viewed trade unions as the vehicles for achieving labor reform primarily by economic action. They saw the party as a mechanism for achieving an almost apocalyptic restructuring of society from capitalist to socialist.[56]

They moved to delete all immediate demands from the platform. As at all future Socialist conventions, the move was defeated.[57]

- 11 -

Internal feuding rent the Socialist party almost immediately. The internecine warfare followed naturally from the heterogeneous composition of its activist cadre, for these members were, from the beginning, products of differing traditions whose social and economic interests were often diametrically opposed.

As early as 1902, it was apparent that the party had contradictory tendencies. One element, centered in the western and prairie states and supported almost entirely by native-born Americans, was essentially Anarcho-Syndicalist in outlook. Its followers had contempt "for forms and conventionalities" and "little use for the wisdom of books." The western Socialists did not comprehend the need for national, international, "or, indeed, . . . any organization whatsoever." They invariably looked askance at technical economics. The eastern Socialists were generally urban, working class, well read, ideological, and foreign-born.[58] Followers of this tendency were dedicated to a simplistic Marxism and recognized the need for organization.

- 12 -

Real control of the party was in the hands of a small cadre of activists who held official positions, served on committees and were the group from which delegates to national conventions were chosen. They differed a great deal from the rank and file in social class and background. Delegates to national conventions between 1904 and 1912 included labor leaders, ministers, publicists, teachers, lawyers, and writers. A majority of the delegates were professionals. The party membership, on the other hand, was composed predominantly of skilled workmen.[59]

That the leadership should come from one social class and the rank and file from another was only natural. Debs's claim that "Jimmie Higgins"—a euphemism for rank-and-file activist—was "the actual maker of out movement the world over" and that he "more nearly than any other is the actual incarnation of the social revolution"[60] avoided the reality of party organization. The average rank-and-file member lacked the time, energy, interest, and commitment to become involved in party policies. Few members retained their interest in the party for any length of time, nor did they have a deep commitment to it. Normally, only one in seven members voted in party referenda. Debs complained that "of the many thousands who join the Socialist Party, but a few remain. . . . They pass through it as water passes through a sieve." Between 1911 and 1913, about 150,000 Americans joined the Socialist party; most soon dropped out.[61]

Party activity—including feuding—was thus primarily a function of the party leadership. The average member was, at most, peripherally involved.

- 13 -

Most Socialists took it for granted that their Utopia was inevitable. They were convinced that they were dealing with laws that were "immutable and fixed in the very nature of the universe . . . laws that are not man-made." They participated in political contests and economic strife with the aim of educating the working class, thus making sure that the new order would be inaugurated by the workers themselves. This would assure that the proletariat would control the new system and use it to free itself of wages and classes—the fetters of all preceding social orders.[62]

Although party members had a virtually unanimous dedication to this simplistic revolutionary-opportunist socialism, serious rifts within the organization threatened to tear the party asunder.

The warring factions appeared more interested in destroying each other than in destroying the capitalist system.

The disagreements were almost all tactical rather than theoretical. Yet these tactical differences—how best to succeed—kept the party in a constant state of strife between its three wings: right, left, and center.

The right-wing Socialists looked upon the party as a purely political movement and assumed that the revolution would begin when the Socialists would win political power in an election. Most right-wingers were active members of the AF of L and had little faith in the revolutionary potential of labor unions except as ancillaries of the political party. Left-wingers considered electoral activity to be, at best, incidental to economic. They were convinced that the revolution would be consummated by economic action—probably a general strike—and the primary duty of the party was to build a revolutionary labor-union movement. Many had joined the Industrial Workers of the World (IWW) during its first six years. Many more had supported it. By 1913 few remained in it; they were disillusioned by the anarcho-syndicalism of its leadership. The centrists, who represented the view of the majority of party members, considered both political and economic action essential to revolution, although they emphasized the former. Most centrists were members of the AF of L.[63]

- 14 -

The party's right wing was dedicated to political democracy, the electoral process, and reform. Victor Berger, the undisputed leader of the faction, proclaimed as early as 1901 that he believed in Eduard Bernstein's reformist revision of Marx. He declared Bernstein's *Evolutionary Socialism* applicable to the United States, where "for the first time in history we find an oppressed class with the same fundamental right as the ruling class—the right of universal suffrage."[64] It was essential for the working class to protect its democratic rights. Socialism was, in fact, seen as a bulwark of democracy. "Personal liberty and economic depotism are incompatible," Berger said.[65] By economic despotism, Berger meant capitalism. Social democracy, which he professed, meant to Berger both social ownership of industry and democratic government. "We mean, therefore, to reserve as much right for the individual as is consistent with the welfare of all," he wrote.[66]

Few right-wingers believed that a Socialist victory at the polls would by itself usher in socialism. Bernard Berlyn's statement that the "election of a Socialist administration—that would be the Socialist revolution itself"[67] was hardly representative of right-wing Socialist thought. Most accepted the so-called Wisconsin idea, which postulated that the advance of socialism would have to be gradual even should a majority favor the cooperative commonwealth.[68] Before they obtained a majority, Social Democrats believed, a Socialist minority could force from the capitalist system significant reforms "that will advance us toward socialism."[69]

The Socialists' role was thus, according to Berger and his associates, to fight for social reform and to propagandize for socialism. Socialist legislators did both. Berger used his congressional seat primarily for the latter. He mailed out copies of the Socialist platform by the hundreds of thousands from his office—as a congressman he had free mail privileges—and sent out millions of copies of speeches he made on the floor of the House, particularly one labeled *The Working Class Must Have Its Own Party to Give Expression to Its Own Class Interests.*[70]

- 15 -

The party's left wing—its adherents called themselves revolutionary or industrial Socialists—was more amorphous than the right wing. Small subfactions within the left wing held positions that the other adherents of the tendency opposed. The faction had no single outstanding leader, although Gene Debs was generally considered its spokesman. Despite its self-portrayal as the party's proletarian segment, most of its outstanding members belonged to the middle and, occasionally, the upper class. Besides Debs, the leading figures of the left wing were two publicists, William English Walling and Robert Rives La Monte; two lawyers, Henry Slobodin and Louis Boudin; and—between 1906 and 1913—one labor leader, William D. Haywood, of the Industrial Workers of the World. Its strength was greatest in the western states and Ohio and Michigan.

The three basic left-wing tenets were the class struggle, the materialist conception of history, and pragmatism. Revolutionists held the class struggle to be the political and economic foundation of the Socialist party. They considered the materialist conception of history to be the party's philosophic base, and they believed pragmatism to be its spirit and method-ological underpinning. In reality, pragmatic considerations dominated the left wing's practice. Revolutionary Socialists "care not for the manner of their emancipation from wage slavery. They want results," one of them wrote.[71]

As pragmatists, the more radical Socialists questioned the effectiveness of the electoral process, although none of them rejected it outright. Most of the left-wingers belittled elections as a means for achieving socialsm, but virtu-ally all of them favored the running of candidates as a means for preventing the machinery of the state from being used against the industrial unions they considered the effective instrumentality for establishing the Socialist commonwealth. Emancipation would require demonstrations, boycotts, and a general strike; elections could serve only to protect these methods of "direct action" from being repressed by the state. Debs, who disagreed with his fellow leftists on the efficacy of elections, agreed with them, however, on their basic assumption that parties were insignificant in the political process, which he considered to be "a life and death struggle between two hostile economic classes."[72]

Leftists were convinced that the electoral process had diluted the workers' battle for class supremacy into a contest for political office. They charged that where Socialists had won political office, the true victors had in-variably been the officeholders and the smaller bourgeoisie. Since "when one class is helped it is to the detriment of the other, and since Socialist vic-tories at the polls invariably profited the petit-bourgeoisie at the expense of the working class," it followed that left-wingers considered electoral victory to be generally an undesirable end for Socialists to seek.[73] Despite their dis-paragement of the election process, no serious support was seen for any sug-gestion that the party withdraw from politics.

Not all left-wing Socialists agreed that the ballot was of secondary impor-tance. Debs, for example, argued that "The working class intends to use its political power through the machinery of popular government and free elec-tions to force compliance with its demands for powerful, legal, and con-stitutional methods to the end that wage slavery may be entirely abolished." But, Debs conceded, "Voting for Socialism is not Socialism any more than a menu is a meal."[74]

The denigration of the electoral process by the left-wingers generally created a tactical vacuum, for they also opposed violence. Boudin declared that "the class struggle theory is peaceful." Debs noted that the social revolution would be gradual and would follow "evolutionary laws which are producing it." The editor of the *International Socialist Review* pointed out that the proletariat would be the chief sufferer in the event of social violence. Even James Connolly, an active Socialist Irishman who would die on the gallows in Dublin in 1916 for leading the rebellion against British rule, argued that new weapons had made armed uprisings untenable. The electoral process alone might be futile, but he contended that in tandem with revolutionary unions, "each resting upon, fortifying and completing each other," they were unconquerable.[75]

The revolutionists, despite their rejection of the electoral process, were, like virtually all other Socialists, dedicated to political democracy. Socialism could not be instituted, almost all left-wingers agreed, "unless a majority of the people are determined to establish it." In their dedication to individual liberty, the revolutionary Socialists were at times theoretically akin to the anti-statism of the Anarchists. "The chief end of government," Debs wrote, "has been and is to keep the victims of oppression and injustice in subjection." William Haywood believed the state was by its nature oppressive and that it would be superfluous once the social revolution had been accomplished. Under socialism, Haywood said, laws would not be needed to govern individuals. The only government that would be needed would be one to administer industry.[76]

Although left, right, and center wings agreed on their definition of socialism, they disagreed on its implementation. Most left-wingers favored "industrial socialism," a system that postulated the restructuring of government on the basis on industry. Under their form of socialism, the postal workers rather than the government would run the post office, teachers would run the schools, railroad workers would run the railroads, and miners would run the mines. All places of employment would be operated by and for the benefit of the workers in each shop. They would get "full value for their social service." Government operation and control—as practiced in the post office or school system—was not, in their view, genuine socialism; they labeled it political socialism.[77]

- 16 -

The centrists were the dominant faction in the national party. They controlled party organizations in the major eastern states.

Much like the left-wingers, they favored electoral activity as a means of educating the workers, thus winning them for socialism. Unlike the left-wingers, however, the centrists assumed that socialism would eventually come into being as the result of a Socialist victory at the polls. They resembled the right-wingers by supporting reform measures, which they favored primarily as a means of preparing the working class to assume power under socialism. Their view of the state as an institution, although ostensibly diametrically opposed to the left-wing position, differed from the latter only semantically.

Hillquit asserted in 1910 that the party's role was primarily educational. He doubted that municipal or state electoral victories would advance socialism. Socialists would have to be in full control before they could begin restructuring society, and that would be in the distant future. Until that time, Socialists should use the electoral process to educate the workers.[78]

Centrists argued that the simplest means for achieving the social revolution was by taking over state power by elections. The state would then become an instrument for the liberation of the working class. They considered the state to be a "reflex of our economic life" rather than the basic force in society. The state under socialism would differ radically from the capitalist state in both form and substance. According to Hillquit: "It is not a class state, it does not serve any party of the population; it represents the interests of the entire community, and it is for the benefit of the community that it levies taxes and makes and enforces the law." It would be a Socialist state, but "a state nevertheless." To call it something other than a state, as the left wing proposed, would gain little or nothing. Nor would the Socialist state be almighty either politically or economically. Hillquit wanted some but not all industries nationalized. Many would be placed under municipal control, some would be operated by cooperatives, others—nonexploitative and agricultural, primarily—would remain in private hands, under government regulation. Upton Sinclair, who was considered a centrist, wrote to John Reed: "I am not . . . anxious to turn all industry over to politicians, whether good or bad."[79]

Neither Hillquit nor any of his followers ruled out an eventual stateless society; none of them believed that socialism was the ultimate social order. "We do not claim perfection under socialism," Hillquit said. "There is no such thing as absolute perfection"; social development is endless, part of an eternal human evolution. Socialism was only "the most humane form of social life which we can conceive today."[80]

Almost all Socialists—certainly all centrists—rejected the old Anarchist motto: "The worse [conditions are] the better [for the revolution]." They believed instead that the better conditions became, the better for the revolution. Each ameliorative measure was thus a step in the direction of the "radical cure." Unlike right-wingers, centrists did not believe that the sum total of all social reform was the "complete cure"; it was merely a force that would help propel the social revolution.[81]

- 17 -

Behind some of the disputes were semantic problems or questions of nuance. Many involved matters of personality. Kate Richards O'Hare, a leading left-wing writer, editor, and orator, despised Hillquit, because he "never knew that the Hudson River was not the West boundary of the United States, with some colonies in Chicago and Milwaukee." She accused him and his followers of being ignorant of American psychology and politics, and she charged that the New York party he dominated was "based entirely on European concepts." On most issues, O'Hare agreed with Hillquit; she disagreed with Victor Berger on Socialist "methods, procedure, techniques, and activities"; but she was personally friendly with Berger because, unlike Hillquit, "there was not one bit of meaness [sic] or venom in Victor."[82] Another possible explanation for the factionalism might be the fact that the party, composed of political activists, was denied any major role in the government. Unable to win political contests in the broad political arena, Socialists created conflicts within the party where victory was possible.[83]

NOTES

1. The date on which the Socialist party was organized is a matter of disagreement. It is often given as 1901, the year in which the various anti-De Leon factions of the American Socialist movements united. The party was, in fact, organized in 1897, as Social Democracy of America, and a Socialist candidate—Eugene V. Debs—ran for president in 1900.

The date for the demise of the Socialist party is also a matter of disagreement. Formally, it dissolved as a political party in 1972. From that year forward, it divided into three Quixotic, minuscule sects (from Left to Right): The Socialist party, USA, which continues the myth of independent political action, under the leadership of former Milwaukee Mayor Frank P. Zeidler; the Democratic Socialist Organizing Committee, led by Michael Harrington, which proposes working within the Democratic party; and Social Democrats, USA, the party's legal heir. At the time of the party's demise, its official records showed that it had fewer than 900 members nationally despite boasting of 18,000. the last Socialist presidential candidate, in 1956, polled only 2,121 votes. See *The New York Times*, December 31, 1972, p. 36.

2. *American Socialist*, January 2, 1915, p. 1; Fiorello LaGuardia was elected to Congress in 1924 on the Socialist ticket from East Harlem in New York City. He served as a Progressive-Republican, however, and never as a Socialist.

3. Norman Thomas, "The Split of 1936," [1956], typescript, Socialist Party of America Collection, Duke University, Durham, North Carolina (hereafter cited as Duke); Frances Perkins, *The Roosevelt I Knew* (New York: Viking Press, 1946), p. 34.

4. Karl Marx to Friedrich Engels, August 19, 1852, in Saul K. Padover, ed. and trans., *Karl Marx on America and the Civil War*, vol. 2, *The Karl Marx Library* (New York: McGraw Hill and Company, 1972), p. 38; Marx to Engels, July 25, 1877, in ibid., p. 42.

5. By 1916 Socialists were conceding that the party had failed politically; see, for example, George B. Leonard to Algernon Lee, November 14, 1916, Algernon Lee Papers, Tamiment Institute Library, New York University, New York City.

6. See, for example, David A. Shannon, *The Socialist Party of America: A History* (New York: Macmillan, 1955); Daniel Bell, "The Background and Development of American Socialism," in *Socialism and American Life*, ed. Donald Drew Egbert and Stow Persons (Princeton: Princeton University Press, 1952), pp. 311–405; John H. M. Laslett and Seymour Martin Lipset, eds. *The Failure of a Dream? Essays in the History of American Socialism* (Garden City, N.Y.: Anchor Press/Doubleday, 1974); James Weinstein, *The Decline of Socialism in America, 1912–1925* (New York: Monthly Review Press [1967]), and Ira Kipnis, *The American Socialist Movement, 1897–1912* (New York: Columbia University Press, 1952). Of particular interest is Werner Sombart, *Warum Gibt es in den Vereinigten Staaten Keinen Sozialismus* (Tubingen: J. C. B. Mohr [P. Siebeck], 1906), available in English translation as *Why is There no Socialism in the United States*, trans. Patricia M. Hocking and C. T. Husbands (London: The Macmillan Press, Ltd., 1976).

7. Morris Hillquit, *Socialism in Theory and Practice* (New York: The Macmillan Company, 1909), p. 11.

8. Karl Marx, "Introduction to the Programme of the French Workers Party," in *Political Writings*, by Karl Marx, vol. 3, *The First International and After* (New York: Vintage Books, Random House, 1974), pp. 376–77.

9. James Keir Hardie, M.P., *From Serfdom to Socialism* (London: G. Allen, 1907), p. 95.

10. Karl Kautsky, *Die Agrarfrage* (Stuttgart: J. H. W. Deitz/nachf g.m.g.h., 1899), p. 477.

11. Jane T. Stoddart, *The New Socialism: An Impartial Inquiry* (London: Hodder and Stoughton, 1909), p. 36.

12. Socialist Party of America, Convention Minutes [Stenographic], Indianapolis, Indiana, July 17–August 1, 1901, following p. 119, typescript, Duke. The name Social Democratic party was changed to Socialist party at that convention.

13. "Socialist Party Platform of 1912," reprinted in Albert Fried, ed., *Socialism in America: From the Shakers to the Third International* (Garden City, N.Y.: Doubleday and Company, 1970), p. 303.

14. Morris Hillquit, Samuel Gompers, and Max Hayes, *The Double Edge of Labor's Sword: Discussion and Testimony on Socialism and Trade-Unionism Before the Commission on Industrial Relations* (Chicago: Socialist Party National Office, [1914]), p. 303.

15. Jessie Wallace Hughan, *What is Socialism* (New York: Vanguard Press, 1928), p. 40.

16. Hillquit, Gompers, and Hayes, *Double Edge*, p. 23.

17. Ibid., p. 25.

18. [Karl Marx and Friedrich Engels], *Manifest der Kommunistischen Partei* (Bishopsgate: Bildings Gessellschaft fur Arbeiter, 1848), p. 16.

19. Socialist Party, Convention Minutes, following page 119.

20. Kipnis, *American Socialist Movement*; Weinstein, *Decline of Socialism*; Shannon, *Socialist Party*; Bell, "Background"; Bernard K. Johnpoll, *Pacifist's Progress: Norman Thomas and the Decline of American Socialism* (Chicago: Quadrangle Books, 1970), especially chaps. 4 and 5.

21. For a definition of federalism, see Kenneth Wheare, *Federal Government* (London: Oxford University Press, 1953), pp. 11–15.

22. See, for example, Henry F. Bedford, *Socialism and the Workers of Massachusetts* (Amherst: University of Massachusetts Press, 1966); Garin Burbank, *When Workers Voted Red: The Gospel of Socialism in the Oklahoma Countryside* (Westport, Conn., Greenwood Press, 1977); Marvin Wachman, *History of the Social Democratic Party of Milwaukee* (Urbana: University of Illinois Studies in Social Science, 1945); James H. Maurer, *It Can be Done* (New York: Rand School, 1938); Oscar Ameringer, *If You Don't Weaken* (New York: Henry Holt and Company, 1940); Ronald Sanders, *The Downtown Jews* (New York: Harper and Row, 1969); James R. Green, *Grass Roots Socialism: Radical Movements in the Southwest, 1895–1943* (Baton Rouge: Louisiana State University Press, 1978). No published studies are available on the Montana, Nevada, Washington, California, or Connecticut parties. Each published a newspaper. See also Robert L. Morlan, *Political Prairie Fire: The Non-Partisan League, 1915–1922* (Minneapolis: University of Minnesota Press, 1955).

23. See chapter 18.

24. The standard biography of Debs is Ray Ginger, *The Bending Cross: A Biography of Eugene Victor Debs* (New Brunswick, N.J.: Rutgers University Press, 1949); a definitive political biography of Victor Berger is still to be written. Sally Miller, *Victor Berger and the Promise of Constructive Socialism* (Westport, Conn.: Greenwood Press, 1973), has interesting insights into Berger; so does Wachman, *History*. Berger's writings and speeches during his long career are in *The Voice and Pen of Victor Berger* (Milwaukee: Milwaukee Leader, 1929).

25. William Macon Coleman, "Socialism in Politics," *International Socialist Review* 3 (February 1903): 178–79. See also "The Social Democracy of America," *Literary Digest* 15 (July 5, 1897): 275; O. Gene Clanton, *Kansas Populism* (Lawrence: University of Kansas Press, 1969), pp. 70, 146–47, 217–18, 222–24, 226, 236.

26. Charles P. LeWarne, "Equality Colony: The Plan to Socialize Washington," *Pacific Northwest Quarterly* 59 (July 1968): 137; Leon Greenbaum, "Socialism in the Middle West," *International Socialist Review* 1 (May 1901): 697.

27. Almont Lindsey, *The Pullman Strike* (Chicago: University of Chicago Press, 1942), pp. 107–10.

28. Ibid., pp. 111–13; Eugene V. Debs, "How I Became a Socialist," *The Comrade* 1 (April 1902): 146–48.

29. Lindsey, *Pullman Strike*, pp. 122–23, 129–35, 139; *New York Morning Journal* October 19, 1896.

30. Lindsey, *Pullman Strike*, pp. 167–213; Caro Lloyd, *Henry Demarest Lloyd, 1847–1903: A Biography* 2 vols. (New York: G. P. Putnam's Sons, 1912), 1: 156.

31. Lindsey, *Pullman Strike*, pp. 276, 295–305; "The Debs Co-operative Colony," *The Outlook* 56 (July 3, 1897): 358; "Collectivism in the United States," *The Spectator* (London), July 17, 1897, p. 70.

32. *The People* 3 (June 25, 1893): 1; E. V. Debs, "Labor Omnia Vincit," *Labor Day Souvenir of Boston Central Labor Union*, in *Debs: His Life, Writings and Speeches* (Girard, Kans.: Appeal to Reason, 1908), pp. 254–55.

33. *The People* 5 (April 25, 1895): 1; 7 (December 12, 1897): 3.

34. *The Social Gospel* 1 (March 1898): 25–26; Frederic Heath, ed., *Social Democracy Red Book* (Terre Haute, Ind.: Debs Publishing Company, 1900), pp. 130–31; "Collectivism in the United States," p. 70; "The Debs Co-operative Colony," p. 539; Morris Hillquit, *History of Socialism in the United States* (New York: Funk and Wagnalls, 1910), pp. 302–3; Caro Lloyd, *Henry Demarest Lloyd*, 2: 60–61.

35. Caro Lloyd, *Henry Demarest Lloyd*, 2: 60–61; LeWarne, "Equality Colony," pp. 138–39; "Collectivism in The United States," p. 70; "The Debs Co-operative Commonwealth," p. 70; Howard H. Quint, "Julius Wayland, Pioneer Socialist Propagandist," *Mississippi Valley Historical Review* 35 (March 1949): 599; *The People* 7 (July 25, 1897): 1; Wachman, *History*, p. 17.

36. Abraham Cahan, *Bleter fun Mein Lebn*, [Leaves from My Life] (Yiddish), 5 vols. (New York: Forward Association, 1926–1931), 4: 487–91.

37. *The Social Gospel* 1 (March 1898): 26.

38. "The Debs Co-operative Commonwealth," p. 540; "Collectivism in the United States," p. 70; *Brooklyn Daily Eagle*, March 22, 1899; Hillel Rogoff, *Meyer London, A Biografie* (Yiddish) (New York: Meyer London Memorial Fund, 1930), pp. 20–21.

39. Wachman, *History*, pp. 12, 15; *Encyclopedia Judaica*, 16 vols. (Jerusalem: Macmillan, 1971), 4: 614.

40. *Encyclopedia Judaica*, 4: 10, 13–14, 19; Heath, *Social Democracy*, p. 39.

41. Frederic Heath, "How I Became a Socialist," *The Comrade* 2, no. 7 (1902); 154–55; Wachman, *History*, pp. 10–11.

42. Wachman, *History*, pp. 26–27; Emma Goldman, *Living My Life* (New York: Alfred A. Knopf, 1931), 2 vols., 2:220; *Social Democratic Herald*, July 9, 1898, p. 1.

43. Heath, *Social Democracy*, pp. 132–33.

44. *The Social Gospel* 2 (February 1899): 28; 3 (January 1900): 21; Heath, *Social Democracy*, pp. 70–71; Wachman, *History*, pp. 11, 21, 23.

45. Morris Hillquit, *Loose Leaves from a Busy Life* (New York: Macmillan, 1933), pp. 7, 8, 17, 18, 31–33, 39–40, 47.

46. Hillquit, *History of Socialism*, pp. 197–301.

47. "Proceedings of the Tenth National Convention of the Socialist Labor Party: Held in the Common Council Chamber at the City of Rochester, New York, January 27, 1900, to February 2, 1900," typescript, Tamiment Institute Library, Second Day's Session, pp. 2–3, 6–7; Fourth Day's Session, pp. 4–6; Fifth Day's Session, p. 3.

48. Ibid., Second Day's Session, pp. 16–17; the Cox-Stedman letter is reproduced following page 18; see also pp. 20, 22, 23.

49. *The Haverhill [Massachusetts] Social Democrat* 1 (March 1900): 1–3, carries virtually complete minutes of the convention. The *Jewish Daily Forward* had equally comprehensive coverage in Yiddish, especially on March 7, 1900, and March 27, 1900, both p. 1. For a discussion of the intricacies of the merger, see Hillquit, *History of Socialism*, pp. 304–9.

50. See, for example, *Proceedings: National Convention of the Socialist Party* [Chicago, May, 10–17, 1908] (Chicago: Socialist Party of America, 1908), p. 291, copy at Tamiment Institute Library; *Social Democratic Herald* 2 (March 10, 1900): 2; (March 17, 1900): 8.

51. *Haverhill Social Democrat* 1 (March 17, 1900): 1; (March 24, 1900): 2; *Jewish Daily Forward*, March 7, 1900, p. 1.

52. *Haverhill Social Democrat* 1 (March 17, 1900): 1; Handwritten insert in "Proceedings, 1900," Sixth Day's Session (not paginated; 6 pages past 10).

53. *Haverhill Social Democrat* 1 (March 17, 1900): 2; *Social Democratic Herald* 2 (March 24, 1900): 1; Edgar Eugene Robinson, *The Presidential Vote, 1896–1932* (Stanford, Calif.: Stanford University Press, 1932), pp. 379–99.

54. Robinson, *Presidential Vote*, pp. 379–99.

55. Hillquit, *History of Socialism*, p. 306; Socialist Party, Convention Minutes, pp. 9–11, 14, 19, 63, 212, 443–44. See also Shannon, *Socialist Party*, pp. 6–7.

56. Socialist Party, Convention Minutes, pp. 120–22.

57. Ibid., pp. 122, 128–33; 136–49.

58. "Lines of Division in American Socialism," *International Socialist Review* 3 (August 1902): 109–14.

59. *National Convention of the Socialist Party Held at Chicago, Illinois, May 1 to 6, 1904* [stenographic report by William E. McDermutt, edited by William Mailly], (Chicago: National Committee of the Socialist Party, [1904]), pp. 301–5; Alexander Jonas to Morris Hillquit, June 23, 1904, Morris Hillquit Papers, Wisconsin State Historical Society, Madison, Wisconsin; "Interesting Convention Statistics," *International Socialist Review* 4 (May 1904): 705; Jessie Wallace Hughan, *American Socialism of the Present Day* (New York: John Lane Company, 1911), p. 354; *California Social Democrat* 1 (May 18, 1912): 1.

60. Eugene V. Debs to Upton Sinclair, September 19, 1918, Upton Sinclair Collection, Lilly Library, Indiana University, Bloomington, Indiana.

61. *The Party Builder*, no. 34 (June 28, 1913): 2; no. 43 (August 30, 1913); *Montana Socialist* 5 (September 23, 1916): 4; William Mailly to Morris Hillquit, March 17, 1906, Morris Hillquit Papers; Louis Boudin, quoted in Hughan, *American Socialism*, p. 222.

62. *National Convention, 1904*, pp. 217, 308; Hughan, *American Socialism*, pp. 171, 251, 255; Marxist [pseudonym], "The Referendum Movement and the Socialist Movement in America," *International Socialist Review* 4 (October 1903): 206; John S. Pyle, "The Philosophy of Socialism," *Socialist Campaign Book* (Toledo, Ohio: Socialist Party of Lucas Party, 1902), pp. 32–33.

63. J. L. Engdahl, "Winning Labor for Socialism," *The Western Comrade* 1 (February 1914): 335; Clarence E. Meilly, "Actual Divisions: Dangers of the Socialist Movement," *Revolt* (San Francisco) 2 (August 19, 1911): 1.

64. *Social Democratic Herald* 4 (October 12, 1901).

65. Quoted in William English Walling, J. G. Phelps Stokes, Jessie Wallace Hughan, Harry W. Laidler et al., *The Socialism of Today* (New York: Henry Holt and Co., 1916), p. 221.

66. *Social Democratic Herald* 4 (August 24, 1901).

67. "Practical Socialism: Is There Any Such Thing," *Saturday Evening Post*, May 8, 1909, p. 9.

68. Ibid., p. 9.

69. William English Walling, *Socialism as It Is* (New York: Macmillan, 1912), p. 182.

70. *Montana Socialist* 1 (March 16, 1913): 1.

71. William English Walling, "The Pragmatism of Marx and Engels," *The New Review* 1 (April 1913): 469; Mary Marcy, "The Milwaukee Victory," *International Socialist Review* 10 (May 1910): 991.

72. Hughan, *American Socialism*, pp. 198–99; Eugene V. Debs, "The Socialist Party and the Working Class," in *Debs: His Life, Writings, and Speeches*, p. 358.

73. Austin Lewis, "The Militant and the Socialist Party," *The World* (Oakland, Calif.), no. 302 (January 6, 1912): 1; Mary E. Marcy, "Can a Socialist Serve 'All the People,' " *International Socialist Review* 12 (September 1911): 150.

74. Debs, quoted in Joseph Medill Patterson, ed., *Socialist Campaign Book* (Chicago: National Executive Committee, Socialist Party, 1908), p. 5; Eugene V. Debs, The Growth of Socialism," in *Debs: His Life, Writings and Speeches*, p. 237; Debs, "The Socialist Party and the Working Class," in ibid., p. 361; Debs, quoted in Walling, *Socialism as It Is*, p. 177.

75. Louis B. Boudin, *Socialism and War* (New York: New Review Publishing Company, 1916), p. 228; "Practical Socialism," p. 8; "Violence and the Socialist Movement," *International Socialist Review* 3 (February 1903): 490–91; James Connolly, "Ballots, Bullets, or . . . ," *International Socialist Review* 10 (October 1910): 356–58.

76. "1913," *New Review* 1 (January 4, 1913): 3–6; Walling, *Socialism as It Is*, p. 436; Boudin, *Socialism and War*, p. 328; B. E. Nilsson, "Unionism and Socialist Politics," *International Socialist Review* 10 (November 1909): 403; Eugene V. Debs, "Speech at Battery D, Chicago, on His Release from Woodstock Jail, November 22, 1895," in *Debs: His Life, Writings and Speeches*, p. 329; Debs, "The Growth of Socialism," in ibid., p. 227; Debs, "Unionism and Socialism," in ibid., p. 119; William D. Haywood, "Socialism the Hope of the Working Class," *International Socialist Review* 12 (February 1912): 462–66. A rare left-winger who was antilibertarian and favored the use of the state's power against anti-Socialists by force was Austin Lewis; see his "The Economic Interpretation of History and the Practical Socialist Movement," *International Socialist Review* 7 (April 1907): 618.

77. Austin Lewis, "The Militant and the Socialist Party," *The World* (Oakland, Calif.), no. 302 (January 6, 1912): 1; B. E. Nilsson, "Unionism and Socialist Politics," *International Socialist Review* 10 (November 1909): 402; Caroline Nelson, "Political Socialism versus Industrial Socialism," *Revolt* 2 (November 18, 1911): 3.

78. Hillquit, *History of Socialism*, p. 364; Morris Hillquit, *What Socialists Have Done* (New York: Socialist Party, 1916), p. 3.

79. Hughan, *American Socialism*, pp. 16, 156–58; William E. Bohn, "Reformer and Revolutionist," *International Socialist Review* 10 (September 1909): 204; Upton Sinclair to John Reed, November 5, 1913, Morris Hillquit Papers; Scott Nearing, Morris Hillquit, Rev. Dr. John L. Bedford, and Frederick M. Davenport, *Should Socialism Prevail* (New York: Rand School of Social Science, 1916), pp. 13, 25.

80. United States Commission on Industrial Relations, Hearings, *Industrial Relations* 11 vols. (Washington, D.C.: U.S. Government Printing Office, 1915), 2 : 1463, 1490.

81. Hillquit, *What Socialists Have Done*, p. 6; Morris Hillquit, *Socialism Summed Up*, (New York: Rand School, 1917), pp. 34, 37, 39; *Industrial Relations*, 2: 1467, 1491.

82. Kate Richards O'Hare to Samuel Castleton, September 16, 1945, in Castleton Collection, Tamiment Institute Library.

83. See, for example, Bernard K. Johnpoll, *The Politics of Futility: The General Jewish Workers Bund of Poland, 1917–1943* (Ithaca: Cornell University Press, 1967), p. 267, for a similar phenomenon in another powerless Socialist party. This factor in factionalism has been generally ignored in the literature about Socialist and other radical movements.

∾ *17* ∾

Decline of the Left

- 1 -

Between 1900 and 1912 the Socialist party showed almost continuous growth. The dues-paying membership increased from fewer than 10,000 in 1900 to 135,364 in April 1912.[1] The national vote rose from 96,116 to 901,032 during the same period.[2] Beginning in 1913, however, the Socialist party began to decline. By 1916 more than 50,000 members had left the party, and only 82,284 dues payers were left. By 1922 the membership had declined to 11,019.[3] The same was true of the national vote. By 1916 it had declined to 590,166.[4] During the period 1910 to 1912, Socialists elected 160 chief executives in American municipalities, including mayors in Milwaukee (1910), Schenectady (1911), Berkeley (1911), and Butte (1911).[5] By 1916 only one of these cities—Milwaukee—elected a Socialist mayor. In all of the others, the Socialists were defeated.[6]

The Socialist fortunes in membership, elections, and power were all closely related. Membership rose as Socialists won elections. Thousands of non-Socialist reformers joined the party, attracted by the "immediate demands" and the assumption that Socialists were the wave of the political future who could make these reforms a reality. Many of them left the party between 1913 and 1916 when they saw "their pet reforms in a fair way . . . realized by Woodrow Wilson and his followers."[7] A large number of politically ambitious young professionals—lawyers, publicists, teachers, writers—joined the party in the anticipation that they could ride to high political office through it. They invariably dropped out when the party failed to live up to their political expectations.[8] A large number of workers joined the party in towns and cities where Socialists had won political control, hoping to obtain municipal jobs. When Socialists lost control of these cities and towns, the workers left for greener pastures.[9] Others left the party after the 1912 convention outlawed the advocacy of sabotage and forced "Big Bill" Haywood from the National Executive Committee. But this was a minor and short-lived cause for the party's decline. by 1915 left-winger Ludwig E. Katterfield reportd that "the party today contains more clear-cut revolutionists than ever before."[10]

The rise and fall of Socialist strength was primarily due to the fact that the party offered attractive, reformist platforms that the major parties or their offshoots subsequently enacted. Socialist platforms offered major reforms of immediate advantage to the working class, and Socialists in state and federal legislatures attempted to have them enacted.[11] Victor Berger, during his congressional career (1911–1913, 1923–1929), fought for agricultural, labor, and election reform, for an antilynching law, and for old-age pensions.[12] Meyer London, while in Congress (1915–1919, 1921–1923), pleaded against the war, for woman's suffrage, and for old-age and disability pensions. Berger and London differed from non-Socialist reformers only in their insistence that reform was a matter of right and not an act of charity.[13]

Socialists who served in state legislatures also found that, once elected, they were limited to reform—socialism was hardly an issue. Socialist state legislators introduced bills that ranged from pension plans to safety regulations to taxation to education, but not a single one for major socialization or nationalization.[14]

The Socialists—Left or Right, moderate or revolutionary—once elected, recognized that they had no alternative but to support reform legislation. Socialism itself was not a viable issue. Even the left-wing *International Socialist Review* conceded that "the most important task that our representatives will have will be to wage a militant fight for the right of all wage-workers . . . to organize and to have a voice in determining the conditions under which they shall work."[15]

These reforms were to be part of the undoing of the Socialist party. Socialists would frame reform legislation; the traditional parties would then adopt these reforms, enact them, and take credit for them. The conservative *Boston Herald* conceded that part of the Socialist platform of 1899 was enacted by Democrats and Republicans by 1912.[16]

In cities where Socialists served on city councils or as mayors, they invariably gave honest, efficient, economic government, generally for the benefit of the working people. The Socialist municipal victories of 1910 and 1911 were due to rebellions against corruption, graft, maladministration, inefficiency, and extravagance or due to the popularity of a candidate. Virtually every Socialist municipal victory exemplified popular rebellions against particular industries that controlled particular cities, or against unfair taxation in which the burden fell most heavily on the working class, or against inefficiency and waste.[17]

The Socialists generally did enact the reforms they promised. In Milwaukee and Schenectady, Socialist administrations ended graft in street paving contracts, saving each city hundreds of thousands of dollars. In Butte, the Democratic city treasurer was forced to return to the city $6,000 interest on city funds he had previously pocketed. In all of these cities, more efficient budgeting and purchasing allowed Socialists to turn deficits into surpluses while raising the wages of municipal employees and improving schools and recreational facilities.[18]

- 2 -

One cause of the demise of the American Socialist party was its failure to win the labor movement to its cause. This failure led to the most strident arguments and rifts within the party.

Virtually all Socialists agreed that labor unions were the "kindergartens of the proletarian movement" from which full-blown Socialists would develop. But they disagreed on how the party and the labor unions should relate to each other. The Right and Center wanted the party to support the existing trade unions, hoping to win them over to socialism and more efficient union organization by industry rather than craft.[19] Left-wingers wanted the whole labor movement reorganized on industrial lines as the vanguard of a revolutionary Socialist movement.[20] The leadership of the American Federation of Labor (AF of L) loathed all Socialists.

From the mid-1890s, Socialists attempted to have the AF of L formally endorse the basic principles of socialism. Samuel Gompers consistently opposed such a declaration. The animosity reached its apex when, in 1903, he denounced the Socialists as enemies of the labor movement, who "looked forward to the promised land" in the "sweet bye and bye" while ignoring the realities of the present.[21] He concluded his diatribe by proclaiming:

I want to tell you, Socialists, that I have studied your philosophy; read your works upon economics, and not the meanest of them, I have heard your orators and watched the work of your movement the world over, I have kept close watch upon your doctrines for thirty years; have been closely associated with many of you and know how you think and what you propose. I declare it to you, I am not only at variance with your doctrines but with your philosophy. Economically you are unsound, socially you are wrong, industrially you are an impossibility.[22]

Thereafter Gompers and the Socialists were in a constant state of conflict. But Socialists invariably lost, never winning over more than one-fourth the delegates to AF of L conventions.[23]

Gompers was hostile to the Socialists, becasue he was basically a syndicalist. He had arranged in 1892 for the AF of L to publish a small book by

Dyer D. Lum, an Anarcho-Syndicalist, which espoused Gompers's own viewpoint. In *The Philosophy of Trade Unions*, Lum argued that "trade unions build no system" but are "an expression of voluntary co-operation and free association" and thus illustrate the possibility of "social administration as a matter of mutual arrangement rather than collective interference."[24] Gompers was "very suspicious of the activities of governmental agencies," and he believed that "the giving of . . . jurisdiction to government and to government agencies is always dangerous to the working people."[25]

- 3 -

Antipathy for Gompers and his associates was universal among party members. The right and center wings, especially in the East and Midwest, favored "boring from within" the AF of L. The basically western left wing favored, instead, the organization of a new, competing labor federation.

Left-winger Gene Debs was the Socialist most responsible for the organization of the Industrial Workers of the World (IWW) and its predecessor, the American Labor Union. Debs believed that the AF of L leadership could not be won to socialism, political action, organization of the unskilled, and industrial unionism. He charged that the average AF of L union cared not a "damn about anyone but itself. It is all hog and no sympathy for the workers." Members of such unions could not be expected to change their leadership. The only solution, Debs argued, was the formation of new unions.[26]

A new labor federation centered in the Western Federation of Miners, a militant pro-Socialist industrial union of employees in metal mines and smelters in Arizona, Colorado, Idaho, Montana, Nevada, New Mexico, and Wyoming, was formed in 1898. The Western Labor Union's (WLU's) aim was to organize the great mass of unskilled western workers ignored by the AF of L. In 1902, at Deb's suggestion, the WLU became the American Labor Union, expanded into the East, and competed with the AF of L nationally.[27] The American Labor Union (ALU) added little strength to either the American labor movement or the Socialists' political power. Its organizing drives were failures.[28] In areas where ALU affiliates were strongest, the Socialists won few elective offices.

In the fall of 1904, with the failure of the ALU apparent, seven pro-Socialist labor figures—Isaac Cowen, representative in the United States of the British Amalgamated Association of Engineers; Clarence Smith, general secretary-treasurer of the ALU; George Estes, president of the United Brotherhood of Railway Employees; W. L. Hall, general secretary of the United Brotherhood of Railway Employees; Father Thomas J. Hagerty, Catholic priest turned militant Socialist who was editor of the ALU's official organ, *Voice of Labor*; Ernest Untermann, German-born Socialist intellectual; and William E. Trautmann, editor of the *Brauer Zeitung*, German-language organ of the United Brewery Workers—conferred on the future of industrial unions in America. They called a secret conference of militant labor leaders for January 1905. Thirty-six were invited; only two—Max Hayes and Victor Berger—refused to attend. That meeting, in Chicago, issued a manifesto that called for the organization of industrial unions open to all workers and prohibiting "initiation fees that force men to scab against their will." The conference called a convention in late June of that year. The Industrial Workers of the World was formed at that convention.[29]

The call for a new labor organization almost split the Socialist party. Berger condemned Debs for lending his name to the new labor organization. "If Debs stays with that crowd," Berger said, "he would lend them some prestige for a little while, but I am also sure that would be the end of Eugene V. Debs."[30]

The first IWW convention had within it the seeds for its failure. Only seventy official delegates attended, ostensibly representing 51,430 affiliated members: seventy-two observers came from organizations with 91,500 members. Sixty-one delegates represented only themselves. More than half the membership was in the Western Federation of Miners. All sorts of radicals, members of the Socialist party, the Socialist Labor party, Anarchists, Syndicalists, were among the delegates. Most vocal among them were the fourteen, led by Daniel De Leon, who represented the old Socialist Trades and Labor Alliance (ST and LA). De Leon had added to his delegation by inflating ST and LA figures. He tried unsuccessfully to dominate the convention.[31]

The leaders of the Western Federation of Miners, refused to join the IWW once the latter was organized. A struggle for control soon broke out between a triumverate composed of De Leon and Anarcho-Syndicalists Vincent St. John and William Trautmann, and Charles O. Sherman, an official of the United Metal Workers and a Socialist party member, who was elected president at the 1905 convention. The triumverate fabricated charges of financial irresponsibility against Sherman to force him from office. At the second convention of the IWW in 1906, De Leon and his "bunch of half-crazed fanatics" obstructed business, spending more than a week in passing on credentials, and deposed Sherman. The few viable unions that had remained in the IWW now left. Most Socialists, including Debs, joined the exodus. By 1908 the De Leon-St. John-Trautmann axis dissolved over a new effort by De Leon to seize control by himself. St. John and Trautmann joined forces temporarily to oust the imperious ruler of the Socialist Labor party remnant. De Leon, charging he had been robbed of control by the "bummery," then organized his own competing IWW, which led a sedentary half-life over the next twelve years.[32]

- 4 -

Despite disagreements with the IWW, Socialists were of great help to the Wobblies—a euphemism for members of the IWW—during their battles for civil liberties, against persecution, and during strikes.

Between 1912 and 1914, Socialists donated more than $60,000 to aid IWW strikers. Victor Berger, then a member of Congress, was instrumental in setting up a special congressional investigation of the IWW strike against the American Woolen Company in Lawrence, Massachusetts. The investigation exposed the needless violence and atrocities committed by police against the strikers. Confessions by police officials were widely publicized and helped win public support for the strikers.[33]

In Spokane, Washington, when the City Council passed ordinances restricting outdoor "soapbox" rallies, particularly those aimed against the unscrupulous employment agencies that preyed upon agricultural and timber workers, the IWW, with the aid of the local Socialists, defied the ban. Hundreds of them were arrested. Despite the arrests, Wobblies continued to speak from soapboxes. As police seized one, another mounted the platform. Some of their leaders were arrested as they walked on Spokane streets; IWW-organized newsboys were seized, beaten, and tortured by police, and their parents were compelled to swear that their youngsters—all under eighteen—were not members of the IWW. All told, more than 300 speakers and their supporters were arrested, tried, and sentenced. But the drive against free speech proved expensive for the city. Local business was hard hit as Socialist miners in nearby Coeur d'Alene, Idaho, declared a boycott of the city; the bars and retail shops suffered severe financial losses because of the boycott. "Needless to say all of these different activities have their result upon the opinion of the taxpayers and the businessmen," Elizabeth Gurley Flynn told the readers of the *International Socialist Review*. "We can appeal to their pocketbooks far more than to their intelligence or sense of justice." The city finally gave up; the restrictive laws were revoked, the Wobblies were freed, the Socialist miners called off their boycott.[34]

In San Diego, Wobblies, Socialists, and Anarchists united in a joint struggle against ordinances limiting free speech. Again, hundreds of Socialists and Wobblies were arrested for defying the local laws. One hundred fifty radicals were forced to dog trot twenty-two miles, after being taken from their jail cells, and then were beaten over their heads by local lawmen posing as vigilantes. Two participants in the struggle were murdered. Anarchist Emma Goldman was forced by a lynch mob to flee her hotel room. Her manager, Ben Reitman, was tarred, feathered, kidnaped, and left for dead twenty miles out of town.[35]

A battle took place in Everett, Washington, in 1916, between Wobblies and a large force composed of sheriff's deputies, the police, and strike-breakers—instigated by sheriff's men. Five of the Wobblies, and two of their opponents were killed in the battle: thirty-one members of the IWW and nineteen others were wounded, and several people—the number was never established—completely disappeared. Shortly thereafter, seventy-four members of the IWW were arrested and charged with murder. The Socialists raised much of the money needed for the defense. All seventy-four were acquitted.[36]

Socialist help for the IWW failed to lessen the strife between members of the two organizations. The strong antipolitical tone of the IWW's pronouncements after 1906, its failure to become a major labor organization, and the irresponsibility of some of its adherents within the Socialist party—as well as the intractability of some of its Socialist opponents—combined to create friction.

The failure of the IWW to form a viable labor organization was a predominant cause of the Socialist disenchantment. Most major IWW strikes were militant and spectacular, but ultimately futile. Because the Wobblies did not believe in contracts between unions and employers, they had no formal instrument to tie the workers to their union. The result was nearly disastrous; IWW membership rose precipitously and then fell, spectacularly, in roller-coaster fashion. It never exceeded 40,000.[37]

- 5 -

The IWW leadership had no compunctions about employing violence to achieve their Utopia, for the Anarcho-Syndicalists the ends justified the means. "If the destruction of property would gain the point for the workers . . . that is the only consideration we would give it," St. John said. The same was true of violence against persons.[38]

IWW spokesmen denied that sabotage and direct action, which they advocated, were forms of violence. One of the leading Wobbly apologists described sabotage as, at worst, the damaging of machinery to prevent strikebreakers from using the equipment during a walkout.[39] But they were being less than candid. Haywood, in a bid for Socialist support, declared: "I despise the law . . . no Socialist can be a law-abiding citizen," and urged Socialists to declare themselves conspirators whose aim would be the replacement of government with industrial society. This was too much even for Debs, who condemned Haywood's statement.[40]

By 1912 the Socialist party leadership decided to rid itself of Wobblies. The party now had more than 100,000 card-carrying members; more than 1,000 of them had been elected to state or city offices, and a Socialist, Victor Berger, sat in Congress. Most were convinced that advocates of sabotage, direct action, or violence could only retard their political progress. An amendment to the party constitution that would bar from membership anyone who advocated crime, violence, or sabotage, therefore, was passed, after an intense debate at that year's national convention.[41]

Haywood defied the amendment. In a New York speech, shortly after the convention, he proclaimed that he had never advocated the ballot as a means for achieving the revolution. He advised his listeners to employ sabotage and direct action instead. The New York state organization, dominated by followers of Hillquit, almost immediately called for his ouster from the National Executive Committee to which he had been elected in 1911. Even some right-wingers considered the reaction too severe. But the majority of those party members who bothered to vote—only about one in three—supported Haywood's ouster, 22,495 to 10,944. Haywood soon left the party. But not a single member, not even Haywood, was ever expelled for advocating crime, violence, or sabotage.[42]

Even Debs had turned against the IWW by 1913. It was, he wrote, "an Anarchist organization in all except name. . . . Anarchism and socialism have never mixed and never will. . . . There are IWW Anarchists who are in the Socialist Party for no other purpose than to disrupt it, and the Socialist Party is right for taking a decided stand against them." As for Haywood, he knew that he had violated the party constitution, and he knew he would suffer the consequences, Debs said. The party, he declared, was correct in taking action against Haywood and the Wobblies.[43]

Even some of its most ardent supporters in 1905 had by 1913 abandoned the IWW. It continued to exist as a minor, albeit romantic, incident in American labor history.

- 6 -

World War I and the Russian revolution of 1917 were two of the most difficult tests American socialism faced. Both came at a time when the Socialist party was in decline, especially in the West. The result was disaster.

Internationalism and abhorrence of international war were two of the universal principles of Socialists—Right, Left, or Center. Party convention resolutions regularly proclaimed internationalism as part of the Socialist creed.[44] Debs had proclaimed that "the thought of thrusting a gleaming bayonet into a piece of quivering flesh" to be wholly distasteful." He called war "one of the grossest relics of barbarism" whose chief victims were workers and their families.[45] Moreover, American Socialists were certain that European Socialists agreed with them.[46]

But they turned out to be naively optimistic. Europe's Socialists had generally supported their countries once war broke out in 1914. The German Social Democrats had, with a few notable exceptions, voted for war credits, French and Belgian Socialists and British Labourites supported their governments in the war. Even George Plekhanov, the Russian Marxist, backed the hated Czar.[47] The Americans were astounded and upset, especially at the Germans. Right-winger Robert Hunter condemned the German Social Democrats, and to a lesser degree the French, and divorced himself from the American party. So did Fred Warren, editor of the 500,000 circulation *Appeal to Reason*, and left-winger Robert Rives La Monte.[48]

Those who stayed in the party between 1914 and 1917 generally remained true to the principles of "Socialist internationalism." The national leadership denounced the war as soon as it was declared. They called for a stop-the-war conference of the world's Socialist parties. The call was largely ignored. They urged President Wilson to mediate the war, but he, too, ignored them.[49]

In May 1915 the National Committee issued a thirteen-point program, which presaged Wilson's "Fourteen Points." The Socialists opposed indemnities, annexations, colonialism, and profit on war material manufacture and sales. They favored an international parliament and court, internationalization of seaways, neutralization of the seas, universal disarmament, universal suffrage, and industrial democracy. Meyer London proposed a resolution in Congress that generally reiterated the program and called for American mediation of the dispute. He too was ignored.[50]

By late 1915 some erosion of the American Socialist position had occurred. George C. Herron became violently anti-German and wanted the United States to support the Allied cause. So did Charles Edward Russell, Upton Sinclair, Frank Bohn, William English Walling, and John Spargo. "There are worse things than war," they argued. Among them "the irruption of Germany."[51] But they were the exceptions. Most Socialists remained genuinely neutral and antiwar on principle.[52]

So strong was the antiwar sentiment in the party that in May 1915, at a time when "preparedness" hysteria was sweeping the nation, Socialists voted 11,041 to 782 to expel any "member . . . elected to an office, who shall in any way vote to appropriate moneys for military or naval purposes."[53] Likewise, after a German submarine sank the British liner Lusitania, with a loss of 1,200 lives, in May 1915, the Socialists, despite disagreements about culpability in the attack, refused to be stampeded into calling for reprisals.[54] During the 1916 campaign, Socialist candidates made opposition to war their dominant theme.[55]

Hours before America declared war, London pleaded with President Wilson to attempt to institute peace talks. His plea was in vain.[56] London was among the leaders of the opponents of a war declaration in the House. "The American people do not want this war . . . they know it is not necessary or justifiable," he declared. London concluded by calling the war "the greatest crime of the centuries."[57] On Good Friday, April 6, 1917, the House of Representatives voted 373 to 50 to declare war; Meyer London was the only New York Congressman to vote "No."[58]

As Congress was voting to declare war, the American Socialists were convening in St. Louis. A large majority of the convention delegates strongly opposed American intervention. They branded the "declaration of war by our government . . . a crime against the people of the United States and the nations of the world."[59]

- 7 -

Within months, most Socialists favored modification or repeal of the St. Louis Declaration against the war. Wilson's issuance of the Fourteen Points won a lot of Socialist support for the war effort. So did the German attack on the new Soviet government.[60] Those who wanted the party to shift its position had virtually all been supporters of the original Declaration. The earlier prowar Socialists left the party and formed their own short-lived Social Democratic League.[61]

Meyer London was one of the Socialist leaders who changed his stance on the war; he pleaded in May 1918 with members of the Amalgamated Clothing Workers to support the war effort. Six of seven New York City Socialist aldermen voted to support the Liberty Bond drive. The International Ladies Garment Union purchased $100,000 in bonds in April 1918, and the United Hebrew Trades of New York pleaded with Jews to purchase bonds. Both were pro-Socialist. Even Eugene V. Debs wanted a new party convention called to rewrite the St. Louis Declaration.[62] State and local organizations also called for a new convention or referendum to change the party's position. The Nebraska state party declared itself in favor of the war in early 1918. Unfortunately, the Wilson administration had passed laws that made it impossible for the Socialists to call a new convention or order a referendum. Under the wartime Espionage and Trading with the Enemy Acts, it was illegal for the antiwar factions to publish and mail their views, thus limiting debate within the party. All that could safely be called was a conference of party state secretaries in August 1918. It had no authority to rewrite the declaration. Instead, the meeting enacted a platform that virtually ignored the war issue. It heard Debs shift his position again and defend the St. Louis Declaration. Even that platform and all copies of the Socialist magazine that printed it were barred from the mail.[63]

- 8 -

When the Socialists at St. Louis proclaimed their opposition to war, they "indulged in the illusion that there would be no harm in expressing 'their doubts' about the conflict."[64] But they were naively mistaken; domestic democracy and justice are almost invariably the first two victims of war.

Even before the United States entered the conflict, Thomas J. (Tom) Mooney and Warren K. Billings, two militant San Francisco trade unionists and Socialists, were convicted, on the basis of contrived evidence, of bombing a Preparedness Day parade in that city in July 1916 in which nine persons were killed.[65]

Once war was declared, the persecutions became frequent. Raids of Socialist headquarters became common. Within a year, at least 1,000 Socialist party branches, primarily those in smaller cities and towns, were raided and destroyed. Except in a few big cities, meetings were impossible. In Chicago, for example, national headquarters were raided in September, and all files and letters were seized.[66]

Even moderately pro-Socialist organizations were persecuted. The People's Council of America for Peace and Freedom was formed by a combination of Socialists, liberals and a sprinkling of pacifists in 1917. It favored (1) an American declaration of war aims; (2) a speedy general peace based on the equivalent of Wilson's Fourteen Points; (3) an end to the draft; (4) protection of civil liberties; (5) protection of civil rights for labor, and (6) a tax on war profits. Despite its moderate position, the People's Council's meetings were broken up by police; its speakers were beaten. Its efforts to hold a national convention were frustrated by authorities.[67] Socialists were jailed and beaten. In Boston soldiers, sailors, and marines assaulted Socialist paraders and barred a meeting on the Common. In Philadelphia sixty-two were arrested for handing out anticonscription leaflets.[68]

The harshest repression was saved for the Industrial Workers of the World. More than 150 of the organization's leading members were sentenced to long prison terms, ostensibly because they conspired to impede the war effort. An IWW organizer, Frank Little, was lynched in Butte, Montana. In Tulsa, Oklahoma, 17 Wobblies were tarred, feathered, and forced out of the state. In Bisbee, Arizona, about 1,000 metal miners were driven into the desert by vigilantes, with secret cooperation of officials.[69]

Under "the guise of defending the United States against German intrigue and espionage . . . [Postmaster General Burleson] sought to exclude from the mails any writings outside the range of his own interests, which were as narrow and limited as those of any Bourbon monarch." His primary target was thus the Socialist press. Within a year after war had begun, twenty-two Socialist newspapers and innumerable books, pamphlets, and leaflets were barred from the mails.[70]

Non-Socialist, pro-Kaiser newspapers—such as the New York *Staats Zeitung*—were untouched. The Socialist *New Yorker Volkszeitung*, which had openly condemned the Kaiser and the German Social Democrats, lost its mailing privileges.[71] So did the official party organ, the weekly *American Socialist*; the Anarchist monthly *Mother Earth*, the left-wing Russian daily *Novy Mir*, the Hungarian pro-labor *Elore*, and the major Socialist dailies, *The Milwaukee Leader* and the *New York Call*.[72] Even the *Jewish Daily Forward*, with a circulation of more than 150,000, was scheduled to lose its second-class permit. Only a plea by prowar Jewish attorney Louis Marshall and a promise by the *Forward*'s editor Abraham Cahan that he would no longer oppose the war saved its mailing privileges.[73]

Hundreds of Socialists were arrested. In February 1918, five leading members of the party—Berger; Adolph Germer, national secretary; J. Louis Engdahl, editor of the official party organ; William F. Kruse, executive secretary of the Young People's Socialist League; and Irwin St. John Tucker, author, clergyman, and leader of the People's Council in Chicago—were arrested on charges of conspiring to violate the Espionage Act. A jury, composed of antagonistic farmers and businessmen, found them guilty, and a "militant patriot and unconventional, latitudinarian judge" Kenesaw Mountain Landis handed down long prison sentences—which were eventually overturned because of the judge's prejudicial behavior.[74]

Rose Pastor Stokes was given ten years for writing a letter to the *Kansas City Star* charging that the government favored profiteers. Party organizer Kate Richards O'Hare, a mother of four, was given a five-year term for denouncing the war. In Ohio, state secretary Alfred Wagenknecht, state organizer Charles Baker, and congressional candidate Charles Ruthenberg were sentenced to a year each for opposing conscription.[75]

The arrests of Stokes, O'Hare, Wagenknecht, Baker, and Ruthenberg so incensed Debs that he decided to challenge the Espionage Act. In a speech to the Ohio state convention, the sixty-three-year-old Debs spoke out against the war. As a result, he was arrested, tried, and convicted of violating the Espionage Act and sentenced to ten years in the federal penitentiary.[76]

The wartime persecution was a travesty on American democracy. It also damaged the party's ability to operate. But it does not explain the party's decline and demise. For the decline had begun much earlier.

- 9 -

Shortly after the United States went into the war against Germany, the first of a series of revolutions swept the hated Czar from power in Russia. In November 1917, the Bolsheviks seized full power and established a dictatorship "of the proletariat."

Socialists of Right, Center, and Left enthusiastically approved of the Bolsheviki. New York Assemblyman Louis Waldman, of the right wing, wanted to make America "more like Russia is today." James Oneal, of the right-center wing, was "unreservedly in support of the revolutionary government established by the workers and peasants of Russia." Morris Hillquit wrote to Debs that "I believe our comrades in Russia are doing the most inspiring work ever attempted in the history of our race."[77]

The left wing was if anything more enthusiastic. A new left wing, composed primarily of foreign-born, often alien, members emerged. This would exacerbate the problems of the party in the next four years, for it came at a time when the strength of the party had declined perceptibly in its old bastions in the West.

The new bastion of the party was now in the East, particularly among New York's Jewish population in the Lower East Side. But this was more apparent than real. Many of the Jews who came to the United States fleeing the oppressive, anti-Semitic Czarist regime in Russia had been members of the Socialist General Jewish Workers Bund in the old country. Most of them had come to the United States during the first ten years of the century. Since an average of about nine to ten years intervened between arrival and citizenship, most were naturalized between 1913 and 1919. Thus the Socialist vote reached its apex in that area during this period.[78]

The apparent shift in power within the party from the West to the East was accompanied by a sharp increase in the size of the foreign-language federations within the party, most of which were centered in the East. Foreign-language branches had existed in the Socialist movement from its earliest years. In fact, the Socialist Labor party considered English-speaking branches the exception. Within the Socialist party and its immediate predecessors, the foreign-language branches were significant as early as 1897 when the New York Jewish organization affiliated with the Social Democracy. By 1907 enough Finnish branches also existed, mainly in Massachusetts and Michigan, to organize a federaton. Three years later, the national party convention gave such federations formal approval and set up machinery for them to operate in the national office. Between 1910 and 1915, fifteen were formed. By 1917 they represented 41 percent of the party's 80,126 members.[79]

These federations were more involved with their homelands than they were with the United States. The Bohemian Federation, for example, officially supported the Allied cause—because the Austro-Hungarian empire stood in the way of an independent Czech republic. The Lettish, Finnish, and Lithuanian federations, on the contrary, opposed the Allies—because Russia was one of the members of that alliance, and Russians were occupying their homelands. The Polish Federation proclaimed that its "main aim was to prepare the revolution in Poland." All the Socialist foreign-language federations were Nationalist, except the Jewish, which opposed Zionism.[80]

The most radical of the federations was the Lettish. It supported the Bolshevik wing of the Russian Social Democratic Workers party. In early 1915, the Lettish organization in Boston decided to "Bolshevize" the Socialist party by organizing a Socialist Propaganda League that early made contact with Bolshevik leaders, including Nikolai Lenin abroad and Nikolai Bukharin and Mme. Alexandra Kollontay in the United States. They soon gathered about them a coterie of militant, generally East European, Socialists resident in the United States. In January 1917 the league began publication of a magazine, *The Internationalist*, and issued a manifesto calling for a new international, an end to parliamentarianism, and the use of more militant tactics to seize power. The manifesto was reprinted in the *International Socialist Review*, the organ of the party's left wing.[81] It became the model for later manifestos as the Socialist party was being torn asunder by internecine warfare.

The 1919 attack from the Left came at a moment when a false sense of optimism permeated the party. Its candidates had done extremely well in Wisconsin, Ohio, and New York elections.

In Wisconsin, Berger had in April 1918 polled 110,487 votes, more than 26 percent of the total, in a special race for the United States Senate seat. But it was hardly a Socialist vote. Both the Republican and Democratic candidates were vehemently prowar and conservative in an antiwar and progressive state. In November, Berger was elected to Congress from Milwaukee, eighteen Socialists were elected to the Wisconsin state Assembly, and five won seats in the state Senate.[82] In New York, the Socialists in 1917 elected ten members to the assembly—the largest Socialist representation in any legislature until that time—and seven members to the New York City Board of Aldermen and a municipal court judge. Morris Hillquit, Socialist candidate for mayor, polled more than 142,000 votes—three times the vote of four years previous.[83]

By 1918 internal dissension contributed to Meyer London's loss of his congressional seat. He was attacked from the Left of the movement for being too patriotic and from the Right for being too internationalist. One left-winger addressed him as "Our Misrepresentative in Congress." The Brooklyn party, dominated by the Left, refused to distribute any of his speeches. In his own district, the Left mustered 56 of 244 votes—23 percent—against his being renominated. On the Right, the Socialist-Zionist *Poale Zion* fought against his election because he refused to support the idea of a Jewish state in Palestine.[84]

It should have been obvious to Socialists generally that their victories were transient. Party membership declined to 74,519 in 1918. Then suddenly, membership rose to 109,589 early in 1919—a gain of more than 38 percent. But almost all of the increase was in foreign-language federations, which now accounted for 57,248 members—53 percent of the total. The most startling increases had been in the Russian, Ukrainian, South Slavic, Lithuanian, and Lettish organizations, which almost doubled their memberships in five months. Most of the newcomers were interested in the revolution in their own countries. Some hoped to return home to reap the fruits of the revolution or to become teachers of socialism to their more benighted brethen. All were enamored of the Bolshevik takeover in Russia; even those who wanted to remain in the United States hoped to emulate the revolution.[85] Moreover, all were co-opted into the pro-Bolshevik wing of the party.

In imitation of the Russian example, they were intent on capturing complete control of the party so it could better serve the needs of the Bolsheviks. By late 1918, the quasi-Bolshevik left wing had captured the Boston organization and had become dominant in Chicago and in the Bronx, Brooklyn, and Queens locals in New York City. Seven of the fastest growing foreign-language federations—Russian, Lettish, Lithuanian, Ukrainian, Hungarian, South Slavic, and Polish—were controlled by the new left wing.[86]

Then the Russian Bolsheviks issued a call for an international convention, which included an invitation to the De Leonite Socialist Labor party and Workers International Industrial Union, "The elements of the Left-Wing of the American Socialist Party (tendency represented by E. V. Debs and the Socialist Propaganda League)," and the IWW. The Socialist establishment was specifically ignored.[87]

By early April, it became apparent that the left wing had become an organized faction within the party—a virtual party within a party. Its members had acted as a unit in seizing branches and enforcing discipline. Then by using corrupt and illegal tactics, the Left elected twelve of the fifteen new members of the National Executive Committee (NEC). The party establishment counterattacked. First, the New York State Committee voted to revoke charters of left-wing locals, beginning with the Bronx. Next, Morris Hillquit wrote in the *New York Call* that it was "better a hundred times to have two numerically small Socialist organizations, each homogenious and harmonious within itself, than to have one big party torn by dissensions and squabbles, an impotent colossus on feet of clay. The time for action is near. Let's clear the decks."[88] Then the National Executive Committee ousted the left-wing foreign-language federations and the left-wing party organizations in Michigan, Massachusetts, Ohio, and Chicago. It invalidated the election to the NEC.[89]

The left-wing leaders called a national conference at which the *Left Wing Manifesto* was issued. It was a call for revolution and the establishment of a dictatorship of the proletariat. But even the left wing could not hold together. It split into two warring factions: a majority that wanted to stay in the Socialist party and capture it and a minority that wanted to form a new Communist party immediately.[90]

Thus when America's Socialists met in conventions in late August 1919, three separate parties emerged: the Socialist party, the Communist Labor party, and the Communist party. The Socialist delegates adopted a militant declaration, but decided against immediate application for membership in the Third—Communist—International. They called instead for formation of a new international open to all Socialist parties "which subscribe to the class struggle." The Communist Labor party (CLP), whose leader John

Reed, a Harvard-educated journalist, had left the Socialist party in 1916 to support Woodrow Wilson, adopted a quasi-syndicalist platform that eschewed electoral politics for "industrial action" and that had only one demand: "The establishment of the dictatorship of the proletariat." The Communist party, composed primarily of East European federations, proclaimed itself the sole true disciple of Lenin and Trotsky and refused any connection with any other party, even the CLP.[91]

All three of the parties were soon rent with internal feuds. The Socialist membership—what was left of it—rejected the convention decision on international affiliation, voting 3,475 to 1,444 to affiliate with Moscow. Louis Boudin and a number of others left the Communist Labor party. Boudin declaimed that he had not "left a party of crooks to join a party of lunatics." The one major English-speaking unit in the Communist party, the Michigan Federation, withdrew at the very outset, because it refused to be subservient to self-proclaimed revolutionary leaders.[92]

The split did not result, as Hillquit assumed it would, in a united party. The issue of international affiliation continued to cause splits and schisms for two more years.

After the party referendum decided in favor of affiliation with the Communist International, Otto Branstetter, the national secretary, sent a formal letter of application. Moscow replied with an open letter to the membership:

WORKERS: Leave the American Socialist Party. It is your enemy and ours. Already in America there is a revolutinary party, the United Communist Party, the American Section of the Communist International. These are our true comrades. . . . This is the party of the revolutionary working class.[93]

Later in 1920 the Communist International announced its Twenty-One Conditions for admission. It specifically called for the repudiation and ouster of Hillquit and for the party to accept the directives of Moscow without question. Delegates to the 1921 convention voted by almost ten to one to refuse the conditions. A number of party members withdrew. So did the Jewish, Finnish, Bohemian, and German federations.[94]

Thousands of members, disgusted by the incessant feuds, left all three parties. By 1921 their total membership was less than 25,000.[95]

- 10 -

The Socialist party during the last half-century was a mere shadow of its old self. By early 1917, even before the United States had entered the war, Oklahoma reported that it had lost more than two-thirds of its members, Nevada reported that 70 percent had left, and North Dakota informed the national office that 75 percent had left. During and after the war, party organizations disappeared in all of New England, except Connecticut, and in Oregon and Washington. All of the others were mere shells.[96]

The Socialist vote, however, gave the appearance of returning to normal. In 1919 the Socialists elected five members of the New York Assembly. Ten were elected to the Wisconsin House in 1920. Meyer London was again elected that year to Congress from New York's Lower East Side for his one postwar term. Victor Berger was defeated in 1920, but he won in 1922 and served in the House until 1929. Debs polled 919,799 votes in 1920, while still in federal penitentiary. Although this was the largest Socialist vote for president, it represented an actual proportionate decline from 1912, when women did not vote except in a few states, and barely equalled the 1916 percentage.[97]

Immediately after the war, persecution was added to the Socialist woes as thousands of radicals were arrested on "blank warrants or no warrants at all," and hundreds were deported. Drunken soldiers, sailors, and hooligans, egged on by "patriotic" officials, attacked Socialists as they walked from a meeting in Boston or a rally in Cleveland, beating them mercilessly. Socialists were arrested. Government agents raided their headquarters in New York, Baltimore, Detroit, Trenton, Cleveland, and many other cities, on spurious pretexts. Ex-servicemen destroyed Socialist headquarters, injuring innocent bystanders. Attackers were arrested occasionally, but all were freed despite testimony by battered policemen and bruised Socialists. A year after the Armistice, the attorney general's office raided and closed the office of the daily *Seattle Union-Record*, because it criticized the illegal acts of ex-servicemen.[98]

Duly elected Socialists were denied their seats in Congress and the New York State legislature. After the 1918 election, which he won, Berger was refused his place by the House of Representatives. At a special election, held after the House action, Berger was again elected, by a clear majority of the votes cast. He was again refused admission. Berger was finally seated in 1923 after winning the 1922 election. He served in the House until 1929—the year he died in an accident.[99]

In New York, the five Socialists elected to the assembly, in 1919, all of them right-wingers, were denied their seats by the members of the assembly. The Bar Association of the City of New York protested. Charles Evans Hughes, Republican candidate for president in 1916 and future chief justice of the United States, was prevented by the Republican leaders of the legislature from speaking against the ouster at the hearing. He was also barred from distributing a brief. Outcries from other prominent Americans were ignored.[100]

By 1922 the Socialists could no longer elect a single member to any New York office. For the next fifty years, the party was electorally insignificant except in Milwaukee, Reading, Pennsylvania, and Bridgeport, Connecticut, where Socialists were elected to local offices. The last Socialist served in a state legislature—in Wisconsin—in 1942.[101]

After 1920 the Socialist party lived a precarious life. No Socialist ran for president in 1924. The party devoted its energies in support of Progressive Robert M. La Follette in the hope that he would help form a labor party in the United States. He polled a respectable vote, but no labor party emerged.[102] Debs and London died in 1926, Berger in 1929, and Hillquit in 1933. The new leader of the party was Norman Thomas, a graduate of Princeton, Union Theological Seminary, and a Presbyterian minister. His socialism was a mixture of Social-Gospel Christianity, pacifism, and militancy. Thomas attracted a coterie of intellectuals, but few workers, to the party.[103]

Between 1928 and 1948, he was the party's candidate for president six times. His highest vote, 884,781, in 1932, represented only 2.5 percent of the total cast that year. In other elections, his vote varied from 267,420 in 1928 to 80,426 in 1944. Thomas's activities dealt primarily with labor organization, civil liberties, and opposition to war. He was a founder of the American Civil Liberties Union; he defied Mayor Frank Hague's ruthless, corrupt, anticivil libertarian regime in Jersey City, and he led the fight for social justice for tenant farmers in Arkansas in the face of planter vigilantes. Thomas also opposed both world wars—departing from his basic pacifism only to support the United States after it had declared war against Hitler and the Spanish Loyalists in their struggle against Franco's totalitarian regime.

The party disintegrated finally during Norman Thomas's leadership. But it was not primarily his fault. The Socialist party's demise lasted fifty-six years, from 1916 to 1972. Some of its failure, no doubt, can be attributed to internal party squabbling; much of it can be blamed on government persecution, especially during and immediately after World War I. But most of the fault lay in the party program, for it tried to be both revolutionary and reformist at the same time. Its revolutionary call for a Socialist system failed to attract any major interest among ordinary working people, who made up the constituency to whom the Socialists had to appeal. So party leaders emphasized amelioration; reforms, in the end, could be adopted by non-Socialists who could actually effectuate them through a major political organization.

At Thomas's death in 1968, the Socialist party was in its final agonies. Four years later, it died almost unnoticed.

NOTES

1. Party membership statistics compiled from *California Social Democrat* 3 (December 20, 1913): 2; *Proceedings, National Convention of the Socialist Party, 1912* (Chicago: Socialist

Party, 1912), p. 219; William English Walling, J. G. Phelps Stokes, Jessie Wallace Hughan, Harry W. Laidler et al., eds., *The Socialism of Today* (New York: Henry Holt and Company, 1916), p. 191; *The Party Builder*, quoted in *International Socialist Review* 14 (August 1913): 113.

2. "The Socialist Vote, 1900–1916," *International Socialist Review* 16 (February 1917): 507.

3. J. Louis Engdahl, "the Death of the Socialist Party," *The Liberator* (October 1924): 12; *American Labor Year Book*, vol. 5, 1923–1924 (New York: Rand School of Social Science, 1924), p. 125.

4. David A. Shannon, *The Socialist Party of America: A History* (New York: Macmillan, 1955;) *American Labor Year Book*, vol. 5, 1923–1924, p. 125.

5. Robert F. Hoxie, "The Rising Tide of Socialism: A Study," *The Journal of Political Economy* 19 (October 1911); 613; Jessie Wallace Hughan, *American Socialism of the Present Day* (New York: John Lane, 1911), pp. 44–45; Frank Bohn, "The Socialist Party and the Government of Cities," *International Socialist Review* 12 (November 1912): 276.

6. *California Social Democrat* 5 (April 8, 1916): 1.

7. "Back to First Principles," editorial, *International Socialist Review* 14 (August 1913): 113.

8. Henry L. Slobodin, "The State of the Socialist Party," *International Socialist Review* 17 (March 1917): 539–41.

9. Mary Lowndes, "What is the Matter With Butte, Montana," *International Socialist Review* 17 (March 1917): 539–41.

10. L. E. Katterfield, "The 1915 National Committee Meeting," *International Socialist Review* 16 (July 1915): 56–58.

11. See, for example, "Report of the Committee on State Program, Convention of 1912," in Walling et al., *The Socialism of Today*, pp. 210–11; "Oklahoma State Platform, 1912," in ibid., p. 217; "Socialist Party Platform, [1912]," in ibid., pp. 203–4; Hughan, *American Socialism*, p. 175; *National Convention of the Socialist Party Held at Chicago, Illinois, May 1 to 6, 1904* [Stenographic report by Wilson E. McDermutt, edited by William Mailly] (Chicago: National Committee of the Socialist Party, [1904]), pp. 213–20.

12. "Berger's Fine Record in Congress," *California Social Democrat*, September 3, 1911, p. 7; Victor Berger, "Old Age Pensions" (Speech, House of Representatives, August 7, 1911), in *Voice and Pen of Victor L. Berger* (Milwaukee: The Milwaukee Leader, 1929), pp. 637–45.

13. Harry Rogoff, *An East Side Epic: The Life and Work of Meyer London* (New York: Vanguard Press, 1930), pp. 8, 85–88; *Congressional Record*, 64th Cong., 1st sess., pp, 358, 7475, 7477–78, 8422, 8460, 8465–66, 8468; *California Social Democrat* 5 (December 1915).

14. Carl D. Thompson, "Fighting for Labor in State Legislatures," *The Western Comrade* 1 (July 1913): 116–17; Ethelwyn Mills, *The Legislative Program of the Socialist Party* (Chicago: The Socialist Party, 1914), pp. 5–6, 10–21.

15. "The Work of the Socialist Party," *International Socialist Review* 13 (October 1912): 364.

16. Winfield E. Gaylord, "A Legislative Program" (Chicago: Socialist Party, 1911), handbill, Tamiment Institute Library, New York University, New York City. *Boston Herald*, cited in Henry F. Bedford, *Socialism and the Workers of Massachusetts, 1886–1912* (Amherst: University of Massachusetts Press, 1966), pp. 106, 233.

17. Hoxie, "The Rising Tide," pp. 615, 618–19.

18. Carl D. Thompson, *Have the Socialists Made Good?—What They Have Done in Municipalities* (Chicago: National Office of the Socialist Party, [1913]), no pagination.

19. Robert Hunter, "The Power of Unionism," *Socialist Handbook* (Chicago: The Socialist Party, [1916]), p. 43; Ida Crouch-Hazlett, "The Other Side," *International Socialist Review* 5 (August 1904): 91; *National Congress of the Socialist Party Held in Masonic Temple, Chicago, Ill., May 15–21, 1910* [Stenographic report by Wilson E. McDermutt] (Chicago: The Socialist Parry, [1910]), pp. 277–279; Victor L. Berger, "Labor Leaders in the School of Experience," in *Broadsides* (Milwaukee: Social Democratic Publishing Company, 1913), pp. 163–65; *Montana Socialist* 1 (May 25, 1913): 1.

20. Charles H. Kerr, "The Editor's Chair," *International Socialist Review* 10 (October 1909): 360; Eugene V. Debs to Adolph F. Germer, March 4, 1904, Adolph Germer Collection, Wisconsin State Historical Society, Madison, Wisconsin; Eugene V. Debs, *Debs: His Life Writings and Speeches* (Girard, Kan.: *Appeal to Reason*, 1908), pp. 127, 137, 385, 390; Eugene V. Debs, "The Western Labor Movement," *International Socialist Review* 3 (November 1902): 257; *Proceedings of the First Convention of the Industrial Workers of the World, Founded in Chicago, June 27–July 8, 1905* (New York: New York Labor News Company, 1905), pp. 142–43.

21. *Report of Proceedings of the Twenty-Second Annual Convention of the American Federation of Labor Held at New Orleans, Louisiana, November 13 to 22, 1902* (Washington, D.C.: The Law Reporter Co., 1902), pp. 18–182; *Report of the Proceedings of the Twenty-Third Annual Convention of the American Federation of Labor Held at Boston, Massachusetts, November 9 to 23 inclusive, 1903* (Washington, D.C.: The Law Reporter Co., 1903), pp. 100, 120, 126, 188–91.

22. *Proceedings, 1903*, p. 198.

23. William M. Dick, *Labor and Socialism in America: The Gompers Years* (Port Washington, N.Y.: Kennikat Press, 1972), pp. 69, 76.

24. Dyer D. Lum, *Philosophy of Trade Unions* (New York: American Federation of Labor, 1892), pp. 17–19.

25. Morris Hillquit, Samuel Gompers, and Max J. Hayes, *The Double Edge of Labor's Sword: Discussion and Testimony on Socialism and Trade-Unionism before the Commission on Industrial Relations* (Chicago: Socialist Party, National Office, [1914]), pp. 100, 106.

26. [Eugene V.] Debs to Fred [Warren], January 3, 1913, Warren Collection, Lilly Library, Indiana University, Bloomington, Indiana.

27. Hillquit, *Industrial Relations*, 11: 10569–72; J. W. Sullivan, *Socialism as an Incubus From on the American Labor Movement* (New York: Volunteer Press, 1909), pp. 31–35; Algie M. Simons, "The Western Federation of Miners," *International Socialist Review* 6 (May 1906): 642–43.

28. Debs, "The Western Labor Movement," p. 258; G. A. Hoehn, "The American Labor Movement," *International Socialist Review* 3 (January 1903): 41–411.

29. Hazlett, *The Other Side*, p. 87; Vincent St. John, *The IWW, Its History, Structure and Method*, rev. ed. (Chicago: Industrial Workers of the World, 1919), pp. 2–10.

30. Victor Berger to Morris Hillquit, March 27, 1905, Hillquit Papers, Wisconsin State Historical Society, Madison, Wisconsin.

31. Charles O. Sherman to Morris Hillquit, February 2, 1907, Morris Hillquit Papers; St. John, *The IWW*, pp. 3–10; Algie M. Simons, "The Industrial Workers of the World," *International Socialist Review* 6 (August 1905): 65–66; *Proceedings of the First Convention of the Industrial Workers of the World*, pp. 476, 595–97. The total voting membership according to the published *Proceedings* was 51,231. Charles O. Sherman to Morris Hillquit, February 2, 1907, Morris Hillquit Papers.

32. Victor Berger to Morris Hillquit, March 27, 1905, Morris Hillquit Papers; Charles O. Sherman to Morris Hillquit, February 2, 1907, Morris Hillquit Papers; Paul F. Brissenden, *The IWW: A Study of American Syndicalism* (1919; reprint ed. New York: Russell and Russell, 1957), pp. 136–42, 149–51, 222–23; Editorial, *International Socialist Review* 7 (October 1906): 243.

33. *American Labor Year Book, 1916* (New York: The Rand School of Social Sciences, 1916), pp. 122–23; *The World* (Oakland, California), no. 308 (February 17, 1912), and no. 312 (March 9, 1912).

34. Elizabeth Gurley Flynn, "The Shame of Spokane," *International Socialist Review* 10 (January 1910): 613–18; "Spokane Passes Street Speaking Ordinance," *International Socialist Review* 10 (April 1910): 947–48.

35. *Revolt* 3 (February 24, 1912): 1; (April 16, 1912): 1, 3; (March 23, 1912): 1; *San Diego Herald*, quoted in Vincent St. John, "The Fight for Free Speech in San Diego," *International Socialist Review* 12 (April 1912): 649; *California Social Democrat* 1 (February 17, 1912): 1; (March 30, 1912): 1; (April 13, 1912): 1; (April 20, 1912): 1; (April 27, 1912): 1; (May 18, 1912)l 1; (September 10, 1912): 1; *The Citizen* (Los Angeles) 6 (May 17, 1912): 1, 3; (May 24, 1912): 1, 5.

36. *International Socialist Review* 17 (February 1917): 499; Walker C. Smith, "The Voyage of the Verona," *International Socialist Review* 17 (December 1916): 340–46; St. John, *IWW*, pp. 30–33.

37. Frank Bohn, "Is the I.W.W. to Grow?" *International Socialist Review* (July 1911): 42–43; Fred Thompson, *The I.W.W.: Its First Fifty Years, 1905-1955* (Chicago: Industrial Workers of the World, 1955) p. 111.

38. *Industrial Relations*, 2; 1446–47, 1455–59; 11: 10574–75.

39. Andre Tridon, *The New Unionism* (New York: B. W. Huebsch, 1913), pp. 43, 45–49; *Proceedings, 1912*, p. 131.

40. William D. Haywood, "Socialism: The Hope of the Working Class," *International Socialist Review* 12 (February 1912): 467; Eugene V. Debs, "Sound Socialist Tactics," *International Socialist Review* 12 (February 1912): 482.

41. *Proceedings, 1912*, pp. 125, 127, 130, 133.

42. "Bill Haywood," *The Iconoclast* 1 (January 24, 1913): 1–2; "Result of Referendum D 1912, Vote closed, February 26," *Weekly Bulletin*, March 1, 1913, mimeographed, copies in Socialist Party of America Collection, Duke University Library, Durham, North Carolina; and Tamiment Institute Library. States opposing the recall were Nevada, Oregon (by 323 and 321 votes), South Carolina, Tennessee, Texas, Utah, Washington, Montana, and West Virginia.

43. "An Open Letter By Eugene V. Debs," *Montana Socialist* 1 (May 19, 1913): 1; see also E. V. Debs to William English Walling, March 5, 1913, reprinted in Walling et al., *The Socialism of Today*, pp. 387–88.

44. Hughan, *American Socialism*, pp. 154–55; *The Iconoclast* 3 (August 21, 1914): 2.

45. Eugene V. Debs, "The Gunmen and the Miners," *International Socialist Review* 15 (September 1914): 161; *Haverhill Social Democrat* 1 (January 20, 1900): 3; Morris Hillquit to W. H. Short, June 12, 1911, in "Who Are the Peacemakers," broadside (Chicago: National Office, Socialist Party, 1912), n.p., copy in Socialist Party of America Collection.

46. Eugene V. Debs to Claude [G.] Bowers, January 29, 1912, Bowers Papers, Lilly Library.

47. Julius Braunthal, *History of the International, Volume II, 1914-1943* (New York: Frederick A. Praeger, 1963), p. 1; Oscar Ameringer, *If You Don't Weaken* (New York: Henry Holt and Company, 1940), p. 302.

48. Carl D. Thompson, "Liebknecht's Stand Against Militarism," [1915], mimeographed, copy in Socialist Party of America Collection; "Biography of Robert Hunter, 1874-1942, as prepared for a forthcoming volume of *The National Cyclopedia of American Biography*, James T. White Company Publishers," typescript, Hunter Papers, Lilly Library; *Montana Socialist* 5 (September 16, 1916): 2; Fred Warren, "The Little Old Appeal," typescript, Warren Collection; Robert Rives LaMonte and Louis C. Fraina, "Socialists and War: A Debate," *The Class Struggle* 1 (July–August 1917): 72–73. LaMonte voted for Wilson in 1916, helped organize the pacifist Union Against Militarism, and then resigned from that organization to support American intervention in 1917.

49. Alexander Trachtenberg, ed., *American Socialists and the War* (New York: The Rand School of Social Science, 1917), pp. 3, 8–9, 11–14; "Statement of the Socialist Party of America at the Outbreak of War in Europe," *New Review* 2 (September 1914): 523–24; Mary E. Marcy, "The Real Fatherland," *International Socialist Review* 15 (September 1914): 177–78; *The Iconoclast* 2 (August 28, 1914): 1; Socialist Party, National Executive Committee—Victor L. Berger, J. Stitt Wilson, James H. Maurer, Adolph Germer, Lewis J. Duncan; attested by Walter

Lanfersiek, executive secretary, September 24, 1914, "Call for International Socialist Peace Conference" [also in French as *Appel pour une Session Extraordinaire du Congress Socialiste International*, and in German as *Aufruf zu einer auserordentlichen Tagung des Internationalen Sozialisten-Kongresses*], copy in Socialist Party of America Collection; the call appeared in the *New York Call* of August 12, 1914. It was issued by the National Committee on Immediate Action, the group that was in charge of the party's day-to-day operations. Trachtenberg, *American Socialists*, pp. 8–9.

50. Trachtenberg, *American Socialists*, pp. 15, 18–19; Walling et al., *The Socialism of Today*, pp. 622–23; "Suggestions for Peace Program offered by the Peace Committee of the Socialist Party," [1947], and "Socialist Peace Program," [1915], typescripts, Socialist Party of America Collection; Trachtenberg, *American Socialists*, p. 21; "Socialist Terms of Peace in Congress," *New Review* 4 (January 1, 1916): 18.

51. George D. Herron, "The Outlook in Europe," *The Western Comrade* 3 (January-February 1915): 13; George D. Herron to Morris Hillquit, November 9, 1914; George D. Herron to Morris Hillquit, April 5, 1915; George Herron to Morris Hillquit, February 16, 1916, all Morris Hillquit Papers; *The World* (Oakland, California), no. 310 (February 24, 1912); Charles Edward Russell, "Big Business and War," in *WAR*, by Walter Thomas Mill and Charles Edward Russell (Chicago: Socialist Party, 1915), pp. 29–30; Charles Edward Russell, *Facts About War* (New York: Socialist Party, [1914]), broadside, Tamiment Institute Library; Charles Edward Russell to "Dear Comrade [Carl D.] Thompson," January 15, 1915, Socialist Party of America Collection; "Dissension in Socialist Party Concerning Preparedness," *New Review* 3 (December 15, 1915): 368–369; *The World*, no. 511 (January 8, 1916); Eugene V. Debs to Upton Sinclair, June 12, 1916, Upton Sinclair Collection, Lilly Library; Frank Bohn, "Whose War," *International Socialist Review* 17 (March 1917): 539; W. J. Ghent to Algernon Lee, April 30, 1916, Lee Collection, Tamiment Institute Library; Louis C. Fraina, "The Future of Socialism," *New Review* 3 (January 1915): 16; William English Walling, "The Remedy: Anti-Militarism," *New Review* 3 (February 1915): 83; W[illiam] E[nglish] W[alling], "The Peace Program of the Socialist Party," *New Review* 3 (June 15, 1915): 90; Emma [Goldman] to "My Dearest Anna [Strunsky Walling]," June 2, 1915, Anna Strunsky Walling Papers, Bancroft Library, University of California, Berkeley; John Spargo, "The Case for Russian Victory," *New Review* 3 (June 15, 1915); John Spargo to Morris Hillquit, November 13, 1914, Morris Hillquit Papers; Jerome Hall Raymond to "Dear Comrade Walling," September 5, 1915, Anna Strunsky Walling Papers; William English Walling, J. G. Phelps Stokes, Walter E. Krusli, W. J. Ghent, Charles Edward Russell, Harper Leech, John Russell, and Edward H. Gobl, "Letter," *Minneapolis Tribune*, March 28, 1917, reprinted in *Montana Socialist*, March 31, 1917.

52. Hillquit, quoted in "American Socialists and the War," *New Review* 2 (October 1914): 616; Morris Hillquit to Carl D. Thompson, January 6, 1915, Socialist Party of America Collection.

53. William E. Bohn, "Socialism and the Citizen Army," *International Socialist Review* 16 (February 1916): 460–61; Trachtenberg, *American Socialists*, p. 21; *California Social Democrat* 5 (January 22, 1916): 9.

54. "The American Socialist Press and the Lusitania Affair," *New Review* 3 (June 1, 1915): 69.

55. Trachtenberg, *American Socialists*, pp. 26–30; *Socialist Handbook* (Chicago: The Socialist Party, [1916]), pp. 3, 7; *California Social Democrat* 5 (March 25, 1916): 1; (April 8, 1916): 1.

56. "Down With War" (Chicago: National Office of the Socialist Party, [1917]), broadside, Socialist Party of American Collection; *Montana Socialist* 5 (April 14, 1917): 1.

57. *The New York Call*, April 6, 1917, p. 1.

58. *The New York Call*, May 7, 1917, p. 2.

59. William E. Bohn, "An International Policy," *International Socialist Review* 17 (March 1, 1917): 563–65; Leslie Marcy, "The Emergency National Convention," *International Socialist Review* 17 (May 1917): 665; *The American Socialist* 4 (July 14, 1917): 4.

60. Will Herberg, "The Jewish Labor Movement in the United States," *American Jewish Year Book*, vol. 53, 1952 (New York: American Jewish Committee and Philadelphia: Jewish Publication Society, 1952), p. 33; James Oneal, "The Socialists in the War," *American Mercury* 10 (April 1927): 424; *The National Office Review* 1 (March 1918): 7; Jessie Wallace Hughan, quoted in "Notes on Tenth Annual Convention," *Intercollegiate Socialist* 7 (February-March 1919): 28.

61. [Harry W. Laidler], "Notes on Socialist and Labor Movements," *Intercollegiate Socialist* 7 (October-November 1917): 29.

62. *New York Call*, April 14, 1918, p. 2; April 18, 1918, p. 3; April 19, 1918, p. 5; May 17, 1918, p. 1.

63. Laidler, "Notes on Socialist and Labor Movements," p. 30; Morris Hillquit, *Loose Leaves from a Busy Life* (New York: Macmillan, 1934), p. 235; *American Labor Year Book, 1919–1920* (New York: Rand School of Social Science, 1920), p. 403; *New York Call*, May 11, 1918, p. 1.

64. Oneal, "The Socialists in the War," p. 418.

65. *New York World*, August 31, 1919, clipping, Lusk Collection, New York State Library, Albany.

66. Oneal, "The Socialists in the War," pp. 423, 425; *American Labor Year Book, 1919–1920*, p. 401, 467.

67. H. C. Peterson and Gilbert C. Fite, *Opponents of War, 1917–1918* (Madison: University of Wisconsin Press, 1957), pp. 74–80; John Bach McMaster, *The United States in the World War* (New York: D. Appleton and Company, 1918), pp. 393–94; "The Pacifist Pilgrims," *Literary Digest* 55 (September 15, 1917): 16–17; H. Rogoff, "Der Pipls Kansil" (Yiddish), *Zukunft* 22 (September 1917): 513–14.

68. McMaster, *United States*, pp. 387, 392–93.

69. H. W. L. [Harry W. Laidler], "Our Ninth Convention," *Intercollegiate Socialist* 6 (February-March 1917): 18–19; Patterson and Fite, *Opponents*, p. 176; Oneal, "The Socialists in the War," p. 423.

70. William L. Chenery, *Freedom of the Press* (New York: Harcourt, Brace and Company, [1951]), p. 190; Oneal, "The Socialists in the War," p. 423.

71. Oneal, "The Socialists in the War"; *New York Tribune*, October 7, 1917, p. 2; October 11, 1917, p. 7.

72. *American Labor Year Book, 1919–1920*, p. 401; *Jewish Daily Forward*, October 3, 1917, p. 1; October 4, 1917, p. 1; October 5, 1917, p. 1; *New York Tribune*, October 9, 1917, p. 14.

73. *Jewish Daily Forward*, October 7, 1917, p. 1; October 13, 1917, p. 1; October 16, 1917, p. 1; Charles W. Ervin, "Lessons from New York's Labor Daily," *Labor Age* 11 (August 1922): 10; *New York Tribune*, October 3, 1917, p. 1; October 4, 1917, p. 4; October 9, 1917, p. 1; October 1917, p. 2.

74. Reels 6, 7, and 8 of the microfilm edition of the Socialist Party of America Collection (Microfilm Corporation of America) are replete with instances of arrests. See also, for example, *New York Call*, May 7, 1918, p. 3; May 10, 1918, p. 1; June 22, 1918, p. 6; Minutes of the Joint Conference of National Executive Committee and State Secretaries, August 10, 11, 12, 1918, p. 7, copy in Socialist Party of America Collection; *American Labor Year Book, 1919–1920*, pp. 400–403; *National Office Review* 1 (March 1917): 2; *New York Call*, April 30, 1918, p. 5; Joint Legislative Committee of the State of New York to Investigate Seditious Activities, *Revolutionary Radicalism*, 4 vols. (Albany: J. B. Lyon, 1920), 1: 548–52; Victor Yarros, "The Chicago Socialist Trail," *The Nation* 108 (January 25, 1919): 116–18.

75. New York State Legislature, Assembly Committee of the Judiciary, *Proceedings of the Judiciary Committee of the Assembly in the Matter of the Investigation by the Assembly of the State of New York as to the Qualifications of Louis Waldman, August Claessens, Samuel A. DeWitt, Samuel Orr, and Charles Solomon to Retain Their Seats in Said Body* [Legislative Document No. 35, State of New York] (Albany: J. B. Lyons Company, Printers, 1920), p. 1615; *New York Call*, June 4, 1918, p. 1; February 7, 1918, p. 2; May 11, 1919; J. Louis

Engdahl, *Debs and O'Hare in Prison* (Chicago: Socialist Party, [1919]), pp. 29–30; *National Office Review*, December 1917, p. [3].

76. Hillquit, *Loose Leaves*, p. 235; *National Office Review* 1 (March 1917): 7; "The Trial of Eugene V. Debs," *The Survey* 40 (September 21, 1918): 695–96; *The New York Call*, September 12, 1918, p. 1; September 13, 1918, p. 1; September 15, 1918, p. 1.

77. *Proceedings, Judiciary Committee* (Hereafter cited as Judiciary Proceedings) p. 312; James Oneal and Robert Minor, *Resolved That the Terms of the Third International Are Inacceptable to the Revolutionary Workers of the World* [Debate held at the Star Casino, New York, January 16, 1921] (New York: The Academy Press, 1921), p. 3; Morris Hillquit to Eugene Debs, June 30, 1920, Morris Hillquit Papers.

78. See especially Herberg, "Jewish Labor," p. 15; Milton Doroshkin, *Yiddish in America: Social and Cultural Foundations* (Rutherford, Madison, and Teaneck, N.J.: Fairleigh Dickinson University Press, 1969), pp. 161–63.

79. *Social Democratic Herald* 2 (September 9, 1899): Shannon, *Socialist Party*, pp. 44–45; *American Labor Year Book, 1916*, pp. 129–30.

80. Minutes of the Joint Conference, Socialist Party of America Collection, 122–26, 133–34; *American Labor Year Book 1916*, pp. 130–32, 136, 141, 143–44. *The Socialist World* 1 (July 1920): Supplement, pp. 2–4; *The Socialist* 1 (June 18, 1919): 6, 8. On Jewish Socialist Federation and Zionism, see Minutes of the Joint Conference, Socialist Party of America Collection, p. 137.

81. "The Lettish Socialists in America," *The Revolutionary Age* 1 (January 4, 1919): 4; Julius Falk, "The Origins of the Communist Movement in the United States," *The New International* 21 (Fall 1955): 158–59; "Manifesto of the Socialist Propaganda League of America" [adopted at a meeting in Boston, November 26, 1917], *International Socialist Review* 17 (February 1918):483–85; "A Program for Revolutionary Socialism," *The Revolutionary Age* 1 (March 8, 1919): 8. This article errs on the date of the founding of the Socialist Propaganda League.

82. *New York Tribune*, October 23, 1917, p. 3; *New York Call*, February 27, 1918, p. 3; April 4, 1918, pp. 1–2; November 5, 1918, p. 1; April 2, 1918, p. 2; *American Labor Year Book, 1919–1920*, p. 402; Evans Clark, "The 1918 Socialist Vote," *Intercollegiate Socialist* 7 (December 1918-January 1919): 19–20; Charles D. Stewart, "Prussianizing Wisconsin," *Atlantic Monthly* 113 (January 1919): 99–105.

83. William M. Feigenbaum, "The Socialists in the New York Assembly," *American Labor Year Book, 1919–1920*, p. 427; Evans Clark and Charles Solomon, *The Socialists in the New York Board of Aldermen* (New York: Rand School, 1918).

84. Clark, "The 1918 Socialist Vote," pp. 17–18; Maximilian Cohen, "The Growth of the Left Wing," *The Revolutionary Age* 1 (March 8, 1919): 7; J. S. Hertz, *Di Idishe Sotsialistishe Bavegung in Amerika* (Yiddisn) (New York: Der Wecker, 1954), p. 169; *New York Call*, June 28, 1918, p. 3; Rogoff, *An East Side Epic*, pp. 102–3, 121–23; L. Shpizman, *Geshikhte fun der Tsionistiher Arbeter Bavegung in Tsofn Amerika* [History of the Zionist Labor Movement in North America], (New York: Yiddisher Kempfer, 1955), p. 382. Shpizman pointed out that Debs, a non-Jew, supported the establishment of a Jewish homeland in Palestine, p. 381.

85. "Membership by States from January to and Including July 1919," typescript, Socialist Party of America Collection; Adolph Germer to the National Executive Committee, May 24, 1919, Lusk Collection; Minutes of the Joint Conference, Socialist Party of America Collection, p. 132; Hans Pikkor, organizer Esthonian Branch, Philadelphia, to "Com[rades] of Correspondence Department, [Rand School of Social Sciences]," October 1, 1918, Lusk Collection.

86. Theodore Draper, *The Roots of American Communism* (New York: Viking Press, 1963), pp. 131–47; "The Chicago Communist Propaganda League," *Revolutionary Age* 1 (February 8, 1919): 6.

87. "The Bolshevik Call for an International Communist Congress," *Revolutionary Age* 1 (March 1, 1919): 1.

88. Draper, *Roots*, pp. 156–57; Germer to National Executive Committee, Lusk Collection; Morris Hillquit, "The Socialist Task and Outlook," *New York Call*, May 24, 1919, p. 7; *Judiciary Proceedings*, pp. 1257–65.

89. Draper, *Roots*, p. 158; Harry W. Laidler, "Present Status of Socialism in America," *The Socialist Review* 8 (December 1919): 36; "Meeting of the National Executive Committee of the Socialist Party, May 26, 1919," pp. 15–16, 18–26, Lusk Collection; *New York American*, May 30, 1919; *New York Mail*, May 30, 1919; *The New York Times*, May 30, 1919; May 31, 1919; *New York Journal*, May 30, 1919. The news stories are in clippings in Lusk Collection, the most complete record of original documents regarding the birth of the American Communist movement.

90. Draper, *Roots*, p. 164; Laidler, "Present Status," pp. 36–37; "The Hold Up," *The Socialist* 1 (April 29, 1919): 3. A copy of the original *Left-Wing Manifesto* is in Lusk Collection; the authors are John Reed, Bertram D. Wolfe, and Maximillan Cohen. Wolfe was a teacher; Reed, a journalist; and Cohen, a dentist who was an alien.

91. *American Labor Year Book, 1919–1920*, pp. 410–11; Laidler, "Present Status," pp. 107–16.

92. *Judiciary Proceedings*, p. 365; Laidler, "Present Status," p. 108; John Keracher,

93. Laidler, "Present Status," p. 107; "Relations With the Communist International," *Socialist World* 2 (May 1921): 4; Otto Branstetter to G. Zinovief, March 12, 1919, Socialist Party of America Collection; *Socialist World* 2 (April 15, 1921): 4.

94. Morris Hillquit, "The American Socialists and Moscow," *The New York Times Current History* 13 (October 1920): 16; "The Twenty-One Points," *The Socialist World* 2 (May 1921): 3; "The Convention Agenda," *Socialist World* 2 (February 15, 1921): 9; J. Louis Engdahl, "A Ship on the Rocks," *Workers' Council* 1 (September 15, 1921): 108; "Farewell to the Socialist Party! And Appeal to Its Remaining Members! Statement by the Committee for the Third International of the Socialist Party," *Workers' Council* 1 (September 15, 1921): 105; *Workers' Council* 1 (September 15, 1921): 106.

95. Adolph Germer to the National Executive Committee, August 27, 1919, Socialist Party of America Collection; Benjamin Glassberg, "Program Suggestions for the Socialist Party Convention," *Workers' Council* 1 (June 15, 1921): 93; *American Labor Year Book, 1923–1924*, pp. 125, 159–60. Of a total Communist party membership of 15,233, more thatn 14,000 were in foreign-language federations in 1923; less than 1,200 were in English-speaking branches.

96. "Membership, 1917," typescript, Socialist Party of America Collection.

97. *American Labor Year Book, 1923–1924*, p. 125; *Judiciary Proceedings*, p. 2034.

98. *A Political Guide for the Workers* [Socialist campaign handbook, 1920] (Chicago: Socialist Party of the United States, 1920), pp. 113–14; *The Revolutionary Age* 1 (May 10, 1919): 1–3; *New York Herald*, August 28, 1919; November 11, 1919; *New York Sun*, November 11, 1919; *New York World*, October 10, 1919; *The New York Times*, November 10, 1919; *New York American*, November 10, 1919. Clippings in Lusk Collection; Zachariah Chafee Jr., *Free Speech in the United States* (Cambridge: Harvard University Press, 1942), p. 104; Louis Waldman, "The Cossack Raid," *The Socialist* 1 (July 28, 1919).

99. Victor L. Berger, *Voice and Pen of Victor L. Berger: Congressional Speeches and Editorials* (Milwaukee: The Milwaukee Leader, 1929), pp. 575 (note), 598; *New York Tribune*, October 25, 1919; *New York World*, October 25, 1919; *New York Herald*, October 25, 1919; Oswald Garrison Villard, "The Berger Victory," *The Nation* 109 (December 27, 1919): 820–21; *Political Guide*, pp. 118–19.

100. *The New York Times*, November 6, 1919; *New York Tribune*, November 6, 1919; *New York Sun*, November 11, 1919; *New York Herald*, November 6, 1919, all clippings in Lusk Collection; *Judiciary Proceedings*, pp. 3–8, 737–39, 2034; "The Albany Trial—A Digest," *Socialist Review* 8 (April 1920): 304–5; "Suspension of the Assemblymen," *Socialist Review* 8 (February 1920): 176–79.

101. *American Labor Year Book, 1923–1924*, p. 137; *The Call*, November 20, 1942.

102. Kenneth C. MacKay, *The Progressive Movement of 1924* (New York: Columbia University Press, 1947), pp. 149, 199, 202–3; *New Leader,* July 12, 1924; July 26, 1924; November 8, 1924; December 13, 1924; February 28, 1925; *New York Herald Tribune,* February 21, 1925; February 22, 1925.

103. Bernard K. Johnpoll, *Pacifist's Progress: Norman Thomas and the Decline of American Socialism* (Chicago: Quadrangle Books, 1970).

≈ *18* ≈

The Politics of Duplicity

- 1 -

For more than sixty years, a spectre has been haunting America—the spectre of communism. Politicians have assailed it; professional patriots have declaimed against it; clergymen have anathematized it. But the object of their fury has hardly been worth the effort; like most spectres, it has been more shadow than substance, and the noises it has made have been examples of gaseous fury rather than revolutionary power. American Communists have, their vociferous antagonists to the contrary, never been a genuine threat to America's economic, social, or political system. They constituted a small sect with great visibility but little influence or following. At its height, in 1938, the Communist party, U.S.A., had at most 70,000 members, thousands of whom were in fact spies for federal, state, and municipal law-enforcement agencies.[1]

Even in those segments of American society in which the party was believed to have had a following—the literati and trade unions—its influence has proven to be illusory. The allegiance of both to the Communist movement was fleeting and transitory. In 1932 some of the nation's leading authors and critics—including Sherwood Anderson, Malcolm Cowley, John Dos Passos, Granville Hicks, Langston Hughes, Matthew Josephson, Lincoln Steffens, and Edmund Wilson—identified openly with the Communist party. Eight years later, the party leadership found it virtually impossible to claim the support of a single respectable American writer.[2]

So also in the labor unions was Communist support more apparent than real. Between 1930 and 1950, many unions were led by Communists or pro-Communists, and many others had Communists or fellow travellers among their leaders. This was especially true in the Congress of Industrial

Organizations (CIO). Communists also controlled several key union locals, particularly in the International Ladies Garment Workers Union, and shared in the leadership of the United Automobile Workers. By 1950 almost all of these unions either had rid themselves of the Communists among their leaders or had lost their membership to competing unions led by non-Communists.[3] The American working class had been willing to support Communist control of their unions only when the alternative was either no union at all or a corrupt, racketeer-ridden organization. Given a choice between an honest union led by non-Communists and a union whose officials had pledged their fealty to the Communist party, the workers almost always chose the former. Despite more than a decade of intense activity, the Communists had failed to win the allegiance of rank-and-file unionists.

The failure of the American Communists to become relevant to the social, political, and economic life of the United States has been primarily due to their slavish adherence to foreign control and to the persistent changing of party doctrine to serve the foreign and domestic needs of the rulers of the Union of Soviet Socialist Republics. The party tailored its statements and actions according to shifting ideological patterns dictated from Moscow. The Communist party was, in fact, little more than an agency of the Soviet Union. As such, its stance changed from the militantly revolutionary to the passively quasi-Progressive. The determining factor for each change was the whim of the Soviet ruling elite at a given moment.

Seven major shifts in the Communist line occurred between 1919, when the party was organized, and the present:

First, the party's gestation and birth pangs, from 1918 to 1921, was a time when left-wing Socialists and Syndicalists, heady with the Bolshevik victory in Russia, prepared for the expected apocalyptic coming of a revolution to America within a matter of months, at most. Small groups of radical New York waistmakers, Seattle longshoremen, and Philadelphia tailors formed "soviets" at that time and played at "revolution," emulating the Russian Bolsheviks.

Much of the literature of this period now reads like comic-opera; much of it was—the posturing, the factionalism, the long-winded theoretical debates. To its participants, however, the literature was anything but ludicrous, for they were convinced that it reflected the real work of revolution. They were attempting to bring revolutionary success to the Socialist movement in America—a movement that had, in its twenty years, accomplished little except reform. They believed they were truly building the party of socialism without compromise, and they could point to Soviet Russia, where the revolution had actually been accomplished, as their guide.[4]

Second, by 1921 it was apparent that the world revolution would not come immediately; the Soviet Union was too involved in its internal difficulties to export revolution. Germany, which was expected to emulate Russia, turned instead to "bourgeois" democracy. Poland had repelled

Trotsky's Red Army on the banks of the Vistula. In America "normalcy" was returning under Warren G. Harding. The party in America under the tutelage of two emissaries from Moscow—Joseph Pogany, alias John Pepper, and Sergei Gusev, alias P. Green—dropped some of its more apocalyptic rhetoric, abandoned syndicalism and its concommitant dual unionism and attempted unsuccessfully to be accepted into the mainstream of trade unionism and progressive politics. But soon internal Soviet politics intervened: Lenin died and a struggle for power ensued. Stalin, who emerged victorious in that struggle, ordered a shift to the Left. The American party, as usual, followed his orders.[5]

Third, the Period 1928 to 1935 was one of the most bizarre in America Communist history. It reflected events in Russia and to a lesser degree in Germany, but it was totally irrelevant to America. The Socialists, then at their lowest point, and the pitifully weak American Federation of Labor and the trade-union movement generally, became the chief targets for Communist assault. Socialists were labelled "Social Fascists," and the established trade unions were denounced as organized betrayers of the working class. Socialist meetings were the targets for physical onslaught by "Red Guard," *lumpenproletariat* toughs attracted to the Communist party by the rhetoric of violence, which was adopted during the third period. Moscow ordered the organization of dual unions, and they were again the mode; the party's propaganda machine within the labor movement, the Trade Union Educational League, became a new, minuscule labor federation, the Trade Union Unity League (TUUL). William Z. Foster, who had only four years ealier condemned dual unions, now headed the TUUL. From 1933 until 1935, when the third period ended, the New Deal was denounced as a "tool of hunger, fascism, and imperialist war."[6]

Fourth, Stalin's competitors in the struggle for control of the Soviet Union suddenly were all defeated and destroyed. The internal danger was gone, but a new, external threat to Stalin's hegemony arose—Adolf Hitler. The needs of Soviet Russia had thus changed—it was now necessary to form an alliance between the so-called democracies of Western Europe and North America and the Soviet Union—and so had the policies and tactics of the American Communists. They now toned down talk of revolution; they now proposed united action with the hated Socialists. The "united front" was no longer aimed—as it had been during the third period—at the destruction of the Socialist party by weaning away "honest rank-and-filers" from their "misleaders." In 1934 the Communists had used force to disrupt and destroy a Socialist mass rally against Austrian Fascism in Madison Square Garden. Barely a year later, in the same auditorium, Earl Browder pleaded in saccharin tones with Socialist party leader Norman Thomas for unity. In fact, the Communists had by 1936 expanded the idea for a united front to the point where it included not only Socialists and other radicals but also liberals and even some conservatives.[7]

The "popular front," the name by which this strange united front was known, had only one prerequisite: the non-Communist partner was required to favor collective action by all Western nations—including the United States—against Hitler. Behind the popular front was the assumption that Hitler planned the destruction of the Soviet Union and that only joint action by the Western democracies and the Soviet Union could save Soviet Russia. To achieve this popular front, the Communists eschewed revolution and proclaimed their ideal to be "Twentieth-Century Americanism." The New Deal and Franklin D. Roosevelt, which they had damned as Fascist and imperialist only two years earlier, now became "Progressive." The Communists supported Roosevelt coverty in the 1936 elections; in 1938 that support became overt.[8]

Some of the party's members and supporters may actually have been convinced of the correctness of that line; many hoped for its permanence, but they were soon rudely shocked.

Fifth, on August 23, 1939, after long, secret negotiations, Stalin and Hitler signed a pact that freed the German dictator to open his war for the conquest of Europe. Again, the party line changed. The reasonableness of the popular front was replaced by revolutionary rhetoric and militancy. The Western Allies were condemned as imperialists by the American Communists; they ceased their attacks on Hitler; his atrocities were ignored. Now that it suited the purposes of the Kremlin, the slogans became "Keep American Out of the Imperialist War" and "The Yanks Are Not Coming."

For almost two years, between September 1939 and late June 1941, the Communist party opposed any American involvement in the war. It was the most militant antagonist of the Allied cause in America. Its leaders found even Norman Thomas's pacifism and isolationism too pro-Allied. Elizabeth Gurley Flynn, the leading woman Communist, proclaimed that she "didn't raise my boy to be a soldier for Wall Street"; Earl Browder, running for president on a platform that condemned the Allies, told his audiences that there was "no future in Flanders Field"; and Communist girls proclaimed that "We ain't knittin' for Britain." On June 8, 1941, the Communist-run Artists and Writers Congress passed an unanimous resolution that condemned the Allied cause as a struggle for empire, profits, and markets; on June 22, 1941, Communist youths picketed the White House to protest any effort to help the Allies in their war against Hitler. The party's credibility was virtually destroyed by the Hitler-Stalin Pact period. Then on June 23, 1941, Russia was invaded by her erstwhile ally—Hitler.[9]

Sixth, the moment Soviet Russia became involved in the war, the Communist line shifted 180 degrees. In place of "The Yanks Are Not Coming!" the Communist cries became, "Open a Second Front!" and "Attack Hitler Now!" All talk of revolution was abandoned. Workers, who had only a few days previously been urged to display militancy, were now called upon to show extreme restraint. Strikes were an anathema, and the party leaders, never wedded to democratic processes, called for repression of strikes and jailing of strike leaders. Even the issue of racial equality, long a key Communist demand, was shunted aside. The Communists became almost indistinguishable from the professional patriots. In 1944 the party dissolved itself into the Communist Political Association, which eschewed revolution and talked in terms of reform within the context of the existing social and economic order. The association openly supported Roosevelt and Truman—"Win-the-War" candidates in 1944.[10]

Seventh, as soon as the war was won, Germany defeated, and the threat to Soviet Russia dissolved, the Communists again changed their tune. A foreign Communist leader—Jacques Duclos of France—in an article in a foreign journal, *Cahiers du Communisme* of Paris, assailed the Communist Political Association (CPA) and its political position. The long-winded diatribe bore Duclos's signature, but the old party leadership recognized Stalin's handwriting. They all cried *mea culpa* in unison. The party was revived—after the CPA was unceremoniously buried—and the Communist leaders were again preaching revolution.

Soon union after union, as a result, ousted pro-Communist leaders. The United Automobile Workers, for example, replaced its president R. J. Thomas, who tolerated Communists as his aides, with Walter Reuther, an anti-Communist and ex-Socialist. Workers left Communist-led unions in droves; the United Electrical Workers lost more than half of its membership to the new CIO-organized, anti-Communist International Union of Electrical Workers. The Mine, Mill and Smelter Workers Union was absorbed into the conservative United Steelworkers of America.

The party still had one "last hurrah." In 1948 it supported Henry A. Wallace, on the basis of his anti-Cold War stance, for president. He polled more than a million votes, but within two years, even he turned against the Communists. By 1952 the Communist party was in a state of near-total collapse.[11]

Even its persecution by the government was mitigated by its own duplicity. The party was dying of an incurable political disease—lack of credibility. In 1941 Communists cheered the Justice Department when it prosecuted American Trotskyite leaders under the Smith Act. Six years later, the Communists were, themselves, the victims of the same "antisubversive" law. During the late 1940s and the 1950s, many party leaders and bureaucrats went to prison under the act.[12] But it really didn't matter; the party was already virtually dead. By 1960 American communism was little more than a discredited ghost. The *Daily Worker* had expired and was eventually replaced by *The Daily World*, whose chief support came from a bequest of an old, wealthy party member who had died some years earlier. It had virtually no circulation. The Communist literary organ *New Masses* and its successor *Mainstream* had been abandoned for lack of support. Communists, most of them now well beyond middle age, played little if any role in the Civil Rights struggle of the 1960s. They had virtually no influence on the student rebellion of that decade; the aging leader of Communist youth, Gil Green, condemned the New Left as Anarchist.[13] Occasional newswriters still discovered Communists, but this was mere sensationalism. The party was no longer viable; time had passed it by.

- 2 -

A careful study of the Communist party and its innumerable front organizations would prove that the "parent" organization was totally without scruples; it was totally unethical in its behavior to its followers as well as to its enemies. Nowhere is this better demonstrated than in its treatment of organizations such as the National Student League, the International Labor Defense, the Friends of the Soviet Union, the Unemployed Councils, the International Workers Order, the American League Against War and Fascism, the American League for Peace and Democracy, and the American Peace Mobilization, among others. Occasionally, these front organizations served as transmission belts where valuable individuals were recruited into the party itself. This was particularly true of the National Students League. But in most cases, they served primarily as sources of supply for party funds or as the basis for inflated claims of support for party projects.

The Communist party was an extremely expensive organization to operate. It published a daily newspaper (at one time, two dailies), a large weekly magazine, two large monthly magazines, and operated two publishing houses—one for pamphlets, another for pamphlets and books—and it employed a huge bureaucracy.

Other expenses included annual hegiras to Moscow by party leaders and the cost of running elections in which propaganda was the chief object. One former Communist official estimated that it cost more than $5,000,000 a year to run the party. The expenses were so high that the membership itself, even when it reached 70,000, was uable to meet them. Other sources of revenue were necessary, and the party used diverse means to obtain money.

Former Communist leaders now concede that some money did come from the Soviet Union. But tales of Moscow gold dominating the party's coffers are not borne out by the evidence.[14] It is likewise true that party members gave large sums to the organization. But given the small size of the party and the constant turnover of membership, this was unreliable. The greatest source of revenue was the front organizations—and they supplied the funds without the consent or approval of the average member.[15]

The front organizations' other major function was to give party policies a facade of great support. Thus, for example, when the Communist party advocated collective security, it used the American League for Peace and

Democracy as a vehicle. Communist leaders of innumerable fronts affiliated their organizations with the league (itself a front) and by duplicate membership lists gave the impression that millions of Americans favored collective military security. Likewise, after Stalin signed his pact with Hitler, the Communists founded the American Peace Mobilization (APM). An effort was again made to create the illusion of mass support—and again the Communist front leaders faithfully lent the support of their organizations. Thus in 1940 the International Workers' Order (IWO)—a heavily Jewish Communist insurance and educational front organization—joined the anti-Allied APM. More than 80 percent of its members then left the organization.[16] This mattered little to the party: the IWO still helped to serve the Soviet interest by creating an illusion of mass American support for Stalin's foreign policy.

- 3 -

Each twist of the Communist line created upheaval in the movement's ranks. Party organs denied that a shift had actually occurred and proclaimed that an old stance had merely been refined in view of changed conditions. But party members knew better, for it was soon apparent that the party press had been less than truthful with them. The telltale signs of the change in the party line were soon apparent. No sign was more visible than the internal purge. Each shift of position required a scapegoat. Leadership carried with it the permanent threat of disgrace, and this fall from grace required no reason. It was based on caprice and was ordered from Moscow. It could not be appealed. Although they appear diametrically opposed, the denial of error in the first place and the punishment for that same error were, in fact, both segments of the same Communist dictum: the Kremlin could do no wrong.

Ouster from leadership generally meant that a former leader became a pariah whose name was erased from Communist consciousness. In a few rare cases, when the victim had been involved in secret work for the Soviet secret service, and happened to be in Moscow at the time, he or she paid with his or her life. The most prominent such case involved Juliet Stuart Poyntz, a party leader and Soviet secret agent, who vanished and was slain in Russia during the 1930s.

Even the most cursory examination of party history indicates the nature of the Communist need for scapegoats. In 1922, when the party was shifting from its first period of revolutionary fervor to one of "pragmatic" politics, the scapegoat was to have been Louis C. Fraina. But he withdrew from the party before he could be purged and thus avoided the trauma of ouster. Charles A. Ruthenberg was to have been the scapegoat for the shift to the violently revolutionary "third period" in 1928, but he died in 1927, and the victim was, somewhat belatedly, his trusted lieutenant Jay Loveston. Beginning about 1934, the scapegoats were the followers of Leon Trotsky, who were accused of being agents of Hitler (despite the fact that almost half of them were, like their leader, Jewish). In 1945 Earl Browder was blamed for adoption of a policy—dictated from Moscow—that aimed at cooperation with the United States government in defense of the Soviet Union.[17]

The hunt for scapegoats was little more than a weak carbon copy of the Soviet purges. Only the fact that the party in the United States had no power of life or death over its members kept the purge here from being equally bloody. The American party duplicated the paranoia of the Stalinist organization in Soviet Russia in other ways. Like the Russian party, the American party imagined enemies from within and enemies from without the radical labor movement. The external foes were inherent in the capitalist system—employers, who feared Communist organizers; Fascists, who aimed at slaughtering all Communists; and the agents of the capitalist class, the police and the courts. Their fear of these external foes were not totally without basis. Communists were generally considered outlaws by employers, police chiefs, and judges. Communists also were murdered by Fascist dictators. But the internal enemies were creatures of their own fertile imaginations. For years the chief of these enemies were the leaders of the Socialist party whom they called Social Fascists.

- 4 -

That Soviet control of the American Communist party inhibited intellectual inquiry can be evidenced by the lack of original scholarship by party members. The "theoretical" writings by Communists were little more than rote reaffirmations of Soviet interpretations of Marx and Lenin. In this sense, the party was basically anti-Marxist, for it stifled the theory portion of Marx's "unity of theory and practice." In the old Socialist party, from which the Communist party evolved, a veritable flood of works on Socialist theory came out between 1900 and 1919, ranging from the doctrinaire, if simplistic, works of Louis B. Boudin and Morris Hillquit to major modifications of Marxian theory by thinkers such as moderate Christian Socialists George D. Herron and J. Stitt Wilson and revolutionary "Industrial Socialists" Robert Rives La Monte, Frank Bohn, and William English Walling. Such intellectual analyses are totally missing in Communist journals, books, and pamphlets. They were invariably little more than reiterations of positions previously declared valid by the Moscow hierarchy. Each "theoretical" work published by a party-controlled journal or publishing house required a covert Soviet *imprimatur* and *nihil obstat*. When an occasional lapse did occur, it was followed by almost immediate retraction and expulsion of the offender. A reading of the official and semiofficial Communist "intellectual" periodical press is an expedition through monolithic political, social, and economic mediocrity.

This total inhibition of independent thinking was responsible for the tremendous turnover of intellectuals within the party. Genuine scholars and intellectuals found the atmosphere of the party stifling. Those few who remained in the party found it necessary to advance ideologies they often found to be objectionable. Not a single significant work in philosophy, economics, history, or political science was produced by a scholar who was at the time also a member of the Communist party, for where independent research ran counter to the party line of the given moment, scholarly findings had to yield to party dogma. The result generally meant repetition of sycophancy by Communist scholars.[18]

- 5 -

Most of those who joined the Communist party were genuine idealists. But few remained in the party very long. They were almost invariably repelled by the cynicism that dominated the party's higher echelons, by the bureaucratic control of the party, or by the persistent shifting of the party line.

No authentic statistics about Communist party membership are available, nor has a serious study ever been made of its social makeup. Official statistics that appeared in party journals—*The Communist, Political Affairs,* or *Party Organizer*—are inflated or deflated (depending upon which best suited the leadership of a given moment). "Statistics" issued by the Federal Bureau of Investigation and congressional committees were always exaggerated; their aim was primarily to create public hysteria and thus assure themselves inflated appropriations. Autobiographies also suffer from inaccuracies. The authors were either Communist leaders who recanted and turned violently anti-Communist, paid informers who "led three lives" and lost touch with reality, or party leaders intent upon defending their position. Studies of Communist membership and personnel must thus be educated guesses or deductions based on other verifiable data.

Two facts are known about Communist party membership: first, party membership had a high turnover; second, the membership of the Communist party, U.S.A., never went beyond 70,000 at any given time. It averaged 20,000 between 1930 and 1950, although approximately 500,000 Americans joined the party during that twenty-year period. Average length of membership was thus less than one year. Most of those who joined the party dropped out in a matter of months.

Most party members were idealists when they first became affiliated with it. They knew then that they faced economic and social hardships because of their membership in a hated, radical political organization. Once in the party, they would be ostracized by their friends, their co-workers, and often their families. Moreover, many unions ousted Communists from membership with little or no appeal, and employers had no compunctions about firing Communists—and labelling them troublemakers. Students also faced disabilities, albeit not nearly so sharp as those suffered by working people. Courts were not likely to defend the rights of Communists to jobs or to fair treatment at universities. Only those genuinely interested in a classless society would face the hostility and sufferings that being a Communist meant.

New members soon found, however, that socialism or communism was at best a facade for bureaucratic power. Instead of intellectual discussion, the new members found repetition of slogans by rote. Instead of work for the assumed needs of the working class, most found themselves performing petty, useless tasks unrelated to principles. Those who read the party press soon learned that it was written in jargon that perverted the truth.

Moreover, the party exerted stringent discipline. Members were expected to devote long hours to tedious tasks or had to serve on committees that were supposed to implement orders from above without question. These committees held long and boring meetings at which regional and local functionaries pontificated while rank-and-filers had to offer total obeisance. Being a Communist meant a complete loss of individual identity and an absolute surrender to the will of the party. It meant an unquestioning acceptance of orders and a restructuring of ones life to meet the desires of the official hierarchy. Idealists would thus find that their commitment to an imagined better world was insignificant when compared to their commitment to a bureaucratic machine. Most found it unacceptable and soon dropped out of the movement.[19]

Those who remained were co-opted. They were themselves bureaucrats. The Communist party had an immense staff—probably as many as one functionary for each three members. George Charney, who was himself a party official for many years, recalls in his autobiography *A Long Journey* that more than 700 party aides were from Manhattan alone at a meeting he addressed in 1956. This was at a time when the party was at low ebb and when fewer than 2,000 members were in Manhattan! It was almost impossible for party bureaucrats to break with it. Their lives were completely bound up with it; their spouses were usually members, and party loyalty was often considered superior to family loyalty. Whatever friends they had were also party people; their non-Communist friends were long abandoned.[20]

- 6 -

Government investigators and prosecutors have almost always overstated the party's threat and its potential for undermining the American system. The Communists were at no time capable of seizing power—by force and violence or otherwise. Their total following—members, fellow travellers, and inactive sympathizers—never exceeded one-fifth of 1 percent of America's population. Moreover, this support existed in the most powerless sections of American society: alienated middle-class intellectuals, students, and generally unskilled foreign workingmen. Yet it would be naive to refuse to recognize that a few Communists were recruited from the party to perform espionage for the Soviet Union. The Rosenberg case is the most sensational of the spy dramas involving party members—and the most questionable. Other cases were less sensational but more substantive. Most notable was the case of Bronx-born Morris Cohen, a one-time football star at Mississippi State University, who as Peter Kroger was sentenced in 1961 in Britain to twenty years in prison for his espionage. He was recruited into the Soviet Secret Service by a Russian agent in his local Communist party unit during the late 1930s.[21] Other, similar cases also are known.

So, too, does ample verification now exist for the charge that the Soviet rulers gave the American Communists direct orders and controlled their activities. Even a cursory examination of Soviet foreign policy and the party's positions would prove beyond a reasonable doubt that the party's policies followed directly from Russian needs. It was assumed until recently that the Communists received only broad outlines of their policy indirectly from Moscow and that their day-to-day directives came from the American leadership. It is now known that every policy decision was dictated directly in Russia. Philip J. Jaffee in *The Rise and Fall of American Communism*, which is based on secret, official party records of Earl Browder, the party's general secretary from 1930 to 1945, confirmed the use of coded radio transmissions by the Russian rulers to command their American comrades. Browder and the other party leaders were, in fact, little more than delivery boys for Moscow's orders—a fact Browder admitted to Norman Thomas during the early 1960s.[22]

An investigation into specific cases of espionage by Communists, or of foreign control for alien purposes of the party, might serve a valuable purpose. But the investigations into communism since 1920 have almost invariably been self-serving, useless, and counterproductive. The most notorious of the congressional investigators of Communists was Senator Joseph McCarthy of Wisconsin. A man of unbounded ambition and limited ethics, McCarthy made outlandish charges that he then tried to prove by besmirching his opponents. Except for gaining innumerable headlines and a notoriety that raised him from a local judge to a national figure, McCarthy did little to expose the Communist party, its workings, or its nature. The most important Communist "traitor" he unearthed was a dentist in an insignificant military facility. In achieving his notoriety, McCarthy disrupted the workings of American foreign policy for five years and ruined the lives of many capable and dedicated non-Communist government officials.

Other congressional "Red hunters" included Martin Dies, the first chairman of the House Committee on Un-American Activities; John Rankin, J. Parnell Thomas; and a young congressman named Richard M. Nixon. None of them contributed anything toward the exposure of a single major Communist spy, nor did any find genuine subversion. At least two of the leading congressional "anti-Communists" proved the adage that patriotism is the last refuge of the scoundrel. J. Parnell Thomas went to prison for political corruption, and Nixon was forced to resign from the presidency in disgrace.

Nor was the anticommunism of J. Edgar Hoover any more significant or enlightening. He and his Federal Bureau of Investigation (FBI) made a great show of its role in the crusade against the Communists, but a careful investigation of the record indicates that it was merely a facade. Most FBI cases against alleged spies and others involved in illegal activity were so poorly drawn that they could rarely overcome judicial review.[23] Where convictions were upheld—as in the cases of the Rosenbergs and Alger Hiss—careful examination of the methods and evidence obtained by the FBI raises some question as to the guilt of those convicted. Hoover's war against the Communists proved to be "full of sound and fury signifying nothing."

- 7 -

The failure of investigative agencies to unearth any genuine Communist subversion was not surprising; in fact, no such subversion of the American system occurred. Nor was Communist party policy directed at replacing capitalism with some form of socialism. Its revolutionary rhetoric was merely a facade. Investigations would have proven fruitful had the probers inquired into the allegience of Communists to a foreign power. The party was, in fact, an organization whose primary function was to further the foreign policy of the Soviet regime. Its constant change of line precluded the American Communist party from becoming an effective revolutionary organization. Even when the opportunity presented itself, the Communists failed to construct a consistent, revolutionary movement. During the period 1935-1940, many young Communists reached positions of responsibility in major labor unions. Had the Communist party been genuinely revolutionary, its leadership would have directed these young people to use their positions to organize, educate, and agitate for a new social order. Instead, they were directed to support continually shifting positions based upon the needs of Soviet foreign policies rather than upon the exigencies of American reality.

Thus in 1928, when revolutionary possibilities were at their lowest ebb in the United States, the party adopted a program of extreme radicalism. In 1935, when there was an upsurge of militancy in the country, the party became a paragon of respectability and moderation. This dilemma was further exacerbated by the twists and turns the party engineered during World War II, from left-wing hysteria in 1940 to American Legion-type patriotism after the invasion of the Soviet Union in 1941.

The fact that several of its members performed acts of espionage for the Soviet regime is further proof of the nonrevolutionary nature of the Communist party. The spies were not acting to instigate American revolution;

they were rather employed in the service of another country. It is possible that they entered the Soviet secret service on the assumption that the Soviet Union was the vanguard of the social revolution, and espionage in its service was a revolutionary act. But this assumption is itself a negation of an immutable revolutionary law first enunciated by Karl Marx: "the emancipation of the working classes must be achieved by the working classes themselves." It follows, therefore, that the American working class would have to achieve its own emancipation in the United States.

In truth, the Communist party was neither revolutionary nor Marxian. It was in fact a negation of both Marx and the ideal of a free Socialist society.

NOTES

1. National Secretary Earl Browder claimed a party membership of 75,000 in 1938; and he reported to the House Committee on Un-American Activities that it had risen to 100,000 a year later. An analysis of his report indicates the actual figure was less than 72,000. See especially, United States, House of Representatives, Special Committee on Un-American Activities, *Hearings, Investigations of Un-American Propaganda Activities In the United States*, vol. 7, September 5, 6, 7, 8, 9, 11, 12, and 13, at Washington, D.C. (Washington, D.C.: U.S. Government Printing Office, 1939), p. 6; In 1944 Browder, testifying before another House committee, conceded the exaggeration and placed the 1939 figure at 55,000. United States, House of Representatives, *Investigation of Campaign Expenditures*, September 19, 1944, p. 66.

2. Daniel Bell, "The Background and Development of Marxian Socialism in the United States," in *Socialism and American Life*, 2 vols., ed. Donald D. Egbert and Stow Persons (Princeton: Princeton University Press, 1942), 1: 354; William Thorp, "American Writers and the Left," in ibid., p. 354; Irving Howe and Lewis Coser, *The American Communist Party* (New York: Frederick A. Praeger, 1962), pp. 282, 315.

3. Howe and Coser, *The American Communist Party*, pp. 372–73, 457–63, 467–69; Bell, "Background," p. 357; Joseph R. Starobin, *American Communism in Crisis, 1943–1957* (Cambridge: Harvard University Press, 1972), pp. 10–11.

4. The best archive of early Communist documents is the Lusk Collection, at the New York State Library, Albany. It is ignored by most "scholars." See, for example, Cornelia Davis to Maximilan Cohen, June 16, 1919, Lusk collection; "To the Striking Longshoremen," broadside, Communist Party of America, 1919, Lusk collection.

5. See especially, Charles W. Ruthenberg and Isaac E. Ferguson, *A Communist Trial* (New York: National Defense Committee, 1922); "Next Tasks of the C.P. of A." (Thesis, Executive Committee of Communist International), in *Charles E. Ruthenberg v. People of the State of Michigan, United States Supreme Court: Records and Briefs*, October Term 1926, Documents numbered 42 to 46, pp. 158–69; citation is from Document 44; Alexander Bittleman, *Parties and Issues in the Election Campaign* (Chicago: Workers [Communist] Party, 1924); C. E. Ruthenberg, *The Workers (Communist) Party: What it Stands for; Why Workers Should Join* (Chicago: Workers Party, 1926); Regarding Green and Pepper, see Theodore Draper, *American Communism and Soviet Russia* (New York: Viking Books, 1960), especially pp. 38, 140–42; see also Howe and Coser, *The American Communist Party*, pp. 100, 115. The membership of the party at that time was almost totally foreign-born. Of 15,233 members claimed in 1923, only 1,192 belonged to English-speaking branches; the other 14,041 were members of foreign-language units. Thus less than 10 percent spoke English as their primary language. See *The American Labor Year Book, 1923–1924*, p. 159.

6. See, for example, Howe and Coser, *The American Communist Party*, pp. 144–300; Draper, *American Communism and Soviet Russia*, pp. 330–400; on origins of the "Third

Period," see Theodore Draper, "The Strange Case of the Comintern," *Survey* 18 (Summer 1972): 131–37; Franz Borkenau, *World Communism: A History of the Communist International* (Ann Arbor: University of Michigan Press, 1962), especially pp. 332–56; for the "Third Period" at its most banal, see William Z. Foster, *Toward Soviet America* (New York: Coward McCann, 1962); "Vote Communist," 1931 handbill, Chicago Communist Party, copy in Polemic Collection, New York State Library, Albany; Earl Browder, *The Meaning of Social Fascism* (New York: Workers Library, 1934); on the Trade Union Unity League, see Nathaniel Honig, *The Trade Union Unity League Today* (New York: Workers Library Publishers, 1934). Honig later testified against the party.

7. See Howe and Coser, *The American Communist Party*, pp. 319–86; Georgi Dimitroff, "The Threat of Fascism in the United States," *The Communist* 16 (October 1935); Earl Browder, "The United Front—The Key to Our New Tactical Orientation," *The Communist* 14 (December 1935); Clarence Hathaway, *Collective Security: The Road to Peace* (New York: Workers Library, 1938); *Acceptance Speeches: Communist Candidates in the Presidential Election* (New York: Campaign Committee of the Communist Party, 1936); Earl Browder, *The Communists in the People's Front* (New York: Workers Library, 1937); Norman Thomas and Earl Browder, *Which Way for American Workers, Socialist or Communist* (New York: Socialist Call, 1936).

8. See especially, Earl Browder, *The Communist Position in 1936: Radio Speech Broadcast March 5, 1936* (New York: Workers Library Publishers, 1936); "Third Term for the New Deal," *New Masses* 31 (July 11, 1939); "Voters: Save Your Home and Family," broadside (New York: Women's Committee of the New York State Communist Party, 1938), copy in library of Vassar College, Poughkeepsie, New York.

9. See Earl Browder, *The Second Imperialist War* (New York: International Publishers, 1940), especially pp. 17, 42, 93, 125; Earl Browder, *An American Foreign Policy for Peace* (New York: Workers Library Publishers, 1940); Michael Gold, *The Hollow Men* (New York: International Publishers, 1940); "And the American Communists Follow," *New Republic* 53 (September 13, 1939): 143; Howe and Coser, *The American Communist Party*, pp. 387–95. A seven-volume documentary history of the Communist party by the author of this book is scheduled tentatively for 1982 publication by Greenwood Press.

10. William Z. Foster, *American Democracy and the War* (New York: Workers Library, 1942); *Attack Hitler Now* (New York: New York State Committee, Communist Party, 1942); William Z. Foster, *The Trade Unions and the War* (New York: Workers Library Publishers, 1942); "The Strike Wave Conspiracy," *The Communist* 20 (June 1943): 483–94; Earl Browder, *Teheran* (New York: Workers' Library Publishers, 1944); William Z. Foster, "Labor Day in 1944," *The Communist* 23 (September 1944): 771–72; *The Role and Function of the C.P.A* (New York: National Organization Committee, Communist Political Association, 1944).

11. William Z. Foster, *The Menace of a New World War* (New York: New Century, 1946); "The U.A.W. Convention," broadside (Detroit: National Auto Commission, Communist Party, 1946); *New York Herald Tribune's 23 Questions About the Communist Party Answered by William Z. Foster* (New York: New Century, 1948); William Z. Foster, *Labor and the Marshall Plan* (New York: New Century, 1948); Eugene Dennis, *The Third Party and the 1948 Elections* (New York: New Century, 1948); *Not Twelve Men on Trial . . . But Everybody!* (New York: Communist Party, 1949).

12. Philip Jaffe, *The Rise and Fall of American Communism* (New York: Horizon Press, 1975), pp. 50–53; see also Michael R. Belknap, *Cold War Political Justice: The Smith Act, the Communist Party, and American Civil Liberties* (Westport, Conn.: Greenwood Press, 1977).

13. Gil Green, *The New Radicalism: Anarchist or Marxist* (New York: International Publishers, 1973).

14. Draper, *American Communism and Soviet Russia*, p. 208.

15. Ibid., p. 204.

16. The records of the IWO, seized by the attorney general of New York State in 1957 when the order was dissolved, are in the Cornell University Library, Ithaca, New York. They are in poor condition. See also, Howe and Coser, *The American Communist Party*, pp. 348-55.

17. On Poyntz, see Bell, "Background," p. 346 (note 220); On Ruthenberg and Lovestone, see Draper, *American Communism and Soviet Russia*, pp. 243-47, 251-53, 405-40; on the Trotskyites, see Howe and Coser, *The American Communist Party*, pp. 167-68 (Lovestone led the early war against the Trotskyites before he was himself ousted); also see Earl Browder, *Traitors in American History* (New York: Workers Library, 1938); Alexander Bittleman, *Trotsky the Traitor* (New York: Workers Library, 1937); M. J. Olgin, *Trotskyism* (New York: Workers Library, 1935); on Browder, see Starobin, *American Communism*, pp. 278-79; Jaffe, *Rise and Fall*, pp. 77-83.

18. See, for example, Scott Nearing, *The Making of a Radical: A Political Autobiography* (New York, Harper Colophon Books, 1972), pp. 146-54.

19. On Communist party membership figures, see Browder testimony in U.S. House of Representatives, Special Committee on Un-American Activities, *Hearings*, (September 5-13, 1939), pp. 4266, 4283-84; for the "revolving door" syndrome, see Ibid., p. 4458; on party life, see, for example, Stuart Browne (pseudonym), "A Professor Quits the Communist Party," *Harpers* 175 (July 1937): 133-42; Anonymous, "Why I am Not an Active Communist," *New Masses* 27 (May 17, 1938); 13-14.

20. George Charney, *A Long Journey* (Chicago: Quadrangle Books, 1968), see especially pp. 232-33, 245-46.

21. See *New York Times*, March 19, 1961, sect. IV, p. 6; March 23, 1961, p. 2.

22. Jaffe, *Rise and Fall*, pp. 40, 44-47; interview with Norman Thomas, October 1963.

23. The classic case involves Judith Coplon, see *New York Times*, December 6, 1950, p. 1.

❦ *19* ❦

The New Left

- 1 -

The New Left, the radical movement that dominated the 1960s was a tragic, short-lived phenomenon, lasting only five years. The rhetoric of the New Left was a compound of Lenin, Trotsky, Stalin, Mao Tse-tung, and Herbert Marcuse. Its tactics were those of Johann Most and Burnette G. Haskell and its morality that of Machiavelli's *The Prince*.

In fact, the New Left was neither "new" nor "left." It was, at best, an arrogant collection of pseudointellectuals who saw in the movement a chance to achieve greater power, if only among other less able student activists. Some of the academicians who pandered to the movement used the pandering to rise to higher positions as university administrators, forced tenure for themselves, or became political operators closely tied to the "beautiful people."

The apex of the New Left's strength came during the American involvement in the war in Viet Nam. That war created a threat to the lives and well being of American youth, and it was that immoral war that attracted so many young people to the pseudoradical movements.

- 2 -

The leading organization of the New Left was the Students for a Democratic Society (SDS). It was the offspring of the League for Industrial Democracy (LID), one of the few remnants of the Old Left still operational during the late 1950s and 1960s.

The Old Left was in a shambles during the 1950s. Most old radicals had abandoned the revolution by then. Those few who remained were too tired, too old, and too disillusioned to offer youthful rebels any direction. Even

Socialist stalwarts such as Norman Thomas and Upton Sinclair had virtually given up the fight. Both had become staunchly anti-Soviet, and both supported the cold war.[1] Their position was reflected in the LID.

The League for Industrial Democracy, during the 1950s, was a shadow of its old self. Formed in 1905 as the Intercollegiate Socialist Society, it had barely survived World War I, was revived in 1921, and lost it largest segment to the Communist Lorelei song of "united front" fourteen years later when it was merged into the American Student Union, an amalgamation of the Student League for Industrial Democracy (SLID) and the Communist-front National Student League. The new student organization died in 1941, a victim of the Hitler-Stalin pact.

When the SLID was reorganized in 1946, it had at most a few hundred members. Most of them were hardly radical, preferring to identify themselves as liberals or progressives. Then in 1960 came the black student sit-ins against segregation in southern states led by the Students' Non-Violent Coodinating Committee (SNCC). Members of the SLID cooperated with SNCC and became involved in organizing community action. That year the SLID also changed it name to Students for a Democratic Society-League for Industrial Democracy and began a gradual turn to the Left.

First the SDS decided at its annual meeting in 1960 to move from intellectual discussion and community action to serious national activism. Then in 1962, at its annual meeting in Port Huron, Michigan, the SDS issued the "Port Huron Statement," which called for participatory democracy and an end to the cold war—which it blamed on the United States as well as the Soviet Union; it invited Communist youth organizations to send observers to its meeting. The LID disagreed on all three counts, and so began the long process of dissociation between the two organizations.[2]

The New Left of 1965–1970 was composed almost entirely of students on campus or "in movements deriving from the campus." Its members were interested primarily in action on concrete issues and had little interest in ideology. Most were "moralistic" and viewed issues on grounds of right and wrong. Few accepted the possibility of a middle road. Moreover, "SDS is a very middle-class conscious movement." It was almost totally devoid of any normally moderating working-class element.[3]

What moved the SDS to the Left was the war in Viet Nam and, to a lesser degree, the failure of the Democratic National Convention of 1964 to accede to the demands of the Mississippi Free Democrats, a liberal, heavily black wing of the state party, that they, rather than the racist state party, be recognized.[4]

In 1965 the SDS was finally separated from the LID. Once separated the SDS opened its doors to well-organized Communist groups, particularly the pro-Mao Progressive Labor party. In a matter of weeks, the Maoists began tearing the SDS apart. Under pressure from the Progressive-Laborites (PL), they went "directly to the only existing body of prepackaged revolutionary doctrine—Marxism-Leninism." When the PL leadership proved more adept at rote declamations from the works of Marx, Lenin, Stalin, and Mao, the old SDS leadership, to prove its militancy, turned to violence as preached by "Che" Guevara, Rene Debray, Johann Most, and other revolutionary romantic heroes.[5]

The June 1969 convention of the SDS spelled the doom of the society. It was the scene of long and dull debates about issues of Marxian dialectics. Several physical battles broke out. The minority physically ousted the majority (because the latter did not sufficiently support the revolution in Albania!) The two factions threw *Little Red Books*—of Mao Tse-tung's revolutionary platitudes—at each other.[6] Almost immediately after the convention, open warfare between the two factions erupted.

At New York University, they fought with chains; ten members went to the hospital. At Harvard and MIT others were hurt: At the United Front Against Fascism convention—organized jointly by the anti-PL SDS and the militant Black Panthers, PL members who attempted to speak or distribute handbills were so severely beaten that several required hospitalization. The meeting's sponsors brooked no dissent. Women delegates who dared object to a long and boring address by pro-Communist party historian Herbert Aptheker were handled roughly by the guards from the Panthers.[7]

Except for the violence-prone "Weatherman" faction, the SDS virtually disappeared within a year. The factions themselves had begun to splinter almost immediately after the 1969 convention. Progressive-Laborites returned to their own political movement. Most other factions disintegrated under the pressure of internal feuding. Four students participating in an antimilitary rally at Kent State University in Ohio were murdered by National Guardsmen, thus frightening off many of the remaining campus radicals.[8]

Only the Weatherman faction remained. Its few members—fewer than 200 nationally—began a Quixotic "revolutionary struggle" to seize power. In Pittsburgh, for example, "Weatherwomen" took over the offices of the pacifist American Friends Service Committee by threatening the workers with karate chops. While in control of those offices, they turned out mimeographed handbills urging high school students to rebel. In Detroit they assaulted high school students and teachers.[9] They published a newspaper that was filled with "turgid, propagandistic writing; quotations from Lin Piao, General Giap, Nguyen Van Troi, and Chairman Mao, articles advocating armed struggle in the United States. . . . One story glorified a five-year-old boy who derailed a passenger train with a rock."[10]

The explanation for the violence was simple. No "serious political change has ever come about without violence, and I am interested in serious political change," one sympathetic writer declaimed. Others argued that the

Weatherman's role was to educate the American people and "prepare them . . . to wage a determined struggle with arms in hand to destroy imperialism in its lair."[11] Moreover, the Weatherspeople were in a hurry; they wanted a revolution immediately.

The faction's theoretical bombast was a combination of simplistic Machiavellianism and arrogant pretensions. "Political questions are questions of tactics," a leading Weatherman announced. Since the objective was a violent revolution that would replace capitalism with a soviet system, the SDS leadership hoped for more and more government repression, thus assuring that only violence could be used to overthrow the system. "Our task is not to avoid or end repression," an official proclamation declared; "that can always be done by pulling back, so we're not dangerous enough to require smashing." Such repression, the proclamation argued, would awaken the American people to the need for a violent revolution and thus advance the cause.[12]

Weatherman members disagreed with Johann Most's Social Revolutionaries on only two key issues. The 1960s "revolutionists" considered the organized workers to be class enemies of the revolution. They favored formation of a political vanguard, "led by a party of revolutionaries organized on the basis of democratic centralism" to lead the forthcoming revolution. The Social Revolutionaries of the 1880s had pinned their hopes on the labor unions and expected mass support for their revolution.

The prime task of the Weatherman was thus to organize such a vanguard and to develop an American detachment of an international revolutionary army. The aim would be "armed struggle as soon as possible."[13]

Most of the vanguard would, of course, come from the students of the middle class. But they would eschew the old struggle for student power for "student power struggles (are) essentially struggles of the privileged for more privileges." Instead, students would fight for the revolution and would thus get the "best education," since it would be about the "movement, the enemy, the class struggle."[14]

In late 1969, members of the Weatherman faction tried to put their rhetoric into practice. They turned to violence in the street with an "uprising" in Chicago labelled "Days of Rage." The first phase of the "revolution" was the bombing of the memorial to the police killed at Haymarket eighty-three years before. Then they marched through the Loop area smashing windows and attacking passersby and police. An assistant district attorney was paralyzed by the attackers. The Weatherman followers hailed race riots in Newark, Detroit, and Los Angeles as "a PEOPLE's WAR OF LIBERATION."[15] They proclaimed the Chicago riot to be a signal victory, because "the streets are no longer safe for enemies of the people."[16] But it was merely a delusory dream: in 1970 a bomb factory in a town house in Greenwich Village exploded. Three Weatherman leaders were blown to bits. The others fled. Except for occasional crank bombings by individuals who called themselves "Weather Underground," and the surrender to the police of the former leadership, nothing was left of the SDS—or any of its factions—by 1971.

- 3 -

A new element entered the New Left during the 1970s. But it had little to do with the movement of the 1960s. This new set of "movements" used its self-proclaimed radicalism as an excuse for simple criminality. Susan Saxe, an honors graduate of Brandeis University, joined with another woman and two male criminals in an escapade of crime that left a policeman, the father of nine children, dead and all of the participants, except for Susan Saxe's female partner, in prison.[17]

On the West Coast, a group of prison escapees were joined by upper middle-class student "radicals" in the Symbionese Liberation Army. Their leader, a black convict, Donald De Freeze, took the high-sounding title of Generalissimo Cinque. Their first action was the murder of a black school superintendent in Oakland, whom they called "an enemy of the revolution." Then they kidnapped Patricia Hearst, daughter of a San Francisco publisher. Eventually, most of them died in a Los Angeles shoot-out with police.[18]

- 4 -

The New Left exaggerated all of the weaknesses of the old and had none of its positive characteristics. The New Leftists spoke of the poor, the oppressed, and the exploited, but they were invariably the pampered members of the upper class. They spoke of egalitarianism, but they represented the epitome of elitism. They proclaimed their opposition to war as inhumane, but many of them participated in violent, even murderous, activities. They spoke of the need for clarity, but most New-Left theory, such as it was, was a collection of platitudes and cliches couched in virtually incomprehensible jargon. Their political accomplishments have been minimal. They had, at best, a peripheral effect on the American alienation from the war in Viet Nam. Otherwise, their influence was minor and negative.

- 5 -

At the end of the 1970s and beginning of the 1980s, virtually no left-wing movement was evident in America. Three heirs apparent to the mantle of the Socialist party of yore were still around. But between them, they had fewer then 5,000—probably fewer than 2,000—members. The Communist party continued to represent the interests of the Soviet Union in the United

States, but it was a mere shadow of its old self; no one took it seriously. A multitude of Trotskyite and Maoite and Hoxhaite political movements took place—all of which held their conventions in convenient telephone booths. Daniel De Leon's weather-beaten Socialist Labor party continued to debate fine points of the "master's" teachings whenever two or three of them could be gathered together in his name. Eighty and ninety-year-old Anarchists could still be heard extolling the virtues of Most or Warren, and a few university professors, determined to prove they have not forgotten their working-class great-great-grandparents, still belonged to the Industrial Workers of the World (IWW) or wrote lengthy romantic tomes about it. But none of these examples nor all of them taken together, equalled a movement. Except as a bit of nostalgia, the American Left was dead.

Any obituary of the Left must concede its contribution to American life. Although its ultimate aim proved to be unrealizable, it helped develop many of the most significant concepts that have come to permeate American life.

NOTES

1. See, for example, Upton Sinclair to Peter Gulbrandsen, March 23, 1951, Gulbrandsen Papers, Bancroft Library, University of California, Berkeley.

2. Bernard K. Johnpoll and Mark Yerburgh, comps., *The League for Industrial Democracy: A Documentary History* (Westport, Conn.: Greenwood Press, 1980), pp. 49, 57; Edward J. Bacciocco, *The New Left in America* (Stanford, Calif.: Hoover Institution Press, 1974), pp. 109-11, 113-14, 116-17, 122-26; this is the most accurate study of the New Left extant; Andre Shiffrin, "The Student Movement of the 1950s: A Reminiscence," *Radical America* 1 (May-June 1968): 27-28; Wilson Carey McWilliams, Review of *SDS* by Kirkland Sales, *New York Times Book Review*, May 6, 1973, p. 5; Paul Feldman, "L.I.D. and the Student Movement," *L.I.D. News Bulletin* 6 (Winter 1966): 5-7.

3. Hal Draper, "In Defense of the 'New Radicals,' " *New Politics* 4 (Summer 1965) 5-7, 18.

4. Ibid., p. 12.

5. Irwin Unger (with the assistance of Debi Unger), *The Movement: A History of the New Left* (New York: Dodd Mead, 1974), pp. 95-96; Jack Newfield, "SDS: From Port Huron to La Chinoise," *Evergreen Review* 13 (December 1969): 17.

6. Newfield, "SDS," p. 16.

7. Ibid., p. 16; Mark Rudd, "The U.F.A.F. Conference," *New Left Notes*, 4 (July 24, 1969): 1-2.

8. Sanford Pinsker, "Erasing the Sixties—Or, Whatever Happened to Mark Rudd?" *Dissent* 27 (Winter 1980): 101.

9. Newfield, "SDS," p. 15.

10. Ibid., p. 15.

11. J. Kirkland Sale, "Political Violence: Awakening from the American Dream," *Evergreen Review* 15 (May 1971): 59; "Proposed S.D.S. Unity Principles," *New Left Notes* 4 (July 8, 1969): 2; Howard Machtinger, "Principles, Schmiciples: Weatherman Replies," *Fire!* 1 (November 21, 1969): 3.

12. "You Don't Have to be a Weatherman to Know Which Way the Wind is Blowing," in "Debate Within SDS: RYM II vs. Weatherman," mimeograph, p. 29, copy in Tamiment Institute Library, New York University.

13. Les Coleman, "Notes on Class Analysis," in ibid., p. 10

14. Mike Klonsky, Noel Ignatin, Marylin Katz, Sue Sanet, and Lex Coleman, "Revolutionary Youth Movement II," in ibid., p. 13.

15. "SDS—Bring the War Home" (Four-page tabloid-size handbill, 1969), copy at Tamiment Institute Library; "Pretext for Repression," *New Left Notes* 4 (August 1, 1969): 4.

16. "Enemies of the People: Dick Nixon! S. I. Hayakawa! Will be Dining at Hotel Hilton," 1969 SDS Handbill, copy at Tamiment Institute Library.

17. *The New York Times*, March 28, 1975, p. 54.

18. *The New York Times*, January 17, 1974, p. 26; February 5, 1974, p. 1; see especially, Gilbert Geis, "Women and Violence: The SLA," *The Nation* 118 (June 29, 1974): 812-13.

Ideals and Reality

- 1 -

Werner Sombart posed too narrow a question when he asked, in 1906, *Why is There No Socialism in the United States?* He might better have inquired, *Why is There No Socialism Anywhere?* That was a valid question when Sombart propounded the narrower one; it is valid today and probably will be valid seventy-five years after these lines are written. Nowhere was socialism a reality in 1906, nowhere is socialism a reality in 1981, and on the basis of empirical historical evidence, it seems irrefutable that nowhere will socialism be a reality in the year 2056. Socialism, the ideal society in which the means of production and distribution are socialized, thus creating a world of economic, political, and social equality, has proven to be a mirage.

So, too, have anarchism and syndicalism proven to be illusory. Supporters of both made the same basic assumptions as did the true believers of socialism. They argued that private ownership of socially productive property was the root of all evil and that the destruction of such exploitation for personal gain of what should be communal had to be the aim of any just political or economic movement. The Anarchists argued that the state was the evil genius behind the inequities that capitalism represented. The Syndicalists argued that the state was an irrelevant political issue interposed into a basically economic problem. But both agreed with the Socialists that socialization was the answer, and that with socialization would come an end to the state. They agreed with Engels that socialization would lead to the end of the governing of men and its replacement with the administration of things. The net result of this would be absolute equality and total freedom.

One of the prerequisites for such a transformation of society would have to be political democracy. On this, virtually all Socialists, Anarchists, and Syndicalists agreed. To achieve their Nirvana would require free discussion, and such discussion would be impossible under a dictatorship—even of the proletariat. In fact, those who considered themselves to be true Marxists invariably interpreted his call for a dictatorship of the proletariat to mean a democratic state in which workers would hold sway.

It was only after the Russian Revolution of November 1917 that radicals turned to dictatorship as a means of achieving their ends. Although some revolutionists talked in terms of a "reign of terror" against the capitalists—who believed in avenging millenia of wrongs in one violent assault against the exploiters under a transitional state—few radicals paid them much heed. Except for this minuscule rhetorically revolutionary minority, left-wingers of all types believed in an immediate and permanent expansion of the democratic right to dissent.

- 2 -

In Western Europe where Socialists assumed power by democratic, parliamentary means, they soon learned that immediate issues of economic crisis or postwar instability precluded construction of an Utopia. In Germany, they also discovered that their assumption that a majority would vote them into power once World War I had come to a conclusion was delusory. Authoritarians of Right and Left, and Democrats who favored capitalism, proved to hold a continued grasp on society. When economic crisis occurred, the Germans generally opted for the more strident anti-Democratic voices. The same was true in interwar Austria, Poland, and Italy.

In Scandinavia, the Socialists took power at a time of economic distress. They considered their first humanitarian objective to be amelioration of the distress in which the working class found itself. The result was an advanced group of welfare states. The British Labour party had much the same experience, although it did attempt a great deal of socialization—in coal, steel, electricity, and railroads. The only lasting achievements of Labour's rule have been its acts assuring that no Englishman, Scot, or Welshman went hungry or wanted for medical attention or housing.

In those countries that have proclaimed themselves to be Socialist republics, socialism is a chimera and a myth. In all of Eastern Europe—except Yugoslavia—they were forced to accept "Socialist" rule imposed by an invading Soviet Red Army, posing as liberators. The result has been autocratic rule by lackeys reminiscent of medieval despotisms. In China, an effort was made to force a Socialist society into being. But even that had to yield to reality and develop into an industrial state under a powerful bureaucracy of technicians and managers. The underdeveloped "Socialist" states of Asia, Africa, and Latin America have simply exchanged one set of oligarchs for another as they have attempted to enter the modern industrial era.

Although the American Left's history is merely a part of an overall study of the failure of a flawed idea, its telling requires explanation. Partly, the American story is worth telling because the failure here was more obvious and more complete and is thus simpler to pinpoint. The failure of the American Left did not preclude changes from occurring that virtually duplicated those in democratic nations in which Socialists have held sway. Nor was the role of the radicals any less in achievement of these changes than in nations where it was more obvious. Only the alienation of the Left has been more severe.

- 3 -

From the very outset, American radicals assumed they had the final solution for all social, economic, and political problems that beset this country. Robert Owen was confident that he needed only to demonstrate the workability of his ideal society and the world would come flocking to him to design perfect communities. Unfortunately, he underestimated the capriciousness of individuals, and his ideals were ignored. Admittedly, he had impressive listenership, including an American president and America's Congress. But he failed to achieve even the most rudimentary of his ideals. His own small colony at New Harmony died a dismal failure. Although he tried by all means available to achieve the perfect society, perfection, the socialist society, eluded him.

It would be unfair, however, to ignore the major contributions of Robert Owen to American life. His ideal may have been ignored, but his postulate—that environment is the basis for all of humanity's actions—was at the root of much American reform legislation. The arguments for better schools, slum clearance, and social legislation generally are all based on Owen's environmentalist view of intelligence.

As for the offshoots of Owen, the Individualists and the Workies, their contribution is even more monumental than their mentor's. The Individualists, for all their faults, were among the first to object to laws that encroached upon a human's right to lead any type of life he or she desired so long as it did not encroach upon the well being of another human being. They were among the first to warn of the grave danger to life and liberty posed by big government and bureaucracy. The voluntarism and antiorganization attitude in the past century is due to their influence. The political laissez faire they preached may have been too broadly drawn, but they kept the ideal of civil freedom alive against the growing encroachment of church and state.

As for the Workingmen's parties of New York, Pennsylvania, and Massachusetts, their accomplishments were monumental, although their ideals were never achieved. In New York, they were responsible for the enactment of the mechanics lien law, which protected a workingman's earnings. They were in great part responsible for the public school system, the modification of the jury system, and liberalization of the militia laws. The ideals that William Heighton and Thomas Skidmore propagated were ignored. Distribution of wealth in absolutely equal proportions was never accomplished, nor does it appear that it ever will be. Nor has the guardianship education proposal of Robert Dale Owen or Frances Wright ever been considered seriously. But the agitation for both of these ideas led to increased equitability in the law and in education. In Massachusetts and Rhode Island, Seth Luther's agitation raised the issues of political equality and exploitation of children. Political rights were won by rebellion in Rhode Island, and exploitation of children for profit was ended, gradually, as the seed Luther and his colleagues sowed first in Massachusetts bore fruit.

Nor should the radicals' contribution to racial and sexual equality be ignored. Admittedly, Frances Wright's Nashoba was a failure. But this was due more to her own naivete and the radical more's of white men than to her own failings. She proved that black men and women were humans with the same capabilities and shortcomings as all other people.

As for women, the radicals were among the first to struggle for their acceptance as equals. Fanny Wright had the leading role in the early years of that struggle. She was far ahead of the suffragettes in insistence on equal social, political, and economic treatment. Virginia Woodhull and Tennessee Claflin, for all of their eccentricities, led in the fight for equality during the latter half of the nineteenth century. Although Woodhull is famous primarily because she was the first woman to run for president of the United States, her importance goes far beyond that. She was, in fact, among the first women to declare openly for equality in all matters: social, economic, political, and sexual.

The roster of radicals who were active in securing equality between the sexes is legion; it includes men as well as women. The radical movements often suffered because of their work for woman's suffrage. Socialists who won suffrage for women in California and New York, particularly, were hurt politically by their action. Even after it became apparent that support of women's suffrage would be to their party's disadvantage, Socialists continued to work for it.

The contribution of the Fourierites, at Brook Farm particularly, was more cultural than political or economic. Horace Greeley was far less a radical than conservative poseur.

Of all of the labor reformers of the Civil War and immediate post-Civil War period, the most important were Wendell Phillips, Ira Steward, and

William Sylvis. Phillips proved that the struggle for equality was continuous and endless. Ira Steward's struggle for the eight-hour day, which bore fruit sixty years afterward, is one of the outstanding examples of the slow process of revolution by reform. William Sylvis proved that working people would join together against exploitation by their employers. He also proved that labor politics to succeed required that it be nonpartisan.

Of the latter day radicals, the greatest contributions have been made by the Socialist party, the Christian Socialists, and the Bellamy Nationalists. The Socialist party, despite its stated ideology, was essentially militantly reformist. It used the rhetoric of Marxism, but it never deluded any voters into suspecting that once elected it would institute Utopia. Its accomplishments in state legislatures, in city halls, and in Congress were almost all reformist in nature. Franklin D. Roosevelt (FDR) apparently did understand this—as Frances Perkins has noted—and patterned many of the more lasting New Deal reforms on Socialist immediate demands. True, FDR's social compound had other significant elements, but the role of the Socialist planks that dated from the 1890s were significant, and examination of the Socialists' 1898 platform would show the wide range of their proposals that have been enacted since 1933.

As for the Christian Socialists, their chief contribution was to add a moral dimension to socialism. To George Herron, William Bliss, Walter Rauschenbusch, Jesse Jones, and Hugh Owen Pentecost, socialism was more than a mere economic system; it was an affirmation of ethics as a part of life. The Christian Socialists declared that man had an obligation to protect "the least of these my brothers." It was this concern that led the American Socialists to fight for noneconomic issues such as civil liberties and civil rights. American Socialists rarely argued for socialism in quasi-scientific terms, because of the Christian Socialist element. Almost invariably, they called for socialism on moral grounds. This marriage to morality helped direct the Socialists toward amelioration rather than revolution. During the party's latter days, it prevented Socialists from accepting the Leninist doctrine that the ends justify the means.

Edward Bellamy's *Looking Backward* was a major propaganda piece that influenced generations of Americans and Europeans from Aneuran Bevan to Norman Thomas. Its most important contribution was, however, in giving American socialism a somewhat different cast from its European comrades. The party's followers—except for those in foreign-language federations—were nurtured on Bellamy rather than Marx. As a result, they spoke in terms that were American rather than in the language of "scientific socialism."

These three movements together helped shape the nature of labor reform in the United States. No Utopia has come of it, nor did all of the radical movements together create a Utopia. But the net result of these movements—Socialist, Anarchist, and Syndicalist—has been a revolution in American life. It has been a revolution that, despite martyrs and occasional repression and betrayal, was achieved with a minimum of violence.

Has the American Left failed? It has not achieved its stated aims; they were unachievable. It has never held political power. Thus its ideals have failed.

But it was instrumental in framing many of the most significant concepts that have come to permeate American life. It helped reform American society. Any obituary for the Left must concede its positive contributions to American life. It has thus succeeded.

❧ Bibliographic Note ❧

Any attempt to include a full bibliography with this book would have caused insoluble problems of space. A full, one-volume, critical bibliography covering the American Left is in preparation; it will be edited by Mark Yerburgh and Bernard K. Johnpoll. That bibliography will cover the same movements, people, and conditions discussed in this book and also will include a number of other radicals, such as Emma Goldman, and the minute Marxist and quasi-Marxist movements of the twentieth century. This short bibliographic note is designed to aid those interested in American radicalism. Only the most pertinent studies have thus been included.

A large number of general works deal with American radicalism. The most important, by far, is the two-volume *Socialism and American Life*, edited by Donald Drew Egbert and Stow Persons and published by Princeton University Press in 1952. The bibliography, which comprises the second volume, is of particular importance for scholars, even though it is out of date, since it was published in 1952. Also of considerable importance is John R. Commons et al., *Documentary History of American Industrial Society*, published in 1911 by Arthur H. Clark. Many significant documents relating to the early years of the radical movement are included. Commons and his associates also wrote an excellent history of the early labor movement in America, which helps place radicalism in proper prospective. Titled *Labor in America: A History*, it was published in 1918 by Macmillan. Lillian Symes and Travers Clement wrote an interesting, if eulogistic, history of American radicalism, *Rebel America* (1934; reprint ed, with an introduction by Richard Drinnon, Boston: Beacon Press, 1972). James Oneal's *The Workers in American History*, 4th ed. (New York: Rand School, 1921), is an interesting example of radical history. Of great interest, primarily for the latter chapters, is Morris Hillquit, *History of Socialism in the United States* (1903; reprint ed. New York: Russell and Russell, 1965). Also of interest is Selig Perlman, *History of Trade Unionism in the United States* (New York: Macmillan, 1922).

August Sartorius (Freiherrn von Waltershausen), *Der Moderne Socialismus in den Vereinigten Staaten von Amerika* (Berlin: Verlag von Hermann Barr, 1890), is a significant, but untranslated, study of the nineteenth-century American Left. Friedrich Sorge wrote a series of articles in the German, Marxist, theoretical journal *Neue Zeit* during the 1890s titled "Die Arbeiterbewegung in den Vereinigten Staaten," which was one of the major studies of American labor and Socialist movements of that period. Werner Sombart's *Warum Gibt es in den Vereinigten Staaten keinen Sozialismus* (Tubingen: J. B. C. Mohr, 1906) has recently been translated by Patricia M. Hocking and C. T. Husbands and published by Macmillan Press, Ltd., of London. It is a classic work. Nathan Fine's *Labor and Farmer Parties in the United States, 1828–1928* (New York: Rand School, 1928) is a pedestrian study. Murray S. Stedman and Susan W. Stedman, *Discontent at the Polls: A Study of Farmer and Labor Parties, 1827–1948* (New York: Columbia University Press, 1950), remedies much that is wrong with Fine's work.

Any discussion of the communitarian movements would be incomplete without mention of John Humphrey Noyes, *History of American Socialism* (1840 reprint ed. New York: Hillary House, 1961). Three speeches delivered by Robert Owen in 1825 and 1826 are reprinted in Oakley Johnson, *Robert Owen in the United States* (New York: Humanities Press for American Institute for Marxist Studies, 1970). Arthur Bestor, *Backwoods Utopias: The Sectarian Origins of the Owenite Phase of Communitarian Socialism in the United States* (Philadelphia: University of Pennsylvania Press, 1950), is the definitive work on the Robert Owen movement in America. J. F. C. Harrison, *Quest for the New Moral World: Robert Owen and the Owenites in Britain and America* (New York: Scribner's, 1969), is also excellent.

The Fourierite movement in America and Brook Farm are both well covered in American social and literary histories. Arthur Bestor's "Arthur Brisbane—Propagandist for Socialism in the 1840s," *New York History* 28 (April 1947), is an interesting study of the leading American Fourierite. Brisbane's *Social Destiny of Man: On Association and Reorganization of Society* (Philadelphia: C. F. Stollmeyer, 1840) and his *A Concise Exposition of the Doctrine of Association* (New York: J. S. Redfield, 1843) are the definitive primary works on Fourierite philosophy in America. Octavius Brooks Frothingham, *Transcendentalism in New England: A History* (New York: G. Putnam's Sons, 1876), should be read for a comprehension of the Brook Farm movement.

The anti-Fourierite communitarians of the 1840s have not been fully studied. Except for a single paper, published by a local historical society, virtually nothing has been published about John A. Collins. Whitney R. Cross, *The Burned-Over District: The Social and Intellectual History of Enthusiastic Religion in Western New York State* (Ithaca, N.Y.: Cornell University Press, 1950), describes the area in which many of these communities developed. John A. Collins wrote the *Preamble and Constitution of the New England Social Reform Society* in 1844. A copy is in the Anti-Slavery Collection at the Boston Public Library. Grosvenor Wells's paper on the *Skaneateles Communal Experiment* is an interesting, albeit narrow, work published in 1953 by the Onondaga Historical Association.

A large collection of books deal with the Oneida Community, John Humphrey Noyes, and the Perfectionists. The best is Marion Lockwood Carden, *Oneida: Utopian Community to Modern Corporation* (Baltimore: Johns Hopkins University Press, 1969). Also of interest is Constance Noyes Robertson, *Oneida Community:*

An Autobiography, 1851–1876 (Syracuse: Syracuse University Press, 1970), and Pierrepont Noyes, *My Father's House* (New York: Farrar and Rinehart, 1937). Robert Allerton Parker, *A Yankee Saint: John Humphrey Noyes and the Oneida Community* (New York: G. P. Putnam's Sons, 1936), is both a biography and a description of the community.

Howard Quint, *The Forging of American Socialism: Origins of the Modern Movement* (Columbia, S.C.: University of South Carolina Press, 1953), is the best work on the pre-1900 Socialist movements. It covers a vast amount of material intelligently and is extremely well written. The New York Workingmen's party is covered well in Frank Carlton's article, "The Workingmen's Party of New York, 1829–1831," *Political Science Quarterly* 22 (September 1907); the Philadelphia party is examined in Louis H. Arky's 1952 University of Pennsylvania dissertation, "The Mechanics Union of Trade Associations and the Formation of the Philadelphia Workingmen's Movement." Part of it later appeared as an article in the *Pennsylvania Magazine of History and Biography* 76 (April 1952). Edward Pessen's 1976 book, *Most Uncommon Jacksonians: The Radical Leaders of the Early Labor Movement* (Albany: State University of New York Press, 1967), and Walter Hugins, *Jacksonian Democracy and the Working Class: A study of the New York Workingmen's Movement* (Stanford, Calif.: Stanford University Press, 1960), are the two definitive works on labor during the Jacksonian era.

On labor reformers of the mid and later nineteenth century, John R. Commons, "Horace Greeley and the Working Class Origins of the Republican Party," *Political Science Quarterly* 24 (1909), is worth perusing. Hyman Kuritz, "Ira Steward and the Eight Hour Day Movement," *Science and Society* 20 (Spring 1956), should be read. Jonathan Grossman, *William Sylvis, Pioneer of American Labor* (New York: Columbia University Press, 1945), is an interesting factual discussion.

Frances Wright's role in the development of the American radical movement is discussed in William Randall Waterman, *Frances Wright* (New York: Columbia University Studies in History, Philosophy, and Public Law). Richard William Leopold, *Robert Dale Owen: A Biography* (Cambridge: Harvard University Press, 1940), is the best work on that midnineteenth-century radical.

The finest work on individualist-anarchists is James J. Martin's excellent, if ignored, *Men Against the State* (Colorado Springs: Ralph Myles Publisher, 1970). On the philosophy of Anarcho-Communists, see Alexander Berkman, *Now and After: The ABC of Anarchist Communism* (New York: Vanguard Press, 1929). Despite its bombast, and its simplistic style, this is the definitive statement by one of the three leading participants in that movement. Emma Goldman, *Anarchism and Other Essays* (New York: Mother Earth, 1917), is a somewhat more sophisticated discussion. On Johann Most, see Frederic Trautmann, *The Voice of Terror: A Biography* (Westport, Conn.: Greenwood Press, 1980). On Haymarket, see Henry David, *The History of the Haymarket Affair* (New York: Farrar and Rinehart, 1936). See also A. R. Parsons, *Anarchism: Its Philosophy and Scientific Basis* (Chicago: Mrs. A. R. Parsons, 1887), and August Spies, *Autobiography: His Speech in Court, and General Notes* (Chicago: Nina Van Zandt, 1887).

No study of Burnette G. Haskell has ever been completed, although several dissertations about him have been undertaken. On Bellamy, see Arthur E. Morgan, *Ed-*

ward Bellamy (New York: Columbia University Press, 1944). Bellamy's *Looking Backward* (New York: Modern Library, 1951) remains a classic. His columns have been reprinted in *Talks on Nationalism* (Chicago: The Peerage Press, 1938). On Populism, see John D. Hicks, *The Populist Revolt: A History of the Farmers' Alliance and the People's Party*, and Norman Pollack, *The Populist Response to Industrial America: Midwestern Populist Thought* (Cambridge: Harvard University Press, 1962). Of special interest is George H. Knoles article in the 1943 *Pacific Historical Review*, "Populism and Socialism, with Special Reference to the Election of 1892."

Christian Socialism is discussed in James Dombroski, *The Early Days of Christian Socialism in America* (New York: Columbia University Press, 1936), and Charles Howard Hopkins, *The Rise of the Social Gospel in America* (New Haven: Yale University Press, 1940). Dombrowski's book has some errors that mar its otherwise excellent analysis of the movement. As for De Leon, all of the books published are hagiographic. The best, L. Glen Seretan, *Daniel De Leon: The Odyssey of an American Marxist* (Cambridge: Harvard University Press, 1979), exaggerates De Leon's positive role in the Left of the turn of the century and offers an unsubstantiated conclusion.

A multitude of secondary and primary sources can be found on the Socialist party. Of the histories of the party, David Shannon, *The Socialist Party of America* (New York: Macmillan, 1955), is by far the best. Ray Ginger, *The Bending Cross* (New Brunswick, N.J.: Rutgers University Press, 1949), is the most balanced biography of Debs; Morris Hillquit's *Loose Leaves from a Busy Life* (New York: Macmillan, 1933) is worth studying; Oscar Ameringer, *If You Don't Weaken* (New York: Henry Holt, 1940), is important despite several errors of fact. Garin Burbank, *When Farmers Voted Red: The Gospel of Socialism in the Oklahoma Countryside* (Westport, Conn.: Greenwood Press, 1976), and James R. Green, *Grass Roots Socialism: Radical Movements in the Southwest* (Baton Rouge: Louisiana State University Press, 1978), are both excellent studies. Alexander Trachtenberg, ed., *The American Socialists and the War* (New York: Rand School, 1917), has important documents. On Socialists and Labor, see Stuart Bruce Kaufman, *Samuel Gompers and the Origins of the A.F. of L.* (Westport, Conn.: Greenwood Press, 1973). See also William M. Dick, *Labor and Socialism in America: The Gompers Years* (Port Washington, N.Y.: Kennikat Press, 1972).

On the IWW, despite a flood of titles, very little is available that is of any value. Paul Brissenden, *The I.W.W.: A Study of American Syndicalism* (New York: Columbia University Studies in Economics, History and Public Law, 1920), is still the most perceptive friendly study. Joyce L. Kornbluth's collection, *Rebel Voices* (Ann Arbor: University of Michigan Press, 1964), is a tribute to the Wobblies for their spirit.

The Communist party is also the subject of an infinite number of autobiographies, histories, biographies, and analyses. The best history is Irving Howe and Lewis Coser, *The American Communist Party: A Critical History* (Boston: Beacon Press, 1954). William Z. Foster's "history" is replete with errors of omission and commission. Theodore Draper's two volumes, *The Roots of American Communism* and *American Communism and Soviet Russia*, published by Viking in 1957 and 1963 respectively, are excellent, if limited, in scope.

The best history of the New Left is Edward J. Bacciocco, *The New Left in America* (Stanford, Calif.: Hoover Institution Press, 1974).

A number of books, articles, and dissertations are available that I have not mentioned despite their obvious quality. Generally, these works have dealt with esoteric movements or are not easily available to the average reader. My own books have also been left out. They will all be in the full bibliography mentioned at the beginning of this bibliographic note. Some other books have been deleted because they are inaccurate, misleading, or so seriously flawed as to be useless.

Suffice it to say that a careful reading of the books and articles listed in this note will enable the reader to understand better the whole of the radical movement in America. I doubt that anyone who has already found the way to the absolute truth will benefit from such reading. But it will be extremely useful for the inquiring mind.

∾ Index ∾

Abendblatt, 251, 256, 257

Abolitionist movement: Andrews and, 74; Bray's view of, 123; Collins and, 101; Noyes and, 105; Phillips and, 118; Socialist view of, 116; Spooner and, 79

AF of L. *See* American Federation of Labor

"Agrarian Justice," Paine, 10-11

Agrarians, 31

Alarm, 150, 154, 155

Albany Workingmen's party, 67n

Allen, Devere, 245

Allen, Samuel C., 62

Altgeld, John P., 161

Altorf, Wright, 32

ALU. *See* American Labor Union

Alwato, 74

Amalgamated Clothing Workers, 306

America, Jones' view of, 231

American Anti-Slavery Society, 101

American Communists. *See* Communist party, U.S.A.

American Constitution, Spooner's view of, 80

American Destiny-What Shall it Be, Republican or Cossack?, Bray, 122

American Fabian, 237, 247n, 257

American Fabian Society, 237

American Federation of Labor (AF of L), 5, 133, 160; and Communists, 325; Debs' view of, 300; and Social Democratic party, 282; and Socialist Labor party, 258-60; and Socialist party, 299-300; Socialists in, 287

American Labor Union (ALU), 300

American League Against War and Fascism, 328

American League for Peace and Democracy, 328-29

American Left, 3-11, 115-16, 338-39, 342-43; Christian Socialists and, 229, 232, 242, 245; failure of, 347-50; Owen and, 16, 24

American Letter Mail Company, 79

American Peace Mobilization (APM), 328 329

American Railroad Union (ARU), 278, 279-80

American Socialist, 111, 307

American Socialist party, 60

American society, Socialist view of, 123

American Student Union, 339

Anarchism, 5-8, 345- Bliss' views of, 236; of Collins, 103; Haskell's view of, 185; individualist, 4, 5, 70-71, 74, 80-81; of IWW, 304; legalistic, of Spooner, 78-80; Most and, 148-49; Owen and, 24; of Wright, 37-38

Anarchist-Communists, 143, 150-56; and Haskell, 185

Anarchists, 343; and Socialist Labor party, 252

Anderson, Sherwood, 323

Andrews, Stephen Pearl, 5, 73-78, 80-81, 83n, 116; Anarchist-Communists and, 151; view of Greeley, 91

Antinomianism, 106

Anti-Semitism: of De Leon, 256; Populist, 221, 228n
Appeal to Reason, 221, 278, 305
Aptheker, Herbert, 340
Arbeiter Zeitung, 157, 158, 160, 162, 255, 256, 282
Arbeiter Zeitung Publishing Association, 255-56
Arbeiterbund, 129
Arizona, IWW in, 307
Artists and Writers Congress, 326
ARU. *See* American Railway Union
Ashton, Thomas G., 197
Association for the Protection of Industry and for the Promotion of National Education, 41
Association movement, 86-88, 95; Godwin and, 92-93
Association of United Workers of America, 133
Aveling, Edward, 166

Baker, Charles, 308
Bakhunin, Mikhail, 131
Ballou, Adin, 116
Barry, James H., 197-98
Barth, William, 156
The Battle Axe, 106
Baxter, Sylvester, 213, 216
Beard, Charles A., 208
Befreiungsbund, 129
Bellamy, Edward, 5, 6, 205, 208-10, 245; Bliss and, 235; and Bryan, 222; and De Leon, 265; *The Duke of Stockbridge*, 209, 224n; *Equality*, 222; *Looking Backward*, 193, 195, 197, 207-8, 209-13, 215, 219, 233, 250, 349; and Marxism, 216-18; and Nationalist movement, 213-14, 218; and Populist movement, 219-23; and Socialism, 205, 222-23
Bellamy, Rufus, 208
Bentham, Jeremy, 32
Berger, Victor, 221, 222, 273, 276, 277-78, 281, 301, 314; arrest of, 308; candidacy of, 313; in Congress, 298, 310, 313; and Debs, 280; and IWW, 302; O'Hare and, 292; and right-wing Socialism, 287-88; and Social Democracy, 281-82
Berkeley, California, Wilson as mayor, 244-45
Berkman, Alexander, 4, 8, 161
Berliner, Louis, 134, 135

Berlyn, Bernard, 288
Bernhard, Karl, 16-17
Bernstein, Eduard, 287
Berrian, Hobart, 31
Bibliography of American Left, 351
Billings, Warren K., 306
Birth control, views of, 59, 107
Bisbee, Arizona, IWW in, 307
Black Panthers, 340
Blaine, James G., Haskell's view of, 186
Blatchly, Cornelius, 15, 55, 57
Blavatsky, Helen, 213
Bliss, W.D.P., 4, 213, 221, 222, 235-38, 349
Blisset, Robert, 169
Block, George C., 174
Boehm, Ernest, 259
Bohemian Federation, 309
Bohn, Frank, 305, 330
Bolsheviks, 308, 309, 310-11
Bonfield, James, 160
Bonfield, John, 158
Boston: Nationalist Clubs in, 213, 214, 225n; Socialists in, 255, 307, 309
Boston Eight-Hour League, 120
Boston Herald, 298
Boudin, Louis, 288, 289, 312, 330
Bowers, Charles E., 213
Boyle, James, 105, 106
Branstetter, Otto, 312
Bray, John Francis, 116, 121-25, 126, 133, 143
Brentwood community, 73
Bridgeport, Connecticut, Socialists in, 277, 314
Brisbane, Albert, 85-87, 95, 97n; and Greeley, 87-88
British Labour party, 346
Brook Farm, 87, 93-95, 348
Brook Farm School, 93-94
Brotherhood of Locomotive Firemen, 278
Brotherhood of the Co-operative Commonwealth, 280
Browder, Earl, 325, 326, 330, 333
Brown, Corrine, 214
Brown, Paul, 22-23
Brownson, Orestes, 26, 37, 40, 43-46, 56
Bryan, William Jennings, 222, 237; Debs' view of, 280
Buchanan, Joseph R., 191, 261
Burned Over District, 100, 105, 111
Burt, Johnathan, 107

Butler, Benjamin, 77, 119; Socialist support of, 167-68
Butte, Montana: IWW in, 307; Socialist administration in, 299
Byllesby, Langdon, 26-28

Cahan, Abraham, 176, 209, 218, 251, 307; and De Leon, 256
California: Christian Socialists in, 244-45; labor organizations in, 188-89; Nationalists in, 218-19; Socialists in, 180-82, 183, 277
California Federation of Labor, 188
California People's party, 198
Cameron, A. C., 117
Capital, Gronlund's view of, 173
Capitalism: Anarchist view of, 8, 150, 345; Bellamy's view of, 211, 217; Berger's view of, 288; Bray's view of, 123-24; Brown's views of, 23; Christian Socialist views of, 230-31, 235, 239, 245; Collins' view of, 103; De Leon's views of, 250, 265, 267; Fourierism and, 96; Gronlund's view of, 206; Heighton's view of, 52-54; Nationalist movement and, 214, 217; Noyes'; view of, 111; Owen's view of, 40; Phillips' view of 119; and radical Left, 116; Sorge's view of, 137; Steward's view of, 120
Carey, James C., 282
Casson, Herbert, 266
Catholic Church, and George, 179n
Cator, Thomas V., 197, 198
Central Labor Federation, 262, 263; and AF of L, 258-59
Central Labor Union, 168, 258; and George, 169, 170
Channing, William H., 95, 96
Charney, George, 332
Chartists, Bray and, 122
Chicago: German Socialists in, 141; International Working People's Association in, 150; Socialist Labor party in, 147-48; Socialist political action in, 140; Weatherman riot in, 341
Chicago Daily Mail, 156
Chicago Times, 158
Chicopee Falls, Massachusetts, 208
Child labor, 61, 63, 66, 348
Childbearing, Noyes' view of, 109
Children: in Brisbane's communities, 87; in Oneida Community, 109

China, Socialism in, 346
Chinese immigrants, opposition to, 132, 140-41, 184, 191
Christian Commonwealth, 242-43
Christian communities, 15, 242-43; communistic, 9
Christian Labor Union (CLU), 230-32
Christian Socialism, 205, 229
Christian Socialist, 244
Christian Socialist Fellowship, 244
Christian Socialists, 229-45, 349; and Populist movement, 221; and Socialist Labor party, 252, 253
A Christian View of Socialism, Strobell, 244
Christianity: Brownson's view of, 44-45; Herron's view of, 242; Pentecost's view of, 233; Phillips' view of, 118; Rauschenbusch's view of, 240; and social revolution, 4
Christianity and the Social Crisis, Rauschenbusch, 238
Church: Brownson's view of, 45, 46-47; Pentecost's view of, 233; Rauschenbusch's view of, 239; Wright and, 38
Church Association for the Advancement of Interests of Labor, 235
Church Socialist Union, 244
Cincinnati, Ohio, Socialists in, 232
CIO. *See* Congress of Industrial Organizations
Civil rights struggle, 339; Communists and, 328
Civil War: Andrews and, 76-77; Bellamy and, 208; radical Left and, 116
Civil War in France, Marx, 6
Claflin, Tennessee, 77, 348
Class distinctions: Anarchist-Communist view of, 150; Bray's view of, 123; De Leon's view of, 264-65; Greeley's view of, 91; of Nationalist movement, 213, 215, 217; in New Harmony community, 21; in Oneida Community, 110; in Phalanxes, 87; Steward's view of, 120
Class struggle: Anarchist-Communist view of, 151; Godwin's view of, 92; Jones' view of, 230; labor movement and, 115; left-wing Socialist view of, 288; Nationalist views of, 217; Rauschenbusch's view of, 239; Syndicalist view of, 7; Weitling's view of, 129
Class war: Bray's view of, 123-24; Brownson's view of, 45; Christian

Socialist views of, 231; Godwin's view of, 92; Noyes' view of, 111; Wright's view of, 37-38

Classless society, 7

Cleveland, Grover: Haskell's view of, 186; Socialists and, 168

CLU. *See* Christian Labor Union

Coast Seamen's Union, 188

Coastwise Sailors Union, 192

Cohen, Morris (Peter Kroger), 333

Coin's Financial School, 278

Colden, Cadwallader, 35

Coleman, George D., 186

Coles, Edward, 34, 47n

Collectivism, Socialist party and, 274-75

Collegiate Mennonites, 9

Collens, T. Wharton, 80, 230, 246n

Collins, John Anderson, 100-104, 112, 113

Colonial governments, 9

The Coming Age, Bray, 122

The Coming Revolution, Gronlund, 205

Committee of Fifty, 56-57

Common Sense party, 196

Communal ownership, 6

Communes, *see* Communities

Communications, mass, Warren's view of, 71

Communism: in America, 323-35; Christian, 9; frontier, 9; and Gronlund's Socialism, 206-7; Jones' view of, 230; of Oneida Community, 110; Woodhull and, 77-78

Communist front organizations, 328-39

Communist International, and American Socialists, 312

Communist Labor party, 311-12

Communist line, 324-27, 329, 331

Communist Manifesto, Marx and Engels, 6, 184, 206; Anarchist-Communists and, 150-51; first publication of, 83n

Communist party, U.S.A., 311-12, 323-35, 342-43; finances of, 328; membership of, 331-32, 335n

Communist Political Association (CPA), 327

Communistic Workingmen's Educational Society of St. Louis, 149

Communists, and SDS, 339-40

Communitarians, 14-15

Communities: Brisbane's Phalanxes, 86-87; Brook Farm, 87, 93-95, 348; Christian, 242-43; Kaweah Co-operative Colony,

192-95; Modern Times, 73-74, 115; Nashoba, 34-37, 348; New Harmony, 19-23, 28, 40-41, 69; Owenite, 19-24

Complex marriage, 107

Congress of Industrial Organizations (CIO), 323-24

Congressmen, Socialist, 273; *see also* Berger, Victor; London, Meyer

Connecticut, Socialists in, 277, 313, 314

Connolly, James, 289-90

Constitution, American, Spooner's view of, 80

Cooper, Peter, 136

The Co-operative Commonwealth, Gronlund, 205-7, 209, 213, 250; and Kaweah, 192

Cooperative communities, De Leon's view of, 265

Cooperatives, producer's formed by labor, 116

Cowen, Isaac, 300

Cowley, Malcolm, 323

Cox, Jesse, 214, 283

CPA. *See* Communist Political Association

Crocker, Harry, 194

Curran, Thomas, 268

Dacus, J. A., 138

Daily Sentinel, 42

Daily Worker, 327

Daily World, 327

Dana, Charles, 94

Darrow, Clarence, 214

D'Arusmont, Phiquepal Casimir Sylvan, 40

David, Eduard, 131

Davidson, Thomas, 214

Davis, William A., 34

Dawn, 235

Debs, Eugene V., 4, 221-22, 245, 276, 277-82, 314; and electoral process, 289, and Gronlund, 205; imprisonment of, 308; and IWW, 304; and labor unions, 300-301; Socialism of, 288-90; presidential candidacy of, 284-85, 292n, 313; and Social Democratic party, 282-85; and war, 266, 304, 306

Debt imprisonment, 56, 58, 60, 61

De Freeze, Donald, 342

Degan, Mathias J., 159

De Leon, Daniel, 4, 237, 249-50, 264-69, 271n; Debs' view of, 280; and Gompers,

260; and IWW, 301; and Nationalist movement, 215; and Populists, 220; and Socialist Labor party, 252, 254-64; and Socialist party, 276; and Socialist Trade and Labor Alliance, 262-64

Democracy, 346; Andrews' view of, 75-76; Owen's view of, 16; Skidmore's view of, 29

Democratic centralism, Gronlund's idea of, 207

Democratic National Convention, 1964, 339

Democratic party, Bliss' view of, 237

Democratic Socialist Organizing Committee, 292 n

Depression, 1873-1876, 132

Detroit, Weatherman faction in, 340

Devereaux, A. F., 213

Dewey, John, 208

Dictatorship of proletariat, 346

Dies, Martin, 333

Dissent, freedom of, 346

Dorr, Thomas, 65, 91

Dos Passos, John, 323

Doubleday, Abner, 214

Douglas, Frederick, 78, 101

Duane, William, 51

Duclos, Jacques, 327

The Duke of Stockbridge: A Romance of Shay's Rebellion, Bellamy, 209, 224 n

Dwight, John S., 94

Eastern branch, Socialist party of America, 286

Eastern Europe, Soviets in, 346

Economic depression, 1873-1876, 132

Economic reforms, Haskell's demands, 184

Economic system, Gronlund's theory, 206-7

Economic theory: Anarchist-Communist, 150-51; of Andrews, 76; of Warren, 70, 71-72; of Wright, 39

Eddy, Sherwood, 245

Education: Brook Farm School, 93-94; Heighton's view of, 53-54; Luther's view of, 63-64; Most's view of, 153-54; in New Harmony community, 20-21, 22; in Oneida Community, 108; R. D. Owen's views of, 40-42; public, 56, 58, 60, 61-62, 65; state guardianship scheme of, 41-42, 59, 60, 348; Wright's view of, 38-39

Educational and Defense Union, 141-42

Edwards, A. S., 214, 266

Eight Hours, Jones, 230

Eight-hour movement, 117, 118, 120-21; Anarchists and, 150; Haymarket riot, 156; International Workingmen's Association and, 131; Jones and, 230

election campaigns, Heighton's view of, 52

Electoral activity, Socialist views of, 167; *see also* Political action

Electoral process: Haskell's view of, 185, 186; Hillquit's view of, 291; left-wing Socialists and, 289

Elore, 307

Ely, Richard T., 138; view of George, 169

Der Emes, 255

Encyclopaedia of Social Reform, Bliss, ed., 238

End Poverty in California (EPIC), 196, 222; Wilson's support of, 245

Engdahl, J. Louis, 308

Engel, George, 159

Engels, Friedrich, 4, 6, 143, 345; and Bellamyite Nationalists, 215; *Communist Manifesto,* 6, 83 n, 150-51, 184, 206; George and, 175; and Gompers, 259; and Socialist Labor party, 166-67

Environmental influence: Owen's view of, 16, 17; Warren's view of, 70

EPIC (End Poverty in California), 196, 222, 245

Episcopal church, and Christian Socialism, 234-35

Equal Rights party, 65, 78, 89

Equality, Bellamy, 222

Equality: Byllesby's view of, 27; Luther's view of, 63

Equity, 230

Espionage, Communist, 333, 334-35

Espionage Act, Socialists and, 308

An Essay on Commonwealths, Blatchly, 15

Estes, George, 300

Eugenics, Oneida Community experiments in 109

European Socialists, and war, 304-5

Evans, George H., 56, 60

Everett, Washington, IWW in, 302-3

Evolutionary Socialism, Bernstein, 287

Factionalism of Socialist party, 276

Factories, working conditions in, 61, 63, 65-66

Fallenberg, Philip Emanuel von, 42

Family, Most's view of, 152
Farmer's Alliance, 221
Farmer's Alliances, 219
Farmers, De Leon's view of, 264-65
Farmers, Mechanics and Workingmen's Advocate, 59
Federal Bureau of Investigation (FBI), 334
Fielden, Samuel, 154, 158-60
Finch, John, 104
Finney, Charles G., 84
Finnish branches of Socialist party, 309
First Nationalist Club of Boston, 213, 214, 235
Fischer, Adolph, 157, 159
Flower, George, 34
Flynn, Elizabeth Gurley, 302, 326
For the Right, 238
Force, *see* Violence
Ford, Ebenezer, 57, 60
Foreign-born leftists, 4, 129, 147, 148-50, 166; German Marxists, 130, 132; in Socialist Labor party, 250-51; in Socialist party, 308-9
Foreign-language Socialist groups, 166, 250, 277, 283, 309, 310-11
'48ers, 129
Forward, 266
Foster, William E., 222
Foster, William Z., 222, 325
Fourier, François Marie Charles, 85
Fourierism, 86-88, 91-93, 95-97, 100; Brook Farm and, 94-95; Greeley and, 87-88; Peabody's view of, 94; and Skaneateles Community, 104; and transcendentalism, 94-95
Fourteen Points, Wilson's plan, 305, 306
Fraina, Louis C., 327
Free criticism, 108, 113
Free discussion, 346
Free Enquirer, 41, 45
Free love, 77, 78; Noyes' view of, 106-7
Free Press, 52
Freethought, 198
Freiheit, 161
Frick, Henry Clay, 161
Friends of the Soviet Union, 328
Frontier: Anarchism of, 8; communism of, 9

Gall, Ludwig Lampert, 10
Garrison, William Lloyd, 79; Collins and, 101, 104; Phillips and, 118

Gary, Joseph E., 159, 160
Gates, Theophilus, 106
General Grant Tree, 203n
General Sherman Tree, 203n
The Genius of Universal Emancipation, 33, 35-36
George, Henry, 160, 168-70, 178n; and De Leon, 249-50; Pentecost and, 233; Rauschenbusch and, 238; and Socialists, 170-75, 177
German Social Democratic party, 144n, 166
German Socialists, 129-31, 304-5, 346; in U.S., 166, 250, 277, 283
German Workers Educational Association, 131
German-born radicals in America, 4, 11; Socialists, 166, 250, 277, 283
Germany: Anti-Socialist laws in, 147-48; and Soviet Union, 324, 325-26
Germer, Adolph, 308
Ghent, William J., 266
Glyn, Harry, 257
God and Man a Unity and All Mankind a Unity, Bray, 123
Godwin, Parke, 91-93
Godwin, William, 44
Goldman, Emma, 4, 281, 302
Gompers, Samuel, 7, 160, 161, 258; and Pentecost, 233; and Socialists, 259-60, 299-300
Government: Anarchist-Communists and, and, 155; Andrews and, 76-77; Bray's view of, 123; Brownson's view of, 46; Collin's view of, 102, 103; Colonial, 9; force used by, 140, 155-56; Godwin's view of, 92; Grondlund's view of, 206-7; left-wing Socialist views of, 290; Parsons' view of, 152; Skidmore's view of, 29; Spooner's view of, 79-80; Warren's view of, 70; Wright's view of, 38
Government assistance to poor, Greeley's view of, 90
Grand National Consolidation Trades Union, 24
Greeley, Horace, 87-91, 348
Green, Gil, 328
Green, P. (Sergei Gusev), 325
Greenback party, 134, 143
Greenback Labor party, Hewitt's candidacy, 170
Gretsch, Benjamin J., 250

Grey, John, *A Lecture on Human Happiness*, 15
Grinnell, Julius, 160
Grinnell College, 241
Grissom, John, 15
Gronlund, Laurence, 5, 6, 205-7, 213, 223 n, 281; *The Coming Revolution*, 205-6; *The Co-operative Commonwealth*, 192, 205-7, 209, 213, 250; and George, 172-73
Grottkau, Paul, 142, 152, 176
Guardianship scheme of education, 41-42, 59, 60, 348
Guild of the Brotherhood of the Carpenter, 236
Gusev, Sergei (P. Green), 325

Hagerty, Fr. Thomas J., 300
Hague, Frank, 314
Hale, Edward Everett, 213
Hall, Basil, 61
Hall, W. L., 300
Handbook of Socialism, Bliss, 237
The Harbinger, 95, 104
Hardie, James Keir, 274
Harding, Warren G., 325
Harmonia Association of Joiners, 141
Harriman, Job, 283, 284
Harrington, Michael, 292 n
Harrison, Carter, 158
Haskell, Burnette G., 4, 5, 181-200, 213, 261; and Bellamy's *Looking Backward*, 208
Hawthorne, Nathaniel, 95
Hayes, Max, 283, 301
Hayes, Rutherford B., 136; and railroad strikes, 140
Haymarket incident, 156-62, 190; Powderly and, 261
Haywood, William D., 288, 290, 298, 303, 304
Hearst, Patricia, 342
Heath, Frederic C., view of Gronlund, 205
Hegel, Georg Wilhelm Friedrich, Brisbane's view of, 85
Heighton, William, 52-55, 348
Herron, George D., 4, 240-42, 305, 330, 349; and Rauschenbusch, 240
Hess, Christopher, 139
Hewitt, Abram S., 170-72
Heywood, Ezra H., 95

Hicks, Granville, 323
Higginson, Thomas Wentworth, 213
Hillkowitz, Morris, 251-52; *see also* Hillquit, Morris
Hillquit, Morris, 251-52, 276, 277-78, 281, 282, 304, 314, 330; candidacy of, 310; centrist Socialist views of, 290-91; *History of Socialism in the United States*, 183; O'Hare and, 291-92; on Russian revolution, 308; Socialism defined by, 274, 275; and Socialist party, 282-85, 291-92, 311, 312
Hiss, Alger, 334
History of Socialism in the United States, Hillquit, 183
Hitchcock, Roswell D., 231, 246 n
Hitler, Adolph, Communists and, 325-26
Hoan, Daniel W., 276
Holyoake, G. J., Phillips' letter to, 120
Homestead, Pennsylvania, strike at, 218, 237
Hoover, J. Edgar, 334
Hough, Eugene, 196
Howells, William Dean, 213; letter from Bellamy, 209
Hughan, Jessie Wallace, 132
Hughes, Charles Evans, 313
Hughes, Langston, 323
Hunter, Robert, 304-5
Hunter's Federation (*Jaegerverein*), 149

Immiseration thesis, 151
Individualism, 69; Anarchist views of, 152; Andrews' view of, 75-76; Warren's view of, 70-71
Individualist Anarchism, 4, 5, 70-71, 74, 80-81
Individualists, 347
Industrial army, Bellamy's idea of, 211-12
Industrial growth, 19th century, 14, 207
Industrial Socialists, 288-90
Industrial Workers of the World (IWW), 5, 7, 24, 27, 135, 264, 300, 301-4, 343; in North Dakota, 277; repression of, 307; Socialists in, 287
An Inquiry Into the Principles of the Distribution of Wealth Most Conducive to Human Happiness, Thompson, 15-16
Intellectuals, 200; and Brook Farm, 94, 95; and Communist party, 330-31; and labor movement, 96-97; and Nationalist move-

ment, 213; and radical politicians, 7-8;
    and workers, 21, 43, 96-97
Intercollegiate Socialist Society, 339
International Labor Defense, 328
International Ladies Garment Workers
    Union, 306, 324
International Socialist Review, 289, 298,
    302, 310
International Union of Electrical Workers,
    327
International Workers' Order (IWO), 328,
    329
International Working People's Association
    (IWPA), 149-51
International Workingmen's Association
    (IWA), 5, 131-32, 133, 144n; and Na-
    tional Labor Union, 117; San Francisco
    group, 182-92, 199; Woodhull and, 78
The Internationalist, 309-10
Iowa College, 241
Iowa Socialist party, 221
IWA. *See* International Workingmen's
    Association
IWPA. *See* International Working People's
    Association
IWW. *See* Industrial Workers of the World

Jaegerverein, 149
Jaffee, Philip J., *The Rise and Fall of
    American Communism*, 333
James, Charles, 151, 160
Jefferson, Thomas, 10, 32, 33; and Wright,
    34
Jennings, Robert L., 21
Jesus: Bliss' view of, 235; Herron's view of,
    242; and labor movement, 232;
    Pentecost's view of, 233; Rauschenbusch's
    view of, 239; Wilson's view of, 243
Jewish Daily Forward, 256, 280-81, 307
Jewish Socialists, 166, 251, 277, 283, 309;
    in Boston, 255; De Leon and, 256
Jewish Workers League, 171
Jews: Gronlund's view of, 207; Populist
    party and, 221
John Swinton's Paper, 174-75
Johnpoll, Bernard K., 351
Johnson, Quincy A., 102, 104
Jones, Jesse H., 120, 230-32, 349
Josephson, Matthew, 323
The Journal of Commerce, 57
Judiciary, bias of, 50-51, 159-60, 168

Junior Sons of '76, 134
Jury system, modification of, 348
Justice, Spooner's view of, 79

Das Kapital, Marx, 133, 216
Katterfield, Ludwig E., 298
Kautsky, Karl, 274
Kaweah Co-operative Colony, 192-95, 199
Kearney, Dennis, 140-41
Kelley, Florence, 214, 215
Kent State University incident, 340
Kibbutzim, 112, 113
King, Edward, 169
The Kingdom, 241
Knights of Labor, 5, 27, 219, 235; Bray
    and, 125; and Chinese workers, 191; and
    money reform, 134; New York District
    Assembly 49, 250, 261-62; and Socialist
    Labor party, 260-62
Kommunisten Klub, 130
Kroger, Peter (Morris Cohen), 333
Kronberg, David, 135
Kruse, William F., 308
Kuhn, Henry, 250, 256

Labadie, Jo, 185
Labor: Anarchist-Communist view of,
    150-51; Greeley's views of, 88-91;
    Gronlund's view of, 173; Phillip's view
    of, 119, 120
Labor Balance, 230
Labor Enquirer, 161; Haskell and, 191, 192
Labor movement: early 19th century, 50,
    52; and Fourierism, 96; Phillips and,
    118-19; political action of, 116-17; and
    radical Left, 115-17; Socialists and,
    142-43; and Syndicalism, 7; and
    Transcendentalists, 85; Workingmen's
    parties, 50-66
Labor reform movement, 121, 125-26;
    Bray's view of, 124-25; in Massachusetts,
    119
The Labor Standard, 135; and railroad
    strikes, 140
Labor unions, 7, 134-35; Bellamy's view of,
    218; Bliss and, 236-37; and Communists,
    323-24, 325, 327; Haskell and, 188-189;
    Nationalist view of, 217-18; Noyes' view
    of, 111; Pentecost and, 233; political ac-
    tion of, 168; Socialist Labor party and,
    257-68; Socialist party and, 276, 299-304

"The Laboring Classes," Brownson, 45
Labour's Wrongs and Labour's Remedy, Bray, 121, 122
Lafayette, Marquis de, 34-35
La Follette, Robert M., 276, 314
La Guardia, Fiorello, 292 n
Laissez faire capitalism, Bellamy and, 210-11
La Monte, Robert Rives, 288, 305
Land, private ownership of, Paine's view of, 11
Land reform: George's plan, 168-70; Gronlund's view of, 173; Socialists and, 169
Landis, Kenesaw Mountain, 308
Language of Socialists, 166, 178 n, 250, 309
Lassalle, Ferdinand, 131, 144 n
Lassalleans, 133-36
Law: Collins' view of, 103; Haywood's view of, 303; Luther's view of, 64; Parsons' view of, 152; Spooner's view of, 79; Warren's view of, 71; Wright's view of, 38
Lawrence, William, 34
Leacock, Stephen, on Bellamy's *Looking Backward*, 208
Leader, 171
League for Industrial Democracy (LID), 339, 340
A Lecture on Human Happiness, Grey, 15
Lee, Algernon, 214
Leeds Working Men's Association, 122
Left, radical, political, 3-11
Left Wing Manifesto, 311, 321 n
Left-wing Socialists, 287, 288-290; and Russian revolution, 308-11
Legalistic Anarchism, 78-80
Lehr und Wehr Verein, 141-42
Lenin, Vladimir Illyich, 154
Lesueur, Charles, 20
A Letter to Grover Cleveland, Spooner, 79
Lettish branches of Socialist party, 309
Levielle, E., 132
Levy, Moses, 51
LID. *See* League for Industrial Democracy
Liebknecht, Wilhelm, 166
Lien law, 56, 58, 60, 61
Lingg, Louis, 159
Lithuanian Socialists, 309
Little, Frank, 307
Livemore, Mary A., 213
Lloyd, Henry Demarest, 154, 221, 222
Loco-Foco party, 89

London, Meyer, 273, 314; in Congress, 298, 313; and party conflict, 310; and World War I, 305, 306
A Long Journey, Charney, 332
Longbridge, William, 77
Looking Backward, Bellamy, 195, 207-8, 209-13, 222-23, 250, 349; Haskell's view of, 197; Kaweah and, 193; Pentecost and, 233; Populism and, 219; Socialists and, 215
Los Angeles, Nationalist Clubs in, 218
Louisville, Kentucky, Socialists in, 140
Loveston, Jay, 329
Lum, Dyer D., 7, 80; and Haskell, 191; *The Philosophy of Trade Unions*, 300; support of Butler, 167
Lundy, Benjamin, 33, 35-36
Luther, Seth, 62-65, 348
Lynch, Michael, 217

McCarthy, Joseph, 333
McCartney, Frederic O., 282
McCormick Harvester riot, 156-57
MacDonald, George E., view of Haskell, 200
McDonnell, J. P., 135
McGlynn, Fr. Edward, 179 n
McGuire, Peter J., 134, 135-36; and Haskell, 189
Machinists and Blacksmiths Union, 115
McLevy, Jasper, 208
Maclure, William, 20, 24
McNeill, George E., 120, 135, 237
Madison, James, 33, 34
Maguire, Matthew, 253
Mail service, independent, 79
Mailing privileges, restriction of, 306, 307
Mainstream, 328
Man, Owen's view of, 16
Marriage: Anarchist-Communists and, 152; Andrews' view of, 76; Noyes' view of, 106-7; Owen's view of, 18; R. D. Owen's view of, 41; Wright's view of, 36, 39-40
Marshall, John, 33
Marshall, Louis, 307
Martin, Fred E., 257
Martin, J. J., 193-94
Martin, John, 78
Marx, Eleanor, 166
Marx, Karl, 4, 274; and Bray, 121; and Bakhunin, 131; and California, 180; *The*

Civil War in France, 6; *Communist
    Manifesto*, 6, 83 n, 150-51, 184, 206; and
    George, 170; and International Work-
    ingmen's Association, 131; *Das Kapital*,
    133; and National Labor Union, 117
Marxism, 6, 346; and American radicalism,
    11; and Anarchist-Communists, 150-51;
    and Christianity, 238, 240; Communists
    and, 330-31, 335; and Nationalism,
    216-18; Rauschenbusch and, 239; and
    violence, 216-17
Marxist groups, 133; Workingmen's party,
    134-36, 138-41
Marxists: German, 130, 131; and Nationalist
    Clubs, 215; and Populists, 220
Mass communication, Warren's view of, 71
Massachusetts: Finnish Socialists in, 309;
    Industrial Workers of the World strike in,
    302; Luther's reform in, 348; Nationalist
    Clubs, 213, 214, 218, 235; Populists in,
    220; Socialists in, 255, 276, 282, 307, 309;
    Workingmen's movement in, 61-65
Masses, Most's view of, 153-54
Matchett, Charles H., 253
Mayors, Socialist, 273, 297, 298
Mechanics Free Press, 52
Mechanics lien law, 56, 58, 60, 61, 65,
    348
Mechanics Union of Trade Associations, 52,
    54-55
Membership figures: Communist party,
    U.S.A., 323, 331, 332, 335 n; Interna-
    tional Workingmen's Association, 183;
    Knights of Labor, 260' Socialist Labor
    party, 251; Socialist party, 297, 310,
    312-13
Mennonite communities, 9
Michigan: Communists in, 312; Finnish
    Socialists in, 309; New Left in, 339
Middle class: De Leon's view of, 264-65;
    and Nationalist movement, 213, 215; and
    New Left, 339, 341, 342
Military service, universal, Skidmore's view
    of, 30-31
Militia law reform, 56, 58, 60, 61, 348
Miller, Louis, 256
Milwaukee, Socialists in, 175-76, 221, 277,
    281, 282, 310, 314
The Milwaukee Leader, 307
Milwaukee Revolutionary Socialists, 149
Mine, Mill and Smelter Workers Union, 327
Ming, Alexander, Sr., 57

Miscegenation, and Nashoba Colony, 36
Mississippi Free Democrats, 339
Modern Times community, 73-74, 115
Monetary reform movement, 134; National
    Labor Union support of, 117
Money: Byllesby's view of, 27; Warren's
    view of, 72
Monopolies: Bellamy's view of, 211; Sorge's
    view of, 137
Monroe, James, 33, 34
Montana: IWW lynching in, 307; Socialists
    in, 276-77, 299
Mooney, Thomas J. (Tom), 306
Moore, Ely, 65
Moral Physiology, R. D. Owen, 59, 107
Morgan, Thomas J., 161, 215, 266
Morning Courier and *New York Enquirer*,
    57, 58
Most, Johann, 4, 19, 143, 148-49, 161;
    and Anarchist-Communists, 151; and
    Lenin, 154; and revolution, 153; view of
    family, 152; Weatherman faction and,
    340, 341
Mother Earth, 307
Muste, Abraham J., 126, 245

Nashoba colony, 34-37, 348
National Labor Congress of 1880, 121
National Labor Union (NLU), 27, 116-17;
    Lassalleans and, 131
National Student League, 328, 339
National Trades Union, 64
Nationalist movement, 213-18, 220, 222-23,
    245, 349; Bliss' view of, 235; De Leon's
    views of, 250, 266; Haskell and, 195-98,
    199; and Marxism, 216-18
The Nationalist, 219, 227 n
Nationalization of industry, Bliss' view of,
    235
Neebe, Oscar W., 159
Neef, Joseph, 20
Negroes, 253; in Socialist Labor party, 166
Neptune Club, 198
Nevada, Socialist party in, 277, 312
New Bedford Evening Journal, 219
New Deal, 273, 274, 349; Communist views
    of, 325, 326
New Democracy, 77
New England Artisan, 63
New England Association of Farmers,
    Mechanics and Workingmen, 61-62, 64
New England Social Reform Society, 103

New England Workingmen's Association, 96

New Harmony community, 19-23, 40-41, 347; Pentecost and, 232; Skidmore's view of, 28; Warren and 69

New Haven Perfectionist Free Church, 105

New Jersey: Pentecost in, 232; Socialists in, 253

New Lanark, Scotland, 15

New Left, 338-43; Communists and, 328

New Masses, 327-28

The New Nation, 216, 217, 219

New Right, leftist roots of, 80-81

New Socialistic Labor party, 111

New View of Society, Owen, 15

New Views of Society and Manners in America, Wright, 33

New York: Central Labor Federation, 258; Knights of Labor, District Assembly, 49, 250, 261-62; Nationalist Clubs in, 218, 250; population growth, 14; SDS in, 340; Socialist Labor party in, 177, 253; Socialist party in, 277, 310, 313; Socialists in, 140, 147-48; Workingmen's party in, 41, 42, 55-60, 65, 67n, 348

New York Call, 307, 311

New York Morning Journal, 279

New York Society for Promoting Commonwealths, 15

New York Sun, 221; view of Socialist attack on George, 173

New York Times, on Hewitt, 171

New York Tribune, 88

The New Yorker, 88

New Yorker Volkszeitung, 251, 268, 307

Newark, New Jersey, Pentecost in, 232

Nichols, Thomas Low, 22

Nixon, Richard M., 333-34

NLU. *See* National Labor Union

Noah, Mordecai Manuel, 58

North American Phalanx, 95

North Dakota, Socialist party in, 277, 312

Novy Mir, 307

Noyes, John Humphrey, 87, 100, 105-12, 113

Noyes, Theodore, 109

Oglesby, Richard J., 160

O'Hare, Kate Richards, 291-92, 308

Ohio Volkszeitung, 141

Oklahoma: IWW repressed in, 307; Socialist party in, 377, 312

Olney, Richard, 279

Omaha convention of Populists, 220

Oneal, James, 308

Oneida Community, 105-12, 115

O'Reilly, John Boyle, 213

Oregon, Socialists in, 313

Organizatons, Haskell and, 182-83

Osgood, Samuel, 94

Owen, Robert, 4, 15-24, 35, 49n, 347; and Brownson, 44; and Collins, 101; and Heighton, 52; and Skaneateles Community, 104

Owen, Robert Dale, 19-22, 26, 35, 40-43, 55, 348; and Warren, 72; and Workingmen's party, 56-60

Owen, W. C., review of *Das Kapital*, 216

Owen, William, 19, 20

Owenite communities, 19-24, 112; Skaneateles Community, 101-4

Owenite movement, 9, 69

Ownership, communal, 6; *see also* Property, private

Paine, Thomas, 10-11

Pardee, George C., 199

Parsons, Albert R., 139, 140, 148, 162n; determinism of, 151; and Haymarket incident, 157-60; individualism of, 152; and Most, 149; and peaceful revolution, 154

Parsons, Lucy, on violence, 155

Peabody, Elizabeth, 94

Peabody, Nathaniel, 102

Peaceful revolution, Anarchists and, 154

Pennsylvania, Socialists in, 277, 307, 314; *see also* Philadelphia; Pittsburgh

Pentecost, Hugh Owen, 232-34, 246n, 349

The People, 251, 282; De Leon and, 254, 255, 256, 264

People's Council of America for Peace and Freedom, 307

People's party, 205, 219, 221-22; Bellamy and, 218, 220, 265; Christian Socialists and, 237, 243; Nationalists and, 219-23; Socialist Labor party and, 253

Pepper, John (Joseph Pogany), 325

Perfectionism, 15, 105, 113; Noyes and, 105-7

Perkins, Frances, 349

Phalanxes, 86-87; failure of, 95-96

Philadelphia: Nationalist Clubs, 218; population growth, 14; Socialists in, 307; Workingmen's party, 52, 55

Philadelphia Cordwainers case, 50-51

Philadelphia Society for Promoting Communities, 15
Phillips, Wendell, 79, 116, 117-20, 125, 126, 348-49
The Philosophy of Trade Unions, Lum, 299-300
Phonography, 74
Physical science, Wright's view of, 39
Pierce, Julian, 268
Pitman, Isaac, 74
Pitt, Theodore L., 141
Pittsburgh, Weatherman faction in, 340
Pittsburgh Congress, 148-49; Haskell and, 185, 187
"Pittsburgh Manifesto," 185
"A Plan for Gradual Abolition of Slavery in the United States Without Danger or Loss to Citizens of the South," Wright, 33-34
Plekhanov, George, 304
Plockhoy, Christopher, 9-10
Poale Zion, 310
Podeva, Hermann, 157
Pogany, Joseph (John Pepper), 325
Poland, and Russian revolution, 324-25
Polish Federation, 309
Political action: Bray's views of, 124, 133; Debs' view of, 280; De Leon's view of, 263; Haskell's view of, 185, 186, 196; International Workingmen's Association and, 133; by labor movement, 51-60, 116-17; labor unions and, 168; left wing Socialist view of, 289; McGuire's view of, 135-36; Nationalists and, 218-19; Phillips view of, 118-19; Populist, 220; Socialist, 140-41, 147-48, 175-77, 252-53; Socialist Labor party and, 167; Workingmen's party and, 135-36
Political reform, Socialist demands, 176-77
Political theories: of Heighton, 52-54; left-wing, 5-8
Politics: American, left-wing, 3-11; Brisbane's view of, 86
Poor People's party, 58, 59
Popular front, Communist, 326
Population growth, 19th century, 14
Populism of International Workingmen's Association, 183-84
Populist movement, 219-23, 278; Debs and, 280; De Leon's view of, 264-65; and Haskell, 199; Powderly and, 260-61
Port Huron Statement, 339

Post, Elizabeth, 238
Poverty, Paine's view of, 10-11
Powderly, Terrence V., 160, 260-61; and Haskell, 187
Poyntz, Juliet Stuart, 329
Pragmatism of left wing Socialists, 288-89
Prather, Van B., 219
Price, and value, Warren's views of, 71-72
Private ownership. *See* Property, private
Profit: Andrews' view of, 76; Heighton's view of, 53
Progress and Poverty, George, 169, 172-73
Progressive Labor party, 174, 175, 339-40
Property, private, 345; Anarchist-Communists and, 150, 155; Brisbane's view of, 86; Collins' view of, 101, 102-3; Marxist views of, 274; Most's view of, 150; Owen's view of, 17; Paine's view of, 11; Skidmore's view of, 28-30; Socialist view of, 172
Public education, 348
Publications: Communists, 328; Socialist, 251, 255-57
Pullman strikes, 237, 279-80
Putney Perfectionists, 106-7

Quarterly Review, 45
Queen City, 104

Racial discrimination, in Socialist Labor party, 166
Racial equality, 348; International Workingmen's Association and, 132; Socialists and, 138
Racism: of California Socialists, 184; of Haskell, 191
Radical movements, religion and, 229
Radicalism, American, 3-11, 60, 115-16, 347; Byllesby and, 27-28; and Owenite philosophy, 16, 18-19, 24; and R. D. Owen, 43
Railroad strikes, 138-40, 237
Railroad unions, Debs and, 278-79
Rand, Carrie, 241
Rand, Mrs. E. D., 241
Rand School of Social Sciences, 241, 242
Rankin, John, 333
Rappite communities, 15, 32, 112
Rauschenbusch, Walter, 4, 238-40, 349
Raymond, J. E., 238
Reading, Pennsylvania, Socialists in, 277, 314

Reed, John, 311-12; letter from Sinclair, 291
Reform: in American life, 350; De Leon's view of, 267-68; Socialist views of, 275-76, 298
Reid, James P., 268
Reitman, Ben, 302
Religion: and American Left, 229; Brownson's views of, 44-45; Collins' view of, 102; and Nationalism, 214; Owen's view of, 18; R. D. Owen's views of, 41, 42; Phillips' view of, 118; and Utopian communities, 112; Wright's view of, 38
Religious communities, 14-15; early, 9-10; Wright's view of, 32-33
Religious revivals, 100
Republican party, Bliss' view of, 237
Republican Political Association of Workingmen, 55
Die Republik der Arbeiter, 129
Reuther, Walter, 126, 327
Revivalism, 84
Revolution: in America, Marx and, 274; Anarchist view of, 153-54; in Bellamy's *Looking Backward*, 211; Bray's view of, 124-25; Brisbane's view of, 86; Cahan's view of, 251; and Christianity, 4; De Leon's view of, 267-68; Gronlund's view of, 206-7; Haskell's view of, 184-87, 190; Herron's view of, 242; Owen's view of, 16-17; peaceful, Anarchists and, 154; permanently immanent, 4; social, and Communism, 334-35; Socialist views of, 251, 287; Weatherman faction and, 340-41
Revolutionary Socialist party, 148
Revolutionary Socialists, 288-90
Revolutionists, European, in American reform movements, 129
Rhode Island: Nationalist political action in, 219; reform in, 348
Richardson, James, 34-36
The Rights of Man to Property!, Skidmore, 28
Right-wing Socialists, 287-88
Ripley, George, 93-95
The Rise and Fall of American Communism, Jaffee, 333
Roney, Frank, 142, 214; Haskell and, 181, 199
Roosevelt, Franklin D., 273, 349; Communists and, 326, 327
Roosevelt, Theodore, 170, 172, 273
Rose, Ernestine, 102

Rosenberg case, 333, 334
Russell, Bertrand, 6, 7
Russell, Charles Edward, 305
Russia. *See* Soviet Union
Russian Bolsheviks, and American leftists, 311
Russian Jews, and Socialist party, 277
Russian revolution, Americans and, 308-11, 324-25
Russian-born American leftists, 4
Ruthenberg, Charles A., 308, 329
Ryckman, L. W., 96

Sabbatarianism, R. D. Owen and, 42
Sabotage, IWW and, 303
Sailor's Union of the Pacific, 188-89, 198-99
St. John, Vincent, 301, 303
St. Louis, Socialists in, 139
St. Louis Conference, Populist, 219-20
St. Louis Declaration, 305-6
St. Louis Labor, 256
Saint-Simon, Comte Claude Henri de, 85; Brownson and, 44
San Diego, struggles in, 302
San Francisco: Haskell in, 196, 198; Socialist Labor party in, 167, 182
Sanial, Lucien, 253, 254, 258-59, 268
Saxe, Susan, 342
Say, Thomas, 20
Scandinavia, Socialists in, 346
Scapegoats, Communist, 329-30
Scates, Lewis, 282
Schenectady, New York, Socialists in, 277
Schindler, Rabbi Solomon, 213
Schnaubelt, Rudolph, 159
Schools. *See* Education
Schwab, Justus, 4
Schwab, Michael, 159-62
Science of Revolutionary Warfare, Most, 160
The Science of Society, Andrews, 74
Scientific inquiry, Andrews' view of, 74-75
SDP. *See* Social Democratic party of America
SDS. *See* Students for a Democratic Society
SDWP. *See* Social Democratic Workingmen's party
Seattle Union-Record, 313
Second coming of Christ, Noyes' belief of, 105, 107
Sequoia National Park, 194, 199, 203n
Sexual freedom, perfectionist view of, 106-7; *see also* Marriage

Shaker communities, 15, 112
Sharp, J. Howard, 253
Sherman, Charles O., 301
Shevitch, Serge, 215
Shorthand, 74
Simonson, Barton, 158
Sinclair, Upton, 291, 339; EPIC plan, 196,
    222, 245; and World War I, 305
Single tax, 168; Socialists and, 172
Skaneateles Community, 100, 101-4, 111-12
Skidmore, Thomas, 26, 28-31, 55, 348; and
    Workingmen's party, 56-58
Slavery: Bray's view of, 122-23; Brownson's
    view of, 45; Collins' view of, 101; Ger-
    man Socialists and, 130; Gronlund's view
    of, 206; Phillips and, 118; Wright and,
    33-37
SLID. *See* Student League for Industrial
    Democracy
Slobodin, Henry, 288
SLP. *See* Socialist Labor party
Smart, W.G.H., 136-38
Smith, Clarence, 300
Smith Act, Communists and, 327
Smithsonian Institution, 43
SNCC. *See* Students' Non-violent Coordi-
    nating Committee
SNU. *See* Socialist Newspaper Union
Social Crusade, 243-44
Social Darwinism, 80-81; Bellamy's *Looking
    Backward* and, 210-211; Nationalist
    movement and, 214
Social Democratic party of America, 282,
    283-85
Social Democratic Workingmen's party
    (SDWP), 133-34
Social Democracy of America, 280-82, 309;
    Berger's view of, 288
Social Democratic League, 306
Social Democrats, U.S.A., 292n
Social Destiny of Man, Brisbane, 85
The Social Gospel, 229, 243
Social Gospel, 4, 5, 205; Brownson and,
    44; Herron and, 240-42; Phillips and,
    119; Rauschenbusch and, 239
Social reform, 8; Anarchists and, 252;
    Bellamy's view of, 218; Brownson's view
    of, 46; IWPA view of, 150; Socialists
    and, 142, 176, 252-53, 288
Social revolution: Bray's view of, 124; Bris-
    bane's ideas of, 86; centrist views of, 291;
    Fourierism and, 96-97; Godwin's view of,

92-93; IWPA view of, 150; Phillips' view
    of, 118; *see also* Revolution
Social revolutionaries, and Weatherman
    faction, 341
Social science, Andrews' view of, 74-75
Social Security, Socialist support of, 282
Socialism, 5-8, 345-47; and Abolition move-
    ment, 116; and American society, 123-24;
    Americanization of movement, 205,
    222-23; Bellamy and, 216-17; Bellamy's
    :Looking Backward and, 208, 209-10;
    Bliss and, 235-37; Bray and, 123-25;
    Brownson and, 44; Cahan's view of, 251;
    Christian Socialist definitions, 229; De
    Leon's views of, 250, 267-68; Gronlund's
    view of, 206; Haskell's view of, 196;
    Heighton and, 52-54; Jews and, 251; and
    labor reform, 121; and Nationalism, 214,
    216-18; Noyes and, 111; Owen and, 24;
    Rauschenbusch and, 240; and religion,
    229; Socialist definition of, 274-76;
    Sorge's view of, 137-38; of Wilson,
    243-44; *see also* Christian Socialism
Socialist Labor party (SLP), 141-43, 166-68,
    180, 205, 237, 249-69, 343; and AF of L,
    258-60; and Anarchist-Communists, 152;
    and Bellamy's *Looking Backward*, 208,
    215; Christian Socialists and, 232, 236,
    243; Declaration of Principles, 169; De
    Leon and 249-50, 252, 254-57, 260-69;
    election platform, 176-77, 252-53; factions
    of, 282-83; and IWA, 189-90, 192; and
    labor unions, 176, 258-68; and land
    reform, 169; languages of, 166, 178n,
    250, 309; and Nationalist movement,
    215-18, 220-21; and political action,
    147-48, 175-77; press, 251, 257; and
    Social Democratic party, 283-85; and
    United Labor party, 173-74; Western
    groups, 167
Socialist League of Great Britain, 166
Socialist Newspaper Union (SNU), 256-57
Socialist party of America, 223, 273-78,
    285-90, 292n, 297-99, 342, 349; centrist
    faction, 290-91; Christian Socialists in,
    243; and Communists, 311-12; decline of,
    297-300, 313-14; electoral successes of,
    297, 298, 310, 313; foreign-language
    branches, 310; internal disagreements,
    310-12; and IWW, 302, 303-4; and labor
    movement, 299-304; left-wing of, 288-90,
    308, 310-12; membership of, 297, 310,

312-13; National Executive Committee, 311; Pentecost and, 234; persecution of, 306-8, 313, 314; personality conflicts in, 291-92; and reform, 298; right-wing of, 287-88; and social reform, 275, 298-99; and war, 276, 304-8

Socialist platform, 298; "Immediate demands," 285-86

Socialist Propaganda League, 309-10

Socialist Trade and Labor Alliance (ST and LA), 262-64, 268, 301

Socialists, 136-38; Christian, *see* Christian Socialists; and Communists, 325; failure of, 177; and George, 169, 170-75, 177; German, 129-31, 132; and Greenback party, 143; and labor unions, 142-43, 257-58; and Populists, 221; and railroad strikes, 138-140; and Russian revolution, 308-11; and United Labor party, 172-75; and violence, 216-17; in Western Europe, 346; and Workingmen's party, 134

Socialization, 345-46

Society: American, Bray's view of, 123; American, and radical left wing, 3-4, 6; Andrews' view of, 74-75; Brisbane's view of, 86; Godwin's view of, 92

Society of Christian Socialists, 235-36

Sombart, Werner, 345

Sorge, Friedrich A., 117, 131, 136-38; Engel's letters to, 166-67, 175

Sotheran, Charles, 215, 221, 258; and De Leon, 255, 262; and George, 171; view of Socialism, 167

Sovereign, James R., 261-62

Soviet Union: and American Communists, 324-27, 329-31, 333, 334-35; and Eastern Europe, 346

Sozialist, Engel's view of, 167

Sozialistischer Verein, 278

Spanish American war: Christian Socialist views of, 243; Socialist views of, 266

Spargo, John, 305

Spies, August, 4, 147, 148, 162 n; and eight-hour day, 150; Haskell and, 185; and Haymarket incident, 156-60; Marxist theories of, 151; and Most, 149; and revolution, 154, 155

Spies, Communist, 333, 334-35

Spokane, Washington, IWW in, 302

Spooner, Lysander, 5, 78-80, 81; Anarchist-Communists and, 151

Sprague, Philo W., 229

ST and LA, *see* Socialist Trade and Labor Alliance

Stalin, 254

State: Anarchist view of, 345; Bliss' view of, 236; Gronlund's view of, 206-7; Haskell's view of, 197; radical views of, 5, 7, 8; Socialist views of, 291; Syndicalist view of, 345; Wright's view of 48 n; *see also* Government

State guardianship education scheme, 41-42, 59, 60

States' rights, Bray's view of, 122

Steadman, Seymour, 283

Steamship Sailors Union, 188

Steffens, Lincoln, 323

Steward, Ira, 120-21, 135, 348-49

Stirpiculture, 109

Stokes, Rose Pastor, 308

Stone, Lucy, 213

Strikes, 7, 116; Bray's view of, 124; Communists and, 327; De Leon's view of, 263, 267; early, 10, 51-52; Greeley's view of, 89; Haskell's view of, 188; Heighton's view of, 54; by IWW, 302; by Knights of Labor, 261; *Philadelphia Cordwainers*, 50-51; railroad, 138-40; Syndicalist view of, 7

Strobell, George H., 244

Student League for Industrial Democracy (SLID), 339

Students for a Democratic Society (SDS), 19, 155, 338-40; Weatherman faction, 340-42

Students' Non-Violent Coordinating Committee (SNCC), 339

Subversion, Communist, 333-34

Suffrage, 61; colonial restrictions, 9; in Rhode Island, 64-65; for women, 348

Swinton, John, 132, 167; *John Swinton's Paper*, 174-75; view of George, 169

Sylvis, William, 27, 115, 116-17, 125-26, 349

Symbionese Liberation Army, 342

Syndicalism, 5-8, 345; Byllesby and, 27; of Workingmen's party, 135

Tammany Hall, and Workingmen's party, 57-60

Tarbell, Ida M., 210

Taylor, Nathaniel W., 105

Ten-hour day, 56, 61, 65; Utopians and, 96

Theosophists, 213; and Nationalism, 214
218-19
Thomas, J. Parnell, 333-34
Thomas, Norman M., 4, 126, 208, 245,
273, 276, 314, 339; and Communists,
325, 326, 333
Thomas, R. J., 327
Thompson, Jeremiah, 34
Thompson, W. W., 62
Thompson, William, *An Inquiry Into the
Principles of the Distribution of Wealth
Most Conducive to Human Happiness*,
15-16
Tilden, Samuel J., 136
Time Stores, 72
Trade Union Unity League, (TUUL), 325
Trade unions. *See* Labor unions
Trade unions of Boston, 64
Transcendentalism, 84-85, 100; Brook
Farm, 93-95
Transitional dictatorship, 153-54
Trautmann, William E., 7, 301
Trollope, Frances M., 36
Troost, Gerard, 20
Trotsky, Leon, 329-30
Truth, 169, 181, 184-85, 189
Truth Seeker, 234
Tucker, Benjamin, 5, 185, 236
Tucker, Irwin St. John, 308
Tulsa, Oklahoma, IWW in, 307
Turnerbund, 130
Turnverein, 130
TUUL. *See* Trade Union Unity League
Tuskegee Institute, 37
Twain, Mark, 208
Twentieth Century, 233, 234
Tyrell, John, 189

Ullman, Daniel, 91
The Unconstitutionality of Slavery,
Spooner, 79
Unemployed Councils, 328
Unions. *See* Labor unions
United Automobile Workers, and Com-
munists, 324, 327
United Electrical Workers, 327
United Front Against Fascism convention,
340
United Hebrew Trades, 262, 263, 271 n,
282, 306
United Labor party: and George, 170,
172-75; Haskell and, 198; of New York,
168

United States Brotherhood of Carpenters,
135
United Steelworkers of America, 327
United Workingmen, 133
Untremann, Ernest, 301
Upper class, New Left and, 342
Urban growth, 19th century, 14, 207
Utopia, 207, 349; Anarchist, 153; Bellamy's
Looking Backward, 210-13; Gronlund's
idea of, 207; Socialist expectation of, 177,
287; Weitling's idea of, 129-30
Utopian communities, 93, 112, 115; Brook
Farm, 93-95; Kaeah Co-operative Colony,
192-95; Oneida Community, 105-12;
Skaneateales Community, 101-4
Utopianism, 84; and labor movement,
96; of Phillips, 119-120

Value, theories of, 71-72, 150-51
Vanderbilt, Cornelius, 77
Van Patten, Philip, 139, 145 n
Viet Nam war, 338, 339
Views of Society and Manners in America,
Wright, 32
Violence: Anarchists and, 153, 154-56;
Bellamy's view of, 211, 217; Byllesby's
view of, 27-28; Communists and, 325;
Haskell and, 185-87, 189; International
Workingmen's Association and, 190;
IWW and, 303; Jones' view of, 231; left-
wing Socialist view of, 289-90; Marxist
view of, 216; Most and, 149; SDS and,
340; Socialist views of, 141, 167, 216,
251, 304; Sorge's view of, 137; Weather-
man faction and, 340-42
Vocational education, Wright and, 37
Vogt, Hugo, 268
Volkszeitung, 166, 171, 172
Vorwaerts, 251, 266
Voting rights. *See* Suffrage; Women's
rights
*A Voyage from Utopia to Several Unknown
Regions of the World*, Bray, 122

Wagenknecht, Alfred, 308
Wage slavery; Gronlund's view of, 206
Waldman, Louis, 308
Wallace, Henry A., 327
Walling, William English, 288, 305, 330
War: Byllesby's view of, 28; Christian
Socialist views of, 243; Debs' view of,
304; Heighton's view of, 53; *see also*
name of war

Ward, C. Osborne, 131
Ward, William, 158
Warren, Fred, 305
Warren, Josiah, 4, 5, 21, 24, 26, 69-74;
Anarchist Communists and, 151, 152;
assessment of, 80-81
Washington, Booker T., 37
Washington: IWW in, 302-3; Socialist party
in, 277, 313
Wayland, Julius A., 221, 266, 278
Wealth: Anarchist-Communist view of,
150-51; Byllesby's view of, 27; De Leon's
view of, 267; Heighton's view of, 53;
Populist view of, 219; Skidmore's view
of, 28-29; Smart's view of, 137; *see also*
Money; Property, private
Weatherman faction of SDS, 340-42
Weaver, James B., 143, 147
Wedemeyer, Otto, 134
Weeks, Edward, 208
Weinstein, Bernard, and De Leon, 254
Weitling, Wilhelm, 129-30
Welfare states, 346
Western branch of Socialist party, 286
Western Europe, Socialists in, 346
Western Federation of Miners, 300, 301
Western Labor Union (WLU), 300
"What Means This Strike," De Leon, 267
Whitby, Richard, 35
White, Eliot, 248n
Whiton, James, 236
Wilkes, Thomas H., 279
Wilard, Cyrus Field, 213
Willard, Cyrus Field, 213
Williams, Leighton, 238
Wilshire, H. Gaylord, 208, 214, 215, 219
Wilson, Edmund, 323
Wilson, J. Stitt, 241, 243-45, 330
Wilson, Woodrow, 297, 305, 306
Winchester, Marcus, 36
Winchevsky, Morris, 256
Wing, Simon, 253

Wisconsin, Socialists in, 175-76, 221, 277,
282, 310, 313, 314
WLU. *See* Western Labor Union
Wobblies. *See* Industrial Workers of the
World
Women: Andrews' view of, 76; Bellamy's
view of, 212; Bliss' view of, 237;
Brisbane's view of, 87; Gronlund's view
of, 207; Noyes' view of, 109; Owen's
view of, 18; SDS treatment of, 340
Women's rights, 77-78, 348; Greeley's view
of, 91; R. D. Owen and, 42; Perfectionist
view of, 106-7; Socialists and, 138, 142;
Wright's view of, 39-40
Woodhull, Victoria, 77-78, 83n, 348
Woodhull and Claflin's Weekly, 77, 83n
Work, John, 221
Workers: black, 253; Byllesby's view of,
26-27; De Leon's view of, 264-65; and
Fourierism, 96; Greeley's view of, 88-91;
Gronlund's view of, 206; Haskell's view
of, 187; IWA view of, 186-87; Most's
view of, 153; Pentecost's view of, 234;
Phillips' view of, 118
Working conditions, 65-66; in factories, 61,
63
Working Man's Advocate, 58
Workingmen's parties, 52-55, 60-66, 348;
political campaigns of, 55; in
Philadelphia, 52,55
Workingmen's party, 134-36, 138-41; of
New York, 41, 42, 55-60; and railroad
strikes, 138-40
Workmen's Advocate, 215, 266
World War I, Socialists and, 276, 304-7
Wright, Camilla, 31, 32, 34-36
Wright, Frances, 4, 24, 26, 31-40, 41, 56,
348; and Brownson, 45; Greeley's view
of, 91

Yerburgh, Mark, 351

Zeidler, Frank P., 292n

About the Author

BERNARD K. JOHNPOLL is Professor of Political Science at the State University of New York at Albany. His earlier books include *Pacifist's Progress* and *Norman Thomas on War*.